A HISTORY OF INDIA

A History of India presents the grand sweep of Indian history from antiquity to the present in a compact and readable survey. The authors examine the major political, economic, social and cultural forces which have shaped the history of the subcontinent. Providing an authoritative and detailed account, Hermann Kulke and Dietmar Rothermund emphasise and analyse the structural pattern of Indian history.

Revised throughout, the fourth edition of this highly accessible book brings the history of India up to date to consider, for example, the recent developments in the Kashmir conflict. Along with a new glossary, this new edition also includes an expanded discussion of the Mughal empire as well as of the economic history of India.

Hermann Kulke is Professor of Asian History at the University of Kiel. He is the author of *Kings and Cults: State Formation and Legitimation in India and Southeast Asia* (1993).

Dietmar Rothermund is Professor and Head of History at the South Asian Institute, University of Heidelberg. His books include *An Economic History of India* (1993) and *The Global Impact of the Great Depression, 1929–1939* (1996).

Dear Louise
Have a wonderful time!
Happy birthday

A HISTORY OF
INDIA

Love
Laura & Hadi
(2014)
x x x

Fourth Edition

Hermann Kulke and
Dietmar Rothermund

Routledge
Taylor & Francis Group

LONDON AND NEW YORK

First published 1986 in hardback by
Croom Helm Australia Pty Ltd
Second edition first published 1990 in paperback
Third edition first published 1998
by Routledge
2 Park Square, Milton Park, Abingdon, Oxon OX14 4RN

Simultaneously published in the USA and Canada
by Routledge
270 Madison Ave., New York, NY 10016

Fourth edition first published 2004

Reprinted 2006, 2007 (twice), 2008

Routledge is an imprint of the Taylor & Francis Group

© 1986, 1990, 1998, 2004 Hermann Kulke and
Dietmar Rothermund

Typeset in Times New Roman by
Florence Production Ltd, Stoodleigh, Devon
Printed and bound in Great Britain by
MPG Books Ltd, Bodmin

British Library Cataloguing in Publication Data
A catalogue record for this book is available from the British Library

Library of Congress Cataloging in Publication Data
Kulke, Hermann.
A History of India/Hermann Kulke and Dietmar Rothermund. – 4th ed.
p. cm.
Includes bibliographical references and index.
1. India–History. I. Rothermund, Dietmar. II. Title.
DS436.K85 2004
954–dc22   2004002075

ISBN 10: 0–415–32919–1 (hbk)
ISBN 10: 0–415–32920–5 (pbk)

ISBN 13: 978–0–415–32919–4 (hbk)
ISBN 13: 978–0–415–32920–0 (pbk)

CONTENTS

ILLUSTRATIONS

Figures

Maps

PREFACE

India's history is the fascinating epic of a great civilisation. It is a history of amazing cultural continuity. Today, it is the history of one-sixth of mankind. Both Indian and foreign historians have been attracted by this great theme, and each generation has produced its own histories of India. Several histories of India have been written in recent times, thus the present authors may be asked why they have dared to produce yet another account of Indian history.

First, research in Indian history to which both authors have contributed in their own way is progressing rapidly and an adequate synthesis is needed at more frequent intervals so as to reflect the current state of knowledge and to stimulate further inquiries. This kind of up-to-date synthesis the authors hope to have provided here. Furthermore, Indian history from antiquity to the present is such an enormous subject that it requires more than one author to cope with it. Consequently, many surveys of Indian history have been done by teams of authors, but rarely have these authors had the benefit of working together in the same department, comparing notes on Indian history for many years. This has been the good fortune of the present authors who have worked together at the South Asia Institute of Heidelberg University for nearly twenty years.

In the late 1970s they first embarked on this joint venture at the request of a German publisher. The German edition was published in 1982, a revised edition appeared in 1998. The first English edition was published by David Croom of Croom Helm, London, in 1986. Subsequently, the rights were acquired by Routledge, London and, ever since, the Routledge editorial team has been helpful in bringing out new editions of this text which seems to have attracted many readers. Inspired by the interest in their work the authors have submitted this thoroughly revised text for the fourth English edition in December 2003. They updated the text with regard to recent history and also took into account new publications in the field so as to reflect the state of the art in historical research.

The authors have benefited from discussions with Indian, British and American colleagues, many of whom cannot read their German publications.

They are glad to communicate with them by means of this book. However, this text is not restricted to a dialogue among historians, it is written for the student and the general reader. To this reader the authors want to introduce themselves here. Hermann Kulke studied Indology (Sanskrit) and history at Freiburg University and did his PhD thesis on the *Chidambaram Mahatmya*, a text which encompasses the tradition of the south Indian temple city Chidambaram. His second major book was on the Gajapati kings of Orissa. He has actively participated in the first Orissa Research Project of the German Research Council and was the co-editor of *The Cult of Jagannath and the Regional Tradition of Orissa*. He continued to do research on Orissa and became the coordinator of the second Orissa Research Project which is still in progress. He has also worked on Indian historiography and medieval state formation in India and Indonesia and on the Devaraja cult of Angkor. He published a book on kings and cults in India and southeast Asia, edited a volume on *The State in India, 1000–1700* and recently wrote another *History of India* in German. In 1988 Hermann Kulke was called to the new Chair of Asian History at Kiel University. The distance between Heidelberg and Kiel has not reduced the contacts with his co-author.

Dietmar Rothermund studied history and philosophy at Marburg and Munich universities and at the University of Pennsylvania, Philadelphia, where he did his PhD thesis on the history of eighteenth-century Pennsylvania. He then went to India and worked on a history of the freedom movement which was published in German in 1965. He subsequently wrote a book on India and the Soviet Union and a major research monograph on agrarian relations in India under British rule. He also wrote a comprehensive political biography of Mahatma Gandhi in German and then published a shorter version of it in English.

In the 1970s he participated in the Dhanbad Project of the South Asia Interdisciplinary Regional Research Programme. This project was devoted to the history and economy and the social conditions of an Indian coalfield and its rural hinterland. Subsequently, he mostly worked on Indian economic history and published a research monograph on *India in the Great Depression, 1929–1939* (1992) followed by a general text on *The Global Impact of the Great Depression, 1929–1939* (1996).

In the 1990s he turned his attention to the liberalisation of the Indian economy and edited a volume on *Liberalising India. Progress and Problems* (1996). He participated in producing a German series entitled 'Twenty Days of the Twentieth Century', and 'his day' was, of course, 15 August 1947. Taking this date as a point of departure, this book covered the history of decolonisation in Asia and Africa.

In keeping with their respective fields of specialisation the authors have divided the work on the present text. Hermann Kulke has written Chapters 1 to 4. He benefited a great deal from discussions with Martin Brandtner, Kiel, while revising the first chapter. Dietmar Rothermund has written the

Introduction, Chapters 5 to 8 and has also prepared the entire English version of the text. In addition to his contribution to the present text he has also published *An Economic History of India*. Its second edition was published by Routledge in 1993. It was supposed to be a companion volume to *A History of India*, but it seems that students prefer one textbook and do not want to consult two. Due to this, readers missed the economic dimension in *A History of India*. Therefore, the present edition contains some new paragraphs on essential aspects of Indian economic history. Since the text could not be expanded too much, these references are necessarily very brief.

When writing a history of India one is faced with a dilemma with regard to the term 'India'. Before 1947 it refers to an area which is now usually called south Asia and includes, among other states, Bangladesh and Pakistan. The history of the latter states is covered by the present book up to 1947, whereas for the subsequent period it is restricted to the history of the Republic of India. Bangladesh and Pakistan are mentioned to the extent that their development affected that of the Republic of India. Some readers may have liked to see a more detailed treatment of Bangladesh and Pakistan, but this would have been beyond the scope of this text.

The book does not have footnotes but in the bibliographies of the different chapters, there are notes concerning specific quotations included in the text. For the transcription of Indian names and terms the authors have adopted the standard English style and omitted diacritical marks. As a new feature, the present edition has a glossary of Indian terms for ready reference to words which have not been explained in detail in the text. In recent years the names of some major Indian cities have been changed, i.e. the pre-colonial names have been restored. In the present text the previous names have been retained as many readers would not yet be familiar with the changed ones. Moreover, historical names such as Bombay Presidency or Madras Presidency cannot be converted into Mumbai Presidency and Chennai Presidency. The glossary lists the new names for all old names found in the text.

The general emphasis in this book is on the structural pattern of Indian history rather than on the chronology of events. A chronological table has been appended to the text. Several maps have been inserted into the text to help the reader to locate names of places and the shifts of territorial control. As a new feature, illustrations have been added to the present edition which should make the book more attractive as visual representation often transcends the power of words.

Hermann Kulke
Dietmar Rothermund
Kiel and Heidelberg, December 2003

ACKNOWLEDGEMENTS

The authors and publishers would like to thank the following for permission to reproduce material:

Georg Helmes, Aachen (Figure 1.1)
Museum of Indian Art, Berlin (Figure 2.2)
The British Museum (Figure 2.3)
Dinodia.com (Figures 4.1, 5.2, 7.5)
Rietberg Musem (Figure 4.2, 5.1)
The Director, National Army Museum (Figure 5.4)
National Portrait Gallery, London (Figures 5.5, 7.1, 7.2)
India Office Library and Records (Add.Or.888) (Figure 6.1)
Nehru Memorial Museum and Library and National Portrait Gallery, London (Figure 7.3)
Associated Press (Figure 7.4)
AKG London (Figure 8.1)

While every effort has been made to trace and acknowledge ownership of copyright material used in this volume, the publishers will be glad to make suitable arrangements with any copyright holders whom it has not been possible to contact.

INTRODUCTION
History and the environment

Environment – that is a world alive and related to a living centre, the habitat of an animal, the hunting grounds and pastures of nomads, the fields of settled peasants. For human beings the environment is both an objective ecological condition and a field of subjective experience. Nature sets limits, man transgresses them with his tools and his vision. Man progressively creates a specific environment and makes history. In this process it is not only the limits set by nature which are transgressed but also the limits of human experience and cognition. From the elementary adaptation to the natural environment to the establishment of great civilisations, the horizon of experience and the regional extension of human relations constantly expand.

The conception of the environment changes in the course of this evolution. Ecological conditions which may appear hostile to man at one stage of this evolution may prove to be attractive and inviting at another stage. The hunter and foodgatherer armed only with stone tools preferred to live on the edge of forests near the plains or in open river valleys, areas which were less attractive to the settled peasant who cut the trees and reclaimed fertile soil. But initially even the peasant looked for lighter soils until a sturdy plough and draught animals enabled him to cope with heavy soils. At this stage the peasant could venture to open up fertile alluvial plains and reap rich harvests of grain. If rainfall or irrigation were sufficient he could grow that most productive but most demanding of all grains: rice. Wherever irrigated rice was produced, plenty of people could live and great empires could rise, but, of course, such civilisations and empires were very much dependent on their agrarian base. A change of climate or a devastation of this base by invaders cut off their roots and they withered away.

Indian history provides excellent examples of this evolution. Prehistoric sites with stone tools were almost exclusively found in areas which were not centres of the great empires of the later stages of history: the area between Udaipur and Jaipur, the valley of the Narmada river, the eastern slopes of the Western Ghats, the country between the rivers Krishna and Tungabhadra (Raichur Doab), the area of the east coast where the

1

highlands are nearest to the sea (to the north of present Madras), the rim of the Chota Nagpur Plateau and both slopes of the mountain ranges of central India (see Map I.1).

The cultivation of grain started around 7000 BC in southern Asia, according to recent archaeological research. This was a time of increasing rainfall in the region which has always depended on the monsoon. Before venturing into the open plains of the lower Indus the precursors of the Indus civilisation experimented with cultivating alluvial lands on a small scale in the valleys of Baluchistan. There they built stone walls (*gabarbands*) which retained the sediments of the annual inundation. Initially the archaeologists mistook these walls for dams built for irrigation, but the holes in these walls showed that they were designed so as to retain soil but not water. Such constructions were found near Quetta and Las Bela and in the Bolan valley. In this valley is also the site of Mehrgarh which will be described in detail in the next chapter.

Palaeobotanical research has indicated an increase in rainfall in this whole region from about 3000 BC. The new methods of cultivating alluvial soil were then adopted not only in the Indus valley, but also in the parallel Ghaggar valley some 60 to 80 miles to the east of the Indus. This valley was perhaps even more attractive to the early cultivators than the Indus valley with its enormous inundations and a flow of water twice that of the Nile. The builders of the great cities Mohenjo-Daro and Harappa were masters of water management as the systems of urban water supply and sewerage show. So far no village sites have been found in the Indus valley. Perhaps due to the inundations agricultural operations were only seasonal and no permanent villages were established. The cities may have served as organisational centres for such seasonal operations. They were also very important centres of trade. Harappa which was situated near the borderline between agriculture and the pastoral zone served as a gateway city on which the trade routes coming from the north converged. Metals and precious stones came from the mountains and entered international maritime trade via the big Indus cities.

Life in the Ghaggar valley may have been of a different kind. There was a much greater density of settlements there. It was probably the heartland of this civilisation. The site of Ganweriwala, near Derawar Fort, which has been identified but not yet excavated, may contain the remains of a city as big as Harappa. It is surrounded by a large cluster of smaller sites. Perhaps here one could find the rural settlements which are conspicuous by their absence in the Indus valley. Archaeological evidence points to a drying up of the Ghaggar around 1700 BC which may be due to a sudden tectonic change. The river Yamuna which now parallels the Ganga is supposed to have flowed through the Ghaggar valley until an upheaval in the foothills of the Himalayas made it change its course. The distance between the present valley of the Yamuna and the ancient Ghaggar valley is less than

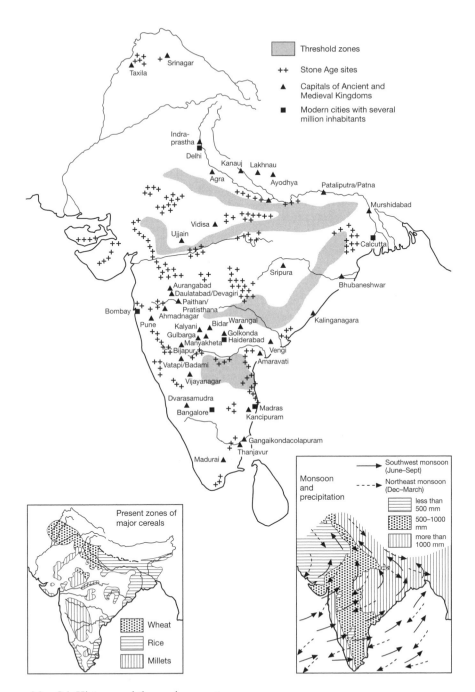

Threshold zones

++ Stone Age sites

▲ Capitals of Ancient and Medieval Kingdoms

■ Modern cities with several million inhabitants

Srinagar
Taxila
Indra-prastha
Delhi
Kanauj
Lakhnau
Agra
Ayodhya
Pataliputra/Patna
Murshidabad
Vidisa
Ujjain
Calcutta
Sripura
Aurangabad
Daulatabad/Devagiri
Paithan/Pratisthana
Bombay
Ahmadnagar
Pune
Kalyani
Bidar
Warangal
Gulbarga
Golkonda
Manyakheta
Haiderabad
Bijapur
Vatapi/Badami
Vengi
Amaravati
Vijayanagar
Dvarasamudra
Bangalore
Madras
Kancipuram
Gangaikondacolapuram
Thanjavur
Madurai
Bhubaneshwar
Kalinganagara

Present zones of major cereals

Wheat
Rice
Millets

Monsoon and precipitation

Southwest monsoon (June–Sept)
Northeast monsoon (Dec–March)
less than 500 mm
500–1000 mm
more than 1000 mm

Map I.1 History and the environment

40 miles in the area between Jagadhri and Ambala. The land is rather flat in this area and even a small tectonic tilt could have caused the shift in the flow of the river. The northward thrust of the subcontinental shelf which threw up the Himalayas causes tectonic movements even today, as frequent earthquakes indicate. Other tectonic upheavals at the mouth of the Indus river may have produced a large lake submerging Mohenjo-Daro. This latter hypothesis is contested by scholars who think that the mighty Indus could never have been blocked for any length of time. However, even one sudden blockage or several seasonal ones would have done enough damage. The drying up of the Ghaggar and the blocking of the lower Indus could thus have ruined the major centres of the Indus civilisation.

There was one region which remained initially unaffected by these upheaveals: the Kathiawar peninsula of Gujarat. This region had been colonised by the people of the Indus civilisation and had emerged as a major link with the outside world. Only a few sites have been excavated there so far. Dholavira is a site to watch. It lies far inside the Rann of Kutch, but it was obviously a seaport like Lothal on the other side of the peninsula. Clearly, Dholavira is an important site. Maritime trade via Oman brought African millets to this region where inland settlements like Rojdi lived on cultivating them rather than wheat and barley which were the mainstay of the Indus civilisation elsewhere. The millets were of great importance for the spread of settled agriculture into the highlands further to the east.

The total area covered by the Indus civilisation was very large. So-called Late Harappan remains have been found even at Daimabad in Maharashtra. Shortugai in Badakshan, Afghanistan, is so far the most northern settlement of the Indus civilisation located by archaeologists. The distance between Shortugai and Daimabad is about 1,500 miles. Such distant outposts, as well as cities not threatened by tectonic upheavals, decayed when the heartland no longer provided trade and cultural supervision. The vigour of the Indus civilisation had thus been sapped long before the tribes of cattle-rearing nomads who called themselves Aryans (the noble ones) descended from the north. The ecological scenario faced by these newcomers was very different from that which had given rise to the Indus civilisation. As nomads they could adjust to a changing environment. Initially the plains of the Panjab provided rich pastures for their cattle until a sharp decrease in rainfall drove them eastwards, to the jungles of the Ganga–Yamuna river system which receded in this period of perennial drought.

THE ROUTES OF ARYAN MIGRATION

The main thrust of Aryan migration was probably south of the Terai region where the tributaries of the river Ganga must have dwindled to the point that they could be easily crossed and where the dry forest could be burned down. The Aryan fire god, Agni, was credited with the feat of colonising this land for the Aryans. They stopped at the river Gandak which enters the plains north of present Gorakhpur and joins the Ganga near Patna. Unlike the other tributaries further to the west, this river seems to have been still full of good water because the Aryans named it Sadanira (everlasting) and their sacred texts report that the land beyond was swampy. Only some daring pioneers crossed the Gandak in due course without the support of Agni.

With the growth of royal authority in the Aryan kingdoms to the west of the river Gandak, escape to the uncontrolled east may have been attractive to those Aryans who preferred the more egalitarian tribal organisation of earlier times to the twin tutelage of kings and their Brahmin priests.

After some time, Brahmins also crossed the river Gandak and were welcome there if they did not insist on subverting the tribal organisation by consecrating kings everywhere. There is much evidence in ancient texts that there were two ideal types of Brahmins in those days, the royal priest or advisor (*rajpurohit, rajguru*) and the sage (*rishi*) who lived in the forest and shared his wisdom only with those who asked for it. The people beyond the Gandak perhaps did not mind sages but were suspicious of the Brahmin courtiers. This suspicion was mutual, because these royal priests had no good words for kingless tribes, whom they thoroughly despised.

The Aryan drive to the east seemed to be preordained by the terms which they used for the four directions. They regarded the sunrise as the main cardinal point, so they called the east 'what was before them' (*purva*). To their right hand (*dakshina*) was the south. But *dakshinapatha*, the way to the south, was obstructed by mountain ranges and a hostile environment. Nevertheless, just as some pioneers crossed the Gandak and explored the fertile eastern plains, other venturesome Aryans proceeded either via the Malwa plateau or further east along the northern slopes of the Vindhya mountains to the fertile region of the Deccan Lava Trap. The rich black soil of this region became the southernmost outpost of Aryan migration. Only small groups of Brahmins proceeded further south in search of patronage, which they found in due course.

Territorial control in the modern sense of the term was unknown to these early Aryans and their kings adopted a very flexible method of asserting their authority. The more powerful chief among them let a sacrificial horse roam around for a year vowing that he would defeat anyone who dared to obstruct the free movement of the horse. If a challenger appeared, he was attacked. If nobody showed up, it was presumed that the king's authority was not questioned. By the end of the year the king could celebrate the horse sacrifice (*ashvamedha*) as a symbol of his victories or of his unchallenged authority. But this pastime of small kings came to an end when a major empire arose in the east which soon annexed the kingdoms of the west.

ANCIENT EMPIRES AND RELIGIOUS MOVEMENTS

The east not only produced the first Indian empire, it also gave rise to new religious movements, Buddhism and Jainism. Both flourished in a region which was in close contact with the Gangetic civilisation of the west but had not been subjected to the slow growth of its royal institutions and courtly Brahminism. Thus, entirely new forms of organisation evolved, like the monastic order (*sangha*) of the Buddhists and the imperial control of trade and land revenue which provided the resources for a greater military potential than any of the Aryan kingdoms could have achieved. Rice was one of the most important resources of this region, because the eastern Gangetic basin was the largest region of India to fulfil the necessary climatic conditions. Well-organised Buddhist monasteries were initially better suited for the cultural penetration of this vast eastern region than small groups of Brahmins would have been. Monasteries, of course, required more sustained support than such small groups of Brahmins, but this was no problem in this rice bowl of India.

The new empire of the east, with its centre in Magadha to the south of the river Ganga, first vanquished the tribal republics in the Trans-Gandak region to the north of the Ganga and then the Aryan kingdoms of the west, showing little respect for their traditions and finally imposing a new ideology of its own. But this empire in turn succumbed to internal conflicts and the onslaught of new invaders who came from the north, where the Aryans had come from more than a millennium earlier. The new invaders arrived when ecological conditions were improving once more in northern India. They also had the benefit of finding readily available imperial patterns which they could adopt very quickly. Aryan royal institutions had taken centuries to mature in the relatively isolated Gangetic basin. In a world of closer connections and wider horizons where Hellenistic, Iranian and Indian models of governance and ritual sovereignty were known to all, a new invader could leap from the darkness of an unrecorded nomadic past to the limelight of imperial history within a relatively short period. Shakas and Kushanas swept in this way across northern India. Their short-lived imperial traditions embodied a syncretism of several available patterns of legitimation. They also adopted Hinduism, not the Vedic tradition but rather the more popular cults of Vishnu and Shiva.

The waves of imperial grandeur which swept across northern India then stimulated the south. But when the first great indigenous dynasty of the south, the Shatavahanas, emerged they did not follow the syncretism of the northern empires but harked back to the tradition of the small Aryan kingdoms of the Gangetic civilisation. The great horse sacrifice was celebrated once more by a Shatavahana king, but the meaning of this ritual was now very different from that of the old flexible test of royal authority.

It was now a great symbolic gesture of a mighty king whose Brahmin advisors must have prompted him to identify himself with the Vedic tradition which they had preserved in the south rather than with the ideologies which great emperors from Ashoka to Kanishka had propagated in the north. This was of crucial importance for the future course of Indian history as well as for the export of the Hindu idea of kingship to southeast Asia.

THE PERIODS OF INDIAN HISTORY

The resurgence of old traditions throughout Indian history prevents the ready transfer of the Western periodisation of history to India. Ancient, medieval and modern history cannot be easily identified in India. For this reason many historians adopted another division for Indian history: Hindu, Islamic and British periods. Hindu historians tended to glorify the golden age of the Hindu period and considered Islamic and British rule as two successive periods of foreign rule. Islamic historians accepted this clear-cut division though they may have had their own ideas about the Hindu period. British historians were equally comfortable with this division as it implied that British rule made such a mark on Indian history that one could very well forget about everything else.

This periodisation, though, has given rise to many misconceptions. First of all, the Hindu period was not at all homogeneous in its traditions and cultural patterns, nor did these Hindu traditions disappear when Islamic rule spread in India nor even when the British controlled the country. Islamic rule in India was of a very heterogeneous character and the cooperation of Hindus and Muslims in many spheres of political, social and cultural life was in many respects more important than the reference to a well-defined Islamic period would indicate. British rule was ephemeral both in terms of its time span and of the intensity of its impact. Due to its fairly recent end it still looms large in our minds, but if we take a long view of history we must regard it as an episode, though a very important one. The younger generation of historians in India has criticised the misleading periodisation of Hindu, Islamic and British, but due to the lack of a better alternative it still lingers on.

We shall adopt in this book a different periodisation and refer to ancient, medieval and modern Indian history in terms of the predominant political structure and not in terms of the religious or ethnic affiliation of the respective rulers.

At the centre of ancient Indian history was the *chakravartin*, the ruler who tried to conquer the entire world. His limits were, of course, his knowledge of the world and his military potential. The ideal chakravartin turned his attention to the elimination or silencing of external challenges rather than to the intensive internal control of the empire. A rich core region and control of the trade routes which provided sufficient support for the military potential of the chakravartin was enough for the maintenance of universal dominance. Many such empires rose and fell in ancient India, the last being the Gupta empire which embodied all the splendour and the problems of this type of ancient Indian political organisation. One important impact of these empires was the dissemination of information about the art of governance, the style of royal or imperial courts, the methods of warfare and the maintenance of an agrarian base. Even though the internal administrative penetration of the various provinces of the ancient empires was negligible, the spread of information certainly was not. At the time of the Maurya empire many parts of India were still so inaccessible that there were natural limits to this spread of information, but by the time of the great Indian campaigns of the Gupta emperors almost all regions of India were receptive to the imperial message. Thus when the empire broke up and India's ancient period drew to an end, numerous regional states arose which set the pattern for India's medieval history. These were concentric states with a royal centre in the core region and a periphery in which the influence of competitors also made itself felt. Intense competition among such concentric states stimulated the political penetration which was so ephemeral in the far-flung empires of the ancient period. A uniform court culture spread to all parts of India. The Islamic rulers who invaded India did contribute new features to this pattern, but to a large extent the rulers were assimilated. Their court culture had a different religious base but it functioned in a way similar to that of the Hindu rulers whom they displaced.

The modern period of Indian history begins with the Mughal empire which was comparable in size with some of the ancient Indian empires but was totally different from them in its internal structure. It was a highly centralised state based on the extensive control of land revenue and of a military machine which could rival that of contemporary European states. In fact, the size of the machine was the reason for the final collapse of this empire which could not meet its financial needs. This was then achieved by the British who conquered the remnants of this empire and continued its administrative tradition and made it much more effective.

CHARIOTS, ELEPHANTS AND THE METHODS OF WARFARE

The course of Indian history which has been briefly sketched here was deeply affected by changes in the methods of warfare. The Aryan warriors relied on their swift chariots which made them militarily superior to the indigenous people but could, of course, also be used for incessant warfare among themselves. Chariots did not lend themselves to monopolisation by a centralised power. But the war elephants on which imperial Magadha based its military strength were ideal supporters of a power monopoly. The eastern environment of Magadha provided an ample supply of wild elephants, but maintenance was of greater importance than supply. Only a mighty ruler could afford to maintain adequate contingents of war elephants. The entrance of the elephant into Indian military history around 500 BC thus made a profound difference to the political structure and the strategy of warfare. Chandragupta Maurya's gift of 500 elephants to Seleukos Nikator was one of the most important military aid transactions of the ancient world.

Indian military strategy is faithfully reflected in the game of chess which is supposed to have been invented by an Indian Brahmin for the entertainment of his king. In this game as well as on the battlefield, the king himself conducts the operations from the back of an elephant. He has to take care not to expose himself too much, because if he is killed his army is vanquished even if it is still in good condition. Therefore the movements of the king are restricted. The dynamics of the battle are determined by the general, the cavalry and the runners. The flanks of the army are protected by elephants which may also be moved into front-line positions as the battle draws to a decisive close. The infantrymen, mostly untrained, slow and armed with very elementary weapons are only important because of their numbers and because of their nuisance value in some critical phases of the battle. This strategic pattern remained more or less the same for more than 2,000 years.

The upkeep of such an army required a regional stronghold of sufficient dimensions. The structure of the Indian environment and the distribution of such nuclear regions predetermined a standard extension of direct rule over an area about 100–200 miles in diameter and a potential of intervention in regions at a distance of 400–500 miles. Direct rule refers to the ability to collect revenue and the potential of intervention is defined as the ability to send a substantial army with war elephants to a distant region with a good chance of defeating the enemy but not with the intention of adding his region permanently to one's own area of direct rule.

If we keep these rules of the game in mind we can delineate three major regions in India which in turn can be subdivided into four smaller sub-regions, each of which theoretically would be able to support a regional ruler. But generally only one ruler in each major region would be strong enough to establish a hegemony over the respective sub-regions, but his resources would not permit him to annex all of them permanently. A ruler who had achieved such a hegemony in his major region might then also have tried to intervene in one or two other major regions. This interaction was conditioned by the location of powerful rulers in the other major regions. It is of great importance in this respect that there was also a fourth region, a vast intermediate area in the centre of India which provided a great challenge to the potential of intervention of aggressive rulers.

THE REGIONAL PATTERN OF INDIAN HISTORY

The first major region of the Indian subcontinent is the alluvial land of the northern rivers which extends for about 2,000 miles from the mouth of the Indus to the mouth of the river Ganga. This belt of land is only about 200 miles wide. The two other major regions are the southern highlands and the east coast. They are separated from the northern region by the large intermediate zone which extends right across India for about 1,000 miles from Gujarat to Orissa and is 300–400 miles wide.

The northern region is subdivided into four smaller regions, the first one being the region of the first great Indian empire in the east, Bengal and Bihar, the second the middle Gangetic basin including the lower Ganga–Yamuna Doab, the third the Agra–Delhi region and the western Doab, and the fourth the Indus region. The intermediate zone is both a mediator and a buffer between the northern region and the two other ones. Its two terminal regions, Gujarat and Orissa, are both separated from the other major regions in specific ways, Gujarat by the desert in the north and Orissa by mountains and rivers which are always in flood in the monsoon season. The interior of the intermediate zone contains four enclaves which are isolated from each other: the fertile plains of Chattisgarh, a region which was called Dakshina Koshala in ancient times; Vidarbha, the area around present Nagpur; the Malwa plateau around Ujjain which was called Avanti in antiquity; and finally the Rajput country between Jaipur and Udaipur. Of course, there have been some contacts among these regions of the intermediate zone and with the other major regions. Furthermore Gujarat and Orissa, predestined by their location on the coast, have been in touch with regions overseas. But for military intervention, this intermediate zone has always been a major obstacle.

The four sub-regional centres of the highland region are the Deccan Lava Trap around Aurangabad and Paithan, the central region around Haiderabad, including the old capitals of Bidar, Manyakheta and Kalyani, the region between Bijapur and Vijayanagara which includes old capitals such as the Badami of the Chalukyas, and finally the region around Mysore, the stronghold of the Hoysalas and later on of Tipu Sultan. The four sub-regions within the east coast region are the Krishna–Godaveri delta, Tondaimandalam around present Madras, the centre of the old Pallava empire, Cholamandalam in the Kaveri delta region, the home ground of the Chola dynasty, and finally Pandyamandala around Madurai, the centre of the Pandyas.

The three last mentioned sub-regions are close to each other, but they are divided from the first east coast sub-region, the Krishna–Godaveri delta, by a stretch of land called *Rayalaseema*. Here the highland comes close to the coast and cuts into the fertile coastal plains. Thus, though Rayalaseema and the region adjacent to it, the Raichur Doab located between Krishna and Tungabhadra, never became an important centre of power, it was fought over frequently. It has a rich cultural heritage and is full of ancient temples, but no powerful ruler ever put up his headquarters there. This may also be due to the fact that Hindu kings did not like to build capitals near the confluence of rivers which are considered to be sacred and must therefore be accessible to pilgrims from everywhere and that means accessible also to enemies.

Another interesting region is Kongunad, the area to the south of present Coimbatore, being the hinterland of the three southern coastal regions. This region was of some importance in antiquity. The many Roman coins found there suggest it may have been an area of transit for important trade routes. However, it never provided a stronghold for an important dynasty, except perhaps for the Kalabhras who dominated the southeast coast from the fourth to the sixth century AD and of whom not much is known so far. The west coast has been omitted from our survey of major regions for good reasons, the small strip of land between the Ghats and the Arabian Sea never provided a foothold for any major power; it only supported some local rulers.

The capitals of the kingdoms which were established in these various regions have, with few exceptions, not survived the decline of those kingdoms. Today we may only find some ruins and occasionally a village which still bears the ancient great name. There are several reasons for this disappearance of the old capitals. First of all they depended on the agricultural surplus of the surrounding countryside and, therefore, on the ruler who managed to appropriate this surplus. Once the ruler was gone, the capital also disappeared and if a new dynasty rose in the same region it usually built a new capital. In the central area of each of these regions there were many places suitable for the location of a capital. In fact, these central areas are demarcated by the frequency of capitals constructed there (see Map I.1).

Only in a very few instances did a unique strategic location compel many dynasties throughout the ages to build their capitals more or less on the same spot. The prime example of this is Delhi, which controls the entrance to the fertile Ganga–Yamuna Doab. The Aravalli mountain range closely approaches the Yamuna here where this river flows in a wide, flat bed. Whoever was in control of this gateway held sway in this part of northern India, or, to put it differently, he who wanted to rule this region had to capture this gateway. Therefore the area around Delhi is, so to speak, littered with the remnants of about a dozen ancient capitals which have been built here for more than two millennia.

Patna, the old Pataliputra, is a strategic place of similar importance. It is located on a high bank of the river Ganga and when the river is in spate in the monsoon season, the city looks like an island in the midst of the flooded plains. Pataliputra emerged as a bastion of Magadha in its fight against the tribal republics to the north of the Ganga. It also controlled the access to the eastern route to the south via the Sone valley and along the slopes of the Vindhya mountains. When the rulers of Magadha moved their capital from southern Bihar into the centre of the valley of the Ganga they naturally selected Pataliputra as their new capital and many of their successors did the same. The highlands and the east coast have no perennial capital sites like that, the regional pattern remained fixed, but the location of the capital was a matter of discretion.

The great distances which separated the regional centres of the southern highlands and the east coast from those of the northern region meant that in many periods of Indian history great rulers of the south and of the north coexisted without ever clashing. Intervention across the wide intermediate zone was always very hazardous, and even more problematic was the attempt at governing a huge empire from two capitals, one at Delhi and the other in the northernmost regional centre of the highlands (Daulatabad/ Aurangabad). But even the regional centres of the highlands and of the east coast were so distant from each other that the potential of intervention was fairly restricted. For instance, Badami (Vatapi), the capital of the third sub-region of the highlands, is about 400 miles from the centres of the first and the second regions of the east coast. The Krishna–Godaveri delta was subjected to frequent intervention from the highlands whenever the foremost ruler of that region had his headquarters around present Haiderabad which is only about 150 miles west of this fertile delta. The only exception to this rule seems to be the establishment of Vengi by the Chalukyas whose home base was at Vatapi at that time.

Within the three major regions the struggle for hegemony continued. The likelihood of conflict between rulers of two major regions was dependent on these 'domestic' struggles. For instance, if the ruler of a southern centre of the highlands was in power and a ruler of the Delhi–Agra region had attained hegemony in the north, there was hardly a chance of their clashing. But if the foremost ruler of the southern highlands was located in the north of this region and the north was in the hands of a ruler of the middle Gangetic basin, a clash was much more likely (for example, the Rashtrakuta encounter with the Gurjara Pratiharas).

The potential for long-distance intervention and conquest grew only when the Islamic invaders of the north introduced the new method of swift cavalry warfare. However, it did not, at first, change the pattern of regional dominance. All rulers quickly adopted the new strategy and thus there was once more a uniform standard of warfare throughout the subcontinent. However, the new strategy had important internal consequences for the political structure of the regional realms. Horse breeding was always a problem in India and good warhorses had to be imported from Arabia and Persia at a high price. This made the maintenance of the military machine more expensive. At the same time the man on horseback was an awe-inspiring collector of land revenue and thus the appropriation of surplus could be intensified. A new military feudalism, hand-in-hand with a military urbanism, arose in this way. Cavalry garrisons were established in the countryside and their commanding officers became local administrators making their headquarters focal points for their respective neighbourhoods. The extraction of surplus from the countryside was delegated to a large extent. These cavalry officers were rarely local notables. They were usually strangers who owed their appointment to the regional ruler, and if they thought of rebellion at all they thought in terms of replacing the ruler himself rather than gaining autonomy over the area which they happened to control.

THE MARITIME PERIPHERY AND THE INTRUSION OF EUROPEAN POWERS

The preoccupation with the cavalry warfare blinded the Indian rulers to the maritime challenge of European powers. They would only take an enemy seriously if he confronted them with large contingents of cavalry. They did not pay any attention to the Indian Ocean as the most important element of the total Indian environment. Nobody had ever invaded India from the sea and, therefore, the rulers were sure that they could neglect the Europeans who, at the most, hired some Indian foot soldiers to protect their trading outposts. They knew the monsoon would not permit a sustained maritime invasion of India, as it only carried ships to India during a few months of the year. Thus a maritime invader would find his supply lines cut within a very short time. Actually the European powers never attempted such an invasion but built up their military contingents in India, drilling infantry troops which were less expensive to maintain but proved to be fatal to the Indian cavalry. At the same time control of the sea and of the maritime periphery provided the European powers with a much greater potential for intervention.

Indian rulers had not always neglected the Indian Ocean. The Chola kings had equipped great naval expeditions and Indian seafarers had a remarkable tradition of long-distance voyages. The Hindu prejudice against crossing the black water (*kala pani*) of the ocean had grown only in the late medieval period and the Mughal emphasis on the internal control of a vast empire had added to India's isolationist tendency. On the other hand India did not conceive of the peripheral foreigners as a serious threat as did Japan, which adopted a policy of deliberate isolation. In this way the British were able to extend their control over India from their peripheral bridgeheads on the coast until they captured the vast land revenue base of the fertile eastern region which had provided the foundation for the first Indian empire more than 2,000 years previously.

In fact, the British conquest of India closely paralleled the pattern of expansion of the Maurya empire. They subjected the Gangetic basin up to the Ganga–Yamuna Doab as well as the east coast and penetrated into the interior of the south where they defeated Tipu Sultan of Mysore. Just like the Mauryas, the British left large parts of the interior untouched. Indirect rule was less expensive in areas which did not promise a high yield of land revenue. But, unlike the ancient Indian empires, the British Indian empire emphasised efficient administrative penetration. The Mughal heritage was already strong in this respect, but the British were able to improve greatly upon it. The Mughal administration was, after all, a military one: the officers who made the decisions were warriors and not bookkeepers. The British replaced the warriors with bookkeepers who were under the strict discipline of a modern bureaucracy. In fact, British bureaucracy in India was far ahead of British administration at home which was both supported and encumbered by British tradition. This new system of bureaucratic administration was both much cheaper and more efficient than the Mughal system. The Mughal warrior administrator spent a large part of the surplus which he appropriated in the region from which it had come, but the British collected more and spent less and could transfer the surplus abroad. This implied a decline of the internal administrative centres which shrank to a size in keeping with their functions in the new system. Only the major bridgeheads on the maritime periphery, Bombay, Calcutta and Madras, grew out of all proportion. They also became the terminal points of the railway network which linked the interior of India to the world market. Thus the old regional pattern of Indian history which has been outlined above was subverted by the British rulers. The pattern was turned inside out. The periphery provided the new regional centres of the three great Presidencies which encompassed the three major regions outlined above. Only some of the capitals of Indian princes who lived on under British paramountcy remained as rather modest centres in the interior of the country until the British rulers decided to revive Delhi as the capital of British India. But this transfer of the capital was more of a symbolic gesture than an effective change in the structure of British rule. Even independent India could not easily change the new regional order of India which was dominated by the great peripheral centres. The rise of new industrial centres in the Indian coal and iron ore belt around Chota Nagpur has not made much difference in this respect. These are industrial enclaves in a very backward region which has never been a nuclear region but rather a retreat for the tribal population.

THE REGIONAL PATTERN OF POPULATION DENSITY

One indicator of the relative changes of the importance of different regions in India is the density of population (see Map I.2). Unfortunately we know

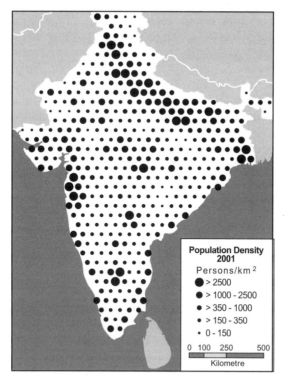

Map I.2 Population density according to the Census of India, 2001

very little about the distribution of population in earlier periods of Indian history. We can only guess that the great rice areas of the eastern Gangetic basin and of the east coast have always been regions with a much higher population density than the rest of India. These conditions remained more or less the same under British rule, because canal irrigation was introduced only in very few areas which could then be expected to support greater numbers of people than previously. Fairly reliable census data are available only from 1881 onwards and since then the Census of India has continued in its decennial rhythm. The late nineteenth century was characterised by a slow but steady population growth which was then checked by the great famines at the end of the century. The 1901 census reflected this stage of development. It thus provides a fairly accurate picture of the regional pattern of population density which must have prevailed for quite some time. The regions of highest population density (more than 150 people per square kilometre) were the following: the first three sub-regions of the northern plains, the first three sub-regions of the east coast, the southern tip of the west coast and a few districts in the fertile plains of Gujarat. This pattern has probably existed also in earlier centuries. Of course, population density must have been less in earlier times, but the relative position of the regions listed here must have been the same. This relative position is still more or less the same at present. But since population increased much more rapidly after 1921, population density is a liability rather than an asset to the respective regions nowadays. The rate of increase has declined in some of these regions and risen in others. The southern rim of the Gangetic basin, the western and southern parts of the highlands, parts of Gujarat and the northern part of the east coast have been areas of above average population increase in recent decades. Particularly the changing structure of population density in the highlands, which had always been below average in earlier years, seems to be of great significance. This may also imply a shift in the political importance of various regions. Hitherto Uttar Pradesh, which encompasses the second and most of the third sub-region of the northern plains, has played a dominant role in India's political history, earlier because of its strategic location and nowadays because of its enormous population which means a corresponding weight in political representation. But this position may not remain unchallenged. On the other hand those regions of India which still continue to be well below the national average in population density are also regions which never played a prominent role in Indian history. These are mainly four zones which cut across the subcontinent (see Map I.1). The first reaches from the great desert in the west to the Chota Nagpur Plateau in the east. The second consists of the Vindhya mountain range. The third extends from the centre of the highlands to the mountain ranges along the northern east coast, and the fourth is the Rayalaseema region and the adjacent area to the west of it. Thus census data help us to support the main conclusions of the regional analysis presented above.

The four areas which we have delineated are also important barriers of communication which limited the spread of regional languages. The border between the Tamil and the Telugu region follows the southern rim of the Rayalaseema region, the northern border of the Telugu language region and thus the border of the Dravidian languages in general more or less follows the third zone. In the western highlands the region of the southernmost Indo-Aryan language, Marathi, is situated between the second and the fourth areas. The area between the first and the second zones is a region of a variety of old tribal languages, but this region has been penetrated by the *lingua franca* of the north, Hindi. But Hindi did not manage to penetrate the area beyond the second zone. Not all borders of language regions in India are marked by such thresholds, but the pattern illustrated here shows a remarkable coincidence of environmental conditions with the spread of languages. History and the environment are interdependent and Indian history owes much to an environment which has a highly differentiated structure and which is in some ways extremely generous but can also prove to be very hostile and challenging to those who have to cope with it.

1

EARLY CIVILISATIONS OF THE NORTHWEST

PREHISTORY AND THE INDUS CIVILISATION

When the great cities of Harappa and Mohenjo-Daro were discovered in the 1920s the history of the Indian subcontinent attained a new dimension. The discovery of these centres of the early Indus civilisation was a major achievement of archaeology. Before these centres were known, the Indo-Aryans were regarded as the creators of the first early culture of the subcontinent. They were supposed to have come down to the Indian plains in the second millennium BC. But the great cities of the Indus civilisation proved to be much older, reaching back into the third and fourth millennia. After ancient Egypt and Mesopotamia, this Indus civilisation emerged as the third major early civilisation of mankind.

Harappa and Mohenjo-Daro show a surprising similarity although they were separated by about 350 miles. In each city the archaeologists found an acropolis and a lower city, each fortified separately. The acropolis, situated to the west of each city and raised on an artificial mound made of bricks, contained large assembly halls and edifices which were obviously constructed for religious cults. In Mohenjo-Daro there was a 'Great Bath' (39 by 23 feet, with a depth of 8 feet) at the centre of the acropolis which may have been used for ritual purposes. This bath was connected to an elaborate water supply system and sewers. To the east of this bath there was a big building (about 230 by 78 feet) which is thought to have been a palace either of a king or of a high priest.

A special feature of each of these cities were large platforms which have been interpreted by the excavators as the foundations of granaries. In Mohenjo-Daro it was situated in the acropolis; in Harappa it was immediately adjacent to it. In Mohenjo-Daro this architectural complex, constructed next to the Great Bath, is still particularly impressive. Its foundation, running east to west, was 150 feet long and 75 feet wide. On this foundation were 27 compartments in three rows. The 15-foot walls of these are still extant. These compartments were very well ventilated and, in case they were used as granaries, they could have been filled from outside the acropolis. At Harappa there were some small houses, assumed to be those of workers or slaves, and a large open space between the acropolis and these buildings.

The big lower cities were divided into rectangular areas. In Mohenjo-Daro there were nine such areas, each about 1,200 by 800 feet. Broad main streets, about 30 feet wide, separated these parts of the city from each other. All the houses were connected directly to the excellent sewage system which ran through all the numerous small alleys. Many houses had a spacious interior courtyard and private wells. All houses were built with standardised bricks. The width of each brick was twice as much as its height and its length twice as large as its width.

But it was not only this excellent city planning which impressed the archaeologists, they also found some interesting sculptures and thousands of well-carved seals made of steatite. These seals show many figures and symbols of the religious life of the people of this early culture. There are tree deities among them and there is the famous so-called 'Proto-Shiva' who is seated in the typical pose of a meditating man. He has three heads, an erect phallus, and is surrounded by animals which were also worshipped by the Hindus of a later age. These seals also show evidence of a script which has not yet been deciphered.

Figure 1.1 Mohenjo Daro, the so-called 'Priest King', late third millennium BC
(Courtesy of Georg Helmes, Aachen)

Both cities shared a uniform system of weights and measures based on binary numbers and the decimal system. Articles made of copper and ornaments with precious stones show that there was a flourishing international trade. More evidence for this international trade emerged when seals of the Indus culture were found in Mesopotamia and other seals which could be traced to Mesopotamia were discovered in the cities on the Indus.

Before indigenous sites of earlier stages of the Indus civilisation were excavated it was believed that Harappa and Mohenjo-Daro were merely outposts of the Mesopotamian civilisation, either constructed by migrants or at least designed according to their specifications. These speculations were strengthened by the mention in Mesopotamian sources of countries such as Dilmun, Magan and Meluhha. Dilmun has been identified as Bahrein and Magan seems to be identical with present Oman. Meluhha may have referred to the Indus valley from where Mesopotamia obtained wood, copper, gold, silver, carnelian and cotton.

In analogy to the Mesopotamian precedent, the Indus culture was thought to be based on a theocratic state whose twin capitals Harappa and Mohenjo-Daro obviously showed the traces of a highly centralised organisation. Scholars were also fairly sure of the reasons for the sudden decline of these cities since scattered skeletons which showed traces of violent death were found in the uppermost strata of Mohenjo-Daro. It appeared that men, women and children had been exterminated by conquerors in a 'last massacre'. The conquerors were assumed to be the Aryans who invaded India around the middle of the second millennium BC. Their warrior god, Indra, was, after all, praised as a breaker of forts in many Vedic hymns.

However, after the Second World War, intensive archaeological research in Afghanistan, Pakistan and India greatly enhanced our knowledge of the historical evolution and the spatial extension of the Indus civilisation (see Map 1.1). Earlier assessments of the rise and fall of this civilisation had to be revised. The new excavations showed that this civilisation, at its height early in the late third millennium BC, had encompassed an area larger than western Europe.

In the Indus valley, other important cities of this civilisation, such as Kot Diji to the east of Mohenjo-Daro and Amri in the Dadu District on the lower Indus, were discovered in the years after 1958. In Kathiawar and on the coast of Gujarat similar centres were traced. Thus in 1954 Lothal was excavated south of Ahmadabad. It is claimed that Lothal was a major port of this period. Another 100 miles further south Malwan was also identified in 1967 as a site of the Indus civilisation. It is located close to Surat and so far marks, together with Daimabad in the Ahmadnagar District of Maharashtra, the southernmost extension of this culture. The spread of the Indus civilisation to the east was documented by the 1961 excavations at Kalibangan in Rajasthan about 200 miles west of Delhi. However,

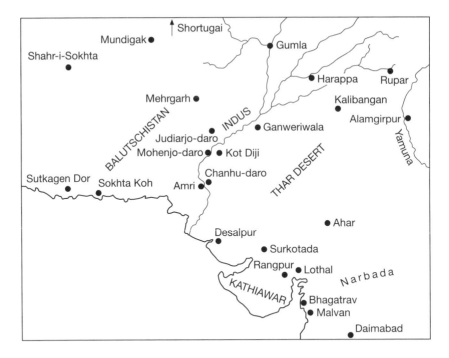

Map 1.1 Indus civilisation

Alamgirpur, in Meerut District in the centre of the Ganga–Yamuna Doab, is considered to mark the farthest extension to the east of this culture. In the north, Rupar in the foothills of the Himalayas is the farthest outpost which is known in India. In the west, traces of this civilisation were found in Baluchistan close to the border of present Iran at Sutkagen Dor. This was probably a trading centre on the route connecting the Indus valley with Mesopotamia. Afghanistan also has its share of Indus civilisation sites. This country was known for its lapis lazuli which was coveted everywhere even in those early times. At Mundigak near Kandahar a palace was excavated which has an impressive façade decorated with pillars. This site, probably one of the earliest settlements in the entire region, is thought to be an outpost of the Indus civilisation. Another one was found more recently further to the north at Shortugai on the Amu Darya.

This amazing extension of our knowledge about the spatial spread of the Indus civilisation was accompanied by an equally successful exploration of its history. Earlier strata of Mohenjo-Daro and Harappa as well as of Kalibangan, Amri and Kot Diji were excavated in a second round of archae-ological research. In this way continuous sequence of strata, showing the gradual development to the high standard of the full-fledged Indus civilisation, was established. These strata have been named Pre-Harappan, Early Harappan, Mature Harappan and Late Harappan. The most important result of this research is the clear proof of the long-term indigenous evolution of this civilisation which obviously began on the periphery of the Indus valley in the hills of eastern Baluchistan and then extended into the plains. There were certainly connections with Mesopotamia, but the earlier hypothesis that the Indus civilisation was merely an extension of Mesopotamian civilisation had to be rejected.

The anatomy of four sites

The various stages of the indigenous evolution of the Indus civilisation can be documented by an analysis of four sites which have been excavated in more recent years: Mehrgarh, Amri, Kalibangan, Lothal. These four sites reflect the sequence of the four important phases in the protohistory of the northwestern region of the Indian subcontinent. The sequence begins with the transition of nomadic herdsmen to settled agriculturists in eastern Baluchistan, continues with the growth of large villages in the Indus valley and the rise of towns, leads to the emergence of the great cities and, finally, ends with their decline. The first stage is exemplified by Mehrgarh in Baluchistan, the second by Amri in the southern Indus valley and the third and fourth by Kalibangan in Rajasthan and by Lothal in Gujarat.

Mehrgarh

Mehrgarh is situated about 150 miles to the northwest of Mohenjo-Daro at the foot of the Bolan Pass which links the Indus valley via Quetta and Kandahar with the Iranian plateau. The site, excavated by French archaeologists since 1974, is about 1,000 yards in diameter and contains seven excavation sites with different strata of early settlements. The oldest mound shows in its upper strata a large Neolithic village which, according to radiocarbon dating, belongs to the sixth millennium BC. The rectangular houses were made of adobe bricks, but ceramics were obviously still unknown to the inhabitants. The most important finds were traces of grain and innumerable flint blades which appear to have been used as sickles for cutting the grain. These clearly establish that some kind of cultivation prevailed in Baluchistan even at that early age. Several types of grain were identified: two kinds of barley, and wheat, particularly emmer. Surprisingly, the same types of grain were found in even lower strata going back to the seventh millennium.

The early transition from hunting and nomadic life to settled agriculture and animal husbandry is documented also by large numbers of animal bones which were found in various Neolithic strata of the site. The oldest strata of the seventh millennium contained mostly remnants of wild animals such as antelopes, wild goats and wild sheep. But in later strata the bones of domesticated animals such as goats, sheep and cows were much more numerous. The domestication of animals must have begun in Baluchistan at about the same time as in western Asia. Sheep were the first animals to be tamed, followed by water buffaloes whose earliest remains, outside China, were discovered here.

Precious items found in the graves of Mehrgarh provide evidence for the existence of a network of long-distance trade even during this early period. There were beads made of turquoise from Persia or central Asia, lapis lazuli from Afghanistan and shells which must have come from the coast 400 miles away.

Next to this oldest mound at Mehrgarh there is another site which contains chalcolithic settlements showing the transition from the Stone Age to the Bronze Age. Ceramics as well as a copper ring and a copper bead were found here. The rise of handicraft is clearly in evidence at this stage. Hundreds of bone awls were found, as well as stones which seem to have been used for sharpening these awls. The uppermost layer of this site contains shards of painted ceramics very similar to those found in a settlement of the fourth millennium (Kili Ghul Mohammad III) near Quetta. When this stage was reached at Mehrgarh the settlement moved a few hundred yards from the older ones. The continuity is documented by finds of the same type of ceramics which characterised the final stage of the second settlement.

In this third phase in the fifth and early fourth millennia skills were obviously much improved and the potter's wheel was introduced to manufacture large amounts of fine ceramics. In this period Mehrgarh seems to have given rise to a technical innovation by introducing a drill moved by means of a bow. The drill was made of green jasper and was used to drill holes into beads made of lapis lazuli, turquoise and cornelian. Similar drills were found at Shahr-i-Sokhta in eastern Iran and at Chanhu-Daro in the Indus valley, but these drills belong to a period which is about one millennium later. Another find at Mehrgarh was that of parts of a crucible for the melting of copper.

At about 3500 BC, the settlement was shifted once more. In this fourth phase ceramics attained major importance. The potters produced large storage jars decorated with geometric patterns as well as smaller receptacles for daily use. Some of the shards are only as thick as an eggshell. Small female figurines made of terracotta were found here and terracotta seals, the earliest precursors of the seals found in the Indus valley, were also found. Mehrgarh must have been inhabited by that time by a well-settled and fairly wealthy population.

The fifth phase of settlement at Mehrgarh started around 3200 BC. The features characteristic of this phase had also been noted in sites in eastern Iran and central Asia. Because not much was known about Baluchistan's protohistory prior to the fourth millennium BC, these features were thought to have derived from those western regions. But the excavations at Mehrgarh show that the early settlers of Baluchistan were not just passive imitators but had actively contributed to the cultural evolution. Long-distance trade certainly contributed to the exchange of cultural achievements in this early period.

The subsequent phases of settlement at Mehrgarh, from about 3000 to 2500 BC and immediately preceding the emergence of Harappa and Mohenjo-Daro, show increasing wealth and urbanisation. A new type of seal with animal symbols, and terracotta figurines of men and women with elaborately dressed hair, seem to reflect a new life style. Artefacts such as the realistic sculpture of a man's head and small, delicately designed figurines foreshadow the later style of Harappan art. The topmost strata of settlements in Mehrgarh are crowded with two-storeyed buildings. Firewood seems to have been scarce in this final period as cow dung was used for fuel, as it still is. Ceramics were produced on such a large scale that archaeologists label it semi-industrial mass production. One kiln was found containing 200 jars which were obviously left there after a mistake had been made in the firing of the kiln.

Sometime around the middle of the third millennium BC the flourishing town of Mehrgarh was abandoned by its inhabitants. However, recent excavations at nearby Nausharo reveal a continuous settlement of population in this area throughout the Harappan period. Towards the end of this period Mehrgarh produced an important graveyard, the cultural assemblage of which shows strong similarities with the culture of central Asia and the famous Cemetery 'H' at Harappa of the early second millennium BC.

Amri

Amri gives us some clues with regard to the transition from the Pre-Harappan to the Mature Harappan culture. This site is located about 100 miles to the south of Mohenjo-Daro on the west bank of the Indus at a point where the hills of Baluchistan are closest to the river. It almost seems as if the people of Amri wanted to keep in touch with the early culture of Baluchistan and considered it as something of a daring venture to settle in the great plains near the river. This new venture was started only about 2,000 years after the early cultures of Baluchistan appeared in places like Mehrgarh. Unlike Mehrgarh, which started in the seventh millennium BC, Amri's earliest strata go back only as far as the early fourth millennium. But Amri and similar sites in the lower Indus valley were inhabited throughout the millennia of the Indus civilisation and, therefore, provide interesting evidence of the cultural evolution in the valley.

The excavations at Amri from 1959 to 1969 were so revealing that the Pre-Harappan culture of the Lower Indus is now referred to as Amri culture.

The four stages of the Indus valley culture are clearly exhibited here at Amri: Pre-Harappan, Early Harappan which is a phase of transition, Mature Harappan and the Jhangar culture which is a regional variation of the Late Harappan. The Pre-Harappan stage at Amri is subdivided into four phases. The earliest phase shows no traces of building but its jars and ceramic shards have patterns related to those of the finds in Baluchistan. There were also some tools made of flint as well as a few items of copper and bronze found. The second and third phases show Amri at the height of its development. Radiocarbon dating points to a period from 3660 to 3020 BC for this flowering of the Amri culture. This coincides with a similar state of development at Mehrgarh. The area of the village had doubled by this time and there were houses constructed of adobe bricks. These houses had interior courtyards and were designed in a more regular fashion as time went by; similarly, the bricks showed a more standardised form. Ceramics were produced on potter's wheels and decorated with geometric patterns of a characteristic style.

Towards the end of this Amri period, there appeared for the first time isolated items with the style characteristic of Early Harappan ceramics. Such items did not, however, replace the indigenous Amri ceramics. This happened only in the Mature Harappan phase at Amri. Probably this new type of ceramics had only been imported into Amri in the Early Harappan period and it was not until the Mature Harappan period that the potters of Amri adopted the style themselves and abandoned their old style altogether. Early in the Mature Harappan period, the new style seems to have come from Mohenjo-Daro and Chanhu-Daro to the Lower Indus, whereas Harappa and Kalibangan stuck to a different northern style. A uniform style, which replaced all regional styles, emerged only at the end of this period, at the height of the Indus civilisation towards the end of the third millennium BC.

The correlation of this stylistic analysis with the pattern of growth and decline of the Amri settlement provides a great deal of insight into the evolution of Indus civilisation. At the beginning of the Early Harappan period, when new influences emanating from Mohenjo-Daro were making themselves felt at Amri, Amri's settled area suffered a remarkable reduction. One of the two mounds of Amri was obviously abandoned at that time. This was followed by a brief period of recuperation when both mounds were occupied. But in the beginning of the Mature Harappan period, when the Amri style was replaced by the style of Mohenjo-Daro, there was another setback and even the main mound was abandoned for some time. In the subsequent phase, Amri was settled again but the smaller mound remained deserted forever. It seems that the rise of Mohenjo-Daro meant a decline for Amri. Perhaps wars and social conflict were at the root of this decline. There are no traces of direct combat at Amri, but there seems to have been some kind of fortification. However, at Kot Diji, a town only

30 miles from Mohenjo-Daro, there were elaborate fortifications even during the Pre-Harappan and Early Harappan periods which ended with a great conflagration in this place. This seems to indicate that the spread of the Mature Harappan culture was accompanied by war and conquest. After the burning down of old Kot Diji there followed a new phase of reconstruction noticeably influenced by Mohenjo-Daro.

Kalibangan

Kalibangan in Panjab experienced a similar upheaval in the latter part of the third millennium. Situated on the then Ghaggar river, this city was next to Harappa and Mohenjo-Daro. What is most interesting about Kalibangan is not its size, but the excellent preservation of its Early Harappan strata. This makes Kalibangan an eminent witness of the circumstances which accompanied the transition from the Early Harappan to the Mature Harappan period.

Kalibangan was founded around 2900 BC and included some features then which later became standard for the cities of the Indus civilisation. For instance, it was a planned city of rectangular shape, about 750 feet long and following a north–south axis. The city was fortified and the houses were constructed with adobe bricks of 10 by 20 by 30 centimetres. The sewerage system was constructed with regular bricks fired in a kiln. Kalibangan's ceramics produced on the potter's wheel were of excellent quality and nicely decorated, their patterns being clearly different from those of the subsequent period. But since this early Kalibangan had so many features similar to those of the later Mature Harappan period some scholars refer to it as Early Harappan rather than Pre-Harappan. Nevertheless this first city of Kalibangan is clearly characterised by a regional style of its own.

Sometime around 2650 BC, when the expansion of the Mature Harappan culture started, Kalibangan was abandoned for reasons which are not yet known. It was reconstructed only 50 to 100 years later and its new pattern reflected the design of Harappa and Mohenjo-Daro. Now for the first time there was a clear distinction in Kalibangan between an acropolis and a separate lower town. The acropolis was built on the ruins of old Kalibangan which had become partly covered by sand. The lower town was situated at a distance of about 120 feet from the acropolis and was about four times larger than old Kalibangan. The acropolis was divided by a wall, the southern part containing what seem to be public and religious buildings, and the northern part, the residential quarters of the dignitaries. The lower city was planned on the same regular pattern as the lower cities of Mohenjo-Daro and Harappa. In fact, standards were extremely rigid: the various streets of the city had a width of 12, 18 or 24 feet according to their relative importance. The bricks, which had been made to strict specifications even in old Kalibangan, were now fashioned according to the uniform measure of Harappa and Mohenjo-Daro (7.5 by 15 by 30 cm).

A special feature of New Kalibangan was a third smaller natural mound at a distance of about 240 feet from the lower city. This mound contained only remnants of fire altars. Perhaps it was a religious centre for the people of the lower city whereas the altars of the acropolis were reserved for its residents. Only further research will provide answers to such questions. The absence of mother goddess figurines in Kalibangan is peculiar, since these goddesses were ubiquitous in all other centres of the Indus civilisation.

New Kalibangan seems to have flourished without interruption until the eighteenth century BC. After a brief period of decline, the inhabitants abandoned the city in the seventeenth century BC. The reasons for its decline seem to be rather obvious: the Ghaggar river had dried up and thus the city lost its agricultural base.

Lothal

The fourth site whose anatomy we want to examine is Lothal near Ahmadabad which is presumed to be the great port of its age. Lothal was founded much later than the other three settlements discussed so far. Construction began here around 2200 BC during the Mature Harappan period. Lothal had the features typical of all towns of the Indus civilisation. Its acropolis was built on a high platform, about 150 by 120 feet, but its city walls surrounded both the lower city and the acropolis. The pattern of streets and alleys was the same as that of Mohenjo-Daro and Harappa.

But Lothal had a unique feature: a large basin, 770 feet long, about 120 feet wide and 15 feet deep, east of the city. The walls were made of hard bricks and had two openings which are believed to have been sluice gates. Four large round stones with holes in their middles were found at the bottom of the basin. It is thought they may have served as anchors for ships which used this basin as a dock. A raised platform between the basin and the city also seems to indicate that this was the dock of a major port, an emporium of trade between the Indus civilisation and Mesopotamia. Critics have doubted this interpretation and have pointed out that the 'dock' may have been a water reservoir which served the city and was also used for irrigating the neighbouring fields. But, regardless of the use of this basin, there seems to be no doubt that Lothal was an important trading centre and a major sea port.

Many tools, stone beads and seals were found in Lothal, among them the famous 'Persian Gulf seal'. Probably Lothal not only served long-distance trade but also supplied the cities on the Indus with raw materials such as cotton from Gujarat and copper from Rajasthan. This would explain why Lothal was founded at a rather late stage when the demand for these raw materials was at its height in Harappa and Mohenjo-Daro.

Although Lothal must have been an important entrepôt, it was not a very large city, only about 900 feet long and 750 feet wide. Its size was thus akin to that of later emporia in the classical period of Indian history. There are no traces here at Lothal of the crisis which had begun to affect the other cities of the Indus civilisation by the beginning of the second millennium BC. But Lothal did not survive the final decline of those cities. Around 1850 BC there was a reduction of the settled area of the town. Perhaps this was due to a decline in the demand for Lothal's products in the great cities on the Indus. This reduction of the settled area was accompanied by a pattern of wild construction when the earlier standards of planning were violated. The end of Lothal came around 1700 BC, at a time when the other great cities were also doomed.

Conclusions

What are the conclusions about the Indus civilisation and its great cities which can be derived from this study of four sites? The new excavations at Mehrgarh show that in this area of Baluchistan there was a continuous cultural evolution from the seventh millennium BC throughout the subsequent five millennia. Earlier it was thought that this evolution started in Baluchistan only in the fifth millennium, but now we must conclude that the transition from nomadic life to settled agriculture occurred in Baluchistan simultaneously with the transition in Iran.

The excavations of Amri show that the decisive step towards the establishment of settlements in the Indus valley was made in the fourth millennium and that it was an extension of indigenous developments and not a mere transfer of a cultural pattern by migrants from Mesopotamia, Iran or central Asia. The discovery of Neolithic settlements in Baluchistan has led to the conclusion that the Indus civilisation was the outcome of an indigenous evolution which started in the northwest of the Indian subcontinent. The many settlements of the fourth millennium which have been traced in recent years provide added evidence for this new hypothesis.

The rise of indigenous crafts obviously led to an increase in long-distance trade with central and western Asia but this trade did not have the unilateral effect of cultural borrowing as an earlier generation of scholars had thought – scholars who were naturally puzzled by the discovery of a mature civilisation which did not seem to have any local antecedents.

Whereas we do have a much clearer idea of the indigenous roots of the Indus civilisation by now, we still know very little about the rise of the specific Mature Harappan culture. The exact date of its rise is still a matter of debate. The dates 2600 to 2500 BC, suggested by those who first excavated the great cities, have not been revised so far, although recent research suggests that the most mature stage of this civilisation is probably limited to 2300 to 2000 BC. Where and how this stage was first attained still remains a puzzle. The archaeologists who initially excavated the two great cities were not very careful about establishing the stratigraphy of the various settlements. Moreover, Mohenjo-Daro, the most important site, is badly affected by groundwater which covers the earliest strata. The original foundations of Mohenjo-Daro are now approximately 24 feet below the groundwater level. The rising of the groundwater level was, presumably, one of the reasons for the decline of that city and it also makes it impossible to unravel the secrets of its birth. This is why it is necessary to excavate parallel strata in other sites of the Indus civilisation which are more accessible and whose age can be found out by means of radiocarbon dating. Future excavations at the newly discovered but yet unexplored vast site of Ganweriwala halfway between Mohenjo-Daro and Kalibangan may lead to new discoveries.

Excavations of Amri and Kot Diji on the Lower Indus show that a new type of ceramic made its appearance there around 2600 BC – a type unknown in Kalibangan at that time. This new type of ceramic and the culture connected with it seem to have arisen at Mohenjo-Daro. Changes in the pattern of settlement reaching from extinction at Mehrgarh to a reduction at Amri and fortification and conflagration at Kot Diji may have been due to this rise of Mohenjo-Daro. The Upper Indus region, Panjab and Rajasthan, with their later centres at Harappa and Kalibangan, were not yet affected by this early development in the south. But they shared the cultural period referred to as Early Harappan.

State formation in Mohenjo-Daro, Harappa and Kalibangan was probably not uniform at this stage, each centre serving as an independent capital of its particular region. But then from about 2500 BC onwards there is evidence for a striking uniformity of all these centres. This was probably achieved at the cost of war and conquest. The sudden extinction of early Kalibangan around 2550 BC and its reconstruction in the uniform Harappan style about 50 to 100 years later seem to point to this conclusion. There was also a spurt of fortification at Harappa at that time where some city gates were completely closed with bricks. Kot Diji witnessed a second conflagration around 2520 BC from which it never recovered. But Lothal and several other settlements which have been found in recent years can also be traced to the Mature Harappan phase of rapid expansion and uniform construction.

All this evidence seems to support the conclusion that this period witnessed a new phase of 'imperial state formation' in southern Asia. Mohenjo-Daro was probably the capital of this earliest state in south Asia which might already have developed certain features of an early empire. Harappa and Kalibangan as subsidiary centres may have enjoyed some regional autonomy; perhaps Mohenjo-Daro held sway over the whole region only for a relatively short period. If this interpretation of the evidence is correct, state formation in the Indus valley proceeded along similar lines as that in the Ganges valley some 1,500 years later. In the Ganges valley, too, state formation in some nuclear areas preceded the establishment of a larger regional context until one of the centres emerged as the imperial capital. But all such questions about early state formation in the Indus valley cannot be finally settled until the script on the Indus seals is deciphered.

The secret of the decline: a change of climate?

Recent research has not only shed more light on the antecedents of the Indus civilisation, it has also helped to explain the reasons for its sudden decline. All excavations support the conclusion that this decline occurred rather suddenly between 1800 and 1700 BC, but they do not support the theory of a violent end as no traces of 'last massacres' were found in any of the centres, apart from Mohenjo-Daro. Moreover, recent research has also exculpated the Vedic Aryans; they most probably arrived in the Indus valley only centuries after its great cities had been extinguished. The excavations have revealed many striking symptoms of endogenous decay in those cities during the Late Harappan period. Some settlements seem to have been abandoned rather suddenly, which would explain why kitchen utensils have been found scattered around fireplaces. Other places were resettled for a short period in a rather rudimentary fashion, before they were finally abandoned. The archaeologists call this the squatter period because there was no planning any longer, broken bricks were used for construction and no attention was paid to a proper sewerage system. There are traces of this period at Kalibangan, Amri and Lothal. But there are no such traces in Mohenjo-Daro and Harappa, perhaps because their last inhabitants simply died out or were exterminated by marauders as in Mohenjo-Daro's 'last massacre'. But the decline of the big cities was obviously due not only to the raids of marauders, but also to other forces, against which man was helpless.

Research in different disciplines has led to the conclusion that the decline of the Indus civilisation was precipitated by a great change in environmental conditions which set in at the beginning of the second millennium BC. Geologists have pointed out tectonic changes which may have thrown up a kind of dam in the lower Indus valley, thus inundating a large part of the plains. This would explain the existence of thick layers of silt in the upper strata of Mohenjo-Daro which are now about 39 feet above the level of the river. Such inundations moreover would have provided an ideal setting for endemic malaria in the Indus plains. The tectonic changes may have caused a very different situation in the plains of the eastern Ghaggar river with its flourishing cities of Kalibangan and Ganweriwala and hundreds of smaller Harappan sites. Apparently it was during this period that the Yamuna river which originally had been flowing into the Ghaggar river shifted its ancient course to its present course in the Ganga–Yamuna Doab.

The annual flooding of the Ghaggar, the life spring of the eastern cities of the Harappans, was thus reduced in a dangerous way. Other scientists have suggested ecological reasons for the decline of the great civilisation: over-grazing, and deforestation caused by the operation of innumerable fireplaces and kilns for firing bricks.

Palaeobotanical research in Rajasthan may provide another amazing explanation of the decline of the Indus civilisation. According to these findings there was a slight increase of rainfall and vegetation in the Indus region in the sixth millennium, and during the third millennium there was a sudden and steep rise in rainfall which reached its peak around 2500 BC. But by the end of the third millennium this rainfall had receded as rapidly as it had increased, and by about 1800 to 1500 BC it had come down to a level well below that of 3000 BC. There was another slight increase of rainfall between 1500 and 1000 BC then it decreased once more. The period around 400 BC was probably one of the driest periods of all. Subsequently, rainfall became more abundant but never again reached the peak which it had attained around 2500 BC. The last 2,000 years up to the present have witnessed a pattern of rainfall and vegetation in southern Asia which conforms to a mean value between the extremes of 2500 and 400 BC.

It is fascinating to see the course of history in the context of these findings. The rise and fall of the Indus civilisation could thus have been strongly influenced by changes in climate, and even the immigration of the Vedic Aryans and their settlement in the northern Indus region could then be attributed to the renewed increase of rainfall and vegetation in the period after 1500 BC. Similarly the decline of the fortunes of the Aryans in that region after 1000 BC and their movement eastwards into the Ganges valley could be explained by means of these climatological data. The dry period would have made the jungles of the Gangetic plains penetrable and when the climate improved again after 500 BC the migrants would have already established their footholds along the Ganges and have started cutting and burning the forest, thus reclaiming fertile lands for agriculture. The improvement of the climate would then have contributed to the second wave of urbanisation which started in south Asia at that time. But only more detailed palaeobotanical research can prove that these hypotheses derived from the findings in Rajasthan are applicable to other regions of southern Asia as well.

In addition to changes in climate and perhaps an inundation caused by a tectonic upheaval, there seem also to have been socio-economic factors which contributed to the decline of the great civilisation. At their height around 2200 BC, the centres of this civilisation had become far removed from their agricultural roots and yet they were more dependent than ever on the land's produce. The traces of destruction at Kot Diji and the abandonment and reconstruction of Kalibangan show that in their prime the great cities were obviously able to hold sway over a vast hinterland. But a perennial control of trade routes and of the agricultural base would have required the maintenance of a large army and of a host of administrators. The excavations have shown no evidence for the existence of such armies. The agricultural surplus of the countryside was probably used for trade or for some kind of religious obligations. Thus, the cities depended on the well-being of their immediate hinterland, and their size was a direct correlate of the agricultural surplus available to them.

When the climate changed and agricultural production declined, the cities were probably in no position to appropriate surplus from farther afield. Under such conditions the people simply had to leave the city and this reduction of the population may have had an accelerating effect on the decline of the cities, the big cities being affected by it earlier and more severely than the smaller ones. Perhaps some inhabitants of the big cities in the Indus valley may have migrated to the new and smaller towns on the periphery, such as the towns of Gujarat. But with the decline of the centres the peripheral outposts also lost their importance and became dependent on their immediate hinterland only. In this way some of the smaller places like Amri and Lothal survived for a few generations in the Post-Harappan time when the big cities were already extinct. Finally these smaller places also lapsed back to the stage of simple villages as urban life had lost its sustenance. This was not a unique event in south Asian social and political development. History repeated itself when the flourishing cities of northern and central India, for instance, Kausambi, started to decline around AD 200 as long-distance trade, the most important factor in their rise, disappeared. It was only several centuries later that the medieval cities, capitals of kings or pilgrimage centres with great temples, signalled a new phase of urbanisation.

IMMIGRATION AND SETTLEMENT OF THE INDO-ARYANS

The second millennium BC witnessed another major historical event in the early history of the south Asian subcontinent after the rise and fall of the Indus civilisation: a semi-nomadic people which called itself *Arya* in its sacred hymns came down to the northwestern plains through the mountain passes of Afghanistan. In 1786 Sir William Jones, the founder of the Asiatic Society of Calcutta, discovered the close relationship between Sanskrit, the language of these Indo-Aryans, and Greek, Latin, German and Celtic languages. His epoch-making discovery laid the foundation for a systematic philological study of the Indo-European family of languages which as we know by now includes many more members than Jones had once assumed. The serious scholarship of the early philologists who discovered these linguistic affinities was later on overshadowed by nationalists who tried to identify the speakers of these ancient languages with modern nations whose origins were to be traced to a mythical Aryan race. In the late nineteenth century, scholars had already agreed that the original home of the Aryans could be traced to the steppes of eastern Europe and central Asia. But in the twentieth century nationalist German historians and also, more recently, Indian nationalists have staked out a claim for their respective countries as the original home of the Aryans. In India this has become a major issue in contemporary historiography.

During the last decades intensive archaeological research in Russia and the central Asian Republics of the former Soviet Union, as well as in Pakistan and northern India, has considerably enlarged our knowledge about the potential ancestors of the Indo-Aryans and their relationship with cultures in west, central and south Asia. Excavations in southern Russia and central Asia convinced the international community of archaeologists that the Eurasian steppes had once been the original home of the speakers of Indo-European language. Since the fourth millennium BC their culture was characterised by the domestication of horses and cattle and by the use of copper and bronze tools and weapons and horse-drawn chariots with spoked wheels. In the third millennium BC this 'Kurgan culture' (named after a special type of grave) spread from the steppes in the west of the Ural eastwards into central Asia. Tribes of this nomadic population located in the area of present-day Kasakhstan which belonged to the timber-grave culture are now considered to be the ancestors of the Indo-Iranian peoples. By the end of the third millennium the Indo-Aryan tribes seem to have separated from their Iranian 'brothers'.

Although the eventual arrival of the Iranian and the Indo-Aryan speaking people in Iran and northwest India is well documented by their respective sacred hymns of the Avesta and Veda, the details and the chronology of their migrations from central Asia are still a matter of controversy among archaeologists, historians and scholars of Indo-Iranian languages. In recent years the 'Aryan question' has given rise to a heated debate among Indian historians as some of them have claimed that the Aryans and the Indo-European family of languages have originated in India and that the Indus civilisation was an Aryan one. Other historians defend the position that the Aryans have been immigrants, but they nowadays tend to agree that there may have been several waves of Aryan immigration. Earlier historians had believed that there was a clearly indentifiable gap of about five centuries (eighteenth to thirteenth centuries BC) between the end of the Indus civilisation and the coming of the Aryans. These scholars concentrated their attention on the Vedic Aryans, but more recent archaeological research has changed our knowledge about this period nearly as dramatically as in the case of our knowledge about the antecedents of the Indus civilisation. The alleged gap between Late Harappan and Early Vedic India is no longer considered to be as clearly defined as it used to be. On the one hand it becomes more and more clear that in some regions of southern Asia Late Harappan traits continued right up to the Early Vedic period, whereas, on the other hand, 'intrusive elements' which are ascribed to early Indo-Aryan migrations into south Asia can be traced in Late Harappan sites. Excavations in Baluchistan (e.g. Mehrgarh VIII and nearby Nausharo III) brought to light a considerable number of new cultural elements around 2000 BC. These findings indicate a close relationship with the contemporary Bronze Age culture of Greater Iran which is known from archaeological sites like Namazga V in southern Turkmenistan and Teppe Hissar III in northwest Iran. This culture may have been controlled by a semi-nomadic elite which is assumed to have belonged to the speakers of the Indo-Iranian languages.

Among the 'intrusive traits' which appear in Late Harappan strata the keeping of horses has to be mentioned which was obviously unknown in the Harappan civilisation before c.2000 BC, as horses were never depicted on its seals. Indian archaeologists claim that there is evidence for fire altars (which were also unknown in Mature Harappan cities) in the upper strata of late Kalibangan and Lothal. New burial rites and offerings of precious items and even treasures are yet another new element which indicates a close relationship with the central Asian and Iranian area. Perhaps the most beautiful item of this kind is the wonderful gold treasure of Quetta – not too far away from Mehrgarh – which was found in 1985 during the construction of a hotel and which shows a clear correspondence with similar items found in Bactria. Of crucial importance among these 'intrusive traits' is the pottery found in cemetery H in Harappa as its painting is totally different from earlier pottery at Harappa. Vats, the excavator of this site, expressed in the 1930s the opinion that these drawings may indicate a Vedic belief in the transmigration of souls and rebirth. However, in view of the much later date of the early Vedas (1300–1000 BC) which had been generally accepted, Vats' idea was rejected by most scholars at that time. But in view of recent findings in Late Harappan strata more and more archaeologists 'are inclined to agree' (Allchin 1995) with Vats' assumption. But if this were correct one would have to think of an earlier date for the Rigveda, too.

In case the Indo-Aryan identity of the people of these early migrations in the early second millennium BC could really be proven, it is evident that some Indo-Aryan groups must have come into a direct and even active contact with the urban civilisation of the Indus cities which was still flourishing at that time. Such an identification however does not necessarily imply that these early Indo-Aryans have to be regarded as the direct ancestors of the (later) Rigvedic people. As will be discussed below, the Rigveda, the oldest Vedic text, reflects a socio-economic and cultural context which does not show any evidence of urban life. Scholars who accept an Indo-Aryan identity of these early central Asian migrants in the Late Harappan period therefore assume that these early carriers of the 'Greater Iranian Bronze Age Culture' (Parpola) were soon absorbed by the Indus civilisation. This hypothesis is corroborated by the observation that the traces of these carriers of the central Asian and Iranian Bronze Age end in northwest India around the sixteenth or fifteenth century BC. However, this 'absorbed' population may have become the upholder of an Indo-Aryan cultural synthesis, combining Indo-Harappan (and therefore perhaps also Dravidian) elements with their central Asian Aryan heritage. It is quite likely that this population was responsible for the continuity of certain traits of Harappan civilisation like the worship of animals and trees which changed and enriched the Vedic culture during the subsequent two millennia.

However, the first clearly documented historical evidence of these Vedic Aryans comes neither from central Asia nor from India but from upper Mesopotamia and Anatolia. About 1380 BC a Mitanni king concluded a treaty with the Hittite ruler Suppiluliuma I in which the Vedic gods Mitra, Varuna, Indra and the Nasatyas were invoked. Moreover, among the tablets which were excavated at Boghazköy, the Hittite capital, a manual about horse training was found which contains a large number of pure Sanskrit words. There can be no doubt about the very direct cultural and linguistic relationship of the ruling elite of the Mitanni kingdom with the Vedic Aryans in India. But this does not necessarily mean that these 'West Asian Vedic Aryans' originated from India. It is more likely that Vedic tribes started more or less simultaneously separate migrations from their mutual homelands in southern central Asia to India and west Asia. As in the case of the Vedic Aryans in India, their 'brothers' in western Asia, too, appear to have had some earlier Aryan predecessors. In the early sixteenth century BC, the names of the Kassite rulers of Babylon may have been of Aryan origin, but they show no link with Sanskrit, the language of Vedic Aryans.

The arrival of several groups of a new population in southern Asia which were speakers of Indo-European languages therefore can be dated quite safely in the first half of the second millennium around 2000 to 1400 BC. The terminal points in time of these movements were, on the one hand, the 'intrusive traits' in Late Harappan strata which indicate a close relationship with the central Asian and Iranian Bronze Age culture of the Namazga V period and, on the other hand, the Rigveda as the oldest Vedic text in India which clearly reveals a semi-nomadic 'post-urban' civilisation. Linguistically and culturally the Rigveda is directly linked with the fourteenth-century evidence from west Asia. But due to a few references to iron, the latest portions of the Rigveda cannot be much older than the eleventh century BC when iron was in use in southern Asia.

The general chronological framework of these migrations has thus been considerably extended in the course of the last decades. But a large number of questions still remain unsettled. This is particularly true with regard to the cultural and historical background of the migration of the Vedic Aryans. Their early hymns do not contain any reference to toponyms of central Asia or Iran while they do mention some names of rivers in eastern Afghanistan and the Northwest Frontier Provinces of Pakistan, e.g. the Kubha and Suvastu rivers which are now known as Kabul and Swat rivers. In this region archaeologists have traced the 'Gandharan Grave Culture' with distinctive traits of new burial rites, fire altars, horses and the use of bronze and copper. But in this case, too, archaeologists are divided on the issue whether these findings can be ascribed to the early pre-Rigvedic Aryans or already to groups of Vedic Aryans who were on their way to the plains of the Indus valley. In this respect the earlier verdict of scholars, who pointed out that there is as yet no evidence which permits us to identify separate pre-Vedic and Vedic waves of migration, is still correct. The Vedic texts, and in particular the Rigveda, still remain our major source concerning the early phases of Vedic culture in northwest India. But we always have to keep in mind that these texts express the priestly world-view of the Brahmins. A critical analysis of these texts will nevertheless provide detailed information about the daily life of the Vedic Age.

The Vedas as a mirror of historical experience

The Vedas are the most important source of information about the Vedic Aryans and at the same time their greatest cultural achievement. This treasure of sacred literature encompasses four categories of texts: holy words (*mantra*), commentaries on the sacrificial rituals (*brahmana*), esoteric philosophical treatises (*upanishad*) and the instructions for rituals, etc. (*sutra*). These categories also reflect the stages of development of this sacred literature in the various phases of cultural evolution and settlement of the Indo-Aryans from their first migration into the plains of the northwest to the reclamation of land in the Ganges valley and the establishment of their first little kingdoms in the sixth century BC.

The dating of these texts and of the cultures that produced them has been debated for a long time by Indologists. The famous Indian nationalist, Bal Gangadhar Tilak, wrote a book on *The Arctic Home of the Vedas* in which he maintained that the Vedas could be dated back to the sixth or fifth millennium BC. He based his conclusions on the interpretation of references to positions of the stars in the text which could be used by astronomers for a detailed calculation of the respective date. The German Indologist Hermann Jacobi independently arrived at a very similar conclusion and suggested the middle of the fifth millennium as the date of the Vedas. It is interesting to note the degree of conformity of these dates with the results of modern archaeology about the origin and age of the Indo-European language family. But another German Indologist, Max Müller, who was teaching at Oxford, projected a much later date. He took the birth of the

Buddha around 500 BC as a point of departure and suggested that the Upanishads, which antedate Buddhist philosophy, must have been produced around 800 to 600 BC. The earlier Brahmana and Mantra texts of the Vedas would then have been produced around 1000 to 800 and 1200 to 1000 BC respectively. Max Müller's chronology of the Vedic literature is still more or less accepted by Indologists, although the date of the Rigveda is extended from 1300 to 1000 BC.

The texts of the Vedas were believed to have originated by divine inspiration and, therefore, they were transmitted orally from one generation of Brahmin priests to another in a most faithful and accurate manner. These well-preserved ancient texts are thus a fairly reliable source of the history of the Vedic period. This is particularly true of the Mantra texts which are regarded in the West as the Vedas as such, whereas in India the Brahmanas, Upanishads and Sutras are also considered to be integral parts of the Vedas. The Mantra texts consist of four collections (*samhita*): Rigveda, Samaveda, Yajurveda and Atharvaveda. The Rigveda is thought to be the most ancient and most sacred text. It is also the best source of information on the daily life of the Vedic Aryans, their struggles and aspirations, their religious and philosophical ideas.

The Rigveda contains 1,028 hymns with, altogether, 10,600 verses which are collected in ten books or cycles of songs (*mandala*). Books II–VII are considered to be the most ancient ones; they are also called 'family books' because they were produced by certain families of sages. Books I and X were composed at a later stage. Book X contains a great deal of philosophical reflection as well as evidence of the caste system which is missing in the earlier books. The early hymns contain older traditions of the migration period but the main corpus was composed when the Vedic culture was still confined to northwestern India and in the Panjab. Later hymns which had their origin probably in the Brahmana period of the first centuries of the first millennium BC reflect an advanced stage of socio-economic development in the Ganga–Yamuna Doab.

The victories of the Vedic people over the indigenous population of northwestern India must have been due to their fast two-wheeled chariots, especially helpful in this dry and flat region, which were also used by other conquerors in western Asia. The wheels of these chariots were so valuable that the chariots were sometimes transported on bullock carts in order to keep them in good condition for their strategic use on the battlefields. In spite of their strategic superiority the Vedic people did not sweep across the Indian plains in a quick campaign of universal conquest. They extended their area of settlement only very slowly. This may have been due to environmental conditions as well as to the resistance of the indigenous people. Moreover, the Vedic Aryans were not the disciplined army of one great conqueror. They consisted of several tribes which frequently fought each other. But the dark-skinned indigenous people who are referred to as Dasas or Dasyus in the Vedic texts were depicted as the ubiquitous foes of the Aryans. They defended themselves in fortified places (*purah*, a word which later referred to a town). These places were surrounded by palisades or walls. Many Vedic hymns praise the chief god of the Aryans, Indra, as a breaker of forts (*purandara*):

> Armed with his bolt and trusting in his prowess he wandered shattering the forts of Dasas.
> Cast thy dart, knowing, Thunderer, at the Dasyu; increase the Arya's might and glory, Indra . . .
>
> See this abundant wealth that he possesses, and put your trust in Indra's hero vigour.
> He found the cattle and he found the horses, he found the plants, the forests and the waters.
>
> (I, 104)[1]

A prominent enemy of the Vedic Aryans seems to have been the Dasa Shambara, whom Indra 'hurled down from a mountain' (VI, 26), whose 'ninety-nine walls he smashed' (VI, 47). In another hymn, a 'hundred stone forts' (IV, 30) are said to have belonged to Shambara. Agni, the fire god of the Aryans and a great patron of the Brahmins who invited him to the sacrificial fire, was also of as much help to them as the mighty Indra. When it is said that Agni weakened 'the walls with his weapons' (VII, 6), this can only mean that wooden fortifications were consumed by fire, with which Agni was identified. The Vedic tribe of the Purus seems to have been particularly successful in this kind of warfare, since one hymn (VII, 5) says:

> For fear of thee forth fled the dark-hued races, scattered abroad, deserting their possessions, when glowing. O Vaisvanara, for Puru, thou, Agni, didst light up and rend their castles . . .
>
> Thou drivest Dasyus from their home, O Agni, and broughtest forth broad light to light the Arya.

But the Vedic Aryans did not only fight the Dasyus, they also fought among themselves because each of their tribes had to defend itself against other tribes – Aryans who came at a later stage and coveted the land which the others had taken away from the Dasyus. On the banks of the river Hariyupiya near the border of Afghanistan a battle was fought between two tribes in which 130 knights in armour were killed. Also, two hymns of the Rigveda (VII, 18 and 33) report a 'Battle of Ten Kings'. This seems to have been a fight between two Vedic tribal confederations. King Sudasa, who belonged to the famous Bharatas, was victorious with the help of Indra, after his enemies had tried in vain to defeat him by opening embankments and causing an inundation.

It is interesting that in this context seven forts of Sudasa's enemies are mentioned although the early Vedic hymns are otherwise silent about Vedic fortifications. At the most there were some fortified shelters for the cows (*gomati-pur*) because cattle was the most precious property of the Aryans.

The antecedents of King Sudasa who is so often mentioned in these hymns are not quite clear. His father's name is given as Divodasa. Another king called Trasadasyu also appears in these hymns and is praised as a great patron of Vedic poets and as a devotee of Indra. The appearance of the terms *dasa* and *dasyu* in these names raises the question whether some tribes of this people had already joined the Vedic Aryans at that time and may have even served as their guides in the course of their immigration. Recently the Finnish Indologist and historian A. Parpola proposed the interesting theory that the Dasas originally belonged to the early pre-Vedic Aryans of southern central Asia. Their names seem to indicate a relationship with Old Iranian in which an etymologically identical ethnic name *daha* is known and *dahyu* has the meaning of 'land'. The Vedic Aryans may have encountered these *daha/dasa* people already in Margiana and Bactria and later on in northwestern India where some of them had already mixed with the indigenous population. This assumption would help to explain the otherwise contradictory evidence that, on the one hand, these Dasas are described in the Rigveda in disdainful words and, on the other hand, some of their chiefs, like the famous Sudasa, are highly praised as allies of the Vedic Aryans whose language they seem to have understood.

The world-view of the migrant Vedic people was simplistic – a characteristic of early cultures. Land and food seem to have been abundant in the early period, because the texts do not mention any problems of scarcity unlike those of later periods when these problems did emerge. With the help of Indra one could always take away from the Dasyus whatever was in short supply. Only the bards were worried about patrons and competitors:

> Bring us the wealth that men require, a manly master of a house, free-handed with the liberal meed.
>
> (VI, 53)

> Let none of thy worshippers delay thee far away from us. Even from far away come thou unto our feast, or listen if already here.
>
> For here, like flies on honey, these who pray to thee sit by the juice that they have poured.
>
> Wealth-craving singers have on Indra set their hope, as men set foot upon a car.
>
> (VII, 32)

The early texts also do not reflect any preoccupation with the meaning of life. It was enough to praise Indra's incessant quest for victory and his enormous thirst for inebriating soma which must have been a very potent drink. A poetic vein appears in the hymns of the Rigveda whenever they are devoted to Ushas, the goddess of the morning dawn:

> With changing tints she gleams in double splendour while from the eastward she displays her body. She travels perfectly the path of Order, nor fails to reach, as one who knows, the quarters.
> As conscious that her limbs are bright with bathing, she stands, as 'twere, erect that we may see her.

(V, 80)

The expansion of Aryan settlements

During the period in which the Rigveda attained its final form the Vedic population extended its settlements from the northwestern mountain passes through which they had descended all the way into the western part of the Ganga–Yamuna Doab. The Yamuna is mentioned twice in the earlier parts of the Rigveda but the Ganga only once in Book X which is supposed to be the latest book of the Rigveda. The Panjab with the Saraswati river seems to have been the heartland of Vedic settlement for quite some time. They held the rivers in high esteem and praised their god for having bestowed this boon upon them: 'Thou hast discovered rivers for the tribes of men' (VI, 61). The river Saraswati on whose banks the Harappan city of Kalibangan had once flourished was considered especially to be sacred, but its 'Seven Sisters' were also praised.

In this land of the rivers the Vedic Aryans obviously made the transition from a semi-nomadic life to settled agriculture. This transition was accompanied by constant fights. Many hymns report the quest for better land or better access to water: 'When two opposing hosts contend in battle for seed and offspring, waters, kine or corn-land' (VI, 25). Stealing cattle seems to have been a popular pastime in those days, because the term *goshati* (getting cattle) was synonymous with warfare. But such fights were probably not just an expression of an aggressive temperament, they may have reflected an increasing pressure on the land. The jungles must still have been impenetrable at that time and this is why the texts mention 'the great struggle for water and sun' (VI, 46) and record a prayer to Indra that he may grant 'undivided fallow land' (VI, 28). After centuries of nomadic life the Vedic Aryans now began to cultivate fertile but semi-arid areas by means of river irrigation and also started to clear the jungle wherever this was possible. The Rigveda reports: 'They made fair fertile fields, they brought the rivers. Plants spread over the desert, waters filled the hollows' (IV, 33).

The cultivation of irrigated arid lands must have been easier than the clearing of dense jungles – a task avoided even by the indigenous people. Of course, the method of slash-and-burn cultivation was known, and Agni, the fire god, was praised for helping them in this endeavour. But this method did not mean a permanent clearing of the jungle. The trees would sprout again and the coveted 'undivided fallow land' could not be acquired in this way. For this, strong axes and ploughs were required. It is not yet known to what extent the immigrant Aryans possessed bronze and copper which had been in common use during the Indus civilisation. However, such metals were better suited for the making of ornaments and arrowheads than for axes and ploughs. The extension of regular cultivation in the Gangetic plains was therefore impossible before iron was used on a large scale.

The Rigveda mentions iron in texts which are thought to date back to the eleventh century BC. This correlates very well with recent archaeological research which dates the first use of iron in northwestern India to the same age. Earlier parts of the Rigveda contain only isolated references to iron as the 'neck' of the tip of an arrow (VI, 75) and as an axe (VI, 8). But references to iron and to the clearing of the forest with iron axes increase in the texts of the period after 1000 BC. The last book of the Rigveda contains a striking example: 'The deities approached, they carried axes; splitting the wood they came with their servants' (X, 28). This seems to be a clear indication of the beginning of a systematic clearing of the jungle. But excavations in northern India have unfortunately not yet produced tangible evidence of this use of iron. The metal seems to have remained rather scarce and was mainly reserved for weapons; axes have not yet been found at all.

The early period of settled agriculture of the Vedic society is generally referred to as the Late Vedic age. Settled life produced a great deal of social change, of intensified conflict with the indigenous population and of internal stratification of the Aryan society itself. Trade and crafts increased, small territorial principalities with small residencies arose, and there was a flowering of philosophical thought. There can be no doubt that the Indian society of the middle of the last millennium BC was fundamentally different from that of the Early Vedic age. This Late Vedic age was in many respects the formative phase of Indian culture.

The transition from semi-nomadic life to settled agriculture in the Late Vedic age after 1000 BC is illustrated by the changing meaning of the term *grama*, which nowadays means 'village' in most Indo-Aryan languages. The German Indologist Wilhelm Rau, who has analysed Late Vedic text for evidence of social and political change in this period, has shown that the word grama originally referred to a nomadic group, its train of vehicles and its band of warriors. The train of vehicles obviously formed a ring or barricade of wagons whenever the group took a rest. This would explain why in one Brahmana text it is mentioned that 'the two ends of the grama came together'.[2] It is also significant that the word *samgrama*, which still means 'war' today, is related to this term. Samgrama must have originally meant a meeting (*sam* – together) of two or more grama, which in the social context of those days always meant a fight. When the Vedic people settled down they moved from carts into houses and the word grama came to refer to a village rather than to a train of vehicles. It is characteristic that in all Rigvedic texts grama still means a train of vehicles or group of warriors and only in the Brahmana texts does it mean a village.

Social differentiation and the emergence of the caste system

Settled life also implied a greater degree of internal social stratification within the tribe or village. Even in Early Vedic times a distinction was made between the ordinary free members (*vish*) of a tribe and the warrior nobility (*kshatriya*), from among whom the tribal chieftain (*rajan*) was selected. The Brahmins as priests were also mentioned as a distinct social group in these Early Vedic texts. When the semi-nomadic groups settled down they established closer relations with the indigenous people who worked for them as labourers or artisans. Colour (*varna*) served as the badge of distinction between the free Aryans and the subjugated indigenous people. Varna soon assumed the meaning of 'caste' and was applied also to the Aryans themselves in order to classify the strata of priests, warriors, free peasants and the subjugated people. A late hymn of the Rigveda contains the first evidence of this new system. It deals with the sacrifice of the mythical being Purusha and the creation of the universe and of the four varnas. This hymn (X, 90) assumed great normative importance for the ordering of Hindu society and legitimising the position of the Brahmin priests at the apex of the social hierarchy:

> When gods prepared the sacrifice with Purusha as their offering
> Its oil was spring, the holy gift was autumn, summer was the wood
> When they divided Purusha how many portions did they make?
> What do they call his mouth, his arms? What do they call his thighs and feet?
> The Brahman was his mouth, of both arms was the Rajanya [Kshatriya] made
> His thighs became the Vaishya, from his feet the Shudra was produced.

The four varnas were originally estates which then served as general categories for various *jatis*, as the individual castes were called because one is born (*jata*) into a caste. But this full-fledged caste system assumed greater importance only at a much later period. Social stratification in the Late Vedic period was characterised by the emergence of a hierarchical order of estates which reflected a division of labour among various social classes. At the top of this hierarchy were the first two estates, the Brahmin priests and the warrior nobility, the second level was occupied by free peasants and traders and the third level was that of the slaves, labourers and artisans belonging to the indigenous people.

The emergence of an internal stratification among the Aryans is shown by the meaning attributed to the terms *gramani* and *gramin*. A gramani was originally the leader of a train of vehicles and warriors and this designation came to refer to the mayor of a village who was usually a Vaishya (member of the third estate). The gramin, however, was the proprietor of a village or landlord, and he was invariably a Kshatriya. It is not known whether these new landlords acquired their rights as patrimonial or prebendal grants from the petty kings who emerged in this period or whether they seized the villages by force and exacted a protection rent from them. But there is no doubt that social conflicts arose in this period which were different from those of the period of nomadic life. Many texts provide insights into this new pattern of social conflict: 'Whenever the Kshatriya feels like it he says: "Vaishya bring me what you have hidden from me." He pillages and plunders. He does what he wants.'[3] But internal differentiation also emerged within the ranks or lineages of the warrior nobility. There was a higher nobility and a lower one (*rajanya*) of which it was explicitly said that it was not entitled to kingship.

Artisans were known even in the Early Vedic period, particularly the cartwrights who were responsible for the making and the repair of the chariots which were of vital importance for the Aryans. But other crafts were hardly mentioned in those early days. In the period of settlement this changed to a great extent. Carpenters, potters and blacksmiths appeared in the texts. Various metals were mentioned: copper (*loha*), bronze (*ayas*), a copper-tin alloy (*kamsa*), silver (*rajata*), gold (*suvarna*) and iron (*shyama* or *krishnayas*).

An important feature foreshadowing the later rigidity of the caste system was in evidence even in this early period: the artisans were despised and mostly belonged to the ranks of the Shudras (the fourth estate). Other early cultures also assigned such a marginal position to artisans. Because of their direct contact with the elements, such as fire and water, artisans, like smiths and millers, were feared as well as despised. But in India there was the additional feature of ritual impurity (*ashuddha*) which meant an exclusion of the Shudra artisan from sacrificial rites (*amedhya*). The fear of ritual impurity was carried to such extremes even in that early stage that certain sacrifices such as the Agnihotra had to be conducted with vessels made by Aryans only: 'It [the *sthali*, an earthen milk-pot] is made by an Arya, with perpendicular sides for the communion with the gods. In this way it is united with the gods. Demonical (*asurya*), indeed, is the vessel which is made by a potter on the potter's wheel.'[4]

This quote from a Late Vedic text is revealing in several respects. It shows that the indigenous people subjected by the Aryans possessed great skills as artisans. Racial discrimination against these dark-skinned people also led to a discrimination against the trades which they plied. The original lack of such skills among the Vedic Aryans was probably one of the most important reasons for the emergence of the caste system, which was designed to maintain the social and political superiority of the Aryans. The text quoted above also indicates that the Vedic Aryans did not bring the potter's wheel along when they entered India but that they found it there. The prejudice expressed in this text against the pottery produced on such a wheel makes it highly unlikely that initially the Aryans themselves produced the famous 'Painted Grey Ware' which was expertly fashioned on the potter's wheel. Archaeologists now tend to regard this Painted Grey Ware as an indicator of settlements of the Late Vedic people. But this type of ceramic probably originated among the indigenous people and was only spread by the Aryans in the course of their migration towards the east.

The Late Vedic period witnessed a great increase in trade (*vanijya*) which was due to the growing commodity production by artisans and the extension of cultivation. Even in this early period of Indian history, traders may have played an important role in finding out about new land and new routes. Long-distance trade in salt and metals and the quest for new deposits of ore would be particularly stimulating in this respect. Crucial to the future development of the social order, trade was not considered to be an impure activity and therefore upper castes could participate in it and Brahmana texts of this period explicitly refer to trade as an activity equal in value with agriculture (*krishi*), priesthood (*brahmacarya*) and royal service (*rajanucarya*). In fact, the upper castes seem to have monopolised trade at this early stage and this explains the relatively high position of the Bania (trader) caste in the Hindu society of a later age.

The role of the king

Political development in the Late Vedic age was of equal importance to the social and economic development which has been discussed so far. A new type of kingship emerged in the small territories of the Gangetic plains. Kings, even hereditary ones, were mentioned already in the Early Vedic texts, but their power was always limited as they had to consult either a council composed of all the male members of the tribe (*vish* or *jana*) or an aristocratic tribal council (*sabha* or *samiti*). Some tribes were governed by such councils only and did not have kings at all. Indian historians of a later age pointed proudly to this ancient 'democratic tradition'.

But this Early Vedic tradition of aristocratic tribal republics was eclipsed in the Late Vedic period. A new type of kingship emerged after the transition from nomadic life to settled agriculture. The new kings were not necessarily more powerful but they owed their position to a new ideology. The early kings, even if they had inherited their rank as lineage elders, always derived their legitimacy from an election by members of the tribe. In the Late Vedic period the king usually emerged from a struggle for power among the nobility and then derived his legitimacy from the ritual investiture by their Brahmin priests. The people participated in this ceremony as mere spectators. This was the time of magnificent royal sacrifices (*rajasuya*) and of the famous horse sacrifice (*ashvamedha*) which testified to the fact that the king had been able to meet all challenges or that no enemy had dared to challenge him at all. The cosmic and magic significance of these royal rites remained of great importance for the next millennium and influenced the kingship ideology of ancient India.

Indologists have done a good deal of research on these royal rites and their meaning. They have highlighted the fact that the king was held responsible for the maintenance of cosmic order and of the fertility of the earth. But they have paid less attention to the social context of this new royal ideology. The apotheosis of the king was due to the increasing internal stratification of Vedic society which gave rise to the mutual interest of kings and Brahmin priests in guaranteeing their respective positions. The Late Vedic texts composed by Brahmins make it quite clear that they were the most ardent supporters of this new idea of sacred kingship because they expected from the king that he would uphold their own eminent position in the caste system. Tribes without kings were mentioned in these texts with disgust. The Brahmin authors of these texts remembered only too well how the lack of patronage in the Early Vedic period forced them to go from one tribe to another in search of support. This could certainly be much better provided by a king whose legitimacy was based on the ritual sanctity bestowed upon him by the Brahmins.

The structure of this early state was reflected in the ceremonies of the royal court. The royal sacrifice (*rajasuya*) was initially repeated every year. The important personages of the royal court had the honorific title *ratnin* (rich in jewels) and the king started the ceremony by paying visits to their houses. The texts state that he had to do this because they were the 'givers and takers of royal power' (*rashtra*). First, the king had to visit his main queen, then the second wife whom he had forsaken because she could not bear children, and then he visited his favourite wife. In each place he had to perform a sacrifice. Further visits and sacrifices were due to the head priest (*purohita*), the commander of his army (*senani*), a member of the nobility (*rajanya*), the heads of villages (*gramani*), the bard (*suta*), the charioteer, the butcher, the cook, the thrower of dice, etc. Some texts also mention the carpenter, the cartwright and the runner.

This peculiar list of the 'jewels' of Vedic kings has given rise to a great deal of speculation because it does not show any specific political order or religious significance. Why was the butcher or the thrower of dice included in this ceremonial list of honour? Indologists who had to provide answers to such questions found a way out by emphasising the symbolic character of the royal sacrifice and the magic functions of those dignitaries. But if we take the social context of these small Vedic realms into consideration we find that this list does, indeed, include all those advisors and servants whose loyalty was of immediate importance to the king. His success and even his survival depended on them. The rajasuya ceremony was most obviously meant to highlight the personal aspect of patrimonial rule in these little kingdoms which were conceived of as extensions of the royal household.

The spread of the new royal ideology preceded the actual development of territorial kingdoms. But there is a good deal of evidence in the texts for the dissolution of tribal organisation and the emergence of a new political order. Once again this can be traced by looking at the changing meaning of words. *Jana*, which used to refer to a tribe, refers to people in general in later texts, and the term *vish*, which indicated a lineage or clan in earlier times, now referred to the subjects of a king. At the same time a new term appeared – *janata* – which meant 'a people'. The area in which such a people was settled was called *janapada*. *Pada* originally meant 'step', so *janapada* was the 'place of a tribe', but it was now used to designate the territory of a people. The new kings called their realm *mahajanapada* (great territory of the people). Another instance of the change from tribal to territorial terms of reference is the name Kurukshetra, the region to the north of Delhi where the famous battle of the *Mahabharata* was fought. Its name, 'field of the Kurus', was derived from the tribe which had settled there.

This process of territorialisation of tribal society was a very slow one which took about half a millennium. The pattern of the proliferation of petty states which was so characteristic of many periods of Indian history was initially designed in this early phase. One reason for this proliferation was the great number of Vedic tribes: about forty of them are mentioned by name in the early Vedic texts and there may have been many more. A hymn of the Rigveda shows how small these tribes must have been when it says: 'Not even in a mountain fort can a whole tribe defend itself if it has challenged Indra's strength' (II, 34). Unlike in western Asia the immigrating Vedic Aryans in India did not encounter mighty enemies and big empires which would have forced them to unite and to establish a more effective political organisation of their own. On the other hand, the small and very mobile tribal units were probably better suited to the enormous task of penetrating the vast plains of northern India.

The world of the *Mahabharata*

India's great epic, the *Mahabharata*, which contains 106,000 verses and is perhaps the most voluminous single literary product of mankind, originated in this period of tribal warfare and early settlement. It depicts the struggle of the fighting cousins, the Pandavas and the Kauravas, for the control of the western Ganga–Yamuna Doab in the Late Vedic age. The Kauravas had their capital at Hastinapura on the Ganga about 57 miles to the north of Delhi and the Pandavas had theirs at Indraprastha on the Yamuna where New Delhi is now located. The *Mahabharata* reports that the 100 Kauravas adopted a stratagem in order to deprive the Pandavas of Indraprastha. They invited them to a game of dice at which the Pandavas lost everything and were exiled to the forest for twelve years and had to spend another year in disguise. When they returned and peace could not be restored, they fought a mighty battle against the Kauravas which lasted for eighteen days. With the support of Krishna, the Pandavas won the battle.

Historians doubted for a long time that the events referred to in this epic had any historical relevance because the text was composed several centuries later. But recent archaeological research has shown that the important places mentioned in the epic were all characterised by significant finds of Painted Grey Ware. This type of ceramic was produced in the period from about 800 to 400 BC, and in some places (e.g. Atranjikhera, District Etah, to the east of Agra) it could even be dated back to 1000 BC. Although this Painted Grey Ware was probably produced by indigenous potters it is now widely accepted as an indicator of Late Vedic settlement because it was frequently found by archaeologists at the places mentioned in contemporary texts.

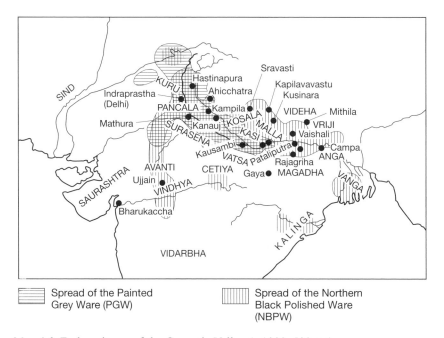

Map 1.2 Early cultures of the Gangetic Valley (*c.*1000–500 BC)

The debate about Painted Grey Ware is still going on, but as far as the historicity of the *Mahabharata* war is concerned, the debate has arrived at some important conclusions. Parts of this epic reflect the poetic imagination of a later age but the basic facts can no longer be doubted. Archaeologists found at several places among the layers of Painted Grey Ware the kind of dice which are described in the epic. The victory of the Pandavas in their battle against the Kauravas may reflect the efficacy of an alliance with indigenous people. Two crucial events referred to in the epic point to this fact. The five Pandava brothers jointly married Draupadi, the daughter of the king of the Panchalas whose realm was east of theirs, and they were supported by Krishna of Mathura whose realm was south of Indraprastha. Polyandry was unknown among the Vedic Aryans, thus the Pandavas' marriage to Draupadi seems to point to the adoption of an indigenous custom, and the dark-skinned Krishna, hero or god of the indigenous people of that area, certainly did not belong to the Aryan immigrants. Whereas the Kauravas were allied with the Vedic tribes to the north of their realm, the Pandavas were obviously in league with the indigenous people who still held sway to the east and to the south of the area of Aryan settlement. The victory of the Pandavas thus meant the emergence of a new synthesis based on marital and political alliances with the indigenous people.

Another fact reported in the *Mahabharata* may shed some light on the expansion of the Late Vedic civilisation to the east. The epic states that the fifth king of the Pandavas who ruled at Hastinapura, after the Kauravas had been deprived of this capital, shifted his capital to Kausambi (near present Allahabad) because a flood of the river Ganga had destroyed Hastinapura. Excavations at Hastinapura have, indeed, shown that a town characterised by Painted Grey Ware was suddenly abandoned after a flood. But the dating of these finds (around the end of the fourth century BC) does not seem to fit in with the statement in the epic which would indicate a much earlier time. However, excavations at Kausambi have shown that this site contains traces of urban settlement in the early centuries of the first millennium BC. Whatever future excavations may show, it is fairly clear even now that the events and movements which occurred in the eighth and seventh centuries BC in the Gangetic plains must have been faithfully reported by bards for several centuries and were then recorded by the poet who composed this part of the *Mahabharata*. The wealth of detailed information which is contained in this epic must have been transmitted by an unbroken tradition which the poet reflected but did not invent.

The culture of the Late Vedic age was a rural one; evidence of an urban culture as in the great cities of the Indus civilisation is totally absent in this period. Even royal 'capitals' like Hastinapura showed neither fortifications nor any traces of city planning. The houses were made of mud and wattling; regular bricks were unknown. There are also no signs of a script in this period. The art of the blacksmith and of the potter were, however, very well developed. Some kinds of vessels which were found in the sites of this period, though unknown in the age of the Indus civilisation, are reproduced in essentially the same fashion today (e.g. the *thali*, a kind of plate; the *katora*, a bowl; and the *lotha*, a small jar). Even the glass bangles which Indian women still wear were known to the people of these Late Vedic settlements.

The essence of wealth was cattle, which was in demand for providing milk, meat and beasts of burden. Heavy soil could often be ploughed only by large teams of oxen. References to such large teams in the texts were thought to be exaggerations, but in parts of India one can see even today about a dozen oxen yoked to one plough – particularly whenever the animals are small and the work hard.

The emergence of Indian philosophy

The world-view in the Late Vedic age was totally different from that in the early period of migration. The simple faith in the power of the Aryans and of their gods gave way to a feeling of insecurity and scepticism. The bard expressed this feeling in moving words: 'I feel depressed by my helplessness, by nakedness and want. My mind wanders like a bird which is chased hither and thither. Like rats gnawing their tails my sorrows are gnawing at me' (X, 33). Questions concerning right conduct troubled the minds of men and are reflected in some of the greatest hymns of the late tenth book of the Rigveda. A typical example is the touching dialogue between the twins Yama and Yami in which the sister asks her brother, in vain, to marry her. There was also doubt about the almighty power of the gods. In its place grew an increasing awareness of an immutable law according to which everybody was accountable for his deeds (*karma*) not only here and now but also in subsequent births (*samsara*). These two ideas of karma and samsara became the key elements of Indian religious life. They may have been derived from the religion of the indigenous people with whom the Aryans became more and more involved. Insecurity and scepticism paved the way for an ever greater reliance on the magic effect of elaborate sacrificial rites which were outlined in the Brahmana texts. These rites and the Brahmin priests who knew the secrets of ritual efficacy became of central importance in this Late Vedic age.

The magic rituals could not satisfy the human quest for an answer to the fundamental question about the meaning of life, however. The emphasis on such rituals may have even stimulated the tendency towards philosophical speculation which no longer remained a privilege solely of the Brahmins. Kings and Vaishyas, even Shudras and women, were reported to have asked the great philosophical questions of this age. These philosophical thoughts were collected in the Upanishads (secret teachings) which were added at the end to the texts of the great Vedic schools of thought. The Upanishads, which originated roughly from 750 to 500 BC, are in many ways connected with the speculations of Brahmin priests about the efficacy of sacrificial rites. But in the Brihadaranyaka Upanishad we find a transition to a deeper philosophical thought, when the meaning of the animal sacrifice is reinterpreted in terms of a cosmic symbolism which is taken as a point of departure for meditation.

The Upanishads document the gradual transition from the mythical world-view of the Early Vedic age and the magic thought recorded in the Brahmana texts to the mystical philosophy of individual salvation. This philosophy led to the liberating insight into the identity of the individual soul (*atman*) with the soul of the universe (*brahman*). This insight is expressed in the famous formula 'that thou are' (*tat tvam asi*). The dualism of mind and matter was not yet accepted by this early philosophy; it attained great importance only later on. The philosophy of the Upanishads, which combined the atman-brahman idea with a belief in rebirth and transmigration, radically changed the old Vedic religion and paved the way both for Buddhism as well as for the later development of Hindu philosophy.

2

THE GREAT ANCIENT EMPIRES

THE RISE OF THE GANGETIC CULTURE AND THE GREAT EMPIRES OF THE EAST

The extension of the Vedic culture into the central and eastern Gangetic plains was as important for the further course of Indian history as the period of their early settlement in the Panjab and in the Ganga–Yamuna Doab. The penetration of the east very soon led to the emergence of the first historical kingdoms and to a second phase of urbanisation – the first phase being that of the Indus civilisation.

It is generally assumed that the eastward migration of the Vedic population was caused by a change of climate. The fertile area in Panjab and Doab became more and more arid and, at the same time, the Gangetic jungles receded and thus became penetrable. The ancient texts show that the tribes were constantly fighting for pasture and agricultural land. In the Brahmana texts, it is stated quite unequivocally that only he who fights on two fronts can establish a settlement successfully, because if he fights on only one front, the land which he has acquired will surely be taken over by the next of the migrating groups. Thus there was continuous warfare both against the indigenous people and against other Vedic tribes.

A further motivation for the movement east may have been escape from royal supremacy and a desire to preserve their earlier republican organisation by settling where the new kings did not yet have power. Heterodox groups and sodalities like the Vratyas which are mentioned in the Atharvaveda may have played an important role in this movement. It is interesting to note that Buddhist texts contain many references to powerful tribal republics which existed in the east in the fifth century BC while the Brahmana texts which originated in the western part of Vedic settlements refer mostly to kingdoms.

Not very much is known so far about the time and the direction of these movements beyond Kurukshetra. There are early references to movements south: 'The people move victoriously to the south.'[1] Avanti, with its capital at Ujjain about 500 miles south of Kurukshetra, was one of the earliest outposts in central India and it showed traces of incipient urbanisation as early as about 700 BC. But groups of Vedic Aryans also moved north. A Brahmana text says: 'Whenever a father resettles a son, he settles him in the north.'[2] Probably those who went north did not stop at the foot of the Himalayas but moved east along the foothills. Indian historians maintain that this route was perhaps one of the earliest passages to the east because there was less jungle there and the many tributaries of the Yamuna and the Ganga could be more easily crossed upstream than down in the plains.

The penetration of the east

The movement east was certainly the most important one. In a text it is clearly stated: 'The people move from the west to the east and conquer land.'[3] It is essential to note that the term for land in this quote is *kshetra* which refers to fields fit for cultivation. There is also a highly instructive text in the Shatapatha Brahmana, the 'Brahmana of the Hundred Paths', which throws light on the extension of the late Vedic civilisation into the eastern Gangetic plains. This text reports the founding of a realm called Videha to the northeast of Patna by a prince, Videgha-Mathava. This prince is said to have started from the river Saraswati in the company of the fire god, Agni-Vaishvanara, of whose fame as a great coloniser we have heard already. Videgha followed him until they came to the river Sadanira (this is now the river Gandak). Here Agni stopped and did not proceed. The text[4] describes this episode very vividly:

Mathava, the Videgha, was at that time on the [river] Sarasvati. He [Agni] thence went burning along this earth towards the East . . . and the Videgha Mathava followed after him as he was burning along. He burnt over [dried up] all these rivers. Now that [river], which is called Sadanira, flows from the northern [Himalaya] mountains: that one he did not burn over. That one the Brahmins did not cross in former times, thinking, 'it has not been burnt over by Agni Vaishvanara'.

Nowadays, however, there are many Brahmins in the East of it. At that time it [the land east of the Sadanira] was very uncultivated, very marshy, because it had not been tasted by Agni Vaishvanara.

Nowadays, however, it is very cultivated, for the Brahmins have caused [Agni] to taste it through sacrifices. Even in late summer that [river] . . . rages along . . .

Mathava the Videgha then said [to Agni] 'Where am I to abide?' 'To the East of this [river] be thy abode!' said he. Even now this [river] forms the boundary of the Koshalas and Videhas.

The events reported here are of great significance. At the time when this text was composed there was obviously still a clear recollection that the land to the east of the river Sadanira (Gandak) was originally unclean to the Brahmins because their great god Agni had not traversed this river. Prince Videgha had nevertheless conquered this country. The term *etarhi* used in the text means 'now' and is obviously a reference to the state of affairs at the time of writing. So, by the time this Brahmana text was written (in approximately the eighth century BC) this land was considered to be acceptable to the Brahmins. But, because the god of the Brahmins had not stepped into this land, it was considered to be inferior to the land in the west. Because of its strong elements of an already highly developed indigenous chalcolithic culture and society this part of the country was suspect and impure to orthodox Brahmins even in the mid-first millennium BC. We can therefore only endorse the statement made by Hermann Oldenberg in his book on Buddhism which was first published in 1881: 'When we think about the origins of Buddhism we must keep in mind that the earliest Buddhist congregations were located in the country or at least at the border of the country into which Agni-Vaishvanara had not crossed on his way to the East, exuding flames.'

Archaeological research sheds more light on the establishment of a Gangetic culture than the stray textual references which cannot be accurately dated. Since India attained independence the Archaeological Survey of India has made great efforts to excavate the early historical cities of northern India. The dating of some sites is still open to debate but there is a consensus that the period from the late seventh to the late fifth century BC was a most decisive phase for the development of Indian culture. It may well be said that the history of the Indian subcontinent actually started at that time.

In this period the first territorial kingdoms were established in the central part of the Gangetic plains, northern India witnessed a second phase of urbanisation, and those parts of the subcontinent which are now included in Pakistan were annexed by the Persian emperor, Dareios the Great. At the end of this period the first historical personality of India, Gautama Buddha, stepped into the limelight of history.

From the numerous small tribal kingdoms (*janapada*) sixteen major ones (*mahajanapada*) emerged in the fifth century BC (see Map 1.2). The emergence of these principalities had a lot to do with agrarian extension, control of trade routes and a new and more aggressive type of warfare. The texts do not necessarily always use the same name for each of these mahajanapadas, but it is possible to list the most important ones which have also been documented by archaeological research. These are: Kamboja and Gandhara located in northern Pakistan; Kuru, Surasena (capital: Mathura) and Panchala in the western Doab; Vatsa (capital: Kausambi) in the eastern Doab; Kasi (capital: Varanasi) and to the north of it, Koshala; Magadha to the south of Patna and the tribal republics of the Mallas and Vrijis to the north of it; and farther east, Anga, near the present border between Bihar and Bengal; in central India there was Avanti (capital: Ujjain) and to the east of it Chetiya. The hub of this whole system of mahajanapadas was the Ganga–Yamuna Doab and the immediately adjacent region to the east.

The origins and the internal organisation of these mahajanapadas are still a matter for speculation. As the earlier tribes were usually rather small, all the inhabitants of a mahajanapada could not have belonged to the tribe that gave it its name. Therefore, they must have been confederations of several tribes. Some of these mahajanapadas had two capitals which seems to be evidence for a fusion of at least two smaller units: Hastinapura and Indraprastha were both located in the land of the Kurus, and Panchala included Kampila and Ahicchatra. The structure of these states was perhaps similar to that of later medieval Hindu kingdoms: the direct exercise of royal power was restricted to the immediate tribal surroundings while other principalities belonging to the kingdom enjoyed a great deal of internal autonomy. The heads of these principalities only joined the king in warfare and plunder and they participated in his royal ceremonies. The only definite borders of such mahajanapadas were rivers and other natural barriers. The extension of royal authority depended on the loyalty of the border tribes which were also able to be influenced by neighbouring kingdoms.

Urbanisation in the Ganges valley

The rise of the mahajanapadas was directly connected with the emergence of the early urban centres of the Gangetic plains in the period after 600 BC. Five of the six major cities in the central Gangetic plains were capitals of mahajanapadas: Rajagriha (Magadha), Varanasi (Kasi), Kausambi (Vatsa), Sravasti (Koshala) and Champa (Anga). Only the sixth city, Saketa, was not an independent capital but was located in Koshala. It must have been the centre of an earlier janapada which merged with Koshala. In central India there was Ujjain (Avanti) and in the northwest there was Taxila (Gandhara) or rather the recently discovered early town which preceded both Taxila and the nearby township on the Bhir Mound which dates back to the period of Persian occupation around 500 BC. There seems to be a correlation between political development and urbanisation in this period of the sixth to the fifth centuries BC.

The most remarkable contrast between the new cities in the Gangetic plains and earlier towns like Hastinapura is that of the system of fortification. Whereas the earlier towns were not fortified, these new cities had moats and ramparts. The ramparts were made of earth which was covered in some cases with bricks from about the fifth century BC onward; later on they were even replaced by solid brick walls. A millennium after the decline of the Indus civilisation, one encounters once more bricks made in kilns.

Kausambi had the most impressive fortification, its city walls are about 4 miles long and at some places 30 feet high. The archaeologist G.R. Sharma, who excavated Kausambi in the 1950s, thought that these walls resembled those of the Indus cities. There were also public buildings like assembly halls in these early Gangetic cities, and after the rise of Buddhism they also contained monasteries and stupas. City planning with regard to the network of streets seems to have started again only in the fourth century BC.

An important indicator of the growth of an urban economy are the punch-marked coins which have been found in those Gangetic cities. There were also standardised weights which provide evidence for a highly developed trade in the fifth century BC. Was there perhaps some cultural continuity right from the time of the Indus civilisation down to this new Gangetic civilisation? This question cannot yet be answered, but it is interesting to note that the weight of 95 per cent of the 1,150 silver coins found at Taxila is very similar to the standardised stone weights of the Indus civilisation.

There was a great demand in this period of the Gangetic civilisation for a new type of ceramic referred to as 'Northern Black Polished Ware'. The centre of production of this was in the Gangetic plains. Just as the earlier Painted Grey Ware was identified with the period of Late Vedic settlement in Panjab and Doab, this new type of ceramic shows the spread of the Gangetic civilisation and its influence on other parts of India opened up by the many new trade routes. Northern Black Polished Ware made its first appearance around 500 BC and could be traced in all the mahajanapadas mentioned above; it even showed up in distant Kalinga (see Map 1.2). In 1981 a city was discovered and partly excavated in western Orissa, which was about 1 mile long and 500 yards wide, surrounded by a solid brick wall. At this site Northern Black Polished Ware was also discovered.

Another important indicator for a well-developed urban culture, a script, has not yet been found in those Gangetic cities. Ashoka's inscriptions of the third century BC still remain the earliest evidence for an Indian script. But since the two scripts Brahmi and Karoshthi were already fully developed, scholars believe that they may have originated in the fifth century BC. Script in India developed probably for the first time under Persian influence. The Persians held sway in the northwest of the Indian subcontinent at that time and Karoshthi, which was written from right to left, was based on the Aramaic script which was the official script of the Persian empire.

The rise of Buddhism

This new Gangetic civilisation found its spiritual expression in a reform movement which was a reaction to the Brahmin–Kshatriya alliance of the Late Vedic age. This reform movement is mainly identified with the teaching of Gautama Buddha who is regarded as the first historic figure of Indian history. The date of his death (*parinirvana*) has always been a controversial issue. Whereas the Buddhist world celebrated in AD 1956 the 2,500th anniversary of his Nirvana (in 544 BC), modern historians and Indologists had generally accepted *c*.483 BC as the date of his death. But in the early 1980s the German Indologist H. Bechert has convincingly shown that none of these dates which are based on later Buddhist chronicles and canonical texts can be taken for granted and that the Buddha may instead have lived and preached about a century later. These findings were generally approved at an international conference at Göttingen in 1988 even though they are not unanimously accepted, especially by Indian historians. As early Buddhist literature, in particular the Jataka stories of the Buddha's previous lives, depict an already flourishing urban society in north India, archaeological evidence also seems to indicate that the Buddha lived in the fifth rather than in the sixth century when urbanisation in the Ganges valley was still in its incipient stage. The Buddha, however, was not the only great reformer of that age. There was also Mahavira, the founder of Jainism, who is supposed to have been a younger contemporary of the Buddha. Jainism, this other great ascetic religion, was destined to have an unbroken tradition in India, especially in the rich merchant communities of western India. Buddhism spread to many other countries later on, but has declined in India itself. It could be said that Mahavira's teachings reappeared in the rigorous ethics of Mahatma Gandhi who was influenced by Jainism as he grew up in a Gujarati Bania family, the Banias being a dominant traders' caste in that region.

Both these ascetic religious movements of the fifth century BC are characterised by a transition from the magic thought of the Vedas and the mystical speculations of the Upanishads to a new type of rationality. This rationality is also in evidence in the famous grammar of the great Indian linguist, Panini. His grammar, India's first scientific treatise, was produced in this period. Buddha's teachings were later on fused once more with mystical speculation and even with magic thought in Tantric Buddhism, but his original quest for rationally enlightened experience is clearly documented by this explanation of the four noble truths, and of the 'eightfold path' of salvation from the burden of human suffering. He had practised penance and experienced the futility of mystical speculation before he arrived at his insight into the causes of human suffering and the way to remove them. The eightfold path of right conduct (in vision, thought, speech, action, giving, striving, vigilance and concentration) which leads to a cessation of the thirst for life and thus stops the cycle of rebirths appears to be a matter of practical instruction rather than the outcome of mystical speculation.

The voluminous Buddhist scriptures throw a flood of light on the life and times of Gautama Buddha. He was born as the son of a Sakhya prince in a region which now belongs to Nepal. He left his family at the age of

29 and spent many years as a wandering ascetic until he experienced his enlightenment at Bodh Gaya. He then preached his first sermon at Sarnath near Varanasi and toured many parts of what is now Bihar and eastern Uttar Pradesh, spreading his teachings and gaining more and more followers. He met the high and mighty of his time – among them King Bimbisara of Magadha.

After his death, a council of 500 Buddhist monks was convened at Rajagriha in order to edit the corpus of his sermons so that his authentic teachings could be preserved. A second council, convened at Vaishali, witnessed a schism: the 'old ones' (*theravadins*) insisted on the ascetic ideal of the community of monks (*sangha*), whereas a new movement stood for a greater accommodation of the lay members and a broadening of the concept of the sangha to include followers other than monks. In keeping with this aim, the new trend was called Mahasanghika. This was the origin of the 'Great Vehicle' (*mahayana*) as the new movement liked to call itself while looking down upon the 'Small Vehicle' (*hinayana*) of the orthodox monks. This schism was undoubtedly of great importance for the later development of Buddhist and Hindu philosophy, but it also predetermined the decline of Buddhism in India itself.

The west under Persian domination

In the sixth century BC, the Persian kingdom of the Achaemenids emerged within a few decades as the first major empire in recorded history. Kyros, the founder of this empire, is said to have sent an expedition to Afghanistan which reached the borders of India, but the conquest of northwestern India was left to Dareios (521 to 485 BC). In the famous inscription of Behistun (*c.*518 BC), he mentions Gandhara as a province of his empire. Other inscriptions add Hindush (Sindh) to this list of provinces only a few years later. The river Indus, which had already been explored by Skylax, a Greek in Persian service, thus had become the border of the Persian empire.

Not much is known about the administration of these Persian provinces on the banks of the Indus, but Herodotus reports that these regions (Indoi) provided the greatest amount of revenue to the Persian empire. This would indicate that under Dareios and Xerxes these regions were thoroughly subjected to Persian administration. News about this altogether novel style of administration must have reached Magadha, whose rulers were on the verge of founding the first major empire on Indian soil. But it is difficult to gauge the extent of Persian influence on Indian history because archaeological evidence is missing and the gold coins of the Achaemenids have not been found in India so far. Only the towns of the Bhir Mound at Taxila and Charsada, west of it, are attributed to the Achaemenids, but no distinctively Persian features have been noted by the archaeologists excavating those sites.

The origins of the early state

A new phase of political development began in the eastern Gangetic plains in the times of Dareios and Buddha. Some of the mahajanapadas of this region established their hegemony over others in the fifth century BC. There emerged a kind of strategic quadrangle: Koshala and the tribal confederation of the Vrijis held sway north of the Ganga; Vatsa, with its capital Kausambi, dominated the confluence of the Ganga and Yamuna; and Magadha ruled the large region southeast of the Ganga.

Koshala and Magadha followed a particularly aggressive policy which was not only aimed at victory over their neighbours but at annexation of their territory as well. Bimbisara of Magadha seems to have started this struggle. During his long reign he laid the foundations for the rise of Magadha as the greatest power in India. An important step towards this aim was the conquest of neighbouring Anga. In this way Magadha could greatly enhance its control over the trade routes of the eastern plains and perhaps also gain access to the trade of the east coast. Bimbisara built a more magnificent capital at New Rajagriha to commemorate his supremacy. There he is also supposed to have met Buddha who converted him to his teachings. Bimbisara died a miserable death, his son Ajatashatru imprisoned and starved him.

Ajatashatru continued the aggressive policy of his father, but soon suffered defeat at the hands of his uncle, the king of Koshala. But this king was soon removed by his own son, Virudhaka. Koshala and Magadha then fought against the northern tribal republics. Koshala vanquished the tribe of the Sakhya, to which Buddha belonged. From then on Koshala held sway from Varanasi to the foothills of the Himalayas.

Magadha's warfare against the strong tribal confederation of the Vrijis is supposed to have continued for fourteen years, and it is said that Buddha himself advised Ajatashatru against starting this war. Magadha for the first time used heavy chariots that were armoured and catapults for hurling huge stones against the enemies in this war. In order to wage war more effectively two generals of Magadha fortified a village, Pataligrama, on the banks of the river Ganga, which soon rose into prominence under its new name Pataliputra (Patna). Vaishali, the capital of the Licchavis, the strongest tribe of the Vriji confederation, is highly praised in Buddhist literature. Its splendour and its multi-storey houses are specifically mentioned. The city is said to have been governed by the assembly of the heads of its 7,707 families who all proudly called themselves rajas. When Ajatashatru had barely established his hegemony over the Gangetic plains he was challenged by King Pradyota of Ujjain (Avanti) in western India who even conquered Kausambi and held it for some time. But Magadha was already so powerful that such challenges could not dislodge it any more from its eminent position.

The meteoric rise of Magadha within the lifetime of two generations has remained an enigma to all historians who have tried to explain the origins of ancient India's first empire. The main problem is not the sudden emergence of a successful dynasty – Indian history is replete with such success stories – but the fact that a vast state of hitherto unprecedented dimensions was born at the periphery of the Gangetic civilisation without any recognisable period of gestation. Historians who believe in the theory of diffusion of imperial state formation from a centre in Western Asia point to the fact that the rise of Magadha closely paralleled the Persian conquest of northwestern India. The knowledge of the new style of imperial administration practised in the Persian provinces on the river Indus must have spread to eastern India, too. But the availability of this knowledge would not suffice to explain the actual rise of Magadha. We have to delve back into India's history in the seventh and sixth centuries BC in order to find clues for the emergence of this new type of state formation.

Early state formation in India usually proceeded in three phases. In the Gangetic region the first phase of this process was characterised by the transition of the small semi-nomadic tribes (*jana*) of the period of Vedic migration to a large number of tribal principalities of a definite area (*janapada*). During the second phase in a period of competition sixteen major mahajanapadas emerged in the late sixth and early fifth centuries BC. The third or imperial phase was reached when one of these mahajanapadas (in this case, Magadha) annexed a few neighbouring principalities and established its hegemony over the others. This three-phase development can be considered as an autochthonous evolution, especially since the first two phases are certainly not due to external influences. They were accompanied by a marked social and political change in the Gangetic civilisation, and it is this change which contributed to the emergence of the empire in the third phase.

Indian Marxist historians insist that the introduction of iron implements in the seventh century BC, which enabled the people to clear the jungle and reclaim the fertile land of the eastern Gangetic plains, led to the rise of the powerful mahajanapadas and finally to the emergence of the great eastern empire. But hitherto there has been little archaeological evidence and there are only a few references in the ancient texts which would clearly support this Marxist thesis of economic change as the main reason for the rise of Magadha. Iron, however, must have indeed played an important yet different role in this period. But it seems that even in this period iron was mostly used for the making of weapons and Magadha may have had a strategic advantage due to its access to the deposits of iron ore in Chota Nagpur and its better armament. Thus it was perhaps no accident that Magadha's first great campaign was directed against neighbouring Anga which was equally close to these deposits of iron ore and perhaps controlled the trade routes through which iron would reach northern India. In this way, Magadha eliminated the most dangerous competitor at the very beginning of its imperial career.

The period of Ajatashatru's successors is not very well documented as yet. Buddhist texts refer to the four rulers who followed him as parricides just as he himself and his contemporary Virudhaka, the king of Koshala, were accused of that crime. These reports may not have been completely reliable but they seem to indicate that a new type of unscrupulous and ambitious ruler emerged at that time. This type was then succinctly described in the famous book on statecraft, Kautalya's *Arthashastra*. Among the rulers of Magadha, Shishunaga deserves special attention because he defeated the Prayota dynasty of Avanti, a major threat to Magadha for quite some time, and annexed its territories of Avanti and Kausambi. In the reign of Shishunaga's son Kakavarna the second Buddhist council was held which has been mentioned above. Kakavarna was assassinated and this time even one of the queens is supposed to have contributed to the violent death of the king.

The usurper who emerged from this intrigue as the new ruler of Magadha was Mahapadma who founded the short-lived but very important Nanda dynasty. Mahapadma was the son of a Shudra woman and later Purana texts refer to him as the destroyer of the Kshatriyas – obviously a reference both to his low birth and his victories over the kings of northern India. Mahapadma energetically continued the aggressive policies of his predecessors. He subjugated most of northern India, parts of central India and even Kalinga on the east coast. He rates as the greatest Indian ruler before the Mauryas and in the royal lists of the Puranas he is the first who bears the imperial title *Ekachattra*, meaning 'he who has united the country under one umbrella', the symbol of overlordship.

Greek and Roman authors report that the Nandas, who had their capital at Pataliputra when Alexander the Great conquered northwestern India, had a powerful standing army of 200,000 infantrymen, 20,000 horsemen, 2,000 chariots drawn by four horses each, and 3,000 elephants. This is the first reference to the large-scale use of elephants in warfare. Such war elephants remained for a long time the most powerful strategic weapons of Indian rulers until the central Asian conquerors of the medieval period introduced the new method of the large-scale deployment of cavalry.

The Nandas could maintain their large army only by rigorously collecting the revenues of their empire and plundering their neighbours. Their name became a byword for avarice in later Indian literature. The legend of their great treasure which they are supposed to have hidden in the river Ganga reminds us of the old German story of the Nibelungen whose treasure was hidden in the river Rhine. Mahapadma Nanda was succeeded by his eight sons; each of them ruled only for a short time until the last one was overthrown by Chandragupta Maurya.

In spite of the very short period of their rule, the Nandas must be credited with having paved the way for their better-known successors, the Mauryas. They united a very large part of northern India under their rule (see Map 2.1). Their army and their administration were taken over by the Mauryas as going concerns. But the empire of the Nandas lacked certain qualities which emerged only under the Mauryas. Just as certain new ideas coming from the West may have contributed to the rise of Magadha in the fifth century BC under Bimbisara, another wave of Western influence may have influenced the transformation of the empire of the Nandas into that of the Mauryas.

The impact of Alexander's Indian campaign

The Indian campaign of Alexander the Great is certainly one of the best-known events of ancient Indian history as far as European historiography is concerned. The historians of the nineteenth and early twentieth centuries have devoted much attention to this event. But Indian sources remain silent about Alexander's campaign. To the Indians he was only one of the nameless conquerors of the northwest who touched this part of India in an endless sequence of raids. The memory of Alexander the Great returned to India only much later with the Islamic conquerors who saw him as a great ruler worth emulating. One of the sultans of Delhi called himself a second Alexander, and the Islamic version of this name (Sikander) was very popular among later Islamic rulers of India and southeast Asia.

Alexander crossed the Hindukush mountains in eastern Afghanistan in the month of May, 327 BC. He fought for more than a year against various tribes in what is now northern Pakistan until he could cross the river Indus in February 326 BC. The king of Takshashila (Taxila) accepted Alexander's suzerainty without putting up a fight. He was a generous host to the Greeks and is reported to have fed them with the meat of 3,000 oxen and more than 10,000 sheep. Then he provided them with 5,000 auxiliary troops so that they could better fight his neighbour, King Poros. King Poros belonged to the tribe of the Pauravas, descended from the Puru tribe mentioned so often in the Rigveda. He joined battle with Alexander at the head of a mighty army with some 2,000 elephants, but Alexander defeated him by a sudden attack after crossing the river Hydaspes at night although the river was in flood. Alexander then reinstated the vanquished Poros and made him his ally.

By this time the monsoon had set in and the rains obstructed Alexander's march east. He was determined to go on, but when his army reached the river Hyphasis (Beas), east of the present city of Lahore, his soldiers refused to obey his orders for the first time in eight years of incessant conquest. Alexander was convinced that he would soon reach the end of the world, but his soldiers were less and less convinced of this as they proceeded to the east where more kings and war elephants were waiting to fight against them. Alexander's speech in which he invoked the memory of their victories over the Persians in order to persuade them to march on is one of the most moving documents of Alexander's time, but so is the reply by Coenus, his general, who spoke on behalf of the soldiers. Alexander finally turned back and proceeded with his troops south along the river Indus where they got involved in battles with the tribes of that area, especially with the Malloi (Malavas). Alexander was almost killed in one of these encounters. He then turned west and crossed, with parts of his army, the desert land of Gedrosia which is a part of present Baluchistan. Very few survived this ordeal. In May 324 BC, three years after he had entered India, Alexander was back at Susa in Persia. In the following year he died in Babylon.

Alexander's early death and the division of his empire among the Diadochi who fought a struggle for succession put an end to the plan of integrating at least a part of India into the Hellenistic empire. By 317 BC the peripheral Greek outposts in India had been given up. Thus Alexander's campaign remained a mere episode in Indian history, but the indirect consequences of this intrusion were of great importance. The reports of Alexander's companions and of the first Greek ambassador at the court of the Mauryas were the main sources of Western knowledge about India from the ancient to the medieval period of history. Also, the Hellenistic states, which arose later on India's northwestern frontier in present Afghanistan, had an important influence on the development of Indian art as well as on the evolution of sciences such as astronomy.

The foundation of the Maurya empire

Alexander's campaign probably made an indirect impact on the further political development of India. Not much is known about the antecedents of Chandragupta Maurya, but it is said that he began his military career by fighting against the outposts which Alexander had left along the river Indus. How he managed to get from there to Magadha and how he seized power from the last Nanda emperor remains obscure. Indian sources, especially the famous play *Mudrarakshasa*, give the credit for Chandragupta's rise to his political advisor, the cunning Brahmin Kautalya, author of the *Arthashastra*.

At any rate Chandragupta seems to have usurped the throne of Magadha in 320 BC. He used the subsequent years for the consolidation of his hold on the army and administration of this empire. There are no reports of his leading any military campaigns in this period. But in 305 BC Seleukos Nikator, who had emerged as the ruler of the eastern part of Alexander's vast domain, crossed the Hindukush mountains in order to claim Alexander's heritage in India. Chandragupta met him at the head of a large army in the Panjab and stopped his march east. In the subsequent peace treaty Seleukos ceded to Chandragupta all territories to the east of Kabul as well as Baluchistan. The frontier of the Maurya empire was thus more or less the same as that of the Mughal empire at the height of its power about 2,000 years later. Chandragupta's gift of 500 war elephants appears to be modest in view of this enormous territorial gain. But this Indian military aid is supposed to have helped Seleukos to defeat his western neighbour and rival, Antigonos, in a decisive battle some four years later.

European knowledge about India was greatly enhanced by the reports which Seleukos' ambassador, Megasthenes, prepared while he was in Pataliputra at Chandragupta's court. The originals have been lost but several classical authors have quoted long passages from Megasthenes' work and, therefore, we know a good deal about what he saw while he was there. Two parts of his report have attracted special attention: his description of the imperial capital, Pataliputra, and his account of the seven strata of Indian society which he observed there.

He reported that Pataliputra was fortified with palisades. This fortification was shaped like a parallelogram measuring about 9 miles in length and about 1.5 miles in breadth and it had 570 towers and 64 gates. The circumference of Pataliputra was about 21 miles and thus this city was about twice as large as Rome under Emperor Marcus Aurelius. If this report is true, Pataliputra must have been the largest city of the ancient world. There was an impression that Megasthenes may have exaggerated the size of the capital to which he was an ambassador in order to enhance his own importance. But the German Indologist D. Schlingloff has shown that the distances between the towers or between a tower and the next gate as derived from Megasthenes' account closely correspond to the distance prescribed for this kind of fortification in Kautalya's *Arthashastra* (i.e. 54 yards).

Megasthenes' description of the society of Magadha seems to be equally accurate. As the first estate, he mentioned the philosophers, by which he obviously means the Brahmins. The second estate was that of the agriculturists. According to Megasthenes, they were exempt from service in the army and from any other similar obligations to the state. No enemy would do harm to an agriculturist tilling his fields. For their fields they paid a rent to the king because 'in India all land belongs to the king and no private person is permitted to own land. In addition to this general rent they give one quarter of their produce to the state'. Megasthenes then named the herdsmen who lived outside the villages, then the traders and artisans 'who get their food from the royal storage'. The fifth estate were the soldiers who, like the war horses and war elephants, also got their food from the royal storage. The sixth estate was that of the inspectors and spies who reported everything to the emperor. The seventh estate was that of the advisors and officers of the king who looked after the administration, the law courts, etc., of the empire.

Although these seven social strata were not listed in any Indian text in this fashion (which does not seem to pay attention to any hierarchical order), there are references to each of them in Indian texts, too. The general impression we get from Megasthenes' report is that of a centrally administered, well-organised state. Of special interest are his categorical assertions that all land belonged to the emperor, that artisans and soldiers were supported directly by the state and that spies reported on everything that went on in the empire. Perhaps these observations were applicable only to the capital and its immediate hinterland which was the area which Megasthenes knew well. But Kautalya's famous account of the proper organisation of an empire also talks about espionage.

The political system of the *Arthashastra*

The *Arthashastra* which is attributed to Kautalya, the Prime Minister and chief advisor of Chandragupta, provides an even more coherent picture of a centrally administered empire in which public life and the economy are controlled by the ruler. Ever since this ancient text was rediscovered and published in the year 1909 scholars have tried to interpret this text as an accurate description of Chandragupta's system of government. There is a consensus that Kautalya was the main author of this famous text and that he lived around 300 BC, but it is also accepted that parts of this text are later additions and revisions, some of which may have been made as late as AD 300.

Kautalya depicts a situation in which several small rival kingdoms each have a chance of gaining supremacy over the others if the respective ruler follows the instructions given by Kautalya. In ancient Indian history the period which corresponds most closely to Kautalya's description is that of the mahajanapadas before Magadha attained supremacy. Thus it seems more likely that Kautalya related in normative terms what he had come to know about this earlier period than that his account actually reflected the structure of the Mauryan empire during Chandragupta's reign. Thus the *Arthashastra* should not be regarded as a source for the study of the history of the empire only but also for the history of state formation in the immediately preceding period. The relevance of the *Arthashastra* for medieval Indian politics is that the coexistence of various smaller rival kingdoms was much more typical for most periods of Indian history than the rather exceptional phase when one great empire completely dominated the political scene.

The central idea of Kautalya's precept (*shastra*) was the prosperity (*artha*) of king and country. The king who strove for victory (*vijigishu*) was at the centre of a circle of states (*mandala*) in which the neighbour was the natural enemy (*ari*) and the more distant neighbour of this neighbour (enemy of the enemy) was the natural friend (*mitra*). This pattern of the *rajamandala* repeated itself in concentric circles of enemies and friends. But there were certain important exceptions: there was the middle king (*madhyama*) who was powerful enough that he could either maintain armed neutrality in a conflict of his neighbours or decide the battle by supporting one side or the other, and finally there was the great outsider (*udashina*) whose actions were not predictable because he did not belong to one of these power circles but was able to interfere with it. He was to be carefully watched.

The *vijigishu* had to try to defeat one after another of his enemies. His ability to do so depended on the seven factors of power which supported his kingdom (*rajya*). These factors were, first of all, the qualities of the king, then that of his ministers, his provinces, his city, his treasure, his army and last, but not least, his allies. The main aim of the *Arthashastra* was to instruct the king on how to improve the qualities of these power factors and weaken those of his enemy even before an open confrontation took place. He was told to strengthen his fortifications, extend facilities for irrigation, encourage trade, cultivate wasteland, open mines, look after the forest and build enclosures for elephants and, of course, try to prevent the enemy from doing likewise. For this purpose he was to send spies and secret agents into his enemy's kingdom. The very detailed instructions for such spies and agents which Kautalya gives with great psychological insight into the weakness of human nature have earned him the doubtful reputation of having even surpassed Machiavelli's cunning advice in *Il Principe*. But actually Kautalya paid less attention to clandestine activities in the enemy's territory than to the elimination of 'thorns' in the king's own country.

Since Kautalya believed that political power was a direct function of economic prosperity, his treatise contained detailed information on the improvement of the economy by state intervention in all spheres of activity, including mining, trade, crafts and agriculture. He also outlined the structure of royal administration and set a salary scale starting with 48,000 panas for the royal high priest, down to 60 panas for a petty inspector. All this gives the impression of a very efficiently administered centralised state which appropriated as much of the surplus produced in the country as possible. There were no moral limits to this exploitation but there were limits of political feasibility. It was recognised that high taxes and forced labour would drive the population into the arms of the enemy and, therefore, the king had to consider the welfare and contentment of his people as a necessary political requirement for his own success.

The history of the Maurya empire after Chandragupta's defeat of Seleukos and the acquisition of the northwest remains a matter for conjecture. Since at the time of Ashoka's accession to the throne in 268 BC the empire extended as far as present Karnataka, we may conclude that either Chandragupta or his son and successor Bindusara (*c.*293 to 268 BC) had conquered these southern parts of India. Old Jaina texts report that Chandragupta was a follower of that religion and ended his life in Karnataka by fasting unto death, a great achievement of holy men in the Jaina tradition. If this report is true, Chandragupta must have started the conquest of the south. At Bindusara's court there were ambassadors of the Seleukids and of the Ptolemaeans but they have not left us valuable reports as Megasthenes did a generation earlier.

Ashoka, the Beloved of the Gods

Ashoka's reign of more than three decades is the first fairly well-documented period of Indian history. Ashoka left us a series of great inscriptions (major rock edicts, minor rock edicts, pillar edicts) which are among the most important records of India's past. Ever since they were discovered and deciphered by the British scholar James Prinsep in the 1830s, several generations of Indologists and historians have studied these inscriptions with great care. The independent Republic of India selected Ashoka's lion pillar as the emblem of the state.

According to Buddhist tradition Prince Ashoka started his political career when he was appointed governor of Taxila in the northwest where he successfully suppressed a revolt. He was then transferred to Ujjain, the famous capital of the earlier kingdom of Avanti in central India. The precise date and the circumstances of Ashoka's accession to the throne are not yet

Figure 2.1 Sarnath, capital of an Ashoka-pillar, third century BC, now the coat of arms of the Republic of India

(Courtesy of Hermann Kulke)

known. Buddhist texts mention that Ashoka had to fight against his brothers and that he was crowned only four years after his de facto accession. But the Dutch Indologist Eggermont thinks that these are only legends which were invented later by the Buddhists, and he feels confident about dating Ashoka's reign from 268 to 233 BC.

The first important event of Ashoka's reign led to a crucial change in his life: in 261 BC he conquered Kalinga, a kingdom on the east coast which had resisted Maurya expansionism for a long time. In his inscriptions Ashoka told the cruel consequences of this war: '150,000 people were forcibly abducted from their homes, 100,000 were killed in battle and many more died later on.' Due to this experience Ashoka abjured further warfare and turned to Buddhism. In his famous thirteenth rock edict he stated: 'Even a hundredth or a thousandth part only of the people who were slain, killed or abducted in Kalinga is now considered as a grievous loss by Devanampiya [Beloved of the Gods, i.e. Ashoka]',[5] and he also stated that he now only strove for conquest in spiritual terms by spreading the doctrine of right conduct (*dhamma*).

He became a Buddhist lay member (*upasaka*) and two years after the Kalinga war he even went on a 256-day pilgrimage (*dhamma-yata*) to all Buddhist holy places in northern India. On his return to Pataliputra he celebrated a great festival of the Buddhist order and in the same year (258 BC, according to Eggermont) began his large-scale missionary activity. In numerous rock edicts strategically placed in all parts of his empire he propagated the principles of right conduct and, to all countries known to him, he sent ambassadors to spread the message of right conduct abroad. He instructed governors and district officers to have the principles of right conduct inscribed on rocks and pillars wherever possible, thereby producing a series of smaller rock edicts in which Ashoka openly confessed his Buddhist faith.

In the following year, 257 BC, he had the first four of altogether fourteen large rock edicts cut into rocks in the frontier regions of his empire. Eight more or less complete versions of these have been discovered so far. More recently two fragmentary versions came to light. One of them, a Greek–Aramaic bilingual, was found even in far-off Kandahar in Afghanistan. In these edicts Ashoka ordered all citizens of his empire to desist as far as possible from eating meat and he also prohibited illicit and immoral meetings. He indicated his goodwill to all neighbours beyond the borders of his empire: to the Cholas, Pandyas, Satyaputras, Keralaputras and to Tambapani (Sri Lanka) in the south and to King Antiyoka of Syria (Antiochos II, 261 to 246 BC) and his neighbours in the west. Further, he ordered different ranks of officers to tour the area of their jurisdiction regularly to see that the rules of right conduct were followed.

Ashoka's orders seem to have been resisted right from the beginning. He indirectly admitted this when, in the new series of rock edicts in the

thirteenth year after his coronation he stated: 'Virtuous deeds are difficult to accomplish. He who tries to accomplish them faces a hard task.' In
order to break the resistance and to intensify the teaching of right conduct
he appointed high officers called *Dhamma-Mahamatras* that year. They had
to teach right conduct and supervise the people in this. They also had to
report to the emperor, and he emphasised that these officers were to have
access to him at all times even if he was having his meals or resting in his
private rooms. These officers were 'deployed everywhere, in Pataliputra as
well as in all distant cities, in the private rooms of my brothers and sisters
and all of my relatives'.

In the same year in which he appointed these special officers he also
sent ambassadors (*duta*) to the distant countries of the West. As a unique
event in Indian history the kings of these distant countries are mentioned by
name in the thirteenth rock edict: the king of the Greeks (Yona), Antiyoka
(as mentioned above), Tulamaya (Ptolomaios II, Philadelphos, 285–247 BC),
Antekina (Antigonos Gonatas of Macedonia, 276–239 BC), Maka (Magas
of Cyrene, *c.*300–250 BC), Alikasudala (probably Alexander of Epirus,
272–255 BC). The independent states of southern India and Sri Lanka were
once again visited by ambassadors and also some of the tribes in areas within
the empire (e.g. the Andhras). The frequency of inscriptions in the border
regions of the northwestern and southern provinces is an eloquent evidence
of Ashoka's missionary zeal.

This activity of imperial missions was unique in ancient history. Of
greater consequence than the establishment of direct contact with the
Hellenistic world was, however, the success of missions in the south and
in Sri Lanka. There Ashoka's son Mahinda personally appeared in order to
teach right conduct. The northwest was also deeply affected by this
missionary zeal. From southern India, Buddhism later travelled to southeast Asia and from northwest India it penetrated central Asia from where
it reached China via the silk road in the first century AD.

Ashoka did not neglect his duties as a ruler while pursuing his missionary
activities. In spite of his contrition after the conquest of Kalinga, he never
thought of relinquishing his hold over this country or of sending back the
people abducted from there. As an astute politician, he also did not express
his contrition in the rock edicts which he put up in Kalinga itself (Dhauli
and Jaugada). Instead of the text of the famous thirteenth rock edict we
find in the so-called 'separate edicts' in Kalinga the following words:

> All men are my children. As on behalf of my own children, I desire
> that they may be provided by me with complete welfare and happi-
> ness in this world and in the other world, even so is my desire on
> behalf of all men. It may occur to my unconquered borderers
> to ask: 'What does the king desire with reference to us?' This alone
> is my wish with reference to the borderers, that they may learn that

the king desires this, that they may not be afraid of me, but may have confidence in me; that they may obtain only happiness from me, not misery, that they may learn this, that the king will forgive them what can be forgiven. (Ashoka orders his officers:) For you are able to inspire those borderers with confidence and to secure their welfare and happiness in this world and the other world.

Ashoka's inscriptions also provide a great deal of important information about the organisation of the empire which was divided into five parts. The central part consisted of Magadha and some of the adjacent old maha-janapadas. This part was under the direct administration of the emperor and, though not much is said about its administration, we may assume that it was conducted more or less in line with what had been mentioned by Megasthenes and Kautalya. Then there were four large provinces governed by princes (*kumara* or *aryaputra*) as governors or viceroys. The viceroy of the northwest resided at Taxila, the viceroy of the east at Tosali in Kalinga (near Bhubaneswar, the present capital of Orissa), the viceroy of the west at Ujjain, and the viceroy of the south at Suvarnagiri (near Kurnool in the Rayalaseema region of Andhra Pradesh). As a newly discovered minor rock inscription at Panguraria in Madhya Pradesh is addressed by Ashoka to a kumara, this inscription is interpreted as an indication of the existence of a fifth province. But as the site of this inscription is only about a hundred kilometres away from Ujjain, the famous capital of the western province, the kumara addressed in this inscription may well have been the viceroy of Ujjain.

The large provinces were divided into fairly extensive districts, headed by *mahamatras*. The mahamatras were probably the high officers mentioned by Megasthenes. They were responsible for the relation between the centre and the provinces. In provincial towns they also were appointed as judges (*nagara-viyohalaka*). In addition to the mahamatras the inscriptions mention the following ranks of officers: *pradeshika*, *rajuka* and *yukta*. The latter were petty officers, probably scribes and revenue collectors. The pradeshikas were in charge of administrative units which could be compared to the divisions of British India which included several districts. Whether the rajuka was a district officer is not quite clear. The fourth pillar inscription belonging to the twenty-sixth year of Ashoka's reign mentions that the rajuka is 'appointed over many hundred thousands of people' and was given special powers of penal jurisdiction, but the same inscription also states that the rajukas had to obey orders conveyed by royal emissaries (*pulisani*) who, as Ashoka emphasised, knew exactly what he wanted done.

References of this kind have often been used to show that Ashoka was running a highly centralised direct administration of his whole empire. But the pillar inscriptions which contain these latter references have so

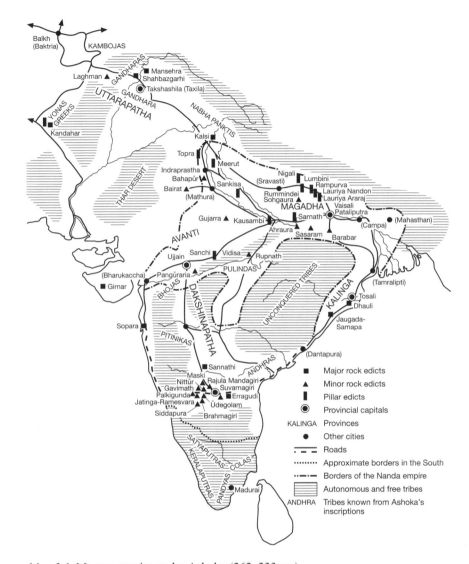

Map 2.1 Maurya empire under Ashoka (262–233 BC)

far been found only in central Gangetic region and the Ganga–Yamuna Doab. Similar inscriptions may still be found at other places, but the pillar inscriptions discovered so far seem to indicate that this specific type of administration prevailed only in the central part of the empire, and that the provinces had a greater degree of administrative autonomy. However, recently conquered Kalinga may have been an exception. In its rock edict,

69

the district administration of Samapa (Jaugada) was addressed directly without reference to the district's viceroy (*kumara*) at Tosali.

In modern historical maps Ashoka's empire is often shown as covering the whole subcontinent, with the exception of its southern tip. But if we look at the sites where Ashoka's inscriptions have been found, we clearly see a definite regional pattern (see Map 2.1). These sites demarcate the five parts of the empire. It is striking that the major rock edicts have so far been found only in the frontier provinces of the empire and not at its centre. Three were found in the northwest (Shahbazgarhi, Mansehra and Kandahar), two in the west (Girnar and Sopara), two in the south (Erragudi and Sannathi), two in the east (Dhauli and Jaugada), and one at the border between the central region and the northwestern province at Kalsi. It is also important to note that ten small rock edicts form a cluster in the southern province and that a good number of pillar inscriptions are concentrated in the central part of the empire and in the upper Ganga–Yamuna Doab. Moreover, the region around the provincial capital of Ujjain once must have formed another cluster, although only fragments of a pillar at Sanchi with Ashoka's famous 'schism edict' and the newly discovered minor rock edict of Panguraria have survived. This high incidence of inscriptions in certain main parts of the empire and on the frontiers contrasts with the vast 'empty' space of the interior of the subcontinent where no inscriptions have been found which can be attributed to Ashoka.

Of course, it is not impossible that some may be still discovered but after more than a century of intensive research in this field it seems highly unlikely that the regional pattern mentioned above would have to be completely revised. This means that large parts of present Maharashtra and Andhra Pradesh as well as Kerala and Tamil Nadu were not actually included in the Maurya empire.

South of the Vindhya mountains the Mauryas mainly controlled the coastal areas and some of the interior near present Mysore which they probably coveted because of the gold which was found there (Suvarnagiri means 'gold mountain'). For the empire it was essential to control the major trade routes. Most important was certainly the northern route which led from Pataliputra through the Gangetic plain and the Panjab to Afghanistan. Another led from Pataliputra west via Kausambi and then along the northern slope of the Vindhya mountains via Vidisha (Sanchi) and Ujjain to the port of Bharukacha (Broach). There was a further route from there along the west coast to the area of present Bombay where the great rock edicts of Sopara were found. Southern parts could be reached along the east coast or via a central route from Ujjain via Pratishthana (Paithan near Aurangabad) to Suvarnagiri. The northern portion of this route – at least up to Ujjain – had been known since the late Vedic period as Dakshinapatha (southern route). Large areas of the interior were inhabited by tribes which had not been defeated. The inscriptions explicitly mention such undefeated (*avijita*) neighbours and forest tribes (*atavi*) inside the empire, and one gets the impression that Ashoka regarded these tribes as the most dangerous enemies of his empire.

This revision of the spatial extension of the Maurya empire nevertheless does not detract from its 'All-India' dimensions and that it marked the apex of the process of state formation which had started in the sixth century BC. The hub of the empire remained the old region of the major mahajanapadas in the triangle Delhi–Pataliputra–Ujjain. Campaigns of conquest had added the northwest, Kalinga, and an enclave in the south to the empire. Control of major trade routes and of the coasts was of major importance for the access to mercantile wealth which must have been essential for imperial finance.

Ashoka's greatness was due to his insight into the futility of further expansionist warfare which would not have added much to the empire but would have impeded its consolidation. In order to conquer the vast areas in the interior, Ashoka would have had to fight many more bloody wars. About 2,000 years later the Mughal empire broke under the strain of incessant conquest when Aurangzeb tried to achieve what Ashoka had wisely avoided. In consolidating his empire, Ashoka adopted revolutionary methods. As emphasised by the Indian historian Romila Thapar, he must have realised that such a vast empire could not be based simply on the naked power polities of the *Arthashastra* but that it required some deeper legitimation. Therefore he adopted the doctrine of right conduct as the maxim of his policy. For the spread of this doctrine, he relied on the spiritual infrastructure provided by the new Buddhist community which was in ascendance in those days. But he carefully avoided equating his doctrine of right conduct with Buddhism as such. He also included the Brahmins and the sect of the Ajivikas in his religious policy.

After a period of unscrupulous power politics under the earlier rulers of Magadha, Indian kingship attained a moral dimension in Ashoka's reign. But in the means he adopted, he was influenced by the tradition of statecraft epitomised by Kautalya. The Dhamma-Mahamatras which he put into the entourage of his relatives – from whom challenges to his power would be expected to come – were different in name only from Kautalya's spies. This, of course, should not detract from the greatness of his vision which prompted him to strive for an ethical legitimation of his imperial rule. His success was nevertheless not only due to his ideology and the strength of his army and administration but also to the relative backwardness of central and southern India in his day. When regional centres of power emerged in those parts of the country in the course of an autochthonous process of state formation in later centuries, the course of Indian history was changed once more and the great regional kingdoms of the early medieval period arose. In that period the old tradition of the legitimation of Hindu kings was revived and Ashoka's great vision was eclipsed.

THE END OF THE MAURYA EMPIRE AND THE NORTHERN INVADERS

The history of the Maurya empire after the death of Ashoka is not very well recorded. There are only stray references in Buddhist texts, the Indian Puranas and some Western classical texts and these references often contradict each other. None of Ashoka's successors produced any larger rock edicts. Perhaps the paternal tone of these edicts and the instruction to recite them publicly on certain days of the year had caused resentment among the people. Buddhist texts maintain that there was evidence of the decay of the empire even in the last days of Ashoka but this view is not generally accepted. The more distant provinces probably attained independence from the empire after Ashoka's death. There is, for instance, no evidence in the south or in Kalinga for the continuation of Maurya domination after Ashoka. Perhaps even the central part of the empire in the north may have been divided among Ashoka's sons and grandsons. One descendant, Dasaratha, succeeded Ashoka on the throne of Magadha, and he is the only one whom we know by name because he left some otherwise unimportant stone inscriptions with which he established some endowment for the Ajivika sect at a place south of Pataliputra.

Figure 2.2 Buddha, Gandhara style at Takht-i-Bahai (near Peshawar), second to third century BC

(Courtesy of Museum of Indian Art, Berlin)

The last ruler of the Maurya dynasty, Brihadratha, was assassinated by his general, Pushyamitra Shunga, during a parade of his troops in the year 185 BC. The usurper then founded the Shunga dynasty which continued for 112 years but about which very little is known. No inscriptions of this dynasty have ever been discovered. Pushyamitra is reported to have been a Brahmin and it is said that his rise to power marked a Brahmin reaction to Buddhism which had been favoured for such a long time by previous rulers. Pushyamitra once again celebrated the Vedic horse sacrifice. This was certainly a clear break with Ashoka's tradition which had prohibited animal sacrifices altogether.

There is some other evidence, too, for the inclination of Indian kings to violate the rules established by the Mauryas and to revive old customs which had been forbidden by them. King Kharavela stated in an inscription of the first century BC near Bhubaneswar that he had reintroduced the musical festivals and dances which were prohibited under the Mauryas. There were reactions against the religious policy of the Mauryas, indeed, but this does not necessarily imply that Buddhism was suppressed and that the Shungas started a Brahmin counter-reformation as some Buddhist texts suggest. Several Buddhist monasteries, for instance the one at Sanchi, were renovated and enlarged under the Shunga rule. At Bharhut, south of Kausambi, they even sponsored the construction of a new Buddhist stupa. The Shunga style differed from the Maurya style, which was greatly influenced by Persian precedent. Old elements of folk art and of the cult of the mother goddess reappeared in the Shunga style which was 'more Indian' and is sometimes regarded as the first indigenous style of Indian art.

Immediately after taking the throne, Pushyamitra had to defend his country against the Greek invaders from Bactria who came to conquer the Indian plains. Pushyamitra prevented their complete success but nevertheless the whole area up to Mathura was finally lost. His son, Agnimitra, is supposed to have been posted as viceroy at Vidisha near Sanchi before ascending the throne. This was reported by the great poet Kalidasa, several centuries later. Towards the end of the second century BC the Greek ambassador, Heliodorus, who represented King Antialkidas, erected a tall Garuda pillar at Besnagar, very close to Vidisha. In his inscription on this pillar, Heliodorus calls himself a follower of the Bhagavata sect of the Vaishnavas and mentions a king by the name of Bhagabhadra who seems to have been a member of the Shunga dynasty. So Vidisha was probably still under the control of the Shungas, but they had obviously lost Ujjain, the old provincial capital situated about a hundred miles further to the west. The last king of the Shunga dynasty was murdered around 73 BC by a slave girl and, it is said, instigated by the king's Brahmin minister, Vasudeva.

The short-lived Kanva dynasty, which was founded by Vasudeva after the Shunga dynasty, witnessed the complete decline of Magadha which relapsed to its earlier position of one mahajanapada among several others.

The political centre of India had shifted to the northwest where several foreign dynasties struggled for supremacy. In 28 BC the last Kanva king was defeated by a king of the Shatavahana (or Andhra) dynasty of central India. This fact not only signalled the end of the Magadha after five centuries of imperial eminence but also the rise of central and southern India which continued throughout the subsequent centuries.

Greek rulers of the northwest

When the Maurya empire was at the height of its power it could thwart all attempts of the Seleukids to claim Alexander's heritage in India. Chandragupta had repulsed Seleukos Nikator at the end of the fourth century BC and a later king of the same dynasty, Antiochos III, who tried to conquer the Indian plains about one century later was equally frustrated. But this was due less to the efficacy of Indian resistance than to the great upheavals which had occurred in Bactria, Persia and southern central Asia in the meantime.

Around 250 BC the Parthians, under King Arsakes, had won their independence from the Seleukids. After a century of tough fights against their former masters and against central Asian nomadic horsemen, they had established hegemony over western Asia. Until their final defeat about AD 226 they remained the most dangerous enemies of the Romans. At about the same time that Arsakes won independence from the Seleukids, the viceroy of Bactria, Diodotos, did the same and established a kingdom of his own. But only the third Greek king of Bactria, Euthydemos, was able to get formal recognition from the Seleukid king, Antiochos III, when he was on his Indian campaign which has been referred to above.

The history of the Greek kings of Bactria became a part of Indian history when the successors of Euthydemos once again tried to follow Alexander's example. They are referred to as 'Indo-Greeks' and there were about forty such kings and rulers who controlled large areas of northwestern India and Afghanistan. Their history, especially during the first century BC, is not very well recorded. Of some of these kings we know the names only, from coins. There are only two inscriptions in India to give us some information about these Indo-Greeks. They appear as *Yavanas* in stray references in Indian literature, and there are few but important references in European sources. In these distant outposts, the representatives of the Hellenic policy survived the defeat of their Western compatriots at the hands of the Parthians for more than a century.

In India the history of the Indo-Greeks is particularly associated with the name of their most prominent king, Menander, who conquered a large part of northern India. This Indian campaign was started by King Demetrios and his brother Apollodoros with the help of their general, Menander, who subsequently became a king in his own right. There is a debate among historians about whether these three military leaders conquered almost the whole of northern India jointly within a few years after 180 BC, or whether this was achieved in two stages, the second stage following the first by about three decades and exclusively managed by Menander. Menander also annexed most of the Ganga–Yamuna Doab and perhaps even reached Pataliputra. Some 150 years later Strabo reported in his *Geography*:

> The Greeks who occasioned its revolt (Bactria's) became so powerful by means of its fertility and the advantages of the country that they became the masters of Ariana and India. Their chiefs, particularly Menander if he really crossed the Hypasis to the East and reached Isamus [i.e. Yamuna] conquered more nations than Alexander. The conquests were achieved partly by Menander, partly by Demetrius, son of Euthydemus, king of the Bactrians.[1]

According to the findings of the British historian W.W. Tarn, Demetrios crossed the Hindukush mountains about 183 BC only shortly after Pushyamitra Shunga had seized power at Pataliputra. Demetrios conquered Gandhara and Taxila and established his new capital at Sirkap near Taxila. He continued his campaign down the river Indus and captured the old port, Patala, which he renamed Demetrias. His brother Apollodoros then marched further east in order to capture the ports of Gujarat, especially Bharukacha which was later known as Barygaza to the Romans who had a great deal of trade with this port.

The unknown seafarer who left us the famous account, *Periplus of the Erythraean Sea* in the first century AD reported that he had seen coins of Apollodoros and Menander at Barygaza. It is presumed that this port was in the hands of the Greeks for some time. Apollodoros proceeded east and conquered the area around Gwalior and probably also the old provincial capital, Ujjain. In a parallel move Menander, who was then still a general of King Demetrios, marched down into the Gangetic basin and reached Pataliputra. Whether he really conquered this capital and held it for some time, as Tarn assumes, or not, we know that Pushyamitra Shunga was finally able to defeat the Greeks.

But even more than Pushyamitra's resistance it was a revolt in Bactria which forced the Greeks to withdraw. Eukratides, a Greek adventurer with the mind of a genius, managed to seize power in Bactria. Thereupon Demetrios appointed Apollodoros and Menander as viceroys of the Indus region and of the Panjab and rushed back to Bactria where he was killed in the civil war. Eukratides then also defeated Apollodoros, but Menander was able to hold on to his territory further east. In subsequent decades the kingdom of Eukratides and his successors came under increasing pressure from the Parthians. Weakened by this constant warfare, this Greek kingdom finally succumbed to the Shakas, a central Asian tribe, between 141 and

128 BC. But in northwest India the period of Indo-Greek rule continued for some time and this was, in fact, a period of great splendour.

The greatest of the Indo-Greek rulers was undoubtedly Menander, who is called Milinda in Buddhist texts. The dates of his reign are still open to debate. Tarn suggests 166 to 150 BC, the Indian historian A.K. Narain prefers 155 to 130 BC. He was the only Indo-Greek ruler commemorated in Indian literature. The famous text *Milindapanho* records a dialogue between Menander and a monk, Nagasena, who introduced him to the Buddhist doctrine. This dialogue is justly praised for the incisive questions asked by Menander and it is regarded by the Buddhists as equal in value to their canonical scriptures. It is not certain whether Menander was actually converted to Buddhism, but he seems to have taken a deep interest in it. Some of his coins show a wheel similar to the Buddhist chakra. Plutarch reports that after Menander's death his ashes were distributed to all cities of his kingdom where monuments were then constructed to contain them – a kind of commemoration which was in tune with Buddhist practice.

After Menander's death, his large kingdom broke up into several small ones which survived for several generations. This survival, far removed from the Hellenistic polity, is a remarkable historical event. The pillar of Heliodoros, mentioned above, is an impressive testimony of this Greek presence right in the heart of India. The political influence of the Indo-Greek states on the further course of Indian history was negligible, but they did make an impact on the subsequent foreign invaders who came to India in quick succession. The most important legacy of the Indo-Greeks was Gandhara art which embodied a synthesis of Greek, Roman and Indian features that are reflected in the image of Buddha which then radiated from India to all other parts of Asia.

Another Indo-Greek contribution, of great importance for historians, is their highly developed coinage. Whereas the Maurya emperors had only produced simple punch-marked coins, even petty Indo-Greek kings issued splendid coins with their image. No period of Indian history is richer in impressive coins than this fairly short period of the Indo-Greeks. This style of coinage was followed by later dynasties and set the pattern for all coins of ancient India. Only some slight changes were made when the Kushanas adopted Roman standards for the weight of their coins and the Guptas then introduced an Indian standard. For the historians this new source proves to be often more reliable, at least for the identification and dating of rulers, than inscriptions and literary texts. For the Indo-Greek kings this coinage was not just an instrument of propagating their own importance, but a practical means of fostering regional and inter-regional trade which was so important for the maintenance of their rule. This combination of domination and commerce was copied from the Indo-Greek precedent by the Shakas and Kushanas who became their heirs in northern India.

The Shakas: new invaders from central Asia

In the last centuries of the first millennium BC northwestern India was once more subjected to a new wave of immigration from central Asia. In Bactria several tribes clashed in the second century BC and pushed each other towards the fertile lowlands in the south. This migration began around 170 BC in the eastern region of central Asia when the nomadic Xiongnu (Hiung-nu) (probably the ancestors of the latter-day Huns) defeated the Yuezhi (Yue-chi) who then moved west where they hit upon a third nomadic tribe, the Sai Wang or Shakas, who in turn moved to the west. According to Chinese reports some of these Shakas directly crossed the mountains and entered the Indus plains whereas others invaded Bactria and eastern Iran. Together with their kinsmen, the Scythians, they became a major threat to the Parthian empire and two Parthian rulers lost their lives in fighting against them. But in the reign of Mithridates II (123 to 88 BC), the Shakas seem to have recognised Parthian suzerainty and some of them settled down in Sakastan (Sistan) in what is now southern Afghanistan. There they inter-married with Scythians and with the local Parthian nobility. Other clans of the Shakas appeared as conquerors in India where they dominated the political scene of the northwest for nearly a century.

The first Shaka king in India was Maues. There are various estimates of the dates of his reign, ranging from 94 BC to AD 22. Under him and his successor, Azes I, the Shakas established a large Indian empire including the northwest and parts of central India from Gandhara down to Mathura and Ujjain and all the way to the coast of Saurashtra. The Shakas wiped out the Indo-Greek kingdoms but largely adopted their culture with which they had already become familiar in Bactria. The Shaka kings translated their Iranian title 'King of Kings' into Greek (*basileus basileon*), used the Greek names of the months and issued coins in the Indo-Greek style.

A Jaina text of a later period, the *Kalakacharyakathanaka*, reports that Kalaka went from Ujjain to the country of the Shakas. Kings were called Shahi there and the mightiest king was called Shahanu Shahi. Kalaka stayed with one of those Shahis and when this one, together with ninety-five others, incurred the displeasure of the Shahanu Shahi, he persuaded them to go to India. They first came to Saurashtra, but in the autumn they moved on to Ujjain and conquered that city. The Shahi became the superior king of that region and thus emerged the dynasty of the Shaka kings. But some time later the king of Malwa, Vikramaditya, revolted and defeated the Shakas and became the superior king. He started a new era. After 135 years, another Shaka king vanquished the dynasty of Vikramaditya and started another new era.[2]

Despite this story of the origins of the two Indian eras, the Vikrama era, which started in 58 BC and the more important Shaka era beginning in AD 78 (adopted officially by the government of independent India), historians are still debating the issue. They generally agree that there was no king by the name Vikramaditya of Malwa. The Vikrama era is now believed to be connected with the Shaka king, Azes I. The beginning of the Shaka era is supposed to coincide with the accession to the throne of the great Kushana emperor, Kanishka, the dates of whose reign are still debated.

In other respects the Jaina text seems to reflect the situation in the Shaka period of dominance fairly accurately. The Shaka political system was obviously one of a confederation of chieftains who all had the Persian title Shahi. The text mentions that there were ninety-five of them. The Indian and Persian titles were 'Great King' (*maharaja*) and 'King of Kings' (*shahanu shahi*, or, in Sanskrit *rajatiraja*) which the Shakas assumed may have reflected their real position rather than an exaggerated image of their own importance. They were *primus inter pares* as leaders of tribal confederations whose chieftains had the title Shahi. The grandiloquent title 'King of Kings' which the Shakas introduced into India, following Persian and Greek precedents, thus implied not a notion of omnipotence but rather the existence of a large number of fairly autonomous small kings. But the Shaka kings also appointed provincial governors called Kshatrapas and Mahakshatrapas (like the Persian *satraps*), though it is not quite clear how they fitted into the pattern of a tribal confederation. Perhaps some of them – particularly the Mahakshatrapas – may have been members of the royal lineage, but there may also have been local Indian rulers among them whom one accommodated in this way. Such a network of Kshatrapas may have served as a counterweight to too powerful tribal chieftains.

In the last decades BC the Shaka empire showed definite signs of decay while the provincial governors became more powerful. Azes II was the last great Shaka king of the northwest. About AD 20 the Shakas were replaced by the short-lived Indo-Parthian dynasty founded by King Gondopharnes who reigned until AD 46. He seems to have been a provincial governor of Arachosia in southern Afghanistan. Though he managed to conquer the central part of the Shaka domain, the eastern part around Mathura seems to have remained outside his kingdom because the local Shaka Kshatrapas in this region had attained their independence. The same was true of Saurashtra where independent Shaka Kshatrapas still held sway until the time of the Gupta empire.

Gondopharnes appeared in third century AD Christian texts as Gunduphar, King of India, at whose court St Thomas is supposed to have lived, converting many people to Christianity. According to Christian sources of the third century AD which refer to St Thomas ('Acts of St Thomas'), the saint moved later on to Kerala and finally died the death of a martyr near Madras. These southern activities of St Thomas are less well documented, but there can be no doubt about early Christian contacts with Gondopharnes. In a further mutation of his name (via Armenian 'Gathaspar') Gondopharnes became 'Kaspar', one of the three *magi* or kings of the east who play such an important role in Christian tradition.

The Kushana empire: a short-lived Asian synthesis

While in the early first century AD Indo-Parthians, Shakas and the remnants of the Indo-Greeks were still fighting each other in India, new invaders were already on their way. The Yuezhi under the leadership of the Kushanas came down from central Asia and swept away all earlier dynasties of the northwest in a great campaign of conquest. They established an empire which extended from central Asia right down to the eastern Gangetic basin. Their earlier encounter with the Shakas whom they displaced in central Asia has been mentioned above. The Xiongnu, their old enemies, did not leave the Yuezhi in possession of the land they had taken from the Shakas but pushed them further west. Thus they appeared in Bactria only a few decades after the Shakas and took over this territory in the late second century BC. Here in Bactria they seem to have changed their previous nomadic life style and settled down in five large tribal territories with a chieftain (*yabgu*) at the head of each.

Around the time of the birth of Christ, Kujala Kadphises, Yabgu of the Kuei-shang (Kushana) vanquished the four other yabgus and established the first Kushana kingdom. The history of the further development of this kingdom is recorded in the chronicles of the contemporary Han dynasty of China which were compiled in the fifth century AD. These chronicles report that Kadphises, after uniting the five principalities, proclaimed himself king, attacked the Parthians, crossed the Hindukush and conquered Gandhara and Ki-pin (Kashmir). When he died at the age of 80 years, his son Vima Kadphises, so the chronicles state, proceeded to conquer India where he appointed a viceroy. Numismatic research has confirmed these statements in recent times. Several coins of Kadphises I were found, which show on one side the name of the last Greek ruler of the valley of Kabul, Hermaios and, on the reverse, his own name, Kujala Kada, Prince of the Kushanas. Since the later coins of Kadphises I no longer refer to him as Yabgu but as king (*maharaja*), historians assume that Kadphises had earlier

Figure 2.3 Kushana gold coin. Obverse: Kanishka in central Asian dress. Reverse: Buddha ('Buddo'), Greek script *c.*100 AD

(Courtesy of The British Museum)

recognised the suzerainty of Hermaios until the Parthians or Kadphises himself had defeated this monarch.

Kadphises I was followed by a 'nameless' king who was known only from his coins which referred to him as *soter mages* (great saviour). In 1993 a most important stone inscription of Kanishka was discovered in Rabatak in northern Afghanistan, which contains an unambiguous genealogy of the early Kushana rulers. Kadphises was followed by Vima Takto, Vima Kadphises II and Kanishka. Accordingly, Vima Takto is the king who had so far been nameless. The monumental sculpture at Mat/Mathura which bears the incomplete inscription 'Vima Tak' thus represents Vima Takto. Vima Takto and Kadphises II continued the aggressive policy initiated by Kadphises I and conquered northern India down to Mathura or even Varanasi. Kadphises II changed the standard of the coins which had so far been of the same weight as the Indo-Greek ones by following Roman precedent. The gold of these coins seems to have been procured by melting down Roman coins (*aurei*), which were pouring into India in increasing quantities ever since the Greek seafarer Hippalos had explored the swift monsoon passage across the Arabian sea in the first century BC. The Kushana coins are of such high quality that some historians believe that they must have been made by Roman mint masters in the service of the Kushana kings.

Whereas Kadphises I seems to have been close to Buddhism – he calls himself on his coins 'firm in right conduct' (*dharma thita*) – Kadphises II seems to have been a devotee of the Hindu god Shiva. There were some other Kushana rulers during this age. Inscriptions and coins refer to those kings but do not record their names. Thus, an inscription was found at Taxila of a king with the grandiloquent title 'Great King, King of Kings, Son of God, the Kushana' (*maharaja rajatiraja devaputra Kushana*). Other coins announce in Greek language a 'King of Kings, the Great Savior' (*basileus basileon soter mages*). It is assumed that some of these inscriptions and coins were produced on behalf of the 'nameless' king, i.e. Vima Takto, or by the viceroys whom Kadphises I had appointed in India and who have been mentioned in Chinese chronicles. The titles adopted by the Kushanas show that they valiantly tried to legitimise their rule over all kinds of petty kings and princes. 'Great King' (*maharaja*) was an old Indian title, 'King of Kings' (*rajatiraja*) was of Persian origin and had already been adopted by the Shakas, but the title 'Son of God' (*devaputra*) was a new one. Perhaps it reflected the Kushanas' understanding of the Chinese 'mandate of heaven'. The Greek titles *basileus* and *soter* were frequently used by the Indo-Greek kings of northwestern India.

Vima Kadphises II was succeeded by Kanishka, the greatest of all Kushana rulers. The first references to Kanishka were found in the eastern parts of the Kushana empire in the Ganga–Yamuna Doab, which was probably under the control of rather autonomous viceroys. In two inscriptions of the second and third year of his reign which have been found at Kausambi and Sarnath in the east, he merely calls himself Maharaja Kanishka. Yet in an inscription of the seventh year of his reign at Mathura he gives his title as Maharaja Rajatiraja Devaputra Shahi, a designation which is repeated in an inscription of the eleventh year of his reign in the central Indus valley. All this would indicate that Kanishka first came to power in the east and, after he had seized the centre of the empire which was probably at Mathura, he adopted the full titles of his predecessors.

The vast extension of Kanishka's empire cannot be adequately outlined. It probably reached from the Oxus in the west to Pataliputra in the east and from Kashmir in the north via Malwa right down to the coast of Gujarat in the south. Not much is known about his hold on central Asia, but there is a reference to the defeat of a Kushana army by the Chinese general, Pan-Chao, at Khotan in the year AD 90 where coins of all early Kushana kings have been found. The kings wanted to control the trade routes connecting India with Rome, i.e. those land and sea routes which would enable this trade to bypass the Parthians' routes. This trade must have been very profitable to the Kushanas. Pliny (VI, 10) laments in those days: 'There is no year in which India does not attract at least 50 million sesterces [Roman coins].' Yet though fifty-seven out of the sixty-eight finds of Roman coins in the whole of southern Asia were found in south India, none at all were found in the area of the Kushana empire. This must be due to the fact that the Kushanas as a matter of policy melted down and reissued them. After the debasement of Roman silver coins in AD 63 in the reign of Nero, gold became the most important medium of exchange for the Roman trade with India, and this must have greatly contributed to the rise of the Kushanas to prosperity and power.

Kanishka's fame is not only based on his military and political success but also on his spiritual merit. The Buddhists rank him together with Ashoka, Menander and Harsha as one of the great Buddhist rulers of India. The great stupa near Peshawar is rated as his greatest contribution to Buddhist monumental architecture. Several Chinese pilgrims have left us descriptions of this stupa and have stated that it was about 600 feet high. When archaeologists excavated the foundations of this stupa at the beginning of the twentieth century they found that it was 286 feet in diameter. Therefore it must have been one of the great miracles of the ancient world. Kanishka is also supposed to have convened a Buddhist council in Kashmir which stimulated the growth of Mahayana Buddhism. For the development of Indian art it was of great importance that Kanishka not only favoured the Gandhara school of Buddhist art which had grown out of Greek influences but also provided his patronage to the Mathura school of art which set the style of Indian art. This school produced the famous statue of Kanishka of which, unfortunately, only the headless trunk has survived. His dress here shows the typical central Asian style.

Kanishka's religious policy is reflected in the legends and images of his coins. His far-flung empire contained so many cultures and religious traditions that only a religious syncretism could do justice to this rich heritage. Accordingly Kanishka's coins show Hindu, Buddhist, Greek, Persian and even Sumerian–Elamite images of gods. Personally Kanishka seems to have shown an inclination towards Buddhism but also towards the Persian cult of Mithras. An inscription at Surkh-Kotal in Bactria which was discovered in 1958 maintains that after Kanishka's death in the thirty-first year of the era which he had started with his accession to the throne, he himself became identified with Mithras. This was probably an attempt by the adherents of Mithras to claim the religious heritage of the great emperor for their cult. Kanishka's syncretism reminds us of that of Ashoka in an earlier and of Akbar in a later age. Great emperors of India who had a vision beyond the immediate control of the levers of power were bound to try to reconcile the manifold religious ideas represented in their vast realm in the interest of internal peace and consolidation.

Another important element of Kanishka's heritage was the introduction of a new era which influenced the chronology of the history of India, central Asia and southeast Asia. The inscriptions of Kanishka and of his successors are dated according to this new era for the ninety-eight years which followed his accession to the throne. But dating this new era is a knotty problem and historians have yet to reach agreement. Several international Kushana conferences, in London in 1913 and 1960, at Dushanbe in Soviet central Asia in 1968 and in Vienna in 1996, have not settled the debate on this date. In 1913 there was a tendency to equate the beginning of this era with the Vikrama era. Kanishka thus would have acceded the throne in 58 BC. Then there was a new trend to equate it with the Shaka era which begins in AD 78. But in recent decades there has emerged still another school of thought which maintains that the Kanishka era must have begun sometime around AD 120 to 144.[3]

When and how Huvishka succeeded Kanishka is not yet quite clear. There are two inscriptions dated in the years 24 and 28 of the Kanishka era and found at Mathura and Sanchi respectively which mention a ruler called Vashishka. There is another inscription at Ara in the northwestern Panjab of the year 41 by a king called Kanishka. From the year 28 to the year 60 there exist a considerable number of inscriptions of Huvishka. Since Vashishka did not issue any coins of his own it is assumed that he ruled together with (his brother?) Huvishka. The Kanishka who was the author of the Ara inscription must have been a second Kanishka. This is also confirmed by the fact that he mentions that his father's name was Vashishka. For some years he may have shared a condominium with (his uncle?) Huvishka. Under these rulers the Kushana empire seems to have maintained the boundaries established by the first Kanishka. This is confirmed by the inscription at Surkh-Kotal in Bactria in the year 31 and another one at the Wardak monastery near Kabul in the year 51 which mentions Maharaja Rajatiraja Huvishka.

The Ara inscription of Kanishka II is unique in Indian history because of another feature: he added to the usual titles of Maharaja Rajatiraja Devaputra the Roman title Kaisara. He probably did this following the Roman victory over their common enemy, the Parthians. This victory was achieved by Trajan in the years AD 114 to 117 and Mesopotamia and Assyria became Roman provinces for some time. Trajan himself crossed the river Tigris and reached the Persian Gulf. It is said that when he saw a ship there which was leaving for India he remembered Alexander's campaign and exclaimed: 'Oh, if I were young what would I have better liked to do but to march towards India.' As Dion Cassius reports in his history of Rome, Trajan had heard much about India because he had received many ambassadors of the 'barbarians' and 'especially of the Indians'. Those who advocate the year AD 78 as the beginning of the Kanishka era would find support in this coincidence of Trajan's campaign and the assumption of the title Kaisara by Kanishka II. The date of the Ara inscription (41 Kanishka era) would then correspond to AD 119 when the Roman emperor's success must have been of recent memory in India.

When the Kushanas were at the height of their power in northern India, a branch of the Shakas ruling the area between Saurashtra in Gujarat and Malwa, including Ujjain, in western central India rose to prominence once more. They retained their old Shaka title Kshatrapa and perhaps initially recognised the suzerainty of the Kushanas until they attained a position of regional hegemony under King Rudradaman in the second century AD. Together with the Kushanas in the north and the Shatavahanas in the south, they emerged as the third great power of Indian history at that time.

Rudradaman is known for his famous Junagadh inscription which is the first Sanskrit rock inscription (Ashoka's were written in Magadhi and later ones in Prakrit). In this inscription Rudradaman tells about a great tank whose wall was broken by a storm in the Shaka year 72 (AD 150). This tank, so he says, had originally been built by a provincial governor (*rashtriya*), Pushyagupta, under Chandragupta Maurya, and a canal (*pranali*) had been added to it by a Yavanaraja Tushaspha under Ashoka Maurya.[4] This would indicate that a Yavana king served as a governor under Ashoka (though his name, Tushaspha, seems to be of Persian rather than Greek origin). Rudradaman then goes on to tell about the victories he himself attained over the Shatavahana kings and over the tribe of the Yaudehas near present Delhi. This particular reference to a Rudradaman's northern campaign has been variously interpreted: those who maintain that the Kanishka era began in AD 78 say that the Kushana empire must have declined soon after his death; and those who suggest a later date (around AD 144) for Kanishka's accession to the throne contend that Rudradaman

Map 2.2 India *c.* AD 0–300

could not have conducted this campaign at the time when the Kushanas were in full control of northern India.

The last great Kushana emperor was Vasudeva whose inscriptions cover the period from the year 67 to the year 98 of the Kanishka era. He was the first Kushana ruler with an Indian name, an indication of the progressive assimilation of the Kushanas whose coins show more and more images of Hindu gods. There were some more Kushana rulers after Vasudeva, but we know very little about them. They have left no inscriptions, only coins. Moreover, the knotty problem of the Kanishka era does not yet permit us to correlate foreign reports about India in the age of the Kushanas (such as the Chinese and the Roman ones) with the reign of clearly identifiable Kushana rulers.

In central Asia and Afghanistan the Kushanas seem to have held sway until the early third century AD. In those regions their rule was only terminated when Ardashir, the founder of the Sassanid dynasty, vanquished the Parthians about AD 226 and then turned against the Kushanas, too. Ardashir I and his successor Shahpur I are credited with the conquest of the whole of Bactria and the rest of the Kushana domain in central Asia. Their provincial governors had the title Kushana Shah. In the valley of Kabul local Kushana princes could still be traced in the fifth century AD. In northwestern India some Kushana rulers also survived the decline of the western centre of their empire. The famous Allahabad inscription of the Gupta emperor, Samudragupta (about AD 335 to 375), reflects a faint reminiscence of the erstwhile glamour of the Kushanas: among the many rulers who acknowledged Samudragupta's power he also lists the Daivaputras Shahi Shahanushahis, who were obviously the successors of the great Kanishka.

The splendour of the 'dark period'

The five centuries which passed between the decline of the first great Indian empire of the Mauryas and the emergence of the great empire of the Guptas has often been described as a dark period in Indian history when foreign dynasties fought each other for short-lived and ephemeral supremacy over northern India. Apart from Kanishka's Indo-central Asian empire which could claim to be similar in size to Han China, the Parthians of Persia and to the contemporary Roman empire, this period did lack the glamour of large empires. But this 'dark period', particularly the first two centuries AD, was a period of intensive economic and cultural contact among the various parts of the Eurasian continent. India played a very active role in stimulating these contacts. Buddhism, which had been fostered by Indian rulers since the days of Ashoka, was greatly aided by the international connections of the Indo-Greeks and the Kushanas and thus rose to prominence in central Asia. South India was establishing its important links with the

West and with southeast Asia in this period. These links, especially those with southeast Asia, proved to be very important for the future course of Asian history.

But India itself also experienced important social and cultural changes in this period. For centuries Buddhism had enjoyed royal patronage. This was partly due to the fact that the foreign rulers of India found Buddhism more accessible than orthodox Hinduism with its caste barriers. The Vedic Brahmins had been pushed into the background by the course of historical development although Hinduism as such did not experience a decline. On the contrary, new popular cults arose around gods like Shiva, Krishna and Vishnu-Vasudeva who had played only a marginal role in an earlier age. The competition between Buddhism, which dominated the royal courts and cities, and orthodox Brahminism, which was still represented by numerous Brahmin families everywhere, left enough scope for these new cults to gain footholds of their own. Of great importance for the further development of Hinduism and particularly for the Hindu idea of kingship was the Kushana rulers' identification with certain Hindu gods – they were actually believed to attain a complete identity with the respective god after their death.

Religious legitimation was of greater importance to these foreign rulers than to other Indian kings. Menander's ashes had been distributed according to the Buddhist fashion, and Kanishka was identified with Mithras, but Wima Kadphises and Huvishka were closer to Shiva as shown by the images on their coins. Huvishka's coins provide a regular almanac of the iconography of the early Shiva cult. The deification of the ruler which was so prevalent in the Roman and Hellenistic world as well as among the Iranians was thus introduced into India and left a mark on the future development of Hindu kingship.

Another feature of crucial importance for the future political development of India was the organisation of the Shaka and Kushana empires. They were not centralised as the Maurya empire had been, but were based on the large-scale incorporation of local rulers. In subsequent centuries many regional empires of India were organised on this pattern.

The best-known contribution of the 'dark period' was, of course, to Indian art. After the early sculptures of the Mauryas which were greatly influenced by the Iranian style, a new Indian style had first emerged under the Shungas and their successors in the Buddhist monuments of Bharhut and Sanchi which particularly showed a new style of relief sculpture. The merger of the Gandhara school of art, with its Graeco-Roman style, and the Mathura school of art which included 'archaic' Indian elements and became the centre of Indo-Kushana art, finally led to the rise of the Sarnath school of art. This school then set the pattern of the classical Gupta style.

Less well-known, but much more important for the future development of Hindu society, was the compilation of the authoritative Hindu law books (*dharmashastra*), the foremost of them being the Code of Manu which probably originated in the second or third century AD. After the breakdown of the Maurya and Shunga empires, there must have been a period of uncertainty which led to a renewed interest in traditional social norms. These were then codified so as to remain inviolate for all times to come. If we add to this the resurgence of Sanskrit, as testified by Rudradaman's famous rock inscription of the second century AD, we see that this 'dark period' actually contained all the elements of the classical culture of the Gupta age. Thus the much maligned 'dark period' was actually the harbinger of the classical age.

THE CLASSICAL AGE OF THE GUPTAS

Like the Mauryas a few centuries earlier, the imperial Guptas made a permanent impact on Indian history. In his Allahabad inscription, Samudragupta, the first great ruler of this dynasty, mentions one Maharaja Shri Gupta and one Ghatotkacha as his ancestors. But, except for these names, nothing else is mentioned in any other Gupta inscription nor have any coins been found which bear their names. They were probably local princelings somewhere around Allahabad or Varanasi. The Puranas report that the early Guptas controlled the area along the Ganges from Prayag (Allahabad) to Magadha. But Pataliputra and the centre of Magadha were certainly not within their reach.

The dynasty stepped into the limelight of history with Chandragupta I (AD 320 to about 335) who married a Licchavi princess. This marriage must have greatly contributed to the rise of the Guptas because the Licchavis were a mighty clan controlling most of north Bihar ever since the days of the Buddha. Chandragupta's coins show the king and his queen, Kumaradevi, and on the reverse a goddess seated on a lion with the legend 'Licchavi'. Samudragupta was also aware of the importance of this connection and in his famous Allahabad inscription he called himself 'son of the daughter of the Licchavi' rather than 'son of the Gupta'. Chandragupta introduced a new era starting with his coronation in AD 320 and he also assumed the title 'Overlord of great kings' (maharaja-adhiraja).

Chandragupta's son, Samudragupta (c. AD 335–375), earned a reputation as one of the greatest conquerors of Indian history. This is mainly due to the fact that his famous Allahabad inscription on an old Ashokan pillar withstood the ravages of time and thus preserved a glorious account of his deeds.[1] The inscription, which is undated, was perhaps initially located at Kausambi. It contains a long list of all kings and realms subdued by Samudragupta. Only half of the names on this list can be identified, but the rest provide us with a clear picture of Samudragupta's policy of conquest and annexation. In the 'land of the Aryas' (aryavarta) he uprooted (unmulya) many kings and princes between west Bengal in the east, Mathura in the west and Vidisha in the southwest and annexed their realms. The old kingdom of Panchala north of the Ganges and many Naga (Snake) dynasties which had arisen in the area from Mathura to Vidisha after the decline of the Kushanas were eliminated in this way. The conquest of Pataliputra was also achieved in this first great campaign.

The most famous campaign of Samudragupta was aimed at southern India. Altogether twelve kings and princes of the south (*dakshinapatha*) are listed among those whom he subdued at that time. Many of them are known only due to their inclusion in this list which is thus one of the most important documents for the early history of southern India. In Dakshina Koshala he defeated King Mahendra, then he crossed the great forest region (Kalahandi and Koraput Districts of western Orissa) so as to reach the coast of Kalinga. In this region he defeated four rulers, among them Mahendra of Pishtapura in the Godaveri Delta and Hastivarman of Vengi. His final great success in the south was the defeat of King Vishnugopa of Kanchipuram. The inscription states that Samudragupta 'defeated, released and reinstated' all these kings thus showing his royal mercy. But this is probably a euphemism typical of the campaigns of early medieval Indian kings who were more interested in conquest as such than in the annexation of distant realms which they could not have controlled anyway. We may therefore assume that those southern kings ruled their realms undisturbed after Samudragupta had returned to the north where he celebrated his imperial round of conquest (*digvijaya*) with a great horse sacrifice (*ashvamedha*). On this occasion he issued gold coins showing the sacrificial horse and on the reverse his chief queen. The coins have the legend: 'After conquering the earth the Great King of Kings with the strength of an invincible hero is going to conquer the heavens.' His grandson, Kumaragupta, praised him many decades later as the great renewer of the horse sacrifice which had been forgotten and neglected for such a long time. This shows that the Guptas consciously strove to renew the old Hindu institutions of kingship.

The Allahabad inscription also lists fourteen realms and tribes whose rulers are described as 'border kings' (*pratyanta-nripati*). These rulers paid tribute (*kara*) to Samudragupta and were prepared to follow his orders (*ajna*) and to show their obedience (*pramana*) by attending his court. The list includes Samatata (southeast Bengal), Kamarupa (Assam) and Nepal as well as tribal chieftaincies in eastern Rajasthan and northern Madhya Pradesh (e.g. Malwas, Abhiras and Yaudehas). Furthermore, some jungle rajas (*atavikaraja*) are mentioned whom Samudragupta had made his servants (*paricaraka*). The jungle rajas probably lived in the Vindhya mountains. Later inscriptions also mention eighteen such 'forest states' in this area. Another group of kings listed in the inscription are those independent rulers who lived beyond the realms of the border kings. The Kushanas (the Daivaputra Shahi Shahanushahi mentioned in the previous chapter), the Shakas, Murundas, as well as Simhala (Sri Lanka) and the inhabitants of 'all islands' are referred to in this context. It is stated that these independent rulers sent embassies to Samudragupta's court, donated girls for his harem and asked him for charters with the imperial Garuda Seal which would certify their legitimate title to their respective realms.

The Shakas or Kshatrapas of western India were subdued only by Samudragupta's successor after a long struggle. The Kushanas in northwestern India, Gandhara and Afghanistan were certainly beyond Samudragupta's reach but they must have been interested in good diplomatic relations with him. The reference to Sri Lanka and the inhabitants of all islands seems to be rather strange in this context, but there is fortunately some Chinese evidence for Sri Lanka's relations with Samudragupta. According to a Chinese report, King Meghavanna of Sri Lanka had asked Samudragupta for his permission to build a monastery and a guesthouse for Buddhist pilgrims at Bodh Gaya. For this purpose Meghavanna must have sent an embassy with presents to Samudragupta which he considered to be a tribute just as the Chinese emperor would have done in a similar context. Diplomatic relations were established in this way without any effect on the actual exercise of political control.

The structure of the Gupta empire

From the very beginning, the Gupta empire revealed a structure which it retained even at the height of its expansion (see Map 2.3) and which served as a blueprint for all medieval kingdoms of India. The centre of the empire was a core area in which Samudragupta had uprooted all earlier rulers in two destructive wars (*prasabha-uddharana*, i.e. violent elimination). This area was under the direct administration of royal officers. Beyond this area lived the border kings some of whom Samudragupta even reinstated after they had been presumably subdued by some of their rivals. These border kings paid tribute and were obliged to attend Samudragupta's court. In contrast with medieval European vassals they were obviously not obliged to join Samudragupta's army in a war. Thus they were not real vassals but, at the most, tributary princes. In subsequent centuries these tributary neighbours were called Samantas and rose to high positions at the imperial court thus coming closer to the ideal type of a feudal vassal.

Between the realms of the border kings and the core region of the empire there were some areas inhabited by tribes which had hardly been subdued. Of course, Samudragupta claimed that he had made all forest rulers his servants, but he probably could not expect any tribute from them. At the most, he could prevent them from disturbing the peace of the people in the core region. Beyond the forest rulers and the tributary kings were the realms of the independent kings who, at the most, entered into diplomatic relations with the Guptas. In the course of further development several regions

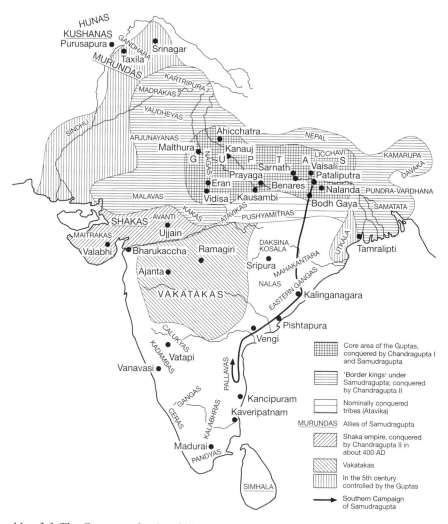

Map 2.3 The Gupta empire (AD 320–500)

of the Gupta empire, e.g. Pundravardhana in Bengal and Avanti with its ancient capital Ujjain, emerged as powerful centres. Some historians therefore prefer to speak of a multicentred rather than a unitary structure of the Gupta state. The subsequent balance of power of medieval regional kingdoms was foreshadowed in this way.

In his southern campaign, Samudragupta passed the circle of forest rulers and border kings and ventured into regions which had been completely outside the Gupta Rajamandala. Although this 'conquest of the four quarters of the world' (*digvijaya*) did not immediately lead to an expansion of the Gupta empire south of the Vindhyas, it did provide a new imperial dimension to Gupta rule. It also contributed to the ideological unification of India in terms of the idea of Hindu kingship. With his great horse sacrifices after his campaigns of conquest, Samudragupta announced his claim to be a universal ruler (*cakravartin*). Therefore the Allahabad inscription praised him in a way which would have been inconceivable in later times when similar inscriptions were much more restrained. The inscription states: 'He was a mortal only in celebrating the rites of the observances of mankind [but otherwise] a god (*deva*), dwelling on the earth.' Samudragupta's royal propaganda influenced his successors, as well as many later rulers of southern and central India who tried to emulate his grandiose style however small their realms might have been.

Subjection and alliance: Shakas and Vakatakas

Under Samudragupta's son, Chandragupta II (*c.* AD 375–413/15), the Gupta empire attained its greatest glory both in terms of territorial expansion and cultural excellence. Chandragupta combined the aggressive expansionist policy of his father with the strategy of marital alliance of his grandfather. His foremost success was his victory over the mighty Shaka-Kshatrapa dynasty and the annexation of their prosperous realm in Gujarat. The date of this event is not recorded but it must have been between 397 and 409: after 397 because for this year coins of the Shaka ruler Rudrasimha III are existent, and before 409 because Chandragupta II that year produced coins of a similar pattern but with the Shakas' Buddhist vihara replaced by Garuda, Vishnu's eagle, the favourite symbol of the Guptas.

Chandragupta's other great achievement was the marriage of his daughter, Prabhavatigupta, with Rudrasena II of the Vakataka dynasty of central India. This dynasty had risen to prominence in the third century AD after the fall of the Shatavahana empire. The founder of the Vakataka dynasty was named Vindhyashakti after the goddess of the Vindhya mountains. His second successor, Pravarasena I, whom his descendants praised as *samraj*, an imperial title, divided his kingdom. His sons ruled over two flourishing independent kingdoms in what is now Madhya Pradesh. The eastern Vakatakas were faced by Samudragupta's expansionism and shifted their capital to Nandivardhana near Nagpur under Rudrasena I. Chandragupta II concluded the marital alliance with Rudrasena's grandson before attacking the Shakas so as to be sure to have a friendly power at his back when invading Gujarat. But Rudrasena II died after a very short reign in 390 and, on Chandragupta's advice, Prabhavatigupta then acted as regent for her two sons, who were 2 and 5 years old. During her regency which lasted for 20 years the Vakataka realm was practically part of the Gupta empire. Under Pravarasena II (*c.*419–455) whose reign is very well documented by many inscriptions, the eastern Vakatakas reasserted their independence. But the relations between the Guptas and the Vakatakas remained close and friendly. Therefore, historians sometimes refer to this whole period as the Vakataka–Gupta Age. The eastern Vakatakas propagated the idea of Hindu kingship by building a veritable state sanctuary at Ramagiri, adorned by monumental temples, whereas the western Vakatakas created the Buddhist marvels of Ajanta. Both dynasties contributed to the spread of Gupta culture in central and southern India.

Chandragupta II controlled most of northern India from the mouth of the Ganges to the mouth of the Indus and from what is now northern Pakistan down to the mouth of the Narmada. In alliance with the Vakatakas, he also controlled a large part of central India. Assam, Nepal, Kashmir and Sri Lanka retained good diplomatic relations with this vast new empire, as did many realms of southeast Asia where a new wave of Indian cultural influence set in. The oldest Sanskrit inscriptions found in Indonesia which testify to the establishment of kingdoms on the Indian pattern can be traced back to this period. The Gupta empire was at its zenith.

Direct access to the eastern and western ports had greatly augmented trade in northern and central India. The large number of beautiful gold coins issued by the Guptas testify to the growth of the imperial economy. Initially these coins, like those of the Kushanas, conformed to the Roman pattern and were accordingly called Dinara. Skandagupta later on diminished the gold content of these coins but at the same time he increased their weight from 7.8 grams to 9.3 grams in keeping with Indian standards. These impressive coins also served as a means of imperial propaganda with their god-like portrayals of the Gupta rulers. Chandragupta II also started producing silver coins following the tradition of the Shakas. At first he restricted this practice to western India, but soon these silver coins circulated throughout the empire. Copper coins and shells served as local currency.

The age of the Guptas was also a prosperous time for the many guilds (*shreni*) of northern India which were often entrusted with the management of towns or parts of cities. There are seals extant of the guilds of bankers (*shreshthin*), traders (*sarthavaha*) and artisans (*kulika*). Sometimes such seals were even combined and there may have been joint organisations which may have performed functions similar to those of chambers of commerce.

Faxian (Fah-hsien), the first of the three great Chinese pilgrims who visited India from the fifth to the seventh centuries, in search of knowledge, manuscripts and relics, arrived in India during the reign of Chandragupta II. As he was only interested in Buddhism his report does not contain much political information, but he does give a general description of northern India at that time:

The region to the South is known as the Middle Kingdom. The people are rich and contented, unencumbered by any poll-tax or official restrictions. Only those who till the king's land pay a land tax, and they are free to go or stay as they please. The kings govern without recourse to capital punishment, but offenders are fined lightly or heavily according to the nature of their crime. Even those who plot high treason only have their right hands cut off. The king's attendants and retainers all receive emoluments and pensions. The people in this country kill no living creatures, drink no wine, and eat no onion or garlic. The single exception to this is the Chandalas, who are known as 'evil men' and are segregated from the others. When they enter towns or markets they strike a piece of wood to announce their presence, so that others may know they are coming and avoid them.[2]

Faxian's report provides an idea of general peace and welfare in Chandragupta's India. He also gives us some glimpses of political and economic affairs. Thus he mentions that all officers of the royal court received fixed salaries – just as Megasthenes had reported about the Maurya court. The method prevailing in later periods of assigning land and revenue in lieu of salaries was obviously unusual in the Gupta age when enough money was in circulation to pay salaries in cash. Faxian also refers to the freedom of the rural people which is in contrast with a later period when land grants often specifically mention the people who will till the soil for the grantee. The Chinese pilgrim also recorded evidence of the caste system as he could observe it. According to this evidence the treatment meted out to untouchables such as the Chandalas was very similar to that which they experienced in later periods. This would contradict assertions that this rigid form of the caste system emerged in India only as a reaction to the Islamic conquest.

Kalidasa and classical Sanskrit literature

The fame of the Guptas rests to a great extent on the flowering of classical Sanskrit literature under their patronage. It was reported in later ages that Chandragupta II had a circle of poets at his court who were known as the 'Nine Jewels'. The greatest jewel among them was Kalidasa who excelled as a dramatist as well as a composer of epic poems. Among his greatest works are the two epic poems *Kumarasambhava* and *Raghuvamsha*, the lyrical poem *Meghaduta* and the great drama, *Shakuntala*. Although we know so much about his magnificent work, we know next to nothing about the poet himself. Indian scholars earlier surmised that he was a contemporary of the legendary ruler Vikramaditya of Ujjain who instituted a new era beginning in 58 BC. But some references to astronomy in Kalidasa's work which show the influence of Greek and Roman ideas seem to indicate that the poet could not have lived before the early centuries AD. Furthermore there is some internal evidence in his work which would seem to corroborate the assumption that he was a contemporary of Chandragupta II. The title of his epic poem *Vikramorvashiya* is supposed to be an allusion to Chandragupta's second name Vikramaditya, and the *Kumarasambhava* which praises the birth of the war god, Kumara, may refer to Chandragupta's son and successor, Kumaragupta. The fourth book of the *Raghuvamsha* which glorifies the mythical dynasty of King Rama could be a eulogy of the deeds of Samudragupta. This transformation of history into myth was in keeping with the programme of the Gupta rulers. Whereas in earlier periods the ruler was seen as executing the immutable laws of a cosmic world order, the Gupta rulers were praised as gods on earth bringing about peace and prosperity by means of their heroic deeds.

Another category of Sanskrit literature which is of lesser literary merit than the great classical works but has nevertheless made an enormous impact on Indian life are the Puranas. These 'Old (Purana) Works' have earlier sources but they most probably attained their final shape in the Age of the Guptas. The Purana contain collections of myths, philosophical dialogues, ritual prescriptions, but also genealogies of northern and central Indian dynasties up to the early Guptas. They are therefore also important as historical sources. For the various sects of Hinduism they provide a storehouse of myths about different gods as well as legends concerning the holy places of the Hindus. There are altogether eighteen Great Puranas and eighteen Lesser Puranas which were frequently amended up to late medieval times. The Vishnu Purana is one of the most important religious books of the Vaishnavas. The devotees of the goddess, Durga, find a magnificent account of her deeds in the Devimahatmya which is a part of the Markandeya Purana. The fight of the goddess against the buffalo demon, Mahisha, is vividly portrayed in this text. The various incarnations (*avatara*) of Vishnu as well as the deeds of Durga are frequently depicted in the sculptures of the Gupta Age.

An age of religious tolerance and political consolidation

During the long reign of Chandragupta's son, Kumaragupta (415–455), the empire remained undiminished but there are no reports about additional conquests. Kumaragupta's rule was obviously a peaceful one and cultural life continued to flourish and to extend its influence into the distant parts of the subcontinent and southeast Asia. Although Kumaragupta was a devotee of Vishnu like his predecessors and had to pay his respects to Kumaraskanda, the god of war and his namesake, his reign was characterised by a spirit of religious tolerance.

Inscriptions registering endowments for the holy places of Buddhism and Jainism as well as for the Hindu gods like Vishnu, Shiva, Skanda and the sun god, Surya, and for the goddess, Shakti, abound in all parts of the empire. Gold coins were donated to Buddhist monasteries with detailed instructions for the use of the interest accruing on the investment of this capital. Thus monks were to be maintained or oil procured for the sacred lamps or buildings were to be added or repaired, etc. The Buddhist monasteries retained their functions as banks in this way. But they were very much dependent on the rich citizens of the cities and towns of the empire. As these cities and towns declined in the late Gupta period this also greatly affected the fortunes of those monasteries. More secure were the donations to Brahmins and Hindu temples which took the form of land grants or of the assignment of the revenue of whole villages. Several such grants inscribed on copper plates were made during the reign of Kumaragupta. Five sets of copper plates, from 433 to 449, were found in Bengal alone. All referred to land granted to Brahmins for the performance of specific rites. One inscription provided for the maintenance and service of a Vishnu temple. Most of these grants referred to uncultivated land which indicates that the grantees had to function as colonisers who not only propagated the glory of their royal donors but also extended the scope of agriculture.

After nearly a century of rapid expansion, Kumaragupta's reign was a period of consolidation in which the administrative structure of the empire attained its final shape. It thus served as the model for the successor states of the Gupta empire. From inscriptions in Bengal we get the impression that the central region of the empire was divided into a number of provinces (*bhukti*) headed by a governor (*uparika*) who was appointed by the Gupta ruler himself. Sometimes these governors even had the title of Uparikamaharaja. The provinces were subdivided into districts (*vishaya*) headed by a Vishayapati. Districts close to the realm's capital were likely to have their heads directly appointed by the ruler. In distant provinces they were usually appointed by the governor. Larger provinces were subdivided into Vishayas and Vithis. But we do not know whether this rather centralised administration in Bengal existed also in other provinces of the Gupta empire.

At the lowest echelon there were the villages and towns which enjoyed a great deal of local autonomy quite in contrast with the instructions of the *Arthashastra*. Bigger cities had Ayuktakas at their head who were appointed by the governor. These Ayuktakas were assisted by town clerks (*pustapala*). The head of the city guilds (*nagarashreshthin*) and the heads of families of artisans (*kulika*) advised the Ayuktaka. In the villages there were headman (*gramika*) also assisted by scribes, and there were the heads of peasant families (*kutumbin*). The district officer rarely interfered with village administration but he was in charge of such transactions as the sale and transfer of land which are mentioned in many documents relating to land grants. The district administration was obviously of great importance and encompassed judicial functions (*adhikarana*).

Internal and external challenges: Pushyamitras and Huns

At the end of Kumaragupta's reign the Gupta empire was challenged by the Pushyamitras, a tribal community living on the banks of the Narmada. Skandagupta, a son and general of Kumaragupta, fought these Pushyamitras and in his later inscriptions he emphasised that the Pushyamitras had shaken the good fortunes of the Gupta dynasty and that he had to try his utmost to subdue them. Obviously such tribes living near the core area of the empire could seriously challenge the ruling dynasty. But Skandagupta may have had good reasons to highlight his role in this affair. He had usurped his father's throne by displacing the legitimate crown prince, Purugupta. As Skandagupta only mentioned his father's but never his mother's name in his inscriptions it can be assumed that his mother was a junior queen or concubine. In later genealogies of the Guptas, Skandagupta's name does not appear. The stigma of the usurper was not removed by the fact that he was a very competent ruler. Coins and inscriptions covering the period from 455 to 467 show that he was in control of the empire in this period and one, dated 458, explicitly states that he posted guards in all parts of the empire.

His vigilance enabled Skandagupta to successfully meet another and probably much more serious challenge to the Gupta empire when the Xiongnu or Huns descended upon India from central Asia where they had fought the Yuezhi in the second century BC. In the middle of the fourth century AD, the Huns invaded the Sassanid empire in Persia and then attacked the Alans and Goths living west of the Volga thus starting the great migration in Europe. Other tribes of the Huns remained in Bactria where they joined with other nomadic tribes and under a great leader, Kidara, who emerged as a powerful ruler towards the end of the fourth century. A new wave of aggressive Huns pushed these people farther south in the beginning of the fifth century. They crossed the Hindukush mountains and descended upon the Indian plains. In about 460, only a few years after the famous Hun ruler, Attila, was defeated in Europe, they seem to have clashed with Skandagupta. In the same inscription in which Skandagupta mentioned his victory over the Pushyamitras he also claims to have vanquished the Huns and in another inscription he again refers to victories over the foreigners (*mleccha*). Sassanid and Roman sources contain no reports of victories of the Huns in India and thus it seems that Skandagupta succeeded in thwarting the first attacks of the Huns on India. But this struggle disrupted the international trade of northwestern India and thus diminished one of the most important financial sources of the Gupta empire.

Skandagupta died around 467, and there was a long drawn-out war of succession between his sons and the sons of his half-brother, Purugupta. The winner of this war was Budhagupta, the son of Purugupta and the last of the great Gupta rulers. During his long reign (467 to 497) the empire remained more or less intact, but the war of succession had obviously sapped its vitality. The successors of Budhagupta, his brother Narasimha and Narasimha's son and grandson, who ruled until about 570, controlled only small parts of the empire. In east Bengal a King Vainyagupta is mentioned in an inscription of 507 and in the west one Bhanugupta left an inscription of 510. It is not known whether these rulers were related to the Gupta dynasty or not, but they were obviously independent of the Guptas of Magadha whose power declined very rapidly.

The Huns must have noted this decline as they attacked India once more under their leader, Toramana. They conquered large parts of northwestern India up to Gwalior and Malwa. In 510 they clashed with Bhanugupta's army at Eran (Madhya Pradesh). Bhanugupta's general, Goparaja, lost his life in this battle. Coins provide evidence for the fact that Toramana controlled the Panjab, Kashmir, Rajasthan and presumably also the western part of what is now Uttar Pradesh. About 515 Toramana's son, Mihirakula, succeeded his father and established his capital at Sakala (Sialkot).

In this way northwestern India once more became part of a central Asian empire which extended from Persia to Khotan. Not much is known about the rule of the Huns in India. There is a Jaina tradition that Toramana embraced that faith. The Kashmir chronicle, *Rajatarangini*, reports that Toramana led his army also to southern India, but since this source originated many centuries later, the accuracy of this report cannot be taken for granted. All sources highlight the cruelty of Hun warfare and of their oppression of the indigenous people: a Chinese ambassador at the Hun court at Gandhara wrote such a report about 520; the Greek seafarer, Cosmas, also called Indicopleustes, recorded similar facts around 540; and finally the Chinese pilgrim, Xuanzang (Hsiuen-tsang), wrote about it from hindsight around 650. Hun rule in India was very short-lived. Yashodharman, a local ruler of Malwa, won a battle in 528 against Mihirakula who then withdrew to Kashmir where he died a few years later. But the final decline of the Huns in India was precipitated by their defeat at the hands of the Turks in central Asia around the middle of the sixth century.

Hun rule was one of the shortest instances of foreign rule over northwestern India, but it had far-reaching consequences. The Huns destroyed what was left of the Gupta empire in the northwest and the centrifugal forces were set free. They destroyed the cities and trading centres of northern India. Not much research has been done on this aspect of the Hun invasion but it seems that the classical northwestern Indian urban culture was eradicated by them. The Buddhist monasteries in the Hun territory also succumbed to this assault and never recovered. A further effect of the Hun invasion was the migration of other central Asian tribes to India where they joined local tribes. The Gurjaras and some Rajput clans seem to have originated in this way and they were soon to make a mark in Indian history. The Classical Age waned and the medieval era began with the rise of these new actors on the political scene of northern India.

THE RISE OF SOUTH INDIA

South India is separated from north India by the Vindhya mountains and the Narmada river and large tracts of barren and inhospitable land. The Deccan, particularly the central and western highlands and the 'far south', the Dravida country, had a history of its own. Cultural influences, however, were as often transmitted from northwestern India via the western highlands down to the south as along the Gangetic valley to eastern India. But, in spite of early influences from the north, the 'far south' remained rather isolated and could develop in its own way. However, in later centuries cultural influences from the south, like the great Bhakti movement, also made an impact on northern India.

The most important impact on the south was, of course, the spread of Late Vedic culture from the north. Scholars refer to this in different terms: Aryanisation, Sanskritisation, Hinduisation. But none of these terms can do justice to the complex transmission of cultural influences. During the early centuries AD north Indian culture had ceased to be a purely 'Aryan' culture and it was transmitted not only by those who spoke Sanskrit; in this early period of the last centuries BC Buddhists and Jainists speaking Pali and Prakrit were as important in this process as Brahmins who propagated various forms of Hinduism. In due course the Dravidian languages of the south absorbed a great many Sanskrit words and became themselves media for the expression of new cultural values.

Brahmin families who continued to transmit sacred texts orally from one generation to another were certainly of great importance in this context. They penetrated the south peacefully and made an impact by setting an example rather than by converting people. But the process of Hinduisation was also accompanied by the oppression and exploitation of former tribal groups as well as pariahs and untouchables within the caste society. Brahmins provided a justification and legitimation for the hierarchical structuring of society which was particularly useful to local rulers who emerged from a tribal status. The Brahmins brought along the ideology of Hindu kingship which such rulers eagerly adopted. The Brahmins literally put the tribal people in their place. They could recite the verses of the *Mahabharata* which state that it is the duty of tribes to lead a quiet life in the forest, to be obedient to the king, to dig wells, to give water and food to travellers and gifts to the Brahmins in such areas where they could 'domesticate' the tribal people.

South Indian geopolitics

The history of south India was determined by the contrast of highland and coastal lowland. At the height of the early medieval period this became very obvious when the great regional kingdoms of the southeast (Pallavas and Cholas) and of the western highlands (Chalukyas and Rashtrakutas) vied with each other for the control of the large rivers flowing from west to east. The fertile delta of Krishna and Godaveri was particularly coveted by rival powers.

Prehistoric finds in northern and southern India mostly indicate that open areas in the interior of the country were preferred by early settlers whereas the early civilisations were based on the great river plains of the Indus and Ganges. The early history of the south was very much influenced by the proximity of the sea and the early historical development in the southeast centred on the coast. Settled agriculture and the growing of rice made the coastal plains around the mouths of the great rivers much more attractive. Social differentiation and political organisation started with the need for defence against raiders. The early nuclear areas along the great rivers were initially isolated from each other by large stretches of forest or barren lands. They could thus give rise to local principalities. At the same time these principalities could profit from maritime trade.

South India was known even in very ancient times as a rich land to which, according to the Bible, King Solomon may have sent his ships once every three years carrying gold, silver, ivory, monkeys and peacocks. Megasthenes reported that in the late fourth century BC the wealth of the Pandya rulers of the south was derived from the trade with pearls. The *Arthashastra* lists shells, diamonds and other precious stones, pearls and articles made of gold as south Indian products. Initially this kind of trade may have been of marginal importance only but in due course it contributed to economic growth. The organisation of trade accelerated the political development of the coastal nuclear areas and the local rulers gradually extended their sway over the surrounding countryside. It is significant in this context that ancient geographers like Ptolemy in the second century AD mention not only the ports of southern India but also the capitals of rulers located at some distance from the coast.

Five types of regional ecology

The pattern of gradual penetration of the hinterland of the southeast coast is clearly reflected in ancient Tamil literature. In the texts of the Sangam period five eco-types (*tinai*) are mentioned again and again. These types are: the mountains, forests and pastures, dry, barren land, the valleys of the great rivers, and the coast. These different eco-types were not only char-acterised by the particular plants and animals found there but also by different modes of economic activity and social structure.[1]

The mountainous region (*kurrinci*) was the habitat of hunters and food gatherers like the tribe of the Kuruvars. Below this region there was the forest and brushland (*mullai*) which also served as pasture for tribes of herdsmen like the Ayar. Agriculture was scarce in this area where only millets would grow. Rice was introduced later and only in the small areas which offered conditions similar to those prevailing in the great valleys.

The Sangam texts indicate that the relations between the hunters of the mountains and the forests and the herdsmen in the adjacent region were often strained. They did share the same religious cults of Muruga, Lord of the Mountains, who was also worshipped as the god of war by the herdsmen. But constant cattle raids were a source of conflict here just as they had been in northern India in the Vedic Age. The Sangam literature abounds with stories about such cattle raids, the term for such a raid being synonymous with that for war.

The third ecotype, the dry, barren land (*palai*) was a transitional zone which often expanded in great droughts. This was a region to which robbers would withdraw and was thus feared by travellers.

The most important of the five types was the fourth one, the river valleys (*marutam*). Natural and artificial irrigation by means of canals, tanks and wells made rice cultivation possible in this area. Artisans and settled agriculturists, like the caste of the Vellalas, lived here and later the kings settled Brahmins in this fertile region who established whole Brahmin villages. These villages were usually located in the region which is below 300 feet above sea level. These river valleys with their well-developed agriculture and high population were the nuclear areas which formed the base of all regional kingdoms of south India.

The fifth eco-type, the coast (*neytal*) was an area where the people made a living by fishing, trading and making salt. Local trade consisted initially only of exchanging fish and salt for rice and milk products, but in the first centuries AD international maritime trade became more and more important for the coastal people. This is why both literary and archaeological evidence point to a higher degree of urbanisation in the coastal region than in the river valleys in this early period.

Sangam literature, just like late Vedic and early Buddhist literature, reflects the transition from tribal society to settled agriculture and early state formation. Even at this very early stage, social stratification in the river valleys of southern India shows traces of a caste system which then becomes increasingly rigid as Brahmin immigrants gain more and more influence and provide the justification for it. But in the early times, even the higher castes were not yet hemmed in by the rigid norms and conventions of a later age. The Sangam texts contain vivid descriptions of the uninhibited life in the early capitals of south Indian rulers, particularly in the Pandya capital, Madurai.

The political development of south India was greatly stimulated by the contact with the first great Indian empire of the Mauryas in the third century BC. The tribal rulers of the south thus gained an insight into new types of administration and large-scale state formation. Trade with northern India added to this flow of information, and so did the migration of Buddhist and Jaina monks who introduced their forms of monastic organisation in central and southern India. Interregional trade and these highly developed monastic institutions often maintained a symbiotic relationship which was of great importance for the emergence of the political infrastructure of these early states of the south.

Kharavela of Orissa and the Andhra Shatavahanas

The history of central and south India in the centuries after the death of Ashoka is still relatively unknown. Thus the dating of the two major dynasties which emerged south of the Vindhyas after the decline of the Maurya dynasty, the Shatavahanas of Central India and the dynasty of Kharavela of Orissa, is as yet very uncertain. It was initially assumed that both emerged soon after the decline of the Maurya empire around 185 BC, but more recent research seems to indicate that they arose only around the middle of the first century BC.

Kharavela, one of the great rulers of ancient India, has left a detailed record of his deeds in the inscription found in the Jaina cave at Udaya-giri near Bhubaneshwar. He called himself 'Supreme Lord of Kalinga' (*Kalinga-adhipati*) and he was probably a member of the Chedi dynasty which had migrated from eastern Madhya Pradesh to Orissa. Kharavela was a true chakravartin though he was a Jaina and should have believed in the doctrine of non-violence (*ahimsa*). In his campaign against the rulers of northern India he got beyond Magadha and so frightened a Greek (Yavana) king who lived northwest of this area that he took to his heels. Marching westward, Kharavela entered the realm of the Shatavahana king, Satakarni, and, turning south, he defeated a confederation of Dravidian rulers (*Tamiradeha sanghata*).

The spoils of the many successful campaigns which Kharavela conducted almost every year seem to have made him so rich that by the sixth year of his reign he could afford to abolish all taxes payable by the citizens of towns (*paura*) and the rural folk (*janapada*) in his realm. The inscription also contains the interesting news that Kharavela reintroduced the sixty-four arts of song, dance and instrumental music (*tauryatrika*) which had been prohibited by the Mauryas. This testifies to the fact that Ashoka's Dhamma-Mahamatras had successfully implemented the imperial orders even in distant Orissa.

Kharavela's far-flung realm, which included large parts of eastern and central India, seems to have disintegrated soon after his death as had happened to the Maurya empire after Ashoka's death. Only his son and another member of the dynasty have left us some rather unimportant inscriptions. But it might be this empire about which Pliny the Elder (AD 23–79) wrote in his *Naturalis historia*: 'The royal city of the Calingae is called Parthalis [i.e. Toshali]. This king had 66,000 foot soldiers, 1,000 horses and 700 elephants, always caparisoned, ready for battle.'

The central Indian state of the Shatavahana dynasty showed a much greater continuity and stability than Kharavela's short-lived realm. The Purana texts even maintain that the dynasty ruled for 460 years, but these texts do not always provide reliable historical evidence. Nothing is known about the antecedents of this dynasty which belonged to the great central Indian tribe of the Andhras, according to the Puranas. This tribe is listed among the non-Aryan tribes in the Aitareya Brahmana text of about 500 BC.

Satakarni I, who seems to be identical with the king mentioned in Kharavela's inscription, was the first great ruler of this dynasty. He claimed to have fought against the Greeks and Shakas in the west and northwest and then extended his kingdom to the east along the river Godaveri. His capital, Pratisthana (Paithan), was located on the banks of the Godaveri in what is now the Marathwada region of Maharashtra. Due to this advance along the Godaveri towards the southeast he could proudly call himself 'Lord of the South' (*dakshinapatha-pati*). Pliny reports that in his time the Andarae, as he calls the Shatavahanas, had 30 fortified cities, 100,000 infantry, 30,000 cavalry and even 9,000 war elephants. They were thus the strongest power in southern India. Nevertheless they were deprived of the central part of their realm on the upper Godaveri by the Shakas who were pushed to the south by the Kushanas.

Only King Gautamiputra was able to restore the Shatavahana realm to its earlier greatness in about AD 125. Gautamiputra's son, Vasishthiputra, alias Shri Pulumavi, ruled the Shatavahana kingdom around AD 140 at the time of Ptolemy, who referred to Shri Pulumavi as Shri Polemaios. The Shatavahanas had consolidated their hold on the east while being forced to concentrate on it for nearly a century until they could reclaim the western part once more. As their empire then stretched more or less from coast to coast they became very important for international trade which linked west and east Asia (see Map 2.2).

The Shatavahana inscriptions contain some information about their administrative system, but details are missing. The empire was divided into districts (*ahara*) headed by imperial officers (*amatya*) who probably had functions similar to the Mahamatras of the Maurya empire. We do not know whether there was an additional level of administration or not. In general, the Shatavahanas seem to have copied the Maurya system of administration with the important difference that they tried to take local interests into account and inducted allodial lords into their administration hierarchy. Furthermore, cities and guilds enjoyed a great deal of autonomy under Shatavahana rule. This was an important feature of later south Indian realms, too. The incorporation of local lords into the state hierarchy was a general feature of state formation in early medieval India.

Two other specific features, or perhaps even innovations, of the Shatavahana system were the distribution of military garrisons throughout the empire and the practice of granting land to Brahmins while at the same time providing them with immunities (*parihara*). Both of these institutions were obviously designed to penetrate the countryside with royal agents. The officers (*gaulmika*) heading the garrisons had some local administrative functions and, as the garrisons were to be self-supporting, had to secure the necessary resources from the local people. This in turn made it necessary to exempt Brahmins and Buddhist monasteries, to whom land was granted very specifically, from such exactions by royal officers. Consequently, the grant of such immunities became part and parcel of the land grant.

The Shatavahana system was not based on a centralised bureaucracy but on a network of noblemen who had such grandiloquent titles as 'Great Lord of the Army' (*mahasenapati*). Recent research has established that there were many local and subregional centres which must have formed a kind of federation under Shatavahana rule. Brahmins and Buddhist monasteries probably served as countervailing forces to the potentially centrifugal forces of local magnates. The Shatavahanas were Hindus but they nevertheless provided a great deal of patronage to the Buddhist order. Perhaps the good connections between monasteries and guilds also recommended the Buddhist order to the rulers who benefited from international trade.

Shatavahana power declined in the third century, showing symptoms typical of the final stages of all Indian kingdoms. Local princes strove for independence and finally a series of small successor states emerged. The northern part of the empire remained under the control of one branch of the Shatavahanas for some time until the Vakatakas rose to prominence in this region; they then entered into the alliance with the Gupta empire.

The eastern part of the Shatavahana empire, especially the fertile delta region of Krishna and Godaveri, was then ruled by the short-lived Ikshvaku dynasty. The founder of this dynasty celebrated the great horse sacrifice obviously in order to declare his independence from his Shatavahana overlord. The Ikshvakus continued the policy of the Shatavahanas in extending their patronage both to Brahmins and to the Buddhist order. Inscriptions belonging to the reign of the second Ikshvaku king which were found in the monasteries at Nagarjunikonda show that even the queens made donations to the Buddhists. One of these inscriptions gives evidence of international relations of the monastery: Kashmir and Gandhara, the Yavanas (Greeks) in northwestern India are mentioned, also Kirata in the Himalayas (Nepal?), Vanavasi in western India, Toshali and Vanga (Orissa and Bengal) in the east, Damila (Tamil Nadu), the Island of Tamrapani (Sri Lanka) and even China. This shows to what extent Buddhism added an international dimension to the polity of India's early regional kingdoms.

In the beginning of the fourth century the delta region of Krishna and Godaveri was already in the hands of a governor appointed by the Pallava dynasty of Kanchipuram and the Ikshvakus had disappeared. Not much is known about south Indian history in this period except what Samudragupta reported about his southern campaign in his famous Allahabad inscription. Vishnugopa of Kanchi (Kanchipuram) and Hastivarman of Vengi, probably a ruler of the local Shalankayana dynasty are mentioned in this inscription but we have no other evidence of their life and times.

Cholas, Pandyas and Cheras

The early history of the 'far south' is the history of the three tribal principalities of the Cholas, Pandyas and Cheras. They are mentioned in Ashoka's inscriptions of the third century BC, in some brief Tamil inscriptions of the second century BC (written in Brahmi script like the Ashokan inscriptions) and in Kharavela's inscription of the first century BC. The Sangam literature of the Tamils sheds a great deal of light on this period. Archaeological discoveries and the reports of ancient European authors provide additional evidence, particularly with regard to maritime trade. The chronicles of Sri Lanka contain many references to the fights between the kings of Sri Lanka and the kings of southern India. Compared to the sources available for other regions in early Indian history, this is a wealth of source material. Sangam literature was named after the 'academies' (*sangam*) of Madurai and its environs where poets worked under the patronage of the Pandya kings. Some traditionalist historians have maintained that these works were composed from about 500 BC to AD 500, but more recent research has shown that they were probably composed in the first to the third centuries AD, the second century being the most active period. The famous Tamil grammar, *Tolkappiyam*, is considered to belong to the beginning of this whole period (parts of it date back to *c*.100 BC) and the great Tamil epic poem, *Shilappatikaram*, to its very end, perhaps even to the fifth or sixth centuries AD.

North Indian royal titles (e.g. *adhiraja*) gained more and more currency in the south in this period but the early south Indian kings seem to have derived their legitimation from tribal loyalties and the network of their respective clan. This sometimes implied the division of power among many members of the clan. The Chera kingdom of the southwest coast (Kerala) must have been such a large-scale family enterprise. Kautalya has referred to this system of government in his *Arthashastra*; he called it *kulasangha* and thought that it was quite efficient. Among the Pandyas and Cholas the monarch seems to have played a more important role. This was particularly true of the Chola king, Karikala, who ruled over a relatively large area around AD 190 after he had vanquished a federation of the Pandyas and Cheras. Even about 1,000 years later the Chola rulers still referred to this great ancestor and they attributed to him the building of dikes along the banks of the Kaveri and the decoration of Kanchipuram with gold. Karikala's policy was obviously aimed at extending the territorial base of the Cholas at the expense of the other tribal principalities, but this policy seems to have alienated the people who threatened to flee from Karikala's domains so that he had to make concessions to them.

At the end of the Sangam era the development of the three southern kingdoms was suddenly interrupted by the invasion of the Kalabhras. Historians have called the period which started with this invasion the 'Kalabhra Interregnum'. It ended only when the Pallava dynasty emerged as the first major regional power of south India in the sixth century. Nothing is known about the origins or tribal affiliations of the Kalabhras. In early medieval Tamil literature they are depicted as 'bad kings' (*kaliarashar*) who disrupted the order of the tribal kingdoms of coastal south India and in the river valleys. It is said that they destroyed legitimate kings and even cancelled land grants to Brahmins. Buddhist literature, however, contains some information about a Kalabhra king, Acchutavikkanta, under whose patronage Buddhist monasteries and poets prospered. A Jaina grammarian quoted some of Acchutavikkanta's poems even in the tenth century. The Kalabhras were probably a mountain tribe of southern India which suddenly swooped down on the kingdoms of the fertile lowlands. The kings who headed this tribe must have been followers of Buddhism and Jainism. In a later period of south Indian history a similar process occurred when the Hoysalas, a highland tribe, emerged at the time when the Chola empire declined. They were also at first depicted as highwaymen who disturbed the peace of the settled Hindu kingdoms. But, unlike the Kalabhras, once the Hoysalas had established their rule they turned into orthodox supporters of Hinduism.

International trade and the Roman connection

An important aspect of early south Indian history was the flourishing trade with Rome. The first two centuries AD were an important time for the trade links between Asia and Europe. In addition to earlier Greek reports, the Roman references to the trade with India provided the information on which the European image of India was based. The European discovery of India in the late medieval period by people like Marco Polo was in effect only a rediscovery of that miraculous country which was known to the ancient writers but had been cut off by the Arabs from direct contact with the West for several centuries. Hegel commented on the trade with India in his *Philosophy of History*: 'The quest for India is a moving force of our whole history. Since ancient times all nations have directed their wishes and desires to that miraculous country whose treasures they coveted. These treasures were the most precious on earth: treasures of nature, pearls, diamonds, incense, the essence of roses, elephants, lions etc. and also the treasures of wisdom. It has always been of great significance for universal history by which route these treasures found their way to the West, the fate of nations has been influenced by this.'[2]

For India itself the trade with the West flourished most in ancient times. But when India's trade with Rome declined in the third and fourth century AD, India, and especially southern India, turned to southeast Asia where Indian influence became much more important than the vague impression which India had made on the nations of the West.

Indian trade with the countries around the Mediterranean goes back far into the pre-Christian era. But this early trade was probably conducted mainly by isolated seafaring adventurers even though the Ptolemies of Egypt had tried for some time to gain access to the trade in the Indian Ocean. It was only under Emperor Augustus (30 BC to AD 14) that this trade suddenly attained much greater dimensions. The Roman annexation of Egypt opened up to the trade route through the Red Sea. Furthermore, after a century of civil war, Rome experienced a period of greater prosperity which increased demand for the luxury goods of the East, a demand which could not be met by means of the old cumbersome method of coastal shipping. Hippalus' discovery early in the first century AD that the monsoon could take a ship straight across the Arabian Sea shortened the trade route and greatly eased access to the goods of the East. In subsequent years there was a great spurt of trading activity which was paralleled only many centuries later by the renewed European trade with India after Vasco da Gama's voyage of 1498.

A comparison of Strabo's geography which was written at the time of Augustus (edited and amended between AD 17 and 23) with the *Periplus of the Erythraean Sea* which was written by an anonymous Greek merchant in the second half of the first century AD shows a great increase in Roman trade with India. Strabo was more interested in northern India and in the ports between the mouth of the Indus and present Bombay and he reported next to nothing about southern India, Sri Lanka and the east coast of India. The author of the *Periplus*, who probably visited India personally, described in detail the ports of the Malabar coast. When Ptolemy wrote his geography around AD 150 Roman knowledge of India had increased even more. He wrote about the east coast of India and also had a vague idea of southeast Asia, especially about 'Chryse', the 'Golden Country' (*suvarnabhumi*) as the countries of southeast Asia had been known to the Indians since the first centuries AD. However, recent research has shown that this so-called Roman trade was integrated into an already flourishing Asian network of coastal and maritime trade.

The most important port of the Malabar coast was Muziris (Cranganore near Cochin) in the kingdom of Cerobothra (Cheraputra), which 'abounds in ships sent there with cargoes from Arabia and by the Greeks'. The *Periplus* reported on Roman trade with Malabar:

> They send large ships to the market-towns on account of the great quantity and bulk of pepper and malabathrum [cinnamon]. There

are imported here, in the first place, a great quantity of coin; topaz, thin clothing, not much; figured linens, antimony, coral, crude glass, copper, tin, lead, wine, not much, but as much as at Barygaza [Broach]; realgar and orpiment; and wheat enough for the sailors, for this is not dealt in by the merchants there. There is exported pepper, which is produced in quantity in only one region near these markets, a district called Cottonora [north Malabar?]. Besides this there are exported great quantities of fine pearls, ivory, silk cloth, spikenard from the Ganges, malabathrum from the places in the interior, transparent stones of all kinds, diamonds and sapphires, and tortoise shell; that from Chryse Island, and that taken among the islands along the coast of Damirica [Tamil Nadu]. They make the voyage to this place in favourable season who set out from Egypt about the month of July, that is Epiphi.[3]

This provides evidence for a great volume of trade in both directions. It also indicates that the south Indian ports served as entrepôts for silk from China, oil from the Gangetic plains which was brought by Indian traders all the way to the tip of southern India, and also for precious stones from southeast Asia. But, as far as the eastern trade was concerned, the Coromandel coast to the south of present Madras soon eclipsed the Malabar coast. To the north of Cape Comorin (Kanya Kumari) there was the kingdom of the Pandyas where prisoners were made to dive for precious pearls in the ocean. Still further north there was a region called Argaru which was perhaps the early Chola kingdom with its capital, Uraiyur. The important ports of this coast were Kamara (Karikal), Poduka (Pondichery) and Sopatma (Supatama) (see Map 2.2). Many centuries later European trading factories were put up near these places: the Danes established Tranquebar near Karikal, the French Pondichery, and the British opted for Madras which was close to Supatama.

The British archaeologist Sir Mortimer Wheeler discovered in 1945 the remnants of an ancient port near the fishing village Arikamedu about 2 miles south of Pondichery. The great number of Roman items found there seems to indicate that this was Poduka of the Periplus, called 'New Town' (*Puducceri*) in Tamil. Brick foundations of large halls and terraces were found, also cisterns and fortifications. Shards of Roman ceramics were identified as Red Polish Ware which Wheeler tried to trace to Arezzo in Italy where it was produced between 30 BC and AD 45. The finds of Arikamedu conjure up the image of a flourishing port just like Kaveripatnam as described in an epic poem of the Sangam era:

The sun shone over the open terraces, over the warehouses near the harbour and over the turrets with windows like eyes of deer. In different places of Puhar the onlooker's attention was caught by the sight of the abodes of Yavanas, whose prosperity never waned. At the harbour were to be seen sailors from many lands, but to all appearances they live as one community.[4]

This Kaveripatnam situated at the mouth of the Kaveri was probably identical with the emporium of Khaberis described by Ptolemy.

The trade with Rome brought large numbers of Roman gold coins to southern India. In contrast with the Kushanas who melted down all Roman coins and reissued them in their own name, the rulers of south India did not do this but simply defaced the coins. A sharp cut across the face of the Roman emperor indicated that his sovereignty was not recognised but his coins were welcome and would be accepted according to their own intrinsic value. Just as in later periods, the Indians imported very few goods but were eager to get precious metals, so the quest for Roman gold was a driving force of India's international trade in ancient times. The Periplus reported this influx of coins and a text of the Sangam era highlights this, too: 'The beautifully built ships of the Yavanas came with gold and returned with pepper, and Muziris resounded with the noise.'[5] Thus it is no accident that the largest number of Roman gold hoards have been found in the hinterland of Muziris. In the area around Coimbatore, through which the trade route from the Malabar coast led into the interior of southern India and on to the east coast, eleven rich hoards of gold and silver Roman coins of the first century AD were found. Perhaps they were the savings of pepper planters and merchants or the loot of highwaymen who may have made this important trade route their special target.

3

THE REGIONAL KINGDOMS
OF EARLY MEDIEVAL INDIA

THE RISE AND CONFLICTS OF
REGIONAL KINGDOMS

Until about 500 the history of India was primarily north Indian history. The great empires of ancient India from the times of the Mauryas to the Guptas were based on the north of India. They rarely made much of a direct political impact on the south. These great empires were fascinating, but the millennium between the decline of the Gupta empire and the rise of the Mughal empire deserves attention too. Early modern historiography tended to depict the history of early medieval India as a period of political fragmentation and cultural decline and devoted to this period just as many pages as to Alexander's India campaign and the Indo-Greek kings. Only in recent decades has more research been done on this neglected millennium during which important regional kingdoms vied with each other for supremacy. This period is interesting not only in terms of regional history but also because of the contribution which it has made to Indian history in general.

Central and south India were equally as important as north India in this medieval period. This absence of political unity contributed in many ways to the development of regional cultures which were interrelated and clearly demonstrated the great theme of Indian history: unity in diversity. The period of the early Middle Ages which will be discussed here encompasses the Hindu kingdoms before the advent of Islamic rule.

Harsha and the dawn of medieval India

King Harsha of Kanauj was the great ruler who stood at the threshold of early medieval India. In his long reign (606 to 647) he once more established an empire nearly as great as that of the Guptas. This empire extended from the Panjab to northern Orissa and from the Himalayas to the banks of the Narmada. The high standard of classical Sanskrit culture at his court and the generous patronage bestowed on Hindu and Buddhist religious institutions alike seemed to show that the glory of the Gupta age had been

109

revived once more. We are well informed about Harsha's life and times because Bana, one of the greatest Sanskrit writers, composed a famous biography, *Harshacharita*, in classical prose with which he immortalised the deeds (*carita*) of his royal patron. At the same time the Chinese pilgrim, Xuanzang, reported in great detail about India in the days of Harsha. He spent thirteen years (630 to 643) in India, and eight of these thirteen years in Harsha's realm, before he returned to China with 20 horses loaded with 657 Buddhist texts and 150 relics. He translated 74 of these texts into Chinese himself. As a keen observer, he reported many facts which give a vivid impression of Harsha's times. No other Indian ruler after Ashoka and before the later Islamic rulers about whom we know from many chronicles emerges so clearly from the shadows of the past as Harsha does due to Bana's and Xuanzang's writings.

The size and splendour of his empire make it appear as if Harsha were a latter-day replica of the great Gupta rulers. But this was not so. At the height of their power the Guptas had no rivals in India. Harsha, however, was faced with many rivals who could hold their own against him. He had succeeded to the throne after his elder brother had succumbed to an intrigue of Shashanka, King of Bengal. Although Harsha was able to find an ally

Figure 3.1 Nymph at Gyaraspur, Madhya Pradesh, ninth century AD

(Courtesy of Hermann Kulke)

in the King of Kamarupa (Assam) he was unable to vanquish Shashanka. Only after Shashanka's death about 621 was Harsha able to conquer large parts of eastern India and Orissa. When he then turned to the south and ventured beyond the Vindhyas like Samudragupta had done he met a crushing defeat about 630 at the hands of his great contemporary, Pulakeshin II (610–642), of the Chalukya dynasty of Badami in Karnataka. Xuanzang hinted cautiously at the discomfiture of his royal patron:

> His subjects obey him with perfect submission but the people of this [Chalukya] country alone have not submitted to him. He has gathered troops from the five Indies, and summoned the best leaders from all countries and himself gone at the head of his army to punish and subdue these people, but he has not yet conquered their troops.[1]

Pulakeshin therefore proudly proclaimed in his Aihole inscription:

> Harsha, whose lotus feet were arrayed with the rays of the jewels of the diadems of hosts of feudatories, prosperous with unmeasured might, through Him (Pukaleshin) had his mirth (*harsha*) melted away by fear, having become loathsome with his rows of lordly elephants fallen in battle.[2]

After Pulakeshin's victory over Harsha no ruler of northern India ventured to conquer the south for nearly 600 years until the sultans of Delhi ushered in a new era. The hegemony of the north over the whole of India which was a characteristic feature of ancient Indian history had definitely come to an end. Thus, later Chalukya rulers praised the victory of their predecessor, Pulakeshin II, as a victory over the 'Lord of the Entire North' (*sakala-uttara-patheshvara*). The Deccan (derived from *dakshina*, originally meaning 'south') had become of equal importance to the north (see Map 3.1).

But Pulakeshin II was by no means the lord of the entire south. In Kanchipuram near Madras the Pallavas had established their capital and had emerged at the end of the sixth century AD as a great regional power in Tamil Nadu. The Pallava kings, Mahendravarman (*c*.600–630) and Narasimhavarman (630–668), were engaged in constant warfare with Pulakeshin II. But neither side was able to gain supremacy over the entire south. Initially Pulakeshin seemed to be getting the upper hand by fighting the Pallavas in alliance with their reluctant tributaries, the Pandyas and the Cholas. After defeating Harsha, Pulakeshin also annexed the Krishna–Godaveri delta region in present-day eastern Andhra Pradesh and installed his brother as viceroy at Vengi. This brother was the ancestor of the dynasty which later became known as the 'Eastern Chalukyas', whereas the main branch of this dynasty is often referred to as 'Western Chalukyas'. Pulakeshin's hegemony over the south seemed to be an established fact, but suddenly Narasimhavarman attacked Badami and Pulakeshin died while defending his capital which succumbed to the Pallava assault. For twelve years the Chalukyas seem to have disappeared from the political scene until Pulakeshin's son, Vikramaditya I, restored their fortunes and sacked Kanchipuram, the Pallava capital, in revenge for the Pallava assault.

The rise of regional centres

The contours of regional centres of power which clearly emerged in the seventh century AD remained of importance for Indian history in subsequent centuries. The triangular contest of Harsha, Shashanka and Pulakeshin in north, east and central India and the rivalry of Pulakeshin's dynasty, the Chalukyas and the Pallavas in the south were repeated in similar patterns over and over again.

When Harsha selected the holy city of Kanauj as his capital, he shifted the centre of north Indian hegemony from the east farther to the west. Patna (Pataliputra) had been an important centre of both the Maurya and the Gupta empires: the lower Gangetic plains could be controlled from there. Kanauj was in the middle of the Ganges–Yamuna Doab ('Land of Two Rivers').

Harsha's empire collapsed soon after his death but one century later Kanauj became once more the capital of a great conqueror, Yashovarman. His realm was soon destroyed by an even greater conqueror, Lalitaditya of Kashmir, whose far-flung empire also collapsed after his death. Lalitaditya made an important contribution to Indian history by defeating the Arabs who had conquered Sind and parts of the Panjab after 711. In spite of its rapidly changing fortunes, Kanauj remained the coveted 'imperial centre' of northern India for several centuries. The mighty dynasty of the Gurjara Pratiharas ruled most of north India from Kanauj until the late tenth century AD.

The shift of the centre of political power from Patna to Kanauj enabled the rulers of eastern India to rise to prominence. Shashanka had made a beginning, others followed soon. From the late eighth to the early twelfth century AD the Pala dynasty controlled large parts of Bihar and Bengal and was for some time the premier power of the north. In Bengal they were succeeded by the Sena dynasty in the twelfth century AD. Even under Islamic rule Bengal retained a great amount of independence as a sultanate in its own right until it became a province of the Mughal empire. When that empire declined Bengal reasserted its independence only to succumb to Britain in the eighteenth century and become its first territorial base.

The western Deccan remained an important region even after the decline of the Chalukyas of Badami. The Rashtrakutas of Malkhed emerged as the premier power of the Deccan in the eighth century AD. Under their rule in the ninth century, the central Deccan briefly even became the hub of political power for the whole of India. In the tenth century, the Chalukyas of Kalyani ruled the Deccan. In the northern region of the Deccan where once the Shatavahanas had founded their empire the Yadava dynasty established a regional kingdom in the twelfth and thirteenth centuries AD. When Islamic rulers penetrated the Deccan in the early fourteenth century they established the Bahmani sultanate whose centres at Gulbarga and Bidar were close to those of the Rashtrakutas of Malkhed and the Chalukyas of Kalyani. At the southern rim of the Deccan not far from the Badami of the early Chalukyas, Vijayanagar was established in the fourteenth century as the capital of the last great Hindu empire which encompassed most of southern India.

On the southeast coast the three dynastic nuclear areas of the Pallavas, Cholas and Pandyas in the major river valleys remained perennial centres of political power in the 'far south'. The nuclear area of the Pallavas was Tondaimandalam with its capital at Kanchipuram near present Madras. They were the premier power of the south from the sixth to the ninth centuries AD. When their power declined the ancient Cholas emerged once more and ruled the south from Thanjavur (Tanjore) in Cholamandalam (Coromandel), the central nuclear area at the Kaveri river, until the middle of the thirteenth century when the Pandyas of Madurai in their southern nuclear area became for a short time the premier power until they succumbed to the assault of the generals of the sultan of Delhi. In addition to the four major regional concentrations of political power in medieval India in north, east, central (Deccan) and south India there were some important intermediate centres which only occasionally interfered with the struggles of the great regional powers. One of these was the mountainous region of southern Karnataka where the western Ganga dynasty had ruled since the fifth century AD and the Hoysala dynasty in the twelfth century; another one was Orissa which was often isolated but under the eastern Gangas and the Gajapatis served as the base of realms which controlled for some times almost the whole east coast from Bengal to Madras. In the northwest there was Kashmir which rose to prominence in the eighth century when Lalitaditya conquered large parts of northern India. In the northeast Kamarupa (Assam) remained fairly isolated and independent throughout this period. But, though these other centres were powerful at times, in general the fate of India was decided in the four major regions mentioned above.

The confusing history of India from about 600 to 1200 with its many regional kingdoms and often rather short-lived dynasties falls into a pattern: the major political processes occurred only within the four central regions outlined above, and there was usually one premier power in each of these regions and none of them was able to control any of the other three regions for any length of time. Interregional warfare was mostly aimed at the control of intermediate regions or simply at the acquisition of goods. There was a balance of power which was determined both by the internal strength of the respective regions and the inability of the rulers to extend their control beyond their respective regions. Their military equipment, their administrative machinery and their strategic concepts were all more or less the same. Due to this balance of power there was a great deal of political stability within the regions which fostered the evolution of distinct regional cultures. At the same time this balance gave rise to frequent confrontation and sometimes multiple interregional clashes which were so characteristic of medieval Indian history. An examination of several of these confrontations gives a better understanding of the system of regional centres (see Map 3.2).

From the late eighth to the end of the ninth century interregional confrontations were particularly intense. The Gurjara Pratiharas in the north, the Palas in the east and the Rashtrakutas on the Deccan emerged as powerful dynasties almost at the same time. Vatsaraja, the founder of the Gurjara Pratihara dynasty conquered large parts of Rajasthan and of northwestern India around 783 while the early Palas, Gopala and Dharmapala (c.770–821), extended their sway from Bengal westward. A clash was then inevitable. Vatsaraja defeated the Pala king near Allahabad. In the meantime the Rashtrakutas had consolidated their hold on the Deccan and were looking northward. The third Rashtrakuta king, Dhruva (c.770–793), invaded the Gangetic plains with a large army and defeated both Vatsaraja and Dharmapala. After Dhruva's death, when Rashtrakuta power was eclipsed for some time, Dharmapala took his chance and captured Kanauj; he held court there and many kings 'bowed down before him with trembling crowns and showered their praise upon him', as it is proclaimed in one of his inscriptions.

But soon Vatsaraja's son, Nagabhata, restored the glory of the Gurjara Pratiharas, recaptured Kanauj and then proceeded to vanquish Dharmapala. This victory made the new Rashtrakuta king, Govinda III, very jealous. He pounced upon Nagabhata who had to flee to the desert of Rajasthan while Dharmapala quickly annexed Kanauj once more. In the following generation of rulers, Dharmapala's son Devapala (c.821–860) was the most prominent. He could extend his sway as the contemporary Gurjara Pratiharas and Rashtrakutas were weak rulers. But in the ninth century the Gurjara Pratihara kings, Bhoja (836–885) and Mahendrapala (885–910), proved to be more powerful than their contemporaries of the other two dynasties whom they defeated several times. Kanauj then emerged as the main focus of power in India.

Towards the end of the ninth century the Rashtrakutas gained in strength once more under their kings Indra III and the great Krishna III (939–968) whose power made an impact on all major regions of India. Whereas the

Rashtrakutas had so far mostly intervened in the affairs of the north, Krishna turned to the south and vanquished the newly powerful Cholas who had only recently defeated the Pallavas. In an inscription of 959 which Krishna left in Tondaimandalam he stated:

> With the intention of conquering the South (*dakshina-dig*) he uprooted the Chola dynasty and bestowed the lands of their realm on his own relatives. The mighty overlords of the Mandalas, like the Cheras and Pandyas and others as well as the ruler of Simhala (Sri Lanka) he reduced to the status of tributaries (*kara-da*). He established a column of victory at Rameshvaram (a South Indian temple-city facing Sri Lanka).[3]

This inscription shows that there were exceptions to the rule that the king of one region was perhaps able to replace a king of another region but could not extend his administrative control over it. Krishna obviously tried to do just that and there seemed to be the beginnings of a new centralised inter-regional empire. But unlike the large empires of ancient India, the medieval regional kingdoms had evolved their own structure and could not be easily controlled from a distance. If the distant ruler wished to retain his hold on another region he had to be prepared for frequent intervention and this was costly and diminished the resources of his own region which would in turn become vulnerable to intervention by third parties or to subversion from within. The latter happened to the mighty Rashtrakuta empire only six years after the death of Krishna III. Taila, the governor of a large province of the empire, usurped the throne of the Rashtrakutas and, in 982, the grandson of Krishna who had tried in vain to recapture the throne ended his life by fasting himself to death. Taila, who claimed to be an offspring of the early dynasty of the Chalukyas of Badami, had risen to prominence in the service of Krishna III, who had entrusted him with the defence of the north of the empire while he himself was devoting all his energy to the subjection of the Cholas. The dynasty founded by Taila was called the Chalukyas of Kalyani.

When the Chalukyas of Kalyani gained control over central India the political situation in two of the other major regions had drastically changed. By the end of the tenth century the mighty Gurjara Pratiharas were almost forgotten. After fighting against many enemies, among them the Arabs of Sind, their power had dwindled. Al-Mas'udi, a traveller from Baghdad who visited Kanauj in the early tenth century, reported that the Pratiharas maintained four large armies of about 700,000 to 900,000 men each. One army was specifically assigned the task of fighting against the Muslim ruler of Multan in the Indus valley and another one had to deal with the Rashtrakutas whom Al-Mas'udi regarded as the natural enemies of the Pratiharas. The maintenance of such large armies with their thousands of horses, camels and elephants must have placed a heavy burden on the people. When their power dwindled, the Gurjara Pratiharas still managed to retain their capital, Kanauj, but most of their territory was usurped by former tributary princes, particularly by the Rajputs. The decline of political unity in northern India was hastened by the annual invasions of Mahmud of Ghazni in the period from 1001 to 1027. He looted all regions from Gujarat to Varanasi (Benares) and destabilised the whole political system. North India did not recover from this onslaught until it was finally conquered by the Turks from Afghanistan in the late twelfth century.

The political development of southern India took an entirely different course. After Taila had usurped the throne of the Rashtrakutas, the Cholas could recover their position in the south. In the beginning of the eleventh century, Chola power was at its zenith under the great kings Rajaraja I and Rajendra I. For the first time the 'far south' became the main focus of Indian history. The Cholas pursued a systematic policy of expansion and extended their sway not only at the expense of the Chalukyas of Kalyani, they also conquered Sri Lanka and sent their troops and fleets to the Ganges and to Indonesia and Malaya. The struggle for the control of Vengi and the Krishna–Godaveri delta region which had continued for nearly four centuries was finally decided in favour of the Cholas due to a marital alliance. Kulottunga of Vengi, a member of the dynasty of the eastern Chalukyas and a relative of the Cholas, usurped the Chola throne and thus united the whole southeast coast under his rule.

Chola power continued until the thirteenth century. Then several local tributary princes emerged as independent kings, among them the Pandyas of Madurai, the Hoysalas of the southern mountains and the Kakatiyas of Warangal. But in due course they all fell prey to the superior military strategy of the Delhi sultanate in the early fourteenth century just about one century later than the rulers of northern India.

Having discussed the interrelations of the major historical regions of India, we can now turn to a closer examination of some of the important medieval dynasties. The details of their numerous confrontations are omitted unless such facts are of direct relevance to the fate of the respective dynasty.

The rise of the Rajputs

When Harsha shifted the centre of north Indian history to Kanauj in the midst of the Ganga–Yamuna Doab, the tribes living to the west of this new centre also became more important for the further course of Indian history. They were first and foremost the Rajputs who now emerged into the limelight of history. Thus the origin of the mighty dynasty of the Gurjara Pratiharas can be traced to the Pratihara clan of the Gurjara tribe of the Rajputs. The antecedents of these tribes are unknown. Because the Rajputs always insisted on ritual purity and valiantly fought against the Arabs and against the sultans of Delhi an Indian historian in the days of the freedom movement staked a determined claim for their descent from the Vedic Aryans. But it is also possible that some of these tribes came from central Asia in the wake of the invasion of the Huns and became part of local tribes. The route of Gurjara migration, for instance, can be traced by looking at the names of districts and places which they traversed from the Panjab down to Rajasthan until they finally settled down near Jodhpur and to the west of the Aravalli Mountains. In this mountain range there is the famous Mount Abu with its great Jaina temples. There is a tradition that in the year 747 a great fire ceremony was held on Mount Abu by which all Rajput clans were purified and admitted to the status of Kshatriyas. The Paramaras, for instance, mentioned in their inscriptions that they belong to the Agnikula ('fire family') purified by the Rishi Vasishta at a great fire sacrifice on Mount Abu. By tracing their origin to the fire they wanted to be on a par with the great legendary lineages of the Sun and the Moon (Suryavamsha, Chandravamsha) which go back to Rama and Krishna respectively.

The rise of the Rajputs in the vast area of Rajasthan seems to have been connected with an extension of settled agriculture and with the displacement of indigenous tribes like the Sabaras, Pulindas and Bhils. The constant division of Rajput tribes into small exogamous clans led to the development of a complicated network of marital alliances. This in turn produced a fusion of the leadership of the Rajputs and gave rise to a common Rajput culture which is still characteristic of Rajasthan today.

The strength of the Gurjara Pratihara dynasty was based to a large extent on the integration of the various Rajput tribes and clans into the imperial system. When Gurjara Pratihara power declined after the sacking of Kanauj by the Rashtrakutas in the early tenth century many Rajput princes declared their independence and founded their own kingdoms, some of which grew to importance in the subsequent two centuries. The better-known among those dynasties were the Chaulukyas or Solankis of Kathiawar and Gujarat, the Chahamanas (i.e. Chauhan) of eastern Rajasthan (Ajmer and Jodhpur), and the Tomaras who had founded Delhi (Dhillika) in 736 but had then been displaced by the Chauhans in the twelfth century. Rajput descent was also claimed by the Chandellas of Khajuraho and the Kalachuris of Tripuri (Madhya Pradesh). With their martial lifestyle and feudal culture which was praised by bards for many centuries throughout northern and central India, the Rajputs made a definite impact on Indian history in the late Middle Ages. Even in distant Orissa several of the princely lineages still trace their descent from the Rajputs. The Rajas of Patna-Bolangir in western Orissa, among them the former Chief Minister of Orissa, R.N. Singh Deo, even proudly claim to belong to the lineage of Prithviraj Chauhan, the great hero who valiantly defended India in 1192 against the Muslim invaders at the head of a Rajput confederation. Historians have referred to this spread of

Rajput culture as 'Rajputisation'. It became of added importance at the time of the Mughal empire when many Rajput families rose to high positions in the imperial service. In fact, due to intermarriage the later Mughals were themselves partly Rajputs. One of the most important contributions of the Rajput dynasties to Indian culture was their patronage of temple building and sculpture. The Chandellas who commissioned the building of the magnificent temples of Khajuraho are a good example of this great age of Rajput culture.

The Pala dynasty of east India

The most important dynasty of east India were the Palas. The founder of this dynasty, Gopala, was not of royal lineage. It is said that he was elected by the people in order to put an end to the general chaos which had prevailed in the country. His son, Dharmapala, stated in an inscription that his father was elected so as to put an end to 'the state of the fishes' and he was supposed to 'touch the hand of fortune'. The 'Law of the Fishes' (*matsyanyaya*) which states that the big are devouring the small in a state of anarchy (*a-rajaka*, i.e. kingless period) is frequently referred to in old Indian writings on the principles of government. The political and philosophical ideas of Hobbes were thus anticipated in India, and if the reports are true then Gopala owed his kingship to the kind of rational contract between the ruler and the ruled which Hobbes had in mind.

Gopala's dynasty rose to great prominence under his two great successors, Dharmapala (*c.*790–821) and Devapala (821–860), who intervened with great success in the political affairs of north India. But after these two great rulers the Palas lapsed back into insignificance for some time. Their power was restricted to their immediate domain around Patna and they completely lost their hold on Bengal. Only Mahipala (988–1038) restored the greatness of Pala rule, although he was temporarily affected by the northern expedition of the Chola king, Rajendra I. Under his successors Pala power was reduced by constant fights with the Kalachuris who ruled the eastern part of what is now Madhya Pradesh. It seems that the Palas even recognised the suzerainty of the Kalachuris for some time. While they were thus confronted with powerful rivals in the west they also faced difficulties in the east where the allodial lords of the tribe of the Kaivartas put up a valiant resistance to the Pala penetration of Varendra (northeast Bengal). Three Kaivarta rulers had controlled large parts of Varendra until Ramapala put an end to Kaivarta power by cementing an alliance with various neighbouring rulers. In this way he was able to restore Pala glory for some time, but his weak successors could not stop the decline of the dynasty.

As usual a tributary prince emerged and put an end to Pala rule from within. He was Vijayasena, the founder of the Sena dynasty, who first defeated all other princes who wanted to claim the heritage of the decaying Pala realm and finally did away with the last Pala ruler, too. Vijayasena's successors, Vallalasena and Lakshmanasena (1179 to 1205), guaranteed peace and stability for Bengal while they sent their troops to Bihar, Assam and Orissa. But by the end of the twelfth century tributary princes again emerged as independent rulers. In this period of internal crisis Muhammad Bakhtyar Khalji, who had earlier conquered Bihar, suddenly captured the Sena capital, Nadiya, and drove away Lakshmanasena who held on to east Bengal but could not prevent the establishment of the sultanate of Bengal under the Khaljis.

The importance of the Pala dynasty for east India is also due to the role which the Palas played in the religious and cultural life of the country. Several centuries of Hindu counter-reformation had greatly reduced the hold of Buddhism on other parts of India, but the Pala dynasty continued the tradition of royal patronage for Buddhist religious institutions. The Palas' control of the major holy places of Buddhism was very important for India's relations with Buddhist countries abroad. In Bengal Mahayana Buddhism attained its specific Tantric form which was influenced by the cult of the mother goddess who is still predominant there in her manifestation as Kali. Mystical and magical cults also grew in southeast Asia and in Tibet in this period under royal patronage and the Palas perhaps set this style. The old Buddhist university of Nalanda retained its international reputation under Pala rule and the new Buddhist university of Vikramashila was founded by Dharmapala. Vikramashila mostly attracted Tibetan monks who translated Indian texts into Tibetan there; Nalanda remained the 'Mecca' of Buddhist scholars of southeast Asia. Balaputra, the Shailendra king of Shrivijaya, arranged for the construction of a monastery for monks from his realm at Nalanda around 860, and Dharmapala granted five villages to this monastery in the thirty-ninth year of his reign. With the spread of Mahayana Buddhism in Tibet and southeast Asia the style of Palal art also made an impact on those countries. The painting of Thangkas in Tibet and the sculptures of southeast Asia provide evidence for this impact of the Pala style.

The Chalukya dynasty of Badami

The Chalukyas had originally been tributary princes under the Kadamba dynasty which ruled the Kanara coast from about the fourth century. In the sixth century, the first Chalukya king Pulakeshin I established his capital at Vatapi (Badami) and celebrated the great horse sacrifice so as to declare his independence from the Kadambas.

The Chalukyas emerged as great patrons of art and architecture. Whereas earlier scholars have often regarded them as mere brokers or mediators who copied northern styles in the south, more recent detailed studies have shown that Chalukya art was very creative in its own right. Perhaps one may even say that the Chalukya sculptors were among the greatest creators of Hindu iconography. Many figures of Hindu mythology were portrayed by them for the first time in beautiful stone sculptures along the lines of the Late Gupta style. Three beautiful cave temples were cut out of the rock near the fortress of Badami and decorated with a wealth of sculptures. The dancing Shiva (Nataraja) and Vishnu-Trivikrama, who recovers the universe from the demons in his dwarf-incarnation, were figures which directly influenced Pallava art as shown by the sculptures of the 'Rathas' (chariots) at Mahabalipuram which were cut out of solid rock at the behest of the Pallavas soon after they had captured Badami in 642. But the Pallavas soon had an opportunity to pay back this artistic 'debt'. When the Chalukya king, Vikramaditya II, captured the Pallava capital, Kanchipuram, in 740 he took some Pallava artists back with him who constructed two famous temples in 746 to 747. These temples in turn influenced the art of the Rashtrakutas who displaced the Chalukyas. The Rashtrakuta king, Krishna I (c.756 to 773), got the enormous Kailasa Temple of Ellora cut out of rock and it showed definite traces of the Pallava style. This is a good example of the mutual impact which the regional styles of medieval India made on each other.

The Pallava dynasty of Kanchipuram

The Pallavas were the first south Indian dynasty which succeeded in extending political control beyond the initial nuclear area – Tondaiman-dalam – which served as the base of their power. Their antecedents are unknown. Some historians maintain that their origin could be traced to the Pahlava (Parthians) of northwestern India. But it is more likely that their name is derived from the Sanskrit equivalent (*pallava*, meaning 'leaves', 'foliage') of the Tamil word *tondai* which designates their original domain: Tondaimandalam. On the other hand there is a legend that the first Pallava was a stranger who married a native Naga princess. The Nagas (snakes) are symbols of fertility and indigenous power. Similar stories of the rise of Hindu dynasties abound also in southeast Asia.

The Pallavas certainly did not belong to the ancient tribal lineages of the Cholas, Pandyas and Cheras and they owed their rise to their defeat of the Kalabhras who had crushed these old lineages. Perhaps the Pallavas would never have been able to gain supremacy over these ancient lineages if the Kalabhras had not paved the way for them. King Simhavishnu, the founder of the Pallava dynasty, extended his realm after defeating the Kalabhras to the north up to the mouth of the Krishna and to the south into the heart of the Chola country in the Kaveri valley. Under his successors, Mahendravarman and Narasimhavarman, the Pallavas confronted the Chalukyas.

Mahendravarman has the reputation of a very talented ruler who composed Sanskrit poetry and constructed the first great Hindu cave temples of southern India. It is said that he had adhered to Jainism originally but was then converted to Shivaism by Appar, one of the early Bhakti saints. Narasimhavarman who was also known as Mahamalla (Great Wrestler) was associated with the construction of the port Mahabalipuram (Mahamallapuram). Some of the most beautiful rock temples there, especially the 'Rathas', and the huge relief of the 'Descent of the Ganga' were completed during his reign. But the greatest builder of the Pallavas was Narasimhavarman II (c.680–720) who is supposed to have ordered the construction of the two magnificent Shiva temples, the Shore Temple of Mahabalipuram and the Kailasanath Temple of Kanchipuram. The southern style of the temple tower, a steep pyramid, was perfected here and was soon transmitted to southeast Asia, especially to Java, where temples of the Pallava style were constructed only a few decades later.

Kanchipuram flourished as the royal capital of the Pallavas and though they were Hindus they also extended their patronage to the Buddhists. The Chinese monk Xuanzang who visited the Pallava kingdom in the reign of Narasimhavarman I reported that there were about 100 monasteries with 10,000 monks all studying Mahayana Buddhism. To the south of Kanchipuram there was a large monastery which was visited by many

Figure 3.2 Rock relief of the late seventh century AD at Mahabalipuram, showing the descent of the Ganga and the penance of Arjuna

(Courtesy of Hermann Kulke)

Figure 3.3 Shore Temple at Mahabalipuram, early eighth century AD
(Courtesy of Hermann Kulke)

foreign scholars who wished to participate in learned debates. Xuanzang also saw eighty Hindu temples in Kanchipuram, and he also reported that down south in the Chola country Buddhism was nearly extinct:

> The disposition of these men is naturally fierce: they are attached to heretical teachings. The sangharamas [monasteries] are ruined and dirty as well as the priests. There are some tens of [Hindu] Deva temples.

The resurgence of the Chola dynasty

The comeback of the Cholas in the ninth century was achieved in a way with which we are by now familiar: they served as tributary princes under the Pallavas and reasserted their independence when Pallava power declined due to the constant confrontation with the mighty Rashtrakutas. While the Pallavas were busy in the north, the Cholas defended the Pallava realm against the southern Pandyas until Aditya took his chance around 897 and challenged his Pallava overlord on the battlefield. The encounter took the usual heroic form of a duel in front of the two armies. Aditya (the Sun) won and he and his son Paratanka (907 to 955) consolidated their hold on the south. While doing this they also had to confront the Rashtrakutas,

122

who defeated them. Thus the Cholas had to restrict their activities to their original nuclear area in the Kaveri valley for several decades.

Towards the end of the tenth century Uttama Chola and finally his son Rajaraja I restored Chola power with a vengeance by extending their territorial boundaries beyond their original 'homeland'. Rajaraja vanquished the Pandyas and Cheras, conquered Sri Lanka and sacked the venerable old capital, Anuradhapura, and at the end of his reign he even captured the distant Maldive islands. His son Rajendra I, whom he had asked to share the responsibilities of ruling the expanding empire in 1012, continued this aggressive policy with equal vigour. He conquered Vengi, captured the capital of the Chalukyas of Kalyani, sent his fleet again to the Maldives in 1017 and then in 1022 to 1023 he launched his great campaign which was to make him the 'Chola who conquered the Ganges', a feat which he commemorated by naming his new capital 'Gangaikondacholapuram'. In an inscription he reported that he had defeated the Pala king, Mahipala, and that he had ordered the defeated princes of Bengal to carry the holy water of the Ganges to his new capital, where he built a huge tank containing this water as a 'liquid pillar of victory'. Three years later he sent his fleet on the famous expedition to Sumatra and Malaya where his army then defeated the mighty Shrivijaya empire and all its tributary princes.

There are many theories about the causes of the sudden expansion of the Chola empire under these two great rulers. Did they just follow the old injunction of conquering the world (*digvijaya*) so as to prove their valour as universal rulers (*chakravartin*)? Were they mainly interested in plunder, as one American historian has suggested? Were their maritime expeditions part of a deliberate policy to establish a monopoly of trade which was obstructed by a similar policy followed by the Shrivijaya empire which had the strategic advantage of controlling the Malacca and Sunda Straits through which eastern trade had to pass? The south Indian historian K.A. Nilakanta Sastri has emphasised this latter point. But perhaps all these motives may have influenced their actions. The transfer of the Ganges water fits in very well with the first theory. The long list of jewels and gold which the Chola kings and generals donated to the imperial temples at Thanjavur (Tanjore) and at Gangaikondacholapuram provide evidence for the second theory. As far as their maritime interests were concerned, Nilakanta Sastri is certainly right. Moreover, these Chola maritime expeditions were by no means the first south Indian endeavours to intervene in the affairs of southeast Asia. In the reign of the Pallava king Nandivarman III (*c*.844–866), a Pallava officer left an inscription at Takuapa on the Isthmus of Siam recording that he had a tank constructed there which he then entrusted to a guild of south Indian merchants who were living in a military camp at this place. Probably these merchants and their troops were already at that time engaged in an endeavour to break the stranglehold of

Shrivijaya with Pallava aid by diverting the trade route via the Isthmus of Siam so as to avoid the Straits.

The Cholas tried to enhance their maritime strength also by gaining control over all strategically important coastlines. They captured the southwest coast of India and almost the entire Indian east coast up to the mouth of the Ganges; they also seized the Maldives, Sri Lanka and perhaps the Andamans. In keeping with this line of policy, they finally took on Shrivijaya. But this must also be seen in the context of increasing diplomatic activities at that time. The Chinese had sent embassies to the 'Countries of the South' in the late tenth century indicating their interest in an increase of trade. Shrivijaya had responded by sending six delegations to the Emperor of China in the brief period from 1003 to 1018. In 1015 and 1033 the Cholas had also sent embassies to China and the Chinese emperor recognised the Chola kingdom as one of the great tributary states, which was a mark of distinction in Chinese eyes. The southeast Asian states were as eager to have good relations with the Cholas as with the Emperor of China. Around 1005, the Shailendra king of Shrivijaya endowed a Buddhist monastery at Nagapatam for which Rajaraja provided some land grants. When Rajendra inherited his father's throne he immediately confirmed the grant made to that monastery. In 1015, after the Chola diplomatic mission had stopped over in Shrivijaya on their way to China, and again in 1019 the ruler of Shrivijaya sent rich presents for this monastery which Rajendra acknowledged in his inscriptions.

Cambodia also established diplomatic relations with the Cholas in 1012. King Suryavarman I, who expanded the kingdom of Angkor so as to encroach upon Shrivijaya's sphere of interest in Malaya, sent a chariot as a present to the Chola ruler in order to protect his own royal fortune (*atmalakshmi*). It is difficult to decide whether the king of Cambodia felt threatened by the emerging power of the Cholas or by their southeast Asian rival in Shrivijaya. There was obviously an increasing competition for trade and trade routes that was stimulated by the Chinese embassies. The Cholas and the southeast Asian rulers probably vied with each other for shares of the market. Rajendra's inscriptions indicate that Chola relations with Shrivijaya and Cambodia were friendly in the period from 1014 to 1019. The reasons for the Chola expedition of 1025 against Shrivijaya can, therefore, only be explained if more relevant sources are discovered. But this military venture was certainly the climax of a period of intense competition. It was obviously 'a continuation of diplomacy by other means', to quote the famous dictum of the Prussian general Karl von Clausewitz.

Rajendra's exploits in the Gulf of Bengal and in southeast Asia did not lead to permanent annexations of territory there. But the influence of the Cholas and of south Indian merchants was felt in southeast Asia throughout the eleventh century. In 1068 to 1069, after Shrivijaya had again sent an embassy to China, the Chola fleet intervened once more in the affairs of the island empire. A Chola inscription recorded that their troops conquered a large part of Malaya 'at the behest of the king who had asked for help and to whom the country was returned'. It seems that the Cholas had taken sides in a dynastic struggle, supporting the claims of the legitimate ruler. The Chinese got a wrong impression of this whole affair and mentioned the Cholas as tributary princes of the Shrivijaya empire in the Chinese imperial annals in subsequent years. Perhaps they were deliberately misled by ambassadors of Shrivijaya. The misunderstanding was corrected only in 1077 when the Chola ruler, Kulottunga I, dispatched an embassy of seventy-two merchants to China. A Tamil inscription of 1088, unfortunately badly damaged, provides evidence for the presence of a south Indian merchants' guild in Sumatra at that time.

In the following year the ruler of Shrivijaya sent two ambassadors to the Chola court and at their request Kulottunga specifically reconfirmed the donations made to the monastery at Nagapatam, which had been established in 1005. Diplomatic relations with Cambodia were also resumed. The king of Angkor, presumably Suryavarman II, the builder of Angkor Vat, sent a precious jewel to Kulottunga who then donated it to the temple of Chidambaram in 1114. Even the Burmese king, Kyanzittha (1086–1113), wrote a letter on golden leaves to a Chola prince. All these bits and pieces of information show that Kulottunga's long reign (c.1070–1120) was a time of peaceful diplomatic relations with southeast Asia which must have enabled the great merchant guilds of southern India to conduct their international business undisturbed.

The great merchants of south India

Indian merchants had participated in international trade since ancient times. But sources of information about those ancient times are restricted to archaeological finds and occasional references in literary texts which tell little about the activities of merchants. For the medieval period there are many more sources including many inscriptions, some of which were even recorded by the merchants themselves. In south India a distinction was made between merchants operating locally (svadeshi) and internationally (nanadeshi). The merchants had their own urban settlements (nagara) with autonomous institutions of local government. The great ports (pattana or pattinam) also had their guilds and autonomous institutions but they were much more under the control of royal officers who, of course, had to try to get along with the local people. The great guilds operating in 'many countries' (i.e. nanadeshi) had emerged as an important power factor in the south Indian polity in the days of the Pallavas. They not only financed local development projects and the construction of temples, they also lent money to the kings. Thus, the rulers did their best to accommodate the guilds because of the benefit which they derived from their trade. Due to their international connections, the troops they employed and the immunities they enjoyed, such guilds almost constituted a state within the state.

Among the most powerful guilds were the Ayyavole and the Manigramam. The Ayyavole, whose name was derived from a former capital of the Chalukyas, Aihole, dominated the trade of the Deccan whereas the Manigramam were based in Tamil Nadu. The international connections of the Ayyavole extended to western Asia while the Manigramam concentrated on the trade with southeast Asia. The inscription at Takuapa in southern Thailand mentions this latter guild specifically. The Tamil inscription of 1088 on Sumatra was also produced by a guild from Tamil Nadu. But there was no strict division of the spheres of trade between these guilds. Thus, for instance, Nanadeshi traders from the Malabar coast (Malaimandalam) established a Nanadeshi-Vinnagar Temple, devoted to Vishnu, at Pagan in Burma in the thirteenth century.

In the trade with western Asia the traders of the southwest coast obviously had some advantage. Ethnic connections were helpful in this respect, too. Arab and Jewish merchants who settled on the Indian southwest coast corresponded with their colleagues even in far-off Cairo. Letters and papers found in an old synagogue of Cairo give ample evidence of the many contacts which the medieval merchants of Cairo had with those of southern India. The respect which the Jewish traders enjoyed in southern India is shown by a royal grant inscribed on copper plates in favour of one Issuppu Irappan (Joseph Raban). He obtained princely privileges, exemption from all taxes and the grant of the revenue of a traders' quarter of the port of Cranganore on the Malabar coast.

The following passages of a lengthy inscription recorded by the guild of the Ayyavole merchants in 1055 tells much about that time. This inscription shows that these merchants had a rather high opinion of themselves and that the negation of the world and the spirit of introspection which were so prevalent in the times of the Upanishads and of Gautama Buddha were not of the same relevance in the Indian Middle Ages.

> Famed throughout the world, adorned with many good qualities, truth, purity, good conduct, policy, condescension, and prudence; protectors of the vira-Bananju-dharmma [law of the heroic traders] having thirty-two veloma, eighteen cities, sixty-four yoga-pithas, and asramas at the four points of the compass; born to be wanderers over many countries, the earth as their sack, the eight regents at the points of the compass as the corner tassels, the serpent race as the cords, the betel pouch as a secret pocket, the horizon as their light;
>
> visiting the Chera, Chola, Pandya, Maleya, Magadha, Kausala [Bihar], Saurashtra, Kamboja [northwest India], Gauda [Bengal], Lala [Gujarat], Parasa [Persia] and Nepala;

and by land routes and water routes penetrating into the regions of the six continents, with superior elephants, well-bred horses, large sapphires, moonstones, pearls, rubies, diamonds, lapis lazuli, onyx, topaz, carbuncles, coral, emeralds and various such articles: cardamoms, cloves, sandal, camphor, musk, saffron and other perfumes and drugs; by selling which wholesale, or hawking about on their shoulders, preventing the loss by customs duties, they fill up the emperor's treasury of gold, his treasury of jewels, and his armoury of weapons; and from the rest they daily bestow gifts on pandits and munis; white umbrellas [royal paraphernalia] as their canopy, the mighty ocean as their moat, Indra as the hand-guard, Varuna as the standard-bearer, Kubera as the treasurer, the nine planets as a belt, Rahu as a tassel, Ketu as a dagger, the sun and moon as the backers, the thirty-three gods as the spectators;

like the elephant they attack and kill, like the cow, they stand and kill, like the serpent, they kill with poison; like the lion they spring and kill; wise as Brihaspati, fertile in expedients as Narayana; perfect in disputes as Narada-rishi; raising a fire, they seize like death, the gone Mari [or epidemic] they make fun of, the coming Mari they face, the tiger with a collar on they irritate; on the moving cart they place their feet; clay they set fire to, of sand they make ropes; the thunderbolt they catch and exhibit; the sun and moon they draw down to earth;

they converse about the frontal eye and four arms of Isvarabhattaraka, the loud laughter of Brahma, and the madness of Bhagavati. In the case of a sack which bursts from the contents collected from the points of the compass, an ass which runs away [laden] with grain, a bar of gold that has been seized, a tax that has been evaded, a cry of looting, an assembly connected with caste customs, a bargain that has been made, – they are not ones to fail.

Be it as it will. To the Five Hundred svamis of Ayyavole, possessed of all titles, having made prostration with the eight members, salute with joined hands raised to the head, pull out that sack, and present offerings of food, O Setti! To the Five hundred svamis of Ayyavole present the tambula in a tray, wishing them all good fortune.[4]

KINGS, PRINCES AND PRIESTS: THE STRUCTURE OF HINDU REALMS

The survey of the development of several important Indian dynasties has shown some basic structural similarities in these medieval regional kingdoms. Ever since the days of the Guptas the style to be followed by a Hindu ruler was fairly well set. The Maharaja, be his realm large or small, had emerged as a distinct cultural type. The spread of this style across the subcontinent and on to southeast Asia was due not only to direct imitation but also to the transmission of its values by the Brahmins who acted as royal advisors and priests to the royal families or to the many temples established by means of royal patronage.

The incessant confrontation of many rulers which was a concomitant of the universal spread of the royal style has distracted attention from the basic continuity of regional cultures which prospered in the medieval period. Within the respective regions the rise and decline of dynasties was only an epiphenomenon. As we have seen, the regional pattern remained rather stable and where one dynasty was eclipsed another one took over. At the most there were slight shifts in the relative importance of nuclear areas. If such a nuclear area were at the centre of a mighty realm it could often benefit from the tribute exacted from other areas. Whenever power shifted to another area that area in turn would attract the tributes. In this way many different areas got a chance to flourish at some time and to develop their regional culture. Thus, the system of medieval kingship had a distributive effect.

In this chapter the basic features of the structure of medieval Hindu realms are highlighted. We shall start with an examination of Harsha's empire which was no longer akin to the empires of ancient India but already showed the characteristics of the medieval period.

Harsha and the Samantas: a new pattern of Indian feudalism

In its dimensions Harsha's vast realm was very much like the Gupta empire, but its internal structure was quite different from that empire. The central area of the realm, the Doab between Kanauj and Prayag (Allahabad) and east of Varanasi (Benares) seems to have been firmly under Harsha's control. This central part of the empire was quite large. Harsha was even in a position to cancel the land grant of a Brahmin at a place which was at a distance of about 250 miles from Kanauj, because the Brahmin could produce only a forged document (*kutashasana*); his land was promptly transferred by the royal chancellor to another grantee. This seemed to be very much like the central control exercised by the Guptas.

But in other respects the organisation of Harsha's realm was much more decentralised. Magadha, for instance, was under the control of Purnavarman, a member of the Maukhari dynasty which Harsha had displaced at Kanauj. Purnavarman ruled that part of the country on Harsha's behalf but probably enjoyed a great amount of autonomy. Bengal was divided between Harsha and his ally, King Bhaskaravarman of Kamarupa (Assam), after Shashanka's death. But there is no evidence of Harsha's direct rule over Bengal. The Guptas had appointed governors and even district officers in Magadha and Bengal but Harsha was obviously not in direct control of those areas.

But it was not only the more restricted area under central control which distinguished Harsha's realm from the Gupta empire. There was also a different type of control within the central core area which showed a definite change in the structure of the state. An inscription of 632 concerning a land grant which Harsha gave to two Brahmins at Madhuban, north of Varanasi, throws light on the structure of the internal administration of this central part of the empire.[1] The inscription mentions 'Great Neighbours' (*mahasamanta*), 'Great Kings' (*maharaja*), 'Guardians of the Royal Gateway' (*dauhsadika*), judges (*pramatara*), vice-regents (*rajasthaniya*), ministers belonging to the royal family (*kumaramatya*), governors of provinces (*uparika*), district officers (*vishayapati*), regular and irregular troops (*bhata, cata*), servants and the local population (*janapada*) as all those who are duly notified and thus guarantee the validity of the grant. The donation was made on behalf of a royal officer named Skandagupta, and it was executed by Ishvaragupta, the royal chancellor (*mahakshapatalika*). Skandagupta was addressed as Mahasamanta and Maharaja whereas Ishvaragupta was only called Samanta and Maharaja. This list of dignitaries does not start with the governor of the province or a royal prince as one would have expected but with a mahasamanta. The institution of the samanta was the main innovation which distinguished the medieval Hindu kingdom from the ancient empires. The term *samanta* originally meant 'neighbour' and referred to the independent ruler of an adjacent territory. The 'border kings' (*pratyanta-nripati*) mentioned by Samudragupta in his Allahabad inscription were such samantas in the original sense of the term. But by the end of Gupta rule and definitely by the sixth century a new meaning of the term had gained universal currency. Samanta had come to mean a subjected but reinstated tributary prince of a realm.

The rise of the samantas was a distinctive structural feature of the growth of medieval realms. Whereas in the ancient empires administrators had been imposed from above by imperial appointment, the medieval realms were controlled by princes who had once been subjected but then reinstated and were then obliged to pay a tribute and to serve the king loyally. In the late Gupta period, this type of administrator was occasionally found in the border provinces but in Harsha's time and later on they became powerful figures even in the core area of the empire. They enjoyed a great deal of autonomy within their territory and soon surpassed the old type of provincial governor in wealth and prestige. In order to integrate these too powerful subjects into the hierarchy of the realm they were often given high positions at the court of the king. Thus the king of Valabhi in western India who was defeated by Harsha not only gained recognition as a mahasamanta but rose to the high positions of a 'Guardian of the Royal Gateway' (*mahapratihara*) and 'Royal Field-marshal' (*mahadandanayaka*). Conversely, the high officers of the central court demanded similar recognition as the defeated kings and princes and obtained it in due course. But the magnificent title alone would not do, the officers also wanted some territory to go with it. This then was the process of the 'samantisation' of the realm which we may regard as the Indian variety of feudalism.

This process was accelerated by two factors: the lack of cash for the payment of salaries and the new idea that royal prestige depended on the size of a king's 'circle of tributary princes' (*samantacakra*). Old treatises on the art of government, like the *Arthashastra*, provide detailed lists of the salaries of officers and Xuanzang reported that high officers received their salaries in cash even in the seventh century. But the recession of international trade and the reduced circulation of coins made it necessary for officers to be paid by the assignment of the revenue of some villages or of whole districts which they held as a prebend. Medieval texts like the *Kathasaritsagara* tell us that kings were eager to cancel such assignments, particularly if the officer concerned had displeased the ruler. But in general the process of samantisation was stronger than the will of the central ruler.

Samantisation slowly eroded the power base of the ruler even in the core area of his realm as this assignment of prebends diminished the area directly controlled by the central administration. This process of the fragmentation of central power occurred in other countries, too, but in India it became a legitimate feature of kingship: the great emphasis placed on the samantachakra made a virtue out of necessity. Medieval inscriptions and texts are full of enthusiastic descriptions of the glitter of the crowns and jewels of the samantas who surrounded the king when he held court. The durbar, or court, emerged in this way as a special feature of the display of royal glory: the greater the number of samantas and mahasamantas who attended the durbar, the greater the fame of the overlord. Such a samantachakra was, of course, inherently unstable. As soon as the power of the central ruler declined a mahasamanta would strive for independence or would even dream of stepping into the centre of the samantachakra.

The emergence of regional kingdoms

So far we have only highlighted the negative effects of this process by referring to the fragmentation of royal control in the core regions of the ancient empires in northern India. But the development of political institutions in eastern, central and southern India must be seen in a different light. In those regions local rulers emerged who became regional kings using the new royal style as a model for the integration of local and tribal forces. In some ways this 'development from below' was similar to that of state formation in the Gangetic plains in the seventh to the sixth centuries BC.

There were usually three stages of this process: initially a tribal chieftain would turn into a local Hindu princeling, then this prince would become a king surrounded by samantas and thus establish an 'early kingdom', and, in the third stage, great rulers of 'imperial kingdoms' would emerge who controlled large realms and integrated the samantas into the internal structure of their realm. The transition of tribal chieftains to Hindu princelings is not very well documented, but it is known that there were many petty Hindu principalities in central and south India in the period after the decline of the Gupta empire. These petty rulers controlled only small nuclear areas. Once they transcended these areas and defeated their neighbours, the second phase began. This was often accompanied by agrarian extension, an increased appropriation of agrarian surplus in the nuclear area and the displacement of tribal people who were either pushed into barren or mountainous tracts or incorporated into the caste system as Shudras. In this second phase, the kings of these early kingdoms also invited more and more Brahmins, endowing them with land grants and immunities and often establishing whole Brahmin villages (*agraharas*). By such formal grants the extraction of surplus revenue was often defined for the first time in an exemplary fashion as immunities granted to Brahmin donees in areas which had not yet come under full control of the ruling dynasty. The most important features of the second phase were the promotion of trade and the subjection of neighbouring rulers whose territory was, however, not annexed but was treated as a tributary realm. These tributary princes attended the court of the victorious king but did not yet play any significant role in the administration of the nuclear area of his realm. Trade was encouraged by the king because it augmented his revenue income and helped him to acquire prestigious goods for his court.

The great regional or imperial kingdom of the third phase was based on the conquest and annexation of at least one other early kingdom and of some principalities which existed in intermediate regions. The appropriation of the surplus within such an extended core area of the realm was necessary in order to defray the cost of the army, of a larger number of retainers and Brahmins and of the 'imperial temple' which usually marked the centre of such an imperial kingdom. Subjected rulers of early kingdoms would surround the ruler of such an imperial kingdom as his mahasamantas and they in turn would have some princelings as their samantas. Marital alliances often served as a means to keep the samantachakra together. In spite of their large size, which could well be compared to that of medieval European kingdoms, these imperial kingdoms of medieval India were not in a position to install a centralised administration beyond the confines of the extended core area. Within this area, however, they sometimes achieved a high degree of direct central administration as recent research on the core area of the Cholas in the eleventh century has shown.

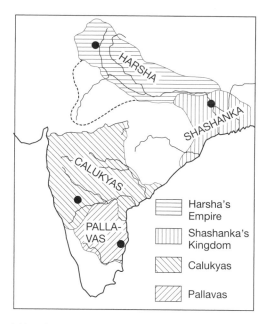

Map 3.1 Regional kingdoms in the early seventh century

Orissa: a case study of the evolution of a medieval polity

The history of medieval Orissa provides an interesting illustration of the stages of development 'from below' of a regional kingdom (see Map 3.3). Orissa had been a province of the north Indian empires under the Nandas and Mauryas, and under Kharavela it had even served as the base of a major kingdom. But these were not instances of indigenous political development but of a kind of development which was either imposed from above or imported from some other region (e.g. Dakshina Koshala). It was only several centuries after the decline of Kharavela's short-lived realm that indigenous state formation of the first phase, i.e. the emergence of princi-palities, was seen in Orissa.

Samudragupta's Allahabad inscription provides some information about the petty rulers whom he vanquished there. He met with four independent rulers when proceeding, via Kalinga, towards the Krishna–Godaveri delta, covering a distance of about 200 miles. None of these rulers claimed any suzerainty over any of the others. But perhaps Samudragupta's intervention did initiate the second phase of state formation there, because immediately after he had returned to the north the Mathara dynasty, which had its base

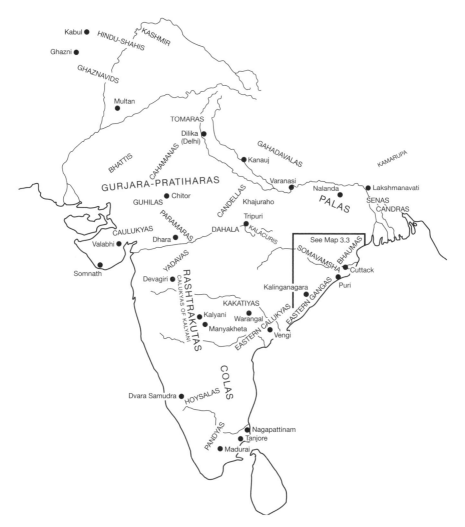

Map 3.2 Regional kingdoms of the early Middle Ages (*c.*900–1200)

in the northern Godaveri delta, extended its sway all the way north to the mouth of the Mahanadi.

In central Orissa, however, the transition to the second phase began only after the decline of the Gupta empire, when the Shailodbhava dynasty emerged in the seventh century after defeating several small principalities and establishing an early kingdom in the southern part of central Orissa. The rise of this dynasty can be traced back to the fifth century and the legend connected with this rise is typical for the origin of such dynasties. A Shailodbhava inscription of the seventh century recorded the following

Map 3.3 Territorial development of Orissa (*c.*600–1400)

story: Pulindasena, a ruler of Kalinga, was tired of ruling his realm and, therefore, prayed to God that he install a new young ruler instead. God granted him this wish; a rock split open and out of it stepped a young man whom Pulindasena called Shailodbhava and whom he made the founder of a new dynasty.[2] This legend and the names of the two kings clearly point to the tribal origin of state formation in this area. The Pulindas were a tribe which had been known to Ashoka, and Pulindasena must have been a war chieftain (*sena*) of that tribe. His successors whose dynaslic name means 'Born of the Mountain' (*saila-udbhava*) must have descended from the mountains to settle at the Rishikulya river. But several generations passed before a member of that dynasty could celebrate the great horse sacrifice and extend his sway into the neighbouring nuclear area, the southern Mahanadi valley. The

Shailodbhava legend shows that even the Hindu kings of a later age proudly referred to their tribal origin. They also continuedto worship the great mountain, Mahendragiri, as their 'family mountain' (*kula-giri*).

The further political development of Orissa is characterised by a constant territorial expansion of the regional kingdom which incorporated several nuclear areas. But this process was not one of 'expansion from within' but of 'addition from without', not one of centrifugal expansion but of a centripetal quest for the more highly developed and more prosperous rice-growing nuclear region at the centre by forces emerging at the periphery. It owed its dynamics to a sequence of conquests of the kingdom's centre by mighty neighbours who then added their own nuclear areas to the expanding kingdom. In the eighth century the Shailodbhavas were dislodged in this way by the Bhaumakaras who united their nuclear area north of the Mahanadi delta with the Shailodbhava area in southern Orissa. In the tenth century the Somavamshi kings of western Orissa conquered the coast and added two of their own nuclear areas to the regional kingdom. The Somavamshis came from Dakshina Koshala on the upper Mahanadi and had slowly worked their way downstream conquering in due course the small but important nuclear area of the Bhanja rulers of Khinjali Mandala. Altogether the new regional kingdom now contained five nuclear areas, three at the coast and two in the hinterland. In the beginning of the twelfth century a ruler of the Ganga dynasty whose base was in Kalinga captured the regional kingdom of Orissa and united it with his own homeland in present northern Andhra Pradesh. The fate of this imperial kingdom of Orissa in the late Middle Ages will be described in the next chapter.

The administrative structure in these principalities and early kingdoms seems to have evolved gradually in keeping with local requirements. Thus the inscriptions of the Matharas of the fifth century did not yet contain long lists of royal officers and there seems to be only a vague indication of district administration (*vishaya*). The villages seem to have enjoyed a considerable degree of autonomy. Mathara land grants only mention the peasants (*kutumbin*) themselves as witnesses. This seems to indicate that in Orissa these small kingdoms in the second phase of development were alliances of princelings under the suzerainty of the strongest among them. A centralised administration probably did not even exist in the nuclear area of the chief ruler at this stage.

A distinct change can be noticed when the Bhaumakara dynasty established its hold over coastal Orissa. The land grants of this dynasty, recorded on copper plates, contain the full list of mahasamantas, maharajas, princes, ministers, governors and district officers and a host of other royal officers. Interestingly enough, the grants also contain a short list of the important people in the villages concerned which seems to indicate that the villages continued to enjoy a large amount of autonomy even at this stage of the development of the regional kingdom.

Figure 3.4 Bhubaneswar, Orissa. Sungod Surya, eighth century AD
(Courtesy of Hermann Kulke)

Another aspect of the rule of the Bhaumakaras is the existence of a circle (*mandala*) of tributary neighbours. The mandala rulers were the Shulkis, Nandas, Tungas and Bhanjas. They have all left inscriptions of their own in which they referred to their Bhaumakara overlords but otherwise acted rather independently. The mandala lords' strong position was due to the fact that they represented important tribal units with their own distinct territorial base. The Shulkis probably belonged to the tribe of the Shaulikas which has been mentioned in the inscriptions of central Indian kings. They worshipped a tribal 'Goddess of the Pillar' (*stambheshvari*), a goddess who is still worshipped today in the former tribal areas of Orissa. Nevertheless, the Shulkis also built magnificent Hindu temples in their capital. These tribal rulers can be compared to the allodial lords of medieval Europe who did not hold a fief bestowed upon them by the king but had grown 'from a wild root'. It was an important element of state formation in early medieval India that such mandala lords extended their sway into the surrounding mountainous regions where tribes lived who were as yet untouched by Hindu influences. The Shulkis, for instance, called themselves 'First Lords of the entire Gondama country' and the Tungas referred to themselves as 'First Lords of the eighteen Gondamas'. Gondama is the area inhabited by the tribe of the Gonds who, even today, live in the mountainous region of western Orissa and eastern Madhya Pradesh. Agrarian extension through local irrigation and large-scale settlement of Brahmins was another significant feature of these early kingdoms, particularly in eastern India. Brahmin settlements were instrumental in spreading agricultural know-how and extending control over rural resources.

The art of controlling the samantas

The expansion of medieval regional kingdoms and the rise of the samantas created problems which could not be solved by means of the usual patrimonial arrangements made by the ancient kings. The main problem was the control of the outer circle of samantas. Outright conquest and annexation of their territories would not only have required more resources and administrative capacity of the central dynasty but also a change in the royal ideology which measured the Hindu kings' prestige in terms of the number of tributary princes attending their court. Such princes were, of course, always eager to regain their independence and, if the central king suffered any kind of setback, they would try to increase their autonomy and cut the tribute due to him. Contemporary texts therefore describe the samantas as potential enemies of the king and their military contingents as the weakest link in the king's defences.

Accordingly, the success of the ruler of a regional kingdom depended, to a large extent, on his abilities to curb the power of his samantas and to instill some loyalty in them. But the inscriptions do not provide much evidence of a successful control of the samantas. Few kings were able to compel their samantas to send a permanent representative to his court or to receive a royal emissary as a permanent watchdog at their court. The Rashtrakuta king, Amoghavarsha, hit upon an interesting method of solving this problem: he sent thousands of dancers and courtesans as spies to the courts of his samantas. These ladies had to be maintained by the samantas but had to report to the royal ambassador at the court of the samanta who would then pass on the news to Amoghavarsha. It is not known whether this interesting experiment of the ninth century was also tried by other kings elsewhere.

A striking example of the way in which a king had to depend on his samantas in crucial times was provided by King Ramapala when he was looking for support against the Kaivartas of north Bengal. Ramapala claimed that the country occupied by the rebellious Kaivartas was his own (*janaka-bhu*) and, to recover it, he made the round of his samantas, asking for help and giving them presents. The contemporary text *Ramacharitam* describes in detail how Ramapala had to visit the chieftains of forest tribes (*atavika*) and how he had to woo his samantas to aid him with elephants and troops giving them gifts and land grants. Other medieval kings probably experienced similar calamities.

In view of the instability of the samantachakra the king could really depend only on the core area directly controlled by him, but even this area explicitly reserved for the 'enjoyment of the king' (*raja-bhoga*) was affected by the institutional changes in the medieval regional kingdoms. Rulers had to compensate in other ways for the revenue lost by assignment to royal officers in lieu of salary. In the twelfth century some instances of rulers obliging provincial governors to keep a certain number of troops for the use of the king have been found. Rulers also tried to see to it that the revenue assignments to their officers were made in such a way that there would not be a dangerous concentration of regional power in their hands. Thus a king of the north Indian Gahadavala dynasty of the twelfth century granted his Brahmin minister and his son the revenue of eighteen villages but saw to it that the assigned villages were located in eighteen different districts. In order to get more resources rulers could also raise the taxes in their immediate domain and encroach upon the territory of their samantas. Both of these courses of action were dangerous, the peasants would flee if their burden was too pressing and the samantas could rebel and bring about the downfall of the dynasty.

The Brahmins and the ritual sovereignty of the king

The precarious position of the king with regard to both the control of his central area and his relations with his samantas called for a specific emphasis on the legitimacy of kingship to enhance his personal power. This was done by means of highlighting his divine mission and his ritual sovereignty. The Brahmins were instrumental in providing the necessary ideology for this purpose. Many documents recording land grants to Brahmins show this very clearly. In the Gupta empire such land grants had often been made in distant, uncultivated areas where the Brahmins were obviously meant to act as missionaries of Hindu culture. But from the tenth century onwards land grants followed a rather different pattern. Kings adopted the practice of granting land, or rather the revenue of whole villages, to Brahmins sometimes even in the territories of their samantas. Such a grant was really at the expense of the samanta rather than the king who gained a loyal follower, because the Brahmin would look upon his royal patron as his true benefactor. The samantas could not object to such grants as they were sanctified by tradition. There was another important change in the policy of granting land to Brahmins. Whereas previously single families or, at the most, small groups had received such grants, the records of the tenth and eleventh centuries suddenly mention large numbers of Brahmins. A ruler of the Gahadavala dynasty, for instance, granted one and a half revenue districts with more than a hundred villages to 500 Brahmins in 1093 and 1100. The area concerned was in the immediate vicinity of Varanasi (Benares) which was the second capital of the Gahadavalas. The king was obviously keen to strengthen his hold on this newly conquered region and did not mind the substantial loss of revenue which he incurred in this way.

This new function of the land grants became even more obvious in the south in the context of the rise of the great royal temples which symbolised the power and religious identity of the respective realm. From the eleventh to the thirteenth centuries such large temples were built in various regional kingdoms of India. They were often three to four times bigger than earlier temples. Some important examples are the Kandariya Mahadeva Temple at Khajuraho (around 1002), the Rajarajeshvara Temple at Thanjavur (Tanjore) (around 1012) and the udayeshvara temple at Udaipur, the capital of the north Indian kingdom of the Paramaras (c.1059–80). Orissa can boast of a particularly impressive sequence of such temples: the Lingaraja Temple at Bhubaneshwar (around 1060), the Jagannath Temple of Puri (c.1135) and the great Sun Temple (c.1250). So far these temples have mainly attracted the attention of the historians of art and architecture and they have not been placed into the context of political history.

The construction of these temples coincided with the increasing samantisation of the regional kingdoms of India. The temples were obviously supposed to be a counterweight to the divisive forces prevailing in those kingdoms. In order to fulfil this function they were endowed with great grants of land often located near the capital but also sometimes in distant provinces and even in the territories of the samantas (see Map 4.2). For the performance of the royal ritual hundreds of Brahmins and temple servants were attached to these temples. The very detailed inscriptions of donors at the great Temple of Thanjavur tell us exactly from which villages the 137 guards of the temple came. The inscriptions contain instructions to the respective villages to supply the guards coming from those villages with rice. Samantarajas and royal officers were obliged to perform special services in the temple. The personal priest of the king, the Rajguru, was also the head priest of the royal temple and the manager of its enormous property.

Although the construction of such great temples was very expensive they soon became self-supporting and were of great benefit to the king. Thus Rajaraja, the king who built the great Temple at Thanjavur, donated altogether the equivalent of 502 kg of gold to this temple until the twenty-ninth year of his reign (1014). But the annual deliveries of grain to the temple from the land granted to it were worth about the same amount. Surplus funds of the temple were lent to villages in the core area of the realm for agricultural development projects at the rate of 12 per cent interest per annum.

The economic and political functions of the temple were realised in the role of the king in the royal ritual. The Linga, the phallic symbol of Shiva, in the sanctum of the temple was often named after the king who had donated it, e.g. the Udayeshvara-Linga or the Rajarajeshvara-Linga in the temples established by Udayaditya and Rajaraja in their respective capitals. Paintings in the temple and sculptures outside it showed the king depicted like a god and the gods in turn were decorated with royal attributes. In order to gain additional legitimation some kings even solemnly transferred their realm to the royal god and ruled it as the god's representative or son (*putra*). In this way they could use the royal temple and its staff as instruments of government and could threaten disobedient samantas with the wrath of the royal god if they did not obey the king's orders.

The settlement of Brahmins and the establishment of royal temples served the purpose of creating a new network of ritual, political and economic relations. This network was centred on the king and was thus an antidote to the centrifugal tendencies of the samantachakra. But in the long run this policy did not solve the problems of the constant power struggles in medieval regional kingdoms. More and more resources were diverted to the Brahmins and temples and thus were not available for other urgent tasks of the state such as infrastructure, agrarian extension, administration and defence. This was particularly true of kingdoms where one king after another established a great temple of his own and more and more land and wealth passed into the hands of the managers of temple trusts. The people were pressed by the burden of taxation and the samantas were driven to rebellion by the very measures which were designed to keep them in check. Thus a dynasty would fall and would be replaced by another one whose strength was mainly based on the as yet undivided resources of its own nuclear region.

GODS, TEMPLES AND POETS: THE GROWTH
OF REGIONAL CULTURES

Four factors characterise the early medieval period in India and indicate its importance for the evolution of Indian culture in general: the emergence of regional kingdoms, the transformation of 'Brahminism' into a new kind of popular Hinduism, the evolution of regional languages and, as a result of all this, the growth of regional cultures. This heritage of the early Middle Ages was in many ways enriched by the influence of Islam and continued to be of relevance in the Mughal empire, in the later realms of the Rajputs, Marathas and Sikhs and even today. We now turn to the transformation of Hinduism.

The new systems of Indian philosophy

The history of Hinduism in the second half of the first millennium was influenced by two tendencies which seemed to contradict each other but whose synthesis actually led to the emergence of the kind of Hinduism which still exists today. On the one hand this period witnessed the rise of the great philosophical systems which were formulated in constant debates with Buddhists and Jains in the course of what has been termed a 'Brahmin counter-reformation'; on the other hand the same period produced the great popular movements of the Bhakti cults which often explicitly rejected Brahmin orthodoxy and monist philosophy and aimed at salvation by means of pure devotion to a personal god. There were six classical philosophical systems of which the Karma Mimamsa, which addressed itself to the theory of right conduct and the performance of sacrifices, and classical Sankhya, which postulated a duality of mind and matter, were of particular significance. But the most influential of these systems was Vedanta (the end, i.e. *anta*, of the Vedas) which was greatly emphasised by the Neo-Hindu thinkers of the nineteenth and twentieth century and which is therefore often regarded as the very essence of Indian philosophy.

The great philosopher Shankara (788–820) renewed and systematised Vedanta philosophy by stressing its main principle of monism (*kevala-advaita*, or absolute non-duality). Shankara is regarded by some of his followers as an incarnation of Shiva. He was born the son of a Nambudiri Brahmin of Malabar (Kerala), composed his main work, the commentary on the Brahmasutras at Varanasi (Benares) and, according to later tradition, travelled throughout India in order to engage Buddhist and Jain scholars in debates. It is said that he defeated many of them by the power of his arguments. He also tried to unify the different rites and traditions of various groups of Brahmins. Four holy sees (*matha*) were established in the four corners of India, perhaps by Shankara or by his followers who attributed their foundation to him. These holy sees were then occupied by the Shankaracharyas who propagated his doctrines after his death and continue to be important to Hindus today. The Shankaracharya of Shringeri in Karnataka enjoys special reverence; one of his predecessors is supposed to have played an important role in the establishment of the Vijayanagar empire.

Shankara formulated an impressive theory of knowledge based on the quintessence of the philosophical thought of his age. He referred to the philosophical teachings of the Upanishads about the unity of the individual soul (*atman*) and the divine spirit (*brahman*). He taught that the individual soul as embodied in a living being (*jiva*) is tied to the cycle of rebirths (*samsara*) because it believes that this world is real although it is only illusion (*maya*). This belief is due to ignorance (*avidya*) which prevents the soul (*atman*) from realising its identity with the divine spirit (*brahman*). Only right knowledge (*jnana*) leads to the realisation of this identity and to salvation (*moksha*) from the cycle of rebirths.

Shankara's philosophy was in many ways akin to Buddhist thought in highlighting the need to overcome the attachment to the cycle of births by self-realisation. He contributed to the elimination of Buddhism by evolving a Hindu philosophy which could account for everything which the Buddhists had taught in an equally systematic way. But he also provided some scope for popular Hinduism by allowing for a 'lower truth' which embodies the manifold appearance of the world and implies the existence of a divine creator (*ishvara*). In this way he reflected similar ideas of the Upanishads and of Mahayana Buddhism and was able to combine popular Hinduism with orthodox Brahmanism in a lofty philosophical system. Everybody could find his own level in this magnificent synthesis of 'lower' and 'higher' truths.

The Bhakti movement

While Shankara evolved his monist system which gave a new lease of life to orthodox Brahmanism, a popular movement emerged outside the confines of orthodoxy and sometimes even challenged this orthodoxy deliberately. This Bhakti movement emphasised the love of god and childlike devotion to him. In contrast with the Brahmin emphasis on right action (*karma-marga*) and the philosopher's insistence on right knowledge (*jnana-marga*) the path of love and devotion (*bhakti-marga*) aimed at self-effacing submission to the will of god. Earlier evidence of this mystical devotion can be found in the *Bhagavadgita* when Krishna says to Arjuna: 'He who loves me will not perish . . . think of me, love me, give sacrifices to me, honour me, and you will be one with me' (IX, 31; 34). The Bhakti movement started in the sixth century in Tamil Nadu where it had decidedly heterodox origins. It then spread to other parts of southern India and finally also to northern India, giving an entirely new slant to Hinduism. The protagonists of this movement were sixty-three Shaivite and twelve Vaishnavite saints, the Nayanars and Alwars. Among the Shaivite saints Appar is praised as one of the most famous: he is said to have defeated many Buddhists and Jains in learned discussions in the early seventh century and to have converted the Pallava king, Mahendravarman, to Shaivism.

Other great saints are Appar's contemporary, Sambandar, then Sundaramurti and Manikkavasagar, eighth and ninth centuries AD respectively. The writings of these saints were collected in the 'Holy Scriptures' (Tirumurai) of the Tamils, which have also been called the 'Tamil Veda'. These scriptures are the quintessence of the Shaivite religious literature of southern India. The eighth book of this collection is Manikkavasagar's Tiruvasagam. The twelfth book, added much later, is the Periya Puranam. Composed by the poet Shekkilar at the behest of the Chola king, Kulottunga I, in the early twelfth century, it is devoted to the lives of the Tamil saints and is still very popular in Tamil Nadu.

The nature of the Bhakti mysticism which inspired these saints can best be explained by referring to their writings. Manikkavasagar, whose life was spent in a continuous pilgrimage to the sacred places of southern India, describes his love for Shiva in these moving words:

> While Indra, Vishnu and Brahma and all the other gods have to line up in heaven in order to get a glimpse of Shiva he has come down to this earth, he has come to me who is of no use, he has shown his great love for me as only a mother would do. He has made my body as soft and tender as wax and has put an end to all my deeds, whether I was born as an elephant or as a worm. He came like honey and milk, like sugarcane, he came as a king who gives precious gifts and he has graciously accepted my service as his slave.[1]

The early Bhakti mystics rejected Brahmin scholarship and ritual sacrifices in which the lower classes could not, in any case, afford to participate. They also rejected, or at least played down, the caste system. Of the sixty-three Nayanar saints only a few were Brahmins. Mostly they were traders and peasants (*vellalas*), people of such low caste as washermen, potters, fishermen, hunters and toddy tappers; in addition, there were a few kings and princes and also a woman among them. One of the few Brahmins thus honoured was Sundaramurti, who married a temple dancer and a girl of the Vellala caste. With the characteristic simplicity of Bhakti writings, the Periya Puranam reports how Shiva had to mediate between the two jealous wives of Sundaramurti – a task to which the god applied himself without pride or prejudice.

Brahmins did not find it easy to accept Bhakti mysticism as an integral part of Hinduism. Thus the Periya Puranam tells an interesting story about a Brahmin whom the Chola king appointed as priest of one of the great temples. On returning from a day of dealing with the crowd of Bhakti devotees, this Brahmin tells his wife: 'When the god appeared in public today, I also went to worship him. But as people of all castes thronged around him I got polluted and I must at first take a bath before performing my rites here at home.'[2] But at night the priest dreamed of Shiva, who told him that all the townspeople were his divine bodyguards. Next day everybody appeared to the Brahmin as divine, and he was ashamed of his prejudice.

It is typical of the Bhakti tradition that this Brahmin was included among the Nayanar saints. First, Shiva had appeared to him. Second, he had repented the old prejudice that Brahmins would become polluted by contact with the masses when serving as temple priests. (The *Mahabharata* tells us that Brahmins serving in temples were considered to be the 'Chandalas' – low-caste untouchables – among the Brahmins.)

Brahmins living at royal courts or in pure Brahmin villages (*agrahara*) could afford to look down upon temple priests and could also disregard the Bhakti movement for some time. Although the Nambudiri Brahmin landlords of Malabar obviously remained unaffected, in most parts of India the movement gained more and more adherents and 'public' temples were constructed to accommodate the many devotees.

The idea of holy places which would attract pilgrims was deeply linked with these popular religious cults. The Vedic gods of the Brahmins never had any definite abode on earth – at best, they could be invoked by priests at the time of a sacrifice. But gods such as Vishnu and Shiva, both of whom were worshipped by Bhakti devotees, manifested themselves at numerous places on earth as well as in their heavenly abodes (Shiva on Mount Kailash and Vishnu on the snake encircling the universe). In the beginning a Bhakta (devotee) might have seen them in a tree or a stone or a hermitage. The traditions of many great temples recorded in later times still refer to such an immediate local origin of the gods worshipped in them. Legends of this kind are called *sthala mahatmya* and are supposed to emphasise the sanctity and greatness (*mahatmya*) of the designated temple. The statues (*arca*) worshipped by the Bhaktas are considered to be incarnations (*avatara*) of gods who had appeared before the people in tangible form. The Bhakta sees and worships his god in this *archa-avatara* and this is why Manikkavasagar exclaimed: 'He has come to me who is of no use.'

Once the great gods were worshipped in terms of such local manifestations, lesser gods and even village gods (*gramadevata*) also claimed admission to the rapidly expanding Hindu pantheon. Many a local god then made a great career by becoming identified with one of the great gods and being served by Brahmin priests. Such local gods – previously often worshipped in primitive non-iconic forms such as rocks – then underwent a process of 'anthropomorphisation', culminating in the installation of fully Hinduised icons in temples constructed at sites reputed to be holy. Legends grew up which justified this transformation and referred to the descent of a great god from heaven or to the visit of a great saint. The cults were 'sanskritised' and related to the 'great tradition'; they were also incorporated in the great circuit of pilgrimages which covered the whole of India. Often pilgrims made a vow to visit a certain number of temples sacred to their favourite god, and a temple would recommend itself by being identified with such a god rather than exclusively with an unknown local deity.

The emergence of India's temple cities

The history of the temple city of Chidambaram illustrates this transformation of a local to a regional sacred place whose fame spread throughout India. Chidambaram is identified with the cult of Shiva as the 'King of Dancers' (Nataraja). The origin of the cult seems to have been the worship of a stone at a pond which subsequently became the temple tank. The stone was later identified as a Shiva lingam and was worshipped as *Mulasthana* ('The Place of Origin'). There was also the cult of a goddess whose shrine was called *Perampalam* ('Great Hall'). In addition, there was a *Cidampalam* ('Little Hall'), associated with a cult similar to that of Murugan, a god served by priests who dance in a state of trance. The whole sacred complex was called *Puliyur* ('Tiger town') in Tamil.

There is no reference to Chidambaram in the early Sangam literature of the first to fifth centuries AD or in the early epic Sanskrit. The identification of the local dancing god of Chidambaram with Shiva seems to have been established by the sixth century at the latest: Appar and Sambadar refer to the dance of Shiva in the Little Hall at Chidambaram in the early seventh century. The Chidambaram Mahatmya composed in the twelfth century provides insights into the subsequent evolution of the cult and also shows the process of Sanskritisation. The upgrading of the cult of the lingam and the Sanskritisation of the name of the temple town were the first achievements. Both were accomplished by inventing a legend according to which a north Indian Brahmin, Vyagrahapada, a devout Bhakta of Shiva, came to Chidambaram in order to worship the Mulasthana lingam. A Brahmin by that name – meaning 'Tiger foot' – was mentioned in Late Vedic texts and so, by making this saint the hero of the legend, the Tamil name *Puliyur* ('Tiger town') was placed in a Sanskrit context.

In the tenth century the 'King of Dancers' was adopted by the Chola kings as their family god, which meant that the reputation of the cult of the dancing Shiva had to be enhanced by inventing a new legend. Vyagrahapada's worship of the Mulasthana lingam was now regarded as a mere prelude to the worship of the divine dancer who manifested himself at Chidambaram by dancing the cosmic dance, *Ananda Tandava*. The fact that the cult had originated in the 'Little Hall' while the neighbouring hall of the goddess was called the 'Great Hall' was felt to be somewhat embarrassing; the legend had to correct this imbalance. The Tamil word *Cid-ampalam* ('Little Hall') was therefore replaced by the Sanskrit word *Cid-ambaram* ('Heavenly Abode of the Spirit') – nearly a homophone, but much more dignified in meaning. Shiva's cosmic dance performed for both Chola kings and humble Bhaktas now had a new setting in keeping with the greatness of the god. This etymological transformation, so typical of Hinduism's evolution, then provided striking metaphysical perspectives. Chidambaram was praised to be the heart of the first being (*purusha*) ever created and at its innermost centre (*antahpura*) was the Brahman, the impersonal cosmic essence. By alluding to the Vedic myth of the Purusha – whose sacrifice had engendered the universe – and by equating this Purusha with the human body, the priest could now interpret the divine dance of Shiva as taking place in Chidambaram, the centre of the cosmos, as well as in the hearts of the Bhaktas. By this kind of Sanskritisation the autochthonous cult of a local god was placed within the context of the 'great tradition'. At the same time the heterodox Bhakti movement was reconciled with the philosophical system of the Brahmins, who had taken over the control of the temple.

In a similar way other local gods emerged as major figures of the Hindu pantheon. Minakshi, the 'fish-eyed' goddess of the Pandyas of Madurai, remained the dominant deity. Her incorporation into the patriarchal Sanskrit tradition was achieved by identifying her with Shiva's wife, Parvati, and making the marriage of Shiva and Parvati the central feature of the cult of Minakshi. This marriage is still celebrated every year by a great procession.

While Chidambaram and Madurai are thus associated with Shiva, the other great god, Vishnu, has his major south Indian centres at Tirupati and at Srirangam, where he is worshipped as Shri Venkateshvara and Shri Ranganatha respectively. On the Deccan, at Pandharpur, many pilgrims are attracted by the cult of Vithoba similarly associated with Vishnu.

Also on the Deccan are the pastoral gods such as Khandoba, whose great temple at Jejuri near Pune attracts many high-caste Hindu devotees, as well as the tribe of the Dhangars, shepherds of the highlands. In former times Maratha rulers also worshipped this god whose impressive temple was built at the behest of the Holkars of Indore. In eastern India Jagannath of Puri is another striking example of the transformation of a tribal god into a great deity of the Hindu pantheon. The icon of this god is made of a big log of wood and some of his essential priests still belong to a local tribe. As 'Lord of the World' (*Jagannatha*), however, he has been identified with Vishnu and as such attracts pilgrims from many parts of India. The best-known example of this transformation of a local god into an incarnation of Vishnu is, of course, Krishna, who was originally a god of the herdsmen around Mathura in northern India.

Divinity and territory: the gods and their samantas

As well as having definite local connections and being rooted in a place where they 'live' or 'dance' or have otherwise manifested themselves, the gods of the Bhakti cults often also have a 'territory' – a region in which their influence is particularly strong and with whose traditions they are intimately related. As incarnations of great gods like Vishnu and Shiva, they are part and parcel of the 'great tradition'; in their particular manifestation, however, their power (*shakti*) and sanctity (*mahatmya*) radiate only within certain limits. This power is most concentrated at their site (*kshetra*) or seat (*pitha*) and the Bhakta can feel it almost as a physical sensation. Towards the periphery of the territory their power diminishes and the power of neighbouring gods takes over. Beyond these limits a god is neither feared nor worshipped.

This territorial radiation of regional gods prompts comparison with the territorial sway of the medieval kings of India's regional kingdoms. The king was also thought to embody the power and cosmic functions of one or the other of the great gods. Many kings were celebrated as *chakravartins* (conquerors of the whole world), but their actual power was limited: near a realm's border, the influence of the neighbouring 'conqueror of the whole world' made itself felt. In both instances we are faced with a kind of confined universalism.

Furthermore, the hierarchy of gods also reflects the levels of government. Even today all villages have their village gods (*gramadevata*), whose power does not extend beyond the village. At the next level we often find sub-regional gods who were sometimes the tutelary deities of local princes. They can be traced back to autochthonous gods, whose influence was felt in a larger area even prior to their adoption as patrons of local princes. The cults of such sub-regional gods have been more or less integrated into the general sphere of Hinduism. However, often their priests are still of local, even tribal, origin and their icons are crude (stones, pillars, etc.). Brahmins were sometimes consulted only for special rites, and not for the daily worship of this type of god. At the next level were regional gods whose rise to that position was often due to their being the 'family gods' (*kuladevata*) and later the 'gods of the realm' (*rashtradevata*) of a royal dynasty. Sometimes such a god was even considered to be the territory's actual overlord (*samraja*).

'Royal' gods owed their career to the dynasty with which they were associated and their cult was usually completely Sanskritised. Nevertheless, the legends about their origin and the shape of their icons often showed clear traces of their autochthonous descent. These traces were at the same time the mainspring for the development of a distinctive regional culture. The special traits of such gods were highlighted and embellished by many legends which formed the core at regional literature and enriched the regional tradition. There was a great variety of ways and means by which regional, sub-regional and local gods could be associated with each other. Like great kings, the regional gods held court surrounded by sub-regional gods, who were the family gods of the king's samantas. The sub-regional gods again rallied the village gods around them, just as headmen were occasionally invited to attend the court of a prince. Many scholars have written about the deification of kings, but for medieval India the converse evolution of a 'royalisation of gods' is as important. The legitimacy of a ruler was enhanced in this way. The more 'royal' the cult of the territorial god, the more legitimate the claim of the king – represented as the deity's temporal embodiment – to rule that territory on behalf of the god. The Bhakti cults contributed to this devotion to gods and kings in medieval India.

The institution of pilgrimage has remained a central and most vital element of Hinduism. It links holy places of the local, regional and all-Indian level. Such holy places were known even in Vedic times. The Early Vedic term for such a holy place was *tirtha*, which originally meant 'ford'. With the spread of Vedic culture, the number of such holy places increased. However, they were usually visited only for special purposes – for example, the sacrifice for the ancestors at Gaya. Longer pilgrimages (*tirtha-yatra*) to several holy places became known only in the early centuries with the rise of the great temples and the belief in the divine presence in the icons (*arca-vatra*), whose worship was considered to be a path to salvation (*moksha*) comparable with other paths. Later additions to the Mahabharata and almost all Purana texts include detailed descriptions of such pilgrimages and outlines of the routes followed.

The literature which is most characteristic of the temple cults of the Bhakti movement are the Mahatmya texts of individual temples. They served as pilgrim guides and were recited by the temple priests. These priests tried their best to prove that 'their' Mahatmya belonged to one of the eighteen great Purana texts in order to show that their temple was one of the great centres of pilgrimage in India. The Skandapurana in this way absorbed many such Mahatmyas of regional holy places until the late Middle Ages. From the end of the first millennium onwards, India was thus crisscrossed by many routes of pilgrimage which greatly helped to enhance the cultural unity of the country at a time of increasing regionalisation.

The quest for philosophical synthesis in medieval India

After several centuries of highly emotional Bhakti cults and their emphasis on devotion to a personal god, a new wave of intense philosophical speculation appeared at the beginning of the second millennium. The early philosophical systems were deeply influenced by the debate about the prevalence of an impersonal law or the domination of the world by the will of an omnipotent god. Those who believed in the impersonal law were not simply atheists – they held it to be irrelevant whether there is a god or not, as he too would be subjected to the impersonal law. Shankara's monism had reconciled non-theist and theist claims: the Brahman, as universal essence, is identical with the individual soul and encompasses both the impersonal law and the divine manifestation which may appeal to the individual believer. Thus Shankara had established a peaceful coexistence between a highly abstract philosophical system and a variety of faiths. The great god worshipped by the Bhakta – Mahadeva – was also part and parcel of Shankara's system. But in the strict sense of Shankara's philosophy, everything perceived as reality – including the Hindu pantheon – was illusion (*maya*), and this was unacceptable to the Bhakta, who saw in this world the manifestation of a divine creator. The tree, the stone, or whatever he may have worshipped, were intensely real to the Bhakta. Philosophical speculation in the wake of the Bhakti movement therefore rejected Shankara's strict monism. Whereas analogous philosophical debates had previously not been conducted along sectarian lines, medieval Indian philosophy became more and more identified with particular sects within the Hindu fold. Shiva, Vishnu or the goddess were worshipped as the highest god by their respective devotees. The Shivites tended to be in sympathy with Shankara's monism; the Vaishnavites, on the other hand, emphasised the reality of this world as a manifestation of the divine will.

The most important representative of the new Vaishnavite school of thought was Ramanuja, who lived in Tamil Nadu around 1100. He combined Shankara's Advaita philosophy with the Vaishnava Pancharatra theology, the latter claiming that Vishnu is the very foundation of the universe. This philosophy became the doctrine of the Shri Vaishnavas. Ramanuja advocated a 'qualified monism' (*vishishthadvaita*), according to which god is all-encompassing and eternal but not undifferentiated. The individual souls (*cit*) and inanimate matter (*acit*) are his divine 'qualities' (*vishishtha*) and thus both real and divine. The individual souls are at once one with god and separate from him. Salvation consists of a unification (*sayujya*) of the soul with god. This can be achieved only by leading a virtuous life and acquiring knowledge of the secret of differentiation by which the individual soul is kept apart from god. The final consummation of this spiritual marriage is possible only by means of devotion (*bhakti*) and by the grace of god.

Thus Ramanuja reconciled the Brahmin doctrine of right conduct, as well as metaphysical speculation, with the fervour of the popular Bhakti movement. In this way he also provided a justification for a process which had been going on for some time: the conversion of Brahmin intellectuals to the ideas of the Bhakti movement. The impact of Ramanuja's writings and his long service as head priest of the famous Vishnu temple at Srirangam made his ideas widely known among the Vaishnavites and he is justly regarded as the founder of Shri Vaishnavism. It is no accident that Ramanuja's message was spread at the time when Bhakti centres of pilgrimage emerged everywhere in southern and central India, with kings and princes building temples in such places so as to convert them into veritable temple cities.

The cults of Krishna and Shiva

The further development of Vaishnavism is characterised by the rise of the Krishna cult. Krishna was no longer regarded as only one of the incarnations (*avatara*) of Vishnu, but as the highest god himself. The Bhagavata Purana, perhaps the greatest of all Puranas, which was composed in the tenth or eleventh century, was devoted to this elevation of Krishna. The mysticism of the Krishna cult found its most vivid expression in the poet Jayadeva's *Gitagovinda*, composed around 1200 either in Bengal or Orissa. The poet describes in emotional and erotic terms the love of Radha and Krishna. The quest of the soul (Radha) for the unification with god (Krishna) is symbolised in this way. At the same time, god is visibly attracted to the soul – hence his being praised as Radhakrishna, the god who is identified by his love.

Nimbarka and Vallabha, two south Indian Brahmins, settled down at Mathura (near Brindaban) which is associated with Krishna's life on earth. Here they pursued their metaphysical speculations concerning this relationship between Radha and Krishna. To them, Radha became a universal principle which enables god (Krishna) to communicate with this world. Not much is known about Nimbarka's life. Vallabha lived from 1479 to 1531. He was the founder of the Vallabhacharya sect, which became known for its erotic Radhakrishna cult.

Vallabha's contemporary was Chaitanya (1485–1533), who is still revered today as the greatest saint of the Vaishnavites. Born in Navadvipa, Bengal, he was the son of a Brahmin and was worshipped even in his lifetime as an incarnation of Krishna. He spent the last two decades of his life at Puri in Orissa, devoting himself to the ecstatic worship of Jagannath, the highest form of Krishna. Often in a state of trance for hours, he would also swoon or rave in emulation of Radha distressed by Krishna's absence. After his death he is said to have merged with the statue of Jagannath.

Neither a teacher nor a philosopher, Chaitanya left it to his followers to record his sayings. At his behest Mathura was chosen by his disciples as the centre of the Krishna cult. This was a very important decision because, in this way, northern India emerged from several centuries' eclipse by the rapid development of Hinduism in southern and central India. The region now began to regain religious importance. During the reign of the Great Mughal, Aurangzeb, the Rana of Mewar secretly removed the statue of Krishna from Mathura in order to install it more safely near his capital,

Udaipur, where the temple of Nathdvara is still one of the greatest and richest centres of pilgrimage in India, even today. The head of this temple is regarded as the highest priest among the Vaishnavites.

Shaivism also gave rise to many popular sects. They all agreed that the 'Great God' (*Mahadeva*) was the very foundation of the universe, but they gave different answers to the great question about the relation of god to the individual soul and to inanimate matter. They also had very different rites with which they distinguished themselves from each other, as well as from the Vaishnavites. In northern India the most prominent school of thought was Kashmir Shaivism, founded by Vasugupta, a renowned teacher, in the early ninth century. Vasugupta advocated a kind of monism which, in contrast to that of Shankara, did not regard the real world as illusion; rather, it was an emanation of the divine spirit. Shiva becomes compared to a painter who creates the image of the world within himself and needs neither canvas nor colours. Because this school of thought aims at the recognition of Shiva in this image created by him, it is referred to as the 'philosophy of recognition'. It is said that this cosmology was also influenced by Mahayana Buddhism. The most prominent exponent of Kashmir Shaivism was Abhinavagupta, who lived in Kashmir in the eleventh century and was also known for his writings on the theory of Sanskrit literature. Kashmir Shaivism was nearly eradicated in its birthplace when Islamic conquerors overran Kashmir in the fourteenth century. But even today many *pandits* belong to this school of thought which provides an unparalleled combination of monist philosophy, the practice of yoga and the worship of the Great God.

South Indian Shaivism – originally shaped by the thought and poetry of the Nayanars – produced in later medieval times the school of Shaiva Siddhanta and a famous reform sect, the Lingayats. Shaiva Siddhanta ('the definitive system of Shaivism') can be traced back to the Nayanars, but it attained its final form only in the thirteenth and fourteenth centuries. With this new system the Shaivites could match the overpowering influence of Ramanuja's Vaishnavite philosophy which had put them on the defensive for quite some time. This system served the same purpose of reconciling earlier orthodoxy with the ideas of the Bhakti movement. But even though both Vaishnavism and Shaivism had now achieved a new synthesis, the conflict between Brahmins and heterodox popular movements arose again and again in the course of the Middle Ages and spawned new sects. Whereas the Christian church in Europe fiercely suppressed such sectarian movements (e.g. the Albigensians), Hinduism usually absorbed or reintegrated these sects. The Lingayat sect is an exception to this general rule.

The Lingayats arose as a radical movement against the caste system and Brahmin orthodoxy; they were to retain this radicalism for centuries. Their founder was Basava, a Brahmin who was a minister at the court of the Kalachuri king of Kalyani in western central India around 1160. The name

Lingayat is derived from the fact that all devotees carry a small lingam like an amulet as a sign of their exclusive adherence to their Shaivite faith. Their other name – Vira Shaiva ('heroic devotees of Shiva') – also emphasises this belief. The Lingayats do believe in the authority of the Vedas, but reject the caste system and Brahmin hegemony of ritual. Of course, they could not prevent becoming a caste or community themselves, as it was essential to retain their solidarity; nevertheless, they still prohibit child marriage and allow the remarriage of widows. Because the Lingayats believed that adherence to their faith would automatically save them from the cycle of rebirths, they buried rather than burned their dead – something otherwise reserved for ascetics and holy men. Although they were radical in many respects, the Lingayats were very conservative as far as their moral standards were concerned: strict vegetarians, they emphasised *ahimsa* (non-killing) and shunned the sexual excesses so common among some other contemporary sects.

Literature and language

The regionalisation of Indian culture had begun with the emergence of the great regional kingdoms. This change of political structure was then paralleled by a religious transformation. The more or less unified Brahminical Hinduism of an earlier age was disrupted by the rise of popular religious movements, which in turn led to the formulation of new philosophical doctrines. At the same time regional languages produced a rich literature which challenged the monopoly of Sanskrit literature. In the period from about 1000 to 1300, the Indo-Aryan languages of north, central and east India attained their specific regional identity, among them Marathi, Bengali, Assamese and Oriya. Their early development and their relationship to the Middle Indian Sanskrit dialects, Prakrit and Apabhramsha, is surely as fascinating a subject for research as the rise of the various European literary languages which took place at almost the same time.

In India the various sects and religious movements made a great impact on this development of regional languages and literatures. Some of the founders of these sects did not know Sanskrit at all and therefore expressed themselves in the respective regional languages. However, even the Brahmins among them who knew Sanskrit were eager to communicate with the people and therefore preferred the regional languages. Moreover, many of the saintly poets who inspired these movements created great works of literature and thus enriched the regional languages.

In addition Sanskrit texts, starting with the great Puranas, had to be translated into the regional languages. The Bhagavata Purana was very important for the Vaishnavites in this respect. Such translations were often the first great works of literature in some of the regional languages. The free rendering of the *Ramayana* in Hindi by Tulsidas (1532–1632) is a prime example of this development. In the midst of the fifteenth century Sharala Das translated the *Mahabharata* into Oriya and thus paved the way for the rise of Oriya literature in the sixteenth.

Two other types of literature should be briefly mentioned in this context: the chronicles of temples and of dynasties. All great temples and centres of pilgrimage produced Sanskrit collections of their legends, the Mahatmyas, but these were soon translated into the respective vernacular language and recited by pilgrims everywhere. Priests who were sent out to recruit pilgrims for these centres in distant parts of the country also contributed to the spread of this kind of literature. The chronicles of kings (*rajavamshavali*) and local rulers had a similar function. They were often produced by bards to provide patrons with an impressive genealogy reaching back into antiquity, or even into the age of mythical heroes. Such chronicles also often contain legends about the temples which the respective dynasties had founded. Only their final chapters are devoted to the deeds of historical rulers. The historian and the literary critic may find these works deficient from many points of view, but they were certainly of great importance in establishing a regional identity which showed much local colour while maintaining a link with the 'great tradition'.

INDIA'S IMPACT ON SOUTHEAST ASIA: CAUSES AND CONSEQUENCES

The transmission of Indian culture to distant parts of central Asia, China, Japan, and especially southeast Asia is one of the greatest achievements of Indian history or even of the history of mankind. None of the other great civilisations – not even the Hellenic – had been able to achieve a similar success without military conquest. In this brief survey of India's history, there is no room for an adequate discussion of the development of the 'Indianised' states of southeast Asia which can boast of such magnificent temple cities as Pagan (Burma; constructed from 1044 to 1287), Angkor (Cambodia; constructed from 889 to *c*.1300), and the Borobudur (Java; early ninth century). Though they were influenced by Indian culture, they are nevertheless part and parcel of the history of those respective countries. Here we will limit our observations to some fundamental problems concerning the transmission of Indian culture to the vast region of southeast Asia.

Who spread Indian culture in southeast Asia?

Historians have formulated several theories regarding the transmission of Indian culture to southeast Asia: (1) the 'Kshatriya' theory; (2) the 'Vaishya' theory; (3) the 'Brahmin' theory. The Kshatriya theory states that Indian warriors colonised southeast Asia; this proposition has now been rejected by most scholars although it was very prominent some time ago. The Vaishya theory attributes the spread of Indian culture to traders; it is certainly much more plausible than the Kshatriya theory, but does not seem to explain the large number of Sanskrit loan words in southeast Asian languages. The Brahmin hypothesis credits Brahmins with the transmission of Indian culture; this would account for the prevalence of these loan words, but may have to be amplified by some reference to the Buddhists as well as to the traders. We shall return to these theories, but first we shall try to understand the rise and fall of the Kshatriya theory.

It owed its origin to the Indian freedom movement. Indian historians, smarting under the stigma of their own colonial subjection, tried to compensate for this by showing that at least in ancient times Indians had been strong enough to establish colonies of their own. In 1926 the Greater India Society was established in Calcutta and in subsequent years the renowned Indian historian R.C. Majumdar published his series of studies, *Ancient Indian Colonies in the Far East*. This school held that Indian kings and warriors had established such colonies and the Sanskrit names of southeast Asian rulers seemed to provide ample supporting evidence. At least this hypothesis stimulated further research, though it also alienated those intellectuals of southeast Asia who rejected the idea of having once been 'colonised' by India. As research progressed, it was found that there was very little proof of any direct Indian political influence in those states of southeast Asia. Furthermore, it was demonstrated that southeast Asian rulers had adopted Sanskrit names themselves – thus such names could not be adduced as evidence for the presence of Indian kings.

The Vaishya theory, in contrast, emphasised a much more important element of the Indian connection with southeast Asia. Trade had indeed been the driving force behind all these early contacts. Inscriptions also showed that guilds of Indian merchants had established outposts in many parts of southeast Asia. Some of their inscriptions were written in languages such as Tamil. However, if such merchants had been the chief agents of the transmission of Indian culture, then their languages should have made an impact on those of southeast Asia. But this was not so: Sanskrit and, to some extent, Pali words predominated as loan words in southeast Asian languages. The traders certainly provided an important transmission belt for all kinds of cultural influences. Nevertheless, they did not play the crucial role which some scholars have attributed to them. One of the most important arguments against the Vaishya theory is that some of the earliest traces of Indianised states in southeast Asia are not found in the coastal areas usually frequented by the traders, but in mountainous, interior areas.

The Brahmin theory is in keeping with what we have shown with regard to the almost contemporary spread of Hindu culture in southern and central India. There Brahmins and Buddhist and Jain monks played the major role in transmitting cultural values and symbols, and in disseminating the style of Hindu kingship. In addition to being religious specialists, the Brahmins also knew the Sanskrit codes regarding law (*dharmashastra*), the art of government (*arthashastra*), and art and architecture (*shilpashastra*). They could thus serve as 'development planners' in many different fields and were accordingly welcome to southeast Asian rulers who may have just emerged from what we earlier described as first- and second-phase state formation.

The dynamics of cultural borrowings

What was the role of the people of southeast Asia in this process of cultural borrowing? Were they merely passive recipients of a culture bestowed upon them by the Indians? Or did they actively participate in this transfer? The passive thesis was originally emphasised by Indian advocates of the 'Greater India' idea, as well by as European scholars who belonged to the elite of the colonial powers then dominant in southeast Asia. The concept of an earlier 'Indianisation' of southeast Asia seemed to provide a close parallel with the later 'Europeanisation' under colonial rule. The first trenchant criticism of this point of view came from the young Dutch scholar J.C. van Leur.

Van Leur highlighted the great skill and courage of Indonesian seafarers and emphasised the fact that Indonesian rulers themselves had invited Indian Brahmins and had thus taken a very active role in the process of cultural borrowing. Van Leur's book on Indonesian trade and society was published posthumously, in 1955. In the meantime, further research has vindicated his point of view.

The Indian influence is no longer regarded as the prime cause of socio-cultural development; rather, it was a consequence of a development which was already in progress in southeast Asia. Early Indonesian inscriptions show that there was a considerable development of agriculture, craftsman-ship, regional trade and social differentiation before Indian influence made itself felt. However, indigenous tribal organisation was egalitarian and pre-vented the emergence of higher forms of political organisation. The intro-duction of such forms required at least a rudimentary form of administration and a kind of legitimation of these new governmental forms which would make them, in the initial stages, acceptable to the people. It was at this point that chieftains and clan heads required Brahmin assistance. Although trade might have helped to spread the necessary information, the initiative came from those indigenous rulers. The invited Brahmins were isolated from the rural people and kept in touch only with their patrons. In this way the royal style emerged in southeast Asia just as it had done in India.

A good example of this kind of development is provided by the earliest Sanskrit inscription found in Indonesia (it was recorded in eastern Borneo around AD 400). Several inscriptions on large megaliths mention a ruler whose name, Kundunga, shows not the slightest trace of Sanskrit influence. His son assumed a Sanskrit name, Ashvavarman, and founded a dynasty (*vamsha*). His grandson, Mulavarman, the author of the inscriptions, celebrated great sacrifices and gave valuable presents to the Brahmins. Of the latter it is explicitly stated that 'they had come here' – most likely from India. After being consecrated by the Brahmins, Mulavarman subjected the neighbouring rulers and made them 'tribute givers' (*kara-da*). Thus these inscriptions present in a nutshell the history of the rise of an early local Indonesian dynasty. It seems that the dynasty had been founded by a son of a clan chief independently of the Brahmins, who on their arrival consecrated the ruler of the third generation. With this kind of moral support and the new administrative know-how, the ruler could subject his neighbours and obtain tribute from them.

The process paralleled that which we have observed in southern and central India. In its initial stages, however, it was not necessarily due to Indian influence at all. Around the middle of the first millennium AD several of such small states seem to have arisen in this way in southeast Asia. They have left only a few inscriptions and some ruins of temples; most of them were obviously very short-lived. There must have been a great deal of competition, with many petty rajas vying with each other and all wishing to be recognised as maharajas entitled to all the Indian paraphernalia of kingship. Indian influence increased in this way and in the second half of the first millennium a hectic activity of temple erection could be observed on Java and in Cambodia, where the first larger realms had come into existence.

Though it is now generally accepted that southeast Asian rulers played an active role in this process of state formation, we cannot entirely rule out the occasional direct contribution of Indian adventurers who proceeded to the East. The most important example of this kind is that of the early history of Funan at the mouth of the Mekong. Chinese sources report the tale of a Brahmin, Kaundinya, who was inspired by a divine dream to go to Funan. There he vanquished the local Naga (serpent) princess by means of his holy bow and married her, thus founding the first dynasty of Funan in the late first century. We have heard of a similar legend in connection with the rise of the Pallava dynasty and this may indicate that Kaundinya came from southern India where the Kaundinyas were known as a famous Brahmin lineage. A Chinese source of the fourth century describes an Indian usurper of the throne of Funan; his name is given as Chu Chan-t'an. 'Chu' always indicates a person of Indian origin and 'Chan-t'an' could have been a transliteration of the title 'Chandana' which can be traced to the Indo-Scythians of northern India. Presumably a member of that dynasty went to southeast Asia after having been defeated by Samundragupta. In the beginning of the fifth century another Kaundinya arrived in Funan and of him it is said in the Chinese annals:

He was originally a Brahmin from India. There a supernatural voice told him: 'You must go to Funan.' Kaundinya rejoiced in his heart. In the South he arrived at P'an-p'an. The people of Funan appeared to him; the whole kingdom rose up with joy, went before him and chose him king. He changed all the laws to conform to the system of India.[1]

This report on the second Kaundinya is the most explicit reference to an Indian ruler who introduced his laws in southeast Asia. In the same period we notice a general wave of Indian influence in southeast Asia, for which the earliest Sanskrit inscriptions of Indonesia – discussed above – also provide striking evidence. We must, however, note that even in this case of early Funan there was no military intervention. Kaundinya had obviously stayed for some time at P'an-p'an at the Isthmus of Siam, then under the control of Funan, and he was later invited by the notables of the court of Funan to ascend the throne at a time of political unrest.

The contribution of the Buddhist monks

So far we have discussed the contribution of Brahmins to the early transmission of Indian culture to southeast Asia. Buddhist monks, however, were at least as important in this respect. Two characteristic features of Buddhism enabled it to make a specific impact on southeast Asia: first, Buddhists were imbued with a strong missionary zeal; and, second, they ignored the caste system and did not emphasise the idea of ritual purity. By his teaching as well as by the organisation of his monastic order (*sangha*) Gautama Buddha had given rise to this missionary zeal, which had then been fostered by Ashoka's dispatch of Buddhist missionaries to western Asia, Egypt, Greece, central Asia, Sri Lanka and Burma.

Buddhism's freedom from ritual restrictions and the spirit of the unity of all adherents enabled Buddhist monks to establish contacts with people abroad, as well as to welcome them in India when they came to visit the sacred places of Buddhism. Chinese sources record 162 visits to India of Chinese Buddhist monks for the period from the fifth to the eighth century. Many more may have travelled without having left a trace in such official records. This was an amazing international scholarly exchange programme for that day and age.

In the early centuries the centre of Buddhist scholarship was the University of Taxila (near the present city of Islamabad), but in the fifth century when the University of Nalanda was founded not far from Bodh Gaya, Bihar, the centre of Buddhist scholarship shifted to eastern India. This university always had a large contingent of students from southeast Asia. There they spent many years close to the holy places of Buddhism, copying and translating texts before returning home. Nalanda was a centre of

Mahayana Buddhism, which became of increasing importance in southeast Asia. We mentioned above that King Balaputra of Shrivijaya established a monastery for students of his realm at Nalanda around 860 which was then endowed with land grants by King Devapala of Bengal. But the Sumatran empire of Shrivijaya had acquired a good reputation in its own right among Buddhist scholars and from the late seventh century attracted resident Chinese and Indian monks. The Chinese monk I-tsing stopped over at Shrivijaya's capital (present-day Palembang) for six months in 671 in order to learn Sanskrit grammar. He then proceeded to India, where he spent fourteen years, and on his return journey he stayed another four years at Palembang so that he could translate the many texts which he had collected. In this period he went to China for a few months in 689 to recruit assistants for his great translation project (completed only in 695). On his return to China he explicitly recommended that other Chinese Buddhists proceeding to India break journey in Shrivijaya, where a thousand monks lived by the same rules as those prevailing in India. In subsequent years many Chinese Buddhists conscientiously followed this advice.

Prominent Indian Buddhist scholars similarly made a point to visit Shrivijaya. Towards the end of the seventh century Dharmapala of Nalanda is supposed to have visited Suvarnadvipa (Java and Sumatra). In the beginning of the eighth century the south Indian monk Vajrabodhi spent five months in Shrivijaya on his way to China. He and his disciple, Amoghavajra, whom he met in Java, are credited with having introduced Buddhist Tantrism to China. Atisha, who later became known as the great reformer of Tibetan Buddhism, is said to have studied for twelve years in Suvarnadvipa in the early eleventh century. The high standard of Buddhist learning which prevailed in Indonesia for many centuries was one of the important preconditions for that great work of art, the Borobudur, whose many reliefs are a pictorial compendium of Buddhist lore, a tribute both to the craftsmanship of Indonesian artists and to the knowledge of Indonesian Buddhist scholars.

The link between southeast Asia and south India

Indian historians have conducted a heated debate for many decades about the relative merits of different Indian regions with regard to the spread of Indian influence in southeast Asia. Nowadays there seems to be a consensus that, at least as far as the early centuries are concerned, south India – and especially Tamil Nadu – deserves the greatest credit for this achievement. In subsequent periods, however, several regional shifts as well as parallel influences emanating from various centres can be noticed. The influence of Tamil Nadu was very strong as far as the earliest inscriptions in southeast Asia are concerned, showing as they do the influence of the script prevalent in the Pallava kingdom. The oldest Buddhist sculpture in southeast Asia – the famous bronze

Buddha of Celebes – shows the marks of the Buddhist sculptures of Amaravati (Coastal Andhra) of the third to the fifth centuries. Early Hindu sculptures of western Java and of the Isthmus of Siam seem to have been guided by the Pallava style of the seventh and eighth centuries. Early southeast Asian temple architecture similarly shows the influence of the Pallava and Chola styles, especially on Java and in Cambodia.

The influence of the north Indian Gupta style also made itself felt from the fifth century onwards. The centre of this school was Sarnath, near Varanasi (Benares), where Buddha preached his first sermon. Sarnath produced the classical Buddha image which influenced the art of Burma and Thailand, as well as that of Funan at the mouth of the Mekong. The art of the Shailendra dynasty of Java in the eighth and ninth centuries – of which the Borobudur is the most famous monument – was obviously influenced by what is termed the Late Gupta style of western central India, as manifested in the great cave temples of Ajanta and Ellora. An inscription at the Plaosan temple in central Java (c.800) explicitly refers to the 'constant flow of the people from Gurjaradesha [Gujarat and adjacent regions]' – due to which this temple had been built. Indeed, the temple's sculptures show a striking similarity with those of the late Buddhist caves of Ajanta and Ellora.

In later centuries southeast Asia was more and more influenced by the scholars of the University of Nalanda and the style of the Pala dynasty, the last of the great Indian dynasties which bestowed royal patronage on Buddhism. The influence of Mahayana Buddhism prevailing in Bihar and Bengal under the Palas was so strong at the court of the Shailendras of Java that a Buddhist monk from 'Gaudi' (Bengal), with the typical Bengali name of Kumara Ghosh, became rajguru of the Shailendra king and in this capacity consecrated a statue of Manjushri in the royal temple of the Shailendras in 782. Bengal, eastern Bihar and Orissa were at that time centres of cultural influence. These regions were in constant contact with southeast Asia, whose painters and sculptors reflected the style of eastern India in their works. Typical of this aesthetic was the special arrangement of figures surrounding the central figure: this type of arrangement can be found both in Indonesian sculptures and in the temple paintings of Pagan (Burma) during this period.

In the same era south Indian influence emerged once more under the Chola dynasty. Maritime trade was of major importance to the Cholas, who thereby also increased their cultural influences. The occasional military interventions of the Cholas did not detract from this peaceful cultural intercourse. At the northern coast of Sumatra the old port of Dilli, near Medan, had great Buddha sculptures evincing a local variation of the Chola style; indeed, a magnificent locally produced statue of the Hindu god Ganesha, in the pure Chola style, has recently been found at Palembang. Close to the famous temple of Padang Lawas, central Sumatra, small but very impressive Chola-style bronze sculptures of a four-armed Lokanath and of Tara have been found. These sculptures are now in the museum of Jakarta. They are dated at 1039 and a brief inscription containing Old Malay words in addition to Sanskrit words – but no Tamil words – proves that the figures were not imported from India but were produced locally.

Nevertheless, Chola relations with southeast Asia were by no means a one-way street. It is presumed that the imperial cult of the Cholas, centred on their enormous temples, was directly influenced by the grand style of Angkor. The great tank at Gangaikondacholapuram was perhaps conceived by the Chola ruler in the same spirit as that which moved contemporary Cambodian rulers who ordered the construction of the famous Barays (tanks) of Angkor, which are considered to be a special indication of royal merit.

In the late thirteenth century Pagan (Burma) was once more exposed to a strong current of direct Indian influence emanating from Bengal, at that time conquered by Islamic rulers. Nalanda had been destroyed by the end of the twelfth century and large groups of monks in search of a new home flocked to Pagan and also to the Buddhist centres of Tibet. The beautiful paintings in the temples of Minnanthu in the eastern part of the city of Pagan may have been due to them.

Islamic conquest of northern India cut off the holy places of Buddhism. A millennium of intensive contacts between India and Buddhist southeast Asia had come to an end. But there was another factor which must be mentioned in this context. In 1190 Chapata, a Buddhist monk from Pagan, returned to that city after having spent ten years in Sri Lanka. In Burma he led a branch of the Theravada school of Buddhism, established on the strict rules of the Mahavihara monastery of Sri Lanka. This led to a schism in the Burmese Buddhist order which had been established at Pagan by Shin Arahan about 150 years earlier. Shin Arahan was a follower of the south Indian school of Buddhism, which had its centre at Kanchipuram. Chapata's reform prevailed and by the thirteenth and fourteenth centuries Burma, Thailand and Cambodia had adopted Theravada Buddhism of the Sri Lanka school. In Cambodia this shift from Mahayana to Theravada Buddhism seems to have been part of a socio-cultural revolution. Under the last great king of Angkor, Jayavarman VII (1181–1218), royal Mahayana Buddhism had become associated in the eyes of the people with the enormous burden which the king imposed upon them in order to build the huge Buddhist temples of Angkor Thom (e.g. the gigantic Bayon).

Even in Indonesia, however, where Tantrist Buddhism with an admixture of Shaivism prevailed at the courts of rulers all the way from Sumatra down to Bali, direct Indian influence rapidly receded in the thirteenth century. This was only partly due to the intervention of Islam in India, its other cause being an upsurge of Javanese art which confined the influence of

Indian art to the statues of deified kings erected after the death of the ruler. The outer walls of the temples were covered with Javanese reliefs which evince a great similarity to the Javanese shadow play (*wayang kulit*). The Chandi Jago (thirteenth century) and the temples of Panantaran (fourteenth century) show this new Javanese style very well. It has remained the dominant style of Bali art up to the present time. A similar trend towards the assertion of indigenous styles can also be found in the Theravada Buddhist countries. The content of the scenes depicted is still derived from Hindu mythology or Buddhist legends, but the presentation clearly incorporates the respective national style.

The impact of Islam

After the conquest of northern India in about 1200 and central India and its harbours in about 1300 by Muslim rulers, Islam also spread to southeast Asia via the maritime trade routes which connected India with the spice islands of the East. We find the first traces of Islam in Atjeh (north Sumatra) at the end of the thirteenth century and in Malaya in the early fourteenth century. In the fifteenth century Islam penetrated the interiors of the respective countries, whereas it had hitherto been mostly confined to the coasts. Just as rulers at an earlier stage of southeast Asian history had found it convenient to adopt an Indian religion, they now found the Islamic creed more helpful in many respects.

India once more became an important transmitter of cultural influences under the new dispensation. Indian Sufism played an important role in the early spread of Islam in Indonesia. The oldest tombstones of Muslim rulers and traders in southeast Asia point to an influence from western India, mainly Gujarat, whose traders played a major role in the spice trade from Indonesia via India to the ports of western Asia. But Muslim traders of the Coromandel coast were also active in this connection. In 1445 Tamil Muslim traders even staged a coup at Malacca, installing a sultan of their choice. In this way they greatly enhanced their influence in an area of great strategic importance. However, a few decades later the Portuguese conqueror of Goa, Albuquerque, captured Malacca with nineteen ships and 800 Portuguese soldiers. Thus, after a millennium of intensive intercourse, the era of European influence started for India and southeast Asia at about the same time.

4

RELIGIOUS COMMUNITIES AND MILITARY FEUDALISM IN THE LATE MIDDLE AGES

THE ISLAMIC CONQUEST OF NORTHERN INDIA AND THE SULTANATE OF DELHI

The year 1206 marks an important turning point in Asian history. In this year a Mongol chieftain united the various Mongol tribes and embarked on a campaign of conquest. His name, Chingis Khan, was soon known by many peoples in Asia as well as in Europe. In the same year Qutb-ud-din Aibak – a Turkish slave of the sultan of Afghanistan and, on behalf of his overlord, ruler of a large part of northwestern India – declared his independence and founded the sultanate of Delhi. Whereas in the following centuries most countries of Asia succumbed to the Mongol tempest, the sultanate of Delhi withstood this onslaught and deeply influenced the course of Indian history.

After having developed relatively undisturbed by outside influences in the early Middle Ages India was now subjected once more to the impact of central Asian and Near Eastern forces. This new impact can only be compared to that made by the British from the eighteenth to the twentieth centuries. The former, however, was in many respects more intense, because the British never became Indian rulers; Qutb-ud-din's declaration of independence, on the other hand, meant that the sultans of Delhi had staked their fate on India, as did the Great Mughals later on. Although these new rulers of India did identify with the country they had conquered, their faith nevertheless remained distinctly alien and this led to conflict and tension hitherto unknown.

Even so, Indian culture was enriched by the encounter with Islam which opened up new connections with west Asia, just as Buddhism had linked India with east Asia. The Islamic countries of the west also transmitted Indian ideas to Europe as, for example, the Indian numerical system which was adopted in Europe as an 'Arab' one. In a similar way the famous game of chess travelled from India via Persia to Europe.

Arab rulers in India

The sultanate of Delhi was not the first Islamic state on Indian soil. In 712, a few months after the Arabs had captured Gibraltar and started their conquest of Spain and a year after Bokhara in central Asia had succumbed to Islamic conquerors, an Arab conqueror had also established a bridge-head in Sind at the mouth of the Indus. This conquest of Sind had started with an insignificant episode: a ship in which the king of Sri Lanka had sent Muslim orphans to the governor of Iraq had been captured by pirates; when the raja of Sind refused to punish those pirates the governor of Iraq launched several punitive expeditions against him until finally the governor's son-in-law, Muhammad Ibn Qasim, conquered most of southern Sind. In this campaign the governor of Iraq had enjoyed the full support of the caliph, but when a new caliph ascended the throne he recalled Ibn Qasim and had him executed. This did not, however, put an end to the policy of conquest: in 725 other Arab commanders successfully extended their campaigns into Kathiawar and Gujarat as far as southern Rajasthan. The valiant Arabs seemed to be poised for a rapid annexation of large parts of India, just as they had swept across all of western Asia.

But in this period the rulers of India still proved a match for the Islamic conquerors. Chalukyas and Rashtrakutas stopped their progress in western India and finally the Gurjara Pratiharas prevented their conquest of northern India. As we have seen earlier, the Muslim traveller Mas'udi, who was in India around 915, reported on the great number of troops which the Gurjara Pratiharas had earmarked especially for the defence against the Arabs. Sulayman, another Muslim historian, listed the Rashtrakutas along with the caliph, the emperor of China and the emperor of 'Rum' (the Byzantine emperor of the Rome of the East, Constantinople) as the four mightiest rulers of the world.

Initially Sind and the Panjab remained under the direct control of the caliph, who appointed the various governors himself. This direct control ended in 871, when Arab princes in Mansura (Sind) and in Multan (the Panjab) established independent dynasties of their own. These rulers seem to have followed a policy of peaceful coexistence with the Hindu population. It is said that the rulers of Multan even carefully protected the temple of the sun god at Multan in order that they might threaten the Gurjara Pratiharas with its destruction if they were attacked.

The destructive campaigns of Mahmud of Ghazni

In the year 1000 this more or less peaceful balance of power in northern India was shattered when Mahmud of Ghazni waged a war of destruction and plunder against India. From that date until 1025 he launched a total of seventeen campaigns of this sort and captured places as far distant as Saurashtra of Gujarat and the capital of the Gurjara Pratiharas, Kanauj.

Mahmud's father, a Turkish slave from central Asia, had seized on the decline of the realm of the Saminids to conquer a large territory which covered most of central Persia and had its eastern boundary at the Indus. His capital was at Ghazni to the south of Kabul. When Mahmud succeeded his father in 998, at the age of 27, he already possessed an enormous power base which he then extended very rapidly. Mahmud's Indian campaigns invariably began in the dry season; his return to Afghanistan was always made before the monsoon rains filled the rivers of the Panjab, which would have cut off his route while his troops were loaded with loot.

The Hindu Shahi dynasty ruling the territory around the Hindukush mountains was the first to feel the pressure of the Ghaznavids while still ruled by Mahmud's father. But the kings of this dynasty managed to resist for about twenty-five years, supported as they were by other Indian kings of the north Indian plains. Finally, however, they succumbed and soon the once so powerful Gurjara Pratiharas of Kanauj shared their fate. The Chandellas of Khajuraho and the Rajput rulers of Gwalior were also defeated and their treasures looted. Mahmud did not hesitate to mete out the same treatment to the Muslim ruler of Multan whose territory blocked his way.

The Hindus were particularly affected by the destruction and looting of their holy places at Thaneshwar, Mathura and Kanauj. The climax of these systematic campaigns was Mahmud's attack on the famous Shiva temple at Somnath on the southern coast of Kathiawar in Gujarat. After a daring expedition across the desert Mahmud reached this temple in 1025. Chronicles report that about 50,000 Hindus lost their lives in defending the temple. Mahmud destroyed the Shiva lingam with his own hands and then is said to have returned through the desert with a booty of about 20 million gold dinars (about 6.5 tons of gold). Many of his troops did not survive the journey.

Mahmud was greatly honoured by the caliph for this feat; to the Indians however, he came to signify the very embodiment of wanton destruction and fanaticism – much like Attila and Chingis Khan for the Europeans. Even Muslim historians find it difficult nowadays to explain his deeds – especially as he did not show the slightest intention of establishing an empire in India, although, given his valour and resourcefulness, he could easily have done so. Some historians suggested that he used India as a treasure trove in order to acquire the means for consolidating his central Asian empire – but he regarded that with as much indifference as he did India and only paid it attention at times of unrest.

His capital, Ghazni, was the only place which definitely profited from his enormous loot. He made it one of the finest cities of the day. Many scholars and poets surrounded him at his court, among them Firdausi, the author of the famous historical work *Shahnama*, and Alberuni, who composed the most comprehensive account of India ever written by a foreigner before the advent of the Europeans. Mahmud's fanaticism was not directed exclusively against the Hindus and other infidels; he attacked Muslim heretics with equal ferocity. Thus he twice waged hostilities against Multan, whose ruler, Daud, was an Ismaili. During his second onslaught on Multan he killed many local Muslims because they had not kept their promise of returning to orthodox Islam.

Whatever one may think of Mahmud, he was certainly one of the few people who made a lasting impact on Indian history. His great military successes were, however, not entirely due to his own skill and valour. The political situation in north India around 1000 was very favourable to a deter- mined invader. The perpetual triangular contest between the powers of northern, eastern and central India had weakened all of them. It had partic- ularly sapped the strength of the Gurjara Pratiharas and no leading power had arisen in early eleventh-century north India to take their place in defending the northern plains against Mahmud's incursions. The greatest Indian dynasty of that time, the Cholas, were so remote from the scene of Mahmud's exploits that they hardly noted them. But there may have been a deeper reason for the vulnerability of India to Mahmud's attacks. Alberuni, who knew and admired India, commented in the first chapter of his book on the national character of the Indians:

> The Hindus believe that there is no nation like theirs, no kings like theirs, no religion like theirs, no science like theirs. They are by nature niggardly in communicating that which they know, and they take the greatest possible care to withhold it from men of another caste among their own people, still much more, of course, from any foreigner. Their haughtiness is such that if you tell them of any science or scholar in Khurasan or Persia, they will think you both an ignoramus and a liar. If they travelled and mixed with other nations, they would soon change their mind, for their ancestors were not as narrow-minded as the present generation is.[1]

After Mahmud's death India gained a respite of more than a century before new invaders once more descended upon the plains from Afghanistan. The Indian rulers had not taken advantage of this reprieve to mend their fences. On the contrary, after the fall of the Gurjara Pratiharas many Rajput king- doms had arisen in northern India whose rulers were often closely related to each other due to marital alliances, but who nevertheless – or perhaps just because of that fact – jealously guarded their respective prestige. The Rajputs, with their code of honour and their proverbial valour, were heroic fighters when pitted against their equals in a duel; however, they were no good at coordinating their efforts or at outwitting the strategy and tactics of the invaders. The Rajput cavalry consisted of freemen who would not take orders easily, whereas the cavalry of the central Asian invaders consisted of specially trained slaves who had practically grown up with their horses and were subjected to a constant drill. Rushing towards the enemy and turning their horses suddenly, they would then – unobstructed by the heads of the horses and at a moment when they had stopped dead in their tracks – shoot a volley of well-aimed arrows before disappearing as quickly as they had come. The performance would be repeated else-where, thus decimating and confusing the enemy without great losses on the Muslim side.

But the Indians were not vanquished just by the superior strategy and tactics of the invaders; they were simply not in a position to organise a concerted defence effort. Caste distinctions and the general separation of the rulers from the rural folk prevented the kind of solidarity which would have been required for such a defence effort. Neither religious wars nor any other wars involving fundamental principles had ever been waged in India. War was a pastime of the rulers. The troops recruited for such wars were either kinsmen of the rulers – particularly so among the Rajputs – or mercenaries who hoped for their share of the loot which was usually the main aim of warfare. Fighting against the troops of the Muslim invaders was both dangerous and unprofitable, as their treasures were not within easy reach. The invading troops, on the other hand, could expect a good deal of loot in India and their imagination was also fired by the merit attached to waging a 'holy war' against the infidels.

Moreover, Islamic society was much more open and egalitarian than Hindu society. Anybody who wanted to join an army and proved to be good at fighting could achieve rapid advancement. Indian armies were led by kings and princes whose military competence was not necessarily in keeping with their hereditary rank; by contrast, the Muslim generals whom they encountered almost invariably owed their position to their superior military merit. Even sultans would be quickly replaced by slaves-turned-generals if they did not know how to maintain their position. This military Darwinism was characteristic of early Islamic history. The Ghaznavids and the Ghurids and then the sultans of Delhi were all slaves to begin with. Such slaves would be bought in the slave markets of central Asia, would subsequently make a mark by their military prowess and their loyalty and obedience, and, once they had risen to a high position, often did not hesitate to murder their master in order to take his place. The immobile Hindu society and its hereditary rulers were no match for such people.

Muhammad of Ghur and the conquest of northern India

The final struggle for India in the twelfth century was again preceded by momentous events in Afghanistan and central Asia. In 1151 Ghazni, with all its magnificent palaces and mosques, was completely destroyed. The rulers of Ghur in western Afghanistan emerged as new leaders from this internecine struggle. In 1175 Muhammad of Ghur conquered Multan, and in 1186 he vanquished Mahmud of Ghazni's last successor, who had withdrawn to Lahore. Using the Panjab as a base for further conquest Muhammad of Ghur pursued his aim of annexing as much of India as he could. Unlike Mahmud of Ghazni he was determined to rule India and not just to plunder it. In 1178 he was not very successful in an encounter with the Chalukya ruler of Gujarat, but in 1191 and 1192 he waged two decisive battles of Tarain, to the northwest of Delhi, the region in which other famous battles of Indian history had been and were yet to be fought. The first battle of Tarain was won by the Rajput confederacy led by Prithviraj Chauhan of Delhi. But when Muhammad of Ghur returned the following year with 10,000 archers on horseback he vanquished Prithviraj and his army.

After winning this decisive battle, Muhammad conquered almost the whole of northern India within a few years. In 1193 he defeated the mighty Gahadavala dynasty and captured Kanauj and Varanasi. Soon he also captured Gwalior, Ajmer and Anhilwara, at that time the capital of Gujarat. In this way most Rajput strongholds were eliminated. Many of these victories were due to the slave-general Qutb-ud-din Aibak, whom Muhammad then installed as his viceroy in Delhi. Eastern India, however, was conquered by another lucky upstart, Muhammad Bakhtiyar Khalji, who had risen to the rank of a general within a very short time. He captured Bihar, destroyed the University of Nalanda and, in about 1202, defeated King Lakshmana Sena of Bengal. This latter attack was so swift that it is said that Lakshmana Sena was taking his lunch when it came. Bengal became a sub-centre of Islamic rule in India which every so often defied the overlords in Delhi. This was so right from the beginning, as Bakhtiyar Khalji was more or less running his own government there. He also tried to annex Assam, but had to retreat after incurring severe losses.

In northern India Muhammad held almost unlimited sway even though he did not manage to capture Kashmir. He also faced trouble in central Asia, where the ruler of Chwaresm rose to prominence and defeated his army in 1205. The next year Muhammad was murdered near the Indus and his vast empire seemed on the verge of disintegration: Hindu princes had raised their heads again, Gwalior and Ranthambor were once more in Hindu hands. After the death of his master Muhammad, Qutb-ud-din took the decisive step of declaring his independence from the Ghurids.

Iltutmish, Qutb-ud-din's son-in-law, succeeded him in 1210, and in 1229 he was solemnly consecrated as sultan of Delhi by a representative of the Abbasid caliph of Baghdad. He won this recognition only after hard-fought battles against Qutb-ud-din's colleagues, the great slave-generals who controlled most of northwestern India. He also had to face Rajput resistance: though he recaptured Gwalior and Ranthambor, several other Rajput leaders (for example, the Guhilas of Nagda near Udaipur, and the Chauhans of Bundi to the south of Agra) defied him successfully. Only shortly before his death in 1236 he subjected Bengal to his control after having subdued the followers of Bakhtiyar Khalji in Bihar. This general had been murdered in 1206, but his companions had held on to his territory.

In addition to these problems of the internal consolidation of his realm, Iltutmish also had to defend it against the Mongols who now appeared in India. In hot pursuit of the son of the Chwaresm Shah whom he had defeated, Chingis Khan reached the Indus in 1221. Iltutmish's success in keeping the Mongols out was due to the fact that he had wisely refrained from taking sides when Chingis Khan attacked the Chwaresm Shah, although this shah could lay claim to Iltutmish's support as a fellow Muslim. Chingis Khan left some troops in the Panjab, which remained a thorn in the side of the sultanate of Delhi throughout the thirteenth century. But the sultans and their troops proved a much better match for the Mongol hordes than had the Hindu princes, whose old-fashioned and cumbersome methods of warfare were no longer appropriate to the new requirements of an effective defence of India.

The sultanate of Delhi: a new Indian empire

The main achievement of Qutb-ud-din Aibak and Iltutmish was that they once more established an empire which matched that of the Guptas or of Harsha (see Map 4.1). These two sultans were also the founders of Delhi as their capital city. From its former status of small Rajput stronghold, Delhi now emerged as an imperial capital. The seven cities which, from the thirteenth to the seventeenth centuries, grew up one after another in the large area now covered by Delhi and New Delhi, symbolise a certain continuity in Indian history. The most splendid of these cities was perhaps that of the Great Mughal Shah Jahan, situated in the present 'Old Delhi' and incorporating the magnificent mosque and Red Fort. In the twentieth century the British were to add an eighth city, New Delhi, which now extends all the way from Qutb-ud-din's tall Qutb Minar in the south to the walls of Shah Jahan's Old Delhi in the north. Qutb-ud-din and Iltutmish also inaugurated Indo-Islamic art and architecture, their buildings ranking with those of the Lodi sultans and of the Great Mughals as among India's most magnificent monuments. In addition to the famous Qutb Minar, the Quwwat-ul-Islam ('Power of Islam') mosque and the tomb of Iltutmish are indicative of these early architectural achievements: Iltutmish's tomb was the first of the great sequence of tombs erected for Islamic rulers in India.

The three decades after Iltutmish's death were a time of incessant struggle among the generals, governors, slaves and descendants of the sultan. Iltutmish's daughter Raziyyat ruled the realm for three years. The contemporary chronicle *Tabaqat-i-Nasari* describes her as a wise ruler and

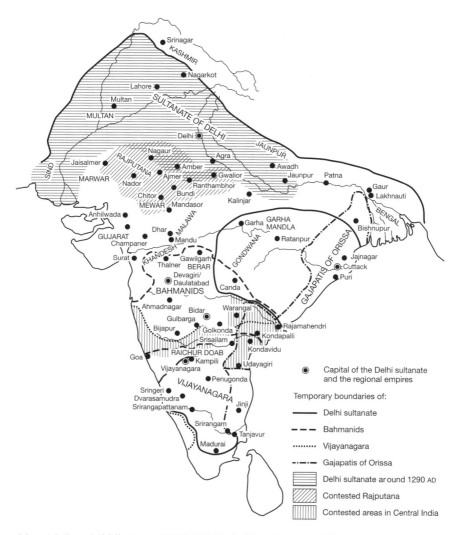

Map 4.1 Late Middle Ages (1206–1526): Delhi sultanate and late regional empires

competent military leader: 'She had all the admirable qualities befitting a ruler. But of what use were these qualities to her as fate had denied her the favour of being born as a man?' She was deposed by the courtiers and when she made an attempt to regain the throne with the help of one of them, she was killed. In subsequent struggles the influential 'Group of the Forty', mostly powerful Turkish slaves of Iltutmish, gained more and more influence until finally one of them seized power after all male descendants of Iltutmish had died. This new sultan, Balban, was notorious for his cruelty.

He had earlier crushed the rebellious Rajputs and he now murdered all the other members of the 'Forty'. He then organised the defence against the Mongols, who were defeated by his son Muhammad in 1279. He also fought against a Turkish officer who, as sultan of Bengal, had declared his independence from Delhi. This self-appointed sultan and his entire family were brutally killed and Balban's descendants then ruled Bengal until 1338, when Bengal once more became an independent state.

After Balban's death in 1286, a member of the Turkish clan of the Khaljis emerged victorious from the struggle for the throne. This man, Jalal-ud-din Khalji, became the founder of the short-lived Khalji dynasty (1290–1320). Jalal-ud-din was soon eliminated by his nephew and son-in-law, Ala-ud-din, who ascended the throne in 1296 and became the greatest and most powerful sultan of Delhi. He invaded southern India, successfully defended the country against the Mongols and introduced administrative reforms which helped him to raise the money for his military ventures.

The invasion of south India and the defence against the Mongols

During the first century of its existence the sultanate of Delhi was a north Indian realm. Furthermore, the Mongols controlled the Panjab for most of this time and Bengal was usually quite independent. But now Ala-ud-din launched a great campaign of conquest around 1300 and managed to extend his sway over India in an amazing fashion. He wanted to be a second Alexander (*Sikander Sani*). His coins showed this title and he also ordered that it should be mentioned in public prayers. Even before ascending the throne he had defeated the Yadava king of Devagiri, capturing his famous fortress which until then had been considered impregnable as it was built on a steep rock of the northern Deccan (near Aurangabad). In 1298 he conquered Gujarat and in 1301 and 1303 he captured the famous Rajput forts of Ranthambor and Chitor. Mandu and Chanderi in Malwa were captured in 1305. Two years later Ala-ud-din once more attacked Devagiri to force the Yadava king to pay the tribute he had promised when first defeated. Ala-ud-din took this king as a prisoner to Delhi, but later reinstated him on condition that he pay his tribute regularly.

In 1309 Ala-ud-din launched his campaign against southern India 'in order to seize elephants and treasures from the rulers of the South', as it is stated in the chronicle *Tarikh-i-Firoz Shahi*. The first target of this campaign was Warangal, the capital of the Kakatiyas in present-day Andhra Pradesh. An earlier attack on Warangal in 1304 had been unsuccessful. Now, however, the great general Malik Kafur, a converted Hindu slave from Gujarat, captured Warangal for Ala-ud-din. The Kakatiya king was then reinstated in the same way as the Yadava king. Malik Kafur is supposed to have returned to Delhi with such an amount of loot that he needed 1,000 camels to carry it. The famous Koh-i-Nur diamond is said to have been among these treasures. In 1310 Malik Kafur penetrated deep into the south. With the support of the Yadava king he rushed to Dvarasamudra, the capital of the Hoysalas, and captured it. The Hoysala king, Ballala III, was at that time away fighting a war against the Pandyas of Madurai; on his return he accepted the same conditions as the Yadava and Kakatiya kings had done before him. Malik Kafur then attacked the Pandya king himself and burned down his capital, Madurai; he also looted some of the great temple cities, such as Srirangam, and once more returned to Delhi loaded with treasures and accompanied by 612 elephants. This whole southern campaign had taken him just eleven months.

At the same time as Ala-ud-din launched his southern campaigns he also successfully fought against the Mongols in the north. In 1296–7 the Mongols had conducted their usual campaigns of plunder in northwestern India, but in 1299 Qutlugh Khvaja, a descendant of Chingis Khan, came with an army of 200,000 men. He obviously wanted to subject the sultanate of Delhi but was defeated by Ala-ud-din. Four years later, when Ala-ud-din was returning from Chitor and many of his troops were in Andhra Pradesh trying to capture Warangal, the Mongols returned with 120,000 men on horseback. The invaders swept through the streets of Delhi but could not capture Ala-ud-din's fortified military camp there. Two months later the Mongols disappeared as quickly as they had come. Further Mongol attacks in 1306–7 were also repulsed successfully. In his methods of warfare and in his cruel acts of revenge Ala-ud-din was certainly on a par with the Mongols. Thousands of Mongol prisoners were trampled to death by elephants in Delhi while the sultan's court watched and, in true Mongol tradition, a pyramid composed of the heads of vanquished Mongols was erected outside the city gate of Delhi.

Ala-ud-din's administrative reforms

Ala-ud-din's victories as the mightiest warlord in Indian history were based to a large extent on his efficient administration. As his administration reforms were of some importance also in the context of the structural prob-lems of Hindu kingdoms which we have discussed earlier we shall analyse these reforms in some detail.

Ala-ud-din's predecessors had based their rule mainly on the strength of their army and the control of a few important towns and fortresses. They derived their financial resources from loot, from taxes imposed on the markets of Delhi, from the land revenue of the area around Delhi and from the tribute of subjected kings. Land revenue and tribute were not always paid very regularly. The rural people were still mostly Hindus; the Muslims lived in the cities and towns where sometimes whole castes of artisans had embraced Islam so as to overcome the stigma of low caste status. The few

Muslims who lived outside the big cities and towns spent their time in the small fortified administrative centres (*qasba*). The countryside and agricultural production were controlled by the traditional Hindu authorities, the headmen of the villages. The sultan depended on them as they were the middlemen through whom he controlled the rural people. Ala-ud-din considered the haughtiness and the direct or indirect resistance of these Hindu middlemen to be the main difficulty besetting his rule. In a dialogue with a scholar, Ala-ud-din vividly described this problem which was more or less the same in all medieval Indian states, whether they were ruled by Hindus or Muslims:

> I have discovered that the khuts and mukkadims [local tax collectors and village headmen] ride upon fine horses, wear fine clothes, shoot with Persian bows, make war upon each other, and go out for hunting; but of the kharaj [land revenue], jizya [poll tax], kari [house tax] and chari [pasture tax] they do not pay one jital. They levy separately the khut's [landowner's] share from the villages, give parties and drink wine, and many of them pay no revenue at all, either upon demand or without demand. Neither do they show any respect for my officers. This has excited my anger, and I have said to myself: 'Thou hast an ambition to conquer other lands, but thou hast hundreds of leagues of country under thy rule where proper obedience is not paid to thy authority. How then wilt thou make other lands submissive?[2]

Ala-ud-din was also quite realistic when he mentioned that his order would be obeyed only up to a distance of about 100 miles from Delhi; beyond that limit military intervention was required if he wanted to impose his will on the people. Another problem which all sultans had to face was the constant babble of conspiracy in the capital and at the court. Ala-ud-din felt that the many feasts and drinking bouts of his courtiers and officers were the mainspring of such intrigues.

After some initial conspiracies and revolts at his court and Hindu rebellions in the rural areas in the early years of his rule, Ala-ud-din decided to get at the root of this problem by introducing reforms which were also intended to secure the support of a large standing army and assure the food supply of his capital. He first of all confiscated all landed property from his courtiers and officers. Revenue assignments were also cancelled and the revenue was collected by the central administration. Henceforth, 'everybody was busy with earning a living so that nobody could even think of rebellion'. The sale and consumption of alcohol was strictly prohibited and the courtiers were no longer permitted to hold private meetings or feasts. Spies were posted everywhere in order to report on any transgression of these orders. Furthermore, Ala-ud-din asked the 'wise men of his realm' to 'supply some rules and regulations for grinding down the Hindus, and for depriving them of that wealth and property which fosters rebellion. The Hindu was to be so reduced as to be left unable to keep a horse to ride on, to carry arms, to wear fine clothes, or to enjoy any of the luxuries of life.'

He also ordered a new revenue survey of all land and decreed a uniform rate of assessment for all rural classes, namely half of the standing crop. There was also a special revenue imposed on pastures. But Ala-ud-din also ordered that no other taxes should be imposed on the poor people. The Hindu middlemen were treated mercilessly by Ala-ud-din's officers:

> The people were brought to such a state of obedience that one revenue officer would string twenty khuts, mukkadims, or chaud-haris [who were responsible for the tax collection] together by the neck, and enforce payment by blows. No Hindu could hold up his head and in their houses no sign of gold or silver or any super-fluity was to be seen. These things which nourish insubordination and rebellion were no longer to be found.

This is mentioned in the chronicle *Tarikh-i-Firoz Shahi*.

The constant fight against the Mongols required the maintenance of a large standing army. In order to be able to hire more soldiers for the same amount of money, Ala-ud-din lowered the men's pay. At the same time he also decreed low fixed prices so that the soldiers could make ends meet. For this purpose Ala-ud-din promulgated the following ordinances:

1 All prices for specific foodstuffs were to be fixed.
2 A high officer with a staff of spies was appointed who had to oversee the markets of Delhi so as to guarantee the fixed prices.
3 Large storages for grain were established in Delhi which were filled with the produce of the directly assessed land (*khalsa*) of the Doab (Land of the Two Rivers, Yamuna and Ganges) where the revenue was paid in kind.
4 Grain trade and transport were controlled by the government. Transport workers were forced to settle with their families at specified distances along the Yamuna in order to guarantee a swift transport of grain to Delhi.
5 Peasants and traders were prohibited from storing grain themselves so as to prevent the rise of a black market.
6 The collection of revenue in kind and government procurement of grain were to be done in the field so as to eliminate any private storage of grain.
7 Daily reports on market prices had to be submitted to the sultan. The overseer of the markets and the spies had to report separately. If these reports differed, the sultan would make further inquiries.

The passages of the *Tarikh-i-Firoz Shahi* where its author, Barani, describes these measures are among the most fascinating accounts of pre-modern administrative reforms in India. This is the only known systematic attempt by a medieval Indian ruler to establish a centralised administration and to interfere directly with market forces. Similar prescriptions are contained only in the old *Arthashastra* and it is possible that Ala-ud-din knew about the *Arthashastra* and tried to implement its suggestions. It is also interesting to note in this context that Ala-ud-din, much like the author of the *Arthashastra*, maintained that the interest of the state was the only norm which the ruler should adopt. Ala-ud-din explicitly rejected the idea of following strict Islamic injunctions in this respect. In the dialogue with a scholar he stated:

> Although I have not studied the science or the Book, I am a Musulman of Musulman stock. To prevent rebellion in which thousands perish, I issue such orders as I conceive to be for the good of the State and for the benefit of the people. Men are heedless, disrespectful, and disobey my commands; I am then compelled to be severe to bring them into obedience, I do not know whether this is lawful or unlawful, whatever I think to be for the good of the State, or suitable for the emergency, that I decree.

The famous chronicle of Kashmir, *Rajatarangini*, also provides some evidence of the fact that Ala-ud-din's measures were in keeping with earlier Indian traditions and do not need to be attributed to west Asian influences. Written in the twelfth century by the Brahmin Kalhana, this chronicle attributes the following sentiments to King Lalitaditya, whose exploits have been described earlier:

> Those who wish to be powerful in the land must always guard against internal dissension. Those who dwell there in the mountains difficult of access, should be punished even if they give no offence, because sheltered by their fastnesses, they are difficult to break up if they have once accumulated wealth. Every care should be taken that there should not be left with the villagers more food supply than required for one year's consumption, nor more oxen than wanted for the tillage of their fields. Because if they keep more wealth, they would become in a single year very formidable Damaras [chiefs] and strong enough to neglect the demands of the king.[3]

The Hindu text and Muslim practice show striking similarities. Ala-ud-din is said to have stated:

The Hindus will never become submissive and obedient till they are reduced to poverty. I have, therefore, given orders, that just sufficient shall be left to them from year to year, of corn, milk, and curds, but they shall not be allowed to accumulate hoards and property.

Although Ala-ud-din had the indisputable merit of having saved India from being overrun by the Mongols, the Hindus naturally disliked him because he oppressed them intentionally. Hindu historians have, therefore, criticised him just as they criticised Aurangzeb. But they tend to forget that Ala-ud-din was rather impartial in his oppression, his measures being aimed at Muslim courtiers just as much as against Hindu notables and middlemen. If we can rely on Barani's account, we can even state that the poor Hindus in the rural areas were explicitly exempted from some of the sultan's stern measures. The complaint that Ala-ud-din, by demanding revenue amounting to 50 per cent of the standing crop, asked for much more than any Hindu ruler had done before him is also not entirely correct. We should not forget that, in addition to the usual one-sixth which was supposed to be the king's share according to the ancient code of Manu, kings, princes, middlemen and headmen collected a great deal of additional taxes or subjected the peasants to irregular exactions. Ala-ud-din explicitly prohibited all such additional collections, imposed a direct assessment and limited it to the above-mentioned amount.

Whether Ala-ud-din was really successful in implementing these measures is difficult to ascertain. Barani reported several decades later that the fact that Delhi was fully supplied with food was regarded as one of the great miracles of that time. Other measures were less successful. Barani described at length how illicit alcohol was produced and sold in Delhi, a report which reminds one of Chicago in the days of Prohibition. The fixed prices which Ala-ud-din decreed were circumvented by many traders who used smaller weights and measures. At any rate, all these decrees were probably implemented only in the capital and extended only as far as places within a radius of 100 miles around the capital, as Ala-ud-din himself had indicated. Beyond that core area of his realm, no Indian ruler – whether Hindu or Muslim – could hope to exercise direct influence.

Ala-ud-din died in 1316. He was succeeded by two of his sons and by a converted outcaste Hindu, Khusru Khan. None of them died a natural death. In 1320 the courtiers made Ghiyas-ud-din Tughluq the new sultan. His father was a Turkish slave who had served Balban; his mother was a Jat woman from India. Ghiyas-ud-din became the founder of the Tughluq dynasty. He had to conduct campaigns against Warangal, which had become independent once more, and against Bengal, which had always been difficult to control. When returning from Bengal he entered a reception hall, built at his own request by his son in celebration of the sultan's victory.

But this hall was constructed in such a way that it collapsed and buried Ghiyas-ud-din, thus paving the way for his son's quick succession. Again one is reminded of ancient Indian treatises on statecraft which recommend the construction of easily inflammable reception halls as a means of eliminating an enemy. Muhammad Tughluq's device differed from this only in terms of the more solid material which he used. For their toleration of this murder he compensated the courtiers with valuable presents; he ruled for twenty-seven years, until 1351.

Muhammad Tughluq's ambitious plans

In the beginning of his reign Muhammad Tughluq seemed to continue the tradition of expanding the realm, and in this he was even more successful than Ala-ud-din. But his unbridled ambition finally led to the downfall of the sultanate of Delhi. Ala-ud-din had been satisfied with subjecting the kings of the south; Muhammad Tughluq wanted to annex their territories, too. As a crown prince he had conducted the campaign against Warangal and he had probably also reached Madurai, which had been sacked by Malik Kafur some decades earlier. Soon after his accession to the throne he conquered Kampili in the area where Vijayanagar was later to be constructed. The northern part of the Hoysala kingdom was also annexed at that time. In order to rule his vast empire from a more central capital Muhammad Tughluq built a new one at Daulatabad, the old Yadava capital at Devagiri. Barani reported:

> The second project of Sultan Muhammad which was ruinous to the capital of the empire and distressing to the chief men of the country, was that of making Deogir [Devagiri] the capital under the title Daulatabad. This place held a central position. Without any consultation, without carefully looking into the advantages and disadvantages on every side, he brought ruin upon Delhi, that city which for 170 or 180 years had grown in prosperity, and rivalled Baghdad and Cairo.[4]

Barani's description of the suffering inflicted on the people who were forced to leave Delhi for Daulatabad is fully confirmed by the detailed report of the famous north African traveller Ibn Battuta, who was in India during Muhammad's reign. Though it made sense to have a more centrally located capital, the whole venture not only failed but contributed to the downfall of the sultanate. In later years the Mughal empire was to suffer the same fate after Aurangzeb established his new capital at Aurangabad only a few miles from Daulatabad. After shifting to Daulatabad, Muhammad Tughluq lost his control over north India, without being able to consolidate his hold on the south. When he finally returned to Delhi this was taken as a sign of

176

weakness and independent states arose in the south. In 1334 the governor at Madurai declared his independence, calling himself 'Sultan of Ma'bar'; four years later Bengal followed suit and in 1346 the Vijayanagar empire was founded. In central India the Bahmani sultanate was established in 1347. The old regional centres of Indian history thus once more emerged very clearly, just as they were to do about four centuries later following the death of Aurangzeb.

Taking Ala-ud-din's example Muhammad Tughluq had also introduced economic and administrative reforms in order to support his policy of expansion. He tried to extend the system of direct administration, which Ala-ud-din had implemented only in the core region of the sultanate, to all provinces of his vast empire. But whereas Ala-ud-din had collected a great deal of revenue in kind from the core region in order to secure a reliable food supply for Delhi, Muhammad insisted on cash in order to transfer anticipated provincial revenues to his capital. This was before the time when silver flowed into India from the West and therefore Muhammad hit upon an idea which was totally incompatible with Indian tradition. The nominal value of Indian coins never deviated very much from their intrinsic value. But now Muhammad issued copper coins, a token currency which was despised by the people. As the intrinsic value of these coins was low, counterfeiters could make a huge profit and contemporary reports indicate that 'every house was turned into a mint'. Muhammad had to withdraw his currency only three years after he had launched this ill-advised experiment. In order to divert attention from these blunders he announced two great campaigns against Persia and central Asia which, in the end, literally got nowhere.

After all his ambitious plans had failed, Muhammad Tughluq's rule degenerated to a reign of terror of which Ibn Battuta has given a detailed account. Oppression and exploitation had to be borne by the rural Hindu population. The main victims of Muhammad's reign of terror, however, were mostly Muslims and sometimes even learned divines whom he did not hesitate to eliminate if their views displeased him.

The twilight of the sultanate of Delhi

The last important sultan of Delhi was Muhammad Tughluq's cousin, Firoz Shah, who succeeded him in 1351 and enjoyed an unusually long reign of thirty-seven years. Firoz consolidated once more the position of the sultanate as a north Indian realm and made no attempt to reconquer central and southern India. He did, however, try to reassert his control over Bengal, but his campaigns of 1353–4 and 1359 were, with the exception of a victory in Orissa, unsuccessful. In 1362 he embarked on a campaign against Sind and Gujarat which almost ended in disaster. For six months no news of the sultan reached Delhi and it was assumed that he had perished in the desert.

It was Firoz's good fortune that in this trying time Delhi was in the hands of his loyal follower, Jahan Khan, a converted Hindu from Telengana.

Firoz was a great builder of mosques, forts and canals. Firoz Shah Kotla, the multi-storeyed citadel of his capital, still exists in Delhi. There he installed two Ashoka pillars which he had transported with great difficulty from distant provinces. He consulted Brahmins in order to decipher the inscriptions on these pillars, but even they could not read the ancient script. Like his predecessors, Firoz also introduced some reforms: he abolished torture and extended the poll tax (*jizya*) to Brahmins who had hitherto been exempt from it. He made a point of having slaves sent to him from the provinces converted to Islam and to reward converts in and around Delhi with presents. This was obviously a deliberate policy aimed at securing the support of loyal Muslims in and around his capital.

When Firoz died in 1388 the sultanate of Delhi soon disintegrated. Two of his relatives indulged in a futile struggle for the succession from their strongholds in two citadels of the capital. Meanwhile, almost all provincial governors attained the de facto status of independent rulers.

The sultanate of Delhi was finally shattered in 1398, when Timur swooped down on India and sacked Delhi after his conquest of Persia (1387) and final capture of Baghdad (1393). For three days Timur's soldiers indulged in an orgy of murder and plunder in the Indian capital. The Hindu population was exterminated; the Muslims were spared, although presumably their property was not. The deeds of these Turkish warriors shocked even Timur, who wrote in his autobiography that he was not responsible for this terrible event and that only his soldiers should be blamed. At any rate after Timur had left Delhi remained uninhabited for quite some time.

The sultanate of Delhi virtually ceased to exist for fifteen years after Timur's raid. Gujarat, Malwa and Jaunpur near Varanasi emerged as sultanates in their own right. In the west, Lahore, Multan and Sind remained under the control of descendants and successors of Timur. From 1414 there was again a sultanate of Delhi under the Sayyid dynasty, but its influence was restricted to the Doab. In 1451 Buhlul Khan of the Afghan clan of the Lodis established a new dynasty in Delhi, which once more asserted its control over northern India. Buhlul Khan himself conquered the sultanate of Jaunpur and his successors – Sikander and Ibrahim – subjected Gwalior and Bihar. The Lodi sultans and particularly the short-lived dynasty of Sher Shah established an efficient administration in the central region of their realm which later provided a good foundation for the Mughal machinery of government. In order to control Gwalior and the Rajput country, Sikander built a new capital at Agra; this also served the Mughals well at a later stage. Sikandara near Agra, where Akbar's tomb is situated, is named after Sikander Lodi. In the Lodi Gardens in New Delhi the stern, heavy-edificed tombs of the Lodi sultans are the last monuments of the sultanate; they are in striking contrast to Humayun's tomb nearby: built only a few decades later, the latter shows the influence of the new Persian style which characterised Mughal art and architecture.

The problems of administrative penetration

The sultans of Delhi never managed to consolidate an empire comprising a large part of India. Although they certainly had the military means to subdue India, they were unable to establish an adequate administration through which they could have penetrated the country and strengthened their rule. We have discussed similar problems with regard to the regional Hindu kingdoms. The personal and patrimonial organisation prevailing in these medieval realms could never serve the purpose of controlling distant provinces. Occasional military intervention or a reshuffle of Hindu rajas or Muslim governors did not make much difference in this respect. The new feature of the sultanate was that the sultans based their power on, or even shared this power with, an alien military elite bound together by Islam and certain tribal affinities.

In the mid-thirteenth century Sultan Balban established this network of Turkish foreign rule over India with special vigour. But it was a system that could not last long: it was very brittle, for the sultans were unable to penetrate the Hindu rural sector in this way. Ala-ud-din tried his best to solve the problem by introducing a direct revenue assessment and curbing the power of rural middlemen. However, he could do this with some success only in the core region of his empire, where the continuous military presence of his standing army would silence all attempts at resistance. The reproduction of this system in the provinces would have been possible, but would have raised the danger of powerful governors turning against the sultan – something they were often prone to do in any case. Muhammad Tughluq's move to locate his capital in a more central place to facilitate control of the distant provinces was quite logical in this context, but it was doomed to remain an isolated measure unless the administrative penetration was also improved. His experiment with copper currency so that he could transfer the provincial revenues in cash to his capital likewise made sense, but it proved to be an even more dismal failure for the reasons discussed above. Actually, these two arbitrary measures – the relocation of the capital and the introduction of a new currency – show in an exemplary manner how isolated responses to the challenge of the administrative penetration of a vast empire are bound to make matters worse and do not help to solve the basic problem of an inadequate system of government.

The establishment of military fiefs (*iqta*) was another aspect of this problem. Initially the Islamic conquerors found the granting of such fiefs to be an easy method of satisfying the greed of their high officers who had helped them to conquer the country. At the same time this system helped to establish a rudimentary control over the rural areas. But to the extent

179

that such fiefs became hereditary, there was always the danger of too powerful subjects rebelling against the sultan. Ala-ud-din therefore cancelled these fiefs and paid his officers fixed salaries from his treasury. Muhammad Tughluq wanted to continue this system, but found that to do so he would have to raise the revenue demand and convert it into cash – which made him embark on his fateful currency policy. After all these ruinous experiments Firoz Shah returned to the old system of granting military fiefs. Thus a military feudalism of a prebendal type was firmly established. The feudal lords belonged to an alien elite distinct from the rural society which they controlled – a phenomenon which similarly characterised other countries and other periods of history when feudalism did not grow from below but was imposed from above by conquerors. This alien elite of the sultanate did not co-opt local notables – not even Indian converts to Islam – and it looked down upon Indians as an inferior kind of people. This may have enhanced the solidarity of this ruling elite; it certainly impeded the administrative penetration of the country.

Some historians have maintained that the main reason for the failure of the policies of the Delhi sultans was their rabid persecution of the Hindus. It is true that several sultans indulged in cruel excesses. More than these excesses and the emphasis on conversion, the permanent aloofness of the ruling elite prevented an integration of Indians – even Indian converts – into the political system of the sultanate. The Mughal system as it developed in the reign of Akbar was quite different in this respect: it offered many opportunities of advancement to the Indians and thus also achieved a much higher degree of administrative penetration. But we must also emphasise that the Delhi sultanate made a definite impact on Indian history by transgressing regional boundaries and projecting an Indian empire which in a way became the precursor of the present highly centralised national state. These transgressions were intermittent only, but they certainly surpassed anything achieved by the early medieval Hindu kingdoms.

THE STATES OF CENTRAL AND SOUTHERN INDIA IN THE PERIOD OF THE SULTANATE OF DELHI

The history of India from 1192, when Muhammad of Ghur conquered north India, to 1526, when the Great Mughal Baber did the same, has often been equated with the history of the sultanate of Delhi. But this sultanate was only a north Indian state for most of the time. Some Hindu states continued to exist throughout this period and new Hindu and Muslim states independent from the sultanate of Delhi arose in central and southern India after Muhammad Tughluq relinquished Daulatabad and returned to

Delhi. The most important states of this kind were the Hindu kingdom of Orissa, which survived all Muslim onslaughts until 1568, the Bahmani sultanate of central India, and the Vijayanagar empire of southern India.

The Bahmani sultanate of the Deccan

Soon after Muhammad Tughluq left Daulatabad, the city was conquered by Zafar Khan in 1345. Independence from Delhi was immediately declared and Khan established a sultanate of his own. Zafar Khan, a Turkish or Afghan officer of unknown descent, had earlier participated in a mutiny of troops in Gujarat. He probably did not feel too safe in Daulatabad, so he shifted his capital two years later to Gulbarga (Karnataka). This town is located in a fertile basin surrounded by hills. The mighty citadel of the sultan exists to this day. Not far from this place was the capital of the Rashtrakutas, Malkhed or Manyakheta, which shows that this area was ideally suited as a nuclear region of a great realm.

Zafar Khan, also known as Bahman Shah, became the founder of an important dynasty which ruled the Deccan for nearly two centuries. He had to fight various remnants of Muhammad Tughluq's troops, as well as the Hindu rulers of Orissa and Warangal who had also expanded their spheres of influence as soon as Muhammad had left the Deccan. The rajas of Vijayanagar had established their empire almost at the same time as Bahman Shah had founded his sultanate; they now emerged as his most formidable enemies. The Bahmani sultans were as cruel and ferocious as the Delhi sultans, at least according to contemporary chronicles. Bahman Shah's successor, Muhammad Shah (1358–73), killed about half a million people in his incessant campaigns until he and his adversaries came to some agreement to spare prisoners-of-war as well as the civilian population.

Despite their many wars, Sultan Muhammad Shah and his successors could not expand the sultanate very much: they just about managed to maintain the status quo. Around 1400 the rulers of Vijayanagar, in good old *Rajamandala* style, even established an alliance with the Bahmani sultans' northern neighbours – the sultans of Gujarat and Malwa – so as to check his expansionist policy. But in 1425 the Bahmani sultan subjected Warangal and thus reached the east coast. However, only a few years later the new Suryavamsha dynasty of Orissa challenged the sultanate and contributed to its downfall.

In the fifteenth century the capital of the Bahmani sultanate was moved from Gulbarga to Bidar. The new capital, Bidar, was at a much higher level (about 3,000 feet) than Gulbarga and had a better climate in the rainy season, but it was also nearly 100 miles further to the northeast and thus much closer to Warangal. Bidar soon was as impressive a capital as Gulbarga had been. Anastasy Nikitin, a Russian traveller who spent four years in the sultanate from 1470 to 1474, left us a report which is one of the most important European accounts of life in medieval India. He high-lighted the great contrast between the enormous wealth of the nobility and the grinding poverty of the rural population.

The most important personality of this Bidar period of the Bahmani sultanate was Mahmud Gawan, who served several sultans as prime minister and general from 1461 to 1481. He reconquered Goa, which had been captured by the rulers of Vijayanagar. The sultanate then extended from coast to coast. Gawan also introduced remarkable administrative reforms and controlled many districts directly. State finance was thus very much improved. But his competent organisation ended with his execution, ordered by the sultan as the result of a court intrigue. After realising his mistake the sultan drank himself to death within the year, thus marking the beginning of the end of the Bahmani sultanate.

After Gawan's death the various factions at the sultan's court started a struggle for power that was to end only with the dynasty itself: indigenous Muslim courtiers and generals were ranged against the 'aliens' – Arabs, Turks and Persians. The last sultan, Mahmud Shah (1482–1518) no longer had any authority and presided over the dissolution of his realm. The gover-nors of the four most important provinces declared their independence from him one after another: Bijapur (1489), Ahmadnagar and Berar (1491), Bidar (1492) and Golconda (1512). Although the Bahmani sultans lived on in Bidar until 1527, they were mere puppets in the hands of the real rulers of Bidar, the Barid Shahis, who used them so as to put pressure on the other usurpers of Bahmani rule.

Bijapur proved to be the most expansive of the successor states and annexed Berar and Bidar. Ahmadnagar and Golconda retained their inde-pendence and finally joined hands with Bijapur in the great struggle against Vijayanagar. Embroiled in incessant fighting on the Deccan, Bijapur lost Goa to the Portuguese in 1510 and was unable to regain this port, even though attempts at capturing it were made up to 1570. The armies of Vijayanagar were a match for the armies of Bijapur. However, when all the Deccan sultanates pooled their resources Vijayanagar suffered a crucial defeat in 1565. Subsequently the Deccan sultanates succumbed to the Great Mughals: Ahmadnagar, being the northernmost, was annexed first; Bijapur and Golconda survived for some time, but were finally vanquished by Aurangzeb in 1686–7.

The Deccan sultanates owed their origin to the withdrawal of the sultanate of Delhi from southern India and they were finally eliminated by the Great Mughals who had wiped out the sultanate of Delhi some time earlier. The role which these Deccan sultanates played in Indian history has been the subject of great debate. Early European historians, as well as later Hindu scholars, have highlighted the destructive role of these sultanates which were literally established on the ruins of flourishing Hindu king-doms. Muslim historians, by contrast, have drawn attention to the fact that these sultanates produced an admirable blend of Indian and Persian culture in art and architecture – indeed, Anastasy Nikitin's report praised Bijapur as the most magnificent city of India.

These sultanates certainly contributed to the further development of India's regional cultures. In this context we should also mention the sultanates of Bengal (1338–1576), Malwa (1401–1531), Gujarat (1403–1572/3), and Kashmir (1346–1568). Some of these sultanates made important contributions to the development of the regional languages. The sultans of Bijapur recognised Marathi as a language in which business could be transacted, a sultan of Bengal commissioned the poet Krittibas to translate the *Ramayana* into Bengali – a translation of great literary merit. Around 1500 the Muslim governor of Chittagong similarly commissioned his court poet, Kavindra Parameshvara, to translate the *Mahabharata* into Bengali. The sweeping conquest of India by Islamic rulers, epitomised by the far-flung military campaigns of the Delhi sultans, was thus in direct contrast to the regionalistic aspect of the above-mentioned ventures. The coexistence of Islamic rule with Hindu rule in this period added a further dimension to this regionalisation.

The mighty Hindu contemporaries of the sultanate of Delhi were the realm of the Gajapatis ('Lords of Elephants') of Orissa, and the empire of Vijayanagar ('City of Victory') in the south. The Gajapatis had controlled the east coast from the mouth of the Ganges to the mouth of the Godaveri from the thirteenth century onwards. In the fifteenth century they temporarily extended their sway down the coast, almost reaching as far as Tiruchirappalli to the south of Madras. From the fourteenth to the sixteenth centuries, the empire of Vijayanagar encompassed nearly all of southern India to the south of the Tungabhadra and Krishna rivers. The existence of these two Hindu states led to an uncontested preservation of Hindu institutions and customs in eastern and southern India quite in contrast to the areas of northern and western India, which had come under Muslim influence in the thirteenth century.

The Gajapatis of Orissa

The history of the late medieval regional kingdom of Orissa begins with King Anantavarman Chodaganga. He belonged to the Ganga dynasty of Kalinganagara and in *c.*1112 conquered the fertile Mahanadi delta of central Orissa from the Somavamsha king. Ten years later, following the death of the last great Pala king of Bengal, Rampala, Anantavarman extended his sway all the way up to present-day Calcutta in the north and to the mouth of the Godaveri in the south. At the end of his long life he built the famous Jagannath temple of Puri. At the beginning of the thirteenth century Anantavarman's successors clashed with the new Muslim rulers of Bengal; nevertheless, the Muslim could not make any inroads into Orissa. King

Anangabhima III (1216–39) proudly praised his Brahmin general, Vishnu, in an inscription:

> How are we to describe that heroism of Vishnu during his fight with the Muslim king, while all alone he shot dead many excellent soldiers? . . . [The display of heroism] became a grand feyst to the sleepless and unwinking eyes of the gods who were the interested lookers-on in the heaven above.[1]

King Narasimhavarman I (1239–64), the builder of the great sun temple at Konarak, was one of the few Hindu rulers of his time who did not manage simply to defend himself against the superior military forces of the Muslims, but who also launched an offensive against them. When in 1243 the Muslim governor of Bengal wanted to increase his autonomy and extend his sway after the death of Iltutmish, an army from Orissa attacked him in his capital, Lakhnaur, in central Bengal. The following year the Hindu forces scored another success in Bengal. Narasimhavarman's grandson was to record the event in an inscription commemorating his ancestor's deed: 'The Ganga herself blackened for a great extent by the flood of tears which washed away the collyrium from the eyes of the Yavanis [Muslim women] of Radha and Varendra [west and north Bengal] whose husbands have been killed by Narasimha's army.'[2]

Narasimhavarman's offensive policy probably warded off a Muslim attack on Orissa for more than a century. Only in 1361 did the sultan of Delhi, Firoz Shah, suddenly assault Orissa on his way back from Bengal, 'extirpating Rai Gajpat (Raja Gajapati), massacring the unbelievers, demolishing their temples, hunting elephants, and getting a glimpse of their enchanting country',[3] as it is reported in the contemporary chronicle *Tarikh-i-Firoz Shahi*. The sultan had rushed through northern Orissa where he had destroyed the Bhanja capital, Khiching, and he had then taken the Gajapati Bhanudeva by surprise at Cuttack. Bhanudeva fled but was reinstated on condition that he pay a regular tribute to the sultan. The *Tarikh-i-Firoz Shahi* then goes on to report: 'The victorious standards now set out for the destruction of the temple of Jagannath. This was the shrine of the polytheists of this land and a sanctuary of worship of the unbelievers of the Far East. It was the most famous of their temples.'

Firoz Shah's assault had no lasting consequences as far as Orissa's status as an independent Hindu kingdom was concerned. The payment of tribute to the sultan was soon stopped. But the Ganga dynasty of Orissa had lost its glamour in the conflict and visibly declined in subsequent years. Finally, at the death of the last king of that dynasty, Bhanudeva IV, the grandson of an officer (*nayaka*), Kapilendra, seized the throne and founded the Suryavamsha dynasty in 1435. Kapilendra had to fight for some years against the followers of the dynasty which he had replaced: he abolished the salt tax in order to gain popular support. In his inscriptions in various temples he threatened his adversaries with dire consequences and the confiscation of their property. After overcoming these initial difficulties, however, Kapilendra soon became the greatest Hindu ruler of his day, extending his realm all the way into Bengal in the north and, temporarily, to the mouth of the Kaveri in the south.

Kapilendra's successors could not defend such an enormous realm and Orissa soon lost most of the territories in the south to Vijayanagar and the Bahmani sultanate. Kapilendra's sons waged a war of succession from which Purushottama (1467–97) emerged victorious. He was able to recover at least all the territory down to the Krishna–Godaveri delta and Orissa enjoyed a period of peace and prosperity, along with a flourishing cultural life, in his long reign.

The third ruler of the Suryavamsha dynasty, Prataparudra, had to face three mighty foes at once. In the north, Hussain Shah (1493–1518) had founded a new dynasty in Bengal and had rapidly increased his power. In the south the greatest ruler of the Vijayanagar empire, Krishnadeva Raya, ascended the throne in 1509. Three years later the sultanate of Golconda emerged as an independent sultanate which was a much more immediate threat to Orissa than the more distant Bahmani sultanate had been. In addition to these external enemies, internal conflict troubled the court of the Gajapatis. The tributary Garhjat states in the mountainous hinterland and rebellious generals in the core of the realm destabilised the rule of the king. Finally, in 1568, the Afghan sultan of Bengal swooped down upon Orissa just as Firoz Shah had done two centuries earlier. In the wake of this attack the ferocious general, Kalapahar, marched towards Puri, desecrated the temple and with the help of a Hindu detected the idols which had been hidden, took them away and had them burned. This could have been the end of both Gajapati rule and of the Jagannath cult. But a few decades later a local princeling, Ramachandra, managed to restore the cult and to win the support of Akbar, who needed a loyal Hindu ally against the sultan of Golconda. The descendants of this Ramachandra still live on as rajas of Puri, spending their time in the shadow of Jagannath as his royal servants.

The close relationship of the Gajapatis with the cult of Jagannath is a peculiar feature of the history of Orissa. The idols worshipped in the great temple in Puri are crude wooden logs, they are renewed from time to time in a special ritual in which tribal priests still play an important role, thus indicating the tribal origin of this cult which was only later identified with Vishnu-Jagannath. The cult achieved historical significance with King Anantavarman Chodaganga, who was a Shaivite like all his ancestors, but who obviously fostered this cult in order to gain the support of the people of central Orissa, an area which he had just conquered. He was related to the Cholas (Chodaganga = Cholaganga) and emulated their example by building the great temple of Puri, which has exactly the same height as the royal temple of the Cholas at Thanjavur (Tanjore).

Subsequently, in 1230, King Anangabhima III announced that Jagannath was the overlord (*samraja*) of Orissa and that he was his son (*putra*) and general (*rauta*) governing the country on behalf of the god. Some of his successors even referred to the years of their reign not in their own name, but in the name of Jagannath. Kapilendra, a usurper, was in need of special legitimation and gave generous presents to the priest of Jagannath, who duly recorded in the temple chronicle that Jagannath himself had appointed Kapilendra as king of Orissa. Kapilendra called himself the first Servitor of Jagannath and equated any resistance to his royal orders with treason (*droha*) committed against Jagannath.

The longevity of Gajapati rule had other, more mundane, reasons. In the third phase, the evolution of an 'imperial' regional kingdom, the Ganga dynasty had managed to subject a fairly large and fertile territory to its direct control. About 250 miles of coastline and the fertile Mahanadi delta were practically free from potential rivals – at least, they do not appear in any inscription. In the pre-Gajapati period the term *Mandala* had referred to the territory of quasi-independent princelings who were known by the title 'Lord of the Mandala' (*mandaleshvara*). Under the imperial Gajapatis they were invariably replaced by an appointed governor (*pariksha*) which is a clear indication for a more centralised government.

There was also another new feature of administration under Ganga rule: the rise of military officers as local magnates. This in a way anticipated the later development in the Vijayanagar empire. An inscription from south Orissa of 1230 contains a long list of such military officers (*nayaka*), who seem also to have had some administrative functions in Ganjam and Kalinga. Kapilendra was the grandson of such a nayaka, as we have seen. The title nayaka was not unknown in earlier periods, but the sudden increase in the number and their importance in several parts of Orissa in the early thirteenth century, and even more so in the fourteenth century, seems to be a clear indication of the militarisation of Hindu states in the late Middle Ages. The nayakas also held fiefs, the inscription referred to above lists in detail the places to which the respective nayakas belong, an altogether novel feature at that time which shows some similarity with military prebendalism or even military feudalism. We may attribute this to the impact of the Delhi sultanate which had been founded only a few decades earlier. If this is correct, it would show that Hindu realms were able to respond very quickly to such new challenges.

The foundation of the Vijayanagar empire

While the development of the regional realm of Orissa was due to a continuous process of state formation which lasted for several centuries,

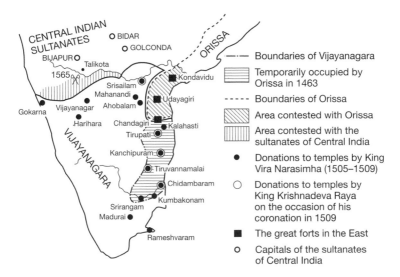

Map 4.2 Temple donations and ritual policy in Vijayanagara (1505–9)

the Vijayanagar empire was founded in 1346 as a direct response to the challenge posed by the sultanate of Delhi. The empire was founded by several brothers, Harihara and Bukka being the most important among them. Their dynasty was named after their father, Sangama.

There is a long and acrimonious debate about the antecedents of these brothers among Indian historians. According to some (mostly those from Tamil Nadu and Andhra Pradesh), the brothers fled from Warangal (Andhra Pradesh) after its capture by the Muslims; they then settled at Kampili, a small realm close to what was to become the city of Vijayanagar, where they were taken prisoner by the sultan's army in 1327. They were taken to Delhi and converted to Islam, whereupon the sultan sent them back to control Kampili on his behalf. Then they came under the influence of the Hindu monk Vidyaranya, who reconverted them to Hinduism. They soon headed the Hindu rebels against Muslim rule and founded a new realm with a capital at a strategic place south of the Tungabhadra river, where Harihara was crowned in 1336. It was probably also due to Vidyaranya's influence that the early rulers of Vijayanagar regarded themselves as the representatives of the god Virupaksha, to whom the main temple of Vijayanagar is dedicated. Later rulers even signed documents in the name of Virupaksha. After defeating the Hoysala king, whose power had been weakened by fighting both against Delhi and Madurai, in 1346 Harihara held a great celebration in the monastery of Sringeri, the seat of the Shankaracharyas, and thus also obtained the necessary ritual sanction.

This story is challenged by other historians, mostly from Karnataka, who claim that Harihara and Bukka were local warriors of Karnataka whom the Hoysala king Ballala III had posted at the northern border of his realm to defend it against Muslim attacks. They also maintain that Harihara ascended the throne only in 1346 – after the death of the last Hoysala king, Ballala IV.

Until recently the first and more dramatic of the two stories was generally accepted, even by historians outside India; the more plausible account of the local origin of the founders of Vijayanagar was rejected as mere wishful thinking on the part of Karnataka's regional historians. Recent research and the interpretation of inscriptions which were not known to earlier historians tend to support the theory that the founders of Vijayanagar were local princelings in the service of the Hoysala kings. Several inscriptions prove that the brothers were already dignitaries in the service of the Hoysala king a decade before their supposed flight to Kampili. An inscription of 1320 records that King Ballala III founded the town of Vijayavirupaksha Hoshapattana on the spot which was later to become Vijayanagar. After the death of Ballala IV, Ballala III's widow seems to have participated in the coronation of Harihara in 1346. In an inscription dated 1349 her name is mentioned before that of King Harihara, indicating that Harihara derived his legitimation from being a kind of devoted heir of the Hoysalas.

In the light of this new information we should also re-examine how the establishment of the Vijayanagar empire was influenced by the monk Vidyaranya and the monastery at Sringeri, which was supposedly founded by Shankara in the early ninth century. Vidyaranya, who has been described as the catalyst for the foundation of this empire, obviously emerged as an important actor on the Vijayanagar scene only several decades after the empire had been founded. But this does not detract from his great merit as a reformer of Hinduism. Vidyaranya, whose name was Madhava before his initiation as an ascetic (*samnyasin*), and his brother Sayana pursued a deliberate policy of a religious and cultural revival in southern India after the impact of the Islamic invasion. They wanted to highlight the importance of the old Vedic texts and Brahmanical codes. Sayana's commentary on the Rigveda is regarded as the most authoritative interpretation of this Veda, even today. His brother Vidyaranya emphasised Shankara's philosophy which provided a unified ideology of Hinduism. It may be that he invented the story of Shankara's great tour of India and of the establishment of the four great monasteries in the four corners of the country. If he did not invent it, he at least saw to it that it would gain universal currency and that the Shankaracharyas, as the abbots of these monasteries were called, would emerge as guardians of the Hindu faith. The fact that Vidyaranya's monastery at Sringeri was supposed to be one of Shankara's four original establishments, coupled with its position close to the old Hoysala capital, was certainly of great importance for the legitimation of the new rulers of Vijayanagar favoured by Vidyaranya's blessing.

Harihara I was succeeded by his younger brother, Bukka I, in 1357. Bukka initiated the rapid expansion of the empire. He defeated and killed King Rajanarayana Sambuvaraya, who had been reinstated as ruler of Tondaimandalam by Harihara when he had needed an ally in his fight against the sultan at Madurai. Bukka also fought against Muhammad Shah Bahmani in order to gain control over the Raichur Doab, the land between the rivers Tungabhadra and Krishna. In a peace treaty of 1365 this Doab was ceded to Bukka and the Krishna became the boundary between the two realms. Some revenue districts to the south of the Krishna were to be administered jointly. However, this Doab remained a battleground into future years. In 1370 Bukka won the war against the sultan of Madurai, whom he defeated and killed. This put an end to the history of this southernmost of all India's sultanates. When Bukka died in 1377, Vijayanagar was the largest regional realm of southern India ever to have existed: it had been established and consolidated within a few decades.

Harihara II (1377–1404) and Devaraya I (1406–24) augmented and preserved the power of the empire. They could defend the Doab against the Bahmani sultans, though this was achieved at the cost of many casualties. Harihara II also extended the influence of the empire to the northeast by fighting against the Reddi princes of Kondavidu (coastal Andhra) and the Velama dynasty of Warangal. In due course this drive to the northeast led to a clash with the Gajapatis of Orissa. A first encounter of Gajapati Bhanudeva IV with Devaraya I seems to have ended in an agreement for peaceful coexistence; under Devaraya II (1426–46), however, Vijayanagar waged several wars against Orissa and this struggle for supremacy continued for about a century. The two major Hindu realms thus undermined each other's resistance to Muslim rule and, as far as Orissa was concerned, the downfall of the Gajapati kingdom was certainly precipitated by this internecine struggle. Whenever the Gajapati was strong and the ruler of Vijayanagar weak – as in the case of Kapilendra and Malikarjuna (1446–64) – Vijayanagar's control of the east coast was challenged. Around 1450 Kapilendra conquered Rajahmundry and Kondavidu (coastal Andhra) and installed his son, Hamvira, as governor of this region. Hamvira conquered the east coast all the way down to Tiruchirappalli in the Kaveri valley in 1463. Kapilendra later withdrew his troops from there and after his death the Gajapatis lost control of coastal Andhra.

At the same time, however, the Sangama dynasty of Vijayanagar also declined. The last king, Virupaksha II (1464–85), was unable to prevent his too powerful subjects from indulging in a struggle for power. It was against this background that Narasimha, a prince of the Saluva clan and son of the commander of the fortress of Chandragiri in eastern Andhra, emerged as the saviour of the empire. At first he fought the various warlords on behalf of Virupaksha II but then he deposed him and usurped the throne. Narasimha died while his sons were still small and the regent whom he had appointed, Tuluva Narasa – a high nayaka officer of the realm – did not wish to relinquish his power. The Saluva princes were murdered and Narasa's son, Narasimha, usurped the throne. This epoch of the usurpers was a period of constant crisis for Vijayanagar. The empire survived only because its enemies were also in trouble: the Bahmani sultanate disintegrated and the power of the Gajapati was waning.

Vijayanagar's glory and doom

Krishnadeva Raya (1509–29), Narasa's younger son and the greatest ruler of the Tuluva dynasty, put an end to this crisis and once more restored Vijayanagar to its great glory. He proved to be both a great warrior and an astute politician. In the first year of his reign Muhammad Shah Bahmani pounced upon him with a mighty army of all the Deccan sultans. Krishnadeva won the battle and reinstated his wounded enemy, thus keeping the rivalry of the Deccan sultans alive. For this shrewd move he earned the strange title of 'Master of the Foundation of the Sultanate' (*yavana-rajya-sthapana-acarya*). Krishnadeva then tried to regain control over coastal Andhra and is supposed to have captured even Cuttack, the capital of Orissa. The vanquished Gajapati gave his daughter to Krishnadeva in marriage and thus retained coastal Andhra. This secured a permanent peace as long as Krishnadeva was alive; it could not, however, save Orissa from its northern enemies.

In addition to his great successes as warrior and administrator, Krishnadeva is also remembered as a great builder. Almost all the big temples of southern India (e.g. Chidambaram) have some temple towers which were erected in Krishnadeva's time. He was also a great patron of Telugu literature and composed poems himself. He was praised as 'Andhra Bhoja' because he could rival the great eleventh-century Paramara king, Bhoja, who had been one of the greatest patrons of literature in Indian history.

After Krishnadeva's death the internal struggles which had earlier engulfed Vijayanagar emerged once more. His successors – Achyutadeva Raya (1529–42) and Sadashiva (1543–5) – were weak rulers who lived under the shadow of Krishnadeva's ambitious son-in-law, Rama Raya, who acted as a regent but was the de facto ruler of the empire. The sultans of the Deccan, especially the sultan of Bijapur, were often involved in the internal intrigues of Vijayanagar. During Sadashiva's reign Vijayanagar also clashed for the first time with the Portuguese. They had destroyed Hindu temples and this led to encounters near Goa and St Thome (Madras), but a peace treaty was signed and Vijayanagar continued to enjoy the vital supply of war horses which the Portuguese imported into Goa from the Gulf region.

While the conflict with the Portuguese remained an episode, the struggle with the Deccan sultans became more and more virulent. For some time Vijayanagar could benefit from the mutual rivalry of the four successor

Figure 4.1 Virupaksha Temple at Vijayanagara, reconstructed by Krishnadevaraya in the early sixteenth century AD

(Courtesy of Dinodia.com)

states of the Bahmani sultanate. In the process of adopting the Muslim methods of warfare which had so greatly contributed to the rise of Vijayanagar, the Hindu rulers now also did not mind recruiting Muslim soldiers and letting Muslim officers rise to high positions in their army. This gave the sultans access to all the information they wanted about Vijayanagar though it might, by the same token, have helped Vijayanagar to keep in touch with the affairs at the courts of the sultans.

Finally Vijayanagar was surprised by an alliance of the sultans, who had realised that their own internecine warfare was to the benefit of Vijayanagar and had often been fostered by intrigues emanating from the Hindu court. The Muslim chronicler Ferishta reports that the sultans eventually united because of the destruction of mosques by the Vijayanagar army. Towards the end of 1564 the combined forces of the sultans rallied near the Vijayanagar fortress of Talikota on the banks of the Krishna. As leader of the Vijayanagar army Rama Raya must have realised what was at stake: he mounted a determined attack with all the forces at his disposal.

When battle was joined in January 1565, it seemed to be turning in favour of Vijayanagar – suddenly, however, two Muslim generals of Vijayanagar changed sides. Rama Raya was taken prisoner and immediately beheaded.

His brother Tirumala then fled with the whole army, including 1,500 elephants and the treasures of the realm, leaving the capital city to the wrath of the victorious Muslims. The victors destroyed Vijayanagar, thus taking revenge for Krishnadeva's devastation of the old Bahmani capital of Gulbarga in 1520. There are few comparable instances in history of such a sudden defeat and of such a wanton destruction of a large imperial capital: Vijayanagar was even more thoroughly sacked than was Delhi by Timur's army.

Tirumala and his descendants continued to rule for some time in the south, but this Aravidu dynasty – the last dynasty of the once-mighty empire – could not restore Vijayanagar to its former glory. In 1568, only three years after the downfall of Vijayanagar, the realm of the Gajapatis also succumbed to Muslim conquerors. These years mark the end of the great medieval Hindu kingdoms of India. With Akbar's accession to the throne of the Great Mughals in 1556 there started a new process of conquest which led to the extinction of all southern states in the course of the subsequent 150 years. In this way the Islamic state reached its zenith in India.

The Amaranayakas and military feudalism

In contrast to all earlier Hindu realms whose history we know only from inscriptions, Vijayanagar is very well documented, which permits us to get an insight into the daily life, the administrative structure and the social organisation of the late medieval Hindu state. There are Hindu chronicles, one example being the *Achyutarayabhyudaya*, which deals with the life of King Achyuta Raya, there are many Muslim chronicles, and there are the extensive reports of European travellers who started visiting Vijayanagar soon after the Portuguese conquest of Goa in 1510. Unlike Hindu authors, who took so much for granted, the Muslim chroniclers and the European travellers recorded many details.

The Europeans admired the impressive organisation of the empire and their reports show that this was a state run along the lines of 'military feudalism', in a rather efficient manner. Domingo Paes, a Portuguese who visited Vijayanagar in 1522 during the rule of mighty Krishnadeva, provides us with the following information:

> this king has continually a million fighting troops, in which are included 35,000 cavalry in armour, all these are in his pay, and he has these troops always together and ready to be dispatched to any quarter whenever such may be necessary. I saw, being in this city of Bisnaga (Vijayanagar), the king dispatch a force against a place, one of those which he has by the seacoast, and he sent fifty captains with 150,000 soldiers, among whom were many cavalry. He has many elephants, and when the king wishes to show the strength

of his power to any of his adversaries amongst the three kings bordering on his kingdom, they say that he puts into the field two million soldiers; in consequence of which he is the most feared king of any in these parts. . . .

Should any one ask what revenue this king possesses, and what his treasure is that enables him to pay so many troops, since he has so many and such great lords in his kingdom, who, the greater part of them, have themselves revenues, I answer thus: These captains whom he has over these troops of his are the nobles of his kingdom; they are lords and they hold the city, the towns and the villages of the kingdom; there are captains among them who have a revenue of a million and a million and a half pardaos, others two hundred, three hundred or five hundred thousand pardaos, and as each one has revenue so the king fixes for him the number of troops which he must maintain, in foot, in horse, and elephants. These troops are always ready for duty, whenever they may be called out and wherever they may have to go; and in this way he has this million of fighting men always ready. . . . Besides maintaining these troops, each captain has to make his annual payments to the king, and the king has his own salaried troops to whom he gives pay. He has eight hundred elephants attached to his person, and five hundred horses always in his stables, and for the expenses of these horses and elephants he has devoted the revenue that he receives from this city of Bisnaga.[4]

The linchpin of the imperial administration was obviously the nayaka, whom Paes calls 'captain'. We have seen that such nayakas were also of great importance in Orissa. As far as Orissa is concerned, we could only surmise that they held military fiefs because the names of the places to which they belonged were explicitly mentioned. The reports on Vijayanagar clearly tell us about revenue assignments (*amara*) which were held by these nayakas and of their obligation to maintain a certain number of troops in keeping with such assignments. This was exactly the system of the Delhi sultanate, where such assignments were called *iqta*; the same system was subsequently adopted by the Mughals, who provided for a hierarchy of *mansabdars* to whom revenue assignments (*jagir*) were given. In earlier Hindu kingdoms such dignitaries were often local men, but the *amaranayakas* of the Vijayanagar empire were imposed on the respective locality from above; under the later dynasties they were often Telugu warriors. They had not only military duties, but also administrative and judicial ones and in times of weakening central control they could convert their assignments into patrimonial holdings or even emerge as warlords.

Many historians agree that this system may be termed one of 'military feudalism'. Even those Indian historians who reject the applicability of the

European concept of feudalism to other periods of Indian history have seen in the amaranayaka system of Vijayanagar a close parallel to such a social structure. In more recent years the American historian Burton Stein has vehemently denied that this system could be called a feudal one, because important elements – such as homage and vassalage – are missing in the Indian case and there is even no proof of any kind of tributary relationship either. Indeed, no indigenous documentary evidence has been found for any transfer of tribute from the nayakas to the king. The Portuguese reports, so Burton Stein argues, should be discounted in this respect, because their use of the term 'feudal' must be understood in the context of their own experience and their desire to explain Indian affairs to their European readers in words which were familiar to them. According to Stein, the strength of the Vijayanagar empire consisted in the ability of its rulers to turn local dignitaries into imperial officers and to impose on many districts Telugu nayakas from above. The military effectiveness of the empire was based on a large army, the use of new firearms and the establishment of swift cavalry units in which Vijayanagar was greatly helped by Muslim and European mercenaries and the trade with the Portuguese.

The rulers of Vijayanagar based their empire not only on brute force, they also pursued a religious policy quite akin to that of the Gajapatis of Orissa. They endowed various temples, cultivated the heads of religious communities, gave presents to priests and enlisted their moral support for the struggle against Muslim rulers as well as against Hindu rebels. An inscription of Krishnadeva Raya provides a good insight into this kind of policy: it lists the temples which he endowed at the time of his accession as well as those which his father had endowed before him. If we look at Map 4.2 we see that all the fourteen temples listed there are located either in the northern border region, or in regions which had only recently been conquered (e.g. Srisailam), or in those regions in the southeast between Tirupati and Rameshvaram which had been invaded by the troops of the Gajapati and had since been troubled by intrigues and rebellions. Such endowments could not directly contribute to the military strength of the empire, but they did enhance the loyalty of the Brahmins and of the people in areas where the rulers of Vijayanagar had only a precarious hold.

There was another aspect of this policy of utilising religious prestige and loyalties for the strengthening of the imperial system: the rulers appointed many Telugu Brahmins from their own homelands as commanders of fortresses (*durga dandanayaka*) in all parts of the empire. The traditional symbiotic relationship between Hindu rajas and Brahmins became an additional element of the loyalty which bound an officer to his king. The fortresses commanded by Brahmins were veritable pillars of the realm. The policy of ritual sovereignty which was so important for the consolidation of Hindu kingdoms was clearly demonstrated in this way. As we have seen, the late medieval Hindu realms of Orissa and Vijayanagar were trying to meet the Muslim challenge by a militarisation of their whole structure and by a stronger emphasis on the religious legitimation of the ruler as a representative of god. The Brahmin-commanded forts symbolised this process in a very striking manner indeed.

5

THE RISE AND FALL OF THE MUGHAL EMPIRE

THE GREAT MUGHALS AND THEIR ADVERSARIES

A new age begins with the unification of India under the Great Mughals. The achievements of this dynasty, which produced a rare sequence of competent rulers, were due to a particular constellation of historical circumstances. These conditions are exemplified by the striking career of Baber, who conquered India for the Mughals. Baber had the great gift of a quick presence of mind. His fate forced him to make incessant use of this gift. The Uzbeks who swept down from central Asia to Samarkand deprived him of his ancestral kingdom. With Persian support he could briefly reclaim his patrimony. The Persian connection remained of importance to him and his successors. Coming from a borderland wedged in between the Persian empire and the horsemen of the north, he was equally impressed with Persian culture and the martial spirit of his northern adversaries. He wrote Persian poems and from the Uzbeks he learned military strategy and tactics which, later, were to help him conquer India. The rising power of the Uzbeks compelled him to go east. He left his country and conquered Afghanistan; from there he made several forays into India before he finally embarked on his great campaign, which gave rise to the Mughal empire.

His success in India was chiefly determined by his use of firearms and artillery, which the Turks had brought to Asia from the west. Baber was a contemporary of the Ottoman sultan Selim I and of the Safavid ruler of Persia, Shah Ismail. They laid the foundations for the three major gunpowder empires of Asia. The speed of the proliferation of the new strategy based on a mobile field artillery was amazing. It guaranteed instant superiority on the battlefield as Selim demonstrated when conquering Syria and Egypt in 1517. Baber's victory in India followed nine years later. Baber's successors jealously guarded the new technology to which they owed their success and did not even share it with their faithful allies, the Rajputs, who mastered it only much later.

It was Baber's unique contribution that he knew how to combine the deployment of these new weapons with the strategy of cavalry warfare,

196

which he had learned from the Uzbeks. This achievement is the more surprising as these firearms were entirely new to him. He himself was trained as an archer and knew how to use his bow and arrows very well. Nevertheless, he managed not only to grasp the strategic function of the new weapons, but also to plan battles so as to integrate the use of artillery and cavalry. He did this so perfectly that he surpassed many generals of later periods who, because they were men on horseback unable to discern the proper use of the mobile guns, often lost touch with the artillery. When Baber besieged the fortress Bajaur on the northwestern border of India in 1519, the appearance of the innovative muskets amused the defenders of the fortress, as Baber reports in his memoirs. They soon ceased to be amused when Baber's marksmen shot down some of their number, and dared not show their faces again.

Seven years later, on the traditional Indian battlefield near Panipat, Baber encountered the great army of the sultan of Delhi, Ibrahim Lodi. The latter's forces were ten times more numerous than Baber's, who, however, had carefully deployed his artillery on the eve of the battle. The light field artillery was posted behind small ramparts and the guns were tied together with leather thongs so that the cavalry of the enemy could not make a quick dash at them. Marksmen with muskets were also at hand. The army of the sultan – with its thousands of elephants, horsemen and footmen – came to a halt in front of the artillery while Baber's archers on horseback bypassed the enemy and then, in the manner of the Uzbeks, attacked the unwieldy army from the rear. Caught between gunfire and showers of arrows the sultan's huge forces were defeated within a few hours. Lodi and most of his men died on the battlefield.

Thereafter, Baber repeated this performance in a battle against the leader of the Rajputs, Rana Sangha of Mewar. In this confrontation Baber gave his artillery an even more frightening appearance by placing wooden dummy guns between the real ones. In addition, he managed to move the whole artillery, dummies and all, further ahead while the battle was raging.

Such victories on the battlefield were followed by successful sieges of the fortresses in which Baber's stricken enemies took refuge. He invested as much as he could in his miraculous artillery. When he moved further to the east in order to combine his forces with those of the governor of Bengal against Afghan rebels in Bihar, he put his guns on barges and shipped them down the Ganga. The treasures of the sultan of Delhi, seized by Baber, were quickly spent on this costly kind of warfare, and the first Great Mughal was soon obliged to levy special taxes.

Sticking to his guns: the secret of Baber's success

Baber's mobile artillery was a striking innovation for India. Big guns used in the siege of fortresses had been known in India for some time. The

Figure 5.1 Baber hunting a rhino. Babur nama, late sixteenth century AD
(Courtesy of the Rietberg Museum)

Mongols had introduced them during their raids, and the sultans of Delhi had, accordingly, been forced to increase their fortifications. But light field artillery and muskets were new to India, and they gave Baber a decisive advantage over his adversaries.

Baber was also sticking to his guns in another sense of the term: his army was composed of more or less autonomous units led by generals whom Baber could impress with his strategic genius, but not necessarily with his ambitious long-term plans. These generals and their troops wanted to go home with their loot; Baber, on the other hand, was determined to claim India as his patrimony, as the country had once been conquered by his ancestor Timur. From the very beginning he treated Indians as his subjects and not as his prey, and he severely punished marauders among his own soldiers. When Timur had come to India, however, he had returned after a short victorious campaign; Baber's generals expected him to do likewise. Baber, though, had made up his mind to stay on. He treated his generals in a diplomatic way, consulted them before every battle, and parted amicably with those who wanted to leave. Thus, he achieved what he could not have done by simply giving orders: many generals decided to stay with him.

Baber's son Humayun, whom he loved very much, had participated in the battle of Panipat as a young man. Later Baber had sent him to Afghanistan to hold the fort there. As luck would have it, Humayun returned to Delhi when his father was seriously ill, but then he himself became sick. Baber prayed to God that he should take his life and save Humayun's; God, it seems, responded and Humayun succeeded to the throne. His succession was by no means a foregone conclusion: according to Mughal custom all royal princes were equally entitled to inherit power, which led to many rivalries in later years when Mughal princes fought each other until the most competent, the most ruthless, or simply the luckiest ascended the throne.

When Humayun succeeded Baber it was due to his good luck, for a powerful minister had sponsored another prince and Humayun had returned just in time to stake his claim as his father's favourite son. This luck soon deserted him, however. After some daring campaigns of conquest, Humayun was deprived of his empire by the Afghan Sher Shah and, like Baber in the wake of his defeat by the Uzbeks, Humayun travelled abroad as a landless fugitive. On one of these travels Humayun's son, Akbar, was born in Sind in 1542. Humayun left him with his brother and rival in Afghanistan and went on to Persia, where he lived in exile for several years. After Sher Shah's death he reconquered India in 1555 with Persian support. But only a year later he died after falling down the steps of his library at Purana Qila in Delhi.

In the very short period of his reign Humayun had made an interesting attempt to systematise the administration that he had taken over as a going concern from Sher Shah, himself a very competent administrator. Humayun used the four elements as categories of classification: fire for the army; water for the department of irrigation; earth for agriculture and revenue; and air for religion and science. This truly elementary division did not last long. Akbar soon improved upon it. But the style of a systematic division of functions was, thus, set by Humayun.

Akbar's expansion and reform of the empire

Akbar was only 13 years old when his father died. During the years of Humayun's exile in Persia, Akbar had grown up among tough warriors in Afghanistan and he had never learned to read or write. He remained illiterate throughout his life, in contrast with his highly educated father and grandfather; nevertheless, he surpassed both in his great intellectual capacity. His sharp memory helped him to store an enormous amount of information which he could combine with whatever caught his attention. The fact that he could not read prevented him from absorbing conventional wisdom and made him eager to discuss new ideas with all kinds of people who came to his court. In this way he merged theory and practice in an unusual manner.

In the first year of his reign he was faced with a challenge by a Hindu usurper, Hemu, who called himself Vikramaditya and almost succeeded in putting an end to Mughal rule. Hemu had been prime minister under one of Sher Shah's successors and had won many battles for his master. He was, thus, a dangerous challenger for young Akbar whose accession to the throne he wanted to prevent. At the decisive battle Hemu fell when an arrow hit him and Akbar was urged by his general to cut off Hemu's head. In later years he became a great conqueror and wise ruler. He married the daughter of the Rajput maharaja of Amber (Jaipur) and soon vanquished the last Rajput prince who still dared to resist him. Indeed, he practically emerged as the leader of the Rajputs, many of whom served him faithfully. He did not force his religion on them and they remained Hindus throughout his reign. Akbar also abolished the *jizya* – the poll tax which Islamic rulers imposed on all non-Islamic subjects. This made him even more popular with the Hindus of India.

After conquering Gujarat in 1574 and Bengal two years later, Akbar found himself in command of a huge empire. He was just 34. The dream of all Great Mughals – the recovery of Samarkand and the restoration of Mughal rule in the homeland whence the Uzbeks had ousted Baber – was also in Akbar's mind. But his Uzbek counterpart, Abdullah, was of equal stature, and Akbar was prudent enough not to risk his Indian empire for a doubtful adventure in central Asia. Instead, he became a master at playing off the Uzbeks against the Persians, and vice versa. These two constantly fought each other and each tried to enlist Akbar's support. Abdullah offered Akbar a share of Persia if he would join him in a campaign against that

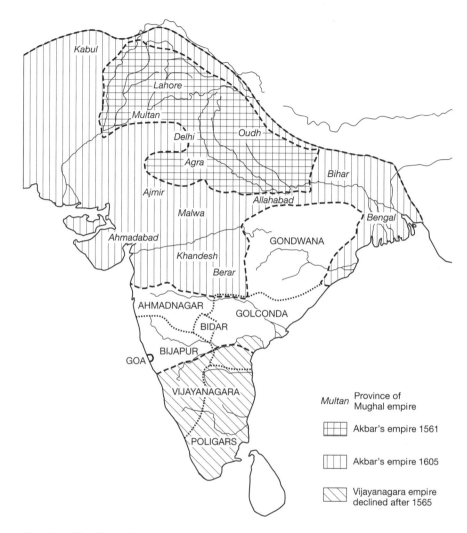

Map 5.1 The Mughal empire

country; the shah of Persia, for his part, tried to entice Akbar into a joint campaign against the Uzbeks, promising the return of Samarkand as a prize of victory.

Although Akbar kept in touch with both of them, he did not get involved in any rash action and so managed to maintain the balance of power in the whole region. In this way he also snatched back from the Persians Kandahar, a territory he had been forced to give up in the early years of his reign. Thus, the Helmand river became the western border of his empire.

The Persians, however, still considered the Indus to be the eastern border of their empire and, therefore, always tried to recover Kandahar, which was the crucial key to this area. As long as Akbar lived they did not succeed, because Akbar valued a strong position in Baluchistan and Afghanistan more than any excursion to the northwest. By indulging in the latter policy his successors lost Kandahar once more.

Akbar's prudent foreign policy enabled him to devote most of his energy in the best years of his life to the internal consolidation of his vast empire which extended from the Helmand river in the west, to Orissa in the east; from Kashmir in the north, to Gujarat in the south. He laid the material and moral foundations of the Mughal empire so solidly that his successors could benefit from his achievements for a long time. This, of course, made them take such foundations for granted and they finally destroyed, by their rash actions, the very bases on which their power rested.

In many ways Akbar played a role similar to that of his older contemporary the Ottoman sultan, Suleiman Kanuni (the lawgiver). He also conceived of himself as giving laws rather than only following Islamic law. He emphasised the dynastic charisma of the Great Mughals and his own spiritual leadership. In this way he contributed to the cohesion of his state, which can be compared to the absolutist monarchies emerging in Europe. Attempts have been made to describe his state as a patrimonial–bureaucratic one. But in its structure it was far more complex than the patrimonial states, which are conceived of as extensions of the ruler's household. On the other hand, the term 'bureaucratic' could be misleading, because the Great Mughals did not rely on a civil bureaucracy but on a systematically organised military elite whose structure will be discussed later. In many ways, this elite continued the tradition of military feudalism as described earlier, but with the difference that the imperial officers were part of a hierarchy of service and could be transferred in keeping with the duties assigned to them. 'Bureaucrats' in the usual sense of the term were the 'civil servants' working for the imperial officers who prided themselves on wielding the sword rather than the pen. Most of these 'civil servants' were Hindus who relied on the pen rather than on the sword under Mughal rule.

Like all great land powers of Asia, the Mughal empire was an agrarian state which essentially depended on the land revenue. The intensity of central rule in such a state directly depended on the accurate assessment of this revenue and on its cash transfer to the centre. For this a stable currency was a necessary prerequisite. Sher Shah had put the revenue administration on a solid footing in this respect. He had introduced an assessment based on an accurate measurement (*zabt*) of the fields; he had put a good silver currency in circulation; and he had adjusted the revenue collection to the annual price level. The annual decision on the revenue demand based on this price information was of such importance that only the ruler himself could arrive at it. Akbar was faced with this annual decision, even if he were on a distant battlefield and could hardly devote much thought to it. With the expansion of the empire it became almost impossible to take the regional variations in the price level into consideration. Furthermore, large areas had been granted to military officers and administrators as fief (*jagir*). These officers had to recover their own salary as well as the expenses for their troops and military establishment from the income derived from these fiefs. Unless they had complaints about the inadequacy of their fiefs these officers had no motive to inform the central government about the actual yield of the assigned revenue.

Akbar solved all these problems with one fundamental reform of the revenue system. To begin with he cancelled all fiefs and paid the salaries and expenses of the officers from the central treasury. He then had all land measured and instructed the district revenue officers to compile all data on crops, prices and revenue collections for a period of ten years. After this period was over he fixed an average demand based on the data collected during one decade. In this way he took account of regional differences and also could do without the rather arbitrary annual decision on the rate of revenue. Moreover, when granting fiefs again he knew exactly the value of each fief. He also adopted a system of hierarchical classification (*mansab*) of all military and civil officers. This classification took account of the salary scale (*zat*) as well as of the size of the cavalry contingents (*sawar*) which the officer had to maintain in keeping with his rank. This system was flexible enough to take into account various combinations – e.g. high salary, but only a small or no cavalry contingent at all in the case of civil officers at the imperial court – and it also enabled the ruler to match the promotion to a higher office with the size of the fief. This system provided a high degree of rationality for the prevailing practice of moving officers frequently from one fief to another in order to prevent them from entrenching themselves somewhere. The system worked to a large extent automatically: detailed adjustments could be left to the administrators at various levels and the Great Mughal would interfere only in case of major appointments and transfers.

Akbar appointed each holder of a *mansab* (*mansabdar*) personally, because these officers were co-sharers of his realm. They served as sub-contractors who controlled the military labour market for him. There were about four million troopers of various kinds available in India at that time. It was important to enlist most of them for the Mughal army so that they could not offer their services to challengers of the empire. The *mansabdar* was responsible for those whom he had enlisted, e.g. 7,000 horsemen in the case of the highest rank (*mansab*) or a few hundred in the lower ranks. There were almost 400,000 horsemen in Mughal service at the end of Akbar's reign. The amount required for the maintenance of one horseman was 240 rupees per year. If one multiplies this by the number of horsemen one arrives at the staggering figure of 960 million rupees, and this did not include the expenditure on elephants and artillery. The Mughal war machine was obviously a heavy burden for the Indian peasantry.

The Mughal princes were among those who held the highest positions in the *mansab*-system, but the hierarchy of *mansabdars* did not necessarily reflect military rank of the kind prevailing in a modern army. A governor of a province and a commander of a fortress in that province may well hold the same rank and when a war had to be waged, it was up to the Great Mughal to decide who would lead the army. But Akbar's design of ranks, honours and privileges certainly helped to convert earlier leaders of war-bands into courtiers who would follow imperial etiquette. The system of military slavery, which was so prominent under other Muslim rulers was not followed by the Mughals. With an abundant supply of soldiers who offered their services to them, the Mughals could dispense with this sort of slavery. The wealth of the Mughal court attracted warriors of various ethnic groups from central and western Asia who were eager to obtain a *mansab*.

The artillery which was of special importance to the Mughals was never entrusted to *mansabdars*, it always remained under direct imperial control. Akbar took a personal interest in the technical improvement of guns and muskets. Jesuits who were invited to his court reported that after discussing religious questions with them he showed even more interest in the technology of firearms and was keen to get as much information from them as they could provide. He is credited with designing gun carriages which made his field artillery more mobile and introducing new muskets which had a longer range and could be aimed with more precision than European ones at that time. Indian musketeers were trained as marksmen and not as infantrists who aimed their volleys in the general direction of the enemy and relied on their collective fire-power rather than on individual marksmanship.

There have been debates on the relative importance of artillery and cavalry in Mughal warfare. Had the Mughals really established a 'gunpowder empire' or did they head a cavalry state just as their predecessors had done? In one respect they were certainly continuing the traditions of the cavalry state and making it even more effective by means of the *mansab*-system, on the other hand they based their central power on the control of the field artillery which always accompanied the Mughal armies to the remotest battlefields and was also on display in the camp of the Great Mughal, providing evidence of the superior fire-power of the emperor. The camp was an important institution of the empire. The Great Mughal spent, on average, one-third of his time outside his capital and moved his camp frequently. In this way he showed his power to friends and foes alike and his guns were the most obvious symbol of that power. These guns were very expensive and for that reason they could not easily proliferate. The art of making cheap cast-iron guns was not yet known in India at that time.

The Mughal guns were made of bronze or brass with a very precise bore which permitted them to hit their target very well. Used against horses and elephants on many battefields they were of great value to the Mughal armies. Of course, Baber's famous stratagem with which he defeated Ibrahim Lodi could not be repeated in later years as everybody knew about it and avoided being trapped in this way. But the Mughals constantly found new ways of deploying their guns, such as putting large numbers of them on river boats and overwhelming their enemies in Bengal in this way.

But, in spite of all this ingenuity, the Mughal empire was not invulnerable in the long run. In particular, the *mansab*-system, so skilfully calibrated by Akbar, was corrupted by his successors and thus contributed to the fall of the empire.

The great advantage of the system – its largely automatic operation – proved to be a most dangerous disadvantage as time went by. The stream of silver which poured from central America via Europe into India changed the price level, and the conquest of new territories and the absorption of their elites into the imperial ranking system led to an undue expansion of this system at the very top of the hierarchy – the material resources, however, did not expand in the same way. Nevertheless, the Mughals continued with Akbar's system as if nothing had happened. At the most, some arbitrary corrections were made from time to time, such as cutting down the size of the military contingent to be maintained by the officers in order to cope with inflation. Such arbitrary corrections would lead to either a weakening of military strength or an erosion of the agrarian base or both. In Akbar's day, however, the system worked well and showed its best results. His treasury was filled with a regular revenue income and the burden on the taxpayer was tolerable.

The Great Mughal's predominant reliance on the land revenue did not preclude an interest in trade. The revenue had to be collected in cash in order to support a great empire. This implied the marketing of produce, the monetisation of the economy and the smooth functioning of a trading network. Maritime trade was more or less taken for granted. It followed its own course and supplied the Mughal economy with a flow of precious metals. But overland trade was at least as important in this respect. Akbar built a string of caravanserais to link the trade of his empire with that of Persia and other countries. He was obviously well aware of the fact that a vibrant trade supported his power.

Akbar's contribution to the moral consolidation of the empire was also admirable, but there was some criticism, too. He combined a policy of religious toleration with a cult of the ruler which was aimed at institutionalising the Mughal charisma. His ideal was that of the just ruler for which he found parallels in the Muslim concept of the *mahdi* as well as in the Hindu idea of the legendary king, Rama. Mirroring the doctrine of royal absolutism in the West, Akbar tried to find legitimation by divine grace. But, unlike the

Hindu kings, he did not want to be only an upholder of the eternal law: he wanted to be a lawgiver in his own right. Akbar's ideas were criticised by his more orthodox Muslim contemporaries, whereas his Hindu subjects could understand these notions much better. The ritual sovereignty of the Indian king depended on his identification with a god, which is in keeping with the Hindu ideas of the immanence and transcendence of the divine spirit. The dualism of Muslim thought which juxtaposes the omnipotence of Allah with the complete subjection (Islam) of man under the divine will is incompatible with this approach. Only the mysticism of the Sufis was akin to Akbar's new 'Belief in God' (*Din-i-Illahi*). The promulgation of this new belief and Akbar's emphasis on the greeting Allahu Akbar ('God is great') – which could also be understood as an allusion to his name – coupled with the decree by which Akbar reserved to himself the final decision in matters of faith, were all bound to provoke the resistance of the orthodox. In this way he wanted to establish a synthesis of all religious ideas that appealed to him and prevent sectarian strife as a supreme umpire. He openly opposed the orthodox Islamic scholars (*ulama*) whom he castigated for their medieval outlook. Akbar's bold attempt at creating a new,

Figure 5.2 Mausoleum of Itimad-ud-Daulah, father-in-law and prime minister of Jahangir

(Courtesy of Dinodia.com)

tolerant religion died with him; but the idea of a divine grace which was bestowed on the Mughal dynasty and constituted its charisma remained alive. Even centuries later, some reflection of Akbar's charismatic splendour still cast a halo on his humblest descendant.

Akbar's last years were embittered by the rebellion of his son Salim, the later Great Mughal Jahangir. The fact that there was no clear line of succession and that Akbar's empire was such that its division would have amounted to a sacrilege made his sons struggle for the throne even before the ruler had died. Paradoxically, this dynastic Darwinism did not upset the Mughal system so much as stabilise it. Nobody came to power merely as a result of his being in the line of succession. The internecine struggles for the throne were fatal for the princes, but not for their followers – the victor would always be keen to reconcile the supporters of the vanquished in order to stabilise his own rule. In this way the transition from Akbar to Jahangir took place without any uprooting of the imperial elite. But a new element was added to the system under Jahangir: his beautiful and ambitious wife, Nur Jahan, came from Persia, and introduced Persian culture and a Persian entourage at the Mughal court. Her father became the chief minister of the empire.

Ever since the days of Baber, the Great Mughals had had a special affinity with Persian culture. Its role in India could be compared with that of French culture in Europe at that time. The Islamic states of the Deccan, which even shared the Shia denomination with the Persians, were also deeply influenced by that culture. The shah of Persia, Shah Abbas, made good use of this: flattering Jahangir with many friendly messages, he took sides with the sultans of the Deccan, and, thinking above all of his own interest, plotted to recapture Kandahar which Akbar had gained and preserved. Shah Abbas waited for a suitable moment, which came when Jahangir's son Shah Jahan rebelled against his father just as Jahangir had rebelled against Akbar. Shah Jahan was the head of the Mughal army even during his father's lifetime. Jahangir had bestowed the honorific name Shah Jahan ('Ruler of the World') on him after he had conquered the sultanate of Ahmadnagar on the Deccan. Thus honoured, he soon strove to oust his father but was defeated several times despite his superiority as a warrior. Shah Jahan was forced to depend on the support of the sultan of Golconda and of Shah Abbas, to whom he surrendered Kandahar – probably in order to have a free hand in his struggle for the Mughal throne.

When Shah Jahan ascended the throne in 1627 India was once more ruled by a truly Great Mughal who matched Baber and Akbar both in military valour and in cultural ambition. He was the greatest builder of the empire in every sense of the word. He extended the sway of Mughal rule in the south and he sponsored some of the most beautiful buildings of the Mughal period: the Red Fort (Delhi) and, in Agra, the Taj Mahal, tomb of his wife Mumtaz. Shah Jahan's style was a wonderful blend of Persian and Indian culture; just like the architecture of the imperial Guptas in medieval times, it set the standard for all Indian princes in the subsequent period.

But Shah Jahan was not satisfied with setting the style for India, he also wanted the old Mughal dream to come true: the recovery of Samarkand. A clever diplomat as well as a great warrior, he was able to deprive the Persians once more of Kandahar and yet retain them as his allies who covered his flank when he embarked on the great northwestern campaign against the Uzbeks, their common enemy. Shah Jahan's son Prince Aurangzeb conquered the distant city of Balkh during this campaign, but was then forced to retreat and found himself unable to recapture Kandahar from the Persians, who had snatched it away in the meantime when they saw that the Mughals had not succeeded in their great endeavour. Kandahar was lost forever and Samarkand was not recovered.

This remained a good lesson for Aurangzeb, who turned his attention to the south and gave up all vain ambitions to go to the north once he ascended the throne. According to established precedent he rebelled against his father. He imprisoned him and set out to give a new orientation to the policy of conquest. He had been viceroy of the Deccan before embarking on the futile northwestern campaign. Once he had seized power, he tried to emulate Muhammad Tughluq in uniting north and south India under his rule.

Aurangzeb and Shivaji: the struggle for the south

Aurangzeb stands in striking contrast to Akbar whose empire he extended to its farthest limits, but which he also destroyed in the process. In the five decades of Aurangzeb's reign (1658–1707) the Mughal empire expanded so much that it could hardly be ruled any longer. He conquered the sultanates of the Deccan, the successor states of the large realm of the Bahmani sultans. Despite constant fighting among themselves these states had, nonetheless, shown enough solidarity to be able to defeat the army of Vijayanagar in the decisive battle of Talikota in 1565. One century later they were no longer able to defend themselves against Aurangzeb.

After these southern conquests Aurangzeb tried to integrate the ruling class of these states into his imperial elite. A comparison of the highest ranks (*mansab*) of this latter elite during the first two decades of Aurangzeb's reign with those of the last three decades shows a decisive structural change. In the first period there were 191 officers holding ranks from 2,000 to 7,000; only 32 of them were from the Deccan and 110 belonged to families which had been in imperial service in earlier genera- tions. In the second period the number of these officers of the highest rank increased to 270; 95 of them belonged to the Deccan and only 129 came from families which had been in service in earlier times. The structural change appears even more striking if we look only at the highest officers with a rank of 7,000. There were only 6 of them in the first period, 1 of

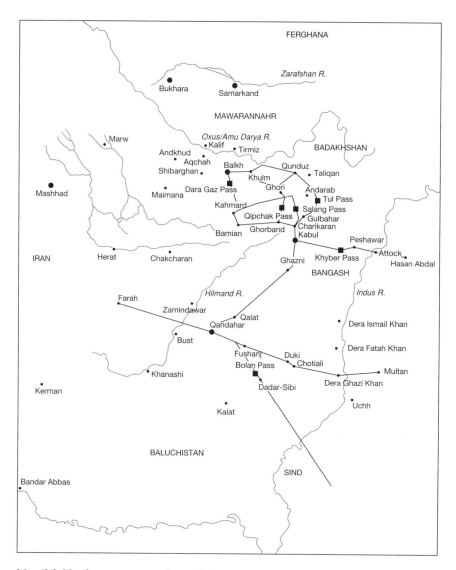

Map 5.2 Northwestern campaigns of the Great Mughals, 1645–8
(Courtesy of Jos Gommans)

them belonging to the Deccan; in the second period there were 14, of whom 9 belonged to the Deccan. In his eagerness to please the elite of the Deccan, Aurangzeb had constructed a rather top-heavy system there. In the north, the ratio of ranks of 2,000 and above to those of 5,000 and above was 8:1; in the Deccan it was 3:1. This was a complete perversion of the system.

Moreover, the financial base of this top-heavy structure was unsound. The newly conquered areas of the Deccan yielded proportionately much less revenue than the fertile plains of the north. Therefore, the expansion of the elite was not accompanied by an increase in resources.

In this way the measures adopted in the south had repercussions also in the north. The large distances made the governance of the overexpanded empire more and more difficult. Therefore, Aurangzeb once again emulated Muhammad Tughluq: he shifted his capital to Aurangabad in the northern Deccan, just a few miles away from Tughluq's Daulatabad. He was confident that his authority would not be challenged in the north and remained in the south in order to control his most formidable adversaries, the Marathas.

At the time when Aurangzeb turned his attention to the south the Marathas had found a leader who was comparable to Baber in terms of courage and presence of mind: Shivaji. The swift horseman and archer Baber would have been a better match for Shivaji than Aurangzeb with his huge, cumbersome army. Since the days of Baber the Mughal army had greatly changed its character. It consisted of thousands of elephants, awe-inspiring numbers of guns, large contingents of cavalry, and a huge crowd of hangers-on. Logistics were a great problem for such an army, whose supply lines could easily be cut by means of guerrilla warfare and surprise attacks of light cavalry units. Shivaji was a past master in these guerrilla tactics and swift cavalry warfare; he had also built a series of fortified strongholds on the table mountains of the western Deccan whose steep slopes were ideally suited for this purpose. Ensconced in these strongholds he could make his forays and escape with impunity. Even when he sacked Surat, the main port of the Mughal empire, he could thus still get away with rich spoils.

Shivaji's father, Shahji Bhonsle, had served many masters as a military officer. He began his career in the service of the sultan of Ahmadnagar, served the Mughals for some time, returned to Ahmadnagar and even ended up in the service of Bijapur. He held a fief at Pune for most of this time, and it was here that Shivaji grew up. Pune was halfway between Ahmadnagar (which had been captured by Shah Jahan) and Bijapur (which was captured by Aurangzeb only after Shivaji's death). The forces of the enemies neutralised each other in this border zone and this is why Shivaji could establish his own base here and challenge the Great Mughal and the sultan.

Aurangzeb took note of Shivaji only after the sacking of Surat in 1664, and sent a large army to subdue him. Faced with the superpower Shivaji had to accept Aurangzeb's conditions. He handed over several of his mountain fortresses and paid Aurangzeb his respects at his court, which was then still in Delhi. Aurangzeb granted him a low rank in the imperial hierarchy (*mansab* of 500) and hoped to have bought him over in this way. But Shivaji escaped from Delhi hidden in a basket; back in Pune, he consolidated his hold on the countryside.

For the time being he had to avoid forays and so, in their place, he introduced a tough land revenue system. The peasants had to deliver half their produce to government storehouses and, when sold, this produce gave a handsome income to the government. But the peasants also got rural credit from the government in order to enhance their production, which would improve their capacity to contribute more revenue. With a good resource base of this kind Shivaji once more expanded his martial pursuits and in 1674 he performed a great coronation ceremony with all the ritual befitting a Hindu king. He consciously emphasised the religious aspect of his military ventures and claimed to fight for the Hindus against Muslim rule.

Aurangzeb, who had given up the tolerant policy of his predecessors and had reintroduced the hated *jizya* (poll tax) for Hindus, exacerbated this religious confrontation. Actually, Aurangzeb did not stop cooperating politically with Hindu princes and he did not spread his faith with his sword. Shivaji on the other hand, did not mind having a Muslim ally when the sultan of Golconda supported his campaign in southern India, where Shivaji's father had held a fief in Tanjore which he claimed as his heritage. But, in general, Aurangzeb and Shivaji were perceived as protagonists of Islam and Hinduism respectively and their confrontation helped to highlight this fact. When Shivaji died in 1680 his ambitions remained unfulfilled: had he lived, he would surely have extended his sway at the expense of Golconda and Bijapur. In the end, it was left to Aurangzeb to conquer these sultanates.

In the year of Shivaji's death Aurangzeb was challenged by his son Akbar. Instead of fighting rebellious Rajputs as Aurangzeb had told him to do, Akbar had fled south and had joined hands with Shivaji's son and heir, Sambhaji. Akbar wanted to depose Aurangzeb with the help of Rajputs and Marathas and restore the tolerant policy of his great namesake. But this proved to be a futile dream. Aurangzeb defeated Akbar and tortured Sambhaji so that he died a painful death; he then extended his southern campaign and annexed Golconda and Bijapur. It was at this stage that he made Aurangabad his capital. Shahuji, Sambhaji's son, lived as a hostage at Aurangzeb's court. He grew up as a mild-mannered courtier in the shadow of the Great Mughal. But later on it was under his guidance that great leaders arose who put an end to the Mughal empire.

Aurangzeb died in 1707 at the age of 89. His modest tomb is at the roadside near Aurangabad. In striking contrast to his predecessors he shunned all pomp and splendour – austere as he had been in his lifetime, he wanted to rest under the open sky after death. But the ambitious military campaigns which he conducted throughout his lifetime had been far from simple and inexpensive. In the century from the accession of Akbar to that of Aurangzeb, India had experienced an epoch of relative peace and prosperity. Trade had expanded and urban centres had grown up everywhere. The agrarian base was strong enough to support the court, the army and the administration in general. Of course, the connection between the

Figure 5.3 Fortress Gwalior built by the Tomar-Rajput ruler Man Singh *c.* AD 1500, subsequently in the possession of the Mughals and the Marathas

(Courtesy of Hermann Kulke)

countryside and the urban centres was a one-way street: the peasants had to yield their surplus and did not receive much in return, even in cultural terms, as their religious values and ideas were different from those of their overlords. The Mughal culture was an urban phenomenon, but within these limitations it flourished very well. Urdu, originally the *lingua franca* of the army camp of the Mughals, emerged as a very flexible element of civilised literary communication. It absorbed elements of Persian favoured by the worldly elite, of Arabic studied by Islamic scholars, and of Hindi, the language of the people. Music, poetry and the fine arts were at their very best. Rebellions against the Mughal regime were few and far between. The Great Mughals knew how to accommodate local and regional elites within their system. Vassals of earlier regimes, tribal chieftains and village headmen, petty kings and princes were all recognised under the general category of landlords (*zamindars*). They retained their rights and privileges as long as they paid their dues to the Mughals.

In Aurangzeb's reign the revenue demand became increasingly oppressive. There were more and more revolts, which were often led by the zamindars who confronted the officers of the Mughal government at the head of their retainers and peasants. Initially these revolts were isolated events; in the course of time, however, a more broad-based solidarity emerged. Ties of kinship like those between the Jats, or religious solidarity like that binding the Sikhs, or a quasi-national feeling like that of the Marathas – all served as common bonds to lend cohesion to the rebellious spirit.

These revolts against the Mughal government were greatly facilitated by the spread of light firearms, which were now handled and produced everywhere. After Baber had introduced these weapons in India they had become very popular with Indian rulers. Sher Shah is supposed to have had 25,000 matchlock men (*toofangchis*) in his service. Whereas the casting of big guns was a complicated and costly affair, even the village blacksmith could learn to make small firearms; even a peasant could manage to shoot with them. The Great Mughals explicitly prohibited the manufacture of firearms in the villages, because they feared that they would be used against the government. The more the agrarian base of the Mughal state was eroded by heavy taxation, the more often the peasants seized their firearms and put up a stiff resistance. Hordes of armed peasants roaming around became as much of a threat to the Mughals as the light cavalry of the Marathas. The Mughal government, with its cumbersome army, was not in a position to suppress this kind of unrest effectively.

Aurangzeb's successor would have had to be a second Akbar in order to cope with this situation and to reconcile the people. But Aurangzeb's son Akbar, who had set out to do just that, had fled and died in exile in Persia. It was Aurangzeb's eldest son, Muazzam, who ascended the throne at the age of 63 and, under the name of Bahadur Shah, ruled for just five years: he was unable to forestall the dissolution of the empire. Trying his best to come to terms with the Rajputs and the Marathas, he installed Shivaji's grandson, Shahu, as raja of Satara. He could not, however, quell the resistance to Mughal rule in this way; rather, he promoted it unwittingly.

Shahu appointed a competent minister (*peshwa*), the Chitpavan Brahmin Balaji Vishwanath, who instilled a spirit of cooperation into the quarrelsome Marathas and put the Maratha state on a sound footing. Balaji's son, Baji Rao, succeeded his father at the age of 19 and held this high office from 1720 to 1740. He proved to be a bold warrior and an eminent strategist of the same calibre as Baber and Shivaji. After some initial infighting in which he defeated the commander (*senapati*) of the Maratha army, he emerged as the supreme political and military leader of the Marathas. Shahu and his successors in Satara were overshadowed by the Peshwa dynasty, which ruled the country like the Shoguns of Japan, the monarch retaining only ceremonial functions. Baji Rao rushed with his cavalry to Delhi, which he captured in a surprise attack only to leave it a few days later. This was a first indication of the fact that the Marathas, though able to destroy the Mughal empire, were unable to hold it on their own.

Baji Rao was not only courageous; he was also clever and calculating. He never got caught in an untenable position. This is why he left Delhi as quickly as he had seized it. His possession of the imperial capital was meant only as a demonstration of his power; when he withdrew from there he built up his position in northern and western India to the south of Delhi. This enabled his generals – Scindia, Holkar and Gaekwar – to emerge as maharajas of Gwalior, Indore and Baroda at a later stage. Baji Rao had a very special relationship with the chief minister (*vezir*) of the Mughal empire, Nizam-ul-Mulk – a politician who was, at times, the greatest rebel against the empire and, at others, its last great supporter. At first the two men hated each other intensely; eventually, they gained more and more respect for each other. Baji Rao several times trapped the chief minister's army and extracted ransom and territorial concessions from him instead of fighting for an empty victory. During such negotiations the old vezir and the young peshwa got to know each other very well. Following Shahu's advice gleaned from his years in the Mughal court, Baji Rao saw in Nizam-ul-Mulk the most important figure on the chessboard of Indian politics. The vezir had the same idea about Baji Rao.

Together, these two men could have prevented Nadir Shah's incursion from Persia into India and his sacking of Delhi in 1739. United, they could have prevented his taking the peacock throne of the Great Mughals and many other treasures. But it was exactly at that time that the vezir chose to embark with all his troops on a campaign against Baji Rao, thus leaving northern India wide open for Nadir Shah's invasion. Baji Rao emerged victorious from this encounter and the vezir had to yield to him most of the territories of the empire to the south of Delhi. After Nadir Shah's campaign and Baji Rao's success not much was left of the Mughal empire. Only a few years later the vezir himself set the pace for the final dissolution of the empire. He left Delhi and settled down in Hyderabad where he established his own dynasty. His successors, the Nizams of Hyderabad, became the most important allies of the British in India and thus they were able to continue their rule until the twentieth century. The peshwas, on the other hand, resisted the British and were eliminated.

INDIAN LAND POWER AND EUROPEAN SEA POWER

When Baber made his first forays into India where his dynasty established one of the greatest landpowers of Asia, Portuguese seapower already controlled the Indian Ocean. The Mughals stuck to the land and never thought of building up a navy to reflect their great power. Even the Mughal ships carrying pilgrims across the Arabian Sea depended on the Portuguese for their protection.

This maritime indifference of the Great Mughals was in striking contrast to the concern of the rulers of Egypt, who dispatched several fleets to the Arabian Sea in order to break the Portuguese stranglehold. This disparity in policy was due to the fact that the Egyptian rulers, after having been challenged by the Christian Crusaders, had followed a protectionist policy which enabled them to control the Red Sea trade route; this trade had become a state monopoly and it yielded a handsome income to the government.

The Mughal state, on the other hand, did not depend on the control of trade, but on the collection of land revenue. For this the influx of precious metals was important because India had no silver mines and only very modest gold mines. Thus, the metal for India's currency had to be obtained from abroad. The Great Mughals were accordingly very much interested in international trade, but they could not care less about the people and the powers involved in it so long as the flow of the precious metals was not interrupted. The European seapowers did not interrupt this flow; on the contrary, they contributed to it in a big way. Only small local rulers along the coast of India, who were themselves interested in trade, had any reason to complain about the Europeans. Such rulers were also in sympathy with the Egyptian maritime intervention. But with the exception of the naval battle of 1508, in which combined Gujarati and Egyptian forces had won a decisive victory over the Portuguese, these interventions were of no avail. For more than a century the Portuguese remained lords of the Indian Ocean and sent many precious shiploads to Lisbon.

The Portuguese seizure of power in the Indian Ocean at the beginning of the sixteenth century proceeded with amazing rapidity. The Portuguese benefited from the fact that they had explored the Atlantic sea routes in the fifteenth century and had gained great skills in navigation and in finding gold and spices. Their little country had been blighted by epidemics and they suffered from shortages of almost everything: their quest for wealth and power abroad was desperate and this made them highly successful. This also meant, however, that their tiny country was a rather slender base for a global maritime empire. They depended entirely on the fortunes of that empire and, thus, on circumstances beyond their control.

The turn of the fifteenth into the sixteenth century was an exceptionally lucky period for the Portuguese. The Turkish empire was increasing its hold on the eastern Mediterranean and locked in conflict with Venice, which operated a system of tight control of the sea route to Egypt and the Levant. The war between Turkey and Venice in 1499 disrupted the European spice trade; it also coincided with the return of the first Portuguese fleet from India. Vasco da Gama, the admiral of this fleet, thus scored a success: the pepper which he had brought along sold at a good profit.

The Portuguese king soon made the pepper trade a royal monopoly, just as he had earlier seized upon the African gold which his explorers had brought home. A comparison of the Portuguese budget in the years 1506 and 1518 shows the striking change in the structure of state finance. African gold yielded the same amount in both years (120,000 cruzados), but the income from the pepper monopoly rose from 135,000 cruzados in the first year to 300,000 in the second (1 cruzado = 3.6 grams of gold). At the same time there seems to have been a general improvement in the economic situation of the country: the income from taxes rose from 173,000 to 245,000 cruzados and the customs duties of the Port of Lisbon increased from 24,000 to 40,000 cruzados. But the pepper monopoly certainly dwarfed all other sources of income. The Portuguese king could thus afford to send, on average, 50,000 cruzados to India every year. In the Mediterranean the Europeans had to spend about ten times that sum in order to buy an equivalent amount of spices. Actually, the king's officers spent only half of the 50,000 cruzados on the spices, the other half being invested in the maintenance of the naval and military establishment which was required to protect this trade. The enormous profit derived from the pepper monopoly made this investment appear rather moderate.

The search for pepper had initially taken Vasco da Gama to Calicut in 1498, because this port of the *Zamorin* (*Samudra Raja* = King of the Sea) was frequented by the Arab traders who conveyed the pepper via the Red Sea to Egypt. The *Zamorin* was a Hindu but he got along very well with the Arab traders and refused to drive them away as Vasco da Gama urged him to do. When Pedro Cabral reached India in 1500 with a big Portuguese fleet he found that the Raja of Cochin, who controlled a port about 100 miles to the south of Calicut, was a better partner. This *raja* was a rival of the *Zamorin* and welcomed the Portuguese as allies. Moreover, his port had a large natural basin with good access to the rivers of the pepper country. In 1505 Cochin became the capital of the Portuguese *Estado da India*. However, it was soon eclipsed by Goa which the Portuguese conquered in 1511 and made their Indian capital in 1535. The Portuguese established further strongholds in Daman and Diu controlling the Gulf of Cambay in Gujarat. At Hormuz they controlled the Persian Gulf and at Malacca they dominated the trade through the Straits. Fort Jesus at Mombasa was their base on the African coast. In this way the armed control of the Indian Ocean trade was relatively easy for the Portuguese. They found a flourishing and unprotected free trade system when they entered this ocean. Except for an occasional pirate bearing rather primitive arms, there was nobody in these waters who had made it his business to use force for the control of trade. The petty rulers who controlled the ports around the Indian Ocean had never tried to use force, because they knew that trade could easily shift to a more hospitable port. For this reason they also had to be moderate with regard to customs duties and similar charges.

With all this flexibility, the free trade system was, nevertheless, very vulnerable. The Indian Ocean trade was not restricted to luxury goods which one could easily forgo if the traffic was interrupted. Of course, gold and ivory, precious textiles and spices did play a major role in this trade. But there was also a considerable division of labour in the course of which some ports had become entirely dependent on long-distance grain shipments. The Portuguese noted with great surprise at Malindi (on the east African coast) and at Hormuz, that these ports were supplied with rice and other produce from distant Gujarat. As no duties and other protection costs distorted the price level in this free trade system, everything was much cheaper here than in the Mediterranean where the Egyptians and the Venetians operated a tight monopoly. The Portuguese projected Mediterranean practice onto the Indian Ocean. They were keen observers and quickly seized upon the strategic points from which they could control the vast network of Asian maritime trade. Their fortified outposts served as customs stations where Asian merchants had to acquire the letters of protection (*cartazes*) which saved them from being attacked and ransacked by the Portuguese on the high seas.

Tomé Pires, the author of the *Suma Oriental* and, subsequently, the first Portuguese ambassador to China, noted as early as 1512 that he who holds Malacca has his hands at the throat of Venice. In the early sixteenth century the Portuguese virtually succeeded in strangling Venetian trade, though they never achieved a complete blockade. For the royal pepper monopoly it was sufficient that supply was tight for Venice, which continued to get pepper via the Red Sea and the Levant. This kept up the prices and assured a high profit. The Portuguese king never wanted to undersell the Venetians, as they had at first suspected. He adjusted his sale price to the Venetian one, while simultaneously forcing his Indian suppliers to part with their pepper at a cheap rate. For the royal monopolist it was an ideal system: buy the pepper at a cheap fixed price in India and sell at a high fixed price in Europe. Once this system was established, it was very well suited for subcontracting – thus saving the king trouble and giving him an assured income. Private merchants could cut in on this trade under a royal lease, which diminished the king's profit somewhat but also placed the entire risk of the voyage on the shoulders of the private investor. This arrangement was predominant in the second half of the sixteenth century when Venetian trade had revived in the Mediterranean and the Portuguese king looked upon his pepper monopoly as a kind of money estate which could be mortgaged to the highest bidder. In fact, the 'Casa da India' – the administration of the royal monopoly – went bankrupt in 1560 because the king had used this method of mortgaging his assets too liberally.

Another source of income which became as important to the Portuguese king as the pepper monopoly was the sale of the offices of captains and customs collectors in the Indian Ocean strongholds. In 1534 the Turks had reached Basra and could thus control the entire caravan route from the Persian Gulf to the Mediterranean. They then became the trading partners of Venice, just as the Egyptian Mameluks had been at an earlier date. Instead of tightening their grip at the throat of Venice, the Portuguese now preferred to collect customs at Hormuz and other places. The offices of those who collected these customs were auctioned by the king at short intervals, usually three years. So this was another royal money estate which yielded income without any risk. In this way the king became a rent receiver rather than a royal entrepreneur. This tendency was even more accentuated when Philip II of Spain inherited the Portuguese throne in 1580. He spent some time in Lisbon after claiming the Portuguese heritage, and could have revamped the Portuguese maritime empire. However, he soon returned to Spain and used the royal money estates of Portugal to fill coffers frequently depleted by a succession of bankruptcies. He forced his creditors, among them the German merchant bankers Fugger and Welser, to take over the pepper monopoly on terms which he dictated to them. The ideal solution for him would have been for them to take over the import monopoly and the entire distribution while giving him a share amounting to about twice the import price as an annuity. But soon after Philip's final bankruptcy and death the pepper monopoly became almost worthless as ships from the Mediterranean brought pepper to Lisbon at a cheaper rate. At this stage only the Portuguese customs at stations around the Indian Ocean still yielded a good income, whereas the pepper trade once more passed into the hands of the Mediterranean merchants. However, this transitional period of a revived Mediterranean trade was very brief: the Dutch invaded the Indian Ocean with dramatic speed at the beginning of the seventeenth century, just as the Portuguese had done a hundred years earlier.

For the Indian landpower the presence of the European seapowers in the Indian Ocean remained politically insignificant. Seapower intervention in the affairs of Indian rulers was of only marginal importance. The case of the sultan of Gujarat, who turned to the Portuguese for help after his defeat by Humayun, was an isolated incident. Once Akbar had reconquered Gujarat in 1574 and had incorporated it into the Mughal empire, there was no repetition of Portuguese intervention: the Portuguese even had to leave their trading post at Hugli when Akbar drove them out of it. He made no further moves against them, although he did send a message to Shah Abbas of Persia – who doubted Akbar's faith in Islam – that they should make common cause against the Portuguese infidels.

As traders, the Portuguese were generally well received by the Indian rulers who granted them the same rights as they did to other merchants but nevertheless disliked their monopsonistic practices. Therefore, the appearance of European competitors in the ports of the Indian Ocean was also welcomed, because these newcomers could be played off against the Portuguese. Their potential for intervention in the affairs of the landpowers was underrated: a century of experience of the Portuguese seemed to have shown that these Europeans stuck to the sea and would not be able to do much on land. Actually, a military expedition into the interior of the country was, in any case, highly unlikely, because the monsoon brought the ships to the Indian shores only during a few months of the year and, thus, the supply lines would be cut quickly by nature itself. Indeed, it was only later, when the Europeans trained Indian mercenaries whom they paid with money brought to India by their ships, that their potential for intervention increased by leaps and bounds.

The Portuguese remained satisfied with strongholds on the coast and never made the sort of daring expedition into the interior of India as had prompted their unfortunate young King Sebastian in Morocco, so causing his death on the battlefield of Kasr-al-Kabir in 1578. It seems that the future of Portugal died with Sebastian on that battlefield. The great drive of the Portuguese to rule the seas was broken; they now merely clung on to what they had gained.

The rise of Dutch and British seapower

At about the same time as the future of the Portuguese began to wane, the future of the Dutch emerged under most adverse circumstances. The union of the seven Dutch provinces was accomplished in 1579 and in the midst of their freedom struggle against their Spanish overlords, who were by then also ruling Portugal, the Dutch dared to invade the Indian Ocean in such a big way that the earlier Portuguese achievements were immediately dwarfed by their success. Several favourable preconditions accounted for this Dutch success. The Dutch had a good educational system and had made much headway in science and technology. This enabled them to acquire nautical information from the Portuguese and to improve upon it in many ways. Although they themselves were later to prove quite secretive about their nautical knowledge, they were past masters at collecting useful information from whatever source. They also already had a huge merchant marine engaged in the Baltic Sea trade; they would be able to draw on this once they decided to embark on their voyages to India. The Baltic Sea link also gave them access to sufficient wood for shipbuilding, thus ensuring that they would never face a shortage of the kind that had seriously injured Venetian shipping in the late sixteenth century.

On the Dutch coast, ships were built so cheaply and quickly that the method of construction almost prefigures that of Henry Ford's twentieth-century assembly line. The standard type of ship was the *fluyt* – a relatively slow vessel, but easy to handle, cheap and sturdy, and with a lot of space for cargo. Investment in ships was popular with the Dutch; even artisans would commit their small savings in fractional shares of ships. Risks were spread in this way and the loss of one ship could be compensated for by the successful return of another. Due to this broad-based pattern of investment, the Dutch East India Company, which was founded in 1602, could immediately send great numbers of ships into the Indian Ocean. In fact, this company was set up not because it was difficult to raise the capital for such voyages but, rather, in order to prevent ruinous competition. Unlike the situation in Portugal, the state had no hand in this business, and the monopoly which was granted to the company referred to spices only. Furthermore, monopoly control stopped once the shipments reached Amsterdam, where the goods were freely auctioned to the highest bidder. Of course, these auctions were sometimes not quite as free as they were supposed to be. The company could store and withhold shipments if the price was going to fall due to a glut on the market. There were also ways and means of arriving at secret deals. But, in general, these auctions provided a good idea of what the market would take, and they also helped to introduce new commodities, such as textiles, which were not covered by any monopoly.

In London, an East India Company was founded in 1600, two years before the Dutch one, and it operated on much the same terms including the sale by auction. The initial stimulus for the establishment of that company was the lack of venture capital for this risky overseas trade. The joint stock subscribed by individual merchants was limited to the investment in single voyages to begin with and it was only when overhead charges for the maintenance of outposts, etc., increased that the joint stock was made permanent.

Throughout the seventeenth century the English East India Company operated on a much smaller scale than its Dutch counterpart. Nevertheless, the Dutch were deeply concerned about British competition and tried their best to ward it off. While fighting against the domination of the seas by the Spanish and the Portuguese, the Dutch had stressed the principle of the freedom of the seas. Their great legal luminary, Hugo Grotius, had published his famous book *Mare Liberum* in 1609, but only a few years later he was sent to London to defend the Dutch claim to the exclusive control of the Indonesian spice islands. The Dutch, so he argued, had to refuse all other powers an access to them because only in this way could the Dutch be compensated for the protection which they furnished.

Whereas the Dutch jealously guarded their territorial control in Indonesia at a very early stage, they showed no such ambitions in India. This was, perhaps, due to the fact that they procured textiles to an increasing extent in India and these were not covered by a monopoly. The textile trade, which became more important to the Dutch, required methods of control other than the physical occupation of the area of production. It was more important in this case to tie down producers and middlemen by means of credit and advances and to organise the acquisition of the right type of textiles which were popular with customers abroad.

The factories of the East India Companies, both Dutch and British, experienced a great deal of structural change as they adapted to the textile trade. Initially, such factories were expected only to store goods for the annual shipment; in due course, however, they became centres whose influence extended far into the interior of the country as they placed orders, distributed patterns, granted and supervised credit, etc. The Dutch, who had many factories on India's east coast, were also represented at the court of the sultan of Golconda whose realm was an important source of textiles for them. The British more or less followed Dutch precedent and, as they had no access to the spice islands, they concentrated on India and on the textile trade to an ever-increasing extent. Nonetheless, in the seventeenth century they were still lagging behind the Dutch even in this field.

The revolution of international maritime trade

The invasion of the Indian Ocean by the western European East India Companies brought about a revolution in international trade which the Portuguese had never accomplished. The flow of commodities in the Mediterranean was completely reversed. The trade of the Levant, following its revival in the late sixteenth century which had meant that ships with spices were even sent from there to Lisbon, experienced a sudden decline. Western European ships now supplied the ports of the Levant with the goods, which had been sent from there to the West only a few years earlier. Venice suffered the same decline, and was soon no more than a regional port of Italy. Asian maritime trade was not as immediately affected by this trade revolution as the Mediterranean trade was. There were great Indian shipowners who dispatched so many ships every year to the ports of Arabia and of the Persian Gulf that they easily outnumbered all the European ships in the Indian Ocean at that time. The Europeans competed with those merchants but also depended on their help as brokers and money-changers. Sometimes they even borrowed substantial amounts from them. European demand for export commodities increased the volume and value of trade and some Indian merchants amassed substantial fortunes. Those merchants who had no ships of their own often entrusted their goods to the Europeans for maritime transport. The Dutch, who were the biggest ship-ping agents in Europe, now also offered their services to Asian merchants. Their ships were sturdy and well armed and could resist ubiquitous piracy. Actually, European piracy also increased in the Indian Ocean as individual 'entrepreneurs' were quick to learn their nautical and commercial lessons. Not all of the European interlopers were pirates – some of them simply earned a living in the 'country trade', as the intra-Asian trade was called. The British private traders were very active in this field, and though the East India Company officially decried the activities of these 'interlopers' – who crossed the Asian seas without any respect for monopoly rights granted by royal charter – there emerged a kind of symbiosis between them and the company. The East India Company concentrated on the intercontinental trade, and the 'country traders' made their deals with the servants of the company and made use of the infrastructure and the protective network provided by the company without contributing to its maintenance. This gave them a comparative advantage in the intra-Asian trade and the company did well in specialising in the intercontinental connection and leaving the 'country trade' to others.

This specialisation was fostered by a characteristic feature of the British East India Company. Unlike the Dutch company, which owned a huge fleet of ships, the British company had given up the policy of building and owning its own ships after a period of initial experimentation; instead, it had adopted the method of leasing ships from private shipowners. Fluctuations in the volume of trade could thus be easily met by hiring fewer ships and the risk of maintaining the vessels had to be borne by the private shipowners. These people tried their best to stay in business by offering the company better and faster ships, for which they could charge high freight rates. These specialised and expensive ships were perfectly suited for the intercontinental run, but their employment in the 'country trade' would have been a waste of money as their freight rates were too high and their speed not much use for the trade between Asian ports. Only if such a ship had missed the monsoon and was forced to stay in Asian waters would an owner try to reduce his losses by arranging for an intra-Asian voyage. In general, however, the company insisted on a strict observance of the timetable, which was fixed for the intercontinental traffic. The captains of these expensive and well-equipped intercontinental ships were about the best-paid employees of their day. They also enjoyed the privilege of taking on board some precious goods on their own account, which gave them a handsome profit in addition to their salary. Many captains also held a share in the ship they commanded. This was, therefore, a very attractive career for intelligent and enterprising people. The British nautical elite was made up of such men, an elite which greatly contributed to British seapower. The specialisation and division of labour which characterised the British system made it much more flexible and efficient than the rather cumbersome Dutch hierarchy, and this is why, finally, even people in Amsterdam bought shares in the British rather than in the Dutch East India Company.

The rapid rise of the West European East India Companies occurred at a time when the Mughal empire was still at its height. Seen from Delhi the Europeans appeared to be rather marginal figures in Asia. But by the end of the seventeenth century there were some indications that these marginal figures had a considerable nuisance value. In 1686 the British waged a maritime war against the Great Mughal knowing full well that he was quite helpless at sea. They managed to block the flourishing trade of Bengal with southeast Asia for some time. Even ships belonging to high Mughal officers and to members of the Great Mughal's family were seized by the British. The victims subsequently withdrew from this trade and probably entrusted their goods to the Dutch or to European country traders, if they still ventured to take part in international trade at all. For the British East India Company this war, which ended in 1688, was of no use: Aurangzeb drove them out of their factory at Hugli and they had to settle further down the river where they held a few villages in a rather unhealthy and inconvenient area. One of these villages was Calcutta, which nobody would then have guessed was destined to become the metropolis of Britain's Indian empire. Madras and Bombay were still much more important in the late seventeenth century. The power of the Great Mughal remained unchallenged in Bengal and it seemed as if the British were only conducting some rearguard action there.

French ambitions and reverses

Another major European power, which was destined to play an important part in the history of India in the eighteenth century, was also still rather insignificant in the Indian context of the late seventeenth century. In 1664 a French East India Company had been founded at the instigation of the energetic finance minister, Jean Baptiste Colbert, who enjoyed the full support of Louis XIV in this venture. Colbert avidly copied Dutch precedent and organised the French company on federal lines. This was counterproductive, because the company was organised by the government and there were no private capitalists who had to be accommodated in federal chambers, like those formed by the merchants of the different Dutch provinces. Colbert had to press the great dignitaries of the realm to subscribe funds for this purpose. They did so reluctantly: it was much safer and more lucrative to invest money at home. The French practice of the sale of offices offered prestige and income to all who had money to invest. Whoever contributed to the French East India Company did so only in order to please the king. The king was indeed pleased, and the first French voyage to India was organised in royal style.

A French viceroy, De la Haye, appeared with a fleet of nine ships off the coast of India so as to demonstrate the power of his king. This was the time of the third Anglo-Dutch war and, therefore, De la Haye hoped for British support against the Dutch in India. But the governor of Madras turned him down, saying that the wars of his king were of no concern to him as he had to obey only the orders of the directors of his company. The bold Frenchman thereupon tried to tackle the Dutch single-handed, but he suffered a miserable defeat, lost all his ships and was sent back to Europe as a prisoner on a Dutch ship. After this misadventure nothing much was heard about the French East India Company for some time. It was only due to the quiet endeavour of one man, François Martin, that the French East India Company gained a foothold in India at all. Martin arrived in India in 1668 and died there in 1706, without ever having left the country in all those years. The French settlement at Pondichery owes its origin to this unique man. His observations and experiences provided guidelines for those ambitious Frenchmen who tried to build a French empire in India in the eighteenth century – the resourceful Governor Dupleix, the daring Admiral La Bourdonnais, and the diplomatic General de Bussy.

The commercial success of the French East India Company was much more limited than the imperial vision of those great Frenchmen. Colbert's son and successor, the Marquis de Seignelay, had re-established the company in 1685 along lines which were much more in keeping with French practice. The board of directors consisted exclusively of high-ranking government officers who received an assured dividend of 10 per cent on the capital which they had subscribed. The trade was managed with bureaucratic precision. The company owned twelve ships, four of which returned from India every year. In peacetime the company could thus make some profit, although it was debarred from the lucrative textile trade because of French mercantilist policy. However, the frequent interruption of this trade due to European wars drove the company to the verge of bankruptcy. It was only when the great financial wizard, John Law, merged the French West Indies Company and the French East India Company in 1719 that France caught up with the new pattern of international trade, which linked Indian Ocean trade with transatlantic trade. The new Compagnie des Indes prospered in this way and also attracted merchant capital which had been lacking at earlier stages.

The European powers and the declining Mughal empire

Europe was the scene of many wars in the first two decades of the eighteenth century: the War of the Spanish Succession, the Nordic War, the war against the Turks. In comparison, the next two decades were rather peaceful. England enjoyed prosperity and stability under the great prime minister Robert Walpole, and in France the regime of Cardinal Fleury produced a similar atmosphere. Therefore, the representatives of both powers enjoyed a quiet time during which they could concentrate on consolidating their respective bases in India.

In India itself, meanwhile, this was the period of the dissolution of the Mughal empire. Baji Rao and Nadir Shah raided Delhi and, in Bengal, a highly competent Mughal governor, Murshid Quli Khan, ruled as if he were an independent prince. Murshid, a Brahmin converted to Islam, had had a meteoric administrative career in the service of the Great Mughal. Following the eclipse of Delhi, he did pretty much what he liked. He built a new capital of Bengal, Murshidabad, and annexed Bihar and Orissa. He organised an efficient centralised administration, eliminated many of the Mughal fiefs and collected the revenue in cash. It may sound paradoxical, but it was he who prepared the ground for British rule in India. Without his efficient system of administration and a large revenue in cash, Bengal would have been useless to the British.

Of course, while Murshid was still alive, the British remained marginal figures in Bengal and were entirely dependent on his pleasure. In 1717 the East India Company had been granted the privilege of free trade and free coinage in Bengal by the Great Mughal, but this grant was an empty promise as far as Murshid was concerned. In order to get along with him, the British had to deal with Murshid's banker, Fatehchand, called Jagat Sheth ('Merchant of the World'). Jagat Sheth obstructed the British by denying them free access to the Mughal mint. He made a good profit by controlling access to the mint and buying up silver at prices dictated by him. But the British wisely decided to work with him and not against him. In this way they gained a key position in the trade of Bengal by making clever use of the existing power structure.

In western India the British position was quite different. Gujarat was of prime importance for international trade, but there was no Murshid Quli Khan in that province, and the dissolution of the Mughal empire immediately affected this region. Surat, the great port of the empire, lost its importance within a few decades. Many merchants fled from this proud imperial port to Bombay where the British offered protection against Mughal and Maratha depredations. Bombay had a good natural port, but its connection with the hinterland was blocked by the Western Ghats and, therefore, it was much less suited for international trade than Surat. Nevertheless, the Indian merchants preferred a safe port to a place where one's life and property were at stake, as the death of Muhammad Ali in 1733 had so clearly shown to everybody concerned.

The tragic fate of this last great merchant of Surat stands in striking contrast with the good fortune of his Bengal contemporary, Jagat Sheth. Muhammad Ali had inherited a veritable trading empire from his grandfather, Abdul Ghaffur. Dozens of ships carried his goods to all the ports of the Arabian Sea. Even the British governor of Bombay envied him because he was a keen competitor. In order to protect himself against the risks of his day Muhammad Ali built a fortified port of his own near Surat. The Mughal commander of the port of Surat did not like this, but had to acquiesce as he owed Muhammad Ali a great deal of money. However, they finally fell out with each other and the Mughal commander imprisoned Muhammad Ali. The great merchant who had lived like a prince died a miserable death in this Mughal prison.

One year after Muhammad Ali's death the British organised a blockade of the port of Surat. They did not mind that they would thus forfeit the privileges bestowed upon them by the Great Mughal. In the following year (1735) the Sidis who commanded the small Mughal navy raided Surat and captured all the ships which were just about to set sail for the Red Sea. They claimed that they did this only because the Great Mughal had not paid them their dues – and thus they abducted the merchant fleet which they were supposed to protect.

The chaotic situation of the declining Mughal empire was such that merchants became an easy prey for robbers and government officers alike. The great web of trade which the Indian merchants had spun was torn apart with a vengeance. The small pedlar who accompanies his goods can escape such depredations more easily. But the great merchant who dispatches huge consignments, maintains agents in many countries, grants and receives credit and places advance orders – he depends very much on political stability. He can survive the sacking of his town as long as the network of trade is not destroyed and stability can be restored.

Thus, Shivaji's raid on Surat in 1664 remained a mere episode, soon forgotten. The city prospered once more and its maritime trade actually experienced its greatest phase of expansion in the early decades of the eighteenth century. In the years from 1720 to 1729 about fifty ships arrived at Surat every year: thirty-three of them belonged to Indian merchants. Of these Indian ships about nine came from the Red Sea, seven from the Malabar coast and five from Bengal and the rest from various other places. After the crucial events of the years 1733 and 1734, which have been described earlier, Surat's maritime trade was reduced by about 50 per cent. In the five years from 1734 to 1738 only about twenty-eight ships arrived at Surat per year; eighteen belonged to Indian merchants. Six of the Indian ships came from the Red Sea, one from the Malabar coast and three from Bengal. The reduction affected almost all routes, but the connection with the Malabar coast seems to have suffered most.

This dwindling trade was a symptom of the decay of political stability. The individual Indian merchant who tried to protect himself after the fashion of Muhammad Ali could find no salvation from this decay: on the contrary, he incited the wrath and the covetousness of those against whom he wanted to protect himself. Only the European companies with their armed ships and fortified factories were able to insulate themselves – very well indeed. Moreover, they could easily shift the scene of their operations to areas which appeared more attractive and profitable. Thus, British trade with Bengal, which was rather marginal in the seventeenth century, suddenly increased in the eighteenth.

The boom of British trade with Bengal began in the second decade of the eighteenth century. In the first years of that decade the British sent annually about £150,000 to Bengal; in the last years the total was about £250,000. Altogether about £2 million was transferred to Bengal in the 1710s, yet this great influx of silver did not lead to a price inflation. There were several reasons for this. First, many of the Mughal officers as well as the great merchants transferred funds from Bengal to northern India. Furthermore, the increasing cash base of the land revenue tied down a great deal of money in the countryside, where it circulated rather slowly. Due to the decay of the central power of the Great Mughal at Delhi, it became more and more difficult for him to get his share of the revenue from Bengal. Later, the British were to profit from this situation when, in the second half of the eighteenth century, they extracted the silver from Bengal which they had pumped in in the early 1700s.

The increasing trade with Bengal also led to the erection of British factories in the interior of the country, where the agents of the company established direct contact with the weavers and so influenced the process of production. Even British artisans were sent to Bengal in order to train their Indian counterparts in the art of producing for the European market. The changing currents of European fashion demanded that the Indian producers adapted their output to the latest fashion as quickly as possible. In spite of this demand there was no investment in the means and methods of production. The weavers remained poor, and the middlemen made the profit. In due course the British eliminated these Indian middlemen and sent their own agents directly to the weavers.

The rulers of Bengal regarded these British activities with mixed feelings: while greatly appreciating the stream of silver which the British brought into the country, they looked askance at the fortified factories and the increasing participation of the foreigners in the inland trade. Even a strong ruler like Alivardi Khan, who governed Bengal from 1740 to 1756, feared the influence of the British and did not trust them. But in his lifetime they could not subvert the political order in Bengal and had to operate within the limits imposed upon them. However, when Alivardi Khan's weak and impetuous successor demanded that the British should remove their fortifications, they defied his order, repulsed his subsequent attack and defeated him. He had feared that the East India Company would grow into a state within the state; now this state within the state soon took over the state itself. The British seapower became an Indian landpower.

THE STRUGGLE FOR SUPREMACY IN INDIA

The British benefited from the 'crisis of the eighteenth century' that impaired the three 'gunpowder empires' which had risen almost simultaneously in the first quarter of the sixteenth century. The Ottomans were defeated by the armies of the Habsburg dynasty and later by the Russian Czar, the Safawids lost their empire completely and the triumph of the usurper, Nadir Shah, who was murdered by his own bodyguard in 1747, was shortlived. The Great Mughals lingered on, although Nadir Shah's sacking of Delhi showed that their power had evaporated. 'Imperial overstretch' was the main reason for this crisis. When imperial control decayed, regional powers could once more rear their heads.

In India the rise of such regional powers was rather spectacular. The huge reservoir of military manpower which has been mentioned earlier, did not disappear, only the unified employment agency of the Mughal empire had vanished. The troopers and horsemen were now available to regional or even local rulers if they managed to raise enough funds. This was an age of the commercialisation of power. Moneylenders and revenue farmers became important partners of rulers and generals. The British with their East India Company fitted in very well with this pattern, because this company was, itself, an integral part of the commercialisation of power at home.

The map of regional powers as they emerged in the eighteenth century showed the following contours. In the north the Afghans who earlier had been vanquished by Nadir Shah once more rose to power. The plains to the east of Delhi were more or less controlled by the Nawab of Awadh (Oudh) who used to be a Mughal governor but had by now become an independent ruler. Bengal was dominated by an equally powerful Nawab. The central highlands were claimed by the Nizam of Hyderabad. Western India was ruled by the Marathas under the overall control of the Peshwa with his headquarters in Pune. In the south various successor states of the erstwhile Vijayanagar empire were ruled by Nayaks who used to be governors of their respective territories but were now as independent as the Nawabs of the north. Wedged in between the Nayaks and the Nizam was the Nawab of Arcot. The Nizam claimed a kind of suzerainty over Arcot and there was a great deal of infighting here which provided openings for the involvement of the European powers. But until the middle of the century, the Europeans

Figure 5.4 Indian soldiers in British service (Gun Lascar Corps, Madras), 1793, sketched by a British officer, presumably Captain Charles Gold

(Courtesy of The Director, National Army Museum)

were still very marginal to the Indian political scene. Their means of military intervention were modest and mainly restricted to their maritime bridgeheads. Indian rulers were much more concerned with the raids of the Afghan Ahmad Shah Durrani, who invaded the Indian plains repeatedly in the 1750s, just as Baber had done in his time.

The real problem of this period was that the Mughal empire, though defunct, did not cease to exist. The Great Mughal still resided in Delhi and everybody tried to manipulate him. Baji Rao is reputed to have said that the way to fell a tree is to cut the trunk – then the branches will come down by themselves. The trunk of the Mughal power, however, was not cut, although it was precariously hollow. Mughal supremacy was no longer respected and ambitious rulers dreamed of becoming heirs to that supremacy: nobody suspected that a European power would claim this heritage.

European military intervention: infantry versus cavalry

The first indications of the growing potential for military intervention by European powers came during the 1744–8 war between the British and the French. The two antagonists were engaged in a global struggle for supremacy which was to last the best part of twenty years (1744–63). In Europe this struggle was suspended from 1748 to 1755; in America and Asia, however, it continued unabated. With the new regional power constellations in India, the British and the French emerged as partners of Indian rulers who waged war against each other. In this way the Europeans were drawn into Indian affairs to an ever-increasing degree. The French governor, Joseph François Dupleix, who assumed his office at Pondichery in 1742 after having served for two decades in the French factory of Chandernagar in Bengal, was a very astute diplomat who knew how to play off Indian rulers against each other.

Although Dupleix's resources were very limited, he put them to good use. He had the excellent idea of having Indian mercenaries trained by French officers as infantrymen adept in the latest methods of European warfare. Such troops, while relatively cheap, could deal a fatal blow to the Indian cavalry. The elite of Indian warriors were daring horsemen used to riding roughshod through the lines of the enemy's ill-equipped and undisciplined foot soldiers; they were, however, mowed down by the European-trained infantry firing with the regular precision of a machine. Just as Baber had founded the Mughal empire on the superior power of muskets and artillery, this type of infantry established the foundation of European power in India. The secret of its success lay entirely in its drill and organisation: the weapons were readily available to Indian rulers, too. But Indian generals were prevented by their cavalry mentality from appreciating the merits of this new type of European-trained infantry. They had respect only for an enemy who would confront them on horseback:

for this reason the European subversion of Indian warfare was even more easily accomplished.

In concentrating on the infantry the Europeans made a virtue out of necessity. Cavalry units had always been very expensive, particularly in India, and the parsimonious directors of the European East India companies – who in any case disapproved of military adventures – would never have sanctioned the funds to maintain cavalry units. But the pay of foot soldiers was minimal in India, and they were courageous and ready to learn if they were properly taught how to fight. In Indian armies they played the same role as the pawns in a game of chess: they shielded the more valuable units of the army and, in straggling along, frequently obstructed the movements of the enemy; by the same token, they might also impede their own units. The armed infantryman (*toofangchi*), who knew how to handle a musket, was represented in Indian armies even in the sixteenth century. The peasants had used similar weapons when rebelling against the Mughal government. However, both the *toofangchi* and the peasant shot in their own individualist manner: they were marksmen, sometimes very good ones, who aimed at their individual target. It was impossible to organise them in regular columns and make them shoot in a disciplined rhythm collectively. After all, this method of infantry warfare was new even in Europe. It was Dupleix's special achievement to adopt it in India. The British were quick to learn this lesson and soon the troops of the two East India companies shot at each other, or at a variety of Indian enemies, in this way.

Initially, Dupleix was not at all keen to get involved in this warfare. When the war started in Europe he actually suggested to his British colleagues in India that they should come to an agreement to keep the peace in India. The British were willing to accept this offer, but indicated that such an understanding would not be binding on the royal troops about to be stationed in India. Thus, Dupleix was forced into hostilities. He was so successful to begin with that it seemed as if the French were going to win the war in India. He called upon the daring Admiral La Bourdonnais, who had organised a small but very effective French navy in the Indian Ocean. In fact, La Bourdonnais was more of a pirate than a regular naval officer. His navy was his own enterprise. Thus, when he managed to capture Madras from the British with Dupleix's support, he was willing to give it back to them if they paid a high ransom. Dupleix, on the other hand, insisted that it should be kept by the French; thereupon La Bourdonnais left India in a huff. Dupleix had to return Madras to the British as a condition of the peace treaty of 1748. However, both he and his British adversaries kept enough troops at hand to continue the game of warfare at which they had become so adept. They were also practically invited by Indian rulers to take sides with them in dynastic infighting or campaigns of regional conquest.

When the 1748 peace treaty was signed in Europe the old Nizam-ul-Mulk died in Hyderabad and his sons started fighting for the succession

230

in true Mughal style. Parallel to this dynastic fight there was a similar one between two sons of the nawab of Arcot, who had been a Mughal governor and had subsequently enjoyed a quasi-independent status under the suzerainty of the nizam of Hyderabad. The French and the British joined the fray, and thus there were two alliances, each composed of one Hyderabad prince, one Arcot prince and one European power. These two alliances waged war against each other for some time. Finally the French ally succeeded in Hyderabad, whereas the British ally succeeded in Arcot and established his independence from Hyderabad's jurisdiction. A young British clerk in the service of the East India Company, Robert Clive, had greatly distinguished himself in this campaign by capturing Arcot and defending this town against the much more numerous forces of the enemy in 1751. Dupleix, however, thought that, because the French protégé had become nizam of Hyderabad, he had won the war; when this nizam died in 1751 the French general, de Bussy, managed to install another French protégé as his successor. Subsequently, de Bussy warded off a Maratha attack on this protégé's realm; he was rewarded by being granted four districts on the east coast, whose revenues he could use to pay his troops.

De Bussy and his master, Dupleix, seemed to have succeeded in securing a major role in Indian politics for the French. In Paris, however, the directors of the Compagnie des Indes took a different view of these activities. The trade of the company had completely stopped during the war and had hardly revived after the peace treaty of 1748. The military exploits of Dupleix and de Bussy seemed to be examples of foolish extravagance, as far as the directors were concerned. Therefore, they fired Dupleix and sent one of the directors to India: he liquidated most of the French possessions there and arrived at an agreement with the British which was very much in their favour. When this happened – in 1754 – the French could not have foreseen that the Seven Years War would soon precipitate another global confrontation with the British. In the interests of cutting the losses of the Compagnie des Indes the measures adopted at the time appeared to be prudent and well considered. The warmongers were made scapegoats, La Bourdonnais was imprisoned; Dupleix died a pauper in France; only de Bussy stayed on in India – but his military potential was now greatly restricted, as he had been forced by his French masters to relinquish the four districts which the nizam had bestowed upon him.

Robert Clive and the Diwani of Bengal

At the same time as Dupleix left India, the young hero of Arcot, Robert Clive, also returned home. Whereas Dupleix was doomed, however, Clive hoped for a political career and aspired to a seat in Parliament. At just 29 years of age he had acquired enough money in India to invest in an electoral campaign: he won the election but lost his mandate when the result was declared invalid. Having spent most of his savings in this political enterprise, he was now forced to return to India in order to recoup his losses: he saw to it that he got a commission as a lieutenant colonel before embarking for India once more.

Clive reached Madras just as the news was received that the nawab of Bengal had attacked the British factories there and he was dispatched with some company troops in order to relieve Calcutta. Siraj-ud-Daula, the young nawab of Bengal, had succeeded his great-uncle, Alivardi Khan, in 1756, and had ordered the British to dismantle their fortifications which had been constructed without due permission. Clive arrived in Calcutta just in time, but, initially, his military operations were not very successful and he had a hard time establishing his credentials with the British officers there. Furthermore, the royal troops who accompanied him and his company troops thought of themselves as very much superior to those mercenaries: consequently, they obeyed his orders only grudgingly. Clive finally managed to relieve the British factories and to capture the French factory at Chandernagar in addition; he also concluded his negotiations with the nawab and should have returned to Madras when his mission was accomplished. He disobeyed those instructions. After having indulged in a secret intrigue with Mir Jaffar, the commander of the nawab's troops, Clive moved to the north in order to challenge the nawab on the battlefield of Plassey. Mir Jaffar was supposed to change sides while the battle was on and Clive would then see to it that he would become the nawab of Bengal. This was a risky gamble. Clive had only 3,000 troops and the nawab's army was far greater; there was also no guarantee that Mir Jaffar would keep his promise. With Clive still hesitating to join the battle, one of his young officers scored a sudden success with his field artillery. Mir Jaffar then did change sides: the nawab was defeated and killed. The traitor duly succeeded to power and rewarded Clive handsomely with a fief and a huge sum of money. Back in Calcutta, Clive got himself elected as governor of Bengal by the company's officers there – a rather unusual procedure, indeed.

At the court of the Great Mughal in Delhi the reaction to this news was quick. The nawab of Bengal had been as good as independent and his defeat was welcome. The Great Mughal thought that he could perhaps restore some of his authority in Bengal by entrusting the British with the civil administration (*Diwani*) of that province so as to curb the influence of the new nawab, who would be left with the military command only. When Clive received this offer in 1758 he was eager to accept. Young Warren Hastings, at that time the company's agent at the court of the nawab in Murshidabad, also recommended it. Nonetheless, Clive also thought that the company would be ill-equipped for this task and wanted the Crown to accept this responsibility, as he clearly foresaw that this would be the beginning of a British empire in India. Clive wrote to Pitt about it, but this astute prime minister rejected the idea. He feared the vesting of too much power and patronage in the hands of the ambitious King George III, which might enable the Crown to circumvent the budgetary control of Parliament by drawing on the rich tribute of Bengal. Pitt, although also enchanted by the vision of empire, did not want to jeopardise the parliamentary system: he advised that the company accept the Diwani of Bengal as it would be better for the tribute of the province to fill the pockets of private citizens rather than the royal treasury. On the other hand, Pitt agreed with Clive's assessment that, following the latter's imminent departure from India, there would be nobody able to cope with this task. Clive did leave India in 1760, without arriving at a decision on the Great Mughal's offer. He was not to know that the course of events would force his return to India only a few years later.

The Seven Years War and the battle of Panipat

The Seven Years War which led to a world-wide confrontation between the British and the French – from the forests of Canada to the east coast of India – was actually only a three years' war in India. By their decision of 1754 the French had given up the position gained by Dupleix and de Bussy; but now when the war began they made a further fatal mistake. Instead of appointing de Bussy as the supreme commander of the French forces in India, they dispatched an arrogant general, Lally, who had no experience of the country at all. The British defeated him in 1760 at the battle of Wandiwash, near Madras. He was made a scapegoat in France and was executed. The dream of an *Inde française* died with him.

From an Indian point of view all these dramatic events were still rather marginal. The battle of Plassey was a mere skirmish compared to the Indian battles of that time and the battle of Wandiwash was an encounter between the British and the French: no Indian interests were involved there. The power of the Marathas was at its zenith in 1760 and their military endeavours dwarfed all these European exploits. Balaji Baji Rao, the Peshwa who had ruled in Pune since 1740, though not a great warrior was a very competent administrator. His brother Raghunath led the Maratha army in north India and had repelled the Afghan Ahmad Shah Durrani several times. Ahmad Shah returned again and again, however, and finally – in 1761 – the Peshwa sent an enormous army to the north which was supposed to meet the Afghan invader on the traditional Indian battlefield of Panipat, where Baber had triumphed over the sultan of Delhi by means of superior firepower and a very flexible strategy. This time the Afghan won his victory over the Marathas for similar reasons. The Maratha general, Sadashiv Rao, relied too much on his heavy field artillery which he had firmly installed on the battlefield. He then got bogged down in a lengthy war of attrition and Ahmad Shah won the final battle by making use of light field artillery mounted on the backs of camels. After his victory Ahmad Shah returned to Afghanistan while the defeated Maratha army returned to the south. The Peshwa died of grief after this defeat.

The paradoxical feature of this great decisive battle of 1761 was that nothing was actually decided by it at the time. With hindsight, it seems to be very clear that the two main contestants for supremacy in India, the Afghans and the Marathas, had neutralised one another in that year and that the British, who had just entrenched themselves in Bengal and had defeated their French rivals at Wandiwash, were bound to benefit from this situation. To contemporary eyes, however, another ruler appeared to be the most immediate beneficiary of the outcome of the battle of Panipat: Shuja-ud-Daula, the nawab of Oudh. He was not only the governor of the largest and most central province of the Mughal empire, he had also attained the position of vezir and the young Great Mughal, Shah Alam, was under his tutelage. Shuja-ud-Daula seemed to emerge as the ruler of north India and had he been able to consolidate his position, the history of the British in India would have been very different.

He decided to challenge the British when he was asked for military support by the nawab of Bengal, Mir Kasim. The British had established a regime of reckless plunder in Bengal following the departure of Clive. After emptying Mir Jaffar's treasury they had seen to it that his richer relative, Mir Kasim, became nawab. After being thoroughly mulcted, Mir Kasim fled to Shuja-ud-Daula. Together they led a large army to the east and confronted the British at Baksar, southwestern Bihar, in 1764. Hector Munro, the commander of the British troops, won the battle; Shuja-ud-Daula was chased all the way to his capital, Lakhnau (Lucknow), and was taken prisoner by the British. In subsequent years he became the main instrument for the establishment of British rule in India. Thus, the battle of Baksar decided what the battle of Panipat had failed to settle. After the major contenders had eliminated each other the British won the crucial round in the struggle for supremacy in India. Clive returned to India and the East India Company assumed the Diwani of Bengal; Shuja-ud-Daula was reinstated in Oudh and had to give some territory to the Great Mughal at Allahabad, where he lived on as a British pensioner.

Clive's doubts about the suitability of the East India Company for the task of the civil administration of Bengal were certainly justified. The two years he spent in India on his third and last assignment (1765–7) did not give him much time for a reorganisation of the administrative machinery of the company, which was, after all, geared exclusively to commercial purposes. Corruption was rampant among the company's officers, who plundered Bengal to their hearts' content. Clive, himself, was certainly not averse to lining his pockets: he disapproved of corruption not on moral grounds, but for strategic reasons. Corruption is individualistic and undermines collective discipline. Therefore, Clive had the bright idea of organising a collective plunder of Bengal by means of a company formed by the servants of the East India Company in Bengal, which would have had a monopoly of the inland trade of Bengal and provided a handsome income to all its members. Bound by this common interest they would have maintained the collective discipline which was necessary for the preservation of British power. However, this plan did not materialise and corruption remained chaotic and undisciplined. The British were lucky that no major challenger appeared on the Indian scene in the wake of Clive's final departure. Otherwise, their future empire could still have been nipped in the bud.

The brilliant young Peshwa Madhav Rao, a great warrior like his ancestor Baji Rao, said at that time that the British had put a ring around India so as to put pressure on the country from all sides. But nobody was able to break that ring: even Madhav Rao would have been unable to do so, although he consolidated the power of the Peshwa once again and achieved several important military successes. Initially, Madhav Rao had a hard time in asserting himself against his ambitious uncle, Raghunath, who was in league with the British. Madhav Rao's aide in this struggle was his diplomatic minister, Nana Phadnavis, who was, similarly, later to check Raghunath's ambitions following Madhav Rao's early death. Instead of concentrating on the defence against the British, Madhav Rao had to turn his attention to another great challenger who appeared in southern India at that time: Haider Ali of Mysore.

Haider had been a general in the service of the maharaja of Mysore, whose throne he usurped in 1761. Within a very short time he had practically subjected the whole of southern India. His swift light cavalry was a formidable force. This upstart was the first Indian ruler who was ready and able to learn from the Europeans. He employed several French officers, built up a strong modern infantry of his own and carefully avoided facing the British infantry with his cavalry units. He also organised a disciplined administration, cancelled all fiefs and paid his officers regular salaries. The horses of the cavalry were also bought and maintained at the government's expense – they were not the property of the individual horsemen, as in other Indian armies. Haider even thought of taking care of the wounded soldiers and established a medical service in his army.

Had this able man entered into an alliance with Madhav Rao, they could have jointly defeated the British; instead, they continued fighting one another. In 1767 Madhav won a decisive battle against Haider; in the same year the British and their ally, the nizam of Hyderabad, confronted Haider. The nizam left the British in the lurch on the battlefield, and from 1767 to 1769 Haider fought several pitched battles against the British. He even threatened to attack Madras and forced the British to sign a peace treaty which was very much in his favour.

It seemed that the British had met a challenger who would put them to a severe test. Their position in India was not very favourable around 1770. Corrupt cliques were ruling the roost in Calcutta and Madras. The governor of Madras, Lord Pigot, who had tried to put an end to corruption there, had been arrested by his own officers and languished in jail, where he died in 1776. With such a chaotic state of affairs a determined Indian ruler could still have broken the British ring around India.

The British, however, were favoured by events. The great Peshwa, Madhav Rao, died in 1772, and Raghunath – as anxious as ever to succeed to this high office – entered into an alliance with the British and thereby split the Maratha forces so deeply that they could no longer hope to win supremacy in India. At the same time the British got a new leader who was going to dominate the Indian political scene for more than a decade: Warren Hastings became governor of Bengal in 1771, and governor general in India in 1774.

Warren Hastings: architect of an empire

Warren Hastings was the main architect of the British empire in India. He was not a warrior, but a great diplomat and a competent administrator. He was only seven years junior to Clive, whose political views he shared. Whereas Clive was daring and ambitious and had once aimed at a seat in Parliament and then received a commission as a lieutenant colonel, Hastings had patiently risen step by step in the East India Company's service. He joined this service in 1750 as a young clerk in Calcutta, in 1756 he was head of the factory at Kosimbazar and had been imprisoned by the nawab, the next year he was sent as the company's agent to the court of the new nawab, and in 1764 he had returned to Britain. Five years later he was appointed as a member of the council of the governor of Madras, where he was in charge of the company storehouses. His knowledge of India and of Indian languages, his diplomatic skills and his experience in commercial activities made him an excellent candidate for the post of governor of Bengal: he was duly appointed at the age of 39. Even so, nobody could have predicted at that time that this man would almost single-handedly turn the wheel of fortune in favour of the British during the subsequent fourteen years of his remarkable career.

The tasks which Hastings faced when he assumed office in Bengal were crushing. Only one year earlier the great famine of 1770 had decimated the population of Bengal and just at this juncture the board of directors in London insisted that the company should 'stand forth as Diwan' (i.e. assume direct responsibility for the civil administration of Bengal). So far the governor of Bengal had delegated this work to an Indian deputy (*naib diwan*) who carried on his business in the old style of the nawabs. This naib diwan had his office in Murshidabad, where the provincial treasury was also maintained until Hastings ordered its transfer to Calcutta. Except for some assertion of British control, however, Hastings could not reform the revenue administration all at once. Moreover, much of his attention was claimed by foreign policy (i.e. relations with Indian rulers).

236

Figure 5.5 Warren Hastings (1732–1818), painting by Joshua Reynolds, *c*.1768
(Courtesy of the National Portrait Gallery, London)

The nawab of Oudh was fighting sometimes against the Marathas and sometimes against the Rohillas, an Afghan community settled in the northern Gangetic plains about 200 kilometres to the east of Delhi. They were horse-breeders and -traders from the country of Roh in eastern Afghanistan, a conglomerate of several Afghan clans. Travelling with their horses to India, they had infiltrated into what came to be known as Rohilkhand where they established their rule when Mughal power declined. They also contributed to settled agriculture in their new home by introducing the method of irrigation by small underground canals of the type prevalent in Afghanistan and Iran. These Rohillas were formidable warriors who could not be easily subdued by the Marathas.

The Great Mughal, who had resided at Allahabad under direct British control, had been lured back to Delhi by the Marathas' promise that they would restore him to his old position of supremacy. The Great Mughal, as an instrument of the Marathas, could be quite dangerous to the British. Hastings stopped British payments to the Great Mughal; at the same time he backed the nawab of Oudh, with whom he concluded an alliance – thus enabling him to beat the Rohillas and to annex their territory. When

Shuja-ud-Daula died in 1775 his successor, Asaf-ud-Daula, was forced by Hastings to surrender the area around Benares (Varanasi) to the British: thus Oudh's acquisitions in the west were paid for in terms of losses in the east.

British landpower expanded, Hastings having no scruples about interfering with the affairs of Indian rulers – a fact which Edmund Burke was later to hold against him when he demanded his impeachment in Parliament. Hastings' methods were no doubt incompatible with the standards of Parliament: as much as MPs were willing to decry his methods, however, no move was made to restore the territories acquired by Hastings to the respective Indian rulers.

In his first years as governor general, Hastings was greatly handicapped in his decisions by the four members of his council who had come directly from London. These men made him feel that they knew much better than he did and regularly outvoted him. It was only when Philip Francis, the most brilliant and most arrogant member, returned to Britain in 1780 that Hastings could recover some freedom of action. Francis was convinced that he would have been a much better governor general than Hastings, and he obstructed Hastings' policy to a great extent. In spite of such obstructions, Hastings managed to pursue his own course rather successfully. He interfered not only with the affairs of his immediate neighbours, but also looked after western India where the governor of Bombay had tied British fortunes to the fate of the ambitious Raghunath, against whom Nana Phadnavis had marshalled the joint forces of the other Maratha leaders. The decisive battle took place in 1779 and Raghunath's army, together with the forces of the governor of Bombay, were defeated by the Marathas before British reinforcements from Bengal could reach the battlefield. Hastings reacted quickly and decided to teach the most important Maratha leader, Mahadaji Scindia of Gwalior, a lesson that he would not forget. In 1781 British troops were sent to Gwalior. They captured Mahadaji's stronghold and when the Maratha leader returned to it they defeated his army. Thereupon, Mahadaji came to terms with Hastings and concluded an alliance with the British. In 1782 the British and the Marathas signed the peace treaty of Salbei. Mahadaji thus emerged as the key figure of Indian politics. As long as Hastings remained in India Mahadaji did not raise his hand against the British: it was only after Hastings had left that Mahadaji briefly assumed a position of eminence unimaginable to Maratha leaders either before or after him.

The peace treaty of Salbei, with which the British returned to the Marathas, the territories in western India which Raghunath had given away to them, has to be seen in the context of British relations with Haider Ali. After Haider had imposed his peace treaty on the British in 1769, he had again rallied his forces in order to drive the British out of India once and for all. He was the only Indian ruler who did not look upon the British as merely one factor in the struggle for supremacy in India: uniquely, Haider saw them as the decisive threat to India in general, and had made up his mind to get rid of them at all costs. The events of 1778, when the British and the French were once more at war with each other and when the British were also challenged by the Marathas, seemed auspicious for his plan. He moved against the British in south India with an army far larger than any army which he had mobilised so far. Even Hector Munro (the victor of Baksar) and Eyre Coote (the victor of Wandiwash) whom Hastings had sent to defeat him, were not able to do so. Therefore, the peace treaty of Salbei served the important purpose of protecting the British in the west so that they had a free hand in the south. Haider got timely support from the French. The French admiral, Suffren, was able to hold his own against the British at sea, and French troops landed in southern India in order to join forces with Haider. At this stage, in 1782, Haider died but his equally brilliant son, Tipu Sultan, continued the war and, in 1784, imposed the peace treaty of Mangalore on the governor of Madras – which was very favourable to him. Hastings was furious when he heard about it. In fact, Tipu achieved this success when the general situation had already once more turned in favour of the British. The French troops under de Bussy – who had returned to India for a final campaign – had left Tipu in 1783 when they received the news that the war against the British had ended in Europe. So Tipu, who had staked his success on the French card, was badly disappointed – and yet he was able to conclude a peace treaty which was to his advantage.

When Hastings left India in 1785 to defend himself in London – he had been impeached by his critics in Parliament – the foundations of the British empire in India which he had laid were not yet secure. Tipu had not been vanquished and Mahadaji now raised his head and challenged the British in a way he had not dared to do as long as Hastings was around. Jointly, Tipu and Mahadaji could have destroyed these foundations; each, however, followed his own course of action and, in the end, the British were bound to triumph. Mahadaji had occupied Delhi in 1771 and had installed the Great Mughal there; for the next eleven years he was fully tied up with the warfare in the Maratha country. But just as the peace treaty of Salbei had permitted the British to concentrate on Haider and Tipu, Mahadaji was now free to consolidate his hold on northern India. In 1785 the powerless Great Mughal made Mahadaji the general administrator of the Mughal empire, and in this capacity Mahadaji dared to ask the British to pay the share of the revenues of Bengal which they owed to the Great Mughal. Mahadaji needed money urgently because he had to maintain a large army in order to control the then turbulent regions of northern India. Sikhs, Jats, Rajputs and Rohillas pursued their respective interests – sometimes fighting each other, sometimes joining forces to oppose an outside enemy. The Great Mughal's jurisdiction had shrunk to the outer limits of his capital. A contemporary saying claimed: 'The empire of Shah Alam extends from

Delhi to Palam.' (Palam is the site of the present airport at Delhi.) But even there he was not safe. In 1788 the Rohillas sacked Delhi and blinded the hapless Great Mughal. Mahadaji, who was just fighting the Rajputs, came too late to his rescue. Even Mahadaji's victory over the Rohillas in 1789 could not restore the central power, however, and when he died (1795) there was nobody left in India who could aspire to a position of supremacy.

In south India, Tipu Sultan had consolidated his position. After the war against the nizam and the Marathas he turned to the west coast and also rallied his forces for a renewed attack on the British. In spite of earlier disappointments he still hoped for French support and, with remarkably bad timing considering the imminence of the revolution, sent ambassadors to Paris. Hastings' successor in India was Lord Cornwallis, who had previously lost the war against the American colonists. Immediately devoting his attention to the campaign against Tipu Sultan, he concluded an alliance with the Peshwa and the nizam and defeated Tipu in 1792. Tipu Sultan had to return the territories which he had earlier taken away from the Marathas and the nizam and he also had to cede to the British some districts to the south of Madras and on the west coast. This was the beginning of British territorial rule in southern India. Cornwallis could have dismembered Tipu's realm completely, had he not wanted to retain him as a counterweight against the Peshwa and the nizam. Because of the latter consideration, Tipu was treated rather leniently, although the British did take away his sons as hostages until he paid the indemnity imposed upon him. Tipu was not satisfied with the limited role cut out for him by the British: he quickly paid up, recovered his sons and prepared for his next attack. In order to do all this he had to increase the land revenue demand, eliminate middlemen and assess the peasants directly. The demand was geared to the productive capacity of the soil and revenue collection was administered with great efficiency. This paved the way for the rather rigorous British revenue settlement of south India in subsequent years.

While preparing for the next attack on the British the indefatigable Tipu once more contacted the French and tried to humour the revolutionary government. In his capital he established a Jacobin club, whose members were entitled to address him as 'Citoyen Tipu' – a truly revolutionary measure for an Indian ruler. But a further turn of events in France prevented the dispatch of French troops to the subcontinent. Instead, Napoleon's Egyptian adventure and reports about Tipu's plans forced the hands of the British. The new governor general, Lord Wellesley, and his brother Arthur (later Duke of Wellington), designed a comprehensive campaign against Tipu. Arthur in a way performed a dress rehearsal for Waterloo at the head of the nizam's forces. Tipu was defeated and died defending his capital, Seringapatam, in 1799. The British annexed north and south Kanara, Wynad, Coimbatore and Dharapuram and, in the much reduced Mysore state, they reinstated the old Hindu dynasty whose throne Haider Ali had usurped. The struggle for supremacy was now clearly decided in favour of the British. Only one major enemy was left: the Peshwa, Baji Rao II, the son of Raghunath. The British isolated him in the following years by making friends with the maharajas of Gwalior, Indore and Baroda, who all retained their territories under British rule. With his influence restricted to the region around Pune, the Peshwa was no longer a serious threat to British power in India.

By the turn of the century the contours of the British empire in India were already firmly delineated. The coasts and the fertile plains of the interior were in British hands. The Indian princes who had made their peace with the British retained some internal autonomy, but could not conduct any foreign policy of their own: they were embedded in the British Indian empire like insects in amber. The only region where British control was still rather precarious was the northwest. The power vacuum that had come into existence here after Mahadaji Scindia's death was filled by the martial Sikhs, who established a kingdom under Maharaja Ranjit Singh at the very time when Tipu Sultan's realm in the south was captured. Just like Tipu Sultan, Ranjit Singh was a very competent military leader who tried his best to learn from the Europeans; in contrast with Tipu, however, he carefully avoided a confrontation with the British. He built up both infantry and artillery units on modern lines, but his main strength was still the Sikh cavalry – which could not always be easily coordinated with those other elements of the army. Under his weak successors Ranjit Singh's realm rapidly decayed and was finally annexed by the British. The pattern of dealing with the Marathas was repeated here. Sikh leaders who were willing to make peace with the British were accommodated and retained some autonomy, but the fertile plains of the Panjab came under direct British rule. This region became the granary of British India and the chief recruiting ground for the British Indian army. Generations of historians have tried to answer the same questions: why were the British able to extend their control over India within a few decades? How did a few isolated bridgeheads on the coast expand into territorial rule over vast areas? The British often tended to agree with those who maintained that this empire was acquired in a fit of absentmindedness. But there were others who used to emphasise that India was conquered by the sword and had to be held by the sword. There is some justification for both points of view.

The conquest of India never loomed large in British public awareness. No great national effort was required in order to gain this huge empire. The battles which the British fought in India were not of very great dimensions and they were fought with Indian mercenaries at no expense to the British taxpayer. Force of arms did play a major role both in the acquisition and in the maintenance of the empire, but it was a very parsimonious use of force. The conquest of India by a trading company meant careful cost-accounting in matters of warfare, just as in everything else. The British did not indulge in hazardous military adventures. They also knew how Indian rulers financed their war efforts: by plunder and land revenue. They learned this lesson very well, and they learned their lessons collectively. The company as an organisation would preserve the experience gained by its brightest and boldest members; hence, even its more mediocre recruits could carry on in the same vein. The affairs of Indian states, on the other hand, often revolved around the individual great man after whose death there was no continuity and very often a serious breakdown. In the most rapid phase of expansion the service of the company offered amazing careers to ambitious young men. The meteoric rise of Clive, from humble clerk to proud lord, could stimulate everybody's imagination – although very few could hope to emulate him.

Even a good organisation and able and ambitious young men, however, would not have guaranteed the success which the British enjoyed in India had there not been several favourable circumstances which contributed to it. The trade in textiles from Bengal was one of these preconditions. Highly specialised and extremely profitable, this trade required an increasing knowledge of the conditions within the country. In the years after 1720 when white cotton cloth from Bengal was exported as a semi-finished good to London where it was used by the new industry of cotton printing, the company had to be very resourceful in finding the right type of cloth and getting it bleached according to the specifications of the printers. Even while the Marathas were ravaging Bengal the agents of the company managed to get this cloth by shifting their supply lines from one district to another. Moreover, many British soldiers recruited for the company's troops in India were weavers who could work as technical experts when they were not engaged in warfare. Another factor which contributed to the British penetration of Bengal was the flow of silver with which they paid for the cotton cloth. This, in turn, facilitated the monetisation of the land revenue and made the Indian rulers look with favour, or at least with tolerance, on the activities of the British. Used to the methods of the counting-house, the British knew how much money the Indian rulers managed to collect. When a weak ruler challenged them and was defeated, they took full advantage of the opportunity thus arising. They were also aware of the importance of military finance, a subject which most Indian rulers never mastered. The great warriors were notoriously improvident and were often left without sufficient troops because they could no longer pay them. This was to some extent also true of Europe in the eighteenth century, where the British gained supremacy mainly because they knew best how to finance wars and how to keep their own engagement limited, getting as much leverage as possible out of the endeavours of other conflicting parties. In India, the British did the same. Here, however, they also annexed more and more territory, whereas they were satisfied with maintaining the balance of power in Europe. In Europe there was a concert of powers; in India there were only soloists who could be tackled one by one. While accomplishing all this, the East India Company still had nothing more than the legal title of 'Diwan of Bengal'. In India, where the personal element is always important, it was difficult to conceive of the new ruler in collective terms and thus a curious expression emerged for this collective entity: 'Company Bahadur' (*bahadur* = hero, an honorific title). 'Company Bahadur' claimed the heritage of the Mughal empire.

6

THE PERIOD OF COLONIAL RULE

COMPANY BAHADUR: TRADER AND RULER

The acquisition of a vast empire by a trading company was certainly a rather strange phenomenon. Contemporary opinion reflected this and those who participated in the endeavour were also puzzled. The royal charter under which the company operated had stated that the Crown claimed all territories which might be conquered by that company, but Parliament saw to it that this clause remained inoperative. Every twenty years the charter came up before Parliament for renewal of the company's privileges. There was a growing feeling that these privileges should be rescinded, the monopoly of trade being an anachronism and territorial rule obviously not the business of a company of traders. As early as 1701 the anonymous author of the *Considerations upon the East India Trade* had suggested the cancellation of the charter and a completely free trade with India. The company's factories, stated the author, should be taken over by the British government and financed by means of customs duties. Clive's offer to Pitt was even more attractive – not only customs duties, but the revenues of Bengal could now be used for government finance. Nevertheless, the risks, too, were high. The British political system could have been disrupted and, furthermore, there was the fear that military expenditure on the defence of the new possessions might soon be greater than the income they provided. Conquest with limited liability was preferable: the privileges of the company were renewed and it remained in control of the new possessions; Parliament was satisfied with an annual tribute of £400,000.

In the nineteenth century, when the trading privileges of the company were finally revoked, it still remained in charge of its territorial possessions. Its only business was to govern India and to get paid very well for this service. This transition could have been made just as well a century earlier. Eighteenth-century private traders, while happy to circumvent the company's monopoly, did recognise their self-interest in making use of the infrastructure and protection offered by the company and, therefore, did not raise a hand against it. More and more of these private traders became company directors and thus gained considerable influence over the conduct of its affairs. Many of these people were actually former servants of the company, and had gone on to establish their own agencies in India. Their interests were opposed to those of the shipowners who leased craft to the company and had also managed to obtain seats on the board of directors. Following the rise of the tea trade these shipowners supplied increasingly specialised and expensive ships to the company; they could not have used these vessels for private trade and were, therefore, deeply concerned about the rights and privileges of the company. Originally the strategy of leasing ships had helped the company to concentrate its capital on trade, but then the capital invested by others in ships compelled them to control the company.

The Regulating Acts

Apart from the shipping interests, there were further reasons for a postponement of the transition from the trading monopoly to the monopoly of territorial rule. In the final decades of the eighteenth century the latter monopoly would not have been a lucrative business. The struggle for supremacy in India cost a good deal of money. The company was heavily indebted and yet the directors insisted on getting their dividend. The government could not prevent this without, at the same time, risking that the directors might abdicate responsibility for territorial rule, thus enmeshing Westminster at a most inopportune moment. The endeavours of Parliament to pass Regulating Acts without abolishing the privileges of the company must be seen in this context.

The company was supposed to act as a buffer, which would shield the British political system from being directly affected by the course of events in India. For this purpose some changes in the management of the company's affairs were required. There should be a centralised command in India but this command should be checked by people who enjoyed the confidence of politicians in Britain. This is why the first Regulating Act of 1773 made provision for the appointment of a governor general and for the establishment of a council composed of four people sent from London who could advise and outvote the governor general. Warren Hastings had to suffer the consequences of this structure. Lord Cornwallis, his successor, accordingly insisted on an amendment of the 1773 Act, as he did not want to share the same fate.

The second Regulating Act of 1784, therefore, gave autocratic powers to the governor general in India; it did, however, also establish a London-based Board of Control, whose president was the precursor of the later Secretary of State for India. Three members of the Board of Control and three directors of the company constituted the Committee of Secrecy, whose decisions were binding on the governor general. The three directors of the company who belonged to this committee were not permitted to divulge its secrets, even to the other directors. This structure was well suited to the political purpose it was designed to serve. The governor general had, more or less, a free hand in India, his freedom being enhanced by the fact that communication between Calcutta and London took more than a year in those days. The Board of Control and the Committee of Secrecy in London laid down the main lines of policy to be followed by the governor general and acted as a mediator between the autocratic system prevailing in India and the British political system. Matters of trade were not discussed by the Board of Control. This arrangement was stable enough to make for a smooth transition from the monopoly of trade to the monopoly of territorial rule. Finally, the trade monopoly was abolished without causing a major disruption of the existing structure.

Although the Regulating Acts reflected a particular political constellation, the arrangements which they embodied evinced a surprising longevity. It was only the Mutiny of 1857 which put an end to the political mandate of the company. But by that time the British government was no longer afraid of shouldering the responsibility of ruling a vast empire.

When Hastings became governor general in 1774 the company was hardly equipped for the task of territorial rule. Just like Hastings himself, most servants of the company had worked in the commercial line and had no experience of revenue administration, which now became the financial mainstay of the company. Nevertheless, the bureaucratic structure of the company – with its covenanted servants who could be freely transferred and who followed a regulated career from junior to senior posts – did provide the administrative infrastructure for a modern system of government. Of course, inexperienced as they were, these British officers had to rely totally on their Indian subordinates and could be easily manipulated by them. At the same time, the British officers of this period were still much more interested in acquiring a thorough knowledge of Indian languages and traditions; they were not yet the arrogant men of a later day who felt that it was their duty to save India from barbaric superstition and moral degradation. Hastings sponsored the beginnings of Indology and welcomed the foundation of the Asiatick Society by Sir William Jones, Justice of the Supreme Court in Calcutta. Jones deliberately chose 'Asiatick' in preference to 'Oriental', because he wanted to study India's civilisation on its own terms rather than looking at it from the Western viewpoint implied by the word 'Oriental'. Such an attitude enabled the British of those days to master the tasks demanded of them by an environment of which they initially knew so little.

As far as the land revenue was concerned the British showed less consideration: even after the cruel famine of 1770 which killed about one-third of the population, they tried their best to squeeze as much money out of hapless Bengal as they could. Hastings adopted a method which had also been employed earlier by the nawab of Bengal: he auctioned the rights of revenue collection to the highest bidder. In this way he hoped to get optimal results with a minimum of administrative effort. But this system collapsed, and the commission of inquiry which Hastings had appointed in order to find out about the land revenue took some time to submit its report. In the meantime, Philip Francis – Hastings' inveterate rival – produced a plan of his own which greatly influenced future debates on the land revenue settlement.

Francis was well read in contemporary economic thought and produced a blend of liberal and mercantilist ideas mixed with precepts borrowed from the French Physiocrats, who taught that a tax on land should be the only one demanded by the state. Governed according to such precepts, Bengal would prosper and pay the tribute to its foreign rulers without much difficulty. First of all, there should be free trade in Bengal and the company should buy goods for export in the free market and no longer tie down producers by means of advances and contracts which made them dependent on the company. Exports from Bengal should consist only of manufactures and not of precious metals. Revenues should be assessed with a view to the needs of good government rather than on the principle of squeezing everybody as much as possible. There should be no tax other than the land revenue, because this revenue was a tax on the society as a whole by virtue of its being passed on to the consumer by means of higher prices. All other taxes could be abolished – especially all duties, which encumbered free trade. The land revenue should be settled permanently and the property on which this revenue would be assessed should be heritable and freely alienable. This last point was especially emphasised by Francis. However, permanent settlement and the emphasis on private landed property made sense only in the context of his other recommendations.

Hastings did not give much thought to his rival's proposals and Francis, who left India in 1780, could do nothing about their implementation. Hastings stuck to the annual assessment of the landlords (*zamindars*) without improving the legal position of their property. He was more concerned about the general problem of the civil jurisdiction of the Diwan of Bengal, for which he was responsible.

British law and Indian law

When Hastings turned his attention to the problem of civil jurisdiction he soon found out that under the benign supervision of his Indian predecessors this jurisdiction did not extend much beyond the city limits of Murshidabad, Dacca and Patna. Within a few years Hastings established eighteen new courts and tried to reform their rules of civil procedure and of appeal to a higher court. Even under Islamic rule this civil jurisdiction (*Diwani Adalat*) was always conducted on secular lines and was handled by special judges and not by the kadi, who could only base his decisions on the Koran. The highest authority of appeal was the diwan himself, but Hastings felt ill-at-ease with this responsibility and asked the presiding judge of the Supreme Court at Calcutta, Sir Eliah Impey, to do this work for him. Impey accepted and drafted rules for civil procedure which were, of course, entirely novel as far as Indian practice was concerned.

The procedures of serving notice on the defendant, the record of the proceedings, the form of the judgment – all these were unheard of before. This was the beginning of the amazing spread of British jurisdiction in India. This was by no means an altruistic measure: it helped to strengthen the foundations of British rule and it contributed to state finance, because the court fees were quite high. Nevertheless, Indian litigants eagerly flocked to these new courts which competed with all kinds of traditional jurisdiction. Impey, the pioneer in this field, was not praised for his work, for his critics pointed out that by accepting a post under the East India Company he had jeopardised his impartiality as presiding judge of the Supreme Court of Calcutta, which was a royal court independent of the company. He was now serving two masters, the Great Mughal, from whose authority the Diwani jurisdiction was derived, and the king, who had appointed him to his high office at Calcutta. In a way all British officers in India served two masters at that time; only in Impey's case it was so very obvious.

Impey's successor, Sir William Jones, went beyond civil procedure and judicial organisation and enquired into Indian legal traditions, which he got translated and codified. This was not just a matter of academic interest but of immediate practical significance. Young British officers with no legal knowledge, who had no idea at all about the intricacies of the Hindu law of inheritance and other subjects of this kind, were appointed as magistrates and had to decide cases which Indian litigants brought before them. These officers needed codified law for ready reference. But codification was actually incompatible with the spirit of tradition, which consisted of a continuous mediation between ancient rules and changing reality. The Brahmins, as guardians of this tradition, had derived much of their influence from this mediating role. A printed code on the shelf of a British judge or magistrate precluded this mediation: it settled all questions once and for all. But this was not what Jones was criticised for by the next generation of legal luminaries who subscribed to the ideology of utilitarianism; he was attacked simply for having produced an inconsistent and unscientific jumble of traditional law, rather than having done away with it altogether and so facilitated social progress through the introduction of modern British law into India. This utilitarian generation not just disregarded, but utterly despised, Indian traditions.

The clash of British legal ideas and judicial practice prevailing in India was even more pronounced in the field of criminal jurisdiction and the penal code. Originally this jurisdiction was not the diwan's responsibility but remained with the nawab in his capacity as military commander (*faujdar*). The nawab was bound to follow Islamic law with all its rigours in this respect. The British were revolted by the mutilation of thieves and other such drastic penalties prescribed by Islamic law. When they took over the responsibility for criminal jurisdiction they had to listen to the advice of Islamic law officers attached to their courts, but they could find ways and means to circumvent the provisions which were repugnant to their principles. However, while they refrained from mutilating convicts they much more readily resorted to capital punishment. After all, death sentences even for thieves and forgers were the order of the day in England at that time, where everything affecting property was treated as an aspect of inviolable public order.

Islamic law was altogether different. There was no public prosecutor, crimes were punished only if the criminal was accused by the aggrieved party, and the law of evidence was hedged in by so many conditions that it was often very difficult to convict a criminal at all. It was only the most blatant crime, which by its very ostentation challenged established authority, that was punished with due severity. The British saw to it that criminal jurisdiction became much more efficient, so many a criminal who would not have been convicted under Islamic law was quickly executed by them.

Absconding peasants and the permanent settlement

The British idea of private property also played an important role in the major reform associated with the name of Hastings' successor, Lord Cornwallis, who ordered the permanent settlement of the land revenue of Bengal as earlier advocated by Philip Francis. This order of 1793 did not just fix the amount of the revenue assessment once and for all; it also bestowed the right of heritable and alienable private property in land on all those who were assessed in this way. These were not the peasants who cultivated the land, but the zamindars or landlords who had, so far, been only revenue collectors who could keep a certain percentage of what they managed to squeeze out of the peasantry. They became landlords in the British legal sense of the term only due to Lord Cornwallis's famous regulation.

Later historians have interpreted Lord Cornwallis's motives in many different ways. Some see in him the executor of Philip Francis's bright ideas; some say he wanted to create a class of squires in Bengal who would play the role of the improving landlord after the fashion of English country squires; others argue that he created something like Irish landlords (i.e. absentee rent receivers) rather than English squires. The debate will probably never be finally settled. A much more practical motive of Cornwallis has been lost sight of in this great discussion.

He certainly was not the executor of Philip Francis's plan: otherwise, he would have adopted Francis's other suggestions, too, because the permanent settlement as a social and economic measure made sense only in the context of the plan as a whole. Cornwallis had a more immediate problem in mind. Since the great famine of 1770 there had been a shortage of cultivators; vagrant peasants roamed around searching for land which they could get on better terms. Zamindars were competing with each other for the services of these itinerants, and when the time came for paying the land revenue they usually complained about absconding peasants from whom they had been unable to collect anything. These complaints were sometimes mere pretexts for paying less revenue; often, however, they corresponded to the facts. In any case, the British authorities were unable to discover the facts. The Regulation of 1793 cut this Gordian knot: the demand was firmly fixed once and for all and the payment was the exclusive responsibility of the zamindar, whose estate would be auctioned if he did not pay his dues at the appointed time. Excuses about absconding peasants were irrelevant under these new provisions, because now only the zamindar paid revenue; the peasants, as his tenants, paid rent to him as their landlord. This payment of rent was a private transaction of no concern to the authorities. If the landlord did not get his rent he could sue his tenant in a court of law. For the state budget this was a great improvement, because the income from revenue could now be predicted fairly well. In 1793 when this measure was implemented, the assessment was not at all lenient; only in later years when the population grew once more and rents could be increased did the zamindars attain some prosperity. Nonetheless, they never became improving landlords but just pocketed the unearned increment, as the British economist David Ricardo called the rent derived from the scarcity of land and the rise in prices in general. In Lord Cornwallis's time the zamindars could not yet dream of this bright future: they could hardly make ends meet. Cornwallis could not afford to treat them leniently as he had spent a great deal of money on fighting Tipu Sultan. In fact, the permanent settlement of 1793 must be seen in the context of this dilemma of rising military expenditure and the uncertainty of revenue collection from absconding peasants. After Tipu had been vanquished in the south, no permanent settlement was introduced by the British in that part of the country; nor did they create landlords, preferring instead the direct assessment of the peasants which Tipu had managed with great efficiency in order to finance his wars.

In addition to the permanent settlement of Bengal, Lord Cornwallis introduced another major reform which was of even greater importance for the future development of India. He changed the terms of service for the East India Company's covenanted servants by raising their salaries substantially so as to place them beyond corruption. Whereas the servants of a trading company could be paid nominal salaries as they were making their real money on private deals, civil servants in charge of the administration of large territories could not be treated in that way. At the same time, this reform meant that these new, well-paid posts would attract more talent –

which was badly needed for the enormous tasks which grew day by day as the policy of conquest greatly extended British territorial rule in India.

The next governor general, Lord Wellesley – a dynamic conqueror indeed – accomplished much in this field within a very short time. Without the new type of civil service he would not have been able to control the new territories which he acquired. He was very conscious of the qualities needed for this type of civil service; accordingly, he established Fort William College, Calcutta, in which the young servants of the company were subjected to some formal education immediately after their arrival in India. Instruction in Indian languages was one of the main priorities of this college, so that the young servants might become competent rulers not entirely at the mercy of interpreters.

The civil servants also influenced Wellesley's plans from the very beginning of his period of office. He operated on the same wavelength as the expansionists among them who felt that their own careers could be advanced in this way. Many of these new servants of the company were military officers rather than traders and they were interested in conquest rather than commercial profit. Wellesley did not mind diverting funds sent to him for the finance of trade to waging wars in India. This displeased the directors of the company and they tried to recall him, but he had friends in high places who protected him. The militarisation of the company progressed rapidly under him. Territorial acquisitions interested him much more than the investment in export commodities. This British Napoleon in India was greatly helped by the imagined threat of the real Napoleon who had, after all, entered Egypt. Wellesley did not take this threat seriously but readily used it as an argument when defending his own strategy.

Changing patterns of trade and Indian enterprise

While 'Company Bahadur', in this way, became more and more of a ruler and less of a trader, the trade itself underwent a major structural change due to political conditions in Europe and the progress of the industrial revolution in England. Napoleon's blockade greatly affected the re-export of Indian textiles to the European continent; at the same time industrial production of textiles in England reduced the demand for Indian textiles in the home market, too. Consequently, the export of textiles from Bengal dwindled – from £1.4 million worth in 1800 to only £0.9 million in 1809. Imports of British goods increased over the same period – from £6 million to £18 million. Under such circumstances the trading monopoly of the East India Company no longer made sense; it was abolished in 1813. The company was now only one among many firms active in the India trade. In fact, this trade was of interest to the company purely as a means of transfer of India's tribute. International financial transactions of various kinds were used for this purpose. For instance, Indian revenues or income

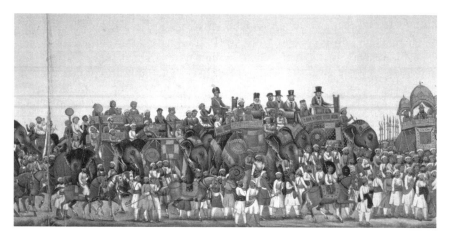

Figure 6.1 Durbar Procession of Great Mughal Akbar II, *c.*1815, painted by an unknown Indian artist. The British Resident and his men (with hats) are more conspicuous than the Great Mughal and his young sons

(Courtesy of the India Office Library and Records (Add.Or.888))

from the company's opium monopoly would be transferred to China in order to buy tea, which was then sold in London; or private traders shipped Indian cotton to China and paid their sales proceeds into the treasury of the company at Canton, obtaining drafts on London or Calcutta in return. Thus, the company had no problem in transferring the tribute to London. In fact, these financial transactions provided additional profit, whereas a direct ship-ment of precious metals from Calcutta to London would have caused a great deal of expenditure.

In India the years after 1813 were a glorious time for the 'agency houses'. They had grown up under the protective shield of the East India Company and had, initially, handled such business as providing European goods to the British officers in India or investing their savings in the 'country trade'. After the company's monopoly was abolished these agency houses entered the indigo trade in a big way, financing indigo cultivation and processing by means of advances, and then exporting the finished product. As there were no regular banks in India as yet, these agency houses also served as their own banks. But the capital at their disposal was limited and the indigo factories in which much of it was invested could not be sold at the time of a crisis in the indigo trade. This trade was very volatile, and in the years after 1830 the agency houses collapsed.

This development coincided with another important event: in 1833 Parliament decided that the East India Company should cease to be a trad-ing company. Consequently, the company had to liquidate all its commercial and industrial assets in India. This included indigo factories and silk-reeling establishments, too. An astute Indian entrepreneur used this opportunity to his advantage: Dwarkanath Tagore, the grandfather of Rabindranath Tagore, the famous poet and Nobel laureate. With a British business partner who had not much capital but good connections, he established the firm Carr, Tagore & Co. He raised the capital for this venture by means of mortgages on his extensive landed property. On his lands he also cultivated indigo and grew mulberry trees for the silkworms. He bought the East India Company's indigo factories and silk-reeling workshops at a price which he could dictate, as these establishments were surrounded by his own property.

Carr, Tagore & Co. was the prototype of the later managing agencies which became so prominent in India. Whenever Tagore thought of a new profitable venture – a coal mine or a steamship company, for example – he sponsored the founding of a new firm for this purpose and put Carr, Tagore & Co. in charge of managing the enterprise. In this way he built up a captive market. For instance, he could sell coal from the mine at a higher rate than the ordinary market rate to the steamship company which he also controlled. He also sponsored a pioneering venture in the banking business by founding the Union Bank together with several other Calcutta merchants. This was supposed to be an independent bank and not subservient to any one company, it was to follow conservative banking principles and was not to get involved in speculative ventures of individual firms. In fact, it did work along these lines quite successfully for several years, although Tagore himself did not refrain from heavily influencing the conduct of the bank's business. But the next economic crisis of 1846–7 swept away both the Union Bank and Carr, Tagore & Co.

Tagore, who died in London in 1845, did not live to see this. After his death no other Indian entrepreneur achieved comparable success, because the favourable conditions which marked the years of his prosperity were not to be found again in later periods, nor had they ever prevailed before his time. Prior to 1830 the East India Company and the agency houses had dominated the scene; after 1847 began a new period of Indian economic development, which was less favourable to Indian private entrepreneurs. The years from 1830 to 1847 were a period of rapid expansion in the export of agricultural produce; the East India Company, which was no longer permitted to trade on its own account, worked like an export bank by financing the business of Indian traders so as to transfer the tribute in this way to London. After 1847 the railway age began in India and British capital was invested in the construction of thousands of miles of Indian railways. The British investors got a guaranteed rate of return of 5 per cent on their investment, which was a very good rate at that time. In India everybody who had some money to spare would expect a higher rate of return in trade or in moneylending. Thus, there was a split capital market and the types of investment which attracted British and Indian capital were clearly set apart.

During these years of economic change the British had penetrated deeply into the interior of India and had organised the revenue settlement of many provinces. The 'permanent settlement' remained restricted to Bengal and Bihar. In the south, Tipu Sultan and the Marathas had established a rather rigorous direct assessment of the peasants; in the north the assessment of zamindars or village communities prevailed. The British continued, nearly everywhere, the type of assessment set up by their immediate predecessors. But they were much more efficient in revenue collection. The Mughal revenue administration clearly differentiated between assessment (*jama*) and collection (*hasil*) and it was taken for granted that the latter would never quite match the former. The Mughal treasury was used to the idea that the budget depended on the rains and other vagaries of men and nature. The British revenue officers held that if the revenue was correctly assessed, it could also be collected without any deficit. They were encouraged by Ricardo's theory of rent in claiming as much as possible of the 'unearned increment'. Ricardo had postulated that rent accrues to the landholder due to the scarcity of land and the rise in prices; according to his definition, rent is influenced by prices and not vice versa. This is just the opposite of what Francis had said when he advocated a tax on land as the only tax on the grounds that this would be passed on to the consumer by means of higher prices. Francis's idea was more in accordance with Indian reality than was Ricardo's theory, because the latter thought of the tenant as a free entrepreneur who will lease land only at the market rate, as determined by the general price level. The Indian peasant, however, was not a free entrepreneur of this type: he paid more or less grudgingly the charges imposed upon him and it did not matter to him whether they were supposed to be rent paid to a landlord or revenue paid to the government. British revenue officers wrote learned notes on rent and revenue and neatly distinguished between the two, whereas in Indian languages no such distinction was made. In the nineteenth century Francis was forgotten and Ricardo's doctrine prevailed – particularly at Haileybury College, where civil servants received their training before being sent out to India.

The uses of education

The arrogant confidence with which a new generation of rulers set out to reconstruct India found its most famous expression in the *obiter dicta* of Lord Macaulay, who was sent to India in 1835 to serve as law member on the governor general's council. Only a few decades before Macaulay's arrival in India, Sir William Jones had shown great respect for Indian traditions; Macaulay, in contrast, simply despised these traditions about which he knew so little. He confidently asserted that one shelf in a Western library would contain more valuable knowledge than all the literature and wisdom of the Orient put together. He recommended that Indians should receive the education of 'gentlemen' to make them faithful replicas of their British rulers in every respect other than blood. In this way he took his stand in the debate between 'Anglicists' and 'Orientalists' then raging in Calcutta. The former, like Macaulay, advocated an English education for Indians; the latter wanted to cultivate the Oriental languages.

This was not just an academic debate: very practical problems were at stake. The company had a small education budget of 100,000 rupees and it had to be decided how to spend this. Moreover, the question of the medium of education and administration had to be settled. The issue was very complex because prominent Indians – for instance, the great Sanskrit scholar Raja Radhakantha Deb, whom one would have expected to side with the Orientalists – thought in practical terms about jobs for the boys and supported the Anglicists, although they would not generally have subscribed to Macaulay's views. The Hindus, especially, were quick to take to English; under Mughal rule they had mastered Persian as the language of administration; they now learned the language of the new rulers as well. The first message of Indian nationalism was articulated in English in the Hindu College, Calcutta, where a young poet, de Rozio, half-European and half-Indian by birth, taught the first generation of English-educated Bengali college boys. They were referred to as Derozians and many of them rose to eminence in later life; in their college days, however, they shocked Indian society by breaking as many of its taboos as possible. The conservative directors of the college – among them Radhakantha Deb – held de Rozio responsible for all this trouble and sacked him. Even so, many generations were to remember him as the harbinger of a new age. The other hero of this new age was Raja Ram Mohan Roy, founder of the Brahmo Samaj sect which formulated the creed of an enlightened Neo-Hinduism akin to Christian Unitarianism, to which he was very much attracted. Roy knew Sanskrit, Arabic, Persian and English, and was a rare mediator between the old and the new in India. He died in 1833 in England, where he had gone as an emissary of the Great Mughal who was still the nominal sovereign of India.

Western college education spread very quickly in India in the first half of the nineteenth century. The pace was set by three government colleges in Calcutta, Madras and Bombay. In Calcutta and Madras they were called Presidency Colleges; in Bombay the government college was named Elphinstone College, in honour of a distinguished governor of Bombay. The Scottish Presbyterians who had done a great deal for education in Britain followed suit with the establishment of the Scottish Churches College, Calcutta, and of Wilson College, Bombay. The graduates of these colleges found good jobs as teachers, lawyers and even as judges on the benches of the British law courts.

The civil service, on the other hand, still remained reserved to British recruits who had studied at Haileybury College in England. This college had been set up in <u>1806</u> by the <u>directors of the East India</u> Company in response to the gauntlet thrown down by Wellesley's establishment of Fort William College, Calcutta. The directors were taken aback by Wellesley's move because the servants of the company were at that time not yet selected by means of a competitive exam, but on the recommendation of directors who usually bestowed this patronage on some poor but promising young relative. If Fort William College could fail such people in examination it would have been a disaster for the directors concerned. Consequently, the functions of Fort William College were reduced to those of a language school and the directors put up their own college in England. If a candidate

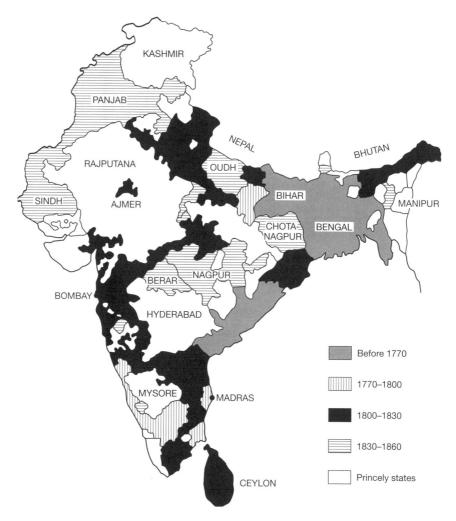

Map 6.1 The British penetration of India (1750–1860)

failed there he would not be sent to India; the director who had recommended him, however, could suggest another name. Haileybury had quite a distinguished staff of professors, among them Thomas Malthus, whose ideas on political economy influenced many civil servants. The number of students was small and the college could not suddenly expand when more civil servants were needed after 1826, due to the acquisition of large territories. The East India Company then established a committee in London to hold competitive exams; finally, in 1853, the company stopped enrolling new students at Haileybury College and introduced freely accessible competitive exams for all posts. It so happened that the last class graduated at Haileybury just a few months before the company lost its mandate due to the Mutiny of 1857.

The Mutiny of 1857

The uprising in northern India, which terminated the existence of the East India Company, almost put an end to British rule in India. While radical Indian nationalists later referred to this uprising as the 'First Indian War of Independence', the British called it the 'Mutiny' because the Indian soldiers who had helped them to conquer India had turned against them. But this revolt of 1857 was neither a national war of independence nor simply a mutiny. It spread over much of northern India and affected many strata of the population. The new educated elite did not participate in it for fear of the chaos or restoration of the old order it might bring. The people who led this uprising had no use for English-educated gentlemen. Apart from the soldiers, the rebels were mostly disgruntled landlords and peasants, and some disinherited princes. The aged Great Mughal in Delhi and the heir of the last Peshwa – forced by the British to stay in Kanpur, northern India, far from his old base at Pune – emerged as the key figures around whom the rebels rallied. The insurgents were not aimless marauders: they did fight for a cause, but this cause was hopeless because the restoration of the old order, which they had in mind, was impossible. The lack of leadership and coordination among the rebels was only a reflection of this deeper problem.

Nevertheless, the rebels managed to continue their struggle for quite some time. The British had no contingency plan for such a revolt, and were completely taken by surprise and slow to react. The risks were high for the British because they were, after all, fighting against people whom they themselves had trained in the art of warfare. Even among the civilian rebels there were dangerous elements – such as the Jats around Delhi, the cowboys of India who were skilful horsemen and courageous fighters. The British had alienated them by assessing their pastures as if they were agricultural land and this over-assessment had nearly ruined them. Rajputs and Gujars were also among the rebels, particularly in areas which had been reached by the British only fairly recently and where the memory of autonomy was still fresh. The rani of Jhansi became the Indian equivalent of Joan of Arc during this revolt. She fought at the head of her troops with fierce determination. The British had annexed her state because her husband had died without a male heir and the adoption of a son by her had not been recognised by them. Whereas the British had tried to maintain friendly relations with Indian princes in the period before the consolidation of their hold on India, they had turned to a policy of annexation in the 1850s and used any available pretext. Lack of an heir was the most convenient excuse, although mismanagement of the state could also be given as a reason for deposing the prince and introducing direct British rule. The latter was done in the case of the nawab of Oudh in 1856 and this caused resentment among those soldiers of the British Indian army who belonged to this state.

All these various causes for dissatisfaction would not necessarily have led to an open revolt had it not been for the mutiny of the soldiers at Meerut on 10 May 1857 and their subsequent march to Delhi. The immediate cause of this mutiny was the distribution of new cartridges greased with animal fat. The handling of these cartridges violated the soldiers' religious taboos and there were rumours that the British were doing this intentionally, in order to convert the soldiers to Christianity after they had been polluted with this grease. Communication between British officers and Indian soldiers was no longer what it had been in earlier days. The social distance between officers and men had increased: no longer the daring and resourceful warriors of old, these officers were people looking for a well-paid job and they treated their soldiers like menial servants. The soldiers, on the other hand, were experienced men who had seen many years of service. They had conquered the Panjab for the British only a few years previously. They had to be handled with some skill and consideration.

The British colonel who commanded the garrison at Meerut was sadly deficient in both. He wanted to pre-empt all resistance to the new cartridges by introducing them in a demonstrative manner. He lined up ninety soldiers, lectured them, had the cartridges distributed and was shocked to see that all but five of the men refused to take them. The resisters were tried for breach of discipline and, in line with British tradition, were judged by their peers, i.e. fellow-soldiers. This caused additional resentment because the accused suspected that their fellow-soldiers would arrive at a judgment which they thought would please the colonel, rather than do justice to them. This was exactly what happened: all culprits were sentenced to long periods of rigorous imprisonment and the colonel lined up his troops in order to witness how the convicts were put in chains.

Next day the mutiny broke out and the mutineers marched immediately to Delhi – no attempt being made to prevent them. The British seemed to be dumbfounded by this unforeseen catastrophe. The Great Mughal around whom the soldiers rallied could not provide much leadership. He finally found an ex-corporal of the British Indian artillery to serve as commander of the troops, who managed to hold Delhi from May to September 1857 and to besiege Lucknow until November 1857. In Kanpur the British asked the Peshwa – of all people – for help and entrusted their local treasury to him. Within a day he also joined the mutineers and expelled the British from Kanpur. For some time almost the whole of northern India seemed to be lost. But then irregular Sikh troops were organised against the rebels. They had an axe to grind because they had only recently been subjugated by the very same army units to which the mutineers belonged, and so gladly fought against them. After Delhi and Lucknow were recovered the scene shifted to Gwalior, which was held by the Peshwa and the rani of Jhansi until June 1858. The rani died fighting while defending Gwalior.

The long and severe fighting left indelible marks. The over-confident liberalism of the British, who had believed that they were bestowing the blessings of civilisation on a grateful India, quickly evaporated. India had proved to be ungrateful and hostile. Of course, the new English-educated elite had remained loyal, but the British did not accord them respect for this and were more impressed with the old feudal leaders, some of whom had valiantly fought against them. From now on they no longer wanted to offend these 'natural leaders of the people'. The majority of princes and zamindars who had not raised a finger thus profited from the fighting spirit of a few. A new 'aristocratic school' of British civil servants dominated the Indian scene in the next decades. They believed that India was conservative and must be governed in a conservative spirit.

In addition to this change of approach, there were also material consequences of the mutiny, which were of immediate importance. The treasury was empty and the East India Company was at the end of its tether. As long as the shareholders could pocket the dividend derived from the tribute of India, everything was fine; but now they were faced with having to raise a good deal of capital in order to foot the bill for the whole affair. Therefore, they gladly left India to the Crown and thus the company ceased to exist in 1858 after 258 years' chequered career. The fears which had prevented Pitt from entrusting British rule in India to the Crown no longer applied: Parliament had consolidated its position, the monarchy was thoroughly constitutional, and the British economy had grown so much that the annual tribute of India – which amounted to about £36 million, was not going to upset the political system because it was only about 5 per cent of the British national income. Moreover, at the time the Crown took over India not much of a tribute could be expected in any case. The future prospects of India were, nevertheless, rated more optimistically. Railway investment was going ahead, India was turned into a typical colonial economy, exporting raw material and importing finished goods. The British empire in India was going to be an asset to the Crown.

THE COLONIAL ECONOMY

Colonial economies were, in general, open economies subjected to the impact of the world market and not national economies, which could determine their own fate and develop their home market. While this was a feature common to all colonial economies, there were also distinctive traits mainly related to the supply of labour and the availability of natural resources. In America, for instance, labour was scarce and African slaves were imported who worked for the most part on large plantations devoted to single crops such as sugar, cacao, coffee and tobacco. In India, labour was abundant and the prevailing mode of agricultural production was that of small peasant households. Plantations existed only for the production of tea in the hills and they recruited their labour in other regions of India. There was hardly any capitalist agriculture. The Indian landlord was a rentier and not an entrepreneur. Under the conditions of the monsoon it was wiser to live on the compulsorily acquired surplus of peasant families rather than to run large farms or plantations with hired labour. Revenue demand or debt service – and very often both of them – forced the peasants to produce for the market. The colonial rulers could profit from the collection of revenue as well as from the cheap supply of cash crops grown by the peasants. On the other hand the colony also provided a market for British goods. There was, of course, a dilemma in this import and export business. Expropriating the surplus value of peasant production would diminish the purchasing power of the peasants.

Colonial economies also provided opportunities of safe investment for citizens of the metropolitan country because political power, the legal system and the control of the currency insured them against risks which they would face in other foreign countries. Accordingly one should have expected that India would attract a large amount of British investment, but actually only about 10 per cent of British overseas investment found its way to India. As we shall see later, the railways were the most important investment project. Indian industry attracted British capital only to a very marginal extent. Indian entrepreneurs could have also turned to the British capital market. But at a time when Indian industrial investment increased in the latter part of the nineteenth century, the depreciation of India's silver currency discouraged Indians from borrowing money in London as the debt service was due in gold, whose value was rising.

The management of the Indian silver currency was the trickiest subject in the period of British colonial rule. Colonies usually coined no currency of their own, they used the currency of their rulers. But India had its well-managed silver currency ever since the days of the Great Mughals and the British had simply taken over the Mughal mints. As long as everybody was free to take silver to the mint and get it coined by paying a very small seignorage, the government actually did not conduct an interventionist monetary policy. But as we shall see when we now turn to the ebb and flow of silver, the Indian silver standard faced crucial problems under British rule.

The ebb and flow of silver

At the time when the crown took over the government of India, silver had once more started to pour into the country due to the investment in the railways. The first half of the nineteenth century, however, had been a period of deflation in India, because the country had been drained of silver by the East India Company. The silver rupee had been made the only legal tender in 1835, but since there was not enough silver around, prices fell to a very low level. Peasants engaged in subsistence agriculture and artisans producing for local markets could survive under these conditions. In southern India the handloom weavers who could buy cheap food and cheap cotton could even compete with industrial products imported from abroad. The Bengal weavers, however, whose production had been geared to the export market were severely hit by this competition. The bones of the weavers were bleaching in the plains of Bengal, as Governor General Lord Bentick had put it. Karl Marx then repeated this dramatic phrase and it has been quoted very often ever since. Actually, this was a local phenomenon which was not characteristic for the whole of India. The less dramatic but more important feature was the general depression of the deflated economy. Buying power was severely restricted. A modern Indian industry could not be expected to grow up under such conditions.

When the flow of silver reached India once more in the 1850s this changed the economic situation substantially. The spread of the railway network will be discussed later on, here it may suffice to state that the money invested in it reflated the Indian economy. The first Indian cotton and jute textile mills were started in the 1850s. The great demand for Indian raw cotton at the time of the American Civil War led to a further inflow of silver. In the 1870s the price of silver started to decline in the world market and India absorbed a huge amount of it, thus helping to support the price of silver. This was greatly welcomed by the silver traders in London. From 1868 to 1887 India imported precious metals (mostly silver) worth 1.8 billion rupees and this amounted to about 18 per cent of India's total imports of commodities in this period. Reflation now turned into inflation, but it was a slow and steady one which contributed to a constant rise in prices for agricultural produce. There was, however, an ever-increasing export of foodgrain towards the end of the nineteenth century. The depression of the gold prices of grain in the world market did not affect India, which was saved from it by the inflow of silver. In fact, India could export grain at the cheapest rate and, at the same time, support the price of silver by absorbing so much of it.

Under such conditions the British were quite happy to keep the Indian mints open to the free coinage of silver, but in doing so they were faced with a crucial dilemma. The 'Home Charges' consisting of pensions, debt service, etc., which the Government of India had to pay in gold could no longer be met by revenues collected in silver. The land revenue, which was settled for long periods (usually 30 years) in most parts of India, could not be suddenly enhanced. Import duties could not be increased, because it would have been castigated as a protective tariff by British industrialists. The income tax was not one of the major pillars of the British–Indian state. Its enhancement would have been resented by a small but very vocal minority. Faced with this quandary, the British finally closed the Indian mints to the free coinage of silver in 1893. From now on the rupee was a token currency maintained at the rate of 1s. 4d. by the Secretary of State for India. He could do so only by subjecting India to a bout of deflation which particulary affected the indebted peasantry whose debts appreciated and thus became more burdensome. Indian grain exports continued throughout this period and the government, which insisted on the principles of free trade, did not interfere even when famines ravaged the country while grain shipments were leaving the ports. The structure of India's export trade had changed dramatically from 1871 to 1901. In 1871 raw cotton and opium were the two major export commodities, which together accounted for 55 per cent of the value of total exports. By 1901 their combined share had dwindled to 18 per cent while other agricultural produce such as wheat, rice and tea now accounted for more than half of the value of exports. On the other hand, cotton textiles and jute products had also emerged as important export commodities. Whereas they had been almost insignificant around 1870 these two industrial products jointly made up nearly a quarter of exports at the end of the century. These industrial products were mostly manufactured in the big port towns, but the huge volume of agricultural produce exported around 1900 owed its outflow to the railway network, which had expanded by leaps and bounds in the last three decades of the nineteenth century.

The spread of the railway network

India was blessed by an early and rapid start of railway expansion mostly due to the fact that the British public was used to investment in railways and the scope for it had been exhausted at home and was also receding in America where British capital had helped to push the railways ahead. It so happened that Governor General Lord Dalhousie who drew up a bold plan for 5,000 miles of railway tracks in India in 1853 had earlier served on the railway board in London. Even before he came out to India, contracts for the construction of the East Indian Railway and the Great Indian Peninsular Railway had been signed in 1849. The Government of India provided generous guarantees to these private companies. They would get 5 per cent return on their capital even if their business was running at a loss. At a time when the general interest rate was 3 per cent, this was a very attractive offer. This also meant that the lines could be extended without looking for immediate economic benefits. The Indian taxpayer had to bear the burden of the railway guarantees and he had no voice in this matter.

After the experience of the mutiny, the government was more interested in the strategic use of the railways for rapid troop movements than in economic gain. Traversing the Gangetic plains and reaching right up to the northwestern frontier was the main aim of this strategic plan. The development of the interior of the country was not of immediate concern. There was no attempt to establish cross-connections within the country. The railway map reflected for a long time the main interest in connecting the big ports with their hinterland. By 1900 the Indian railways had established an impressive 'track record' of 25,000 miles, but they were still in the red as far as their revenue from freight and passenger services was concerned. Indian nationalists criticised this waste of capital which could have been more profitably spent on irrigation works. These critical comments were silenced only much later when the railways finally yielded a profit in the years immediately preceding the First World War. The railways also emerged as India's greatest employer. By 1900 they employed about 400,000 men. The better paid positions were, of course, occupied by expatriates or by Anglo-Indians (sons of British fathers and Indian mothers) who had become somewhat of a 'railway caste'.

The increasing shipment of agricultural produce by the railways had an impact on the rise of prices. As pointed out earlier, the slow but steady inflation pushed up the prices anyhow, but wherever the railway arrived there was a sudden price increase. This was due both to the export demand and to the possibility of inter-regional shipments. Before 1885 agricultural prices reflected the local vagaries of the monsoon, after that they showed a steady upward trend and a decline of seasonal fluctuations. This also contributed to an expansion of rural credit which then increased indebtedness and made the peasants more vulnerable under adverse conditions.

In Great Britain, railway construction had become a second leading sector after the textile industry. Unfortunately, India missed the chance of an industrial take-off again, although Karl Marx had predicted in 1853 that now, since the railways had come to India, the British could not help but industrialise the country due to the linkage effects which the production of rails and engines would have. In fact, in 1865 the first railway engine was produced in India, but then the Suez Canal was opened in 1869 and engines, rails, bridges, etc. could all be shipped to India from Great Britain. Because of the cheap sea transport by steamer even British coal was less expensive in Bombay than Indian coal carried across the country from the coalfields of Bengal. This was due to the freight charges of the Indian railways which showed a rather strange pattern. Shipments from and to the ports could be made at favourable rates whereas cross-country shipments, particularly if they required transfer from one line to another, were much more expensive. India's connections with the world market were, thus, fostered by the railways while Indian industries producing for the home market were at a disadvantage in this respect. The success story of the Indian railways was not without its drawbacks. It was a success for British investors and industrialists, but for the Indians it was less so – and they had to pay for it, after all.

The fate of Indian industry

Railway construction did not lead to an industrial take-off in India as we have seen. But why had it failed to take off earlier? This question has been debated by many Indian economic historians who have argued that British rule had led to a de-industrialisation of India. After all, India had been the major producer of cotton textiles in the eighteenth century before the British experienced their industrial revolution. Actually, both the rise of the industrial revolution in England and the failure of its transfer to India can be explained in terms of the availabilty of labour. England profited from a mercantilist policy which helped it to proceed along a path of import substitution from cotton printing to weaving and spinning, while still conducting a booming re-export trade in printed Indian cotton textiles. In this way it was in touch with a vast market abroad in which it could then sell its own products. The British were a small nation numbering hardly 8m. at the end of the eighteenth century. They also had a booming woollen industry, which could not release labour for the new cotton textile industry. The acute scarcity of labour forced the British to invent labour-saving machinery. This is how the industrial revolution started. Such machinery was not very expensive. It could have been easily reproduced in India, as happened very quickly in continental Europe. But in India there was abundant skilled labour and no need at all for labour-saving machinery.

The large number of Indian artisans actually continued their production throughout the colonial period. Leather goods, tanned hides, pottery, brassware, fine silk – to mention only a few items – were increasingly produced for the market. Commercial capital financed production and distribution. As long as raw materials and food were cheap, the artisans could make both ends meet. When both food and cotton prices rose in the second half of the nineteenth century, India also faced a bottleneck in cotton spinning. It was at this stage that modern spinning mills were set up in India. British makers of textile machinery were eager to sell them to Indian entrepreneurs. Parsis and Gujaratis in Bombay invested their capital in this new line of manufacturing. Indian yarn was even exported to East Asia where it almost replaced British yarn. Industrial yarn was increasingly used by Indian handloom weavers who did survive even when the Bombay millowners established composite spinning and weaving mills. They did this initially so as to be able to use their surplus yarn. In the years before the First World War the Indian cotton textile industry had 6.8m. spindles and 100,000 looms and employed about 250,000 millhands. It had spread beyond Bombay to Ahmedabad and Solapur, but Bombay still housed almost half of the total capacity of this industry.

While this industry was concentrated in western India and was almost completely owned by Indians, Calcutta had, in the meantime, become the centre of an equally important jute industry. Jute could be grown in the ricefields of Bengal. If it fetched a better price it would replace rice. Initially, raw jute was exported to Scotland where the first jute mills were established in Dundee. Scottish entrepreneurs soon saw the point that it would be profitable to establish mills near the jutefields. The peculiar industrial organisations which they built up in Calcutta for running jute mills, coal mines, tea plantations, etc., were called 'managing agencies'. Their mode of operation was somewhat like that of Carr, Tagore & Co. mentioned earlier. Initially, such managing agencies were operating factories on behalf of their owners, earning a commission of about 10 per cent for this. But then these agencies turned into holding companies, floating new firms on the stock market and controlling them while holding only a small percentage of the shares. This was financial wizardry of high calibre. Initially, Indians had no chance to enter into this charmed circle. The predominance of expatriates in this field was also due to the fact that production was geared to the export market and this required close cooperation with partners or agents in London, whereas the Indian industrialists in Bombay were producing for the home market and were usually also linked to distribution networks and to the trade in raw cotton.

The jute mills remained concentrated in Calcutta. There were only about 54 of them before the First World War, but they were larger than the average cotton textile mill of which 211 existed by that time. All these mills required a great deal of textile machinery which was supplied by British firms. The first Indian firm making textile machinery could start production only after 1947. The colonial economy precluded the emergence of linkages in this field, too. Anyway, industrial capital was scarce and whoever had money to spare would rather invest it in another textile mill than in the manufacture of machines.

There was only one industrialist with a vision in India at that time: Jameshed Tata. He had made his money first as a millowner. As a trader in imported steel, he knew about Indian demand for that commodity and had the bold idea of starting an Indian steel mill, since India had both coal and iron ore in abundance. He hired American engineers as he was sure that the British steel industry would not like his plan. In 1907 Tata Iron & Steel Co. started production in Jamshedpur, Bihar. The capital of 23m. rupees invested in this plant would have sufficed for the establishment of more than 23 textile mills and it could have been a costly flop if the First World War had not led to large British orders for Indian steel. Jamshed Tata had died in 1903; he did not live to see the triumph of his ideas. He had also sponsored another important venture: the Indian Institute of Science in Bangalore. Tata was convinced that Indian industrial growth would depend on research and development, but it would take a long time before his dreams came true in this field. The colonial economy was obviously not suited for such visions.

THE REGIONAL IMPACT OF BRITISH RULE

With the transfer of the responsibility for British rule in India to the Crown this vast empire came under the direct influence of the Victorian monarchy. Queen Victoria herself was highly interested in her Indian empire; she took Hindi lessons and invited Indologist Max Mueller to lecture to the royal court. She also took the title Empress of India, which she assumed in 1876, very seriously. The glory of her well-established monarchy was also reflected in the new title of 'viceroy' to be added to the old one of 'governor general'. But the old pattern established under the Regulating Acts remained the same: the viceroy served a five-year term of office, which was rarely extended. His short period corresponded to the life-cycle of Parliament. There was a tacit convention to keep India out of party politics at home, but this did not mean that the appointment of the viceroy was unaffected by party interests. There was always somebody who had to be rewarded and who, for some reason or other, did not quite fit into the cabinet.

At the height of British imperial power it did not really matter who was sent to India as viceroy. Only if there was a major misadventure, such as Lord Lytton's Afghan war, could Indian affairs affect an election campaign at home. Gladstone's 1881 electoral victory, Lord Lytton's subsequent recall and the appointment of the great Liberal, Lord Ripon, was a rare instance of decisive political intervention. The appointment raised high hopes among the educated in India who believed in British liberalism. But they soon found out that one liberal viceroy did not make a liberal empire. In fact, the viceregal impact on the Government of India was usually ephemeral. The term of office was much too short. Also, trapped between the secretary of state at home and the powerful civil servants in India, the viceroy could hardly do more than delay or veto policies which he did not like. Moreover, he could acquire some political weight only if he had the full support of his bureaucracy.

The secretary of state for India, as a cabinet minister backed by the majority in Parliament, was politically much more powerful. Compared with other cabinet ministers, however, he had the serious handicap that most of his subordinates were far away in India and could be reached only via the viceroy. Relations between the secretary of state and the viceroy were very complex. The great distance separating them required an elaborate correspondence, so everything concerning these relations is extremely well documented and has, accordingly, attracted generations of historians who have sometimes made too much of these high-level transactions. The Government of India was dominated by the civil servants who spent their whole career in India. Parliament did not take much interest in the subcontinent. In fact, even this interest declined after India had come under direct British rule. As long as the charter of the East India Company had to be renewed by Parliament at regular intervals, there was an occasion for reviewing everything concerning India in great debates; since this was no longer required, debates on India were few and far between and were mostly conducted by a few specialists who addressed empty benches. Parliamentarians are, after all, most vitally affected by everything concerning the taxpayer's money. The Indian taxpayer was not represented in Parliament and, thus, the secretary of state was rarely asked any serious questions concerning his management of the tribute exacted from India.

Legislation, jurisdiction and administration

Since India was not represented in Parliament there was a need for an Indian legislature after the rule of the East India Company was terminated. In the days of the company the governor general had simply settled all issues by means of regulations. This kind of legislation by the executive was rough and ready and did not quite correspond to the standards of modern jurisprudence. This is why a law member was added to the governor general's council in 1835. Lord Macaulay, and the other law members who succeeded him, did a great deal for the codification and technical perfection of British law as applied to India – but, of course, a law member was no substitute for a legislature.

Such a legislature was established in 1861. Its members were nominated by the governor general; the majority were British civil servants, although a few Indian notables were also included so as to get the benefit of native opinion. Actually, this Imperial Legislative Council just provided a convenient alibi for the executive, which could get passed any law it thought it needed for its purposes. Three independent High Courts in Bombay, Calcutta and Madras had also been established in 1861. The benches of these courts were occupied by highly qualified judges, and Indian judges were also appointed to them. As judges who, in the British tradition, preferred judge-made law based on precedent to the hastily contrived acts of a legislature, these legal luminaries were often at loggerheads with the Imperial Legislative Council and many acts had to be amended after their inconsistencies were exposed in a leading case. The British administrators were not discouraged by judicial criticism and built up an imposing edifice of legislation in India. Some of the acts of the Imperial Legislative Council were even exported to British colonies abroad.

One important line of this legislative work was the enactment of statutes embodying codes of law and unifying legal procedure. Such were the Civil Procedure Code, the Indian Evidence Act and the Transfer of Property Act. There were no great controversies about these acts, which were drafted by expert law commissions. Controversies arose when the administrators passed acts held to contravene such sacred principles as the freedom of contract, which were thought to be blessings bestowed by the British on India. The eviction or rack-renting of tenants and the growing indebtedness of independent peasants to moneylenders, who treated their debtors like tenants-at-will, alarmed the administrators. They feared that the rather brittle imperial structure could never withstand a great wave of peasant unrest. For these political reasons they were prepared to forget about the freedom of contract and to enact restrictions on rent enhancement and on the transfer of land to moneylenders.

Rural India was of great importance to the British administrator who began his career in an Indian district as collector of revenue and district magistrate and usually believed that, having been close to the grassroots, he understood the masses. The British empire in India was a system of foreign domination: India was certainly governed with British and not with Indian interests in view. Nonetheless, the individual British civil servant in India was subjectively convinced that he was trying his best to work for the Indian people in his charge. The British tradition of trusting the 'man on the spot' encouraged and motivated the district officer whose service was, indeed, the mainstay of the empire.

Senior administrators who rose to high positions in the Government of India were deeply influenced in their views on Indian affairs by the experience of their years in the districts, which, of course, belonged to one particular region and province. Imperial structure and its regional impact were interrelated in this way as the Government of India always consisted of administrators who had grown up in a particular regional administrative tradition. This tradition reflected a curious blend of pre-British practices and British adaptations and innovations. A survey of the provinces of British India will illustrate this spectrum of hybrid traditions.

Differential penetration and hybrid traditions

The administrative penetration of India by the British was highly differentiated in many ways. First, there was a time-lag of almost a century between the acquisition of Bengal and the conquest of northwestern India. Furthermore, there were significant differences in the intensity of British administration, largely due to the manner in which the administrative machinery of previous regimes had been geared to the exigencies of colonial rule. Great tracts of the interior of the country were subjected to indirect rule only. In those parts the patterns of British administration were copied by Indian princes in their own peculiar ways. Even in areas under direct British rule the Indian administrative staff carried on most of its earlier style of administration. The British district officer was sometimes completely in the hands of his Indian subordinate staff, but there were also many instances where astute British officers used their own Indian assistants in order to break up the charmed circle of local administration. The fact that these British officers were highly paid and, thus, above the temptations of corruption, and that the pattern of communication among the elite civil service was fairly open and not encumbered with feudal attitudes, helped to establish an efficient administration – efficient at least with regard to the limited purposes which it served, i.e. the maintenance of law and order and the collection of revenue.

Eastern India: the hub of the colonial economy

The region which was exposed to the British impact for the longest period of time was Bengal and Bihar, the area of the 'Diwani' and of the 'permanent settlement'. But the intensity of administration was in many respects rather modest in this area. The permanent settlement had greatly limited the revenue-collecting duties of the district administration: the district officer worked more in his judicial capacity as a district magistrate and the British impact made itself felt more by means of the ubiquitous law courts than by the presence of executive government. Civil servants who grew up in the Bengal tradition normally disapproved of all measures which demanded executive intervention and tended to rely on the working of the courts.

At the same time the spread of English education produced a flood of Indian lawyers who naturally sympathised with this point of view. Local Bar Associations in every small district town with their Bar Library and their professional solidarity became focal points of public opinion in Bengal. Calcutta, with its High Court, its university and its famous colleges, became the hub of this new political culture. Zamindars who enjoyed the fruits of the 'permanent settlement' often became absentee landlords who built palatial houses in Calcutta and sent their sons to the university.

This new elite, the *bhadralok* (people of good families), was highly interested both in English literature and in a revival of Bengali literature. A Bengali Renaissance was hailed by many who combined a new type of philosophical Hinduism with a romantic nostalgia for some of the more popular forms of religion. Some of the representatives of the new Bengali elite looked exactly like the Indian 'gentlemen' whom Macaulay had wanted to produce; now that they actually existed – well dressed and polished and speaking better English than their British masters – the colonial rulers were frightened and looked upon them with disgust. The Bengali 'Babu' was so obviously 'Unindian' that he could not be respected as a true representative of his nation. The humble peasant – illiterate, honest and hardworking – was praised by the British instead. The educated elite was, of course, very small and in eastern India it was largely restricted to the Bengali Hindu upper castes. The Muslim peasantry of east Bengal and the tribal and feudal society of Bihar had not much in common with this Bengali top stratum. In areas outside Bengal the educated Bengali was often resented as 'sub-imperialist' – an instrument to provide the infrastructure of British rule. In this capacity the 'Babu' was, indeed, welcomed by the British, whose own cadre of civil servants was, after all, extremely small. Scores of clerks and bookkeepers were needed to do the rulers' bureaucratic business; it was not so much by the sword as by the pen that the British held India.

In eastern India, Bengal and Bihar became the main areas of production for export cash crops such as indigo, opium and jute, and Assam emerged as a major tea-producer. British firms organised this export trade. They owned tea estates, coalmines, shipping lines, jute mills, etc. India had never attracted European settlers to any great extent. But the staff of the British firms in Calcutta – mostly Scots – emerged as an important pressure group which had a great influence on the Government of India.

Eastern India, with its metropolis, Calcutta, thus provided a classic example of a colonial economy with all its social and cultural concomitants: a poor, exploited peasantry, a small landed and educated elite and an even smaller but very powerful European business community organising the export trade. The export surplus which India always had to have in order to be able to pay its tribute, or home charges, was mostly provided by eastern India.

The evolution of the United Provinces of Agra and Oudh

The adjacent region beyond Benares (Varanasi), which also belonged to the Bengal Presidency, had come under British rule much later than eastern India. Some districts along the rivers Yamuna and Ganga were ceded to the British by the nawab of Oudh in 1803. The administrative penetration of these districts remained fairly slight for some time, but the commercial impact of the East India Company was noticeable as indigo and opium were grown to an increasing extent as export cash crops. Indian merchants participated in this trade, which suffered a severe setback in the 1830s when the agency houses collapsed in Calcutta.

It so happened that at exactly the same time as this trade depression affected the region, energetic British revenue officers descended upon it and imposed a rather tough settlement. This was no longer a permanent settlement, but one which was to be revised at regular thirty-year intervals. The basic rule adopted for this settlement was that half the net rental assets should be claimed as revenue. Rent was assumed to be a function of market prices, but since this did not work in India as smoothly as in Ricardo's theory, the rule was finally overturned. The revenue officers now settled both rent and revenue in such a way that the rent was fixed at about twice the amount of the revenue which the officers thought they could obtain from the land. This made the revenue officer an extremely powerful person in the northwestern province, as this area extending from Delhi to Allahabad was called. Following the annexation of Oudh, the same administrative tradition was extended to that part of the country.

The depression of trade and the tough revenue settlement, combined with a shortage of money, greatly affected this region in the 1830s and 1840s and finally contributed to the revolt, which coincided with the Mutiny of 1857. Earlier, as the heartland of the Mughal empire, this area had been dotted with many towns which housed the local administrative elite and also served as markets. Such centres declined under British rule. Only Allahabad prospered as the provincial capital, and Kanpur emerged as a major industrial centre of northern India.

The Agra Division, as the British administrators called the districts ceded to them by the nawab of Oudh in 1803, was adversely affected by the policies of the new rulers. Reports of itinerant medical doctors in the service of the company show that this was a fertile region with large tracts of forest which helped to maintain its ecological balance. Within a short time the British deforested the area both for security reasons and for obtaining charcoal used for making bricks in innumerable kilns. They also encouraged the growing of cash crops. Combined with the introduction of stiff revenue settlements this led to a rapid exhaustion of the soil. What was once a fertile tract soon became a drought-prone one and by the 1840s the region's degraded soil could no longer support the agricultural regime imposed upon it by the British.

The United Provinces of Agra and Oudh, as they were named in 1901, was a very large and heterogeneous territorial unit of British India. Its eastern part, where rice is the main crop, witnessed a large increase of population and of poverty; its western part, particularly the districts around Meerut where wheat is grown, was more prosperous. The rural areas, in general, were dominated by Hindu folk traditions. The fairly large Muslim minority of the United Provinces (about 17 per cent of the population) was mostly settled in the towns (about 44 per cent of the urban population).

This dichotomy was paralleled in language and literature: Urdu, the *lingua franca* of the Mughal empire, was associated with urban Muslim culture; Hindi and its many dialects was the idiom of the rural Hindus. Movements such as that for the recognition of Hindi in Devanagari script (i.e. the Sanskrit alphabet) as an official language in the Urdu-dominated courts of law (where proceedings were recorded in Persian characters), as well as campaigns for the protection of the sacred cow from the Muslim butcher, merged into a general stream of Hindu nationalism in the late nineteenth century. This development greatly alarmed the Muslims and gave rise to communal conflicts.

The British had certainly not created these conflicts, but they took advantage of them in line with the old maxim 'divide and rule'. After the Mutiny they had not trusted the Muslims; indeed, there was a suspicion of a Muslim conspiracy, which seemed to be confirmed by the role which the Great Mughal was made to play at that time. Towards the end of the nineteenth century this British attitude changed as it became clear that the Muslim minority would look to the British for the protection of its interests against the Hindu majority. Sir Syed Ahmad Khan was a prominent member of the Urdu-educated administrative elite and rose to eminence in British service. He contributed a great deal to this new image of the Muslims as modern loyalists who were no longer sulking because the British had put an end to Muslim rule in India. He established a Muslim college at Aligarh, near Agra, which was designed to impart Western education to Muslims while, at the same time, emphasising their Islamic identity. This college, later called Aligarh Muslim University, became an ideological centre whose influence radiated far beyond the province in which it was established. Challenged by the foundation of a Muslim university, the Hindus soon made a move to start a Hindu university which was eventually established at Benares (Varanasi) and became a major centre of Western education. The reflection of the impact of Western education as introduced by the British in terms of the establishment of two sectarian universities in the United Provinces was characteristic of the political and cultural situation in that part of India.

The Madras Presidency: limitations of the British impact

In the Dravidian south these northern problems and conflicts did not exist. There were only a few Muslims, mostly traders, in the south and there was also no self-conscious Neo-Hinduism. Traditional Indian life was less affected here by the British impact than elsewhere. The districts were huge units in the south, much larger than most districts in the north, and consequently the British district officer and his small staff could hardly make any significant impression. This fact was in striking contrast with the administrative ideology of the Madras Presidency, which had inherited a tradition of a very stern and direct revenue administration from its immediate predecessors. The Madras civil servant, accordingly, grew up in the *ryotwari* tradition of dealing directly with the peasantry. Although this was the dominant tradition, however, nearly one-third of the Madras Presidency was actually under some kind of 'permanent settlement' with zamindars, and

272

some parts which were nominally ryotwari were, in fact, held by landlords such as the *jenmis* of Malabar – Brahmin landlords who had been classified as *ryots* (peasants) for the purposes of the revenue settlement.

With all this medley of traditions and superimposed constructions, the Madras administration managed fairly well to adjust to a great variety of local conditions: the area encompassed the extremely fertile terrain of ancient kingdoms in coastal lowlands near the mouths of the major rivers, as well as barren uplands and mountainous tracts. The Madras administration was known for its masterful inactivity, its reluctance to produce any kind of legislation and its slow responses to any queries from the Government of India. The people were left fairly undisturbed by the administration and reciprocated by showing only rare traces of unrest. Public opinion was dominated for a long time by a small elite of English-educated Brahmins who were rather moderate in their political views. The fact that there were four major Dravidian languages – Kannada, Malayalam, Tamil and Telugu – represented in the Madras Presidency, initially restricted active communication to the few who knew English. (The polyglot nature of this area later led to a demand for provincial boundaries determined by language.)

In economic terms the Madras Presidency was much less 'colonial' than eastern India. Its connection with the world market was slight, as it had hardly any important export commodities to offer. The different fates of the weavers in Bengal and those in the south reflected this situation. In Bengal, where great quantities of textiles were produced for export in the eighteenth century, the change in the demand for textiles due to the industrial revolution in England caused a serious dislocation; the southern weavers, by contrast, produced mostly for the home market and could survive as long as food and cotton were cheap. Even the spinning of yarn still continued in the south at a time when the import of industrially produced yarn had long since replaced indigenous spinning in northern India. Long distances and a lesser density of population reduced the frequency of commercial communication in the south, whereas the populous northern plains with their great rivers were much more accessible even before the railways opened up the interior of India. When the railways were built they also traversed first of all the northern plains and penetrated the interior of south India much more slowly. Thus, the British impact, both in administrative and economic terms, was less intense in the south than in eastern and northern India.

The Bombay Presidency and the 'Gateway of India'

The Bombay Presidency, which encompassed western India from Sindh to Kanara, was also a very complex territorial unit. Its many languages (Sindhi, Gujarati, Marathi, Kannada) precluded active communication and its commercial connections were also handicapped by problems similar to those which have been noted in relation to southern India. Coastal Gujarat always had maritime trade relations, but the thin strip of the west coast in front of the steep Western Ghats was a poor and isolated region. The 'Desh', as the highlands beyond the Ghats are called, was also isolated in its own way. It was sparsely populated and before the railway cut across the Ghats and linked Bombay with this vast hinterland, the 'Desh' remained quite inaccessible. Nevertheless, it was subjected to a rather intensive British impact, because this was the heartland of the Marathas whom the British had finally vanquished in 1818 and whose tough revenue administration they had taken over.

This was the most radical ryotwari system in India and the British took pride in the scientific accuracy of their work in this region. The army, entrusted with the survey work, produced excellent maps on which the settlement officers could base their assessment of the land, analysing the quality of the soil in great detail for this purpose. The Bombay revenue officers were so sure of the scientific accuracy of their settlement operations that remissions of revenue, which were often resorted to in other provinces, were not tolerated by them. They would, at the most, suspend the revenue collection in a bad year; never would they remit the amount once and for all because they believed that this would have been an admission of a faulty assessment. This tough system was mitigated only by the flexibility of the ubiquitous moneylender, who provided credit whenever the revenue authorities threatened to confiscate land for arrears of revenue. This led to large-scale indebtedness and finally to riots against the moneylenders in 1875, greatly to the alarm of the authorities. But as only a few districts near Pune were affected, the system as a whole was not upset. The vast dimensions of India and the variety of regional conditions actually saved the British from any large-scale confrontation with the Indian people. The slow working of the administrative machinery also prevented the emergence of widespread and explosive unrest. In all Indian districts with no 'permanent settlement' revision settlements had to be conducted mostly at intervals of thirty years. However, because the settlement staff could not tackle more than one district per year there was necessarily a differentiation of these settlements due to this time-lag. Therefore, every district had a revenue history of its own and grievances which were noted in one district were absent elsewhere, or at least did not arise at the same time. This was certainly not part of a deliberate policy of 'divide and rule'; in effect, though, it worked as if it had been designed for this purpose.

Economically, the Bombay Presidency was also less 'colonial' than eastern and northern India. Only for a brief period in the 1860s was this region in the limelight as a major centre for the production of cotton which was then in great demand on the world market due to a shortage of American cotton during the Civil War. The fact that the railway had crossed the Ghats and penetrated deep into the 'Desh' around 1860 contributed to this sudden cotton boom. Bombay emerged as a leading port at that time, but when the boom was over and cotton was cheap again, Bombay became India's great industrial centre with a large textile industry which produced some yarn for export but mainly cheap cloth for the Indian home market.

Unlike Calcutta's jute industry – which was exclusively export orientated and dominated by British entrepreneurs – this import substituting textile industry of Bombay was built up by Indian businessmen, particularly Parsis and Gujaratis. The number of foreign businessmen settled in Bombay was small and they never emerged as a pressure group, as was the case with the British community of Calcutta. On the other hand, partnerships between British and Indian businessmen of a kind that hardly existed in Calcutta since the demise of Carr, Tagore & Co. were fairly frequent in Bombay.

This metropolis of western India was very cosmopolitan. It took pride in being the 'Gateway of India' and in this capacity it became more prominent after the Suez Canal was opened and steamships eliminated the need to wait for the monsoon. The fact that for many decades British coal was cheaper in Bombay than Indian coal from the mines near Calcutta shows the commercial importance of this western connection. Of course, this was also due to the freight rates charged by the railways which, while procuring coal cheaply for their own use, made others pay for it dearly. This was not very helpful for the industrialisation of India, and gave the advantage to Bombay, which had access to coal delivered by sea.

The rise of Bombay as an industrial and commercial centre was of great importance for all of western India. This city set the pace in thought and action, and in this respect it was particularly significant that this was not an imperial city like Calcutta but a city of indigenous enterprise. The new elite of this part of India was also very different from that of eastern India. No absentee landlords of large estates had palatial homes in Bombay. An urban middle class dominated the scene. The graduates of Bombay's many colleges came mostly from families with rather modest means: they worked hard to get jobs which enabled them to make a living and perhaps also to get other relatives educated. There was no 'Renaissance' here as in Bengal, but the regional languages and literatures did develop and so did a lively political journalism. Municipal politics also played a great role in Bombay and municipal government was taken very seriously. In spite of Lord Ripon's emphasis on local government and the legislation accordingly introduced by him, this field remains, to this day, rather neglected in India. But the people of Bombay had a sense of civic consciousness and some of the most prominent men of the city were associated with its municipal corporation.

The Panjab and the martial races

The greatest attention was paid by the British to the province which they conquered last: the Panjab. Initially, the Panjab was a 'Non-Regulation

Province' to which the various regulations made by the governor general were not extended. The district officers were, accordingly, very free in dealing with problems as they saw fit. Riding through the countryside and dispensing justice from horseback was considered to be the best style of administration here. Many of the early district officers were not civil servants but ex-army officers. They liked this rough and ready way of governance and claimed that this was what the people of the Panjab were used to. The Sikh government, which had preceded British rule here, was, indeed, a tough one.

The British continued most of the prevalent practices of revenue settlement with peasant proprietors organised in village communities. But, whereas the Sikhs had collected their revenue mostly in kind and took a share of about two-fifths of the produce, the British wanted their revenue in cash and introduced the usual assessment based on long-term averages rather than sharing the risks of each harvest with the peasantry. Accordingly, the moneylender became of crucial significance here, too. Peasant indebtedness and land alienation increased until the British took the drastic step of passing a Land Alienation Act in 1900, which prohibited the transfer of land to non-agriculturists. Experience with legislation in other provinces had shown that it was difficult to define who was an agriculturist and who was not; this Act therefore specified by caste and community those whom the British recognised as agriculturist and those whom they wished to exclude.

The great concern for the agricultural communities of the Panjab was also due to the fact that the British recruited most of the soldiers for the British Indian army from these communities of martial races. In the days before the First World War about one-third of the British Indian army consisted of Sikhs and Panjabi Muslims. The pay received by these soldiers was a major contribution to agricultural investment in the Panjab. Whereas most other provinces received not much in return for the revenue which they paid, the Panjab was certainly in a more advantageous position in this respect. In addition, while they did not do much about irrigation in other provinces, the British did build irrigation canals in the Panjab and settled ex-soldiers in these newly established canal colonies.

British education made an impact on the Panjab only in the late nineteenth century. Government College, Lahore, had been established in 1864 but had a very small staff and few students in its first decade; by the end of the century the college was attended by about 250 students. In the meantime, however, some private colleges had also been established in Lahore, among them the Dayanand Anglo Vedic College sponsored by the Arya Samaj.

Neo-Hinduism had reached the Panjab in the form of the teachings of Swami Dayanand Saraswati, a Gujarati who also had some following in western India. The greatest response to his message came from the Panjab's few educated elites who eagerly joined his Arya Samaj. The odd combination 'Anglo Vedic' in the name of the college reflected the educational programme of the Arya Samaj: modern English education was to be matched with a kind of Vedic fundamentalism. Career prospects and a new feeling of identity were offered to the elite, which was, indeed, greatly in need of both.

Dayanand's emphasis on Hindu solidarity, his criticism of the caste system and the strong stand which he took against Islam and Christianity appealed to the Panjabi mind; at the same time, of course, it alienated the Muslims. The British, too, watched the Arya Samaj with suspicion. The very autocratic government of this province tended in all instances to look askance at anything which seemed to deviate from the straight path of loyalty to British rule. The British impact on this province was certainly of a very special kind.

The role of the army and the 'great game'

The British preoccupation with the Panjab has to be seen in the context of the development of the British Indian army after the Mutiny of 1857. The soldiers of the Panjab had helped the British to defeat the mutineers and to 'hold India by the sword'. The Mutiny had also taught the British the lesson that they had to send more British troops to India, even though this was rather expensive. In the last decades of the nineteenth century the British Indian army consisted of 140,000 Indian and 70,000 British soldiers; despite the disparity in numbers, the expenses for the latter were much higher than for the former. The Indian troops were under the command of British officers whose salaries were twice or three times what they would have been at home. When they returned to Britain on retirement they received high pensions – an important share of the 'home charges', which India had to pay.

At the height of the age of imperialism the British Indian army was frequently in action and military expenditure increased correspondingly. The Afghan war (1878–80), the conquest of Upper Burma (1885), wars against the tribes on the northwestern frontier (1896 and 1898) – all demanded an ever greater military budget which increased from 200m. to 300m. rupees (i.e. from about one-quarter to one-third of the total budget of British India).

The colonial rulers could afford this only because their income had also increased as the composition of the various revenues changed. In 1858 the land revenue made up 50 per cent of all revenue income, 20 per cent was derived from the opium monopoly and 10 per cent from the salt tax, the rest consisting of customs and excise, etc. The salt tax was a very reliable one, as it was based on a government monopoly of the manufacture and collection of salt. At the end of the century only 25 per cent of the revenue income consisted of land revenue, opium was no longer of much significance and the salt tax had been reduced; now, customs duties and excise were of much greater importance. This is why the increased military expenditure could be met.

Recruiting the 'military races' of northwestern India made sense also in the context of the threat perceived by the British in the late nineteenth century, because Russia advanced in central Asia and came closer and closer to India's frontier. The 'great game' of capturing outposts in this region kept the imperialists on tenterhooks. The Russians had conquered Samarkand in 1868. Afghanistan seemed to be endangered and the British tried to convert it into a reliable buffer state. After all, the Great Mughals had always kept Kabul. The British ought to claim this heritage, too. But Lord Lytton's Afghan war ended in a complete disaster. Only one man returned to India, telling about the loss of the entire British expedition corps. The new Amir of Afghanistan, Abdul Rahman, who had won the war, was able to ward off both the British and the Russians. In 1893 he concluded a border treaty with the British emissary Mortimer Durand. The 'Durand Line' became the border between British India and Afghanistan. In 1899 Lord Curzon was sent to India as viceroy. He was the leading British player in the 'great game' and was keen to secure British spheres of influence in central Asia, Persia and Tibet. When Japan defeated Russia in 1905, the Russians opted out of the 'great game' and concluded a treaty with the British in 1907. The British empire in India was now rather secure. It encompassed an enormous area from the Durand Line in the northwest to the eastern border of Burma.

In its territorial dimensions the empire was well settled and faced no major challenges any longer, but its internal order was somewhat of a problem. No further mutinies occurred after 1857, but the 'natives' asserted their rights and demanded constitutional reforms. Although some over-confident imperialists would argue that India was won by the sword and should be held by the sword, the colonial rulers knew that they could never control the millions of India by force alone and had to govern them with their consent.

THE PATTERN OF CONSTITUTIONAL REFORM

In 1885 the Indian National Congress met for the first time in Bombay. It was a fairly small gathering of members of the educated elite from the various provinces of British India. At the provincial level there had been Presidency Associations in Madras and Bombay, as well as the British Indian Association, Calcutta, whose younger and more radical members had then sponsored the Indian Association. This latter group was particularly energetic in its pursuit of the idea of a National Congress.

The admission of Indians to the Indian civil service was one of the main grievances of the members of these associations. Theoretically, admission was unrestricted. Queen Victoria had explicitly promised equal treatment to her Indian subjects in her proclamation of 1858. However, as the age limit for the admission had been fixed at 19 years of age in 1878 and the competitive entrance examinations were held only in Great Britain, hardly any Indian had a chance to enter the 'heaven born' service. Furthermore, British administrators were extremely reluctant to accept Indians as colleagues, probably fearing that it would cramp their style and also, at a deeper level, that the legitimation of British rule would be diminished if Indians proved to be as capable as the British when it came to running this administration.

From this point of view it seemed to be the lesser evil to make some concessions to the Indian educated elite with regard to their representation in the provincial legislatures and in the Imperial Legislative Council. As long as such constitutional reforms did not lead to the control of the British executive by a legislature dominated by a non-official Indian majority, the association of Indians with the legislative process could only enhance the legitimacy of British rule without diminishing the authority of the British administrators.

In 1892 a limited reform of this kind was introduced to meet the demands of the Indian National Congress, which had passed resolutions at each of its annual sessions calling for a greater share of elected Indian representatives in the legislatures of British India. Election was reduced to the right of suggesting a candidate for nomination to the legislature by the governor or the governor general. The nominated British officials still outnumbered the Indian representatives, and these Indians could neither prevent the passing of an act nor throw out a budget: they could only make critical speeches and thus score points in debates which were then reported in the press. Nevertheless, this limited activity absorbed the attention of the Indian leaders who joined the legislatures on these terms; the annual sessions of the National Congress lost much of their earlier zest after 1892.

The Morley–Minto reform and separate electorates

The next constitutional reform came in 1909, after the 1906 Liberal Party victory in the general election in Great Britain and the subsequent appointment of liberal philosopher John Morley as Secretary of State for India. A younger generation of radical nationalists had unleashed a wave of political terrorism in India and Morley was keen to 'rally the Moderates' in India; they, for their part, were equally keen to rally around Morley, of whom they expected much more than he was prepared to give. Furthermore, Morley's decisions were largely determined by the policy of Viceroy Lord Minto and Home Secretary H.H. Risley, who was against territorial representation and parliamentary government for India. Instead, Risley insisted on a representation of communities and interests in keeping with the structure of Indian society as he saw it.

Lord Minto had received a deputation from the Muslim League in 1906 and had promised that he would give due consideration to Muslim demands.

The Muslim League had been founded in that year with the explicit purpose of preventing the emergence of a parliamentary political system in India which would lead to a permanent domination of the Hindu majority over the Muslim minority. The sympathetic attention which the Muslim League attracted among the British administrators in India gave rise to the suspicion that the deputation of 1906 was somehow invited, rather than simply received, by the viceroy.

In fact, the British administrators were in the same boat as the Muslim League: they too did not want to be dominated by an Indian majority in the legislature and therefore they welcomed any support against Morley's democratic preferences. When faced with the Muslim demand Morley wanted to reconcile it with the idea of territorial representation by means of electoral colleges; Risley, however, brilliantly argued the case for separate electorates for Muslims and finally convinced Morley – or at least silenced his opposition – so that this fateful construction became the leading principle of the constitutional reform of 1909.

The Montagu–Chelmsford reform and responsible government

The next constitutional reform was precipitated by the First World War, in which India's support of the British war effort was of major importance in terms of men and money. Indian politicians expected reform, though they could not mount an agitation as long as the war was on. They planned ahead and coordinated their demands, which were aimed at a further enlargement of the legislatures and an increase of their powers. A pact was concluded between the National Congress and the Muslim League in 1916, in which the future distribution of seats in the provincial legislatures was settled in such a manner that the Muslims would be over-represented in the provinces where they were in a minority; in exchange, the League consented to be under-represented in the two Muslim majority provinces – Bengal and the Panjab – a solution which was clearly in the interest of the Muslims in the diaspora.

As long as the future constitution retained the main features of the Morley–Minto reform (i.e. a non-parliamentary system where the legislature acted as a kind of permanent opposition in the face of an irremovable executive), this solution was a fair compromise. However, if the executive were made responsible to the legislature and the members of the executive were to depend on majorities in the legislature, this kind of over-representation and under-representation would cause serious problems – particularly if separate electorates for Muslims were also retained. This is exactly what happened after the British announced a radical new departure in Indian constitutional reform in August 1917. Secretary of State Edwin Montagu declared that the introduction of 'responsible government' would be the direction of future imminent reforms. Montagu had actually suggested the word 'self-government' but this was resented by some of his colleagues in the war cabinet and Lord Curzon, the former viceroy who was now a Conservative minister, had insisted on 'responsible government' – perhaps without due consideration of the technical meaning of this term, which implies the parliamentary principle of an executive responsible to the elected majority in the House of Commons. Montagu, who understood these connotations much better than Curzon, readily agreed and this is why the final declaration contained this loaded phrase. Subsequently, Montagu went to India himself and worked out the reform proposals with Viceroy Lord Chelmsford.

Their report contained the reluctant admission that separate electorates for Muslims, though actually incompatible with responsible government, had to be retained because the Muslims now considered them to be a political right which they were unwilling to sacrifice. To make matters worse, the pact agreed by the National Congress and the Muslim League in 1916 was taken as the basic point of departure for the distribution of seats in the context of this new reform – despite its making no sense in this context at all. Finally, the British authorities noticed that the pact was unfair to Bengal and they unilaterally raised the number of Muslim seats there, completely disregarding the fact that Muslim under-representation in Bengal was originally thought of as a compensation for Muslim over-representation in the Muslim minority provinces.

The Montagu–Chelmsford reforms were also vitiated by the strange construction of dyarchy, whereby the provincial executive was split into two halves – an Indian one responsible to the legislature, and a British one which remained irremovable and 'irresponsible'. The Indian members of the executive were in charge of 'transferred subjects' such as education, health and local government, whereas the British members held the 'reserved' portfolios for home, revenue and finance. The whole design was such that it could only create bitter frustration. The Indian ministers were starved of financial support and, of course, did not dare to ask for new taxes, which would be assigned to their subjects. They were, in any case, faced with a legislature from which they could never hope to get solid support because of the way it was constituted – representing communities and interests in line with the principles of the previous reform, which this new measure had not superseded.

Federalism and the Government of India Act of 1935

The next move came in 1928, when the Simon Commission was sent to India. Secretary of State Lord Birkenhead made this move not because he felt, as Montagu had, that further reform was inevitable, but because he wanted to prevent a Labour government overseeing the next constitutional reform. The Simon Commission included MPs of all parties, but no Indians were associated with it, a fact which was deeply resented in India. Viceroy Lord Irwin, who was taken by surprise at this resentment, later made amends for the omission by sponsoring the idea of Round Table Conferences to be convened in London. It was intended that those conferences would be the forum for British and Indian politicians to arrive at a consensus about a new constitutional reform.

Although the proceedings of the Simon Commission were superseded by these Round Table Conferences, the basic recommendations remained more or less the same: India was to be a federal state which would include the British Indian provinces as well as the princely states; although the centre would retain a great deal of control, power would be shared there in terms of 'dyarchy'; in the provinces dyarchy would be replaced by 'provincial autonomy'. The franchise was to be extended to include about 10 per cent of the population. Property qualifications in terms of certain amounts of rent or revenue paid or, alternatively, some educational qualifications, were made preconditions of enfranchisement. Due representation, however, should also be given to the lower classes such as workers and untouchables. The grant of separate electorates to the latter was recommended by the British, but deeply resented by the caste Hindus who saw in this another dangerous step towards a disaggregation of the body politic in India. The princes, whose representatives at the first Round Table Conference in 1930 were quite sanguine about the prospects of federation, later got cold feet. This was presumably due to the fact that the Political Department of the Government of India, whose task it was to deal with the princes, did not like the idea and told them all about the potential financial consequences they would have to face if they joined the federation.

The Government of India Act of 1935 – the longest act ever passed by Parliament – did make provisions for a federation, but it was to come into being only if at least 50 per cent of the princely states would join it. The second part of the act contained the standard provincial constitution. There was no longer to be 'dyarchy' at the provincial level, but full 'provincial autonomy'. Dyarchy would have been introduced at the centre had the first part of the Government of India Act become operative. Because of the princes' failure to join, however, this was not to be. Winston Churchill, who had waged a furious political campaign against Indian constitutional reform, could be fully satisfied. He had argued that provincial autonomy was enough and that the British hold on the Government of India should remain undiminished. This is exactly what happened. In fact, the power of the viceroy was now greater than ever, because the federal part of the constitution remained inoperative at the same time as interference by the Secretary of State was greatly reduced.

While the end of empire was approaching, imperial structure had attained a rather hybrid final shape. A highly centralised federalism had been

imposed on India and parliamentarianism had, after all, been introduced –
though it was marred by incompatible features such as separate electorates
and the retention of an irremovable executive at the centre. On the one hand,
this provoked an increasing centralisation of the national movement with
its own 'high command'; on the other hand, it led to a movement towards
separatism among those whose segregation had been conditioned by separate electorates. The evolution of imperial structure thus contributed to the
final destruction of the political unity, which had been one of the main
achievements of imperial rule. But the evolution of the national movement
which was directed against that imperial rule also contributed to this end:
national agitation and political interest aggregation could not be promoted
simultaneously. Agitation calls for issues which arouse political passions,
whereas interest aggregation requires the give and take of political compromise – which does not fire anybody's imagination but which is of vital
importance if people are to live together in peace.

7

THE FREEDOM MOVEMENT
AND THE PARTITION OF INDIA

THE INDIAN FREEDOM MOVEMENT

The challenge of imperial rule produced India's nationalism, which raised
its head rather early in the nineteenth century. Among the new educated
elite there were some critical intellectuals who looked upon foreign rule as
a transient phenomenon. As early as 1849 Gopal Hari Deshmukh praised
American democracy in a Marathi newspaper and predicted that the Indians
would emulate the American revolutionaries and drive out the British. Such
publications, for which the author would have been prosecuted for sedition
only a few decades later, were hardly taken note of by the British at that
time. Similarly, the political associations in Bombay, Calcutta and Madras
submitted lengthy petitions to Parliament in 1853 when the renewal of the
charter of the East India Company was due; these did not attract much
attention either, although they contained, among other things, strong pleas
for democratic rights and a reduction of the land revenue. The Mutiny
of 1857 then alarmed both the British and the Indian educated elite. The
British became cautious, suspicious and conservative; the Indian elite
lapsed into a prolonged silence.

Neo-Hinduism and Muslim resentment

In a different field national thought did progress, even in those silent years.
Religious reform movements gained more and more ground. Debates with
Christian missionaries stimulated the quest for a new creed among the
Hindus. Defensive reactions by religious orthodoxy and bold innovations
by Hindu revivalists resulted from this encounter. Modern religious asso-
ciations like the Brahmo Samaj of Bengal and the Arya Samaj of northern
India vied with each other in offering a new sense of identity to the Hindus.
Christian forms of organisation were copied, the Brahmo Samaj sent
missionaries to all parts of India, while the Arya Samajists spoke of a
'Vedic Church' to indicate their feeling that the congregational solidarity
of the Christians was lacking among the Hindus. The various strands of

284

Figure 7.1 Bal Gangadhar Tilak (1856–1920), leader of the 'Extremists' in the National Congress

(Courtesy of the National Portrait Gallery, London)

Neo-Hinduism showed different tendencies – some aimed at a universalism embracing all nations and religions of the world; others were eagerly reconstructing a national tradition in order to achieve a solidarity based on a glorious past. This solidarity traditionalism became a major feature of Indian nationalism – and, as it was based on Hindu traditions, it excluded the Muslims.

The Muslims were suspicious of this Neo-Hinduism and even distrusted its profession of religious universalism. The emphasis on the equality of all religions was seen as a particularly subtle threat to Islamic identity. But while such trends among the educated Hindu elite were merely suspect to the Muslims, more popular movements of Hindu solidarity – such as the cow-protection movement in northern India – were positively resented by them as a direct attack on their own religious practices, which included cow-slaughter at certain religious festivals. The Hindi–Urdu controversy in northern India added additional fuel to the fire of communal conflict. The Hindus asked only for equal recognition of their language – Hindi, written in Devanagari script – as a language permitted in the courts of law, where so far Urdu written in Nastaliq script had prevailed; the Muslims, however, resented this as a challenge to Urdu and identified this linguistic advantage more and more with their existence as a religious community. Even illiterate Muslims whose language hardly differed from that of their Hindu neighbours could be called upon to defend Urdu for the sake of their Islamic identity.

A new generation of liberal nationalists

Liberal nationalists of the educated elite revived vocal political activity in the 1870s. They belonged to a new generation for whom the Mutiny of 1857 was only a vague childhood memory, whereas their experience in England – where many of them had gone for higher studies – had stirred their political consciousness. The old and long dormant associations of the 1850s were now superseded by new organisations of a more vigorous kind. Chief among them were the Indian Association established in Calcutta in 1876 and the Poona Sarvajanik Sabha which was founded in 1870. Mahadev Govind Ranade, the young judge posted in Pune in 1871, emerged as the leading spirit of the Sarvajanik Sabha. Surendranath Banerjea was the mentor of the Indian Association and led an all-India campaign for a better representation of Indians in the Indian civil service. Banerjea was one of the first Indians ever to be admitted to this service, although he had been summarily dismissed from it for some minor mistake. The age limit for admission to the service had also been deliberately reduced from 21 to 19 years of age, thus only Indians who were sent to attend school in England by their parents could ever hope to qualify for admission at all.

Viceroy Lord Lytton, a Conservative, inadvertently fostered the cooperation of Indian nationalists by his reactionary measures; in this he was to be surpassed only by Lord Curzon some decades later. Lytton introduced a Vernacular Press Act in 1878 which subjected newspapers published in Indian languages to a censorship so severe as to be practically tantamount to a suppression of their publication. This raised a storm of national protest in India and was also criticised by Gladstone and his Liberals in Parliament. Henceforth, Indian nationalists believed that the British Liberal Party was their natural ally. They were later disabused of this notion, but for some decades a faith in the Liberals greatly influenced their policy.

Lord Ripon's appointment as viceroy in 1880 gave great encouragement to India's liberal nationalists, who intensified their contacts throughout the country and finally held the first annual session of the Indian National Congress in Bombay in 1885; the second was held in Calcutta, where the Indian Association was in charge of the arrangements (indeed, the Indian Association had wanted to host the first session, and Bombay got ahead of Calcutta only by accident). In subsequent years all major Indian cities vied with each other for the great honour of hosting the National Congress.

There was hardly any activity in the time between annual sessions, nor was there any permanent office. The nationalists of the inviting city and the local chairman of the reception committee did what was necessary; they also decided whom to invite to preside over the session, which was more of a mark of distinction than an onerous duty. An informal group of leaders emerged to coordinate the affairs of the National Congress. For a long time the political boss of Bombay, Parsi lawyer Pherozeshah Mehta, was the mentor of the Congress. He felt that the Congress should work like an Indian branch of the British Liberal Party and was, therefore, at logger-heads with the national revolutionaries, who preferred to fight for Indian independence rather than put their trust in any British party.

The liberal nationalists and the national revolutionaries held fundamentally different views about the Indian nation. The liberals believed in nation-building within the framework of British rule. To them an Indian nation was a promise of the future rather than a fact of past and present. The national revolutionaries felt that the Indian nation had existed from time immemorial and that it only had to be awakened in order for it to shake off foreign rule. These different views had immediate consequences for Indian politics. The liberal nationalists welcomed British constitutional reforms for India and also asked for social reforms legislation; the national revolutionaries thought that any kind of British-granted reform would only serve to strengthen the fetters of foreign rule and make the British the umpires of India's fate. Dissociation rather than association was the watchword of the revolutionaries. Vedanta philosophy, the mainstay of Neo-Hinduism, lent itself to a political interpretation by the national revolutionaries: its emphasis on spiritual unity and on the liberation from illusion could be transformed into a message of national solidarity and of a political awakening which would put an end to foreign rule.

Vedanta, Karmayoga and the national revolutionaries

Vedanta philosophy was certainly an inspiration for the national revolutionaries, but it had one major disadvantage: it was originally aimed at the liberation of the soul by meditation and by the renunciation of worldly preoccupations. Therefore, it was necessary to emphasise the concept of Karmayoga, which implies that action as a sacrifice – as an unselfish quest for right conduct – is as good as renunciation. The crucial proviso is that one should not expect any reward or benefit from such action and must remain completely detached. In this way active self-realisation rather than passive contemplation could be propagated as the true message of Vedanta philosophy.

Swami Vivekananda was the prophet of this new thought. He impressed the Western world when he propounded this message at the World Parliament of Religions in Chicago in 1894; on his return to India in 1897

Figure 7.2 Swami Vivekananda (1863–1902), religious reformer and founder of the
Ramakrishna Mission. Painting by Chintamani Kar

(Courtesy of the National Portrait Gallery, London)

following his spiritual conquest of the West, he greatly stimulated Indian
nationalism. The British rulers had usually looked down on Hinduism as a
ragbag of superstition; Vivekananda's rehabilitation of Hindu thought in the
West was, therefore, considered to be a major national achievement. Even
contemporary liberal nationalists (e.g. Gopal Krishna Gokhale) or socialists of the next generation (e.g. Jawaharlal Nehru) admired Vivekananda
and found his ideas attractive.

Vedanta philosophy and Karmayoga were, of course, of importance only
to members of the educated elite who had looked for a new identity and
found that borrowed British liberalism was not enough of an inspiration
for Indian nationalism. The monism of Vedanta philosophy also provided
this elite with an ideological justification for assuming the leadership of the
masses in the spirit of national identity. For political mobilisation this
imputed identity was, of course, insufficient and attempts were therefore
made to communicate with the masses by way of the more popular symbols
of folk religion. In Bengal the cult of the goddess Kali or the ecstatic
mysticism of the Vaishnava saints provided symbols for an emotional

nationalism. The hymn of the Bengali national revolutionaries, 'Bande Mataram' ('Bow to the Mother'), alluded to an identification of the mother goddess with the motherland. In Maharashtra, Bal Gangadhar Tilak organised festivals in honour of the popular god Ganapati, as well as of the great hero Shivaji, whose fight against the Great Mughal was taken as analogous to the fight against British foreign rule. In northern India the cow-protection movement and the Hindi movement served the purpose of mobilising the masses.

The Dravidian south, however, was not stirred by any movements of this kind. Nationalism remained restricted to the small circles of liberal intellectuals. A number of factors contributed to this situation: the scarcity of urban centres of communication; the plurality of languages; the fact that the south contained several important princely states (Hyderabad, Mysore, Travancore) which provided no scope for nationalist politics; and the social distance between Brahmins and the rest of the population. Although the Brahmins of the south did turn towards nationalism, consciousness of their isolation tended to make them very moderate liberals. Northern liberal nationalists found, in them, faithful allies against the radicalism of a younger generation of national revolutionaries.

The partition of Bengal and the rise of extremism

Radical nationalism was stimulated by the partition of Bengal in 1905. Originally, the partition of this vast province – which at that time still included Assam, Bihar and Orissa, in addition to Bengal proper – was mooted for purely administrative reasons. But when Viceroy Lord Curzon finally executed this administrative act, it was obviously meant to strike at the territorial roots of the nationalist elite of Bengal. The province was split right down the middle: east Bengal and Assam formed one province, and west Bengal, Bihar and Orissa another. Lord Curzon did not hesitate to point out to the Muslims of eastern Bengal that he conceived of this province as Muslim. The Bengali Hindus, on the other hand, noted with dismay that they were in a minority in the new province of Bengal. They mounted a furious agitation in which political terrorism became a prominent feature as young 'Extremists' took to the cult of the pistol and the bomb. The repartition of Bengal in 1911 showed that the administrative needs could have been met in a different way to begin with: Bengal was once more amalgamated and Bihar and Orissa formed a new province. Had the British refrained from splitting Bengal in the first place, they would have saved themselves a great deal of trouble. Terrorism now spread in Bengal and increased with every future instance of repression; without this first partition of Bengal, Indian nationalism might have retained more of its liberal features. The Indian National Congress was greatly embarrassed by the partition of Bengal. Gopal Krishna Gokhale, who was the Congress

Figure 7.3 Gopal Krishna Gokhale (1866–1915), leader of the 'Moderates' in the National Congress

(Courtesy of the Nehru Memorial Museum and Library and National Portrait Gallery, London)

president in 1905, had met leading Liberals in London shortly before that year's Congress, which was held at Benares (Varanasi). He hoped for an advance in Indian constitutional reforms after a victory of the Liberals in the elections and he had even toyed with the idea of contesting a seat on a Liberal ticket himself in order to promote Indian political progress from the floor of the House of Commons. If Indian nationalism now took a radical turn due to the partition of Bengal, this could greatly reduce the chances for a constitutional reform. But Gokhale managed to steer a moderate course at the Congress session and obtained a clear mandate for further negotiations in London, where he arrived once more in 1906 in order to discuss the proposals for constitutional reform with the new secretary of state, John Morley.

Tensions increased in India in 1906; at the same time, the hopes of the liberal nationalists represented by Gokhale also increased. The annual Congress – due to be held in Calcutta, in the heart of radicalised Bengal – posed a major challenge to the 'Moderates' as they were now called in contrast to the 'Extremists'. They met this challenge by inviting the Grand Old Man of Indian nationalism, Dadabhai Naoroji, to preside over this session. Naoroji had been active in Indian politics as far back as the 1850s and in 1892 he had become the first Indian MP after contesting a seat at Finsbury, England, on a Liberal ticket. His famous book *Poverty and un-British Rule in India* had endeared him even to the national revolutionaries; and so because nobody dared to attack him in his venerable old age, Naoroji was able to save the day for the 'Moderates' in Calcutta. A split of Congress was thus avoided – until the following year.

The Congress of 1907 was scheduled to be held at Nagpur. However, as the time for the session approached, the 'Moderates' suspected that the 'Extremists' might steal the show at Nagpur, where disciples of Tilak were very active. Almost at the last minute it was decided to shift the venue to Surat, Gujarat, where there were no 'Extremists'. The 'Extremists' naturally resented this move and decided to attend the session at Surat en masse. Pandemonium broke out when the session opened and finally the two factions met separately: a split was inevitable. Tilak and Aurobindo emerged as the leaders of the 'Extremist' faction. Tilak, however, was sentenced to six years' imprisonment in 1908; Aurobindo escaped arrest only by fleeing to Pondichery in 1910. While he had been a prophet of a fiery nationalism up to this point, he then turned into a religious figure.

The 'Extremists' remained politically isolated while the 'Moderates' controlled the Congress. A new Congress constitution of 1908 established the All-India Congress Committee, composed of elected delegates, as the central decision-making body. 'Extremists' could no longer hope to carry the day by simply crowding the annual session.

The First World War and the Home Rule League

As long as Gokhale and Mehta (the great Parsi politician of Bombay) were alive the Congress continued under the control of the 'Moderates'. Both died in 1915, however, and this gave Tilak a chance to reassert his leadership. Finishing his term of imprisonment in 1914, he recognised that radical politics would be impossible during the war. Thus, for the time being he followed a rather moderate line, though he did not change his views. Another striking leader also appeared on the Indian political scene at that time: Annie Besant, an Irish socialist who had come to India in order to spread the message of Theosophy. On settling in Madras she had become a kind of female Vivekananda, inspiring the Brahmin intellectuals of the south. When she founded an Indian Home Rule League on the Irish pattern, this movement spread like wildfire and eclipsed the National Congress for some time. Tilak founded his own Home Rule League in western India and even Mohammad Ali Jinnah, a brilliant Bombay lawyer who aspired to become a Muslim Gokhale, joined that Home Rule League.

The Indian Muslims, who held the Turkish caliph in high regard, were greatly agitated by the fact that their British overlords were presently fighting the caliph. They were caught on the horns of a dilemma: before the war they had looked to the British for protection of their minority rights; now they came closer to the Indian nationalists. This was also reflected by the political shift made by Jinnah, who now led the Muslim League along nationalist lines. He found a political partner in Tilak and, together, they concluded the Congress–League pact of 1916 (see pp. 280–1, above). The sessions of the Congress and of the Muslim League were held in the same places in those war years in order to be conducted on parallel lines.

During the war it seemed as if such harmony was destined to last for ever. The Congress of 1917 was a unique manifestation of national solidarity. The British rulers had contributed to this cohesion by arresting and then releasing Annie Besant, who thus emerged as a national hero, was promptly elected Congress president, and made the 1917 session a forum for her home rule message. The initial solidarity of 1917 was soon eclipsed by another split of the Congress. Tilak and the Bengal leader C.R. Das were opposed to the Montagu–Chelmsford reforms and demanded an immediate step towards provincial autonomy, whereas the more moderate Congress politicians wanted to work the reforms. Finally, Tilak and Das remained in control of the Congress and the moderate wing left to form the National Liberal Federation. But the debate about the merits or demerits of the impending constitutional reform was suddenly interrupted by an altogether different problem.

As the end of the war approached, the British were anxious to introduce some emergency legislation which would enable them to continue the wartime repression of sedition, should this prove to be necessary. A sedition committee chaired by Justice Rowlatt reported on this and prepared drafts of such emergency legislation, which, though promptly enacted, was never applied due to the storm of protest it provoked in India. The main principles of this legislation were summed up by the people in the short formula: 'No trial, no lawyer, no appeal.' This, then, was the reward for Indian loyalty during the war. The protest against the Rowlatt Acts had to be articulated somehow and a new leader appeared on the scene who knew what to do: Mohandas Karamchand Gandhi. He designed a campaign which came to be known as the 'Rowlatt satyagraha' – the first experiment with non-violent resistance on a national scale.

Gandhi and non-cooperation

Gandhi was born in 1869 in a small princely state of Gujarat. The son of the chief minister, he completed his studies in London and subsequently tried, rather unsuccessfully, to practise law in Bombay. He had then gladly accepted the offer of a Muslim businessman who sent him on some legal business to South Africa. As that country's only Indian lawyer he had emerged as the leader of the Indian minority. In fighting against discriminatory legislation he and his followers had adopted the methods of passive resistance, i.e. deliberate and open breach of those laws. As Gandhi did not like to call this resistance passive, he finally coined the term 'satyagraha' (holding on to the truth). With his carefully designed non-violent campaigns, Gandhi even made an impression on his great adversary, General Smuts, the powerful home and defence minister of the Union of South Africa. When Gandhi returned to India in 1915 he was known to all Indian nationalists as leader of the Indian minority in South Africa, but nobody had any idea of what Gandhi was going to do in India and whether he could be classified as a 'Moderate' or as an 'Extremist'.

Aged 46 at the time of his return to India, Gandhi was no longer a novice, yet he was ready to listen to his mentor Gokhale, whose Servants of India Society he intended to join. Gokhale sent him on a one-year tour of India during which he was not supposed to make any speeches or take a stand in politics: he was merely to see things for himself. Unfortunately, Gokhale died soon after sending Gandhi on this tour and the other members of the Servants of India Society later refused to admit him, suspecting that his views were much more radical than theirs. In this they were quite right and Gandhi accepted their verdict ungrudgingly.

In subsequent years Gandhi devoted his attention to some local campaigns for the peasants of Champaran district, Bihar, and those of Kheda district, Gujarat, and the millhands of Ahmadabad. In these campaigns he gained a great deal of experience and won loyal followers, such as Rajendra Prasad in Bihar and Vallabhbhai Patel in Gujarat. In the last year of the war he even conducted a campaign for the recruitment of soldiers for the British Indian army in Gujarat. He was still a loyalist at that time and thought that the British would honour India's loyalty after the war. The recruiting campaign failed and taught Gandhi the lesson that people will not respond to a leader if he asks them for something which they really are not prepared to give. Knocking at the doors of the peasants of Kheda district – the very ones who had followed him earlier and had appreciated his help – he found no response when he pleaded for support in the British war effort. After this experience he was even more hurt by the passing of the Rowlatt Acts and their plain message that India's loyalty was not respected by the British at all. The method of satyagraha which he had adopted in South Africa seemed to be the right means for articulating the Indian reaction to the Rowlatt Acts. In order to adjust the method to Indian conditions, he called for a 'hartal' – a closing of shops and stopping of all business, on a certain day.

The economic conditions in India after the end of the war were rather chaotic: prices had risen enormously in 1918, and the urban population and the rural poor were badly affected by this. More than a million Indians had participated in the war abroad and most of them returned now as demobilised soldiers. The situation in the Panjab was particularly tense in this respect and the government there was quite nervous. For this reason Gandhi was prohibited from entering this province, and was taken off the train and forced to return to Bombay. This, however, did not improve the situation in the Panjab; on the contrary, uncontrolled unrest flared up and the British military authorities thought that they had to counter with a show of force. General Dyer selected an unauthorised meeting in the Jallianwalla Bagh of Amritsar for this purpose. This is a square surrounded by walls which prevent a dispersal of a crowd, even if given due notice and enough time. General Dyer, in fact, did not give the crowd much of a chance to disperse and ordered his soldiers to fire several rounds until hundreds of people were dead.

The 'Massacre', as it came to be known, conveyed a message quite the reverse of what General Dyer had intended: this was not a show of force, but of a nervousness which indicated the beginning of the end of the British Indian empire. The British depended on the cooperation of the Indians for the continuation of their rule and this was not the way to go about getting it. A campaign of non-cooperation was a fitting answer to this fatal mistake. Gandhi had outlined such a strategy of non-cooperation in his manifesto, *Hind Swaraj*, as early as 1909 when he was in South Africa. Nevertheless, he did not immediately embark on such a campaign. There was a delayed reaction as the events in the Panjab were not yet fully known and two commissions of inquiry were set up in order to discover the facts. One commission was an official British body under the chairmanship of Lord Hunter; the other was appointed by the National Congress and Gandhi was one of its members.

In 1919 the session of the National Congress was held at Amritsar, the site of the massacre, and presided over by Motilal Nehru, the father of Jawaharlal Nehru. The tone of the resolutions was rather moderate and the radical turn which the Congress and Gandhi would take a few months later could not have been predicted from these proceedings. Gandhi and Jinnah even co-sponsored a resolution thanking Montagu for the constitutional reforms. Gandhi supported this resolution by arguing that since the Congress had not rejected the reform outright, it should have the decency to thank Montagu for it.

Two different trends converged in the subsequent months which made Gandhi adopt a much more radical attitude. The first was the rapidly increasing groundswell of the Khilafat movement of Indian Muslims; the second was growing Indian indignation over the British report on the events in the Panjab. In late 1919 Gandhi had still tried to keep these two issues strictly apart. He was in touch with the Bombay Khilafat Committee and had made attempts to communicate the Muslim grievances to the Hindus, as he saw a chance of improving national solidarity in this way. But, for this very reason, he did not want to mix up this issue with the Panjab problem: he felt that the Muslims should not get the idea that the Hindus took note of the Khilafat issue only in order to win Muslim support for a different campaign. Furthermore, Gandhi's contacts were still with Bombay's Muslim traders, who tended to be moderate and would not have sponsored a campaign such as the one for a boycott of foreign cloth – these merchants were themselves selling it. But in 1920 the leadership of the Khilafat movement was assumed by north Indian ulema (Islamic scholars) and journalists like Maulana Azad and the Ali brothers. Azad had spent the war in prison and had already advocated a programme of non-cooperation similar to that envisaged by Gandhi. When they met for the first time in January 1920 they soon agreed on a joint programme of action.

'Swaraj in one year'

In May 1920 a special concatenation of events precipitated Gandhi's decision for a radical course of action. The Congress report on occurrences in the Panjab was published and soon thereafter the official British report also appeared. Gandhi had written a large part of the Congress document and had seen to it that only proven facts were included and all hearsay and polemics were eliminated – in this way the contrasts with the official British version appeared even more striking because that report tried to whitewash many of the misdeeds perpetrated by the Panjab regime. The conditions imposed on the caliph by the Treaty of Sevres also became known at the same time, thus making it impossible any longer to separate the reaction to the Panjab wrongs from the Khilafat movement. Gandhi now outlined the main features of a campaign of non-cooperation: boycott of British textiles, British schools, universities and law courts; rejection of all honours and titles bestowed by the British on Indians. As an afterthought and almost in passing, Gandhi (in June 1920) added to this list the boycott of the forthcoming elections. This last move later proved to be the most crucial decision – the one which set the pace for the future course of the freedom movement.

Whereas the Khilafatists welcomed Gandhi's new policy, most Congress members were sceptical about it. A special Congress was to decide on the adoption of a non-cooperation resolution in Calcutta in September 1920. Tilak, who had avoided taking a definite stand, died in August 1920. When Gandhi received this news he said: 'My strongest bulwark is gone.' This statement has remained an enigma and one can only surmise what Gandhi meant. Far from being his follower, Tilak was, in fact, Gandhi's rival; Gandhi, however, probably assumed that Tilak was bound to support him once he had to take a stand at the Calcutta Congress. Gandhi attended this Congress with mixed feelings: he was not sure whether he would get a majority for non-cooperation. To his surprise the proposal of a boycott of the elections was favoured by many politicians who had already registered as candidates. Perhaps they felt that their chances of success were limited and that the boycott would provide them with a good alibi. The Congress politicians were caught on the horns of a dilemma: the franchise had been extended to many people with whom they had had no contact, and those voters who had been enfranchised earlier would probably vote for the liberals who had left the Congress. Among these liberals there were many prominent politicians who had held seats for quite some time and could not be dislodged very easily. Under such circumstances non-cooperation was the best solution. When Gandhi noticed this unexpected wave of support he forgot about his usual reluctance concerning big words and empty slogans. The Congress members had pointed out to him that his programme referred only to specific issues and did not even mention 'swaraj' (self government). He took the hint, included this term in his resolution and enthusiastically promised 'swaraj in one year' if his programme was fully adopted. But in spite of this enthusiasm the resolution was carried with only a narrow majority.

Between the special Congress of September 1920 and the annual Congress to be held in Nagpur in December 1920, Gandhi had only a very limited time to consolidate his position. He toured the country with the Khilafatists and tried to get support among the young people, whom he asked to leave the schools and colleges set up by the British. He called this whole education system 'satanic' and found a good deal of response among college boys. But he did not spend his time exclusively on agitation; he also drafted a new constitution for the National Congress to include provisions for a permanent Working Committee, a reorganisation of the Provincial Congress Committees along the lines of linguistic provinces and a better representation of rural areas. This reform of the Congress constitution was Gandhi's answer to the Montagu–Chelmsford reform which the Congress had decided to boycott. Actually, the boycott of the elections to the reformed councils proved to be much more important for the consolidation of Gandhi's position than all the other boycotts. The voters had not responded to the boycott as readily as Gandhi had hoped, but the Congress politicians – including those who had been outvoted at the special Congress – had all withdrawn their candidatures. The liberals had captured the seats and the new ministerial positions, which the Congress politicians would also have liked to occupy. Now, however, there was no use looking back: their only option was to support Gandhi's programme wholeheartedly, and thus non-cooperation was endorsed almost unanimously at the Nagpur Congress.

In the course of 1921 this programme lost much of its novelty and attraction and would have petered out completely if the British had not unwittingly contributed to a brief revival by sending the Prince of Wales on a tour of India. Wherever the prince appeared the agitation was renewed, but even this was only a passing phenomenon. The Government of India adopted a skilful strategy in dealing with the movement: they refrained from repression and did not even arrest Gandhi who was actually waiting for his detention. When the movement took a violent turn with a mob burning some policemen alive in their police station in the small north Indian village of Chauri Chaura, Gandhi himself called off the campaign and was then promptly arrested. When he was put on trial Gandhi refused to defend himself and, rather, took this opportunity to explain to the court why he had turned from a loyalist into a rebel. He got the same sentence as Tilak, and accepted it proudly. But whereas Tilak had served his full term of six years, Gandhi was released after two years because his health was failing. His contemporaries thought he had reached the end of his political career: he had had his innings and others would have to direct the movement with new ideas.

The return to the constitutional arena

Gandhi was released in 1924 to find Indian politics in bad shape. The Khilafat movement had lost its meaning as the Turks themselves had done away with the caliph. Hindu–Muslim relations were strained, the agitational alliance was soon forgotten: Gandhi had made a mistake in staking everything on a card which turned out not to be a trump card at all. Jinnah, who had criticised the Khilafat movement and Gandhi's involvement in it, had become isolated, had left the Congress and devoted his energies to the Muslim League which now emerged once more as the Khilafat movement faded away. The rivalry of Congress and League, Gandhi and Jinnah, was to play a decisive role in Indian politics in subsequent years.

The 1920s also witnessed a renewed interest in political Hinduism which had been dormant for some time while Gandhi's movement had prevailed. Pandit Madan Mohan Malaviya, the founder of the Banaras Hindu University, had patiently nurtured a Hindu Sabha movement which he wanted to keep within the Congress fold as a pressure group. A more strident voice was that of Vinayak Damodar Savarkar who published his manifesto 'Hindutva' in 1923. He was, at that time, still in prison where the British kept him for a long time after he had been captured as a young terrorist in London in 1909. According to Savarkar everybody was a Hindu who considered India as his holy land (*punyabhumi*). He wanted to do away with the caste system and to create a broad-based national solidarity of the Hindus. This, of course, excluded the Muslims and was diametrically opposed to Gandhi's attempts at bridging the gap between Hindus and Muslims. Savarkar's disciples founded the Rashtriya Swayamsevak Sangh (National Self-help Association, RSS) in 1925 in the same year when the Hindu Mahasabha was also resurrected, which then emerged as a separate political party in 1928. At that time these circles were still rather isolated, because Sarvarkar's radical ideas did not appeal to the majority of the Hindus. But this was the period when seeds were sown which sprouted in recent times. In the 1920s the National Congress was still the dominant force. It returned to the constitutional arena after Gandhi's movement had failed for the time being.

With Gandhi's reluctant blessing, Motilal Nehru and C.R. Das established a Swaraj Party within the Congress and quite successfully contested the next elections. Many prominent liberals were unseated by unknown Swarajists. In Bengal the old national hero, Surendranath Banerjea, was defeated by a young medical doctor, B.C. Roy, who later became chief minister of Bengal; nobody had heard of him before he achieved this first remarkable success. A new generation of Congress politicians emerged at this time. Many of them had left college or their profession in order to join the non-cooperation movement and had then become full-time political workers.

Gandhi managed to support this new generation because he was not only a great agitator, but also a very successful fund-raiser. Being, himself, a member of a traders' caste he had much better contacts with Indian merchants and businessmen than the Brahmin intellectuals who had dominated the Congress at an earlier stage. The Tilak Swaraj Fund, for which Gandhi collected money during the non-cooperation campaign, amounted to 10m. rupees and this money was available for the support of political workers. Bombay played a major role in financing the freedom movement, as did the Marwaris who were spread all over northern India. G.D. Birla, a leading member of this latter community and a lifetime friend of Gandhi, donated large amounts to Gandhi's All-India Handspinners' Association – although he himself owned textile mills.

Birla knew that the industry did not need to be afraid of the competition of the handspinners. This spinning was of symbolic rather than of practical significance. Gandhi had introduced it because he wanted to add a positive dimension to the boycott of foreign cloth and to encourage active self-help in India. For some time even the membership fee of the Congress had to be paid in kind, i.e. a certain amount of home-spun yarn. But this soon became a routine command performance and Gandhi's message was lost. The handwoven cloth which the Congressmen wore in order to emphasise their faith in self-reliance also degenerated into a kind of uniform – and did not necessarily guarantee the integrity of the wearer.

Among the younger generation of nationalists there were critical voices which dissented from Gandhi's programme and ideas. Jawaharlal Nehru and Subhas Chandra Bose were the mentors of this younger generation. An anti-imperialism based on socialist ideology was propagated by them and they hoped for a simultaneous political and socio-economic emancipation of India. Jawaharlal Nehru had studied in England and had then joined the national movement together with his father, Motilal; following his attendance at the Congress of the Oppressed Nations in Brussels in 1927, he had returned to India with a new radical message. He had joined the League against Imperialism and with Bose had co-founded an Indian Independence League which stood for complete independence and tried to enlist the Congress to this end. Bose, who still worked in close partnership with Nehru at that time, had succeeded C.R. Das as leader of the Congress in Bengal. Das had died in 1925 at a very crucial juncture in Indian politics. Bose was in sympathy with the Bengal tradition of the national revolutionaries who preferred violent action to Gandhi's non-violence. Gandhi, who always had an instinct for political trends, tried his best to tame the young radical opposition in the Congress by getting Jawaharlal Nehru elected as Congress president in 1929.

This Congress session had to arrive at an important decision. The demand for Dominion status had not been met by the British; a draft constitution prepared for this purpose by an All-Party Conference chaired by Motilal Nehru had hardly been taken note of by them. Viceroy Lord Irwin had made a declaration which was so vague and non-committal that it could not satisfy the aspirations of the Indian nationalists. The declaration had been edited in London so carefully that Irwin could state much less than he had originally envisaged. In this atmosphere of mutual frustration the Congress was forced to start a new campaign of national agitation. Everybody looked to Gandhi for a suitable programme. Gandhi now personally moved the resolution demanding India's complete independence – a step he had rejected at the previous session, so that Irwin might still have the chance of offering Dominion status.

Civil disobedience and the Gandhi–Irwin pact

Gandhi was given a general authorisation by the Congress for any kind of campaign which he might suggest, but he took his own time before he announced his new plan. He had not forgotten the lessons of the earlier campaigns. The multitude of boycotts had lessened rather than enhanced the impact of the agitation and it had finally ended in violence. Now he had the brilliant idea of selecting the Government of India's salt monopoly as a suitable target.

The salt tax affected all parts of the population and especially the poor; the law, which ensured the government's monopoly, could be easily and demonstratively broken by picking up some salt near the sea. In order to intensify the dramatic effect of this demonstration, Gandhi recruited a reliable batch of 'satyagrahis' and marched with them over a long distance to the beach at Dandi, Gujarat. The press reported the daily progress of this salt march. After Gandhi finally picked up the first grain of salt, thousands of people from all parts of India did likewise and thus courted arrest. Contemporary observers were surprised at the enormous response which

Gandhi elicited in this way. He had engineered a perfect symbolic revolution: one that pitted the Indians against the British but did not create a conflict of Indian interests.

In addition, he announced an eleven-point programme, which he termed the 'substance of Independence'. These points reflected various Indian interests and thus constituted a common meeting-ground. The abolition of the salt tax was only one of these points; Gandhi also asked for a 50 per cent reduction of the land revenue, for protective tariffs on textiles, for a devaluation of the rupee from 1s. 6d. to 1s. 4d. Several other grievances were similarly highlighted.

When Gandhi started his campaign in April 1930 the impact of the Great Depression had not yet affected India. But while the campaign was in full swing the wheat price fell and landlords and tenants in the wheat-growing regions of northern India came into conflict because the landlords – themselves pressed by their creditors – mercilessly collected their rents, which the tenants found difficult to pay as their income had dwindled. Jawaharlal Nehru and other radical Congress members of northern India advocated Congress support for a 'no-rent' campaign by the tenants. Gandhi and the old guard of the Congress were hostile to the idea because they wanted to avoid a class struggle, which would drive the landlords into the arms of the British. But Nehru made some calculations which foreshadowed the land reform introduced at a later stage. He came to the conclusion that the Congress could very well risk alienating the small group of landlords. In fact, driving them into the arms of the British would be no bad thing: sooner or later they would have to be deprived of their privileges and then it would be much better if they could be attacked as allies of the British, rather than placated as adherents of the freedom movement.

In the winter of 1930–1 the situation became more tense and Lord Irwin, who had so far watched the campaign with equanimity, became worried about the prospect of a peasants' revolt. Gandhi indicated that he would be prepared for a compromise. He was obviously interested in terminating his civil disobedience campaign honourably before it turned into uncontrolled violence as it had done at Chauri Chaura in 1922. Moreover, the first Round Table Conference in London – which the Congress had boycotted – had been successfully concluded in the meantime and the participants had returned to India exuding optimism. Irwin was keen to lend credibility to the next Round Table Conference by involving the Congress. Gandhi, who was not at all interested in British–Indian constitutional reforms because he considered the Congress to be the only political forum in India, was, nevertheless, prevailed upon to attend the second Round Table Conference. The optimism of those who had attended the first – including the representatives of the Indian princes – was one of the reasons for this decision. But even more important were the talks which Gandhi had with Purushottamdas Thakurdas, the great Bombay magnate who had, so far, supported Gandhi's campaign. Bombay, which was the mainspring of Congress finance, had felt the severe pinch of credit contraction in the wake of the Great Depression and could no longer back the freedom movement sufficiently. At the same time, the civil disobedience campaign had swelled the ranks of political workers who depended on Gandhi's fund-raising ingenuity. Under such circumstances it was difficult for Gandhi to make ends meet and he had to arrive at a compromise.

In March 1931, Irwin and Gandhi concluded a pact by which Irwin gained much and Gandhi very little. The civil disobedience campaign was suspended. Irwin released most, but not all, prisoners and permitted the production of salt for individual home consumption. He did not make any further concessions. He pointed out that he was unable to recover the land which was confiscated from peasants who had refused to pay land revenue and which had been auctioned off to others. He also categorically refused to enquire into charges of police brutality in suppressing agitations.

Gandhi appreciated the pact because of its symbolic significance rather than for its specific concessions. The viceroy had negotiations with him on equal terms. Gandhi saw in this 'a change of heart', whereas Winston Churchill – equally aware of the symbolic significance of this pact – deplored it as a disgraceful lowering of British prestige. Jawaharlal Nehru was furious about the agreement and said that had his father Motilal (who had died recently) still been alive, it would never have been concluded. He felt that this pact was a betrayal of the cause of the peasants who had been driven into the arms of the Congress by the Great Depression and who had shown that they were willing and able to put up a fight. They were now let down by the Congress, which had to refrain from all agitation after Gandhi had suspended the campaign. The pact was, indeed, concluded when the peasant movement was at its height. As soon as the landlords noticed that the Congress could no longer support the peasants they pounced on them and observed no limits in the degree to which they exploited them.

Frustration at the Round Table and the Communal Award

Gandhi's participation in the second Round Table Conference was not worth all this sacrifice. Moreover, Gandhi insisted on being sent there as the only representative of the Congress because he did not want to initiate discussions so much as simply to present the national demand. Once in London, however, he became involved in dealing with complicated issues like federal structure and the representation of minorities. He had never wanted to talk about all this and was out of his depth. A couple of constitutional advisors should have accompanied him, given this agenda. Gandhi was completely frustrated, but Irwin – who had got him into this fix and who had returned home by that time after finishing his term as viceroy – remained completely aloof from the conference. The viceroy's Tory colleagues had not liked his pact-making, but he could point out to them that he had thus averted a peasants' revolt in India. Had he also masterminded Gandhi's discomfiture at the conference? He could not, of course, be blamed for the Congress decision to send Gandhi as its sole representative to the conference; but, from a long-term perspective, Irwin's success at getting Gandhi involved in the process of British–Indian constitutional reforms was of great importance. Gandhi's participation in this conference tied the Congress down to British–Indian constitution-making in a way that was not yet obvious to the contemporary observers. Princes and untouchables were in the limelight of this conference. By integrating the princes in a federal British India the British hoped to get a conservative counterweight against the Congress; similarly, by means of separate electorates for the untouchables the policy of 'divide and rule' would gain additional leverage. Gandhi was particularly adamant in resisting this latter proposal but, nevertheless, he signed a document by which the British Prime Minister was called upon to settle the issue by means of a Communal Award.

Gandhi's frustration in London was even more acute for reasons which he could not state. He had hoped to arrive at a pact with the British Prime Minister just as he had concluded a pact with the viceroy as a prelude to this summit meeting. Ramsay MacDonald was a veteran leader of the Labour Party and he was known to be a friend of India. In getting the mandate of the Congress as its sole representative at the Round Table Conference and in restricting his mission to placing the national demand before that conference, he had paved the way for this encounter with the Prime Minister. He was probably prepared to make substantial concessions to him just as he had made concessions to Irwin. If MacDonald had been in a position to make a deal with Gandhi at this stage, Indian history might have taken a different course, but by the time Gandhi finally met him, his Labour government had fallen and he had re-emerged as a captive of his coalition partners in a national government. Gandhi met a sphinx, as he described his impression of this encounter later on. The helpless Prime Minister could not commit himself to anything. He could not even answer Gandhi's question concerning recent British currency policy in India after the British had left the gold standard. But this was due to his ignorance of monetary economics rather than to his political handicap at that time. This must have added to Gandhi's impression that the Prime Minister behaved like a sphinx. The interview was certainly the most notorious non-event in Gandhi's political life.

When Gandhi returned from London he was deeply disappointed and resumed the civil disobedience campaign. In northern India this meant a renewal of the 'no-rent' campaign. The wheat-growing regions which had been in the vanguard in the period up to the Gandhi–Irwin pact were now fairly quiet. In the meantime, the rice price had also fallen and the rice-growing regions – particularly the eastern part of the United Provinces and Bihar – became active in the campaign that got under way in autumn 1931. In Bihar, tensions were largely due to the fact that landlords could deprive tenants of their occupancy tenancy if they fell into arrears of rent. Occupancy rights and the legal restriction of rent enhancement had made this type of tenancy a valuable asset which the landlords were eager to recover. Once the tenant had lost his occupancy status he could be treated as a tenant-at-will, to whom the provisions of the Tenancy Act did not apply. The intense class conflict which prevailed in Bihar led to the rise of a militant peasant organisation (Kisan Sabha) in which socialists and communists were very active. Similar conditions were to be found in the coastal Andhra region of the Madras Presidency, where big landlords held large tracts of land. However, due to different tenancy laws, the tenants in that part of the country were in a better position to face the landlords: the peasant movement was less radical here but, in the short run, more effective than in Bihar. Gandhi still did not like to encourage movements which intensified a class struggle among Indians, but he was preoccupied with a different problem at that time.

He had been imprisoned almost immediately after his return to India and was now confronted with the Communal Award of the British Prime Minister which granted separate electorates to the untouchables but left the parties concerned the option of arriving at an agreement which would settle the representation of the untouchables in a different manner. Gandhi announced that he would fast unto death against this introduction of separate electorates. This 'epic fast' made a great impact on public opinion: temples were thrown open to the untouchables, they were given access to wells which had been denied them before. Dr Ambedkar, the leader of the untouchables, felt the mounting burden of moral pressure and, finally, he had to visit Gandhi in prison in order to conclude a pact with him which replaced the conditions imposed by the Communal Award. The untouchables were compensated for the elimination of separate electorates by a generous number of reserved seats.

This generosity was at the expense of the caste Hindus, many of whom deeply resented this Gandhi–Ambedkar pact. On the other hand, untouchable politicians were also not happy with it because candidates who wanted to win such reserved seats had to be acceptable to the majority of the voters and not only to the untouchables. Special parties of untouchables would not have a chance, whereas untouchable candidates put up by the Congress would win the seats. The Gandhi–Ambedkar pact had a side-effect which was not immediately noticed by contemporary observers: it tied the Congress to the Communal Award, of which it was merely a modification and, in this way, it also obliged the Congress to play the constitutional game according to the rules laid down by the British.

The rise of economic nationalism

When Gandhi had time to read, in prison once more in 1932, he had asked his friend G.D. Birla to get all the reports of the currency commissions for him and he studied them with great care, reporting to Birla about the progress he made in understanding this subject. This was surprising because Gandhi had never taken an interest in economics. He had even called the law of supply and demand a law of the devil and had admitted that he had never read any of the British economists. But at the Round Table Conference in London in 1931 he had made a statement about British high-handedness in handling the Indian exchange rate. Since even Prime Minister Macdonald had not been able to answer his questions, Gandhi decided to study this problem in detail, the more so as India's business community deeply resented British monetary policy.

The economic nationalism of Indian businessmen had emerged after the First World War. During the war the Secretary of State had to permit the Indian exchange rate to drift from 1s. 4d. to 2s., because silver appreciated and India's token coins soon had a metal value which was higher than their official denomination. If the rate had not been adjusted, the coins would have been converted into metal and the currency would have disappeared. After the war, silver depreciated once more. Now, the Secretary of State tried to support the overvalued currency by buying rupees. The gold reserve at his disposal for this purpose was soon exhausted. He then adopted a different strategy. Worn-out coins were simply not replaced with new ones. A gradual deflation then pushed up the exchange rate to 1s. 6d. in 1927. At this stage a currency act was passed, pegging the rupee to the international gold standard at that rate. These measures favoured British creditors and also provided a bonus to British exporters of goods to India; on the other hand they hurt Indian debtors and exporters. The demand for a return to 1s. 4d. became a rallying cry for the Indian business community. G.D. Birla was one of the main protagonists of this campaign.

When the impact of the Great Depression hit India in the second half of 1930, the deflationary effect of the overvalued currency further precipitated the already dramatic fall in prices. When the British abandoned the gold standard and let the pound sterling float in September 1931, the Finance Member of the Government of India recommended that the rupee should be permitted to float, too. The Secretary of State prohibited that as he feared a flight from the rupee. India remained wedded to its high exchange rate which could be easily maintained as a flood of gold poured out of India, providing it with an admirable balance of payments. This was rightly called 'distress gold', because it was sold by innumerable peasants who had to pay land revenue and interest on their debts at the same old rates while their income had been severely reduced by the fall in prices.

The Government of India, which could not help the peasants, tried at least to control the moneylenders, imposing a moratorium on debts and creating debt settlement procedures. The peasants were not much relieved in this way, but the moneylenders now also turned against the government. The leadership of the National Congress made full use of this development and espoused the causes of all those who were hit by the impact of the depression and British policy. Since the 1920s Gandhi had seen to it that the Congress would be adequately represented in the rural areas. This endeavour now yielded a rich political harvest. By now Gandhi was also better equipped to understand the economics behind agrarian unrest. Economic nationalism, which had earlier been debated by educated Indians well-read in economics, had now become a matter of common concern for vast strata of Indian society. The British could very well ignore those earlier debates, but this new groundswell shook the foundations of their empire. From an economic point of view this empire also appeared to be less useful than it used to be. Earlier, the privileged access to raw materials and agri- cultural produce had been a major reason for holding on to colonial rule. Since the depression had led to a dramatic fall in prices of such colonial products, whereas the maintenance of colonial rule proved to be a financial burden, decolonisation seemed to be inevitable. But the colonial rulers were also creditors and wanted to keep their debtors under control. Indian nationalists proclaimed that India should refuse to acknowledge the 'national debt' with which the British had saddled their country. Such proclamations scared the creditors who defended their control so as not to be driven into bankruptcy by their debtors. Therefore, colonial rule became more desperate and high-handed at the time when it was approaching its end. On the other hand, the Indian freedom movement gained added momentum due to its association with economic nationalism.

The fear of a 'fascist compact'

The impact of the Great Depression not only affected the peasantry but also Indian industry and foreign trade. The Japanese, who had joined the gold standard only in 1930, stuck to it firmly even after the British left it, but in December 1931 they also had to give it up. In 1932 their floating currency depreciated by about 60 per cent. This provided an enormous export bonus to them at the time when India's overvalued currency acted as an import bonus. Moreover, the Japanese cotton textile industry had cut costs by increasing productivity. Between 1926 and 1935 the output per Japanese textile worker had more than doubled. The Indian textile industry clam- oured for protective tariffs and the Government of India actually increased customs duties on textiles in several steps up to 75 per cent in 1933. The British textile industry feared that the Indian market would be lost to it and campaigned for 'imperial preference', i.e. preferential tariffs for British goods at generous rates. At this stage Sir Homy Mody on behalf of the Indian textile industry and his British counterpart Lees concluded the

Mody–Lees Pact which amounted to a market sharing arrangement. Indian nationalists, particularly the socialist followers of Jawaharlal Nehru, denounced this arrangement and saw in it the harbinger of a 'fascist compact' between Indian and British capitalists. It was feared the Indian capitalists would give up nationalism and gang up with their British counterparts to jointly exploit the poor people of India. This threat was taken very seriously at that time and greatly contributed to the rise of the socialist movement in India. But, in fact, the interests of Indian and British industrials were irreconcilable. Protectionism suited the Indian industrialists very well, but they wanted to get rid of imperial preference. The experience of the 1930s set the stage for the undiluted protectionism which was then practised by the government of independent India.

Election campaigns and office acceptance

In 1933 the Congress had returned once more to the constitutional arena. Gandhi terminated the civil disobedience campaign and in the following year Congress candidates were very successful in elections to the Central Legislative Assembly (formerly the Imperial Legislative Council). In 1934 the left wing of the Congress established the Congress Socialist Party, which looked upon Nehru as its mentor although he never joined it. Gandhi saw to it that Nehru was once more elected Congress president in 1936. In this capacity he had to lead the Congress into the election campaign under the new Government of India Act of 1935. Nehru was all for winning the elections but was opposed to Congressmen accepting office under this new constitution. The particular federal structure of the new constitution and the bloc of conservative princes were anathema to Nehru and the leftists. The princes, however, were far from unanimous in their policy. The most powerful – those of Kashmir, Hyderabad and Mysore – looked down upon the rest, believing that they were quite safe from all future plans of integration and amalgamation. The politically most active princes were the middling ones (Patiala, Bikaner, Bhopal, Alwar, etc.), although they, too, were subject to rivalries and status conflicts, which made it difficult for them to get together for any concerted action. The more enlightened representatives of princely governments and of the Chamber of Princes were unable to inspire the other princes with their concern for the future, just as they were unable to establish a princely consensus; when the princes found out that the British were not very eager to get the new federation going, they were content to stay out of it and enjoy life as usual.

The elections to the provincial assemblies were a great success for the Congress, which gained a majority in most of them with the exception of the Panjab and Bengal, where regional parties and coalitions prevailed. The richer peasants and occupancy tenants, who were enfranchised for the first time in this election, voted massively for the Congress; the British had hoped that they would provide a social base for their rule. Had it not been for the Great Depression this British plan of enfranchising peasants in order to undercut the Congress would probably have worked quite well; now, however, it had the opposite effect. On the other hand, the peasant electorate also put the Congress under some obligation to accept office in the provinces and legislate in favour of the peasantry.

Jawaharlal Nehru had led the election campaign with great vigour. He wanted to demonstrate that the Congress had the mandate of the people, but he did not favour office acceptance. In this, he came once more into conflict with Gandhi and finally had to accept his judgement. Many contemporary observers were amazed at the fact that these two leaders continued to work together although they so often disagreed. In his autobiography published in 1936 Nehru had written perceptively about Gandhi:

> he does represent the peasant masses of India, he is the quintessence of the conscious and subconscious will of those millions . . . he knows his India well and reacts to her slightest tremors, and gauges a situation accurately and almost instinctively, and has a knack of acting at the psychological moment.

Nehru appreciated this and very often followed Gandhi's instinct rather than his own analytical mind. Nehru and the left wing felt that with office acceptance the Congress would be at the mercy of the provincial governors who could always suspend the whole experiment under the emergency provisions of the constitution. Gandhi tried to solve this problem by asking the governors for a solemn promise that they would not make use of this emergency clause. Such a general promise would have been completely *ultra vires* under constitutional law and thus this was an impossible request.

Due to the Congress's refusal to accept office, minority governments of small splinter parties were formed and the Congress had to witness these governments getting the credit for implementing the Congress programme. Consequently, the right-wing Congress leaders became more and more impatient and when the governor of Madras promised C. Rajagopalachari (the provincial Congress leader) not to make undue use of the emergency provision and to give the Congress a fair chance, this was taken as the signal for office acceptance. Rajagopalachari had special reasons for being eager to form a government. After the previous constitutional reform a non-Brahmin party – proudly calling itself the Justice Party – had come to power in Madras; it had now been trounced in the elections but was back in power due to the Congress's refusal to accept office.

In order to reconcile office acceptance with the aims of the freedom movement, the Congress passed a strange resolution: those who joined the government as ministers had to vacate their positions in the Provincial Congress Committees. The Congress organisation was to carry on the

freedom struggle in which office acceptance made sense only as a tempo-
rary tactical move. Accordingly, the ministers were under the jurisdiction
of the Congress organisation, which could tell them to quit if this was
thought to be necessary in the interest of the movement. The practical effect
of this was that the ministers' rivals, who had just missed getting a ministerial post themselves, took charge of the respective Provincial Congress
Committee and started breathing down the necks of the ministers. Everywhere, there was now a ministerial and an organisational wing of the
Congress and the two usually did not see eye to eye.

This was soon to affect the National Congress as a whole when the
Congress president, Subhas Chandra Bose, decided to stand as a candidate
for a second term against the wishes of Gandhi, who had sponsored the can-
didature of Pattabhi Sitaramayya from Andhra. Bose won the election
because he was supported by the organisational wing. Gandhi announced
that he regarded this as a personal defeat; thereupon the Working Committee
resigned, leaving Bose high and dry. Bose then resigned, too, obviously
hoping to get immediately re-elected. But in this he was disappointed as
Rajendra Prasad was elected in his place. Prasad belonged to the Congress
High Command, together with Maulana Azad and Vallabhbhai Patel. This
High Command was responsible for the control of the work of the Congress
ministries and was, in general, more 'ministerial' than 'organisational' in its
outlook.

The Second World War, the Cripps mission and 'Quit India'

With the outbreak of the Second World War, Congress participation in the
provincial governments came to an abrupt end. Viceroy Lord Linlithgow
had declared India to be at war by signing on the dotted line without even
going through the motions of consulting Indian politicians about it. But
even that had not yet precipitated the decision of the Congress to stop cooperation. The Congress leaders had asked for a declaration of the British war
aims with regard to India and this was not forthcoming. Was this an anti-
fascist war or was it just an imperialist war aimed at maintaining the status
quo – including colonial rule in India? When no reply was given to this
question by October 1939 the High Command ordered the Congress
ministries to resign. Consequently, the British governors took over in those
provinces and only the Panjab and Bengal remained under the government
of regional Muslim parties or coalitions.

The two years of Congress government in the provinces had passed very
quickly and not much of the Congress programme had been implemented
in this short period. Some amendments of existing Tenancy Acts had been
introduced and in some provinces such legislation was prepared for the first
time. The Congress had satisfied some of the expectations of its rural voters.

The resignation of the ministries had also absolved it from the task of tackling some crucial issues and it could later renew its mandate more easily. On the other hand, the resignation also deprived the Congress of all influence on the conduct of Indian politics during the war. A resumption of national agitation was difficult under wartime conditions and Gandhi's campaign of 'individual satyagraha' was a rather weak substitute for a fully fledged civil disobedience campaign.

Viceroy Lord Linlithgow, a faithful standard-bearer for Winston Churchill, was convinced that there was no necessity to make any concession during the war. However, the rapid conquest of southeast Asia by the Japanese and the expectations of the American allies finally forced the British cabinet to make a declaration of its war aims in order to obtain India's full support for the war effort. When Linlithgow saw the draft declaration he immediately tendered his resignation which, of course, the cabinet did not want to accept at this juncture. Churchill was in a fix, but he was suddenly saved from making a difficult choice.

Sir Stafford Cripps appeared as a *deus ex machina* and offered to fly to India as representative of the war cabinet in order to negotiate a viable compromise. Cripps had served as British ambassador to the Soviet Union and was credited with having won that country as an ally. He had just joined the war cabinet and a further success in India could have built him up as a serious rival to Churchill. Thus, Churchill could hardly wish that Cripps should solve the Indian problem; for the time being, however, Cripps's initiative provided a convenient alibi. Cripps took up his mission with great confidence. He was a friend of Nehru and in 1938 he had made some plans for a future transfer of power with Nehru and his Labour Party colleagues. He had then visited India in December 1939 and had clearly stated his sympathy with that country's political aspirations. He now cherished a secret hope that he might be able to dislodge the conservative viceroy with the help of the Congress, or that he would at least be able to dictate the terms according to which the viceroy had to conduct his business.

Although Cripps carefully avoided any conflict with Linlithgow and informed him of every step of his negotiations, the viceroy sensed what was going on and sabotaged the mission at its decisive stage. Cripps had almost succeeded in getting the Congress leaders into a wartime national government, which was to function just like the British war cabinet with the viceroy acting like a constitutional monarch. Of course, the constitution as such could not be changed then and there but within the given framework this kind of national government could be established by convention. If at this stage the viceroy had come forward with a statement that he would be willing to work such a scheme, the Congress would have joined the national government; instead, Linlithgow kept his mouth shut and wrote to Churchill complaining that Cripps intended to deprive him of his constitutional powers.

This killed the 'Cripps offer'; in a final round of talks Nehru and Azad noticed that Cripps could not give definitive answers to specific questions: he had obviously promised more than he could deliver. Cripps, on the other hand, felt that the Congress should have taken the risk of entering the national government, because once they were in it a threat of resignation would have given them enough leverage to keep Linlithgow in line. But Linlithgow, who was in office and who had already threatened to resign, had by far the greater leverage. Cripps returned home embittered and disappointed: he was peeved at the pusillanimity of the Congress leaders. Churchill and Linlithgow, however, were glad to see Cripps's discomfiture. No further declaration was required and Roosevelt had to keep quiet. In fact, Roosevelt's personal representative, Colonel Johnson, had actively intervened in New Delhi at the time of the negotiations in order to help Cripps. Churchill had resented this and had asked Roosevelt about Johnson's mandate – whereupon the US President denied that he had authorised Johnson to intervene in this way. Thus, Churchill had scored another point and the American initiative was stymied.

After the rejection of the Cripps offer the Congress could not remain passive; it had to give a suitable reply. The answer was the 'Quit India Resolution' which called upon the British to leave India while there was still time to save the country from the consequences of a destructive battle with the Japanese, who were daily coming closer. Gandhi was supposed to give emphasis to this resolution by designing a new campaign, but before he could do so he and all the Congress leaders were imprisoned. Linlithgow even proposed to deport all of them to Africa for the duration of the war, but his governors advised him against this because they felt that it would do more harm than good to British rule in India. The arrest of the Congress leaders did not stop the campaign; on the contrary, the younger nationalists who had resented Gandhi's restraining influence now unleashed a violent offensive.

In many parts of India they cut telegraph wires, dismantled rails, stormed police stations and planted Congress flags on government offices. Quite a few districts were completely in the hands of the rebels; in Bihar, especially, the oppressed peasants were ready for violent action and the government could no longer control the situation. But this so-called 'August revolution' did, indeed, not outlast the month of August 1942. Soon thereafter the tide of the war turned in favour of the Allies and the Japanese offensive lost its momentum.

The year 1943 was a very critical one for the Government of India because it had to cope with the distribution of food grains, a task for which it was not equipped. A Food Department had been established only in December 1942 after the Japanese advance had led to price increases which the government had tried to control in vain. There was actually no shortage of supply as all the war years had good harvests, but the market went out

310

of gear as traders hoarded grain in expectation of further price rises. Food grain procurement and storage by government agencies and rationing in the cities were the only effective means of counteracting hoarding and inflationary pressure. British India became an interventionist state in the last years of the war. But before the interventionist machinery was fully established, a terrible man-made famine killed about one million people in Bengal in 1943 and many more died subsequently due to malnutrition and diseases. In the former Congress provinces the British bureaucracy was in full control and could cope with the problems of food administration. But in Bengal there was still an 'autonomous' provincial government which did not want to go against the interests of the grain traders. The new viceroy, Lord Wavell, finally deployed units of the army to distribute grain in Bengal, but by that time the famine had already claimed its victims, many of whom had died within sight of rice bags whose contents they could no longer afford to buy and which they did not dare to snatch because they were used to a regime which maintained law and order very rigorously.

Subhas Chandra Bose, who had escaped to Germany in the hope of enlisting Hitler's support for the Indian freedom movement, was thoroughly disappointed there and by the time he reached Japan – where Hitler had sent him after a great deal of prevarication and delay – there was no longer much scope for Bose's initiative. He organised an 'Indian National Army' recruited from among Indian prisoners-of-war in southeast Asia and some units of this army did actually reach Indian soil at Imphal in the course of the Japanese conquest of Burma. But then the great retreat began and the cause of India's liberation from outside was lost. Bose's heroic endeavour still fires the imagination of many of his countrymen. But like a meteor which enters the earth's atmosphere, he burnt brightly on the horizon for a brief moment only. He died before the war was over, in an aircraft which is thought to have crashed while flying over Taiwan.

In the last years of the war, when they felt sure of an Allied victory, the British in India kept the nationalists at bay. When Gandhi went on a fast in prison in order to protest against British accusations that he was responsible for the 'August revolution', his jailers kept sandalwood ready for his funeral pyre and were not at all alarmed at the prospect of his dying in their custody. Gandhi, however, survived and in May 1944 was released for reasons of health. His talks with Jinnah later that year ended without a result. The freedom movement had been eclipsed in the last years of the war by the debate about the partition of India demanded by Jinnah.

Jinnah, rather than Gandhi, now dominated the political scene. The British were looking forward to the end of the war with some trepidation. The unrest in the aftermath of the First World War was still within living memory, and even more demobilised soldiers were returning to India this time. They had seen a great deal of the world and knew how to handle modern weapons. Postwar economic problems were also going to be difficult to cope with. Gandhi had asked the British to 'Quit India' in 1942. 'Divide and Rule' had been a safe watchword for a long time; now they found another one: 'Divide and Quit'.

THE PARTITION OF INDIA

Like Shylock in *The Merchant of Venice*, Mohammad Ali Jinnah had asked for his pound of flesh; he did not, however, find a Portia willing to concede it to him provided that no drop of blood be spilled by its excision. Much blood was spilled when India was divided. Millions of refugees fled from one part of the country to another. Pakistan, which Jinnah did not himself excise from the body of India but which he made the departing British cut for him, proved to be an unstable construction and a cause of continuous friction in the entire region. The British, who had always taken pride in having established the political unity of India, undid their achievement at the end of their rule. How did this come about?

The partition of India and the foundation of Pakistan was – more than any comparable event in human history – the work of one man. This is why any enquiry into the course of events which led to this end has always concentrated on the career of M.A. Jinnah. When did he finally make up his mind? At what point was he still prepared to compromise? Who prevented such a compromise? Many different answers have been given to these questions. But this retrospective focus on Jinnah detracts attention from the complex and fluid condition of Muslim politics in India which, for a long time, made Jinnah more of a pleader than a leader. He was not a fervent Muslim and not an agitator of the masses; he was a moderate, secular nationalist who looked to Gokhale as a man to emulate in Indian politics. He was also, first and foremost, a brilliant lawyer who knew how to take care of his clients' interests. In the political field the Muslims of India were his clients and even as a young member of the Imperial Legislative Council he scored a big success with the passing of the Waqf Validating Act of 1913, which was of benefit to all Muslims who wanted to establish religious trusts. During the First World War when Muslim opinion became more nationalist, Jinnah could play his favourite role as ambassador of Hindu–Muslim unity. The Congress–League pact of 1916 was the high point of his career in this respect. He, himself, had been a member of the National Congress before he joined the Muslim League and he remained a member of both organisations, as he had been assured that the League membership would not be incompatible with his Congress membership.

The emphasis on provincial politics which started with the introduction of 'responsible government' was a setback for Jinnah. He was a man of the Muslim diaspora, his arena was the Imperial Legislative Council and he had had no contact with the problems of the Muslim majority provinces. The Khilafat agitation which fired the imagination of the Indian Muslims was, to him, a case of false consciousness and his political judgement proved to be right in this respect. Nevertheless, there was little consolation for him in being right but isolated – as he was for a long time after 1919. He always hoped for the emergence of another sequence of events similar to those of 1916, which would enable him to act as mediator between the Congress and the League. But the Congress was strong and did not need him, while the League was moribund. Jinnah grew old, became ill and increasingly bitter.

Jinnah, Rahmat Ali and the idea of Pakistan

The Round Table Conferences in London once more provided a congenial political arena for Jinnah. He actually settled down in London for several years and practised law, making a good deal of money. To many contemporary observers it might have seemed as if he had left Indian politics for good and would spend the rest of his life in England. He was, after all, nearly 60 years old. While he was in England he was confronted with a scheme proposed by another expatriate Indian Muslim, Rahmat Ali, who lived in Cambridge where he had founded the Pakistan National Movement.

Rahmat Ali was a Panjabi who had made some money early in life as a legal advisor to a rich Baluchi landlord; he had then gone to Cambridge as a student. He was inspired by Mohammad Iqbal's call for the establishment of a Muslim state in northwestern India, a proposal which Iqbal had made in his presidential address to the Muslim League session of 1930. But he felt that Iqbal's proposal had been too vague. Moreover, when Iqbal attended the Round Table Conference he had refrained from pressing this issue. Thus, Rahmat Ali felt called upon to spell out more clearly what would be entailed by an autonomous Muslim state in northwestern India; he also found a name for it: Pakistan. This was an acronym composed of the first letters of Panjab, Afghan Province (i.e. Northwest Frontier Province), Kashmir and Sindh and the last syllable of Baluchistan. Issuing a flood of pamphlets, Rahmat Ali saw to it that his ideas were noticed everywhere – particularly in certain British circles and, of course, among his countrymen at home.

Jinnah disliked Rahmat Ali's ideas and avoided meeting him. To Jinnah, himself a diaspora Muslim, this Panjabi scheme must, at this time, have resembled a counsel of despair rather than the bright hope of the future, for it completely disregarded the Muslims in the Muslim minority provinces. In fact, Rahmat Ali had not even considered the other Muslim majority province, Bengal, and only when this was later pointed out to him did he coin the term 'Bangistan' and advocated the establishment of another state like Pakistan. It was an irony of fate that Jinnah, despite his initial abhorrence of the scheme, subsequently had to adopt most of Rahmat Ali's programme without giving him credit for it. But before this happened, Jinnah had hoped for a political comeback under the Government of India Act of 1935; it was only when this hope was disappointed that he changed his views.

Jinnah had been elected once more to the Central Legislative Assembly in October 1934 while he was still in London. His constituency was the Muslims of Bombay and there was no other contestant; he could therefore win this election even *in absentia*. He had earlier intended to enter Parliament on a Conservative Party ticket, but the Tories did not want him and so he went back to New Delhi instead. Here, he pursued a nationalist line: when the elections to the provincial assemblies approached in 1936, he established Parliamentary Boards of the Muslim League in all provinces and practically copied the Congress election programme. In this way, he hoped to recommend himself as the coalition partner he thought the Congress might require in order to form ministries in the various provinces. He also calculated that the separate electorates for Muslims (now operating with an enlarged franchise) would yield a good crop of successful Muslim League candidates. Why should a Muslim vote for a Congress Muslim if a League candidate standing for the same programme was available? To Jinnah's great disappointment this calculation proved to be wrong. In British India as a whole, the Muslim League won only about 25 per cent of the Muslim seats, Congress Muslims obtained 6 per cent and the lion's share of 69 per cent was captured by provincial parties in the Muslim majority provinces. With its overwhelming strength in the Hindu majority provinces the Congress did not need the League as a coalition partner there; in the Muslim majority provinces the League also had to remain in opposition.

With the benefit of hindsight one can state that it would have been an act of wise statesmanship if the Congress had, nevertheless, established coalition governments with the League, thus helping Jinnah to remain what he had been up to this point – a nationalist spokesman for the Muslims in the Muslim minority provinces. But from the perspective of 1936 there were serious obstacles to such a course. The Congress initially had an ambivalent attitude towards office acceptance and the needs of the freedom movement might have called for a resignation of the ministries at any moment. Would the League as a coalition partner have gone along with all this? Moreover, the League was, at this stage, not yet the political force it was to become ten years later. Why should the Congress try to nurse this sectarian party rather than make an attempt to wean the Muslim masses away from it? Thus, Jinnah was left out in the cold and had to turn his attention to the Muslim majority provinces. Rahmat Ali's ideas were growing upon him, whether he liked it or not. The Urdu press had spread these ideas in India: Pakistan was now no longer a strange word but had already become a very familiar slogan.

At the session of the Muslim League in October 1937 Jinnah underwent a fateful metamorphosis which he also expressed outwardly by abandoning his fashionable Western suit and donning, for the first time, a north Indian *sherwani* (long coat) complemented by the typical fur cap which soon became known as the 'Jinnah cap'. In this attire he concluded a pact with the powerful chief minister of the Panjab, Sir Sikander Hyat Khan. This Sikander–Jinnah pact stipulated that the Unionist Party of the Panjab, led by Sikander, would retain full autonomy of the affairs of that province; Jinnah, however, was acknowledged as the leader at a national level. Since the League had only won two seats in the Panjab, Jinnah did not lose much by assuring Sikander that he did not intend to challenge him on his home ground. Sikander, on the other hand, interpreted the pact in his own way and thought that he had Jinnah in his pocket. At any rate, this pact marked the beginning of Jinnah's new role as spokesman for the Muslim majority provinces. He had opted for Pakistan although he did not say so as yet. It was in 1938 that he started talking about national goals for the Muslims and he gladly adopted the title 'Qaid-i-Azam' (Great Leader) bestowed upon him by his followers, whose numbers were increasing rapidly.

The outbreak of the Second World War and the resignation of the Congress ministries pushed Jinnah even more into the arms of the Muslims in the Muslim majority provinces, as political activity in the Muslim minority provinces was now practically suspended in order that British governors might run them much as they had done in unreformed times. At the Lahore session of the Muslim League in March 1940, Jinnah introduced a resolution which included the demand for Pakistan – though the term itself was still avoided. Rahmat Ali happened to be in India at that time but was kept out of the Panjab by Sikander's men, who told him that he would be arrested if he entered the province. Had he been present at Lahore, he would have been surprised to hear Jinnah's speech with its echoes of so much that he himself had written in his Cambridge pamphlets. The Lahore resolution was supported by Sikander and by Fazlul Haq, the leader of the Bengali Muslim peasantry. It soon came to be referred to as the 'Pakistan Resolution' – which must have thrilled Rahmat Ali, who had been so assiduously debarred from witnessing the scene that signalled the triumph of his ideas.

The Lahore Resolution and the Two Nations Theory

Jinnah's assertion at Lahore that the Muslims of India are a nation by any definition of the term – his 'Two Nations Theory', as it came to be known – provided him with a new legitimation as a national leader whose commands ought to be obeyed by provincial Muslim leaders. He soon proved this point when Sikander and Fazlul Haq accepted posts on a National Defence Council which the viceroy had established in 1941.

Jinnah had not been consulted and promptly ordered the two to resign from these posts. They did so reluctantly, but did not dare snub their leader. In this way Jinnah not only taught them a lesson, but also issued a warning to the viceroy, who preferred to deal with Sikander rather than with Jinnah.

Such moves helped Jinnah to consolidate his position as a leader whom nobody could afford to ignore. A most crucial test came for him when Cripps arrived in India in 1942. Had the Cripps mission been successful, Jinnah would have had to join a national government and play second fiddle to Nehru and the Congress. He kept his cards close to his chest, noted with satisfaction that the Cripps offer contained certain concessions with regard to the Pakistan demand, withheld any immediate promise of his cooperation and watched what the Congress was going to do. When the Congress finally refused to accept the Cripps offer, Jinnah rejected it, too. Perhaps he did this with a sigh of relief, because he thus retained a free hand to build up his bargaining position. This he did with great skill during the last years of the war.

In 1944 he held a series of talks with Gandhi in which Gandhi practically conceded the Pakistan demand, although insisting on a treaty to be concluded before partition which would ensure that India and Pakistan would stay together in a kind of confederation. Jinnah accepted the idea of a treaty but said that it should be concluded after partition because only truly autonomous partners could conclude a treaty on equal terms. Legally, Jinnah's point was well taken and Gandhi despaired of reaching an agreement. The talks ended without a result; they also added to Jinnah's political stature. In reality, he was not much interested in these talks – Britain rather than the Congress would concede to the Pakistan demand – but he wished to project an image of a reasonable negotiator who would never refuse to consider an honourable compromise.

The Simla Conference and its aftermath

Jinnah was put to a more severe test a year later when Viceroy Lord Wavell convened a conference at Simla in the hope of getting Indian leaders to agree on the formation of a national government now that the war was almost over. Wavell was keen to get such a government installed to tackle India's immediate postwar problems. What Linlithgow had failed to do at the time of the Cripps mission Wavell wanted to do now. The Congress was ready to enter such a government and Jinnah was, again, afraid of getting into the 'second fiddle' position without any guarantee that the British were going to give him Pakistan in due course. On the other hand, he could not afford to be unreasonable to begin with, so he torpedoed the conference at the end by demanding that the Muslim League should have the exclusive right to nominate all the Muslim ministers of the proposed national government. The conference broke down on this point. But Wavell made another attempt with the blessing of the India Committee of the British war cabinet. He drafted a list of a national government himself. This included no Congress Muslims; only one Unionist Muslim of the Panjab; all other Muslims mentioned were members of the Muslim League. Jinnah rejected this list, too, and as the India Committee had authorised Wavell to show the list to Jinnah and to nobody else, he could neither call Jinnah's bluff nor publicise what had happened. Again, Jinnah emerged with a greatly enhanced political stature from this round of negotiations. He had shown that nothing could be done against his will and the British had unwittingly helped him to demonstrate this point.

This was the state of affairs when a momentous change took place in British politics. Churchill had dissolved the war cabinet at the earliest opportunity, confident of winning the elections and heading a Conservative government. Instead, a Labour government came to power with Clement Attlee as the new prime minister. He could have taken bold steps towards India's independence. A major obstacle – the settlement of India's national debt to Great Britain – had been removed by the war as India had emerged from it as a creditor to the colonial rulers. Substantial sterling balances had accumulated in the Bank of England, which India had earned by producing essential goods for the British.

But the Labour government missed the chance of taking a bold initiative. The fact that this government felt that the Cripps offer was still open actually prevented it from giving much thought to the new developments in India at that time. As a true democrat Attlee believed that elections should be held as soon as possible. The newly elected provincial assemblies could then serve as electoral colleges for the election of a constituent assembly. Elections are certainly the lifeblood of a democratic system, but they can prove to be disruptive in societies with sectarian parties and separate electorates – and this even more so when the electorate is not given any clear idea of the issues at stake. Jinnah had deliberately kept his Pakistan demand rather vague and tall claims were made in the election campaign. Wavell was upset because he was not permitted even to contradict such claims. Indeed, when the viceroy wrote to Secretary of State Lord Pethick-Lawrence that he might suggest an MP asking a question from the floor of the House, which could then be authoritatively answered on behalf of the government, Pethick-Lawrence declined on the grounds that such a course might elicit more embarrassing questions for which the government had no proper answer. This was a striking indication of the Labour government's helplessness.

Left to his own devices Wavell drafted a 'Breakdown Plan' which he wanted to put into effect if the elections reflected the pattern of the Simla Conference in granting Jinnah the power to veto, as Jinnah could then simply wait for the viceroy's next move in order to increase his political leverage. Should there be another deadlock, Wavell wanted to threaten Jinnah that the British would give him a Pakistan restricted to the Muslim majority districts of the Panjab and Bengal only. Wavell also proposed that he would make such a move towards a showdown immediately after the election results for the Panjab were known, without waiting for the results of the other provinces. Wavell thought that everything depended on the fate of the Unionist Party in this respect.

Wavell received no reply from London, but his plan had obviously caused such consternation in Attlee's cabinet that a decision was made to send a cabinet mission to India, composed of Secretary of State Lord Pethick-Lawrence, Sir Stafford Cripps and Lord Alexander. The records provide no clue as to the emergence of this idea. Attlee and his colleagues had been unhappy with Wavell's handling of Indian politics for some time. The names of various potential emissaries were discussed, but it was clear that only a cabinet minister could supersede the viceroy in political negotiations in India. So, finally, three of them were dispatched to India and Wavell was not even informed of the mission's terms of reference.

Had Wavell been a politician, he probably would have resigned at this point; he was, instead, a loyal soldier and did what he thought to be his duty until the bitter end. Attlee, on the other hand, ought to have replaced Wavell with a viceroy of his choice as soon as possible – but he probably did not want to shock the Conservative opposition by what would have appeared to be a partisan appointment. Due to this prevarication British policy with regard to India did not have a clear profile. The cabinet mission did not exactly help to remedy this deficiency. It spent nearly four months in India and evolved a complicated scheme. When it returned home, however, it left Wavell pretty much where he was before the ministers had arrived and it was only when he produced another disastrous 'Breakdown Plan' that he was finally replaced.

The cabinet mission scheme and the advent of partition

When the cabinet mission arrived in India it was confronted with a Congress and a League, which were less prepared for compromise than ever. Both parties had done very well in the elections, provincial parties had been nearly eliminated. A clear-cut, two-party system had emerged in India. This was not, however, due to the principle of interest aggregation as fostered by the majority election system: it was simply a product of the system of separate electorates for Muslims. This time Jinnah's calculations proved accurate and the League had captured about 90 per cent of all Muslim seats. With such a mandate he was sure to get what he wanted. The British, who had themselves created the separate electorates, were now unable to undo the consequences of this fateful system – even though they were genuinely interested in maintaining the unity of India.

The scheme which the cabinet mission evolved for this purpose envisaged three tiers; the provinces, regional groups of provinces and a federal centre charged with a few well-defined central subjects, such as foreign affairs, defence, currency, etc. Jinnah accepted the scheme because he interpreted the regional groups of provinces as a de facto recognition of his Pakistan demand: these groups would have constituent assemblies of their own; the constitution of the federal centre could eventually be designed so that it became a mere agency centre with executive and not legislative powers, and dealt only with matters specifically delegated to it by the federal units. The Congress also accepted the scheme, but for the opposite reason: it took it to be a rejection of the Pakistan demand. It also held that the provinces were free to opt out of a group to which they did not wish to belong. This was particularly important in view of the fact that the Northwest Frontier Province in the proposed Group A had a Congress government, as had Assam in the proposed Group C (Group B contained the Hindu majority provinces). Jinnah, however, interpreted the scheme in terms of compulsory grouping, i.e. the respective provinces would have to join their group first, whether they liked it or not, and if they wished to opt out of it they could do so only at a much later stage when constitution making was completed. There was still a further point of disagreement: the Congress held that once a constituent assembly was convened, it was a sovereign body not bound by the cabinet mission scheme; Jinnah, of course, insisted that this scheme, once accepted, must be binding on everybody concerned.

The cabinet mission scheme was not an Act on the statute book: it was only a suggestion, and the only sanction which the British had in order to make it a success was that they would not quit India before the Congress and the League had made this scheme work. But this sanction was wearing thin as it became more and more obvious that British staying power – in the most literal sense of the term – was diminishing very rapidly. For this reason Wavell was most concerned to get a national interim government going. This time the viceroy did not let Jinnah's veto deter him and he appointed a cabinet with Nehru as interim prime minister.

Jinnah was furious. He resorted to agitation by declaring 16 August 1946 to be the League's 'Direct Action Day', though he did not actually say what was to be done on that day. In most provinces nothing happened. However, in Bengal the Muslim League chief minister, H. Suhrawardy, engineered a communal holocaust in Calcutta. He probably hoped to tilt the city's demographic balance in this way in favour of the Muslims. Calcutta had a large population of Hindu workers from Bihar, and many of them actually did flee to their home province due to the 'Great Calcutta Killing' as this fateful event came to be known. The cabinet mission scheme had conceived of a united Bengal, but there had been indications that if this scheme failed then Bengal would have to be divided and Calcutta might become part of west

Bengal. Jinnah stated that depriving Bengal of Calcutta would be like asking a man to live without his heart. Suhrawardy obviously hoped to cleanse this heart by driving out Hindu blood. When this did not work he turned to seek Hindu support for a united Bengal, which would have become an autonomous dominion along the lines laid down for India and Pakistan. Jinnah would have supported this plan: he stated that such a Bengal would certainly have friendly relations with a Pakistan restricted to 'Group A'. He would have preferred this solution – which reflected Rahmat Ali's plan – to the 'moth-eaten' Pakistan he finally accepted, and for which Rahmat Ali criticised him bitterly. The latter paid his own price for this censure: the man who had given a name to the new nation was never permitted to enter Pakistan; Rahmat Ali died a lonely death in England.

The shock of the 'Direct Action Day' in Calcutta did not prevent Wavell from going ahead with the establishment of the interim government; on the contrary, it made him even more eager to have such a government to share the burden of maintaining law and order in India. Nehru and his cabinet were sworn in on 2 September 1946. Wavell was right in his assumption that Jinnah would soon climb down and agree to League participation in this government. However, Jinnah did not enter the government himself: he deputed his right hand man, Liaquat Ali Khan, to play second fiddle to Nehru. Not wanting to give up the vital Home Ministry, the Congress relinquished the finance portfolio to Liaquat, who soon annoyed the Congress by using his powers to obstruct the working of the ministries run by Congressmen.

In the meantime, Wavell had inaugurated the Constituent Assembly, which was then boycotted by the League. He hoped that in due course the League would join that assembly, too, just as it had joined the interim government. Instead of this, he was faced with a Congress request to dismiss the League ministers, coupled with growing Congress assertiveness in the Constituent Assembly. To his great dismay he also was unable to get any final declaration of the aims of the British government despite his having made repeated requests for such a declaration. In this hopeless situation he worked on another 'Breakdown Plan' which reflected his military mind. He proposed an orderly regional withdrawal of the British Indian army, starting with an evacuation of southern India and ending up with a concentration on the Muslim majority provinces, where he felt the British might still be welcome. Wavell knew that this would be a desperate move and ironically named it 'Operation Madhouse'. Attlee and his colleagues were appalled by this plan; Wavell was dismissed and replaced by Lord Mountbatten.

Operation Mountbatten and 'Plan Balkan'

As a cousin of the king and former Supreme Commander of the southeast Asian area during the war, Mountbatten had a standing which made him generally acceptable and nobody could blame Attlee for making a partisan choice. At the same time, this standing enabled Mountbatten to dictate his terms when accepting the post which he had not solicited. He was asked whether he realised that the powers he requested would make him the superior rather than the subordinate of the secretary of state and he replied, unruffled, that this was exactly what he wanted. Moreover, his appointment was accompanied by the very declaration of the aims of the British government that Wavell had petitioned in vain. The declaration stated that the British were to quit India by June 1948; Mountbatten would be the last viceroy. Only 41 years old when he reached India, Mountbatten was dynamic and sociable and immediately established good relations with Indian leaders. His only drawback was that he did not like paperwork and rarely studied the detailed drafts of constitutional proposals, which were churned out by his own staff and by Indian politicians with increasing frequency in the last few months before independence and partition.

The plan which Mountbatten finally sent home for approval by the cabinet was appropriately called 'Plan Balkan' in official circles. It was more or less a revised version of the cabinet mission scheme, but it was no longer based on the hope of preserving the unity of India. Instead, it aimed to arrive at a reasonable partition. Even Nehru was now convinced that this was the only way out of the impasse, but the version of the 'Plan

Figure 7.4 Negotiations prior to India's independence in 1947. At the table are Jawaharlal Nehru, Lord Mountbatten, Mohammed Ali Jinnah. Behind them are Sir Eric Miéville and Lord Ismay (members of Lord Mountbatten's staff)

(Courtesy of Associated Press)

Balkan' which was shown to him before it was sent to London at least preserved the unity of the Hindu majority provinces ('Group B') and enabled provinces which did not want to stay in 'Group A' or 'Group B' to opt out of them.

The cabinet made some important changes in this plan, probably due to Attlee's preference for a clear statement of the principle of provincial self-determination. Independence would be granted to the provinces and to the princely states and they could then get together in whatever way they wanted. In other words, instead of providing for the exceptional possibility of 'opting out' the plan now put all units on an equal footing and gave them the chance of 'opting in' according to their free choice. Although certainly a more logical proposition, in practical terms it could have disastrous consequences. 'Plan Balkan' could now, indeed, lead to a complete Balkanisation of India.

Mountbatten, who did not pay attention to such details, did not see much of a difference between the plan sent to London and the plan as revised by the cabinet; he was completely surprised when Nehru rejected it outright. Faced with the potential consequences of this plan, Nehru now also pressed for what Jinnah had expected all along: a Pakistan award made by the British. But this Pakistan was to be the 'moth-eaten' one composed of the Muslim majority districts only and not consisting of an undivided Panjab and an undivided Bengal. Taking note of Nehru's reaction Mountbatten swung around to his point of view and worked for this kind of award. Jinnah could not object to it either, even though it meant a substantial reduction of the Pakistan he had hoped for. His hold on the Muslim majority provinces was still rather precarious. He had consolidated his position as a national leader of the Muslims – but if the provincial level were now to re-emerge as the crucial arena of decision-making, his control over the course of events might be diminished.

When Mountbatten saw this consensus emerging he did his best to strike while the iron was hot. Constitution-making was postponed and the Government of India Act of 1935 was suitably revised so as to become the Independence of India Act of 1947. The dates for the inaugurations of two new dominions were fixed for 14 and 15 August 1947. An eminent British jurist whose name had been suggested by Jinnah was commissioned to draw the boundary lines. Mountbatten saw to it that these lines were kept secret until after the inauguration of the two dominions. Perhaps he thought that by conducting the operation under anaesthetic the patient would get over it more easily, and by the time he awoke he would be reconciled to what had happened. In fact, Mountbatten was so sure of this that he took leave and went to the mountains after the inaugurations and was taken by surprise when a storm of violence swept the Panjab once the border line became known. The Sikhs in particular – enraged that their region of settlement had been cut right down the middle – took violent revenge on their

Figure 7.5 Mohammed Ali Jinnah and Mahatma Gandhi
(Courtesy of Dinodia.com)

Muslim countrymen and thus provoked another round of retribution in which many of them died, too.

Mountbatten was in trouble. Initially, he had agreed to stay on as governor general of *both* India and Pakistan, but Jinnah had insisted on becoming governor general of Pakistan and it was only at the request of Nehru that Mountbatten changed his mind and agreed to stay on as governor general of India alone. Now he could no longer control the situation on the other side of the border line which he had disguised so ingeniously until the last minute. Violence in the Panjab was just the first challenge; the next followed immediately.

Gurdaspur district in the Panjab had been awarded to India and this meant that the princely state of Kashmir had a direct link with India. Kashmir had a Muslim majority but a Hindu maharaja who dragged his feet when he was expected to accede to one dominion or the other. Preoccupied with the fate of British India, the cabinet mission had not given much thought to the princely states and Mountbatten had announced the 'Lapse of Paramountcy' quite suddenly. The Pakistan award and the transfer of power to two dominions did not affect the princes. 'Plan Balkan' was still applicable as far as they were concerned and this provided them with a good bargaining position. Of course, only a few of them could actually contemplate independence and use this as a bargaining counter; Kashmir was placed in the most advantageous position in this respect. Pakistan tried to help the maharaja of Kashmir to make up his mind by sending armed rebels across the border. But, instead of coming to terms with Pakistan, the maharaja appealed to India for assistance. Mountbatten insisted on accession before such assistance could be given and the maharaja signed on the dotted line.

The fat was in the fire. Mountbatten had wished to avoid taking sides, but the Kashmir crisis brought him down strongly on the side of India and he advised Nehru to stand firm. The Indian army defended Kashmir against Pakistani aggression. Nehru appealed to the United Nations for it to pass a resolution demanding that Pakistan 'vacate the aggression'. Instead, the United Nations tried to find a political solution and emphasised the necessity of a referendum, as Nehru had promised at the time of accession. Nehru was later to regret this promise and the referendum was never held. It would have been the Indian Muslims' first opportunity to decide whether they preferred to live in India or in Pakistan. No referendum had been held when Pakistan was established.

A referendum in Kashmir would have rejected either the principle on which Pakistan was founded or the principle of the secular state which was so essential for Indian unity. It would have been, in fact, a referendum for or against the 'Two Nations Theory'. Although India was reconciled to the existence of Pakistan, it could never accept the 'Two Nations Theory' because more than one-third of the Muslims of India had remained in India and had not gone to Pakistan. Even Jinnah was forced to revise his theory in this respect. When he was leaving India for Pakistan he was asked by Muslims who had decided to stay what he would advise them to do now: he told them to be loyal citizens of India.

While Jinnah departed with such good advice Gandhi was trying hard to stop the carnage which broke out after partition and to work for good relations between India and Pakistan. When the violence in the Panjab spilled over into India he rushed to Delhi from Bengal, where he had been at the time of partition. With a great fast he attempted to bring his countrymen to their senses. Then the Kashmir conflict led to an undeclared war between India and Pakistan and at this point it was debated how and why the funds of the Indian treasury should be divided between India and Pakistan. Many Hindus felt that Pakistan had forfeited its claim to a share of these funds by attacking India in Kashmir, and that it would be the height of folly to hand over such funds to finance an aggressor's war effort. Gandhi, however, pleaded for evenhanded justice. The Congress had approved of partition and was in honour bound to divide the assets equitably. To radical Hindus this advice amounted to high treason, and one of them, a young Brahmin named Nathuram Godse, shot Gandhi on 30 January 1948.

8

THE REPUBLIC

INTERNAL AFFAIRS AND POLITICAL DEVELOPMENT

Apart from the carnage at the time of partition, the transfer of power was a peaceful affair. The freedom movement had come to an end without a dramatic triumph. There was no revolution. The institutional heritage of British India was taken over as a going concern. The major heritage of the freedom movement was the National Congress itself, which Gandhi had organised with such great skill and devotion. Now that freedom had been achieved, Gandhi advised that the National Congress should be dissolved because he had never thought of it as a party but as a national forum. Free India should now have political parties with their distinct programmes, Gandhi argued. His advice went unheeded and the National Congress survived as a large centrist party, though other parties did emerge on its fringes in due course.

The Congress was the main support of the new republic and it was more or less identified with that state. Since the Great Depression had pushed substantial numbers of peasants into the arms of the Congress, it had a fairly broad social base and tried its best to retain that base. No other country which attained freedom through decolonisation had a political organisation of such dimensions. The Muslim League – which had been successful in the elections prior to partition and could be regarded as the party which had established Pakistan – soon proved to be unstable and ephemeral after its great leader, M.A. Jinnah, died in September 1948. The Congress, on the other hand, was going strong under the leadership of Jawaharlal Nehru and Vallabhbhai Patel.

Nehru, Patel and the making of the Indian constitution

Though Nehru and Patel often did not see eye to eye and were identified with the left and the right wing of the Congress respectively, their different talents actually helped the new republic to get off to a good start. Nehru

325

was able to stir the imagination of the people, to reconcile hopes and reality by making radical speeches but being, nevertheless, cautious and moderate in practical politics. Patel was a superb administrator who could delegate work and inspire trust and confidence in those who had to work with him. As home minister he tackled the princes and made them all accede to the Indian Union so that the spectre of 'Plan Balkan' was soon forgotten. Belonging to a caste of substantial peasants in Gujarat he was close to the main strata, which provided the social base for the Congress. Nehru, as prime minister and minister for external affairs, saw India in a global context and had a vision of the future – but he also knew how to preserve his political power by making compromises in internal affairs, which were largely dominated by Patel until his death in 1950. Many of the aspirations of the freedom movement had to be relegated to the background in order to meet the exigencies of practical politics.

This was quite obvious in the deliberations of the Constituent Assembly, which was inaugurated in December 1946 and worked until the end of 1949. The new constitution was then introduced on 26 January 1950, the twentieth anniversary of the resolution of the National Congress which had first specified an independent republic as the aim of the freedom movement.

Figure 8.1 Dr Rajendra Prasad, President of the Constituent Assembly, addressing the members on 15 August 1947

(Courtesy of AKG London)

Contrary to Nehru's often repeated demand that the Constituent Assembly should be a sovereign body based on adult suffrage, the Indian Constituent Assembly remained the same body which Lord Wavell had inaugurated and which was based on the very limited franchise prevailing in British India. This assembly did not even consider breaking new ground by producing a constitution of its own: it spent three years in amending the existing constitution, the Government of India Act of 1935 in its new guise as the 1947 Independence of India Act. That this would be the fate of this assembly was not apparent from the very beginning: it grew upon the assembly due to external circumstances and, of course, also due to the fact that the government was actually working within the framework of this constitution bequeathed to India by the British.

The conflict with Pakistan greatly contributed to the conservative and centrist attitude of the Constituent Assembly. More democratic ideas – like that of having elected governors rather than governors appointed by the central government – were quickly given up. In fact, the emergency powers which had been so deeply resented by the Congress at the time of office acceptance in 1937 and which had been omitted by the British when they passed the Independence of India Act were now reintroduced as 'President's Rule', a powerful instrument of central control. Whenever a party controls a state which is not identical with the party in power at the centre, there is the danger of its government being toppled by means of this instrument. Of course, the establishment of President's Rule must be followed by elections within six months, but the performance can be repeated if the results do not please the party controlling the central government. The restoration of these emergency powers was, no doubt, due to the reaction to 'Plan Balkan' and the partition. As long as the Congress was in power, both at the centre and in the states, there was no need to utilise this remarkable constitutional device. When this changed after 1967, however, it was used rather excessively.

The only heritage of the freedom movement which was subsequently enshrined in the constitution is the catalogue of fundamental rights. The Government of India Act of 1935 made no mention of fundamental rights because, according to the British tradition, the protection of such rights is left to the due process of law. The draft constitution of the Nehru Report of 1928 did contain a catalogue of fundamental rights, as the secular nationalists held that such rights guarantee a better protection of minorities than the grant of political privileges which only enhances sectarianism. In the Karachi Resolution of 1931 the Congress had extended this catalogue of fundamental rights to include many items of the social and economic programme of the party. The right to work or the right to a living wage had thus been included among the fundamental rights. The Government of India would have had a hard time if it could have been sued in a court of law to guarantee such rights to every Indian citizen. Therefore, the Constituent

Assembly divided the catalogue of fundamental rights into a list of justiciable rights and a list of non-justiciable rights ('Directive Principles of State Policy'). But even the justiciable fundamental rights were so carefully defined and hedged about by emergency provisions, which permitted their suspension, that a Communist Party member of the Constituent Assembly complained that this part of the constitution looked as if it had been drafted by a policeman. He was not too far off the mark with this statement, because Home Minister Patel – the supreme chief of all policemen – was the main architect of this constitution. Law Minister Dr Ambedkar, who had been given this portfolio although he was not a member of the Congress, did not have the sort of political power that would have enabled him to do more than act as the chief draftsman and spokesman – a fact which he himself deplored.

Nehru was drawn into this process of constitution-making only occasionally, when controversial matters were at stake. The persuasive rhetoric with which he could reconcile conservative practice with radical aspirations was in great demand at such times. Thus, he made a great speech in order to assuage leftist disappointment at the paragraph which guaranteed due compensation for private property when it was acquired by the state. This paragraph would prevent all measures of working towards a socialist state, as well as a radical land reform. The right wing of the Congress insisted on this and Nehru diverted the attention of the left by assuring it that the Indian Parliament would not tolerate any move by the courts to set themselves up as supreme umpires whose verdict could not be superseded by the people. In fact, most land reform acts were later introduced as constitutional amendments, as they were incompatible with the paragraph guaranteeing due compensation. In this respect, Nehru's prediction was right.

One subject that deeply interested Nehru was the reform of Hindu law, particularly with regard to the rights of Hindu women, and he found an able supporter in Dr Ambedkar in this work. Afraid of arousing the opposition of Hindu society, the British had been content to codify rather than substantially amend Hindu law. The Indian government now continued the same cautious attitude with regard to Muslim law: it did not want to be accused of tampering with the law of a minority. Therefore, a specific effort was made to modernise Hindu law alone. Critics pointed out that this was incompatible with the idea of a secular state which ought to have a civil law applicable to all citizens, regardless of their creed. But the incongruity of a secular government sponsoring a reformed Hindu law was still preferable to doing nothing at all and giving in to conservative Hindu opinion which was hostile to any reform.

Unreformed Hindu law reflected the structure of a patriarchal agrarian society. A man could marry several wives. This was often done when no son was born. On the other hand, the wife had no right to ask for a divorce. Daughters received a dowry but were excluded from any right of inheritance. Consequently, women were always kept dependent on men and had no rights of their own. Patel supported the conservative opposition to the reform of the Hindu law and Dr Ambedkar was finally so frustrated that he resigned. Nehru, himself, did not give up and completed this reform – though he could not do so by means of one reform code and was obliged to introduce piecemeal legislation, dealing with divorce, right to property and inheritance, etc., separately. He later stated that he considered this to be his greatest achievement in Indian politics.

Patel died in December 1950 when Nehru's reform work was in full swing and Nehru then entered the ring in order to eliminate the conservative challenge to his policy. Purushottamdas Tandon, a conservative follower of Patel, was Congress president at that time. Nehru defeated him by himself standing for election as Congress president. He thus broke with a tradition established in 1937, according to which office acceptance disqualified a Congress member from holding a party office in order to keep ministerial and organisational duties apart. Actually, this was by now an anachronism, although it had been observed until Nehru found it necessary to dislodge Tandon in order to put the conservative opposition in its place.

The mixed economy and the Planning Commission

In addition to the reform of Hindu law, Nehru considered economic planning as one of his major fields of interest. He had chaired the Congress Planning Committee of 1938, but the work of this committee had been interrupted by the war. On the other hand, the war had made the British Indian government – earlier wedded to a laissez-faire attitude – firmly interventionist as it had to coordinate war production and procure and ration food grains, etc. In the last years of the war a group of Indian industrialists, among them Gandhi's friend G.D. Birla and J.R.D. Tata, had drafted a fifteen-year plan for the postwar period. Known as the 'Bombay Plan', it emphasised public sector investment in infrastructure and heavy industry probably with the tacit assumption that the state should foot the bill for intensive, low-return investment, while the private sector could concentrate on more immediately profitable investment. The 'mixed economy' which actually emerged in independent India was clearly foreshadowed in this plan. Whether they wanted it or not, the planners of the Government of India were going to help the Bombay planners to realise their objectives.

According to the Government of India Act of 1935 industry was under the control of the provincial governments. During the war the control of the central government was imposed under the Defence of India Act. This was going to lapse at the end of the war. A Statement on Industrial Policy of the Government of India highlighted this in 1945 and called for legislation which would make industry a central subject. As interim prime minister, Nehru devoted his attention to this problem. A new Industrial

Policy Resolution was produced in 1948 and in 1949 a bill was introduced which was debated for a long time and then passed in 1951 as the Industries (Devevelopment and Regulation) Act. It was frequently amended in later years, but its basic framework remained the same. With this the heritage of war time state interventionism was firmly entrenched in independent India. The legal framework of industrial control was essential for Nehru's policy, but he also needed an instrument of continuous guidance of the process of industrialisation. Therefore, he had seen to it that the Planning Commission was set up by a cabinet resolution of 1950 with the prime minister as *ex officio* chairman. His chief planner for the first two five-year plans was Professor Mahalanobis, who drafted them very much along the lines of the earlier plans of the Soviet Union. Public sector investment in the steel industry and in heavy machine tools was a high priority, especially of the second plan. The scheme soon depleted the sterling balances in the Bank of England which had accumulated due to India's forced saving in the war – when the British had taken away much of India's production on credit – and by 1956 India had to turn to the Western nations for development aid in order to finance the ambitious plans. Nehru believed that a great break-through could be achieved by this massive industrial investment: he saw India close to the famous 'take-off into self-sustained growth'.

There were some basic flaws in Nehru's industrial policy. He believed that a poor nation could not afford competition, which would lead to a waste of scarce resources. He also saw to it that the state would occupy 'the commanding heights of the economy' so as to prevent the rise of monopoly capitalism. Since India had a vast home market he felt that an industry producing goods which had so far been imported had an enormous scope and should have high priority. During his lifetime he witnessed remarkable progress along those lines as industrial production more than doubled from 1948 to 1964. But in the long run his policies proved to be self-defeating. The lack of competition bred inefficiency and corruption, the public sector enterprises operated at a loss, the emphasis on protectionism and import substitution and the neglect of export-led growth deprived Indian industry of stimulating challenges. Nehru did a great deal for starting national research institutes devoted to industrial development, but in the absence of such challenges, they did not perform the tasks assigned to them. The representatives of Western nations who aided India's industrial development after 1957 did not admonish Nehru to change his policies. They were glad to sell their machinery to India and involved their taxpayers in providing 'development aid'.

Another flaw of Nehru's policy was his neglect of Indian agriculture. Since agricultural production was in the hands of millions of peasants, there was hardly any scope for state intervention. Nehru was mainly interested in keeping food prices low so as not to encumber industrial growth with wage rises. There was, nevertheless, a substantial increase of agricultural

production in Nehru's time, but it was due to the extension of the cultivated area. This meant that marginal soils were ploughed which would not
yield any harvests if the rains failed. Nehru died before the great drought
hit India in the mid-1960s and was thus saved from witnessing the collapse
of his policy in this field.

Land reform, which had had a high priority for Nehru ever since he
worked for the cause of the peasantry in the campaign of 1930, remained
more or less at the level predetermined by British Indian Tenancy Acts.
These acts had secured the rights of those peasants who held their land
directly from the landlord (*zamindar*), but had left subtenants and other categories of the rural poor unprotected. With zamindari abolition the only
effective land reform, the already rather extenuated rights of these superior
landlords were done away with and they joined the ranks of their former
tenants, who now emerged as a kind of peasant landlord with perfect freedom to exploit the rural poor. Of course, there were ceilings on landhold-
ings imposed by legislation and there was the prohibition of the subletting
of land. But in the absence of a proper record of rights, breaches of the law
were hard to prove and this type of legislation remained an eyewash.

Moreover, the substantial peasantry was politically powerful and constituted the social base not only of the Congress but also of all other parties
which tried to get a foothold in the countryside. The political mobilisation
of poor peasants holding tiny plots of land or of landless labourers has
never succeeded. The web of rural dependence and servitude is so complex
and tightly knit that it is difficult to unravel and poor people are usually
much too weak in every respect to put up much resistance. Well-meaning
reformers like Vinobha Bhave and his Bhoodan (land gift) movement have
not made much of an impact on the rural scene. Although inaugurated with
high hopes, Community Development has become just another government
department and its officers usually turn into petty bureaucrats.

The spectrum of political parties

Nehru grew impatient with the immobility of India's rural society and
talked of a collective organisation of agriculture. The famous Avadi
Resolution of the National Congress of 1955 stated this goal and it seemed
that the Congress was bent upon a radical new programme to broaden
its rural base. Instead of doing this, however, it only frightened the
substantial number of peasants who had so far supported the Congress.
C. Rajagopalachari, who had been the first Indian governor general after
Mountbatten's departure and before Rajendra Prasad was sworn in as India's
first president, sponsored a new party, the Swatantra Party, which soon
attracted the protest vote of rich peasants disturbed by Nehru's ideas. While
Nehru had so far directed his efforts at taking the wind out of the sails of
his leftist opposition, especially the Communists, he now veered to the right

and saw to it that the Swatantra Party did not erode the social base of the Congress. The structure of Indian society hardly permits a successful alliance of urban people with the lower strata of rural society. Wherever such alliances have been formed – as, for instance, in Kerala – they have remained the exception rather than the rule. Furthermore, the majority election system favours a broad middle-of-the-road party like the Congress and works against smaller parties with a specific ideological profile whose competition even enhances the chances of the Congress candidate. The Congress normally got about 42 to 48 per cent of the national vote, but captured 65 to 75 per cent of the seats in the Lok Sabha (House of Commons). The Socialists, on the other hand, often obtained about 30 per cent of the national vote, but usually got only 10 per cent of the seats.

The Socialists can trace their ancestry to the Congress Socialist Party founded in 1934; pushed out of the Congress by Patel in 1948, they indulged in several splits which did not contribute to their political success. This leaves the Indian Communist Party as the most consistent leftist force in Indian politics. The party's history began in 1920 with the foundation of an expatriate Communist Party of India at Tashkent, where M.N. Roy had rallied a group of radical Indian refugees. Subsequently, a Communist Party was founded on Indian soil in 1925. Repression by the British brought most of these early Communists to jail; the party was then founded once more in 1933 and sponsored a policy of leftist unity with the Socialists. This was a short-lived honeymoon. During the Second World War, when the Communists had to tergiversate due to the Hitler–Stalin pact and Hitler's subsequent attack on the Soviet Union, they lost the respect of all other leftists and found it difficult to recover credibility after the war. They tried to make up for this by adopting a very radical line, but with Nehru's increasing friendship with the Soviet Union they were forced to toe the line and follow the 'parliamentary path'. In this they scored certain regional successes, particularly in west Bengal and Kerala. The Chinese attack on India and the Sino-Soviet schism were a great setback for the Indian Communists. Their party split in 1964. The Communist Party of India, which remained close to Moscow, had its social base mostly in the trade union movement and, therefore, in the big industrial centres; the new Communist Party of India (Marxist) had its base in the regional Communist strongholds in west Bengal and Kerala.

At the other end of the Indian political spectrum was the Bharatiya Jana Sangh (Indian People's Association), which has a Hindu outlook though it denies that it ever was a sectarian party. Its strong emphasis on Hindi as a national language – which, in fact, according to the Indian constitution, it is – has not commended this party to the people of southern India and it remained a northern phenomenon. Its social base consisted to a large extent of the urban traders of northern India and the Panjabi refugees. Its strength as a cadre party was largely derived from the fact that many of its most active members came from the ranks of the Rashtriya Swayam Sevak Sangh (National Self-help Association). This organisation claims to be a cultural and not a political organisation. It was for some time under a cloud, because Nathuram Godse, who shot Gandhi, was one of its active members. In the early years of the Indian republic when the founder of the Bharatiya Jana Sangh, Shyamaprasad Mukherjee, a prominent Bengali Brahmin, was still alive this party got a great deal of tacit support from the right wing of the Congress. It was, therefore, perceived as a serious challenger by Nehru, who knew that the members of the Jana Sangh often expressed what the right-wing Congressmen thought but could not say without violating party discipline.

Federalism and states reorganisation

The three general elections of 1952, 1957 and 1962, which were held when Nehru was the prime minister, resulted in solid Congress majorities at the centre and in all states with the exception of a 1957 Communist victory in Kerala, where Chief Minister E.M.S. Namboodiripad launched a land reform programme and a reform of the educational system; he was soon removed with the instrument of President's Rule. Nehru set a bad precedent by getting rid of an elected state government in this way. In those years elections to the state assemblies and to the central Lok Sabha were held simultaneously. This demanded a particular blend of local and national issues in the election campaigns; the candidates for the assembly seats, who were naturally closer to the people, often carried the Lok Sabha candidate along on their bandwagon.

The ubiquitous Congress easily supported the federal structure of India. There were only some dissenting voices in the south, where the people who were not satisfied with the old administrative boundaries drawn by the British wanted to have them redrawn along linguistic lines. The first unit to be affected was the giant Madras Presidency, which encompassed speakers of all the four Dravidian languages. The Telugu-speaking Andhras were the first to campaign for a state of their own. Their linguistic movement was of long standing and an Andhra University had been established already, under British rule. Gandhi had recognised their claim when he redrafted the Congress constitution in 1920, which also made provision for new Provincial Congress Committees such as the Andhra PCC, the Tamil Nadu PCC and the Karnataka PCC. But the experience of partition and the spectre of 'Plan Balkan' had made Nehru very nervous about such subdivisions and he had, at first, resisted all attempts to redraw boundaries. He had to yield to the Andhras when, after a long fast, one of their leaders died in 1953. A States Reorganisation Commission was then appointed and, subsequently, more linguistic states were established according to its recommendations. One of the most problematic constructions of this kind was the new state of Kerala, which was composed of all Malayalam-speaking districts, some of which had belonged to the princely states of Travancore and Cochin and some to the Madras Presidency.

A much thornier problem than that of the division of the old Madras Presidency was the carving up of the Bombay Presidency, although this seemed to be easier at first sight because there were only two clearcut units left: Gujarat and Maharashtra. The difficulty was that Bombay City was geographically part of Maharashtra but that its industry and trade were in the hands of Gujaratis. For this reason, Gandhi had made provision for a special Bombay City PCC in addition to the Gujarat and Maharashtra PCCs. This could have served as a precedent for establishing a city state, like Hamburg in Germany, but Nehru did not think of such a solution and stoutly resisted the division of the Bombay Presidency until a militant regional party, Samyukta Maharashtra Samiti (United Maharashtra Society), threatened to dislodge the Congress there. Finally, the division was made in 1960 and Bombay became the capital of Maharashtra. The regional party disappeared and Maharashtra emerged once more as a Congress stronghold. Similarly, Andhra (which had started the whole movement) was, in those days, one of the pillars of Congress rule in India. This showed that whenever the Congress came to terms with the federal plurality of India, it gained added strength rather than any loosening of its hold.

The Congress system and Nehru's successors

After Nehru's death in May 1964 the Congress system seemed to be in serious danger. Under his immediate successor, Lal Bahadur Shastri, this did not yet become apparent. Fate would have it that Shastri emerged as a major figure of national integration, as a result of his courageous stand at the time of Pakistan's aggression in 1965 and his conduct at the Tashkent Conference. He would almost certainly have won an election, but died of a heart attack at the end of the Tashkent Conference.

Indira Gandhi, the daughter of Nehru, was selected as Shastri's successor by the old guard of the Congress. This move was designed mainly to forestall Morarji Desai, who had already made it clear that he wanted to become prime minister at the time of Shastri's selection. The new premier appeared to be a weak candidate, not destined to lead the Congress to a great success. Unfortunately, she had to face an election after barely one year in office and the result of that election was poor, the majority at the centre was narrow and several north Indian states had turned down the Congress and were then governed by coalition governments. The year 1967 was a bad year for India in other respects: it was the second year of a devastating drought, which not only meant a great setback for agriculture but also brought about an industrial recession. This long-term recession reduced the chances of thousands of young men who had undertaken an education in engineering in the hope that this would be the profession of the future. Unemployment among the educated increased and, with it, the potential for political protest.

Indira Gandhi was left with a rather brittle political system after the elections of 1967. She used the instrument of 'President's Rule' in order to topple the unstable coalition governments in northern India, but the subsequent election results in those states did not please her either. She then adopted a bold and risky course of action which was ultimately successful and assured her of a position of unchallenged leadership. She split the Congress Party and threw out the old guard. This purge started with the resignation in 1969 of her deputy prime minister, Morarji Desai, who embodied the conservative opposition to her more left-wing attitude. Finally, she separated the Lok Sabha elections from the elections in the states by dissolving the Lok Sabha one year in advance of the elections that had been scheduled for 1972. With the resonant slogan 'Garibi Hatao' ('Beat Poverty'), she ran her election campaign like a national plebiscite. The opposition parties engaged in their customary inter-rivalry and could find a common denominator only in the rather inane battle cry 'Indira Hatao' ('Beat Indira'). In this way they contributed to her resounding victory.

After her victory the steps that had led to it seemed to form a pattern. Had she followed a well-planned strategy? Her break with the old guard, her leftish moves of bank nationalisation and of the abolition of the privy purses of the Indian princes, the bold coup of advancing the national elections – all these now appeared to be calculated steps to the final goal. But, in fact, she had, rather, reacted to challenges of the moment and had followed her political instinct in deciding what to do next at every bend of the road. Bank nationalisation and the abolition of the privy purses had been part of the pre-Indira Congress programme and only had to be implemented. Indira Gandhi was not the driving force in this respect: she merely executed the resolutions of the party. She did, however, make use of the apparently radical tendency implied by these measures in order to project her image.

Moreover, the social groups affected by these measures – the owners of a few big banks and the Indian princes – could easily be taken on: they did not have the political power to hit back. The conservative opposition within the Congress was a more serious challenge. But it soon turned out that the political strength of the right wing was waning. In 1970 the elections for the office of the President of India were due, and the right wing put up one of its most prominent members, the former Andhra chief minister, Sanjiva Reddy. Indira Gandhi then sponsored an old trade union leader, V.V. Giri, as candidate of her wing of the Congress and when Giri won this election she felt confident that she, too, could win an election. This is why she decided on the advanced elections of 1971.

The 'Green Revolution' and the energy crisis

The choice of the year 1971 turned out to be a good move for economic reasons, too. Agricultural production had greatly improved since 1967 and the rich peasants were happy. The previous price policy of the Government of India, which had aimed at keeping food-grain prices low so as to ensure cheap food supplies for the urban population, had completely collapsed due to the drought of 1966–7. Grain prices had soared and those peasants who produced for the market had made a good profit, enabling them to invest in the fertilisers and irrigation required for the high-yield hybrid varieties of rice and wheat. To begin with, this 'Green Revolution' was mostly a wheat revolution and the peasants of the Panjab and of western Uttar Pradesh were the main beneficiaries. The year 1971 marked the peak of radical change in agriculture and this greatly contributed to Indira Gandhi's victory. The successful liberation of Bangladesh in December 1971 similarly added to her stature and one may well say that this year was the high point of her political career.

The energy crisis, which hit India very badly after 1973, also severely affected the prospects of Indira Gandhi's government. The steep rise in the oil price and the enormous inflation which it caused in India made fertilisers much too expensive and also accentuated the industrial recession. Both the 'Green Revolution' and industrial growth were jeopardised. As cheap oil had been available in the world market in the years immediately preceding, India had not pushed ahead the exploitation of its own substantial oil resources; coal mining had also been neglected.

This tendency could not be immediately reversed and the government was faced with a severe crisis, which was made worse by a great railway strike in 1974. A subterranean test explosion of an atomic device in the Rajasthan desert, which signalled India's claim to join the exclusive club of atomic powers, could not detract public attention from domestic troubles for more than a fleeting moment.

In the following year a political crisis was added to the economic one. Indira Gandhi's opponent in the 1971 elections had filed an election petition against her, arguing that she had made inappropriate use of government facilities in her campaign and demanding that her victory should be declared invalid for this reason. In 1975 the Allahabad High Court found against Indira Gandhi. Her immediate inclination was to resign, but she was prevailed upon to remain in office. As she could not constitutionally do this in any other way, she made the President declare a national emergency. Instead of admitting that this was her own personal emergency, she claimed that the economic situation demanded such an extraordinary step and she soon backed this up with a twenty-point programme of economic measures.

The 'Emergency' and the short-lived Janata Party regime

The emergency measures did lead to a certain improvement in the economic situation: no strikes were allowed, inflation was curbed and general discipline greatly improved. But all this was at the cost of the loss of civil liberties, which were, after all, the most cherished heritage of the Indian freedom movement. In addition to all this, Indira Gandhi's son Sanjay increased the political power of his Youth Congress, an organisation which contained many unscrupulous elements whose loyalty and solidarity were mostly based on the lust for power. Sanjay also sponsored a campaign of mass sterilisation in northern India as a shortcut to the solution of India's population problem. Although there is no fundamental opposition to birth control and family planning in India, the radical infringement of individual liberty in the course of the sterilisation campaign was deeply resented by the people. This campaign was not pursued with equal vigour in southern India and, consequently, there was less resentment against it here.

General protest movements against the emergency regime gained strength. Most prominent among them was that led by Jayaprakash Narayan, the veteran socialist who had been an associate of Vinobha Bhave in the Bhoodan movement and who now returned to the political arena with a vengeance. Indira Gandhi had most opposition leaders arrested. The old instrument of preventive detention, which permits the indefinite arrest of people without trial and stipulates only that their names be placed before the Lok Sabha, was used to a large extent at that time.

The elections should have been held in 1976, but Indira Gandhi did not dare to face the people in that year and postponed them. Then, suddenly, at the end of 1976 she announced that elections would be held early in 1977. She released the opposition leaders only a few weeks before the polling date, hoping that they would not be able to organise a proper campaign in this way. At the last minute a prominent supporter of Indira Gandhi, the leader of the untouchables in the Lok Sabha, Jagjivan Ram, broke with her and established his own party – the Congress for Democracy – which joined the opposition parties in an electoral alliance. For the first time in Indian history the opposition had learned the lesson of the prevailing election system and had managed to match every Congress candidate with only one opponent. In spite of having been given no time for running a campaign, this did the trick for the opposition: much to everyone's surprise Indira Gandhi lost the elections.

The question of settling the issue of national leadership proved to be far more difficult than winning the elections. Jagjivan Ram thought he ought to be prime minister, as his last-minute defection had turned the scales in favour of the opposition. But there was also Morarji Desai, the permanent candidate for this post ever since Nehru's death. Charan Singh, a veteran leader of the Jat peasantry in western Uttar Pradesh, was also convinced of his merits. Jayaprakash Narayan, who was soon to die, did his nation a last service by acting as umpire in this contest: he nominated Morarji Desai. Charan Singh agreed to serve as deputy prime minister. The Bharatiya Jana Sangh, a very strong element in the opposition ranks, adopted a low profile and asked only for two cabinet posts. Atal Bihari Vajpayee became minister for external affairs and Lal Advani became information minister.

In due course the Jana Sangh took an even more surprising step when it agreed to merge its identity in the new Janata ('People's') Party, which all the parties forming the government now joined. The Jana Sangh cadres were, by far, the most disciplined element in the new party and the others, particularly the Socialists, did not trust the low profile and the accommodating approach of the Jana Sangh, suspecting that it intended to take over the new Janata Party in due course. But Morarji was proud of his new Janata Party and expected it to have a great future. Although an experienced administrator, he was not a good party leader and thus was unable to prevent the internal bickering which afflicted the Janata Party more and more. Internal conflict was also unchecked by any fear of a potential comeback of Indira Gandhi, who was considered to be finished politically.

The Janata regime succumbed because of a basic incompatibility of the parties, which had only superficially merged their identity. In economic terms the years of the Janata regime were a good time, though this was only partly due to the government's achievements. Agricultural production increased and India's balance of payments showed a comfortable surplus. This was due to a surprising byproduct of the energy crisis: the shift of Indian manpower to the Gulf states and the large remittances to the home country that this produced. Agricultural goods were also exported in a big way to the Gulf states – in fact, shortages were caused in India as produce was syphoned off by the Arabs, who could afford to pay a good price. A serious drawback of the 'Green Revolution' thus became apparent: it was primarily a wheat revolution and had almost completely bypassed all other aspects of agricultural production. The harvest of 1979 failed to remedy the shortfall and the high prices of essential foodstuffs played an important role in the election campaign of 1980.

Indira Gandhi's comeback and end

The result of the election of 1980 was even more surprising than that of 1977. Of course, the Janata Party was split once more and the old disregard for the lessons of the majority election system prevailed. But Indira Gandhi had hardly any party worth the name: she had divided it again in 1978 and many defectors had gone over to the other side – she never forgot or forgave this when she was back in power. On the other hand, Jagjivan Ram now led what was left of the Janata Party and expected the solid support of all Harijans (untouchables). Charan Singh was concentrating on his stronghold in western Uttar Pradesh and, as the election result would show, was very successful there and managed to get more seats in the Lok Sabha for his Lok Dal – a purely regional party – than Jagjivan Ram achieved for his Janata Party, which had conducted a nationwide campaign. It was Indira Gandhi's untiring national electioneering which brought about her comeback: it was a personal plebiscite rather than the campaign of a party.

Once Indira Gandhi had staged her comeback she started the old toppling game in order to eliminate state governments which did not belong to her party. This toppling game was justified with an argument which runs counter to the spirit of federalism. The verdict of the electorate in a Lok Sabha election is equated with its general will and thus a state government which owes its existence to an earlier election at state level is thought to have forfeited its mandate if the composition of that government is at variance with this new verdict. In several cases she was successful, although she did not dare to touch the well-entrenched Communist government of Jyoti Basu in west Bengal. In some state elections she was bitterly disappointed in her expectation – for example, when the Janata Party won the elections in Karnataka and established a government headed by a very competent chief minister, Dr Hegde, whom she could not easily dislodge; or when a new party, Telugu Desam, emerged victoriously in Andhra Pradesh under the leadership of the popular film actor, Rama Rao, whom she did try to remove but who got himself reinstated and thus raised his prestige and lowered hers.

In Assam she was faced with the steady influx of Bengalis, or rather Bangladeshis, as well as other groups of people into an area inviting settlement because of a relatively low population density. The census showed that the population of Assam had grown on average by about 3.5 per cent per year, compared with a national average of about 2.4 per cent. This could only be due to large-scale immigration. The local people became increasingly alarmed and students played a leading role in the anti-immigration agitation. 'Jobs for the boys' would be in danger if the Assamese were to become a minority in their own state. Talks conducted by the Government of India with such student leaders concentrated on fixing an historical date to distinguish bona fide citizens from undesirable aliens, and few were fooled by the discussion's lack of realism. In the midst of all this, Indira Gandhi went ahead with holding elections in Assam. Boycotted by the majority of the voters, the poll thus resulted in the victory of a Congress government, which was duly installed.

In the Panjab, Indira Gandhi faced her worst dilemma. She had actually started her career as prime minister in 1966 with a concession to the Sikhs, whose campaign for a Sikh state under the guise of a Panjabi linguistic state had been resisted by her predecessors. Separating the Hindi-speaking areas of the southern Panjab and creating the new state of Haryana, Indira Gandhi had satisfied the quest for a Panjabi state although she had not conceded a Sikh state, as the Sikhs made up only about 60 per cent of the population of the new Panjab. This delicate balance made party politics in the Panjab an extremely tense and unpredictable affair. The Akali Dal, a Sikh party, oscillated between a radical and a moderate stance. If it wanted to attract the entire Sikh vote in order to get a majority, it had to follow a radical sectarian line; if it looked for non-sectarian alliances, it had to be moderate in this respect. Under the Janata regime the Akali Dal had enjoyed such a non-sectarian honeymoon and had followed a very moderate course. After Indira Gandhi's comeback the Akali Dal was thrown out of office and a Congress government installed.

divide + rule

On top of this the Congress leadership tried to sow sectarian communal discord in Sikh ranks by building up a young fanatic, Jarnail Singh Bhindranwale, who soon outgrew the control of his mentors. In October 1983 'President's Rule' was established in the Panjab, superseding the state's beleaguered Congress government. Even under 'President's Rule' nothing was done to curb Bhindranwale's activities – in fact, in December 1983 he occupied the Akal Takht, the priestly headquarters controlling the access to the Golden Temple. Under his direction this building was made into a veritable fortress and when the Indian army was ordered to storm the Golden Temple in June 1984, it walked right into the trap which Bhindranwale had prepared for it. A retired Sikh general was in charge of the defence of the Golden Temple and an active Sikh general led the attack. Bhindranwale died and was promptly praised as a martyr. Indira Gandhi survived this fateful event by only a few months. She was shot by her Sikh bodyguard on 31 October 1984.

Operation Blue Star

The immediate consequence of her assassination was a pogrom directed against the Sikhs of Delhi and other north Indian cities. It appeared to be a spontaneous reaction, but it was obviously masterminded by politicians who had prepared a contingency plan for this event well in advance. This played into the hands of Sikh extremists who wanted to forestall any compromise that would jeopardise their plan for a Sikh state, 'Khalistan'. The daunting task of achieving this compromise was left to Indira Gandhi's son and successor, Rajiv Gandhi.

The rise of Rajiv Gandhi

Rajiv Gandhi's brother Sanjay had died in the summer of 1980 by indulging in a daring stunt in his private plane. Rajiv, a pilot with Indian Airlines, had never approved of his brother's way of flying nor of his way of conducting politics. After Sanjay's death a reluctant Rajiv was enlisted by his mother, who had obviously made up her mind that she must be succeeded by her son; her tragic death then accomplished what she could not have easily achieved had she remained alive. President Zail Singh, himself a Sikh and very much aware of the immediate problems facing the nation, knew that no other Congress leader could emerge as a symbol of national integration in this crucial hour. He, therefore, set aside all parliamentary conventions and immediately installed Rajiv Gandhi as prime minister, so that this news could be announced to the nation almost simultaneously with the sad message of his mother's assassination.

Rajiv wanted to legitimise his appointment by elections which were held a few months later. The opposition parties were almost completely obliterated, with the exception of the Andhra Pradesh regional party, Telugu Desam, which captured 28 seats in the new Lok Sabha. The overwhelming victory of the Congress Party paved the way for an important step which had been contemplated several times in the past: changing party allegiance while retaining one's mandate was prohibited by legislation.

Defection had been a universal pastime among Indian politicians and the toppling game depended on the availability of people who suddenly found that their conscience moved them to join another party. The new law required that an elected representative who joined another party must immediately seek re-election. Earlier governments had hesitated to introduce this legislation because it would have prevented them from making converts.

Rajiv Gandhi then made another bold move by introducing a budget which provided for tax cuts and heralded a more liberal economy whose aim was to stimulate a new spirit of enterprise. He also seemed to be all set to tackle the Assam and Panjab affairs. In reaching detailed accords with the leaders of the Assamese students and of the Sikhs in 1985 he paved the way for elections in both states. In Assam, the Asom Gana Parishad won the elections and the student leader, Prafulla Mahanta, became chief minister. In the Panjab, Sant Harchand Longowal who had concluded the accord on behalf of the Akali Dal in July 1985 was shot by Sikh extremists in August, nevertheless elections were held in September and won by the Akali Dal. Surjit Singh Barnala became chief minister, but his term of office was cut short in May 1987 when 'President's Rule' was once more imposed on the Panjab. The main reason for the failure of the Panjab Accord was that Rajiv Gandhi was unable to deliver the goods. He had pledged that Chandigarh, a Union Territory housing the capitals of both Panjab and Haryana, would be handed over to the Panjab as its exclusive capital on 26 January 1986. When this did not happen both Gandhi and Barnala lost face. The Haryana government had stymied this part of the accord, and as elections were due in that state in 1987, Gandhi did not dare to alienate the Haryana voters. Ultimately, this did not help and the Congress lost the Haryana elections to the Lok Dal, a regional party. Devi Lal, who became chief minister of Haryana, had roundly abused Gandhi in his election campaign, making much of the corruption scandal connected with the purchase of howitzers from the Swedish firm Bofors.

In this context Gandhi also parted company with V.P. Singh, his efficient finance minister, whom he first transferred to the defence ministry and then forced to resign in 1987. Singh turned against the government, was thrown out of the Congress Party and emerged as the most important leader of the opposition. As India also experienced a severe drought in 1987, this proved to be the worst year for Rajiv Gandhi, but with a very comfortable majority in parliament he could safely neglect all adverse conditions. He finally announced elections, at rather short notice, to be held in November 1989. The major opposition parties, Janata Dal and the Bharatiya Janata Party, agreed not to stand against each other and nominated their candidates for the constituencies accordingly. In this way they succeeded in capturing a large number of seats in northern India whereas the Congress Party remained strong in the south where it routed regional parties such as Telugu Desam in Andhra. But this did not help as far as retaining power at the centre was concerned. The Congress Party won less than 40 per cent of the seats there, Rajiv Gandhi had to resign and V.P. Singh, whose party had obtained about 20 per cent of the seats, formed a new government. According to the usual parliamentary conventions, Gandhi, as the leader of the largest party, should have been able to form a coalition government, but none of the other parties was willing to join such a government as their declared aim had been to oust Gandhi. On the other hand, fundamental incompatibilities prevented the formation of a coalition consisting of all opposition parties. India had gone back to square one, i.e. the position in 1977 when Indira Gandhi was ousted by a similar combination of opposition parties. But at that time these parties had finally agreed to merge so as to support a viable government. This experiment had not proved to be successful and was, therefore, not repeated. Finally, V.P. Singh had to form a minority government tolerated by the Communists on the one hand and by the BJP on the other. The most important factor in this new political equation was the BJP, which had increased the number of its parliamentary seats from 2 to 108. This success was entirely due to the electoral pact with V.P. Singh, which was, however, not an electoral alliance, which would have obliged the BJP to support rather than merely to tolerate V.P. Singh.

Minority governments and the success of the Bharatiya Janata Party

Soon after the elections the BJP embarked on a course which was bound to lead to a collision with V.P. Singh's government. The BJP opted for the Ramjanmabhumi campaign which had been going on before 1989 but which now seemed to provide the victorious party with a popular cause so as to broaden its social base. Ramjanmabhumi (birthplace of Rama) refers to a locality in Ayodhya, the ancient capital of the legendary King Rama where, supposedly, a temple dedicated to him was replaced with a mosque at the behest of Baber, the first Great Mughal. The mosque existed but there was no archaeological evidence as far as the temple is concerned. In fact, scholars still debate whether present Ayodhya is identical with Rama's Ayodhya. However, the firm belief of many Hindus that this is Rama's Ayodhya and that there had been a temple is stronger than the evidence which would satisfy scholars. Moreover, the fact that Muslim rulers did replace temples with mosques has been well documented elsewhere. The Babri Masjid – as it was called – had not been used by Muslims as a place of worship. It was a protected monument and the government had kept it under lock and key to keep both contending parties out of it. Nevertheless, Hindus had managed to install some images of Rama and Sita in the mosque and thus claimed that it had been converted into a temple.

In 1986 the lock had been removed and the people had free access to the place. Rajiv Gandhi sanctioned this as a compensation for a concession which he had to make to Muslim orthodoxy. A Muslim woman, Shah Bano, had sued her former husband for maintenance and the Supreme Court had decided in her favour on the basis of a general law which obliges husbands to support their divorced wives so that they do not become a burden on society. Orthodox Muslims argued that Islamic law regulates this differently and that the Supreme Court has no business to interfere with it. This highlighted once more the problem left unresolved by Nehru when he had not seen to it that a uniform civil code was enacted in India, because he was afraid of losing the Muslim vote. This was also true for Rajiv Gandhi who caved in when faced with the protest of the orthodox. He should have been firm in supporting the decision of the Supreme Court as well as in keeping the Babri Masjid locked; instead he unlocked it and thus opened a Pandora's box. The BJP raised the slogan that the temple of Rama must be resurrected. This implied the destruction of the mosque, but this point was not stressed initially.

The idea to reclaim Ramjanmabhumi was not a new one. It had earlier been advocated by the Vishwa Hindu Parishad (World Council of Hindus), an organisation devoted to the defence of the interests of all Hindus. It has considerable support also among Hindus abroad. Together with BJP and RSS it belongs to the *sangh parivar*, as the group of Hindu organisations is called. In recent years a youth wing, *Bajrang Dal*, has been added to this group. Its name refers to the army of monkeys which helped Rama to fight against Ravana, the demon king. Ramjanmabhumi became a focal point of the activities of this whole group. The leadership of the BJP and the RSS-cadres remain imbued with Savarkar's idea of Hindutva, but they also know that it is difficult to convey this idea to the people. It was much easier to conjure up Rama, the more so as the *Ramayana* had just been the subject of an extremely popular TV series. Hinduism is a non-congregational religion whose traditions depend on the family more than on any other institution. In recent times the family has no longer served this purpose as well as it used to. Young people tend to be more influenced by TV than by the prayers of their parents. The BJP President, Lal Advani, seems to have realised that; he climbed on to a small truck decorated to look like Rama's chariot with a bow in hand which was supposed to represent Rama's famous weapon. Thus, he led a long march of his followers which was supposed to end at Ayodhya in October 1990. But, before he could reach his aim, V.P. Singh had him arrested. Advani himself, thus, did not reach Ayodhya, but his vanguard attacked the mosque at that time. Several men lost their lives and were subsequently celebrated as martyrs. V.P. Singh had taken action at the last moment. Since his minority government depended on the BJP's toleration, he also sealed his government's fate in this way.

There was a hidden agenda behind this confrontation. V.P. Singh had openly favoured the Other Backward Castes (OBC); these included most of the large peasant castes of northern India, which did not qualify as Scheduled Castes (untouchables) and therefore could not claim reserved posts in government service. Several years before, the Mandal Commission had recommended such reservations for the OBCs, but its report had been shelved by the Congress government at that time. V.P. Singh revived these recommendations. The respective reservations amounted to more than a quarter of all posts in government service; together with the reservations for the Scheduled Castes this added up to nearly one half of all such posts. This caused a great upheaval in northern India where the high castes such as Brahmins, Rajputs and Banias were strong and were equally concerned with jobs for their boys in government service. In southern India the peasant castes had long since taken over power and the rather marginal high castes had turned to the private sector for employment. In northern India high caste boys got so excited over this issue that some of them immolated themselves in public and others staged protest demonstrations in major cities. The BJP was mainly supported by the high caste voters of northern India and saw that V.P. Singh was bent on outflanking the BJP after having contributed to its success by the electoral pact of 1989. If the BJP had come out openly against the OBCs, it would have fallen into V.P. Singh's trap. Instead of this it played the Hindu card and confronted him by fighting for Ramjanmabhumi. Taking a stand against the Muslims in this way helped the BJP, which could not hope to get Muslim votes anyhow, while V.P. Singh was relying on Muslim support. Moreover, the easiest way of defining a Hindu is that he is not a Muslim. The OBCs could be rallied to the BJP's cause in this way. The contest for votes between V.P. Singh and the BJP, which expressed itself in those two manoeuvres of outflanking each other, created tensions which deeply affected north Indian society.

Nevertheless, when V.P. Singh's government fell, the BJP did not press for immediate elections. It could not be sure of improving its position since, this time, V.P. Singh would certainly not be prepared to conclude an electoral pact with it as he had done in 1989. The other parties were also not ready for an election as yet. Election expenditure is phenomenal in India and the parties were still in the process of replenishing their coffers, which they had emptied only a year before. Thus, everybody was willing to put up with another minority government led by Chandrashekhar whose political base was insignificant and who depended entirely on the toleration of the National Congress, which could topple his government at any time convenient to it. This was done in February 1991 and an election campaign was launched, in the course of which Rajiv Gandhi was assassinated near Madras in May 1991, obviously by Tamil Tigers from Sri Lanka.

Fiscal indiscipline and political instability ruined India's creditworthiness and plunged it into a serious balance of payments crisis. As India's bankruptcy seemed to be imminent, the non-resident Indians who had parked large funds in India because of the high interest rates prevailing there withdrew their money – a typical case of a self-fulfilling prophecy. The bankruptcy was only averted because the World Bank and the International Monetary Fund bailed out India at the time when the new government took office in June 1991.

The verdict of the electorate had not been clearcut. Once more a minority government had to be installed, but this time it was, again, a Congress government. Rajiv Gandhi's assassination may have provided a sympathy bonus to his party, but it was an open question who should be its new leader. In keeping with the entrenched idea of dynastic charisma, Rajiv's widow Sonia was considered to be a potential candidate. As an Italian Catholic who had only recently become an Indian citizen she was an unlikely choice and she was wise enough to opt out of this game. Instead, a senior politician, P.V. Narasimha Rao, who was ill at that time and was looking forward to retirement, was reactivated and rose to the occasion. He had once been chief minister of Andhra Pradesh before he served under Indira and Rajiv Gandhi as a cabinet minister handling various portfolios for more than a decade. He was the first south Indian to become prime minister. In view of the pressing economic problems which he faced when taking office, he appointed Dr Manmohan Singh as his finance minister. Whereas all previous finance ministers had been prominent politicians, Manmohan Singh was a technocrat without any political base except for the prime minister's trust in him.

As soon as India presented itself under new management, the atmosphere changed immediately and the non-resident Indians sent their money back. A devaluation by about 18 per cent encouraged exports and made foreign investment more attractive. Unfortunately, there was little foreign direct investment and more institutional investment, which gave a boost to the stock market without entering into the primary market. Speculation increased and attracted a trickster who made use of the imperfections of India's financial markets to earn a profit by using other people's money. This scam led to a collapse of the stock market in 1992. The same year was marred by another disastrous event, the destruction of the Babri Masjid of Ayodhya on 6 December 1992 – a tragic day in India's history.

The BJP had resumed its campaign after being stymied by Advani's arrest in October 1990. This time it was in a much better position, because the state government of Uttar Pradesh, in which Ayodhya is located, was formed by the BJP in 1991. Thus, a large crowd could converge on Ayodhya in December 1992. The destruction of the mosque by innumerable hands equipped with only the most elementary instruments was an astonishing feat. It left the nation dumbfounded. Most of those who voted for the BJP were middle-class people who owned some property and were disinclined to upset law and order. This was obviously also in the mind of the Prime Minister when he advised the President to dismiss all four BJP governments and not only that of Uttar Pradesh, which could be held directly responsible for the disaster. The elections held in November 1993 in the four states in which the BJP governments had been dismissed led to decisive losses for this party. Narasimha Rao's calculations seemed to have been right. He reached the zenith of his political power at this stage and was able to entice a splinter party to join his government, which thereupon was no longer a minority government though its majority remained a precarious one.

The next round of state elections at the end of 1994 and the beginning of 1995 went against Narasimha Rao, who campaigned everywhere but to no avail. This did not augur well for the federal elections due in the spring of 1996. Therefore, the programme of economic reform was put on the back burner and all kinds of populist measures aimed at the masses of the voters inevitably led to a new round of fiscal indiscipline. Therefore, some observers look back at the years from 1991 to 1993 when the liberalisation programme was in full swing as a mere episode which was soon followed by a relapse. Others stress that in a democracy like India reforms are bound to be slow, but whatever has been achieved is firmly grounded in democratic consensus and thus more stable than the ephemeral success of autocratic regimes. There is some truth in both of these points of view.

The results of the elections, which were held at the end of April and the beginning of May 1996, finally put an end to the old Congress system. The Congress could no longer maintain its power and its position in the middle of the political spectrum, making use of the polarisation of the opposition parties. The contours of India's political landscape had changed dramatically. Of the 537 seats for which elections had been held, 160 were won by the BJP, whereas the Congress Party was reduced to a mere 136 seats. The most surprising feature was the sudden increase in the number of seats won by small regional parties. Earlier, they had only held, altogether, 58 seats but now they had captured 155. In terms of its spread the Congress still remained the only national party holding seats in more than ten federal states while the BJP was mainly represented in five states in northern and western India, Uttar Pradesh with 52 seats being its major stronghold.

Narasimha Rao could have formed a coalition government but the old aversion against coalitions prevailed. Instead, he wrote a letter to the President, Dr Shankar Dayal Sharma, indicating that the Congress would 'tolerate' a National Front government of the regional parties. This letter reached the President too late. He had already invited the BJP to form a government. The BJP had opted for Atal Bihari Vajpayee as its candidate for the post of prime minister. He was known to be a moderate who could attract the support of other parties. In fact, some regional parties had pledged to support him even before the President had asked him to form a government. But the number of parliamentarians supporting him was insufficient. Finally, Vajpayee resigned even before he had to face a vote of no confidence.

Now the President had to turn to the National Front, but before it could form a government it had to present a candidate for the post of prime minister. The National Front found it very difficult to agree on a candidate. For a brief moment it seemed as if Jyoti Basu, the Communist chief minister of west Bengal, would emerge as a suitable leader. Being the most senior chief minister who enjoyed the respect of his peers he was the obvious candidate, but his party asked him to decline the offer. The CPM of west Bengal was obviously worried that Jyoti Basu's shifting to New Delhi would undermine their control of the state. As Basu was not available, H.D. Deve Gowda, the chief minister of Karnataka, made the grade. He represented the Janata Party, which had once been a national party but had lost its national appeal in the meantime. It had won only 43 seats in the federal elections, of which 15 belonged to Karnataka and 21 to Bihar. With this limited support, Deve Gowda could not dominate his coalition government and depended on the motley crowd of small parties which formed the National Front. The most important element of the stability of his government was the reluctance of all parties to face new elections. The Congress had been humbled and could not hope to improve its position in the immediate future and the BJP had just tested the limits of its support.

The resilience of the Indian political system was once more demonstrated in April 1997, when a sudden crisis led to the fall of Deve Gowda's minority government and a new government, led by Inder Gujral, was formed within eleven days. Deve Gowda had made the fatal mistake of instigating corruption charges against the Congress establishment. He felt that the Congress would be more 'tolerant' if it was cornered in this way. The Congress President, Sitaram Kesri, may have expected that he would also be prosecuted and wished to show that Congress tolerance had its limits. A vote of no confidence toppled the government on 11 April and hectic consultations began which were aimed at reinstating the National Front government with a new leader.

Chandrababu Naidu, the Chief Minister of Andhra Pradesh, convened the leaders of the National Front at Andhra Bhavan in New Delhi. He had not yet consolidated his position in his own state and did not want to become prime minister. When none of those present appeared to be a candidate, they sent for Inder Gujral. Arriving at a late hour, he was tired and asked to be permitted to rest while the others continued their deliberations. After a while they woke him up and announced that he would be the prime minister. He accepted the office which had come to him in his sleep and was proud of this as he had got it without manipulating anybody. His drawback was that he did not have much political clout. He had always served as a minister in the central government and was a wise elder statesman. Being totally dependent on the 'tolerance' of the Congress, he lost his office when the Congress felt that it could call for elections in 1998.

The results were more or less the same as in 1996. The BJP could improve its position slightly. It got 26 per cent of the national vote – just as much as the Congress – but whereas the Congress captured only 141 seats, the BJP had 179. The most surprising result was that the large number of regional parties (excluding the two Communist parties) had won 37 per cent of the national vote and, altogether, 185 seats. Under these conditions, Vajpayee had a better chance to cobble together a coalition than in 1996. The Congress was still adverse to coalition politics. The All-India Anna Dravida Munnetra Kazagham (AIADMK) led by Jayalalitha, the former chief minister of Tamil Nadu, was Vajpayee's most difficult partner. Jayalalitha had prevaricated before she joined the coalition. It was clear that she held the fate of the government in her hands. Sonia Gandhi as Congress president tried to woo her. In April 1999 Jayalalitha left the coalition and Vajpayee was defeated in a vote of no confidence. Sonia Gandhi could now have formed a new coalition, but she failed to do so. She had got used to people coming to her and when no potential coalition partners appeared at her doorstep she made no effort to recruit them. Vajpayee remained acting prime minister, mastered the Kargil war of summer 1999 and won the elections in the autumn of that year. The results were similar to those of 1998 with some minor but significant differences. The BJP retained its position in terms of seats but lost some votes. The Congress party was reduced from 141 to 112 seats, its worst result ever. Regional parties had gained an even greater share of the national vote. Thus, the Telugu Desam Party (TDP) of Chandrababu Naidu increased its parliamentary seats from 12 to 29. The TDP did not join the coalition, which was called the National Democratic Alliance (NDA), but supported it from the 'outside'. However, those regional parties which joined the NDA had also won more seats and the NDA had a comfortable majority of 300 seats.

The decline of the Congress and the rise of regional parties are interrelated. They reflect a fundamental change in the composition of the Indian political elite. Earlier, this had been a national elite inspired by the experience of the freedom movement. It was rooted in a relatively small stratum of salarymen, traders and rich peasants. India's steady growth, in terms of both income and population, then gave rise to a large 'middle class'. India's population trebled since independence, not so much due to high birth rates but to a steep decline in death rates. India managed to feed this growing population and to double the per capita income. Shocking inequalities hide behind these statistical averages. India is home to the greatest number of poor people in the world, but it also has a 'middle class' of 150 to 250 million people. 'Middle class' is actually a misnomer, for these people constitute the upper 15 to 25 per cent of the population. The majority of these people are not very rich, but they have a considerable buying power. They demand goods and services, education and health care, etc. These demands concern the regional rather than the national level and, therefore, this 'middle class' articulates its political preferences regionally. The TDP is a case in point. The Congress has lost the mandate of these people. Its erosion has been a gradual process, but its manifestation has been rather sudden as the decline from 405 parliamentary seats in 1984 to 112 in 1999 has shown. Political sociology alone does not explain this change. The mechanics of the majority election system also have to be taken into consideration. The Congress used to benefit from three-cornered contests, but the astute policy of electoral alliances practised by the BJP spoiled this game. The BJP became the midwife of the regional parties. It then included some of them in the NDA while retaining the 'outside' support of others – and all this at the expense of the Congress, which hoped to revive the game of three-cornered contests by avoiding coalitions. Now the regional parties have come to stay and the Congress has to learn the lessons of coalition politics.

The process of change also caused tensions in Indian society. The Gujarat pogrom of 2002 in which thousands of Muslims were killed was due to such tensions. With only about 9 per cent of the population, the Muslim minority of Gujarat is below the national average of about 11 per cent. In Uttar Pradesh where 17 per cent of the population are Muslims most of them are poor workers and peasants; in Gujarat, however, there is a size-able Muslim middle class. In earlier times, Hindu and Muslim middle classes were fairly well integrated, but in recent years competition seems to have spoiled communal relations. The Hindu middle class turned to the BJP. Narendra Modi, an RSS-leader who had become BJP-chief minister of Gujarat catered to the anti-Muslim mood of the Hindus. The spark that ignited the powder keg was a tragic event which happened near Godhra station in Gujarat. A train carrying Hindus returning from Ayodhya was stopped in a Muslim locality soon after leaving the station. Wagons carrying Hindu women and children were burned, soon thereafter the pogrom started in Ahmedabad. There is circumstantial evidence that this was not an act of spontaneous revenge but a premeditated campaign of arson, plunder and murder. The police did not interfere and the state government prevaricated about calling in the army to restore order. Narendra Modi should have resigned but, instead, he launched a campaign of 'pride' (*gaurav*) throughout Gujarat and won the state elections of 2002 with a big margin. It was the saving grace of Indian regionalism that this terrible affair remained confined to Gujarat and did not spill over into other Indian states. But Modi's uninhibited *gaurav* may inspire likeminded politicians elsewhere. The central leadership of the BJP was embarrassed by Modi's conduct but did not discipline him. The most alarming feature was that members of the Hindu middle class, who normally shun violence as it could hurt their own interests, participated in the pogrom and supported Modi wholeheartedly.

It was to be feared that Modi's methods would be adopted in the next round of state elections in Chattisgarh, Delhi, Madhya Pradesh and Rajasthan, which were due in November 2003. But, except for Delhi, which once more elected a Congress government, the other three states were captured by the BJP without using Modi's stratagems. Two women, Uma Bharati in Madhya Pradesh and Vasundhara Raje in Rajasthan, emerged as chief ministers. It is to be hoped that this augurs well for the future of democracy in India.

EXTERNAL AFFAIRS: GLOBAL AND REGIONAL DIMENSIONS

In his famous *Arthashastra* the wily old Kautilya had outlined the *rajamandala* (circle of kings) in which the neighbour is usually the enemy and his neighbour, in turn, the natural ally of the first king. But he did not stop with that simple pattern. He also mentioned the more powerful 'middle king' who could decide a contest by coming down on the side of one neighbour or the other. He had to be wooed or diplomacy had to aim at keeping him neutral. Then there was the 'heelcatcher' whom one had to watch because he would take the opportunity of attacking from the rear while one was engaged in fighting someone else. Helpful, however, was the 'caller in the back of the enemy' who would raise an alarm if the enemy prepared for an attack. Finally, there was the 'outsider' – a mighty ruler not enmeshed in the *rajamandala* whose interventions were, therefore, unpredictable and who had to be watched with great care.

The republic of India is familiar with all these types, the superpowers playing the roles of the 'middle king' (Soviet Union) and the 'outsider' (US). India's political leaders have gained a good deal of experience in the conduct of foreign affairs in the years since 1947. Of course, they could have learned from the British, who expanded and defended their Indian empire for more than two centuries. But the Indian nationalists did not want to do that: they did not want to be identified with an imperialist foreign policy. In fact, one of the first resolutions of the Indian National Congress

Map 8.1 The Republic of India

of 1885 condemned the contemporary British annexation of Upper Burma and stressed that India wanted to live in peace with all its neighbours. This anti-imperialist attitude also determined all later foreign policy statements of Indian nationalists. Jawaharlal Nehru, who became the most prominent spokesman of the National Congress with regard to foreign affairs, added another dimension to this attitude. He saw the enemy in the capitalist camp of the West and regarded the Soviet Union and, later, also the People's Republic of China as harbingers of peace.

Nehru: the international mediator

When Nehru took over the conduct of independent India's foreign policy he was influenced by the views adopted in the years of the freedom movement. Even though Stalin paid little attention to India and initially thought of Nehru as an agent of British imperialism, Nehru made it a point to send his sister, Vijayalakshmi Pandit, who had served as a minister in the days of provincial autonomy, as India's first ambassador to Moscow in April 1947 when India was not yet independent. Nehru's sceptical attitude to the West was exacerbated by the incipient Cold War and the American policy of 'containment'. On the other hand, he also did not share the Soviet view of the division of the world into 'two camps'. Independent India did not want to be put into any 'camp'. this was not properly appreciated in either western or eastern Europe, but Nehru could base his foreign policy on a broad consensus in India.

The conflict with Pakistan, did, of course, constitute a severe handicap for Nehru's policy of global mediation and peaceful coexistence. At the same time it provided an opening for outside powers to interfere with the affairs of the region. The fact that Pakistan consisted of two wings separated by more than 1,000 miles of Indian territory meant that Pakistan would not be able to challenge India seriously; on the other hand, Pakistan felt that it was at the mercy of India and looked for outside support – this is why it ended up as a military ally of the US in 1954. The Kashmir conflict ruined India's relations with the United Nations, too, although India had been an ardent supporter of the idea of the United Nations all along. The United Nations, bent upon finding a political solution in Kashmir, sent several representatives – among them Americans – to Kashmir. From India's point of view, these delegates tried to interfere with the internal affairs of the country. Consequently, India became extremely jealous of its national sovereignty, an attitude which was at odds with Nehru's deep concern for other people's problems in his quest for world peace.

Nehru could score his first success at international mediation when he wrote to Stalin and to the American secretary of state Dean Acheson, at the time of the Korean war. India, then, could play a very helpful role in solving the difficult problem of the repatriation of Korean prisoners-of-war. The next chance for international mediation came at the end of the Indochina war after France had unsuccessfully tried to re-establish colonial rule and had been beaten by the Vietminh. At the Geneva Conference of 1954 the Indian emissary, Krishna Menon, played a crucial role behind the scenes although India was not officially represented there. Both superpowers thought at that time that a neutralisation of Indochina would be in their interests and India was asked to take up the chairmanship of the International Commission which was charged with the task of controlling their neutrality. But although the US had supported this solution, it simultaneously sponsored the SEATO (southeast Asia Treaty Organisation) as a parallel force to NATO capable of holding the line against Communist expansion in the East. Pakistan promptly joined this organisation. Nehru and Menon were furious about this pact which worked against the principle of neutralising conflict not only in Indochina, but also in its immediate environs. It became obvious to them that international mediation was a thankless task whenever it conflicted with superpower interests. But in 1955 universal harmony seemed to prevail and Nehru was at the height of his political career.

The spirit of Bandung, where the Afro-Asian leaders met, was matched by the spirit of Geneva where Eisenhower and Khrushchev met at an agreeable summit. In the same year Khrushchev and President Bulganin paid a memorable visit to India. Nehru's old vision of a friendly and peace-loving Soviet Union seemed to come true. Moreover, this friendly superpower backed him to the hilt both against Pakistan and against Indian Communists.

The Chinese challenge

The successful year 1955 was, however, soon followed by darker years full of problems. Nehru's strong reaction against Western intervention in Egypt was in striking contrast with his vague words about the Soviet intervention in Hungary. At the same time, India became dependent on Western development aid because the country's sterling balances were exhausted. The Aid to India Consortium met for the first time in 1957 in order to decide about financial help for India's five-year plans.

In those years the border conflict with China also emerged, though it did not yet come into the limelight of public debate. This happened only after the Dalai Lama fled to India in 1959 and Nehru was irked by questions asked in the Lok Sabha, which finally forced him to publish a White Paper that plainly showed how more and more acrimonious notes had been exchanged between the Indian and the Chinese governments for quite some time. A few years later this conflict was to break Nehru's heart. He had been in touch with the Chinese nationalists in the course of the Indian freedom movement and he had great sympathy for the aspirations of the Chinese nation. In his first foreign policy speeches after India attained independence he had referred to Asia as a zone of peace: conflict had started only with the intrusion of imperialism. With the emancipation of Asia peace was bound to be restored. In this optimistic spirit of anti-imperialism he had also welcomed the victory of Mao Tse Tung and had hoped for peace and harmony with the great neighbour. When in 1950 the Chinese occupied Tibet – which had long enjoyed a quasi-independent status – Nehru quickly gave up those Tibetan outposts which India had inherited from the British. These outposts were imperialistic relics to him. In 1954 Nehru concluded a treaty with the People's Republic of China concerning India's trade with Tibet. Except for a few passes which the traders were permitted to cross, there was no reference to the boundary in that treaty. Both sides obviously refrained from touching that subject at that time – Nehru, perhaps, in the hope that the border was considered to be a natural one which was not open to dispute. The five principles of peaceful coexistence (*panchashila*) were embodied in this treaty: (1) mutual respect for each other's sovereignty and territorial integrity; (2) non-aggression; (3) non-interference with the affairs of others; (4) equality and mutual benefit; (5) peaceful coexistence. The Soviet Union and its allies, as well as the non-aligned nations, found this formula very convenient. It contained an implicit rejection of Western interventionism and the American pact system.

The anti-imperialist fraternisation of India and China was a short-lived phenomenon. National interest soon prevailed and led to a tough border conflict. The consolidation of the Chinese hold on Tibet, as well as on other areas of central Asia, was a problem. Military infrastructure was required to maintain it and a ring road was constructed which led from China to Tibet and from there, via the Karakorum Range, to Sinkiang and Mongolia and then back to China. At a crucial point some Indian territory (Aksai Chin) obstructed this connection. Beyond Aksai Chin was the terrible desert, Takla Makan, which was a major obstacle. Faced with the dilemma of violating Indian territory or getting stuck in the desert, the Chinese opted for the first course and quietly built a road through Aksai Chin. In the meantime, they provoked incidents on the northeastern border to divert attention from their real aims. They also published maps which showed the border in Assam at the foot of the mountains rather than on the watershed. The watershed line had been settled by the 1914 McMahon border commission, which had also included a Chinese delegate who initialled the protocol, although it was not subsequently ratified by the Chinese government. Actually, there was no disagreement about the watershed line at that time when debate was focused on a different line, supposed to divide Tibet into an Inner and Outer Tibet on the same pattern as Inner and Outer Mongolia. Inner Tibet was to be under Chinese influence and Outer Tibet under British influence. But Communist China made use of the fact that the agreement had not been ratified and accused India of clinging to the imperialist heritage with regard to the Himalayan boundary.

This harping on the legal position in the northeast was a tactical move made in order to build up a bargaining position with regard to Aksai Chin where the Chinese could not raise similar claims. But Chinese feelers in this direction were always ignored by India. Aksai Chin, although uninhabited, was nevertheless a part of Indian territory which could not be bartered away. When the public came to know about the Chinese roads in Aksai Chin, Nehru was faced with increasingly vocal criticism in the Indian Parliament, and he once angrily asked his critics whether they wanted him to go to war on this issue. The Chinese pursued their aims relentlessly and edged closer and closer to the strategic Karakorum Pass.

Finally, a border war broke out in October 1962. It was a typical demonstration war conducted with great finesse by the Chinese. They completely perplexed the Indian generals by pushing a whole division through the mountains down to the valley of Assam and withdrawing it again as quickly as it had come. The Indian strategic concept of defending the Himalayan boundary by cutting off the supply lines of the enemy if it ventured too far beyond the border could not even be put into operation: the Chinese were gone before their supply lines could be cut. But why did they do this? They wanted to divert attention from their moves in the northwest, where they did reach the Karakorum Pass in a swift offensive and did not withdraw as they had done in the east.

In the years after 1962 there was a conspiracy of silence about the line of actual control established by the Chinese. India did not like to admit the loss of territory as this would have led to acrimonious debates at home. China had no reason to advertise its territorial gains. Subsequent Indian attempts at resuming the dialogue with China were frustrated until Prime Minister P.V. Narasimha Rao visited China in 1993 and signed an agreement whereby both sides respect the line of actual control. Once again no attempt was made to specifiy this in detail or to delineate a border. To this extent the position remains more or less the same as in 1954 when both sides refrained from delineating the border. Nehru had to pay the price for this in 1962. The Indian army smarted for many years under the humiliating defeat in that border war until the more conventional battles with Pakistan in 1965 and 1971 restored its image. Pakistan was an enemy operating on the same military wavelength, whereas Chinese strategy and tactics were too devious for officers trained in the Sandhurst tradition.

Nehru was flabbergasted by the course of events and 1962, in stark contrast with 1961, was the nadir of his political career. At Belgrade the year before, he had been the star at the conference of the non-aligned nations; as their spokesman he had then visited Moscow to impress upon Khrushchev the need for a cessation of Soviet nuclear tests. African nationalists who had found Nehru too moderate at Belgrade were surprised by his decision to liberate Goa from Portuguese rule in December 1961. Nehru had hesitated for a long time before seeking a military solution to this problem. But the Portuguese dictator, Salazar, was in no mood to negotiate a peaceful transfer of power. The Africans felt that Nehru, instead of giving them a lead, was waiting until the Portuguese empire in Africa crumbled and Goa would then fall into his lap – and they said so in no uncertain terms. Talks with Kennedy in America must have given Nehru the impression that this president would not support his colonialist NATO ally when the chips were down. Nehru did not mention a word about his plan to Kennedy, who was annoyed about this after the event – although he did not, indeed, lift a finger to help the Portuguese. Pakistan also kept out of it. And last but not least, the Portuguese governor general of Goa only blasted some bridges; apart from that, he did not attempt to put up a hopeless fight against the Indian army. This was Nehru's last success. The Chinese blow of 1962 struck him hard and his health deteriorated rapidly. After his death in May 1964 his successor, Lal Bahadur Shastri, who was completely inexperienced in the conduct of foreign policy, was faced with a daunting task.

Pakistan's Operation 'Grand Slam' and Soviet mediation

In 1960 the relations between India and Pakistan seemed to be perfect. Ayub Khan, Pakistan's military ruler, was at the height of his power and did not need to point to India as the great threat in order to swing public opinion in his favour. The Indus Water Treaty had finally been signed and Nehru and Ayub met at Murree in a spirit of harmony. However, when India failed to meet the Chinese challenge in 1962 and Nehru's power declined, Pakistan established friendly relations with China in 1963. The ambitious young minister Zulfiqar Ali Bhutto was the main architect of this new alliance. He also pursued a hard line as far as India was concerned and when Nehru died, Ayub and Bhutto thought that the time had come to settle old scores once and for all. Shastri seemed to be a weak man and a little test war in the Rann of Kutch proved that he would walk into any trap which Pakistan laid for him. The Rann is flooded by the sea for several months of the year: Pakistan selected a time to settle a border dispute there by military means and in such a way as to put the Indian troops defending the area at a great disadvantage – they were literally at sea. Shastri then agreed to mediation and the British Prime Minister Harold Wilson was asked to act as the mediator.

After this trial run, Ayub prepared Operation 'Grand Slam' in order to capture Kashmir. In a quick offensive Pakistan's mighty Patton tanks were supposed to cut off the only road which connects India with Kashmir. If Shastri again stuck to local defence only and refrained from opening a second front, Ayub was sure to win. But this time Shastri did not play the game according to the rules set by Ayub. Soon after Operation 'Grand Slam' commenced on 1 September 1965, Indian troops marched towards Lahore. India had stepped up its arms production and defence efforts after the traumatic experience of the Chinese invasion; Pakistan, on the other hand, was not adequately prepared for a full-scale war.

Ayub had put all his cards on a quick first strike and had now lost his gamble. The Chinese were not willing to bail him out, either. Just for show they provoked a border dispute in Sikkim and delivered an ultimatum to Shastri, threatening to open a second front there. Shastri ignored the ultimatum and the Chinese made no move. Left in the lurch by China, Ayub had to arrive at a ceasefire agreement with India while Indian troops held several areas of Pakistani territory. Ayub lost face and Shastri emerged as a courageous leader whom nobody would now dare to call weak.

At this stage the Soviet Union saw a great chance of becoming an umpire in south Asian affairs by acting as a mediator between India and Pakistan. India could not reject the offer of this friendly power and actually hoped to get the Soviet Union involved in the maintenance of the status quo in south Asia. Pakistan was eager to go to any conference table because the withdrawal of Indian troops from Pakistani territory could only be achieved by negotiation as the battle had been lost. In January 1966 Ayub, Shastri and the Soviet prime minister Kosygin met at Tashkent. The negotiations were difficult and protracted. Shastri insisted that Pakistan should sign a declaration never to use force again and he wanted the Soviet Union to act as signatory witness and guarantor that Pakistan would keep its promise. Ayub threatened to leave the conference, but he could not afford to do this because there was no other way of getting rid of the Indian troops. Finally, he signed the declaration and Shastri agreed to withdraw the Indian troops. The Soviet Union refused to get involved in a written guarantee of Pakistan's good behaviour, but Shastri could assume that by bringing about the Tashkent Accord the Soviet Union would be interested in preserving it.

Shastri's death at the end of this strenuous conference was a heavy price paid for a meagre result. Pakistan tried to forget about the declaration as soon as the Indian troops had been removed. For Ayub, any reference to this declaration was only a reminder of his humiliation. As a soldier he had lost a military venture and, on top of that, he had been compelled to promise that he would never do it again. His authority was undermined. He fired Bhutto who had greatly encouraged him in this venture, but this did not help him to restore his authority. On the contrary, Bhutto soon emerged as the leader of the opposition to Ayub's regime and nobody seemed to remember that it was he who had aided and abetted Ayub. Ayub's loss of popular support was hastened by the necessity of restoring Pakistan's military capacity at the expense of the taxpayer. About 300 tanks were lost in 1965 and an arms embargo by the Western powers deprived Pakistan of its usual sources of free supply of military hardware. Consequently, Ayub was happy when the Soviet Union – playing its new role of umpire in south Asian affairs – sent such hardware to Pakistan in 1968 in an attempt to do evenhanded justice to India and Pakistan.

Indo-Soviet friendship and the liberation of Bangladesh

Indira Gandhi had not yet won the respect of the Soviet Union in 1968. These were the days when she was still to make a mark in Indian politics and her protest against Soviet military aid to Pakistan could be easily ignored. But in 1969 several events contributed to a change in the Soviet attitude. The border clashes with China made the Soviet leadership more concerned about security in Asia. Pakistan could not be weaned away from China, in spite of Soviet pressure. India, however, did not need to be converted in this respect and so the Soviet Union and India established closer relations once more. A draft of what later became known as the Indo-Soviet Friendship Treaty was prepared in Moscow in September 1969 and Soviet military aid to Pakistan was stopped in 1970. Indira Gandhi had split the Congress in the summer of 1969, projecting a 'left' image which impressed the Soviet Union. But she was not yet in full control of the political situation and the signing of the Friendship Treaty before she had won the next elections would have been inopportune. Nevertheless, after her great electoral victory of March 1971 she did not rush to sign this treaty. It was only in the context of the deteriorating situation in east Pakistan that she found it useful to enlist the Soviet Union as a potential ally.

In July 1971 President Nixon revealed that Henry Kissinger had secretly flown from Islamabad to Peking in order to prepare the ground for a presidential visit. A Washington–Islamabad–Peking axis seemed to emerge very clearly. Kissinger told the Indian ambassador in Washington that China would surely attack in the event of Indian intervention in east Pakistan, and that there would be no American help for India in this case. On the other hand, the rising influx of refugees from east Pakistan into India and the massive transfer of troops from west to east Pakistan alarmed Indira Gandhi, who was probably convinced by that time that an armed intervention would be necessary. So she sent urgent messages to Moscow, indicating her willingness to sign the treaty as soon as possible. The foreign minister Gromyko was hastily dispatched to New Delhi and the Treaty of Peace, Friendship and Cooperation was signed on 8 August 1971.

The speed at which this was accomplished seems to prove that the text of the treaty had been settled some time earlier. For the Soviet Union this was a major achievement as President Brezhnev had not hitherto found partners for his much advertised Asian security system. Now there was, at least, a treaty with India, and Soviet diplomacy greatly emphasised this treaty in subsequent years, whereas India was not so enamoured of it once the armed intervention in east Pakistan had been successfully completed. The treaty did not provide for a military pact, it only contained clauses which obliged both parties to refrain from entering military alliances which would be harmful to the other. Thus, the treaty was no guarantee of Soviet support for India in the event of India's armed intervention in east Pakistan. But if India had fared badly in such an intervention – and particularly if third parties had joined the fray – the Soviet Union could not have afforded to let India down. For this very reason, the Soviet Union did not encourage India to proceed with this venture.

Before the final showdown Indira Gandhi went on a tour of the capitals of the West in order to ask their heads of government to use their influence to change the course of Pakistan's destructive policy. After two futile and frustrating sessions with Nixon she might as well have gone home without talking to anybody else. However, she persevered with the whole futile round not because she hoped for help, but because she wanted to make sure that nobody could later accuse her of not having tried her best to avoid the intervention. As the conflict drew nearer the Soviet Union became more sympathetic to the Indian point of view – but did not promise to give India full support, regardless of the consequences of the venture. after India finally intervened in east Pakistan at the beginning of December 1971 the Soviet Union vetoed UN resolutions which called for an immediate cease-fire, but a Soviet deputy foreign minister was dispatched to New Delhi in order to warn India that the Soviet Union could not reiterate this veto indef-initely. However, when the Pakistani troops surrendered on 16 December 1971 the Soviet Union was quick to rejoice and a Soviet official at the UN emphasised that this was the first time in history that the US and China had been defeated together.

Indira Gandhi could, indeed, take pride in having been able to defy both these powers successfully. Nixon's policy of threatening an intervention by sending an aircraft carrier into the Bay of Bengal turned out to be mere bluff. The Chinese did not even go that far and made no move to support their Pakistani friends. Indian regional hegemony was firmly established in this way – but this, of course, increased the sense of insecurity experienced by smaller neighbouring states. Indira Gandhi had no talent for making them feel at ease. Even Bangladesh, which she had helped to liberate, soon showed anti-Indian feelings. Although Indian troops had been quickly with-drawn, Indian businessmen moved in and the people of Bangladesh felt that they were exploited by them. The constant quarrel over the division of the Ganges water contributed to this atmosphere of distrust. The Farakka barrage was built on Indian territory and was used to divert water which would have flowed into Bangladesh into the Hugli; the official reason for this measure was that it prevented the silting up of the port of Calcutta. Whereas the Indus Water Treaty had settled similar problems in the west, no immediate solution was found here in the east and it took a long time before the two states settled this problem.

On the other hand, Indira Gandhi did make some progress in normal-ising relations with Pakistan when she met Bhutto, who had emerged as the new leader of that country, in Simla in 1972. Since 90,000 Pakistani prisoners-of-war had to be returned, Indira Gandhi was in a strong position and could have forced Bhutto to recognise the Line of Control in Kashmir as an international boundary. Bhutto argued that he would work for this recognition, but that he would be thrown out of office if Indira Gandhi forced him to recognise it at that particular time. She accepted this plea, but Bhutto did not follow up his promise. He was glad that he had been let off lightly. He recognised Bangladesh fairly soon, but whereas he tried to appear sweet and reasonable, he secretly pursued his old quest to be on a par with India in terms of power and international influence. As this could not be achieved by conventional methods he had to strive for the atomic bomb – particularly as he knew that India was also keeping its nuclear options open.

The Indian atom bomb

In 1974 India surprised the world by exploding a 'nuclear device' in an underground test in the Rajasthan desert. The term 'bomb' was carefully avoided and Indira Gandhi emphasised that India would use this type of device only for peaceful purposes. Nevertheless, India had signalled in this way that it now belonged to the exclusive club of atomic powers. In Jawaharlal Nehru's time the campaign against nuclear tests had been a major item of India's foreign policy and India had been one of the first signatories of the Moscow treaty in 1963 which banned nuclear tests on the ground or in the atmosphere. In 1964 China had blasted its first atomic bomb and this made India shy away from signing the Nuclear Non-proliferation Treaty (1968), which was jointly sponsored by the US and the Soviet Union. There was a general consensus in India that the treaty should not be signed as it only secured the hegemony of the existing atomic powers once and for all. India should keep the nuclear option open. But there were differences of opinion as far as the actual exercise of that option was concerned.

Mahatma Gandhi had called the dropping of the atom bomb on Japan 'the violence of the cowards'. He was deeply upset about it, because in his resistance to violence he had always faced the adversary whereas atom bombs were dropped by remote control. Non-violent courage could not impress those who operated such controls. Homi Bhabha, India's great nuclear physicist, seems to have been influenced by Gandhi's thought when he asked Nehru in 1955 to proclaim India's unilateral renunciation of the bomb. Nehru replied at that time that such a declaration would only make sense if India were actually able to produce such a bomb. Ten years later, Nehru's successor, Shastri, asked Bhabha whether Indian scientists could prepare an underground test. The Chinese had conducted their tests in 1964 and Shastri had asked other powers whether they would be willing to provide a 'nuclear umbrella' for India. Of course, nobody wished to offer such an umbrella, because the risks of doing so would outweigh any benefits from protecting India. This is why Shastri finally asked Bhabha about producing an Indian atom bomb.

A new challenge was introduced by President Nixon at the time of the liberation of Bangladesh. The aircraft carrier which he sent to the Bay of Bengal in December 1971 had nuclear weapons on board. Nixon revealed later on that he would not have hesitated to use them against India if the Soviet Union had helped India. When Bhutto embarked on sponsoring his 'Islamic bomb' in 1972, India was even more concerned about being able to withstand nuclear threats. But Indira Gandhi's solitary experiment in 1974 was all that the world came to know about India's intentions. Her successor, Morarji Desai, was against such experiments and during his period of office there was no further progress in this field. Presumably Indira Gandhi pursued this matter again after 1980. India also made rapid advances in the field of rocketry so as to be able to match atom bombs with an adequate delivery system. It seems that by 1995 the government of P.V. Narasimha Rao was on the verge of testing bombs but then refrained from it due to American pressure. There was the great debate about the signing of the Comprehensive Test Ban Treaty (CTBT) at that time. India refused to sign it because it was another treaty which would discriminate against nuclear have-nots. Perhaps there was an idea of signing the treaty after conducting the tests, but then India continued its policy of 'nuclear ambiguity' without signing the CTBT.

The BJP had all along advocated that India should 'go nuclear'. When it came to power in 1998 it was expected that tests would be conducted immediately. But in his initial statement Prime Minister Vajpayee only repeated the old formula of keeping the nuclear option open. At this stage Pakistan made a very provocative move. It tested a rocket named 'Ghauri' after Muhmmad von Ghor who had once raided northern India. Actually this rocket was made in North Korea and had only been re-baptised in Pakistan. A few days later, on 11 May 1998, Vajpayee shocked the world with an announcement that India had conducted five massive tests of atom bombs. He added that this was done to test those bombs with a view to their military use. While this news shocked many observers abroad, there was a consensus in India supporting the tests. In fact, there was a wave of patriotic frenzy at that time. Most of those who hailed the bomb were, of course, quite ignorant about the horrors of nuclear warfare. Pakistan followed this up with its own tests, which were greeted with equal enthusiasm in that country. Both countries were now faced with American sanctions, which did not affect India very much but were very painful for Pakistan, which was nearly bankrupt. From then on the world had to live with two nuclear powers which were neighbours with a record of continuous hostility. Seen from this perspective, the Cold War appeared to be a time of stability and predictable international relations.

India between the US and the Soviet Union

During the period of the Cold War, India had followed the policy of non-alignment and had tried to maintain 'equidistance' from both superpowers.

Its attachment to democracy actually made India more akin to the US. Initially, India had regarded the US as a friend, because President Roosevelt had tried his best to foster the advance of Indian independence. But in 1949 the US missed a chance to help India at the time of a serious food crisis and Nehru's first visit to the US in that year proved to be a mutual disappointment. When John Foster Dulles subsequently organised the global pact system, which India regarded as a threat to its own security since Pakistan had joined it wholeheartedly, Indo-American relations were at a low ebb in spite of American economic aid for India. The short-lived administration of President Kennedy was a ray of hope. India was considered to be a major partner, the world's greatest democracy, and thus an asset to the free world. But soon after Kennedy's untimely death Indo-American relations deteriorated once more as the Indochina war escalated. After American disengagement in Vietnam, President Nixon wooed China and alienated India at the time of the liberation of Bangladesh. The enthusiastic reception of Brezhnev in New Delhi in 1973 and the explosion of India's nuclear device in 1974 could be interpreted as deliberate acts of defiance by Nixon, whose 'tilt' towards Pakistan was well known. Indira Gandhi's 'emergency' of 1975 received wholehearted support from the Soviet Union and silenced American friends of India who had praised the subcontinent as the world's greatest democracy.

The election of President Carter in November 1976 and the restoration of democracy in India seemed to augur well for an Indo-American rapprochement. The new Indian prime minister, Morarji Desai, had the reputation of being for the West and against the Soviet Union. A major shift in Indian foreign policy was expected. But when Carter visited India, the disagreement about the supply of uranium and the nuclear option spoiled everything. Desai, who did not approve of the 1974 explosion, was, nevertheless, firm in his adherence to the nuclear option and told Carter that he himself should scrap American stockpiles of atomic bombs before he lectured other nations about non-proliferation. Thus, contrary to earlier expectations, there was no rapprochement with the West.

On the other hand, Indo-Soviet relations remained stable as they coincided with the perceived national interest of both partners. Nevertheless, the Soviet Union was somewhat nervous about India's closer contacts with the US and China. Desai's visit to Washington in June 1978 and the February 1979 visit of Indian minister of external affairs, Atal Bihari Vajpayee, to Peking showed a new initiative in Indian foreign policy, which alarmed the Soviet Union. Vajpayee was treated to anti-Chinese harangues by the Soviet leaders when he visited Moscow prior to his Chinese tour and, to their great relief, the Chinese behaved true to type when Vajpayee was in Peking: the Chinese demonstration war against Vietnam was started at that time and the Chinese leaders did not hesitate to stress the analogy of this war with that against India in 1962. Vajpayee left Peking abruptly and the normalisation of India's relations with China was postponed for the time being.

The Soviet invasion of Afghanistan and India's reaction

A completely new political scenario seemed to emerge when the Soviet Union staged a massive invasion of Afghanistan in December 1979. India had very friendly relations with that country and the sudden demise of a non-aligned regime was a severe blow to India, which still considered itself to be a leader of the non-aligned world. Both in terms of global and regional dimensions, this was a serious challenge to India and it was perceived as that. However, this perception was not articulated in public because India had to retain the friendship of the Soviet Union. The events in Afghanistan coincided with the elections in India which brought Indira Gandhi back to power. Prior to her reinstatement she had made some critical remarks about the Soviet invasion; as soon as she came to assume responsibility for the conduct of India's foreign policy, though, she refrained from such statements – the more so since Pakistan emerged once more as the major partner of the US in south Asia. Indian diplomacy was now aimed at quiet mediation with the hope of achieving a political solution in Afghanistan, which would help to ease out the Soviet troops. India emphasised that in the interest of such efforts it would be better not to subject the Soviet Union to futile verbal attacks. But Indian leaders felt very uncomfortable about the whole situation and, as time went by, they realised that they could not do much about a political solution whether they refrained from criticising the Soviet Union or not.

Another issue which alarmed India in this context was the growing military importance of the Indian Ocean, which India would have liked to recognise as a 'Zone of Peace'. Before the Soviet invasion there had been some attempts at coming to an agreement which would provide at least for a 'freeze' of the arms race in this region. The American leaders could afford to think of such a 'freeze' as they were already well represented in the region. The huge American base on the island of Diego Garcia in the centre of the Indian Ocean would remain intact, even under such a 'freeze'. The Soviet invasion, however, put an end to such considerations and the regional arms race was stepped up with a vengeance. Additional American bases were established in Oman, and the Soviet Union gained control of Aden and some bases in the Red Sea.

All these problems were soon forgotten once the Soviet Union withdrew from Afghanistan and collapsed soon thereafter. The old rule that empires must expand or they will implode seemed to be confirmed by the fate of the Soviet Union. India renewed the treaty of friendship with the Soviet

Union in 1991 only a few weeks before that state ceased to exist. It then signed a treaty with the new Russian republic and established diplomatic relations with a host of successor states. But all this could not compensate India for the loss of a fairly stable relationship, which began in 1955 and proved to be useful in many respects.

After the demise of the Soviet Union, India had to get along with the US as the only remaining superpower. The beginning of this period was not very auspicious, because the Gulf War of 1990 greatly embarrassed India, which had exported skilled manpower to this region on a massive scale and had profited from the remittances of the Indians working there. Many of them had to be repatriated when the war started. Moreover, India had good relations with Iraq, which had signed a friendship treaty with the Soviet Union in April 1972, closely following the precedent of the Indo-Soviet treaty signed eight months earlier. Indian foreign policy was also handicapped in 1990 by its internal political instability.

India's balance of payments crisis of 1991, which has been discussed earlier, was triggered by the Gulf War. When India presented itself under new management in the summer of 1991 and embarked on a course of economic reform, the Americans were pleased. The International Monetary Fund (IMF) once more provided India with a big loan. India promptly devalued its currency and introduced measures of structural adjustment. Such measures were usually part of the 'conditionalities' imposed by the IMF, but in India, finance minister Dr Manmohan Singh, an eminent economist, did not need to be told what he was supposed to do. Very soon the Indian currency was made convertible on current account and it was announced that it would soon be convertible on capital account as well. Fortunately, this latter step was postponed and thus India was not affected by the Asian Crisis of 1997, which demonstrated that capital that had inundated several Asian countries could also flow out of them, fatally damaging their economies. The IMF actually deepened the crisis by its inept management. India could be glad that it did not depend on the tender mercies of this institution at this crucial time.

A new era of Indo-American cooperation dawned with President Clinton's visit to India in March 2000. He had imposed sanctions on India and Pakistan after the atomic tests of 1998, but now he was keen to normalise relations with India. From the Indian perspective he appeared to be another Kennedy. There was a profound change in the Indian perception of America even among those who had earlier praised the virtues of non-alignment. This political perception now caught up with the general admiration of America in Indian middle-class society. The community of Indian immigrants in the US, mostly skilled technicians and professionals, had grown by leaps and bounds in recent years. Thus, many Indian families had relatives in America. These ties had, so far, not been reflected in political perceptions, but now India seemed to emerge as a natural ally of the US.

The terrible events of 11 September 2001, which ushered in the global alliance against terror, contributed to even better relations between India and the US. India immediately declared that it wished to join that alliance. Of course, India hoped that the alliance would also help against terror in Kashmir, but in this it was soon to be disappointed. The Americans crushed the Taliban in Afghanistan, but this increased troubles in the region. Moreover, the Americans did not concentrate on pacifying Afghanistan but turned their attention to Iraq. India made it clear that it did not want to get involved in another Gulf War, but it also did not join the chorus of America's more vocal critics. It seems that Indo-American relations were better than ever in 2003. An official spokesman even advocated an axis India–Israel–US. This has highlighted another aspect of Indo-American relations. In earlier times India had always sided with Arab nationalism, but after the Gulf War it had changed sides and had established diplomatic relations with Israel in 1992. Ever since, there has been increasing Indo-Israeli cooperation, which was enhanced by the Indian visit of the Israeli Premier Ariel Sharon in 2003. Such contacts are appreciated by the US.

All these endeavours are prompted by India's concern with its national security in a hostile environment. Nehru's dream of Asia as a zone of peace was shattered a long time ago. Since the Chinese border war of 1962 and the subsequent Pakistani attack of 1965, security has had a high priority in India. In this context India has also paid close attention to its immediate regional environment.

South Asian Regional Cooperation

The problems of regional security have made India a convert to the idea of South Asian Regional Cooperation, which was first mooted by President Zia-ur Rahman of Bangladesh. India had always preferred to deal with its neighbours bilaterally, thus preventing antagonistic 'ganging up' with regard to common grievances. For this very reason Bangladesh – which did not want to be left alone in its dealings with its huge neighbour – emphasised the need for regional cooperation. On the other hand, India also had some interest in keeping in touch with Pakistan and a forum of regional cooperation could serve this purpose too. So, finally, and for a variety of different reasons, the scheme of South Asian Regional Cooperation (SARC) took shape. After a round of meetings at foreign secretary level, a ministerial meeting was arranged in July 1983 in New Delhi. It was here that SARC was formally established. Bangladesh, Bhutan, India, the Maldives, Nepal, Pakistan and Sri Lanka are the seven members of this association. The fact that this was to be an association of states was officially announced at its first summit meeting, when the heads of government met in Dhaka in December 1985. Accordingly, a new name was adopted: South Asian Association for Regional Cooperation (SAARC). It was also decided to establish a permanent secretariat and to hold annual summit meetings.

In subsequent years some dramatic changes occurred in south Asia. Whereas India had been an apprehensive observer of superpower rivalry in the region in earlier years, it now took on the arduous task of policing the region, with the blessings of both superpowers. This caused resentment among India's smaller neighbours, but they had to accept it as a fact of life. Some had reason to be grateful as, for example, the government of the Maldives, which was saved by Indian intervention from being swept away by a coup in 1988. Others complained about a high-handed abuse of power, as Nepal did when it was faced with an Indian blockade in 1989. The most complicated case was India's intervention in Sri Lanka in 1987 which was supposed to be a swift police action by an 'Indian peace-keeping force' but which turned into a long occupation of northern Sri Lanka.

India's involvement began with its support of the Tamil terrorists of Sri Lanka whose activities increased after the Sinhala pogrom directed against Tamils living in the diaspora in southern Sri Lanka in 1983. President Jayewardene's army was only a tiny parade force but he geared it up with the help of various foreign powers in order to seek a military solution. His new army was still no match for the Tamil guerrilla fighters, but when it closed in on Jaffna in 1987, India air-dropped supplies for the beleaguered Tamils. Jayewardene at first protested against Indian interference, but then signed an accord with Rajiv Gandhi in July 1987. The Indian army was now supposed to disarm the terrorists, but it did not succeed. A protracted war ensued which caused severe losses to India in terms of men, money and reputation. Jayewardene's successor, Premadasa, who was under great pressure from right-wing Sinhala terrorists, put an ultimatum to India, asking for a withdrawal of Indian troops by July 1989. This, of course, did not happen; instead a new accord was signed in September which postponed the day of reckoning. At a time when the Soviet withdrawal from Afghanistan in 1989 came as a relief to India, but also obliged it to stand by the Kabul regime, India remained deeply involved in Sri Lanka.

Rajiv Gandhi's defeat in the elections of 1989 made it easier for India to withdraw from Sri Lanka as the new government was not committed to the accord signed in 1987. By the spring of 1990 all Indian soldiers had left the island. A costly and frustrating venture had come to an end. Some Indian experts claim that India was close to achieving a decisive victory just before its troops had to be withdrawn. Perhaps this may explain why the Tamil Tigers assassinated Rajiv Gandhi in May 1991. They may have feared that if he came back to power he would take up the fight against them once more. In the meantime the Indian government has been relieved of further worries by the active policy of Chandrika Kumaratunge who has designed a convincing political solution to the Tamil problem, but also did not hesitate to occupy Jaffna when the Tigers defied her. In 1987 India intervened when Jayewardene attacked Jaffna. This time India did not protest and even supported Chandrika Kumaratunge in her endeavours.

P.V. Narasimha Rao who had served as external affairs minister for a long time in earlier years has, in general, followed a less dramatic line than Indira and Rajiv Gandhi; he defended India's national interest quietly but firmly. The foreign policy of the National Front government then followed more or less the same line. Inder Gujral who was initially the external affairs minister of that government and then became its prime minister in 1997 proclaimed the 'Gujral Doctrine' according to which India would unilaterally accommodate its neighbours so as to remove their misgivings. Earlier, India had preferred to talk from a position of strength in bilateral negotiations, therefore this new doctrine indicated a change of the climate of south Asian diplomacy. Unfortunately, this climate did not prevail very long as new conflicts arose after India and Pakistan became nuclear powers.

Recent conflicts and the prospects of peace

Pakistan had always aimed at parity with India, which it could not achieve in conventional terms. As an atomic power it did achieve this parity and the logic of mutual deterrence seemed to apply here, too. This is what Vajpayee must have thought when he launched a bold 'peace offensive', visiting the Pakistani prime minister, Nawaz Sharif, in Lahore in February 1999. Nawaz Sharif winced when Vajpayee gave him a friendly hug because he knew that General Parvez Musharraf, who was witnessing this scene, had already made preparations for a surprise attack in Kashmir. Musharraf's plan was brilliant, but it eventually misfired. In May he launched an attack across the Line of Control in the Kargil sector. During the winter the Indian troops in this area were concentrated in a few fortified posts only and Musharraf had organised infiltrations in between those posts. He wanted to capture some territory beyond the Line of Control before the Indian posts could be re-enforced by troops reaching this sector from Srinagar via the Zhoji La pass, which was blocked by ice until the end of May. He argued that this was a 'proxy war' because his men were supposed to be Kashmiri freedom fighters. Such 'proxy wars' had been indulged in by atomic powers during the Cold War. The Indians soon found out that they were attacked by regular Pakistani troops. They did not cross the Line of Control from their side so as not to provoke a nuclear escalation. Even with this handi-cap they managed to defeat the Pakistanis and, by June, Musharraf knew that his plan had failed. When his friend and colleague, the American Chief of Staff, General Zinni, visited him in order to persuade him to withdraw his troops, Musharraf quickly agreed, but he saw to it that prime minister Nawaz Sharif was invited to Washington for the final negotiations. This was a clever move, because in this way Nawaz Sharif was responsible for the withdrawal. When he noticed that he had been framed by Musharraf he wanted to remove him but, in the end, it was Musharraf who got rid of Nawaz Sharif and seized power – which he then retained for several years.

Map 8.2 Jammu and Kashmir and the Line of Control

Vajpayee had acted throughout with great restraint although he had been betrayed by Musharraf and was facing an election which he could have lost if India had not won this war. He then won the election, but found it difficult to talk about peace with Musharraf. His position became worse when Pakistani terrorists attacked the Indian Parliament in December 2001. This attack was not planned by Musharraf; on the contrary, it was meant to embarrass him and to upset the 'alliance against terror' – which it certainly did. Vajpayee could not take this lying down, but he could not reach the terrorists who had planned this dastardly attack and had to mass his troops on the Pakistani border. In the summer of 2002 another war between India and Pakistan seemed to be imminent. American mediators flocked to India and Pakistan and finally the crisis was overcome. In 2003 Vajpayee even launched another 'peace offensive' stressing that it would be his last one. Musharraf was under American pressure to reciprocate this gesture, but he, himself, was a target of fundamentalist terrorists. In earlier times, war and peace were made by states, but nowadays states themselves are at the mercy of terrorists who may strike anywhere and at any time. Neither diplomacy nor atom bombs are of much use under such conditions. A new type of vigilance is required – but this may also infringe civil liberties. Perhaps the ideas of Mahatma Gandhi may prove to be relevant in this new context. He always rose to new challenges and trusted in human agency when confronted by the overwhelming force of circumstances which seemed to determine human fate.

PERSPECTIVES

The state of India is based on a great tradition. The small kingdoms of the Gangetic plains, the great empires of antiquity, the regional kingdoms of medieval times, the Mughal empire, the British Indian empire and, finally, the Union of India contributed, each in their own way, to state formation in India. Even the medieval kingdoms, whose history was later regarded as a striking example of centrifugal tendencies, served the purpose of reproducing everywhere a uniform style of government. These early state formations were not conceived of in territorial terms as modern states are. They consisted of networks of towns and temples, warriors, priests and villages. There was a great deal of local autonomy, but the ritual sovereignty of the king enabled him to act as an umpire who could interfere in local conflicts and settle issues.

The modern territorial state in India was introduced by the Great Mughals whose political, military and financial systems were copied by their enemies and successors. The British, who took over the Mughal structure, 'civilised' it by replacing the military officer by the civil servant. This civil service then emerged as the 'steel frame' of the British Indian empire. At the same time they introduced their law and their courts, which soon penetrated the Indian countryside. Local autonomy as well as the royal umpire were superseded by judges. British legislation and jurisdiction made an impact on Indian life. The alternating current of national agitation and constitutional reform then introduced a commitment to the parliamentary form of government. The federalism which the British introduced as a device for the devolution of power in terms of provincial autonomy ran counter to nationalist aspirations but was, nevertheless, retained after independence.

As both the Mughal and the British Indian political traditions were highly centralist, this centralism was emulated by the Indian nationalists. It was enhanced by the partition of India, which highlighted the need for national integration. A further contribution to this centralism was the unbroken tradition of the civil service, which was taken over as a going concern following the negotiated, non-revolutionary transfer of power. The developmental

369

needs of the federal states were not realised as a result of this prevalent centralism, and it is only in recent times that a new awareness of the value of federalism for a vast state like the Union of India is becoming evident.

Another important element of the Indian political tradition is India's secularism. The various religious trends of India, which come under the general rubric of Hinduism, always provided for a large degree of autonomy for the political sphere. When Islamic rulers conquered extensive parts of India, they brought along a different idea of the state as a corporation of Muslims which would, at the most, grant protection to non-believers. But in actual political practice they had to take note of the fact that the majority of the citizens were such non-believers. When the British conquered India they did not make it a Christian empire; similarly, when the Indian National Congress challenged British rule this organisation took great care to retain a secular character. This was not simply a matter of ideology but also of political expediency, because anybody who wanted to build up solidarity on a sectarian platform was bound to become isolated from the mainstream of political life. The British policy of 'divide and rule', the introduction of separate electorates for the Indian Muslims – which finally led to the partition of India – confirmed the Indian National Congress even more in its adherence to secularism, which then also became the guiding principle of the Union of India. Jawaharlal Nehru saw in this secular republic the true school of the Indian nation in which it would grow up in terms of modern national solidarity. In this respect his views closely paralleled those of earlier liberal nationalists such as Ranade and Gokhale, who had hoped for the transformation of the many Indian communities into a modern nation. This process is still going on and there are many problems which have to be overcome by concerted action. Streamlining the nation so as to conform to Hindu nationalism will not solve these problems. Unity in diversity must remain the guiding principle of national integration.

One of the problems besetting the Indian nation is the existence of great regional discrepancies. The states in the western half of India, including Tamil Nadu, are on a par with Latin America as far as their general standard of life is concerned; the states of the east are on the level of the poorer states of Africa. The dynamics of economic development usually do not reduce, but rather enhance, such discrepancies. Thus, the over-populated and under-urbanised areas of the east remain backward, while the west forges ahead. At the same time, however, the backward and densely populated rural districts to the north of Varanasi and Patna – where forty million people live, most of them poor and exploited – also claim immediate attention. Such tasks require a great deal of stamina and resilience from the political system. The record which has been examined here has demonstrated this resilience; it has also provided evidence of many problems which have remained unsolved. These are the challenges of the future.

GLOSSARY OF INDIAN TERMS

Agrahara	Freehold land given to Brahmins
Ahimsa	*Non-killing*, non-violence
Alim	Scholar of Islamic law who is entitled to expound the Koran
Arthashastra	Ancient Indian text on politics (artha) ascribed to Kautilya who was supposedly a minister of Chandragupta Maurya. It contains the doctrine of the circle of kings (**rajamandala**)
Arya	*The noble one*, self-assumed name of the Aryan people
Avatara	*Descent*, incarnation of a god, especially Vishnu
Bhadralok	*People of good family*, a Bengali term which refers to the upper castes of brahmins, kayasths and vaidyas, more specifically to their educated members
Bhakti	*Piety*, devotion to a god
Bhoodan	*Landgift*, i.e. donation of surplus land by rich peasants to landless labourers. The Bhoodan Movement was initiated by Vinoba Bhave, a disciple of Mahatma Gandhi
Bombay	*see* **Mumbai**
Calcutta	*see* **Kolkata**
Chakravartin	*Roller of the disc*, i.e. ruler whose sway extends everywhere, imperial title
Chennai	Previously Madras, a name which referred to a **madrasa** located there. Chennai is the old Tamil name of the locality
Chhatra	*Parasol*, belonging to the royal insignia
Dakshinapatha	*The southern way*, the southern highlands (Deccan)
Danda	*Stick*, symbol of (state) power
Dasa, dasyu	*Slave*, enemy of the **arya**
Desh	*Country*. In Maharashtra the land beyond the **Ghats**
Devanagari	Script in which Sanskrit as well as some modern Indian languages (Hindi, Marathi) are written
Dharma	*That which upholds*, i.e. law, religion, morality

371

Dharma-mahamatra	Superintendant of **dharma**, royal emissary, supervisor of morality under Ashoka
Digvijaya	*Conquest of the four quarters* (of the world)
Din-i-Illahi	*Belief in God*, a kind of religious order established by Akbar. Its members belonged to the imperial elite and acknowledged Akbar as their **pir**
Diwan, diwani	The minister of an Indian ruler, the jurisdiction of a diwan. In the Mughal administration the diwan was the minister in charge of civil and revenue affairs under the **nawab**
Diwani adalat	Customary law administered by the **diwan** (as distinct from Islamic law recorded in the Koran)
Fauj, faujdar	*Army, commander of the army* (*see* **nawab**)
Garibi hatao	*Beat Poverty*, election slogan of Indira Gandhi
Ghat	*Step*. It refers to the mountain ranges on the western coast of India, but also to the steps at the banks of a river or tank
Hartal	A strike, particularly of merchants who close their shops as a token of protest against unjust acts of the government
Hasil	*Collection*, i.e. land revenue collection
Hind Swaraj	*'India's Freedom'*, title of Mahatma Gandhi's political manifesto written in 1909
Hindi	North Indian language, written in the **Devanagari** script. National language of the Republic of India
Hindutva	*Hinduness*. Neologism coined by V.D. Savarkar. Also title of his political manifesto first published anonymously in 1924. In contrast with Hinduism as a religious designation, 'Hindutva' is a political term referring to all those who consider India as their fatherland and their **punyabhumi**
Jagir, jagirdar	*A place, a locality, the holder of such a place*. A Persian term used in Mughal India for revenue assignment in lieu of salary or for the maintenance of troops. The holder of such a jagir was usually a **mansabdar**
Jama	*Land revenue assessment*
Janapada	*Place of the people*, realm, Vedic chiefdom
Jati	*Species, birth*, subcaste, nation
Jizya	Poll tax imposed by Muslim rulers on non-believers, i.e on Hindus in India
Kalif	Spiritual and temporal head of the community of believers (Islam)
Karma	*Action*, acts which condition **samsara**

372

Karmayoga	The acquisition of spiritual merit by proper actions (**karma**). There must be no selfish motive for such actions
Khalsa	Directly assessed crownland
Khilafat	Office of the **Kalif** held by the Ottoman sultans, abolished in 1924
Kolkata	Previously Calcutta. Kolkata is derived from Kalighata, i.e. the **ghat** at the temple of the goddess Kali
Kutumbin	*Householder*, agriculturist
Madras	*see* **Chennai**
Madrasa	Islamic religious school
Mahatmya	*Magnanimity*, medieval text praising the merits of a holy place (**tirtha**)
Mandala	*Circle*, cycle of Vedic hymns, district, **rajamandala**
Mansab, **mansabdar**	*Rank, holder of a rank.* Akbar established a scale of such ranks and allotted a **jagir** to each mansabdar (*see also* **sawar**, **zat**)
Mantra	Sacred formula, Vedic hymn
Mantrin	King's counsellor, minister
Masjid	*Mosque*
Matsyanyaya	*Law of the fishes* (the big ones devouring the smaller ones), concept of ancient Indian political theory
Mleccha	(Impure) foreigner, outcast
Mumbai	Previously Bombay. In the regional language Marathi the original name Mumbai was always retained. It refers to Mumba Devi, a local mother goddess also called Mumba Ai (mother Mumba)
Murid	Religious disciple (of a **pir**)
Nabob	Nickname of servants of the East India Company who had enriched themselves by plundering Bengal (from **nawab**)
Nagara	*City*
Nasaq	Land revenue settlement. Mughal assessment based on estimates or on striking a bargain with the landholders. Initially British revenue 'settlements' were arrived at in the same manner
Nastaliq	Persian script in which **Urdu** is written
Nawab	Governor of a province of the Mughal empire. The nawab was also **faujdar** and as such entrusted with enforcing criminal law
Nayak	Cavalry captain (under the Hindu rulers of southern India), in the Vijayanagar empire also the title of the governor of a province

Panchashila	Five Principles. Guidelines of Jawaharlal Nehru's foreign policy. Initially stated in his treaty with China of 1954
Parihara	Immunities attached to freehold land
Peshwa	Major domus of the Maratha kings (comparable to the Shoguns of Japan), the office was held by several generations of a family of Chitpavan brahmins
Pir	Religious preceptor among Muslims, particularly among the **Sufis**. The position of the pir was often hereditary
Punyabhumi	Land in which one can acquire spiritual merit (punya), *see* **Hindutva**
Pur, **pura**	*Rampart*, fortress, town
Purana	*Ancient*, class of sacred texts
Rajamandala	*Circle of kings*. Doctrine expounded in the **Arthashastra**. Basically each king is surrounded by enemies, the kings in the back of these enemies are his natural friends etc.
Rajya	*Kingship*, **rashtra**
Rashtra	*Kingdom*, country
Ryot (raiyat)	A peasant. In revenue terminology a peasant paying land revenue directly to the government (also called 'government tenant'), *see* **ryotwari**
Ryotwari (raiyatwari)	A system of land revenue settlement under which the **ryot** was directly assessed
Samanta	*Neighbour*, vassal, tributary chief
Samsara	*Wandering through*, transmigration, rebirth
Sangha	*Community*, order of Buddhist monks
Satyagraha	*Holding on to truth*. Neologism coined by Mahatma Gandhi for his non-violent resistance to unjust laws. He did not like the term 'passive resistance' as his campaigns were very active
Satyagrahi	A person practising **satyagraha**
Sawar	Amount stipulated for the number of horsemen to be kept by a **mansabdar**. Initially it used to correspond to his salary scale (**zat**), e.g. 7000/7000, but later on the mansabdar was sometimes permitted to reduce the number of horsemen so as to cope with inflation
Senapati	*Leader of the army*. Title of the commander of Indian armies
Sherwani	North Indian male upper garment, a jacket as long as a coat
Shreni	*Guild*
Swaraj	Self-government, freedom
Tirtha	*Ford, bathing place*. Place of pilgrimage, temple city
Ulama	Plural of **alim**

Upanishad	*Sitting down* (to listen to the reading of a sacred text), philosophical texts added to the **Vedas**, *see* **Vedanta**
Urdu	North Indian language which originated in the camp (urdu) of the Great Mughal as a lingua franca with **Hindi** as its base and many Arabic and Persian loanwords, written in the **Nastaliq** script
Vamsha	*Lineage*, dynasty
Varna	*Colour*, name of the four principal castes
Veda	*Knowledge*. Orally transmitted sacred texts (in Vedic Sanskrit) of the Hindus
Vedanta	*End of the Veda*. Philosophical texts (**upanishad**) composed after the Vedic age. General term for Hindu monism
Vezir	Prime minister (of Muslim realms)
Yavana	*Ionian*, a term originally applied to the Greeks, then to the Muslims and to foreigners in general
Zabt	Physical measurement of land for revenue assessment
Zamin, **zamindar**	*Land, landholder*. In Mughal terminology a zamindar was a local magnate entrusted with the collection of land revenue of which he could keep some amount for his own maintenance. In British terminology a zamindar was a landlord who paid land revenue to the government and collected rent from his tenants
Zat	Salary fixed for a **mansabdar** for his personal maintenance, an additional rate (**sawar**) referred to the number of horsemen whom he had to support from his **jagir**

CHRONOLOGY

BC

*c.*6000	Neolithic settlements in Baluchistan
4th millennium	Settlements in the Indus valley
2800–2600	Beginning of Indus civilisation
2600–1700	Civilisation of the great cities in the Indus valley (Mohenjo-Daro, Harappa), in the Panjab (Kalibangan) and Gujarat (Lothal)
2nd millennium	Immigration of the Indo-Aryans
*c.*1400–900	Early Vedic period (*Rigveda*); settlement of the Aryans in the Panjab and the western Ganga–Yamuna Doab
*c.*1000	Iron in India
900–500	Late Vedic period (*Brahmanas*); settlement of the Aryans in the central and eastern Gangetic plain; emergence of the early Mahajanapadas
800–400	Painted Grey Ware in the area of Vedic settlement
500 onwards	Early urbanisation in the eastern Gangetic valley (Kausambi probably earlier)
*c.*518	Gandhara and Sind satrapies of the Persian empire
*c.*500	Magadha emerges as supreme power of the East
*c.*5th century	The Buddha teaches in northern India
*c.*364	Nanda dynasty under Mahapadma
327–325	Alexander in northwest India
*c.*320	Chandragupta establishes the Maurya dynasty
268–233	Emperor Ashoka
261	Ashoka's conquest of Kalinga and his conversion to Buddhism
256	Buddhist missions in south Asia and the Hellenistic world
*c.*248	Independence of the Greeks in Bactria
*c.*185	Pushyamitra kills the last Maurya and establishes the Sunga dynasty (till 73 BC)
*c.*175	Foundation of the Indo-Greek empire
*c.*155–130	Menander, most important king of the Indo-Greeks ('Milindapanho')
after 141	Shakas conquer Bactria
*c.*94	Maues, Shaka king in northwest India
58	Azes I: beginning of Vikrama era

| 1st century | Emergence of the Shatavahanas in central India and King Kharavela in eastern India (Kalinga) |

AD

*c.*20–46	Gondopharnes, Indo-Parthian king in Taxila
early 1st century	Kujala Kadphises unites the Yüe-chi tribes and establishes the Kushana empire
1st century	Intensive trade connections with the Roman empire
78	Shaka era
between 78 and 144	Kanishka's accession to the throne; heyday of the Kushana empire
after 125	Resurgence of the Shatavahanas under Gautamiputra and Vasishtiputra
150	Rudradaman Shaka Kshatrapa in western India
*c.*250	Disintegration of the Shatavahana kingdom
320	Chandragupta I establishes the Gupta dynasty
335–75	Samudragupta, expansion of the Gupta kingdom throughout north India and temporarily to south India
375–413/5	Chandragupta II; Gupta empire at the peak of its power, conquest of the Shaka kingdom in the west and marriage alliance with the Vakatakas of central India; a new climax of Sanskrit poetry (Kalidasa)
405–11	Fa-hsien (Faxian) in India
415–55	Period of peace and cultural expansion under Kumaragupta
455–67	Skandagupta; first attack of the Huns
467–97	Budhagupta, last important Gupta ruler
*c.*500–27	Huns rule over north India under Toramana and Mihirakula; decline of the classical urban culture of the north
543–66	Pulakeshin I, rise of the Chalukyas of Badami in central India
*c.*574	Simhavishnu, rise of the Pallavas of Kanchipuram, south India
606–47	Harsha of Kanauj
609–42	Pulakeshin II of Badami; hegemony of the Chalukyas over central India
*c.*630	Pulakeshin defeats Harsha of Kanauj; end of northern India's hegemony
630–43	Hsiuen-tsang (Xuanzang) in India
680–720	Zenith of the Pallava kingdom under Narasimhavarman II (shore temple at Mahabalipuram)
711	Arabs conquer Sind
752–6	Dantidurga overthrows the Chalukyas and establishes the Rashtrakuta dynasty
770–821	Gopala establishes the Pala dynasty of Bihar and Bengal, under his successor Dharmapala hegemony over eastern India
788–820	Shankara
783	Vatsaraja establishes the Gurjara-Pratihara dynasty of Rajasthan
late 8th century	Beginning of the great interregional conflicts

836–85	Gurjara-Pratiharas become the most powerful dynasty of India under Bhoja
860	King Balaputra of Sumatra establishes a monastery at Nalanda
871–907	Aditya I overthrows the Pallavas and establishes the Chola dynasty
939–68	Rashtrakutas become the most powerful dynasty under Krishna III; defeat of the Cholas
973	Taila overthrows the Rashtrakutas and establishes the Chalukya dynasty of Kalyani
985–1014	Rajaraja establishes the Chola empire, conquest of south India and Sri Lanka
988–1038	Mahipala, resurgence of the Palas of Bihar and Bengal
1000–27	Mahmud of Ghazni raids north India in 17 'expeditions' (destruction of Mathura, Kanauj and Somnath temple)
1014–47	Rajendra Chola, 'The Great'
1023/3	Chola army advances to the Ganga and defeats the Somavamshis of Orissa and the Palas of Bengal
1025	Conquest of Srivijaya (Sumatra and Malaya) by a maritime expedition of the Cholas
1070–1120	Kulottunga I of Vengi ascends the Chola throne
1077–1147	Anantavarman Chodaganga of Kalinga conquers central Orissa and establishes the Ganga empire
1077–1120	Ramapala, the last important Pala king, reconquers parts of Bengal
1137	Death of the Vaishnava reformer Ramanuja
1179–1205	Lakshmana Sena, last Hindu king of Bengal
1192	Battle of Tarain, Mahmud of Ghur defeats a Rajput confederation under Prithiviraja; in the following years conquest of north and east India by Muslim armies
1206	Aibak establishes the sultanate of Delhi
1210–36	Iltutmish, sultan of Delhi
1246–79	Rajendra III, last Chola king
c.1250	Sun Temple of Konarak
1253–75	Under Jatavarman Vira Pandya, temporary resurgences of the Pandyas of Madurai
1266–87	Balban, sultan of Delhi
1290–1320	Khalji dynasty of Delhi
1293	Marco Polo in south India
1297–1306	Delhi sultanate repulses several attacks of the Mongols
1296–1316	Ala-ud-din, sultan of Delhi, radical administrative reform
1309–11	Conquest of south India by the sultanate of Delhi
1320–88	Tughluq dynasty of Delhi
1325–51	Muhammad Tughluq
1327	Daulatabad in central India temporarily the new capital of the sultanate; beginning of the disintegration
1334–70	Sultanate of Madurai
1338	Separate sultanate of Bengal
1346	Foundation of the Vijayanagara empire
1347	Bahman Shah establishes the Bahmani sultanate, central India

1351–88	Firoz Shah, the last important sultan of Delhi
1361	Firoz Shah raids Orissa
1370	Vijayanagara conquers the sultanate of Madurai
1398	Timur devastates Delhi
1403	Separate sultanate of Gujarat
1406–22	Conquests of the east coast by King Devaraja II of Vijayanagara
1414–51	Sayyids of Delhi
1435–67	Kapilendra establishes the Suryavamsha dynasty of Orissa
1451–1526	Lodi dynasty; renewal of the Delhi sultanate
1463	Kapilendra conquers the east coast up to the Kaveri
1481	Murder of Prime Minister Mahmud Gawan and beginning of the disintegration of the Bahmani sultanate
1489–1505	Sikander Lodi; Agra new capital of the Delhi sultanate
1498	Vasco da Gama in Calicut
1509–29	Krishnadeva Raya, zenith of the power of Vijayanagara
1510	The Portuguese conquer Goa
1526	Baber, the Great Mughal, defeats the sultan of Delhi
1542	Sher Shah conquers north India and introduces a new system of revenue administration
1554	Humayun, the Great Mughal, defeats the successor of Sher Shah and re-establishes Mughal rule
1556	Akbar succeeds Humayun
1565	Battle of Talikota; Vijayanagar army defeated by the joint forces of the successor states of the Bahmani sultanate
1574	Akbar conquers Gujarat
1586	Philip II, King of Spain and Portugal, concludes the pepper contract with the German merchants Fugger and Welser
1600	Foundation of the East India Company in London
1602	Foundation of the Dutch East India Company
1605–27	Jahangir, the Great Mughal, and his wife Nur Jahan preside over the flowering of Persian court culture in India
1615–18	Sir Thomas Roe, the first British ambassador, stays at the Mughal court
1627–58	Shah Jahan, the Great Mughal, conquers large parts of the northern Deccan, builds Red Fort (Delhi) and Taj Mahal (Agra)
1636–44	Mughal Prince Aurangzeb viceroy of the Deccan
1646	Shivaji establishes his strongholds in the region of Pune, Maharashtra
1655	Aurangzeb raids the sultanate of Golconda
1658–1707	Mughal empire at its height under Aurangzeb, the Great Mughal, who brings about its decline by exhausting its resources
1664	Inauguration of the French East India Company
1668–1706	François Martin, the founder of French power in India
1670	Shivaji raids Surat, the port of the Mughal empire
1680	Shivaji dies
1681	Aurangzeb establishes Aurangabad (Deccan) as new capital
1686–7	Aurangzeb annexes the sultanates of Bijapur and Golconda
1707–19	Three weak Great Mughals follow each other in quick succession

1714–20	Balaji Vishwanath, the first Peshwa (chief minister) of the Maratha king, Shahu, establishes a new system of a centralised collection of tribute
1724	Nizam-ul-Mulk Asaf Jah, viceroy of the Deccan and vezir of the Mughal empire, leaves Delhi and establishes a quasi-independent state at Hyderabad, other Mughal provinces (Bengal, Oudh) follow suit
1720–40	Peshwa Baji Rao I extends Maratha rule, raids Delhi
1739	Nadir Shah, ruler of Persia, sacks Delhi and steals the Mughals' peacock throne
1742–54	The French governor, Dupleix, exploits the feuds among Indian rulers and builds up an Indian infantry in French service
1746	The French admiral, La Bourdonnais, captures Madras
1751	Robert Clive captures and defends Arcot
1757	Battle of Plassey, Clive defeats the nawab of Bengal and installs Mir Jafar
1760	Battle of Wandiwash, British troops defeat the French
1761	Battle of Panipat, the Afghan ruler, Ahmad Shah Durrani, defeats the Marathas who withdraw to the south
1764	Battle of Baxar, the joint forces of the Great Mughal and of the nawabs of Bengal and Oudh are defeated by the British
1765	Clive returns to India as governor of Bengal and accepts the grant of civil authority (Diwani) of Bengal from the Great Mughal on behalf of the East India Company
1769	Haider Ali, who had usurped the throne of Mysore in 1761, conquers large parts of southern India
1770	Bengal famine, one-third of the population dies
1773	Regulation Act, Warren Hastings becomes governor general
1782	Haider Ali dies; his son Tipu Sultan continues the fight against the British power in India; Hastings concludes the peace treaty of Salbei with the Marathas so as to concentrate on the south
1784	Second Regulation Act, stronger position of the governor general, establishment of the Board of Control in London
1785	Impeachment of Warren Hastings; his successor, Lord Cornwallis, defeats Tipu Sultan, annexes half of his territory
1793	Permanent Settlement (Land Revenue) of Bengal
1799	Final defeat and death of Tipu Sultan
1803	The nawab of Oudh cedes the southern and western districts of his territories to the British
1818	Final British victory over the Marathas
1843–8	Consolidation of British territorial rule in India; conquest of Sind and of the Panjab
1857	Mutiny of the Indian soldiers of the army of the East India Company and revolt of the landlords of Oudh and of some Indian princes
1858	East India Company dissolved, India under the Crown
1861	Establishment of the Imperial Legislative Council (Indian members nominated by the viceroy)

1877	Queen Victoria assumes the title Empress of India
1880	Defeat in the Afghan war influences British elections, Gladstone sends Liberal viceroy, Lord Ripon, to India
1885	First Indian National Congress meets in Bombay
1892	Reform of Legislative Councils; more Indian members
1905	Partition of Bengal, national agitation, boycott of British goods (Swadeshi campaign)
1906	Foundation of the Muslim League
1907	Split of the National Congress ('Moderates'/'Extremists')
1908	Bal Gangadhar Tilak sentenced to six years' imprisonment
1909	Morley–Minto reform, separate electorates for Muslims
1916	Lucknow (Lakhnau) Pact between National Congress and Muslim League (Tilak–Jinnah)
1917	Montagu declaration on 'responsible government'
1918	Split of the National Congress and establishment of the National Liberal Federation
1919	Rowlatt Acts and Gandhi's Rowlatt satyagraha. Massacre at Jallianwala Bagh, Amritsar
1920	Montagu–Chelmsford reform, dyarchy in the provinces
1920–2	Gandhi's non-cooperation campaign and the Khilafat agitation of the Indian Muslims
1928	Simon Commission visits India
1930	Gandhi's 'salt march' and civil disobedience campaign; first Round Table Conference in London boycotted by Congress
1930–1	Great Depression (fall of agrarian prices) hits India, peasant unrest articulated by Congress
1931	Gandhi–Irwin Pact; Gandhi participates in second Round Table Conference
1932	Resumption of civil disobedience campaign; Gandhi–Ambedkar Pact (reserved seats instead of separate electorates for untouchables)
1933	End of civil disobedience campaign
1934	Elections to the Central Legislative Assembly, Congress wins several seats
1935	Government of India Act
1936	Elections, Congress wins majority in seven provinces
1937	Congress accepts office after initial protest against governor's emergency powers
1939	Second World War begins, Congress ministers resign
1940	Lahore Resolution ('Pakistan Resolution') of the Muslim League, 'Two Nations' theory articulated by Jinnah
1942	Cripps Mission and 'Quit India' resolution; 'August revolution'
1944	Gandhi–Jinnah talks end without results
1945	Simla Conference, national interim government cannot be formed due to Jinnah's demands
1946	Elections, Muslim League very successful; cabinet mission; 'Direct Action Day' of the Muslim League (16 August) and 'Great Calcutta Killing'; interim government: Jawaharlal Nehru prime minister

1947	Independence and partition (Pakistan, 14 August; India, 15 August); Kashmir conflict begins
1948	Assassination of Mahatma Gandhi (30 January)
1950	Constitution of Republic of India inaugurated: Rajendra Prasad (president), J. Nehru (prime minister)
1951	Nehru mediates in the Korean war
1952	First general election, Congress wins
1952–6	First five-year plan
1954	Indian mediation in Indochina; Pakistan joins American pacts
1955	Bandung Conference of Afro-Asian states; Krushchev and Bulganin visit India; States Reorganisation Committee recommends creation of linguistic provinces
1957–61	Second five-year plan, emphasis on industrialisation
1957	Second general election, Congress wins with the exception of Kerala (Communist Chief Minister: E.M.S. Namboodiripad)
1959	'President's Rule' in Kerala; foundation of the Swatantra Party; Dalai Lama flees from Tibet to India; beginning of open confrontation between China and India
1960	Indus Water Treaty with Pakistan, Nehru–Ayub Khan talks; Nehru's attempt at mediation in UN after breakdown of Paris summit; division of Bombay state between Gujarat and Maharashtra
1961	Non-aligned Conference in Belgrade; Nehru–Chou Enlai talks in Delhi; liberation of Goa
1962	Third general election; Congress wins; border war with China
1962–6	Third five-year plan, rapid expansion of heavy industry
1964	Nehru dies; succeeded by Lal Bahadur Shastri
1965	Conflict with Pakistan over the Rann of Cutch; Pakistan's attack on road to Kashmir, Indian counter-offensive directed at Lahore
1966	Conference at Tashkent (USSR); Shastri dies, succeeded by Indira Gandhi; devaluation of the rupee, bad harvests, increase of agrarian prices
1967	Fourth general election, Congress maintains majority position at the centre but loses control of several states
1968	'Green Revolution' begins; fourth five-year plan postponed
1969	Elections in several states, no consolidation of Congress position; Indira Gandhi splits Congress, drops 'old guard'
1971	Elections (centre only), Indira Gandhi's Congress wins; Indo-Soviet Friendship Treaty; Indian army helps in liberation of Bangladesh, Pakistan's troops surrender in Dhaka
1972	Indira Gandhi's meeting with Bhutto at Simla
1974	Oil price rise and bad harvest lead to rapid inflation; strike of railway workers; underground test of a nuclear device
1975	Protest movement led by Jayaprakash Narayan; High Court judgment against Indira Gandhi in election case; Congress defeat in Gujarat; 'Emergency', many opposition leaders arrested
1976	Indira Gandhi first postpones elections and then suddenly fixes election date for March 1977

1977	Indira Gandhi defeated, Morarji Desai becomes prime minister, former opposition parties merge and form Janata Party
1979	Desai resigns, Charan Singh leads caretaker government
1980	Indira Gandhi wins elections; Sanjay Gandhi, Congress secretary general, dies in private aircraft accident
1983	Elections in Andhra Pradesh (Telugu Desam Party: N.T. Rama Rao) and Karnataka (Janata Party: Ramkrishna Hegde) lead to defeat of Congress (I)
1984	Unrest in Panjab, Indian army action in Golden Temple of Amritsar; Indira Gandhi assassinated by Sikh members of body-guard (31 October) and succeeded by Rajiv Gandhi; December elections won by him
1985	Budget signals change in economic policy; Assam and Panjab Accords; elections in Assam won by Asom Gana Parishad, in the Panjab by the Akali Dal
1987	President's Rule in the Panjab, Lok Dal wins election in Haryana; V.P. Singh leads opposition. Gandhi and Sri Lanka President Jayewardene sign accord, Indian peace-keeping force in northern Sri Lanka, unable to disarm Tamil terrorists
1988	Panjab unrest continues, Golden Temple again stormed by Indian army
1989	Conflict with Nepal on foreign policy and migration. Sri Lanka President Premadasa asks Indian troops to quit. Soviet withdrawal from Afghanistan relieves India, but India pledged to support Kabul regime. Elections in November 1989, Congress defeated; Gandhi resigns, V.P. Singh forms government
1990	Indian troops leave Sri Lanka. Ramjanmabhumi campaign, BJP President Advani heads procession to Ayodhya, arrested in October, V.P. Singh's government falls, Chandrashekhar forms another minority government, November
1991	Chandrashekhar's government toppled by Congress. Rajiv Gandhi assassinated in election campaign near Madras, 21 May. P.V. Narasimha Rao forms new minority government (Congress) programme of structural adjustment. Rupee devalued
1992	Destruction of Babri Masjid, Ayodhya, 6 December. Four BJP state governments dismissed
1993	Narasimha Rao visits China, agreement on line of actual control. Elections in Himachal Pradesh, Madhya Pradesh, Rajasthan and Uttar Pradesh. BJP loses votes
1994	Elections in Karnataka, won by Janata Party; Andhra Pradesh, won by N.T. Rama Rao's party Telugu Desam
1995	Elections in Gujarat, won by BJP, and in Maharashtra where BJP and Shiv Sena form a coalition government
1996	Federal elections, April–May, result in hung Parliament. A.B. Vajpayee (BJP) Prime Minister, 15–27 May. H.D. Deve Gowda (National Front) Prime Minister, 1 June
1997	Deve Gowda replaced by Inder Kumar Gujral as prime minister, April

1998	April, Federal Elections. Vajpayee (BJP) forms coalition government. May, Indian atom bomb test followed by tests in Pakistan
1999	Vajpayee visits Lahore to promote peace. April, Vajpayee defeated (vote of no confidence), remains acting prime minister. Pakistan launches attack across Line of Control in Kashmir (Kargil sector). November, Vajpayee's coalition government re-elected
2000	March, President Clinton visits India, new ties of cooperation. August, three new states created: Uttar Anchal, capital Dehra Dun (northern part of Uttar Pradesh); Chhattisgarh, capital Raipur (eastern part of Madhya Pradesh); Jharkhand, capital Ranchi (southern part of Bihar)
2002	Hindu–Muslim clashes in Gujarat, pogrom in Ahmedabad, Chief Minister Narendra Modi stresses Hindu communialism, wins election
2003	Vajpayee announces new peace initiative (Pakistan), visits China
2004	April-May. Federal elections resulted in the emergence of a new coalition government (United Progressive Alliance) led by the Congress Party and including several smaller regional parties, a minority government (217 seats) which depended on the 'outside support' of the two Communist parties and of the Samajwadi Party (altogether 89 seats). Congress Party President Sonia Gandhi renounced her claim to head the government and suggested Manmohan Singh as Prime Minister, she subsequently joined his cabinet. Singh would pursue a policy of economic reform supported by Finance Minister P. Chidambaram. Assembly elections in Andhra Pradesh and Karnataka, which paralled the federal elections, produced contrasting results. In Andhra Pradesh, they led to the fall of Chandrababu Naidu (Telugu Desam Party) and the victory of the Congress Party led by Y. S. Rajashekhara Reddy. In Karnataka, the BJP achieved an unprecedented success (84 seats) but could not form a government as the Congress Party (61 seats) and the Janata Party (56 seats) joined in a coalition

BIBLIOGRAPHY AND NOTES

The first section of the bibliography contains references to general books on Indian history. The subsequent sections refer to individual chapters of this book. Notes are restricted to the sources of quotations inserted in the text. These notes are printed at the end of the bibliography of the relevant sections within chapters.

General works on Indian history

G. Berkemer *et al.* (eds), *Explorations in the History of South Asia. Essays in Honour of Dietmar Rothermund* (New Delhi, 2001)

S. Bhattacharya and R. Thapar (eds), *Situating Indian History. For Sarvepalli Gopal* (Delhi, 1986)

N. Chandhoke (ed.), *Mapping Histories. Essays Presented to Ravinder Kumar* (London, 2002)

B.D. Chattopadhyaya, *Studying Early India. Archaeology, Texts and Historical Issues* (New Delhi, 2003)

J. Gommans and Om Prakash (eds), *Circumambulations in South Asian History. Essays in Honour of Dirk H.A. Kolff* (Leiden, 2003)

D.N. Jha (ed.), *Society and Ideology in India. Essays in Honour of R. S. Sharma* (New Delhi, 1996)

J. Keay, *India. A History* (London, 2000)

H. Kulke, *Indien. Von den frühen Hochkulturen bis zum Untergang des Mogulreiches* (Munich, 2004)

D.D. Kosambi, *Combined Methods in Indology and Other Writings*, ed. by B.D. Chattopadhyaya (New Delhi, 2002)

R.C. Majumdar *et al.* (eds), *The History and Culture of the Indian People*, 11 vols (Bombay, 1951 ff.)

C. Markovits, *A History of Modern India* (London, 2002)

V.A. Smith (ed.), *The Oxford History of India* (Oxford, 1919; 3rd rev. edn, Oxford, 1958)

B. Stein, *A History of India* (Oxford, 1998)

R. Thapar, *Cultural Pasts. Essays in Early Indian History* (New Delhi, 2000)

R. Thapar, *Early India. From its Origins to AD 1300* (London, 2002)

R. Thapar and P. Spear, *History of India*, 2 vols (Harmondsworth, 1966)

The New Cambridge History of India (abbreviation *NCHI*): see references to individual authors

S. Wolpert, *A New History of India* (5th edn, New York, 1997)

385

Area studies

B.D. Chattopadhyaya, *A Survey of Historical Geography of Ancient India* (New Delhi, 1987)

R.G. Fox (ed.), *Realm and Region in Traditional India* (Delhi, 1977)

H. Kulke and D. Rothermund (eds), *Regionale Tradition in Südasien* (Wiesbaden, 1985)

R.L. Singh, *India: A Regional Geography* (Varanasi, 1971)

O.H.K. Spate *et al.*, *India and Pakistan: A Central and Regional Geography* (3rd edn, London, 1967)

General cultural studies

Th. de Bary (ed.), *Sources of Indian Tradition* (5th edn, New York, 1966)

A.L. Basham, *The Wonder that was India* (London, 1954)

A.L. Basham (ed.), *A Cultural History of India* (Oxford, 1975)

C. Breckenridge and P. van der Veer, *Orientalism and the Post-Colonial Predicament. Perspectives on South Asia* (Philadelphia, 1993)

V. Dalmia and H. von Stietencron, *Representing Hinduism. The Construction of Religious Traditions and National Identity* (New Delhi, 1995)

J. Filliozat and L. Renou, *L'Inde classique*, 2 vols (Paris, 1947–53)

W. Halbfass, *India and Europe. An Essay in Understanding* (Albany, 1988)

R. Inden, *Imagining India* (Oxford, 1990)

D.D. Kosambi, *The Culture and Civilisation of Ancient India in Historical Outline* (London, 1965)

N.R. Ray, *A Sourcebook of Indian Civilization*, ed. by B.D. Chattopadhyaya and R. Chakravarti (Calcutta, 2000)

S.A.A. Rizvi, *The Wonder that was India, vol. II (1200–1700)* (London, 1987)

G. Sontheimer and H. Kulke (eds), *Hinduism Reconsidered* (2nd rev. edn, Delhi, 1996)

Literature, religion, art and society

H. Bechert and R. Gombrich (eds), *The World of Buddhism* (London, 1984)

S.K. Chatterji, *Languages and Literatures of Modern India* (Calcutta, 1963)

A. Dallapiccola and S. Zingel Avé-Lallemant (eds), *Islam and Indian Regions*, 2 vols (Stuttgart, 1993)

L. Dumont, *Homo Hierarchicus: The Caste System and its Implications* (Chicago, 1980)

S. Fuchs, *The Aboriginal Tribes of India* (Delhi, 1973)

J. Gonda (ed.), *A History of Indian Literature*, 10 vols (Wiesbaden, 1974 ff.)

F. Hardy, *The Religious Culture of India. Power, Love and Wisdom* (Cambridge, 1994)

J.C. Harle, *The Art and Architecture of the Indian Subcontinent* (Harmondsworth, 1986)

E. Kulke, *The Parsees in India. A Minority as an Agent of Change* (Munich, 1974)

E. Lamotte, *History of Indian Buddhism* (Louvain, 1988)

W.H. McLeod, *The Sikhs: History, Religion and Society* (New York, 1989)

T.N. Madan (ed.), *Religion in India* (Delhi, 1991)

A. Michaels, *Hinduism, Past and Present*, trans. by B. Harshaw (Princeton, 2004)
A. Schimmel, *Islam in the Indian Subcontinent* (Leiden, 1980)
K.S. Singh, *People of India: An Introduction* (Calcutta, 1992)
C. Sivaramamurti, *The Art of India* (New York, 1977)
M. Winternitz, *History of Indian Literature*, 3 vols (New Delhi, 1963–7)
H. Zimmer, *The Art of Indian Asia*, 2 vols (New York, 1955)

Further bibliographical information

H. Kulke, H.-J. Leue, J. Lütt and D. Rothermund, *Indische Geschichte vom Altertum bis zur Gegenwart: Literaturbericht über neuere Veröffentlichungen* (*Historische Zeitschrift, Sonderheft X*) (Munich, 1981)

INTRODUCTION: HISTORY AND THE ENVIRONMENT

K. Davis, *The Population of India and Pakistan* (Princeton, 1951)
P. Nag and S. Sengupta, *A Geography of India* (New Delhi, 1992)
S. Raju *et al.*, *Atlas of Women and Men in India* (New Delhi, 1999)
J. Schwartzberg (ed.), *Historical Atlas of South Asia* (Chicago, 1978)
D.E. Sopher (ed.), *Exploration of India. Geographical Perspectives on Society and Culture* (Ithaca, 1980)
B. Subbarao, *The Personality of India* (Baroda, 1958)

CHAPTER 1: EARLY CIVILISATIONS OF THE NORTHWEST

Prehistory and the Indus civilisation

D.P. Agrawal and D.K. Chakrabarti (eds), *Essays in Indian Protohistory* (Delhi, 1979)
B. and R. Allchin, *The Rise of Civilization in India and Pakistan* (Cambridge, 1982)
S. Asthana, *Pre-Harappan Cultures of India and the Borderland* (New Delhi, 1985)
D.K. Chakrabarti, *The External Trade of the Indus Civilization* (New Delhi, 1990)
A. Ghosh (ed.), *An Encyclopaedia of Indian Archaeology*, 2 vols (New Delhi, 1989)
J.F. Jarrige and M. Lechavellier, 'Excavations at Mehrgarh, Baluchistan: Their Significance in the Context of the Indo-Pakistan Borderlands', *South Asian Archaeology*, ed. by M. Taddei, Naples, 1979, pp. 463–535
J.M. Kenoyer, *The Ancient Cities of the Indus Civilization* (Karachi, 1998)
J. Marshall, *Mohenjo-Daro and the Indus Civilization*, 3 vols (London, 1931)
G.L. Possehl (ed.), *Harappan Civilization* (rev. edn, New Delhi, 1993)
S. Ratnagar, *Enquiries into the Political Organization of Harappan Society* (Pune, 1991)
Vergessene Städte am Indus: Frühe Kulturen in Pakistan vom 8.-2. Jahrtausend v. Chr. (Mainz: R. von Zabern, 1987)

Immigration and settlement of the Indo-Aryans

The Indo-Aryans and their migrations

J. Bronkhorst and M.M. Deshpande (eds), *Aryan and Non-Aryan in South Asia. Interpretation and Ideology* (Cambridge, Mass., 1999)

E. Bryant, *The Quest for Origins of Vedic Culture. The Indo-Aryan Migration Debate* (Oxford, 2001)

G. Erdosy (ed.), *The Indo-Aryans of Ancient South Asia: Language, Culture and Ethnicity* (Berlin, 1995)

A. Parpola, 'The Coming of the Aryans to Iran and India and the Cultural and Ethnic Identity of the Dasas', *Studia Orientalia*, vol. 64, 1988, pp. 195–302

C. Renfrew, *Archaeology and Language: The Puzzle of Indo-European Origins* (London, 1987)

R.S. Sharma, *Advent of the Aryans in India* (New Delhi, 1999)

P. Thieme, 'The "Aryan" Gods of the Mitanni Treaties', *Journal of the American Oriental Society*, vol. 80, 1960, pp. 301–17

T.R. Trautmann, *Aryans and British India* (New Delhi, 1997)

Translations

J. Eggeling, *The Shatapatha-Brahmana According to the Text of the Madhyandina School*, 5 vols (Oxford, 1882–1900)

K.F. Geldner, *Rig-veda: Aus dem Sanskrit ins Deutsche übersetzt*, 4 vols (Cambridge, Mass., 1951–7)

R.T.H. Griffiths, *The Hymns of the Rig-Veda* (Benares, 1896–7)

W.D. Whitney, *Atharva-Veda Samhita*, 2 vols (Cambridge, Mass., 1905)

Archaeology of the Vedic period

D.K. Chakrabarti, *Theoretical Issues in Indian Archaeology* (New Delhi, 1988)

M. Lal, *Settlement History and Rise of Civilization in Ganga–Yamuna Doab, from 1500 BC to AD 300* (Delhi, 1984)

T.N. Roy, *The Ganges Civilization: A Critical Archaeological Study of the Painted Grey Ware and Northern Black Polished Ware Periods of the Ganga Plains of India* (New Delhi, 1983)

B.K. Thapar, *Recent Archaeological Discoveries in India* (Paris, UNESCO, 1985)

V. Tripathi, *The Painted Grey Ware, an Iron Age Culture of Northern India* (Delhi, 1976)

Social and political development

J.C. Heesterman, *The Ancient Indian Royal Consecration* (s'Grafenhage, 1957)

D.N. Jha, *Ancient India. A Historical Outline* (New Delhi, 1998)

W. Rau, *Staat und Gesellschaft im alten Indien nach den Brahmana-Texten dargestellt* (Wiesbaden, 1957)

K. Roy, *The Emergence of Monarchy in North India: Eighth–Fourth Centuries BC as Reflected in the Brahmanical Tradition* (Delhi, 1994)

H. Scharfe, *The State in Indian Tradition* (Leiden, 1989)

R.S. Sharma, *Material Culture and Social Formations in Ancient India* (Madras, 1983)

R.S. Sharma, *Aspects of Political Ideas and Institutions in Ancient India*, (3rd rev. edn, Delhi, 1991)

R.S. Sharma, *The State and the Varna Formation in the Mid-Ganga Plains. An Ethnoarchaeological View* (New Delhi, 1996)

J.W. Spellman, *Political Theory of Ancient India: A Study of Kingship from Earliest Times to circa AD 300* (Oxford, 1964)

R. Thapar, *Ancient Indian Social History* (Delhi, 1978)

R. Thapar, *From Lineage to State: Social Formations in Mid-first Millennium BC in the Ganga Valley* (Bombay, 1984) repr. in *History and Beyond* (New Delhi, 2000)

Notes (pp. 37–42)

1 Quotations from the Rigveda mainly from Griffiths, *op. cit.*
2 Jaiminiya Upanishad Brahmana, 1, 35, 7 (quoted from W. Rau, *Staat und Gesellschaft*, p. 53).
3 Shatapatha Brahmana, 1, 3, 2, 15.
4 Maitrayani Samhita, 1, 8, 3; see also W. Rau, *Töpferei und Tongeschirr im vedischen Indien* (Wiesbaden, 1972), p. 69.

CHAPTER 2: THE GREAT ANCIENT EMPIRES

The rise of the Gangetic culture and the great empires of the east

H. Bechert (ed.), *When Did the Buddha Live? The Controversy on the Dating of the Historical Buddha* (Delhi, 1995)

G. Bongard-Levin, *Mauryan India* (New Delhi, 1985)

S. Chattopadhyaya, *The Achaemenids and India* (2nd edn, Delhi, 1974)

P.H.L. Eggermont, *The Chronology of the Reign of Asoka Moriya* (Leiden, 1956)

G. Fussman, 'Central and Provincial Administration in Ancient India: The Problem of the Mauryan Empire', *Indian Historical Review*, vol. 14, 1987/88, pp. 43–72

E. Hultzsch, *Inscriptions of Asoka*, vol. I of *Corpus Inscriptionum Indicarum* (Oxford, 1925)

J.W. McCrindle, *Ancient India as Described by Megasthenes and Arrian* (Calcutta/London, 1877)

R.C. Majumdar, *Classical Accounts of India* (Calcutta, 1960)

B.N. Mukherjee, *Studies in the Aramaic Edicts of Asoka* (Calcutta, 1984)

U. Schneider, *Die großen Felsen-Edikte Ashokas: Kritische Ausgabe, Übersetzung und Analyse der Texte* (Wiesbaden, 1978)

D.C. Sircar, *Ashokan Studies* (Calcutta, 1979)

R. Thapar, *Asoka and the Decline of the Mauryas* (London, 1961)

R. Thapar, *The Mauryas Revisited* (Calcutta, 1987)

K.N. Wagle, *Society at the Time of the Buddha* (Bombay, 1995)

Urbanisation of the Ganges valley

F.R. Allchin, *The Archaeology of Early Historic South Asia: The Emergence of Cities and States* (Cambridge, 1995)

I. Banga (ed.), *The City in Indian History* (Delhi, 1994)

D.K. Chakravarti, *Ancient Indian Cities* (Delhi, 1995)

G. Erdosy, *Urbanisation in Early Historic India* (Oxford, 1988)

A. Ghosh, *The City in Early Historical India* (Simla, 1973)

H. Härtel, 'Archaeological Research on Ancient Buddhist Sites', *The Dating of the Historical Buddha*, ed. by H. Bechert, vol. 1 (Göttingen, 1991), pp. 61–89

D. Schlingloff, *Die altindische Stadt* (Wiesbaden, 1970)

H. Spodek and D.M. Srinivasan (eds), *Urban Form and Meaning in South Asia – The Shaping of Cities from Prehistoric to Precolonial Times* (Washington, 1993)

V.K. Thakur, *Urbanisation in Ancient India* (New Delhi, 1981)

Arthashastra of Kautalya

R.P. Kangle, *The Kautiliya Arthashastra*, 3 vols (Bombay, 1960–65)

H. Scharfe, *Untersuchungen zur Staatslehre des Kautalya* (Wiesbaden, 1968)

T.R. Trautmann, *Kautilya and the Arthasastra* (Leiden, 1971)

Notes (pp. 50–6)

1 Maitrayani Samhita, 4, 7, 9 (W. Rau, *Staat und Gesellschaft*, p. 13).
2 Jaiminiya-Brahmana, 3, 146 (W. Rau, ibid., p. 14).
3 Katakam, 26, 2 (W. Rau, ibid., p. 13).
4 Shatapatha-Brahmana, 1, 4, 1, 14–16.
5 Ashoka's inscriptions are quoted from E. Hultzsch, *Inscriptions of Asoka*.

The end of the Maurya empire and the northern invaders

G. Fussman, 'Documents, epigraphiques Kouchans', *Bulletin de l'Ecole Française d'Extrême-Orient*, vol. 61, 1974, pp. 1–66

H. Härtel, *Excavations at Sonkh: 2500 Years of a Town in Mathura District* (Berlin, 1993)

K. Karttunen, *India and the Helenistic World* (Helsinki, 1997)

B.L. Lahiri, *Indigenous States of Northern India (circa 200 BC to AD 320)* (Calcutta, 1974)

J.E. van Lohuizen-de Leeuw, *The 'Scythian' Period* (Leiden, 1949)

B.N. Mukherjee, *The Rise and Fall of the Kushana Empire* (Calcutta, 1988)

K.A. Nilakanta Sastri (ed.), *Mauryas and Satavahanas, 325 BC–AD 300, vol. 2 of Comprehensive History of India* (Bombay, 1956)

W.W. Tarn, *The Greeks in Baktria and India* (2nd edn, Cambridge, 1951)

Notes (pp. 75–83)

1 R.C. Majumdar, *Classical Accounts of India* (Delhi, 1960), p. 286.

2   H. Jacobi, 'Das Kalakacarya–Kathanakam', *ZDMG*, vol. 34, 1880, pp. 247–318.
3   For further details of the present debate on the Kanishka era and Kushana chronology, see E. Errington and J. Cribb (eds), *The Crossroads of Asia – Transformation in Image and Symbol in the Art of Ancient Afghanistan and Pakistan* (Cambridge, 1992); G. Fussman, 'L'inscription de Rabatak et l'origine de l'ère saka', in: *Journal asiatique*, vol. 286 (1998), pp. 571–651; M. Alram, D. Klimburg-Salter (eds), *Coins, Art and Chronology. Essays in the pre-Islamic History of the Indo-Iranian Borderlands* (Vienna, 1999); H. Falk, 'The Yuga of Sphujiddhvaja and the Era of the Kushanas', in: *Silk Road Art and Archaeology*, 7 (2001), pp. 121–36.
4   F. Kielhorn, 'Junagadh Inscription of Rudradaman', *Epigraphia Indica*, vol. 8, 1905, pp. 36–49.

The classical age of the Guptas

A. Agrawal, *Rise and Fall of the Imperial Guptas* (Delhi, 1989)
H. Bakker, *The Vakatakas. An Essay in Hindu Iconology* (Groningen, 1997)
B.C. Chhabra *et al.* (eds), *Reappraising Gupta History for S.R. Goyal* (New Delhi, 1992)
S.R. Goyal, *A History of the Imperial Guptas* (Allahabad, 1967)
P.L. Gupta, *The Imperial Guptas*, 2 vols (Varanasi, 1974–9)
S.K. Maity, *The Imperial Guptas and their Times, c. AD 300–550* (Delhi, 1975)
R.S. Sharma, *Urban Decay in India (c.300–c.1000)* (New Delhi, 1987)
B.L. Smith, *Essays on Gupta Culture* (New Delhi, 1983)
U. Thakur, *The Hunas in India* (Varanasi, 1967)

Notes (pp. 87–93)

1   J.F. Fleet, *Inscriptions of the Early Gupta Kings and their Successors*, vol. 3 of *Corpus Inscriptionum Indicarum* (Calcutta, 1888), pp. 1–17.
2   Translated by San Shih, *A Record of the Buddhist Countries by Fa-hsien* (Peking, 1957), pp. 34f.

The rise of south India

V. Begley and R.D. de Puma, *Rome and India: The Ancient Sea Trade* (Delhi, 1992)
M.F. Boussac and J.F. Salles (eds), *Athens, Aden and Arikamedu: Essays on the Interrelations between India, Arabia and the Eastern Mediterranean* (New Delhi, 1995)
L. Casson (ed.), *The Periplus Maris Erythraei* (Princeton, 1989)
K.A. Nilakanta Sastri, *A History of South India from Prehistoric Times to the Fall of Vijayanagara* (Madras, 1955)
A. Parasher-Sen (ed.), *Social and Economic History of Early Deccan: Some Interpretations* (Delhi, 1993)
H.P. Ray, *Monastery and Guild: Commerce under the Satavahanas* (Delhi, 1986)
H.P. Ray and J.F. Salles (eds), *Tradition and Archaeology: Early Maritime Contacts in the Indian Ocean* (New Delhi, 1996)
A.M. Sastri, *Early History of the Deccan: Problems and Perspectives* (Delhi, 1987)

A.M. Shastri, *The Age of the Satavahanas*, 2 vols (New Delhi, 1999)

D.C. Sircar, *Successors of the Satavahanas in the Lower Deccan* (Calcutta, 1939)

B. Stein (ed.), *Essays on South India* (New Delhi, 1975)

N. Subrahmanian, *Sangam Polity: The Administration and Social Life of the Sangam Tamils* (Bombay, 1966)

K.V. Zvelebil, *The Smile of Murugan: On Tamil Literature of South India* (Leiden, 1973)

Notes (pp. 99–108)

1   G. Sontheimer, *Pastoral Deities in Western India* (New York, 1989), pp. 16ff.

2   G.W.F. Hegel, *Vorlesungen über die Philosophie der Geschichte* (Stuttgart, 1961), pp. 215ff.

3   W.H. Schoff (ed.), *The Periplus of the Erythraean Sea* (London, 1912), pp. 44ff.

4   Quoted from M. Wheeler, *Rome beyond its Imperial Frontiers* (London, 1955).

5   Ibid.

CHAPTER 3: THE REGIONAL KINGDOMS OF EARLY MEDIEVAL INDIA

The rise and conflicts of regional kingdoms

B.D. Chattopadhyaya, *The Making of Early Medieval India* (Delhi, 1994)

H. Kulke (ed.), *The State in India 1000–1700* (New Delhi, 1995)

B.P. Sahu (ed.), *Land System and Rural Society in Early India* (New Delhi, 1997)

A.Wink, *The Making of the Indo-Islamic World*, Vol. I (Leiden, 1990), Vol. II (Leiden, 1997)

North India

P. Bhatia, *The Paramaras* (*c.* AD 800–1305) (Delhi, 1970)

R. Chakravarti, *Explorations in Trade and Society in Early India* (New Delhi, 2001)

B.D. Chattopadhyaya, 'Origins of the Rajputs: The Political, Economic and Social Processes in Early Medieval Rajasthan', *Indian Historical Review*, vol. 3, 1976, pp. 59–82

D. Devahuti, *Harsha: A Political Study* (London, 1970; 2nd edn, Delhi, 1983)

H.C. Ray, *The Dynastic History of Northern India, Early and Medieval Period*, 2 vols (Calcutta, 1931–6)

D.R. Sharma, *Rajasthan through the Ages* (Bikaner, 1966)

East India

G. Berkemer, *Little Kingdoms in Kalinga: Ideologie, Legitimation und Politik regionaler Eliten* (Stuttgart, 1993)

Swapna Bhattacharya, *Landschenkungen und staatliche Entwicklung im frühmittel-alterlich Bengalen* (5. bis 13. Jh. n. Chr.) (Wiesbaden, 1984)

D.K. Chakravarti, *Ancient Bangladesh: A Study of Archaeological Sources* (Delhi, 1992)

R.C. Majumdar (ed.), *The History of Bengal*, vol. 1: *Hindu Period* (2nd edn, Patna, 1971)

P.K. Mishra, *Comprehensive History and Culture of Orissa*, 2 vols (New Delhi, 1997)

B.M. Morrison, *Political Centers and Cultural Regions in Early Bengal* (Arizona, 1970)

S.K. Panda, *The State and Statecraft in Medieval Orissa under the Later Eastern Ganges (AD 1038–1434)* (Calcutta, 1995)

Central and south India

M. Abraham, *Two Merchant Guilds of South India* (New Delhi, 1988)

A.S. Altekar, *Rashtrakutas and their Times* (2nd edn, Poona, 1967)

J.D.M. Derrett, *The Hoysalas: A Medieval Indian Royal Family* (Madras, 1957)

K.R. Hall, *Trade and Statecraft in the Age of the Colas* (New Delhi, 1980)

N. Karashima, *History and Society in South India: The Cholas to Vijayanagara* (Comprising *South Indian History and Society* and *Towards a New Formation*) (New Delhi, 2001)

K.A. Nilakanta Sastri, *The Colas* (2nd edn, Madras, 1955)

G.W. Spencer, *The Politics of Expansion: The Chola Conquest of Sri Lanka and Sri Vijaya* (Madras, 1983)

B. Stein, *Peasant State and Society in Medieval South India* (New Delhi, 1980)

B. Stein, *All the King's Mana. Papers on Medieval South Indian History* (Madras, 1984)

G. Yazdani (ed.), *The Early History of the Deccan*, 2 vols (London, 1960)

Notes (pp. 111–27)

1 Hsiuen-tsang (trans. S. Beal), *Buddhist Record of the Western World*, vol. 2 (London, 1906), p. 256.

2 F. Kielhorn, 'Inscription of Pulakeshin II', *Epigraphia Indica*, vol. 6, 1900, pp. 1–12.

3 R.G. Bhandarkar, 'Karhad Inscription of Krishna III Saka-Samvat 88', *Epigraphia Indica*, vol. 4, 1896, p. 278.

4 Translated by K.A. Nilakanta Sastri, 'A Tamil Merchant Guild in Sumatra', *Tijdschrift voor Indische Taal-, Land- en Volkenkunde*, vol. 72, 1932, pp. 321–5.

Kings, princes and priests: the structure of Hindu realms

B.D. Chattopadhyaya, *Aspects of Rural Settlements and Rural Society in Early Medieval India* (Calcutta, 1990)

L. Gopal, 'Samanta – Its Varying Significance in Ancient India', *Journal of the Royal Asiatic Society of Great Britain and Ireland*, 1963, pp. 21–37

D.N. Jha (ed.), *The Feudal Order. State, Society and Ideology in Early Medieval India* (New Delhi, 2000)

N. Karashima (ed.), *Kingship in Ancient India* (New Delhi, 1999)

H. Kulke, *Jagannatha-Kult und Gajapati-Königtum: Ein Beitrag zur Geschichte religiöser Legitimation hinduistischer Herrscher* (Wiesbaden, 1979)

R.S. Sharma, *Indian Feudalism: c.300–1200* (Calcutta, 1965)

R.S. Sharma, *Early Medieval Indian Society. A Study in Feudalisation* (Kolkata, 2001)

D.D. Shulman, *The King and the Clown in South Indian Myth and Poetry* (Princeton, NJ, 1986)

D.C. Sircar (ed.), *Land System and Feudalism in Ancient India* (Calcutta, 1966)

Y. Subbarayalu, 'The Cola State', *Studies in History* (New Delhi), vol. 4, 1982, pp. 265–306

B.N.S. Yadava, *Society and Culture in North India in the Twelfth Century* (Allahabad, 1973)

Notes (pp. 129–34)

1 G. Bühler, 'Madhuban Copper-plates of Harsha', *Epigraphia Indica*, vol. 1, 1882, pp. 67–75.

2 D.C. Sircar, 'Banpur Copper-plates of Ayasobhita II', *Epigraphia Indica*, vol. 29, pp. 32ff.

Gods, temples and poets: the growth of regional cultures

H. Bakker, *Ayodhya*, 2 vols (Groningen, 1986)

H. Bakker (ed.), *The Sacred Centre as the Focus of Political Interest* (Groningen, 1992)

R. Champakalakshmi, *Trade, Ideology and Urbanization* (Oxford, 1996)

D. Eck, *Banaras, City of Light* (London, 1983)

A. Eschmann, H. Kulke and G.C. Tripathi (eds), *The Cult of Jagannath and the Regional Tradition of Orissa* (New Delhi, 1978)

J.C. Galey (ed.), *L'espace du temple*, 2 vols (Purusartha Vol. 8, 10) (Paris, 1985/1986)

H. Kulke, *Cidambaramahatmya* (Wiesbaden, 1970)

H. Kulke, *Kings and Cults: State Formation and Legitimation in India and southeast Asia* (New Delhi, 1993)

R.N. Nandi, *Religious Institutions and Cults in the Deccan, c. AD 600–1000* (Delhi, 1973)

D.D. Shulman, *Tamil Temple Myths* (Princeton, 1980)

G.W. Spencer, 'Religious Networks and Royal Influence in Eleventh Century South India', *Journal of the Economic and Social History of the Orient*, vol. 12, 1969, pp. 42–56)

B. Stein (ed.), *South Indian Temples: An Analytical Reconsideration* (New Delhi, 1978)

K. Sundaram, *The Simhachalam Temple* (Waltair, 1984)

Notes (pp. 143–4)

1 H.W. Schomerus, *Die Hymnen des Manikka-Vashaga* (*Tiruvashaga*) (Jena, 1923), pp. 65ff.

2   H.W. Schomerus, *Sivaitische Heiligenlegenden* (*Periyapurana and Tiruvatavurar-Purana*) (Jena, 1923), p. 131.

India's impact on southeast Asia: causes and consequences

J.G. de Casparis, *India and Maritime South East Asia: A Lasting Relationship* (Kuala Lumpur, 1983)

K.N. Chaudhuri, *Trade and Civilisation in the Indian Ocean: An Economic History from the Rise of Islam to 1750* (Cambridge, 1985)

B.C. Chhabra, *Expansion of Indo-Aryan Culture during Pallava Rule as Evidenced by Inscriptions* (Delhi, 1965)

G. Coedès, *The Indianized States of southeast Asia* (Honolulu, 1968)

K.R. Hall, *Maritime Trade and State Development in Early southeast Asia* (Honolulu, 1984)

H. Kulke, 'Indian Colonies, Indianization or Cultural Convergence? Reflections on the Changing Image of India's Role in South-East Asia', *Ouderzoek in Zuidoost-Azie*, ed. by H. Schulte Nordholt, Leiden, 1990, pp. 8–32

J.C. van Leur, *Indonesian Trade and Society* (The Hague, 1955)

I.W. Mabbett, 'The Indianization of southeast Asia. I. Reflections on the Prehistoric Sources; II. Reflections on the Historical Sources', *Journal of Southeast Asian Studies*, vol. 8, 1977, pp. 1–14; pp. 143–61

H.P. Ray, *The Winds of Change: Buddhism and the Maritime Links of Early South Asia* (Delhi, 1994)

Note (p. 157)

1   P. Pelliot, 'Le Fou-nan', *Bulletin de l'Ecole Française d'Extrême-Orient*, vol. 3, 1903, p. 269.

CHAPTER 4: RELIGIOUS COMMUNITIES AND MILITARY FEUDALISM IN THE LATE MIDDLE AGES

The Islamic conquest of northern India and the sultanate of Delhi

B.D. Chattopadhyaya, *Representing the Other. Sanskrit Sources and the Muslims* (New Delhi, 1998)

U.N. Day, *The Government of the Sultanate* (New Delhi, 1993)

M. Habib, *Politics and Society during the Early Medieval Period* (New Delhi, 1974)

M. Habib and K.A. Nizami, *The Delhi Sultanate*, vol. 5 of *A Comprehensive History of India* (New Delhi, 1970)

P. Jackson, *The Delhi Sultanate. A Political and Military History* (Cambridge, 1998)

S.B.P. Nigam, *Nobility under the Sultans of Delhi: AD 1206–1398* (Delhi, 1968)

K.A. Nizami, *Some Aspects of Religion and Politics in India during the Thirteenth Century* (Delhi, 1972)

T. Raychaudhuri and I. Habib (eds), *The Cambridge Economic History of India*, vol. 1 *c*.1200–*c*.1750 (Cambridge, 1982), pp. 45–101

Notes (pp. 165–76)

1   E.C. Sachau, *Alberuni's India* (Berlin, 1888; reprinted Delhi, 1964), pp. 22ff.
2   Tarikh-i-Firuz Shahi (trans. H.M. Elliot and J. Dowson), *The History of India: as Told by its Own Historians*, vol. 3 (London, 1867f.). The following quotations are from the same volume.
3   M.A. Stein, *Kalhana's Rajatarangini* or *Chronicle of the Kings of Kashmir* (reprinted Delhi, 1961), vol. 1, p. 154.
4   See note 2.

The states of central and southern India in the period of the sultanate of Delhi

Deccan

R.M. Eaton, *The Rise of Islam and the Bengal Frontier, 1204–1760* (Delhi, 1994)

H.K. Sherwani, *The Bahmanis of the Deccan* (Hyderabad, 1953)

H.K. Sherwani and M.P. Joshi (eds), *History of Medieval Deccan 1295–1724*, 2 vols (Hyderabad, 1973/4)

Orissa and Vijayanagara

A. Dallapiccola and S. Zingel-Avé Lallemant (eds), *Vijayanagara: City and Empire – New Currents of Research* (Wiesbaden, 1985)

V. Filliozat, *L'epigraphie de Vijayanagara du début à 1377* (Paris, 1973)

J.M. Fritz and G. Michell, *City of Victory: Vijayanagara – the Medieval Hindu Capital of Southern India* (New York, 1991)

V. Narayana Rao, D. Shulman and S. Subrahmanyam, *Symbols of Substance. Court and State in Nayaka Period Tamilnadu* (Delhi, 1992)

R. Sewell, *A Forgotten Empire* (reprinted New Delhi, 1962)

B. Stein, *Vijayanagara* (*NCHI*) vol. I.2 (Cambridge, 1989)

R. Subrahmanya, *The Suryavamshi Gajapatis of Orissa* (Waltair, 1957)

Notes (pp. 184–93)

1   B.C. Chhabra, 'Chateshvara Temple Inscription', *Epigraphia Indica*, vol. 29, 1952, pp. 121–33.
2   N.N. Vasu, 'Copper-plate Inscriptions of Narasimha II', *Journal of the Asiatic Society of Bengal*, 1896, pp. 229–71.
3   Tarikh-i-Firuz Shahi (trans. H.M. Elliot and J. Dowson), *The History of India: as Told by its Own Historians*, vol. 3 (London, 1867).
4   Quoted from R. Sewell, *A Forgotten Empire* (reprinted New Delhi, 1962), p. 268f.

CHAPTER 5: THE RISE AND FALL OF
THE MUGHAL EMPIRE

The Great Mughals and their adversaries

M. Athar Ali, *The Mughal Nobility under Aurangzeb* (Calcutta, 1966)

M. Athar Ali, *The Apparatus of the Mughal Empire* (Delhi, 1985)

M. Athar Ali, 'Towards an Interpretation of the Mughal Empire', in H. Kulke (ed.), *The State in India, 1000–1700* (Delhi, 1995)

Babur, *Babur-nama*, Engl. trans. by A. Beveridge, 2 vols (London, 1921)

S. P. Blake, 'The Patrimonial-Bureaucratic Empire of the Mughals', *The State in India, 1000–1700* ed. by H. Kulke, Delhi, 1995

S. Chandra, *Parties and Politics at the Mughal Court* (Calcutta, 1959)

V.G. Dighe, *Peshwa Baji Rao I and Maratha Expansion* (Bombay, 1944)

Abul Fazl, *The Akbar-nama of Abul Fazl*, Engl. trans. by H. Beveridge, 3 vols (Calcutta, 1898)

J. Gommans, *Mughal Warfare* (London, 2002)

I. Habib, *The Agrarian System of Mughal India, 1526–1707* (Bombay, 1963)

D. Kolff, *Naukar, Rajput and Sepoy: The Ethnohistory of the Military Labour Market in Hindustan, 1450–1850* (Cambridge, 1990)

A.R. Kulkarni, *Maharashtra in the Age of Shivaji* (Pune, 1969)

S. Moosvi, *The Economy of the Mughal Empire: A Statistical Study* (Delhi, 1987)

G.S. Sardesai, *New History of the Marathas*, 3 vols (2nd edn, Bombay, 1957)

J. Sarkar, *History of Aurangzib*, 5 vols (Calcutta, 1912–52)

J. Sarkar, *The Fall of the Mughal Empire*, 4 vols (Calcutta, 1932–50)

S. N. Sen, *The Military System of the Marathas* (rev. edn, Bombay, 1958)

S. Subrahmanian, *The Political Economy of Commerce: Southern India, 1500–1630* (Cambridge, 1990)

R.C. Varma, *Foreign Policy of the Great Mughals, 1526–1727* (Agra, 1967)

A. Wink, *Land and Sovereignty in India: Agrarian Society and Politics under the Eighteenth-century Maratha Svarajya* (Cambridge, 1986)

Indian land power and European sea power

S. Aiolfi, *Calicos und gedrucktes Zeug: Die Entwicklung der englischen Textilveredlung und der Tuchhandel der East India Company, 1650–1750* (Stuttgart, 1987)

R.J. Barendse, *The Arabian Seas. The Indian Ocean World of the Seventeenth Century* (Armonk, NY, 2002)

C.R. Boxer, *The Dutch Seaborne Empire* (London, 1965)

K.N. Chaudhuri, *The English East India Company: The Study of an Early Joint Stock Company* (London, 1965)

K.N. Chaudhuri, *The Trading World of Asia and the East India Company, 1660–1760* (Cambridge, 1978)

S. Chaudhuri, *Trade and Commercial Organization in Bengal, 1650–1720* (Calcutta, 1975)

A. Das Gupta, *Indian Merchants and the Decline of Surat* (Wiesbaden, 1978, repr. Delhi, 1996)

R. Davies, *The Rise of the English Shipping Industry in the Seventeenth and Eighteenth Centuries* (London, 1972)

H. Furber, *Rival Empires of Trade in the Orient, 1600–1800* (Minneapolis, 1976)

K. Glamann, *Dutch-Asiatic Trade, 1620–1740* (Copenhagen, 1958)

P. Kaeppelin, *La Compagnie des Indes Orientales et François Martin* (Paris, 1908)

B.B. Kling and M.N. Pearson (eds), *The Age of Partnership: Europeans in Asia before Dominion* (Honolulu, 1978)

S. Labib, *Handelsgeschichte Ägyptens im Spätmittelalter, 1171–1517* (Wiesbaden, 1965)

V. Magalhaes-Godinho, *L'Economie de l'empire portugais aux XVᵉ et XVIᵉ siècles* (Paris, 1969)

P. Malekandathil, *Portuguese Cochin and the Martime Trade of India, 1500–1663* (New Delhi, 2001)

P. Malekandathil and T.J. Mohammed (eds), *The Portuguese, Indian Ocean and European Bridgeheads. Festschrift in Honour of Prof. K.S. Mathew* (Tellicherry, 2001)

K.S. Mathew, *Indo-Portuguese Trade and the Fuggers of Germany* (New Delhi, 1997)

M.N. Pearson, *Merchants and Rulers in Gujarat: The Response to the Portuguese in the Sixteenth Century* (Berkeley, 1976)

M.N. Pearson, *The Portuguese in India (NCHI)* (Cambridge, 1988)

M.N. Pearson, *The Indian Ocean* (London, 2003)

T. Pires, *The Suma Oriental: An Account of the East 1512–1515*, Portuguese text and Engl. trans., A. Cortesao (ed.), 2 vols (London, 1944)

Om Prakash, *The Dutch EIC and the Economy of Bengal, 1630–1720* (Princeton, NJ, 1985)

Om Prakash, *European Commercial Enterprise in Pre-Colonial India (NCHI)* (Cambridge, 1998)

T. Raychaudhuri, *Jan Company in Coromandel, 1605–1680* (The Hague, 1962)

N. Steensgaard, *The Asian Trade Revolution of the Seventeenth Century* (Chicago, 1974)

Sanjay Subrahmanyam, *The Career and Legend of Vasco da Gama* (Cambridge, 1997)

The struggle for supremacy in India

F.S. Bajwa, *Military System of the Sikhs* (Delhi, 1964)

J.J.L. Gommans, *The Rise of the Indo-Afghan Empire. c.1710–1780* (Delhi, 1999)

A. Ranga Pillai, *The Private Diary of Ananda Ranga Pillai: A Record of Matters Political Historical Social and Personal, From 1736–1761*, vol. 1 ed. by F. Price (Madras, 1907)

I. Prasad, *India in the Eighteenth Century* (Allahabad, 1973)

P. Marshall, *The Impeachment of Warren Hastings* (London, 1965)

P. Marshall, *East Indian Fortunes. The British in Bengal in the Eighteenth Century* (Oxford, 1976)

P. Marshall, *Bengal: The British Bridgehead in Eastern India 1740–1828 (NCHI)* (Cambridge, 1987)

A. Toussaint, *History of the Indian Ocean* (London, 1966)

CHAPTER 6: THE PERIOD OF COLONIAL RULE

Company Bahadur: trader and ruler

Anon., *Considerations upon the East India Trade* (London, 1701; reprinted in *East Indian Trade: Selected Works, 17th Century*, London, 1968)

A. Nag Chowdhury-Zilly, *The Vagrant Peasant: Agrarian Distress and Desertion in Bengal, 1770 to 1830* (Wiesbaden, 1982)

J. Fisch, *Cheap Lives and Dear Limbs: The British Transformation of the Bengal Criminal Law, 1769–1817* (Wiesbaden, 1983)

S. Förster, *Die mächtigen Diener der East India Company. Ursachen und Hintergründe der britischen Expansionspolitik in Südasien, 1793–1819* (Stuttgart, 1992)

H. Furber, *John Company at Work: A Study of European Expansion in India in the late Eighteenth Century* (London, 1951)

R. Guha, *A Rule of Property for Bengal: An Essay on the Idea of Permanent Settlement* (Paris, 1963)

B.B. Kling, *Partner in Empire: Dwarkanath Tagore and the Age of Enterprise in Eastern India* (Berkeley, 1976)

D. Kopf, *British Orientalism and the Bengal Renaissance: The Dynamics of Indian Modernization 1773–1835* (Berkeley, 1969)

B.B. Misra, *The Central Administration of the East India Company 1773–1834* (Manchester, 1959)

S.N. Mukherjee, *Sir William Jones: A Study in Eighteenth Century British Attitudes to India* (Cambridge, 1968)

C.H. Philips, *The East India Company, 1784–1834* (Manchester, 1940; reprinted Manchester, 1961)

Surendra Nath Sen, *Eighteen Fifty-Seven* (Calcutta, 1958)

B. Stein, *Thomas Munro: Origins of the Colonial State and His Vision of Empire* (Delhi, 1989)

E. Stokes, *The English Utilitarians and India* (Oxford, 1959)

E. Stokes, *The Peasant and the Raj: Studies in Agrarian Society and Peasant Rebellion in Colonial India* (Cambridge, 1978)

L. Sutherland, *The East Indian Company in Eighteenth Century Politics* (Oxford, 1952)

L. Zastoupil, *John Stuart Mill and India* (Stanford, 1994)

The colonial economy

S. Ambirajan, *Political Economy and British Policy in India* (Cambridge, 1978)

S. Ambirajan, *Political Economy and Monetary Management. India 1766–1914* (Madras, 1984)

A.K. Bagchi, *Private Investment in India, 1900–1939* (Cambridge, 1972)

C.J. Baker, *An Indian Rural Economy, 1880–1955. The Tamilnad Countryside* (Delhi, 1984)

Sabyasachi Bhattacharya, *Financial Foundations of the British Raj, 1858–1872* (Simla, 1971)

G. Blyn, *Agricultural Trends in India, 1891–1947: Output, Availability and Productivity* (Philadelphia, 1966)

S. Bose, *Agrarian Bengal. Social Structure and Politics, 1919–1947* (Cambridge, 1986)

R. Chandavarkar, *The Origins of Industrial Capitalism in India: Business Strategies and the Working Classes in Bombay, 1900–1940* (Cambridge, 1994)

R. Chandavarkar, *Imperial Power and Popular Politics. Class, Resistance and the State in India, c.1850–1950* (Cambridge, 1998)

N. Charlesworth, *British Rule and the Indian Economy* (London, 1982)

N. Charlesworth, *Peasants and Imperial Rule: Agriculture and Agrarian Society in the Bombay Presidency, 1850–1935* (Cambridge, 1985)

B.B. Chowdhury, *Growth of Commercial Agriculture in Bengal, Vol. I: 1757–1900* (Calcutta, 1964)

C. Dewey (ed.), *Arrested Development in India. The Historical Dimension* (New Delhi, 1988)

R.W. Goldsmith, *The Financial Development of India, 1860–1977* (New Haven, 1983)

Omkar Goswami, *Industry, Trade and Peasant Society. The Jute Economy of Eastern India, 1900–1947* (Delhi, 1991)

David Hardiman, *Feeding the Baniya. Peasants and Usurers in Western India* (Delhi, 1996)

M.M. Islam, *Bengal Agriculture 1920–1946: A Quantitative Study* (Cambridge, 1979)

T. Kessinger, *Vilyatpur, 1848–1968: Social and Economic Change in a North Indian Village* (Berkeley, 1974)

D. Kumar, *Land and Caste in South India. Agricultural Labour in the Madras Presidency During the Nineteenth Century* (Cambridge, 1965)

D. Kumar (ed.), *The Cambridge Economic History of India, Vol. 2: c.1757–1970* (Cambridge, 1983)

M. Mann, *British Rule on Indian Soil. Northern India in the First Half of the Nineteenth Century* (2nd edn, New Delhi, 2002)

M.D. Morris, *The Emergence of an Industrial Labour Force in India: A Study of the Bombay Cotton Mills, 1854–1947* (Berkeley, 1965)

M.D. Morris and C.B. Dudley, 'Selected Railway Statistics for the Indian Subcontinent, 1853–1946/47', *Artha Vijnana*, vol. 17 (Pune, 1975)

Gyan Prakash, *Bonded Histories: Genealogies of Labour Servitude in Colonial India* (Cambridge, 1990)

D. Rothermund, *Government, Landlord and Peasant in India. Agrarian Relations under British Rule, 1865–1935* (Wiesbaden, 1978)

D. Rothermund, *An Economic History of India* (2nd rev. edn, London, 1993)

T. Roy, *Traditional Industry in the Economy of Colonial India* (Cambridge, 1999)

T. Roy, *The Economic History of India, 1857–1947* (New Delhi, 2000)

A. Satyanarayana, *Andhra Peasants under British Rule. Agrarain Relations and the Rural Economy, 1900–1940* (New Delhi, 1990)

K. Specker, *Weber im Wettbewerb. Das Schicksal des südindischen Textilhandwerks im 19. Jahrhundert* (Wiesbaden, 1984)

D. Thorner, *Investment in Empire. British Railway and Steamshipping Enterprise in India, 1825–1849* (Philadelphia, 1950)

B.R. Tomlinson, *The Economy of Modern India, 1860–1970* (*NCHI*) (Cambridge, 1993)

The regional impact of British rule

B.H. Baden-Powell, *The Land Systems of British India*, 3 vols (London, 1892)

C. Baker, *The Politics of South India, 1920–1937* (Cambridge, 1976)

B.S. Baliga, *Studies in Madras Administration*, 2 vols (Madras, 1960)

H. Banerjee, *Agrarian Society of the Punjab, 1849–1901* (New Delhi, 1982)

I. Banga, *Agrarian System of the Sikhs* (New Delhi, 1978)

C. Bayly, *The Local Roots of Indian Politics – Allahabad 1880–1920* (Oxford, 1975)

C. Bayly, *Rulers, Townsmen and Bazaars: North Indian Society in the Age of British Expansion, 1770–1870* (Cambridge, 1983)

C. Bayly, *Indian Society and the Making of the British Empire* (*NCHI*) (Cambridge, 1988)

C. Bayly, *Imperial Meridian: The British Empire and the World, 1780–1830* (London, 1989)

C. Bayly, *An Empire of Information. Political Intelligence and Social Communication in India, c.1780–1880* (Cambridge, 1996)

M. Frenz, *From Contact to Conquest. Transition to British Rule in Malabar, 1790–1805* (Delhi, 2003)

R. Frykenberg, *Guntur District, 1788–1848: A History of Local Influence and Central Authority in South India* (Oxford, 1965)

H.L.O. Garren and Abdul Hamid, *A History of Government College Lahore, 1864–1964* (Lahore, 1964)

S. Gopal, *British Policy in India, 1858–1905* (Cambridge, 1965)

A. Gupta (ed.), *Studies in the Bengal Renaissance* (Calcutta, 1958)

M.V. Jain, *Outlines of Indian Legal History* (Bombay, 1972)

R. Kumar, *Western India in the Nineteenth Century: A Study in the Social History of Maharashtra* (London, 1968)

J. Lütt, *Hindu-Nationalismus in Uttar Pradesh, 1867–1900* (Stuttgart, 1970)

S. Manickam, *The Social Setting of Christian Conversion in South India. The Impact of the Wesleyan Methodist Missionaries on the Trichy-Tanjore Diocese with Special Reference to the Harijan Communities of the Mass Movement Area, 1820–1947* (Wiesbaden, 1977)

P. Sharan, *The Imperial Legislative Council for India from 1861 to 1920* (New Delhi, 1961)

A. Siddiqui, *Agrarian Change in a Northern Indian State: Uttar Pradesh, 1819–33* (Oxford, 1973)

W. Simon, *Die britische Militärpolitik in Indien und ihre Auswirkungen auf den britisch-indischen Finanzhaushalt, 1878–1910* (Wiesbaden, 1974)

D. Washbrook and C. Baker, *South India: Political Institutions and Political Change, 1880–1940* (Delhi, 1975)

E. Whitcombe, *Agrarian Conditions in Northern India*, vol. 1: *The United Provinces under British Rule, 1860–1900* (Berkeley, 1972)

The pattern of constitutional reform

J. Broomfield, *Elite Conflict in a Plural Society. Twentieth Century Bengal* (Berkeley, 1968)

A.B. Keith, *A Constitutional History of India*, 1600–1935 (London, 1936)

S.R. Mehrotra, *The Emergence of the Indian National Congress* (New Delhi, 1971)

B.B. Mishra, *The Administrative History of India, 1834–1947* (New Delhi, 1971)

R. Moore, *The Crisis of Indian Unity, 1917–1940* (Oxford, 1974)

P. Robb, *The Government of India and Reform, 1916–1921* (Oxford, 1976)

D. Rothermund, *Die politische Willensbildung in Indien, 1900–1960* (Wiesbaden, 1965)

A. Rumbold, *Watershed in India, 1914–1922* (London, 1979)

A. Seal, *The Emergence of Indian Nationalism: Competition and Collaboration in the Later Nineteenth Century* (Cambridge, 1968)

S. Wolpert, *Tilak and Gokhale: Revolution and Reform in the Making of Modern India* (Berkeley, 1962)

S. Wolpert, *Morley and India, 1906–1910* (Berkeley, 1967)

CHAPTER 7: THE FREEDOM MOVEMENT AND THE PARTITION OF INDIA

The Indian freedom movement

D. Arnold, *The Congress in Tamilnad. Nationalist Politics in South India* (London, 1977)

D. Arnold and D. Hardiman (eds), *Subaltern Studies VIII. Essays in Honour of Ranajit Guha* (New Delhi, 1994)

A.K. Azad, *India Wins Freedom. The Complete Version* (Madras, 1989)

S.N. Banerjea, *A Nation in the Making* (London, 1925)

A. Besant, *How India Wrought for Freedom* (Madras, 1915)

G.D. Birla, *In the Shadow of the Mahatma* (Bombay, 1953)

S.C. Bose, *The Indian Struggle, 1920–1934* (Calcutta, 1948)

S.C. Bose, *The Indian Struggle, 1935–1942* (Calcutta, 1952)

M. Brecher, *Nehru. A Political Biography* (London, 1959)

J.M. Brown, *Gandhi: Prisoner of Hope* (Delhi, 1989)

J.M. Brown, *Gandhi's Rise to Power: Indian Politics, 1915–1922* (Cambridge, 1972)

T. Chand, *History of the Freedom Movement in India*, 4 vols (New Delhi, 1961–72)

B. Chandra, *The Rise and Growth of Economic Nationalism in India. Economic Policies of Indian National Leadership, 1880–1905* (New Delhi, 1966)

P. Chatterjee, *The Nation and its Fragments: Colonial and Postcolonial Histories* (Delhi, 1994)

P. Chatterjee and G. Pandey, *Subaltern Studies VII* (New Delhi, 1992)

G.H. Deshmukh (Lokhitwadi), *Satapatren* (Marathi) Aundh 1940 (letter 54, 1849)

C. Dobbin, *Urban Leadership in Western India: Politics and Communities in Western India, 1840–1885* (London, 1972)

M.K. Gandhi, *My Experiments with Truth: An Autobiography* (Boston, 1940)

S. Gopal, *The Viceroyalty of Lord Ripon* (London, 1953)

S. Gopal, *The Viceroyalty of Lord Irwin, 1926–1931* (Oxford, 1957)

S. Gopal, *Jawaharlal Nehru. A Biography. Vol. I: 1889–1947* (London, 1975)

L. Gordon, *Bengal. The Nationalist Movement, 1876–1940* (New York/London, 1974)

R. Guha (ed.), *Subaltern Studies. Writings on South Asian History and Society, Vols I–VI* (New Delhi, 1982–9)

P.S. Gupta, *Imperialism and the British Labour Movement, 1914–1964* (London, 1975)

D. Hardiman, *Peasant Nationalists of Gujarat, Kheda District, 1917–1934* (Delhi, 1981)

S. Hay, *Asian Ideas of East and West. Tagore and His Critics in Japan, China and India* (Cambridge, Mass., 1970)

C. Heimsath, *Indian Nationalism and Hindu Social Reform* (Princeton, 1964)

E. Irschick, *Politics and Conflict in South India. The Non-Brahmin Movement and Tamil Separatism, 1916–1929* (Berkeley, 1969)

G. Johnson, *Provincial Politics and Indian Nationalism: Bombay and the Indian National Congress, 1880–1915* (Cambridge, 1973)

D. Kopf, *The Brahmo Samaj and the Shaping of the Modern Indian Mind* (Princeton, 1979)

R. Kumar (ed.), *Essays on Gandhian Politics: The Rowlatt Satyagraha of 1919* (Oxford, 1971)

R. Kumar, *Making of a Nation. Essays in Indian History and Politics* (New Delhi, 1989)

H.J. Leue, *Britische Indien-Politik, 1926–1932* (Wiesbaden, 1980)

D.A. Low (ed.), *Soundings in Modern South Asian History* (London, 1968)

D.A. Low (ed.), *Congress and the Raj: Facets of the Indian Struggle, 1917–1947* (London, 1977)

R.C. Majumdar, *History of the Freedom Movement in India*, 3 vols (Calcutta, 1962/1963)

C. Markovits, *Indian Business and Nationalist Politics 1931–39: The Indigenous Capitalist Class and the Rise of the Congress Party* (Cambridge, 1985)

P. Moon, *Divide and Quit* (London, 1962)

B.R. Nanda, *Gokhale: The Indian Moderates and the British Raj* (Delhi, 1977)

D. Naoroji, *Poverty and un-British Rule in India* (London, 1901)

J. Nehru, *An Autobiography* (London, 1936)

Nivedita Mohanty, *Oriya Nationalism. Quest for a United Orissa* (New Delhi, 1982)

G. Omvedt, *Dalits and the Democratic Revolution. Dr Ambedkar and the Dalit Movement in Colonial India* (New Delhi, 1994)

G. Pandey, *Ascendancy of the Congress in Uttar Pradesh 1926–1934: A Case of Imperfect Mobilization* (Delhi, 1978)

M. Pernau, *The Passing of Patrimonialism. Politics and Political Culture in Hyderabad, 1911–1948* (New Delhi, 2000)

B. Ramusack, *The Princes of India in the Twilight of Empire: Dissolution of a Patron–Client System, 1914–1939* (Columbia, 1978)

D. Rothermund, 'Traditionalism and Socialism in Vivekananda's Thought', *The Phases of Indian Nationalism and Other Essays*, ed. by D. Rothermund, Bombay, 1970, pp. 57–64

D. Rothermund, *Mahatma Gandhi: Der Revolutionär der Gewaltlosigkeit. Eine politische Biographie* (Munich, 1989)

D. Rothermund, *Mahatma Gandhi: An Essay in Political Biography* (New Delhi, 1991)

D. Rothermund, *India in the Great Depression, 1929–1939* (New Delhi, 1992)

S. Sarkar, *The Swadeshi Movement in Bengal, 1903–1908* (New Delhi, 1973)

S. Sarkar, 'The Logic of Gandhian Nationalism: Civil Disobedience and the Gandhi–Irwin Pact, 1930–1931', *Indian Historical Review*, vol. 3, 1976, pp. 114–46

S. Sarkar, *Modern India, 1885–1947* (London, 1989)

K. Gräfin Schwerin, *Indirekte Herrschaft und Reformpolitik im indischen Fürsten-staat Hyderabad, 1853–1911* (Wiesbaden, 1980)

A. Seal, *The Emergence of Indian Nationalism. Competition and Collaboration in the Later Nineteenth Century* (Cambridge, 1968)

M. Shakir, *Khilafat to Partition: A Survey of Major Political Trends among Indian Muslims during 1919–1947* (New Delhi, 1970)

B. Pattabhi Sitaramayya, *History of the Indian National Congress*, 2 vols (Bombay, 1935–47)

B.R. Tomlinson, *The Indian National Congress and the Raj, 1929–1942. The Penultimate Phase* (London, 1976)

J. Voigt, *Indien im Zweiten Weltkrieg* (Stuttgart, 1978)

David Washbrook, *The Emergence of Provincial Politics: The Madras Presidency, 1870–1920* (Cambridge, 1976)

The partition of India

K.K. Aziz, *Rahmat Ali: A Biography* (Lahore, 1986)

A. Campbell-Johnson, *Mission with Mountbatten* (London, 1953)

P. Hardy, *The Muslims of British India* (Cambridge, 1972)

M. Hasan, *Nationalism and Communal Politics in India, 1916–1928* (Delhi, 1979)

M. Hasan, *Legacy of a Divided Nation* (London, 1997)

H.V. Hodson, *The Great Divide* (New York, 1971)

A. Jalal, *The Sole Spokesman. Jinnah, the Muslim League and the Demand for Pakistan* (Cambridge, 1985)

K. MacPherson, *The Muslim Microcosm. Calcutta, 1919–1935* (Wiesbaden, 1935)

N. Mansergh (ed.), *The Transfer of Power*, vols 3–8 (London, 1971–9)

V.P. Menon, *The Transfer of Power in India* (Bombay, 1957)

P. Moon (ed.), *Wavell: The Viceroy's Journal* (London, 1973)

R.J. Moore, *Churchill, Cripps and India, 1939–1945* (Oxford, 1979)

R.J. Moore, *Escape from Empire: The Attlee Government and the Indian Problem* (Oxford, 1983)

C.H. Philips and W. Wainwright (eds), *The Partition of India: Policies and Perspectives, 1935–1947* (London, 1970)

F. Robinson, *Separatism Among Indian Muslims. The Politics of the United Provinces' Muslims, 1860–1923* (Cambridge, 1975)

I. Talbot, *Provincial Politics and the Pakistan Movement. The Growth of the Muslim League in North-West and North-East India* (New Delhi, 1989)

F. Tuker, *While Memory Serves* (London, 1950)

S. Wolpert, *Jinnah of Pakistan* (New York/Oxford, 1984)

CHAPTER 8: THE REPUBLIC

Internal affairs and political development

G. Austin, *The Indian Constitution: Cornerstone of a Nation* (Oxford, 1966)

C. Baxter, *The Jana Sangh: A Biography of an Indian Political Party* (Philadelphia, 1969)

S. Bose (ed.), *South Asia and World Capitalism* (Delhi, 1990)

P.R. Brass, *The Politics of India since Independence* (*NCHI*) (Cambridge, 1990)

M. Brecher, *Nehru – A Political Biography* (London, 1959)

A.S. Burger, *Opposition in a Dominant Party System: A Study of the Jan Sangh, the Praja Socialist Party and the Socialist Party in Uttar Pradesh, India* (Berkeley, 1969)

H. Erdmann, *The Swatantra Party and Indian Conservatism* (Cambridge, 1967)

F. Frankel, *India's Green Revolution: Economic Gains and Political Costs* (Princeton, 1971)

Government of India, *Report of the States Reorganisation Commission* (New Delhi, 1955)

B. Graham, *Hindu Nationalism and Indian Politics. The Origins and Development of Bharatiya Jana Sangh* (Cambridge, 1993)

A.H. Hanson, *The Process of Planning: A Study of India's Five Year Plans, 1950–1964* (London, 1966)

C. Jaffrelot, *The Hindu Nationalist Movement and Indian Politics, 1925 to the 1990s* (London, 1996)

S. Kochanek, *The Congress Party of India: The Dynamics of One Party Democracy* (Princeton, 1968)

S. Kochanek, *Business and Politics in India* (Berkeley, 1974)

W. Malenbaum, *Prospects for Indian Development* (London, 1962)

V.P. Menon, *The Story of the Integration of the Indian States* (Bombay, 1956)

W.H. Morris-Jones, *Parliament in India* (Philadelphia, 1957)

W.H. Morris-Jones, *The Government and Politics of India* (London, 1964)

E.M.S. Namboodiripad, *The National Question in Kerala* (Bombay, 1952)

G. Overstreet and M. Windmiller, *Communism in India* (Berkeley, 1959)

D. Rothermund (ed.), *Liberalising India: Progress and Problems* (New Delhi, 1996)

D. Rothermund, *The Role of the State in South Asia and Other Essays* (New Delhi, 2001)

M. Weiner, *Party Building in a New Nation: The Indian National Congress* (Chicago, 1967)

External affairs: global and regional dimensions

J.S. Bains, *India's International Disputes* (London, 1962)

R.N. Berkes and M. Bedi, *The Diplomacy of India* (Stanford, 1958)

P.S. Gosh, *Cooperation and Conflict in South Asia* (New Delhi, 1992)

S. Gupta, *Kashmir* (New Delhi, 1966)

C. Heimsath and S. Mansingh, *A Diplomatic History of Modern India* (Bombay, 1971)

R.C. Horn, *Soviet–Indian Relations: Issues and Influences* (New York, 1982)

R.P. Kangle (ed.), *The Kautiliya Arthasastra*, 3 vols (Bombay, 1960–5)

A. Lamb, *The China–India Border* (London, 1964)

K.P. Misra (ed.), *Studies in Indian Foreign Policy* (New Delhi, 1969)

B. Prasad, *The Origins of India's Foreign Policy* (Patna, 1960)

D. Rothermund, *Indien und die Sowjetunion* (Tübingen, 1968)

A. Stein, *India and the Soviet Union: The Nehru Era* (Chicago, 1969)

Ton That Tien, *Indian Foreign Policy in Cambodia, Laos and Vietnam, 1947–1964* (Berkeley, 1968)

INDEX